D0872087

MANUAL OF POLITICAL ECONOMY

MANUAL

OF

POLITICAL ECONOMY

BY

VILFREDO PARETO

Translated by
ANN S. SCHWIER

Edited by
ANN S. SCHWIER AND ALFRED N. PAGE

AUGUSTUS M. KELLEY · PUBLISHERS
NEW YORK 1971

TABLE OF CONTENTS

CHAPTER I.—GENERAL PRINCIPLES.   1

§ 1. Objectives which the study of political economy and sociology may have. — 2, 3. The methods employed. — 4, 5, 6. Uniformities, or laws. — 7. Apparent exceptions. — 8. Uniformities, or laws, are true only under certain conditions. — 9. These conditions are sometimes implicit, sometimes explicit. — 10. We can never know a concrete phenomenon in all its particulars. — 11. We can only have an approximate knowledge of it. — 12. The claim that a theory deviates, on certain points, from the concrete phenomenon is an objection of no significance. — 13. Example. — 14. Successive approximations. — 15, 16, 17. We cannot know the facts by reasoning about the conceptions which we have of them; it is necessary to resort to direct observation. — 18. Reasoning *by elimination*; how it is incorrect. — 19. The results of theory always differ somewhat from reality. — 20. Sciences which can resort to experimentation, and those which must be content with observation. A theory can have no other criterion than its more or less complete accord with reality. — 21. Abstraction: its role in science. — 22, 23, 24. It can assume two forms; they are equivalent. — 25, 26. Science is essentially analytic; practice, synthetic. — 27, 28, 29, 30. The theory of a concrete phenomenon is the theory of only one part of that phenomenon. Science separates the different parts of a phenomenon and studies them separately; practice must bring together the results thus obtained. — 31. The uselessness of merely negative criticism of a theory. — 32. In a theory we sometimes depart from the concrete phenomenon in order to attain greater simplicity. — 33. Historical study of economic phenomena; how it is useful and how it is not. — 34. Evolution. — 35. The uselessness of disputes about the *method* of political economy. — 36. Affirmations which can be verified experimentally and those which cannot. — 37, 38. Science is concerned only with the first. — 39, 40. Anything which has the appearance of a precept, unless it is the form only, is not scientific. — 41 to 44. Confusion between science and faith. — 45. Intuition, its modes and forms. — 46. Universal consent is not a criterion of scientific truth. — 47. The error of metaphysicians who want to convert absolute propositions into scientific propositions which, by nature, are essentially dependent, and in regard to which it is always necessary to understand the condition that they are true within the limits of the time and experience known to us. — 48. It is absurd to want to replace faith by science. — 49, 50. Conclusions deduced from non-experimental premises. — 51. Discovery.

CHAPTER II.—INTRODUCTION TO SOCIAL SCIENCE   29

§ 1. The study of sociology ought to start from certain empirical principles. — 2, 3. Logical and non-logical actions. — 4, 5. Tendency to represent non-logical actions as logical, and to consider all relationships between phenomena as relations of cause and effect. — 6. Objective relations. — 7, 8, 9. How and in what way the subjective relation deviates from the objective relation. — 10, 11, 12. Varieties of relations between real facts. — 13, 14, 15. Relations between imaginary and real facts. — 16, 17. How repeated experiments can bring the subjective and the objective relation closer together. — 18, 19. Some ideas about the theory of non-logical actions. Morality is a subjective phenomenon. — 20. Useful experimental studies which may be made of moral and religious sentiments. — 21. Relation between morality and religion. — 22. Relations between non-logical sentiments in general. — 23. Logical and non-logical relations between morality and religion. — 24 to 40. Examination of logical systems of morality. These are useless constructs containing no reality. — 41. Useful studies which may be made on moral sentiments and other similar sentiments. — 42. These sentiments are essentially subjective. — 43. The interdependence between these different sentiments is not of a logical order, but comes from the fact that these sentiments have remote and common causes. — 44. This dependance varies in time and space, and, within the same society, according to individuals. — 45, 46, 47. There is no one unique morality; there are as many of them as there are individuals. — 48. Contradictions between different non-logical sentiments, for example between moral sentiments and religious sentiments. How an intense faith prevents these contradictions being noticed. — 49. How and why they are not generally perceived. — 50. Man endeavors to establish the logical relations which he thinks ought to exist between these non-logical sentiments. — 51, 52, 53. Certain circumstances favor the development of certain sentiments, certain others inhibit them, and they operate differently depending upon individuals. — 54, 55. How the morals and the religions of different social classes act upon each other. — 56, 57. Historical examples. — 58, 59. This reciprocal action gives rise to rhythmical movements. — 60, 61. Evils which result from the extension of upper class sentiments to the lower classes. — 62 to 74. Historical examples. — 75. The general problem of sociology. — 76 to 79. The Darwinian solution; what is true about it and what is incorrect. — 80 to 82. Solution according to which society is organized so as to satisfy the interest of one social class. — 83. It is useless to investigate whether moral sentiments have an individual or a social origin. — 84. It is important to know, not their origin, but how sentiments arise and change. — 85, 86, 87. Historical examples. — 88. Imitation and opposition. — 89 to 93. How the objective relations which we have just studied are transformed into subjective relations. — 94 to 96. A single objective relation can be expressed under different subjective forms. The persistence of certain social phenomena under completely different forms. — 97. Real and virtual movements. The problem of investigating how certain hypothetical modifications of certain social facts act on other facts. — 98, 99. Examination of this problem. — 100, 101. Subjective and objective difficulties encountered in the study. — 102. Society is not homogeneous. — 103. The circulation of aristocracies. — 104, 105, 106. How the struggle between the different social classes is viewed subjectively. Objectively the concept of equality of men is absurd;

subjectively it has a very important place in social phenomena. — 107. How certain men attempting to move in one direction, go in the opposite direction. — 108. Social and economic theories affect society not by their objective value, but by their subjective value. — 109. The presumption of equality before the law. — 110 to 114. Morality and beliefs vary among men; social utility of these variations. — 115 to 123. How appearances differ from reality in political organization. Historical examples.

CHAPTER III.—GENERAL NOTION OF ECONOMIC EQUILIBRIUM 103

§ § 1, 2. Subject matter of political economy. — 3. Difficulties in the study of the economic problem and how mathematics serves to overcome certain of these difficulties. — 4, 5, 6. Simplification of the economic phenomenon; pure economics. — 7. The three parts of pure economics. — 8, 9, 10. Economic statics. A continuing phenomenon is studied. — 11, 12. Two classes of theories: the first seeks to compare the sensations of one individual; the second seeks to compare the sensations of different individuals. Political economy is concerned only with the first. — 13. How we will make this study. — 14, 15. We will study tastes, obstacles, and how economic equilibrium arises from their opposition. — 16, 17, 18. Economic goods and the sensations which they provide. — 19. The elements which must be combined are tastes and obstacles. — 20, 21. Qualitative and quantitative combinations of economic goods. — 22. Definition of economic equilibrium; real movements and virtual movements. — 23, 24, 25, 26. The data of the problem of equilibrium. — 27. How equilibrium is determined, in general. — 28, 29. Men's tastes; the imperfect notion which economists have of them; *value in use*. — 30, 31. How pure economics arises from the rectification of the erroneous notions in economics. — 32 to 36b. Ophelimity. — 37. Constraints on the conditions of the economic phenomenon. — 38. We will attempt to explain the theories of pure economics without using algebraic symbols. — 39. Direct and indirect effects of tastes. — 40 to 48. Types of phenomena in connection with the effects of tastes; free competition; monopoly. — 49. Socialist type of organization. — 50, 51. How the types are mixed, and how they must be studied. — 52 to 54. Indifference lines of tastes. — 55, 56. Indices of ophelimity. — 57, 58, 59. How the tastes of the individual are represented; the hill of pleasure. — 60, 61. How the condition of a person who has a succession of different quantities of an economic good is represented by a path. — 62, 63, 64. Considerations regarding the paths; terminal points and points of tangency with indifference lines. — 65, 66, 67. Continuous and discontinuous variations. — 68. The obstacles. — 69. The first kind of obstacles. — 70, 71, 72. Transformation of economic goods. — 73, 74. Second kind of obstacles. — 75. Indifference lines of obstacles in objective transformations. — 76. The producer's indifference lines. — 77 to 80. Analogy between indifference lines of tastes and indifference lines of obstacles. — 81. The hill of profit. 82. Competition. — 83. Competition in exchange. — 84. Competition in production. — 85. We must begin by studying a collectivity separated from all others. — 86 to 88. Modes of competition. — 89. Types of phenomena in connection with producers. — 90, 91, 92. Equilibrium in general. — 93 to 99. Equilibrium with respect to tastes; how equilibrium on a path takes place at a terminal point or at a point of tangency of the path and an indifference curve. — 100 to 104. Producer equilibrium. — 105. The lines of maximum profit. — 106 to 111. Equilibrium of tastes and obstacles. — 112 to 115. General theory of the determination of equilibrium points. — 116 to 133. Modes and forms of equilibrium in exchange. Different points of equilibrium. Stable and unstable equilibrium. — 134. Maximum ophelimity. — 135 to 151. Modes and forms of equilibrium in production. The line of maximum profit. Producer competition. — 152 to 155. Prices. — 156, 157. Value in exchange. — 158. The price of one good in terms of another. — 159 to 166. Economic phenomena described making use of the notion of price. — 167 to 174. Prices and the second kind of obstacles. Constant and variable prices. — 175. The budget of the individual. — 176. The budget of the producer. — 177, 178, 179. The cost of production. — 180 to 183. Supply and demand. — 184. Supply curve and demand curve. — 185, 186, 187. Supply and demand depend upon all the circumstances of economic equilibrium. — 188 to 192. The equality of supply and demand at the equilibrium point. — 193. How supply and demand vary. — 194. The equality of cost of production and of selling prices. — 195. Stable and unstable equilibrium; its relation to the notions of supply and demand. — 196 to 204. Equilibrium in general. — 205 to 216. Equilibrium of production and of exchange, in general. — 217, 218. The benefit from the use of mathematics. — 219 to 226. Errors which have arisen from not using mathematics where it was indispensable. — 227. It is fruitless to look for the single cause of value. — 228. Up to now pure economics alone has been able to provide a synthetic notion of the economic phenomenon.

CHAPTER IV.—TASTES 181

§ 1. Purpose of the present chapter. — 2 to 7. Tastes and ophelimity. Only voluntary consumption is considered. — 8. Independent and dependent consumption. Two kinds of dependence. — 9 to 13. Study of the first kind of dependence. It is divided into two sub-types. — 14 to 18. Study of the second kind of dependence. — 19. Hierarchy of goods. — 20 to 23. A way of considering the second kind of dependence. Equivalence of various consumption. — 24. The phenomenon of dependence in consumption is very extensive. — 25. We can only study the economic phenomenon in a small region around the point of equilibrium. — 26 to 28. The indifference curves vary with time and circumstances. — 29 to 31. Differences between the theoretical phenomenon and the concrete phenomenon. — 32. Ophelimity and its indices. — 33, 34. Characteristics of ophelimity for independent consumption. — 35, 36. Dependent consumption. — 37 to 42. Characteristics of ophelimity in general. — 43 to 47. Characteristics of indifference lines. — 48 to 53. Relation between ophelimity or indifference lines and supply and demand. Relations with the income of the consumer. — 54 to 65. Different shapes of indifference lines of exchange. Consideration of the different kinds of dependence. — 66 to 68. The phenomenon of ophelimity in general. — 69, 70. The hill of ophelimity.

CHAPTER V.—THE OBSTACLES 211

§ 1. The study of production is more complex than the study of tastes. — 2 to 7. Division of labor and the enterprise. — 8 to 10. The objective the enterprise strives for. — 11. How, in pursuing a certain objective, it sometimes attains another. — 12. The socialist type of organization. — 13 to 16. The various methods of the enterprise. — 17 to 24. Capital. In what respects this concept is not rigorous, and how it can be made so. — 25 to 29. The theory of economic equilibrium with and without the concept of capital. — 30, 31, 32. Amortization and insurance. — 33. The services of capital. — 34. Material goods and immaterial goods. — 35, 36, 37. The coefficients of production. — 38. Transformations in space. — 39 to 42. Transformations in time. — 43 to 47. The balance sheet of the enterprise and transformations in time. Different ways of considering these transformations. — 48 to 51. The income from capital. — 52 to 57. Net income and its causes. — 58. Net income of diverse capital. — 59, 60. The budget of the enterprise and the income from capital. — 61. The balance sheet of the enterprise, the labor and capital of the entrepreneur. — 62 to 65. The entrepreneur and the owner of economic goods. — 66 to 69. Real enterprises, their profits and their losses. — 70 to 75. Variability of the coefficients of production. — 76 to 77. Possible compensation in the variations of the different coefficients. — 78 to 80. Division of production. — 81 to 87. General equilibrium of production. — 88. Production of capital — 89. Successive positions of equilibrium. — 90. *Rent.* — 91, 92. Acquired rent. — 93, 94, 95. Ricardian rent; its relation to the cost of production. — 96, 97. How this particular case is related to production.

CHAPTER VI.—ECONOMIC EQUILIBRIUM 251

§ § 1 to 18. Examples of equilibrium. The law of cost of production. How competition operates. — 19 to 25. Usual shapes of indifference curves in exchange and in production; goods with increasing cost of production, and goods with decreasing cost. — 26. Equilibrium of tastes and production. — 27 to 31. Equilibrium in general. Closer approximation to the concrete phenomenon. — 32, 33. Properties of equilibrium. Maximum ophelimity. — 34 to 38. Properties of equilibrium in exchange. How maximum ophelimity is obtained. — 39 to 47. Properties of equilibrium in production. How maximum ophelimity is obtained. — 48. Argument in favor of collectivist production. — 49 to 51. How free competition operates to determine the coefficients of production and to attain the equality of all the net income of different capital. — 52 to 61. Economic equilibrium in the collectivist society. — 62, 63, 64. Maximum ophelimity for segments of collectivities. — 65 to 69. The pure theory of international trade. — 70. Equilibrium and prices. — 71 to 79. Quantity theory of money. Variation of prices. — 80 to 89. Relation between equilibrium, the prices of the factors of production, and the prices of products. — 90, 91. Subjective version of the phenomena studied. — 92. Economic circulation. — 93 to 96. Incorrect interpretations of competition between entrepreneurs. — 97 to 101. Erroneous conceptions of production.

CHAPTER VII.—POPULATION 281

§ 1. The economic phenomenon, its starting point and how it ends up with man. — 2. Social heterogeneity. — 3 to 10. The mean type and the distribution of deviations. The curve of errors. — 11 to 17. The income distribution curve. — 18 to 22. Social circulation — 23 to 25. Within certain limits of time and space, changes in the form of the income curve have been very slight. — 26. The lower portion has changed more than the upper portion. — 27 to 31. Theoretical consequences of these facts. — 32 to 45. Relationships between economic conditions and population. — 46, 47. Neglecting consideration of economic crises can lead to serious errors. — 48. Theory of correlation. — 49, 50. Effects of an increase in economic prosperity. — 51 to 56. The effect of variation in wealth can be completely different from the effect of its level. Study of the effect of the latter. — 57 to 60. Production of human capital. — 61. Cost of production of an adult. — 62 to 67. Obstacles to the generative force. Exceptional population increase in the 19th century. — 68 to 70. The means of subsistence and population. — 71 to 80. Nature of the obstacles. Their direct and indirect effects. — 81 to 88. Subjective view of phenomena related to population increase. — 89 to 96. Malthus and his theories. — 97 to 101. Human society in general. The main facts which determine its characteristics are: hierarchy, rise of aristocracies, selection, the average wealth or capital per person. — 102 to 103. Quantitative conditions regarding usefulness to society and to the individual. — 104 to 115. Stability and selection. The principle of stability and the principle of change. — 116, 117. Subjective interpretation of these facts.

CHAPTER VIII.—LAND CAPITAL AND MOBILE CAPITAL 321

§ 1. Land capital. — 2. Competition between segments of land capital. — 3, 4. Main characteristics; *rent.* — 5 to 7. Forms of ownership and relationships between those who own the land and those who work it. — 8. Mobile capital. — 9, 10. Savings. — 11. Production of savings is not determined by the income obtained from savings. — 12 to 16. Different types of savings, classified according to use. — 17 to 21. Income from savings and the social organization. — 22 to 25. Subjective version of these phenomena. — 26, 27, 28. So-called laws of the decline in the return from capital. — 29. Money; different kinds of money. — 30. Roles played by money. — 31 to 34. Foreign exchange. — 35 to 39. Exchange and international trade. A paper currency. Equivalent equilibrium positions. — 40. Gresham's Law. — 41. Bimetallism. — 42. Money substitutes. — 43. Metallic money is a small part of a country's wealth. — 44 and 45. Quantity of money in circulation; industrial consumption of gold and silver. — 46 to 50. Banks. The guaranty of the notes of banks of issue. The discount rate.

CHAPTER IX.—THE CONCRETE ECONOMIC PHENOMENON 337

§ 1. How we move from the study of the abstract phenomenon to that of the concrete phenomenon. — 2. Divergences between the abstract and the concrete phenomenon in consumption. — 3 to 6. Retailing and how its organization is disastrous for society. — 7. Variations in retail prices and wholesale prices. — 8 to 15. Trusts and syndicates. — 16. The collective contract in production. — 17 to 19. One part of the population devotes its efforts to appropriating the goods produced by the other part. — 20 to 22. This uniformity, which has been observed up to the present time, does not tend to disappear; it changes its form. — 23, 24. How and why high prices were looked on as disastrous in earlier times, whereas at present they are considered to be good for society. — 25 to 35. The evolution which leads to the establishment of a new caste. — 36 to 38. How the present, and probably the future, economic organization is a mixture of competition and monopoly. — 39. International trade. — 40. Economic theory of international trade. — 41. Theory of *markets*. — 42 to 52. Ricardo's theory of *comparative costs*. — 53. Export taxes. — 54. Import taxes. — 55. Indirect economic effects. — 56. Distribution effects. — 57. Social effects. — 58, 59. Fiscal effects. — 60. The complexity of the problem of free trade and protection. — 61. It is not enough to know that protection necessarily leads to a destruction of wealth in order to condemn it. — 62 to 66. Grounds for protection. — 62. Political economy does not provide any of these grounds. — 63 to 65. The composition of protectionist leagues. — 66. Opponents and supporters of protection. — 67. Protection cannot be rejected solely because those who demand it and profit from it are appropriating the goods of others. — 68. The effects of protection cannot be determined empirically. — 69. Exception; it confirms the theory. — 70. Empirical errors on the subject of protection. — 71, 72. How the destruction of wealth brought about by protection could be offset in certain cases by an increase in wealth brought about by other causes. — 73, 74. Economic crises. — 75. The crisis is only a particular case of the law of rhythm of economic and social phenomena. — 76, 77. How production adjusts itself to consumption. — 78, 79. Two main types of causes of economic crises. — 80. The upswing and the downswing. — 81. Crises produce less damage than is thought. — 82. Events concomitant with crises are erroneously regarded as the causes of crises. — 83, 84. So-called excess production, high velocity of circulation, use of credit. — 85 to 87. Symptoms of crises. Juglar's and Des Essars' theories. — 88. Jevon's theory.

APPENDIX 391

§ 1. Purpose of the Appendix. — 2 to 4. Indifference lines. — 5 to 7. Differential equation furnished by observation. — 8, 9. The integral of the equation and its correspondence with pleasure. — 10 to 19. How ophelimity can be deduced from observation. — 20, 21. The term ophelimity. — 22, 23. Equilibrium in the case of one individual and two goods. — 24, 25. Several economic goods. — 26, 27. Equation for the obstacles. — 28 to 33. One monopolist. — 34. Free competition. — 35. Comparison of the cases considered. — 36. Three goods. — 37. Prices. — 38. The budget. — 39. Variable prices. — 40. Example. — 41. Equilibrium for one individual, any number of goods, and constant prices. — 42. Ophelimity and the curves of supply and demand. — 43. Economic equilibrium deduced from curves of supply and demand. — 44, 45. Properties of indifference curves. — 46 to 50. Characteristics of the indices. — 51. Complexity of indifference lines. — 52 to 55. General laws of supply and of demand — 56 to 62. The error of economists who have regarded the ophelimity of money as constant. — 63 to 67. General case of exchange with constant prices. — 68. One monopolist and one good. — 69, 70. Two monopolists and one good. — 71. Two monopolists and two goods. — 72 to 76. Considerations regarding these different cases of monopoly. — 76b. Example. — 77. Production. — 78. The coefficients of production. — 79. Costs of production. — 80. Equilibrium of the consumers. — 81. Equilibrium of the enterprises. — 82. Equilibrium of production. — 83. Free competition. — 84 to 88. Monopoly in production. — 89. Definition of maximum ophelimity for a collectivity. — 90 to 92b. Determination of maximum ophelimity from production. — 93 to 100. Example. — 101 to 106. Variability of the coefficients of production. — 107. Division of quantities among the enterprises. — 108. Common errors on the subject of the coefficients of production. — 109 to 115. Properties of economic equilibrium and its relations to maximum ophelimity. — 116. The case of a single individual. — 117 to 120. The conditions for maximum ophelimity. — 121 to 126. Maximum ophelimity involving finite displacements. — 127 to 129. The economic meaning of maximum ophelimity. — 130 to 132. The theory as a whole: the restrictions. — 133. Decomposition of the economic system. — 134 to 136. The index functions. — 137. The indices of ophelimity. — 138. Index functions in general. — 139 to 141. Economic types. — 142. The second derivatives of the index functions. — 143. The system of equations which determines economic equilibrium. — 144. Properties of economic equilibrium; economic antagonisms. — 145 to 150. Maximum ophelimity. — 151. Finite variations. — 152. Different points of equilibrium.

CHAPTER I

GENERAL PRINCIPLES

1. Among the objectives which the study of political economy and sociology may have, the following three may be described briefly: 1° This study may consist of gathering together prescriptions which are useful to private individuals and public authorities in their economic and social activity. In this case the writer simply has this usefulness in mind, just as the author of a tract on raising rabbits merely has the objective of being useful to those who raise these little animals. 2° The writer may believe that he possesses a doctrine, an excellent one in his opinion, which should provide all kinds of benefits to the nation, or even to the human race, and he proposes to divulge it, as an apostle would do, in order to make people happy, or as a hallowed formula expresses it, "to do a little good." The purpose here again is usefulness, but a much more general and less prosaic usefulness. The difference between these two kinds of study is, in general, the difference between a collection of precepts and a treatise on morality. It is exactly the same, though in a less obvious way, when the doctrine which the writer considers the best is not expressly stated, and he declares simply that he studies phenomena in order to promote the good of humanity.[1] In the same way, the

---

[1] In 1904, M. B. deGreef still gives this definition (*Sociologie économique*, p. 101): "Economics is that fundamental part of social science whose object is the study and the understanding of the operation and the structure of the nutritive system of societies, with a view toward their preservation and also their improvement through the progressive reduction of human effort and of dead weight, and through the increase of useful results in the interest and for the common good of the individual and of the species organized into society."

1° First, it is strange that the writer gives us a metaphor (nutritive system) for a definition. 2° Is *economics* concerned with the production of poisons,

1

botanist would study vegetables in order to learn which are useful to man; the geometrist would study lines and surfaces with the measurement of land in mind, etc. It is true that the sciences began in this way. They were arts at first, but little by little they began to study phenomena independently of any other purpose. 3° The writer may intend only to search for the uniformities that phenomena present, that is to say their laws (§4), without having any direct practical usefulness in mind, without concerning himself in any way with giving recipes or precepts, without seeking the happiness, the benefit, or the well-being of humanity or of any part of it. In this case, the purpose is exclusively scientific; one wants *to know, to understand,* no more.

I ought to warn the reader that in this Manual I have in mind this third objective exclusively. It is not that I deprecate the other two; I simply intend to distinguish, to separate the methods, and to point out the one which will be adopted in this book.

I warn him also that I am striving as much as possible — and knowing how difficult it is, I fear I may not always achieve my goal — to use only words which clearly correspond to well defined real things, and never to use words which may bias the reader's mind. It is not, I repeat, that I want to disparage or deprecate that kind of procedure which, on the contrary, I hold to be the only one capable of instilling a belief in a great many individuals, and to which one must necessarily confine himself if he wishes that result. But in this work I am not seeking to convince anyone; I am simply investigating the uniformities of phenomena. Those who have another objective will have no trouble finding an infinity of works which will give them complete satisfaction; they need not read this one.

---

with the construction of railroads, of tunnels for railroads, of cuirasses, etc.? If not, what science is concerned with them? If yes, are all those things eaten by the society *(nutritive system)*? What an appetite! 3° Such a study is made with a practico-humanitarian purpose *(with a view toward);* hence his defininition is that of an art and not of a science. 4° We realize that definitions are not to be debated; neither should they contain a theorem. Our author has inserted some in his. He talks about the improvement which can be obtained by the reduction of *dead weight* (capitalists must make up a part of it, so there they are condemned by definition), and also about the *common good of the individual and of the species.* Thus, by definition, he gets rid of the difficult problem of knowing when this common good exists, and when, on the other hand, the good of the individual is opposed to the good of the species, or vice versa. We could make many more comments about this definition, but we will stop here.

2. In almost all branches of human knowledge phenomena have been studied from the points of view which we have just pointed out. The usual chronological order of these viewpoints corresponds to our enumeration; the first, however, is often intermingled with the second, and for certain very practical subjects the second is rarely used.

The work of Cato, *De re rustica*, belongs to the first type; in the preface, however, he occasionally takes the second point of view. Works published in England towards the end of the 18th century advocating new methods of cultivation belong partly to the second type, partly to the first. Tracts on agricultural chemistry and other similar sciences belong for the most part to the third type.

Pliny's *Natural History* gives prescriptions for physics and chemistry; what is found in books on alchemy are also prescriptions. On the other hand modern works on chemistry belong to the third type.

3. All three methods still are used in the majority of works devoted to political economy; science is not yet separated from art. Not only do people not clearly and frankly take the third point of view in tracts on political economy, but the majority of authors disapprove of the exclusive use of this method. Adam Smith declares plainly that "political economy, considered as a branch of the sciences of the statesman and the legislator, proposes two distinct objectives: first, to provide a plentiful revenue or subsistence for the people, or more properly to enable them to provide this plentiful revenue or subsistence for themselves; and secondly, to supply the state or commonwealth with a revenue sufficient for the public services. It proposes to enrich both the people and the sovereign." This would be taking our first point of view exclusively; fortunately Smith does not restrict himself to his definition and usually takes our third point of view.

John Stuart Mill declares that "economists take as their mission either to investigate or to teach the nature of wealth and the laws of its production and distribution." This definition reverts to the third type, but Mill often takes the second point of view and preaches on behalf of the poor.

M. Paul Leroy-Beaulieu says that he has returned to Adam Smith's method. Perhaps he even goes further: in his *Traité* he usually follows the first method, sometimes the second, rarely the third.

4. Human actions display certain uniformities [*uniformités*], and it is thanks to this property alone that they can be made the subject of a scientific study. These uniformities also have another name. They are called *laws*.

5. Whoever studies a social science, whoever asserts anything at all on the subject of the effects of such and such an economic, political or social measure, implicitly admits the existence of these uniformities; otherwise his study would not have any subject matter, and there would be no basis for his statements. If there were no uniformities, the budget of a state, of a commune, or even of an industrial company could not be drawn up even approximately.

Certain authors, while not admitting the existence of economic uniformities (laws), propose nevertheless to write the economic history of such and such a people; but that is an obvious contradiction. In order to make a choice between the multiplicity of facts which occur at a given time and to separate those to be retained from those to be disregarded, the existence of certain uniformities must be admitted. If we separate the facts A, B, C, . . . from facts M, N, P, . . ., it is because we have observed that the first ones appear together consistently, whereas they do not occur with the second group in a consistent way; and this assertion is the assertion of a law. If someone describing the sowing of wheat does not acknowledge that there are some uniformities, he will have to take up all of the details of the operation: for example he will have to tell us whether the sower has red or black hair, just as he tells us that one sows only after having plowed. Why is the first fact omitted and the second taken into account? Because, it is said, the first has nothing to do with the germination or the growth of the wheat. But what does that mean but that the wheat germinates and grows in the same way whether the sower has black or red hair, that is, that the combination of these two facts displays no uniformity. On the other hand a uniformity does exist between the fact that the ground has or has not been plowed and the other fact that the wheat comes up well or poorly.

6. When we assert that A has been observed at the same time as B, we ordinarily do not say whether we consider this simultaneity as fortuitous or not. Those who wish to formulate a system of political economy, while at the same time denying that it is a science, depend upon this ambiguity. If you point out to them that by asserting that A accompanies B they admit that there is a uniformity, a law, they reply: "We are simply recounting what took place." But after having secured acceptance of their proposition in this sense, they employ it in another, and declare that in the future A will be followed by B. But if, from the fact that the economic or social phenomena A and B have been united in certain cases in the past, one infers that they will be united in the future as well, he is clearly

asserting a uniformity, a law; and after that, it is ridiculous to deny the existence of economic and social laws.

If one does not admit that there are such uniformities, knowledge of the past and of the present is a mere curiosity, and nothing can be deduced from it about the future; the reading of a novel about chivalry or the *Three Musketeers* is as good as reading Thucydides's history. On the other hand, if one pretends to draw the slightest deduction about the future from knowledge of the past, this is admitting, at least implicitly, that there are uniformities.

7. Properly speaking, there can be no exceptions to economic and sociological laws, no more than to other scientific laws. A non-uniform uniformity does not make sense.

But scientific laws do not have an objective existence. The imperfection of our mind does not permit us to consider phenomena in their entirety,[2] and we are obliged to study them separately. Conse-

---

[2] At the time the Italian edition was published, a writer of great talent, M. Benedetto Croce, offered some criticisms which it is appropriate to note here, not with the object of polemics, for that is generally not very worth while, but because they can serve as examples to clarify the general theories.

The author just named observes: "What is this *imperfection* of the human mind? Could we know, by chance, *a perfect mind*, in comparison with which we can establish that the human mind is imperfect?"

We could reply that if the use of the term "imperfect" is licit only when one can, by contrast, point out something "perfect", the term "imperfect" must be banished from the dictionary because we will never find occasion for its use, perfection being not of this world, as they say.

But this reply would be only formal. We must get to the bottom of things and see what lies behind the words.

M. Croce, being Hegelian, evidently felt offended by the ill-sounding epithet of *imperfect* coupled with the human mind. The human mind could not be imperfect since it is the only thing which exists in this world.

But if one wants to take the trouble to investigate what the terms of our text express, he will perceive immediately that the meaning remains absolutely the same if, instead of saying "The imperfection of our mind does not permit us, etc.," we would say "The nature of our mind does not permit us, etc." In an objective rather than verbal discussion, it is useless then to cling to this term *imperfection*.

Then, he could protest, since you recognize that this term imperfection is not essential to express your idea, why not strike it out of the French edition? Thereby you would, at little expense, satisfy the admirers of the human mind.

That calls for some general observations which it is well to make once and for all.

The use of ordinary language, rather than the technical language which certain sciences possess, has great drawbacks, not the least of which is lack of precision. But it also has several advantages; and, while suffering the former, it is well to profit from the latter. Among these latter is the ability

quently, instead of general uniformities, which are and will always remain unknown, we are forced to consider an infinite number of partial uniformities, which overlap, are superimposed upon, and contradict one another in a thousand ways. When we consider one of these uniformities, and the fact that its effects are modified or hidden by the effects of other uniformities which we do not intend to consider, we ordinarily say, although the expression is inappropriate, that the uniformity or the law under consideration admits of exceptions. If this manner of speaking is accepted, physical laws and even mathematical laws[3] permit exceptions, just as economic laws do.

According to the law of gravity a feather thrown in the air must fall toward the center of the earth. But it often goes the other way due to the influence of the wind. One could say then that the law of gravity permits exceptions; but that is an improper statement which physicists do not employ. We are simply faced with other phenomena which are superimposed on those which the law of gravity considers.[4]

8. A law or a uniformity is true only under certain conditions which serve to indicate precisely which phenomena we wish to detach from the whole. For example, chemical laws which depend on affinity are different depending on whether or not the temperature remains within certain limits. Up to a certain temperature two

---

[3] Assume that a mathematician is able to observe Euclidian space and non-Euclidian space at the same time. He will note that the geometric theorems which depend on the postulate of Euclid are not true in the latter case, and consequently, accepting the manner of speech in question in the text, he will say that these theorems admit exceptions.

[4] *Systèmes*, II, p. 75 *et seq.* [Pareto's *Les systèmes socialistes*, 1902, reprinted in 1926 and 1965.]

---

to suggest by a word additional considerations, which, if developed at great length, would divert attention from the principal subject which one has in mind.

The use made here of the term imperfection suggests that it is a case of something capable of being more or less imperfect, and which varies gradually. Indeed, men are able to consider a more or less extensive portion of phenomena; certain synthesizing minds encompass a greater portion than other minds more inclined to analysis; but in any case, no one can grasp more than a part, often very limited, of the whole.

These considerations are accessories. They may find a place in a note; they cannot be inserted in the text without doing serious injury to the clarity of the discussion.

substances do not combine; above that temperature they do combine, but if the temperature increases again above a certain limit, they separate.

9. Some of these conditions are implicit, others explicit. Among the first should be included only those which are readily understood by everyone and do not have the slightest ambiguity. Otherwise it would be a riddle and not a scientific theorem. There is no proposition which cannot be guaranteed true under some set of conditions. The circumstances surrounding a phenomenon are an integral part of the phenomenon and cannot be separated from it.

10. We do not know and we can never know a concrete phenomenon in all its details. There is always a residue.[5] Now and then this is brought home to us in a striking way. For example, we thought we knew the composition of the atmosphere completely, and one fine day argon was discovered. And a little later, once on the track, many other gases in the atmosphere were discovered. What is simpler than the falling of a body? And yet we do not know nor will we ever know all the particulars.

11. Many consequences of great importance follow from the preceding observation.

---

[5] Here M. Croce asks: "And who will know it if not man?" All believers are punctilious on the subject of their faith; M. Croce must have seen here again (§ 7, note 1) a new blasphemy against the human mind. But truly, I had no evil intention of that kind. It is sufficient to read this paragraph, even very superficially, to see that it simply says that new details of a given phenomenon are continually coming to our attention. The example of the atmosphere seems to me to express this clearly.

Perhaps M. Croce believed that I wished to resolve in passing the grave question of the objective world. The partisans of the *existence* of an exterior world will express themselves by saying that argon existed before it was discovered; partisans of the existence of human concepts alone will say that it *existed* only from the day when it was discovered.

I ought to warn the reader that I do not at all intend to devote myself to this type of discussion. Hence one should not search through what is written in this volume for any solution to those problems, which I abandon entirely to the metaphysicians.

I will repeat that I only fight the invasion by the metaphysicians of the territory of the θεωρία φυσιχή,— this term being understood as all that is real —; if they stay outside, beyond the θεωρία φυσιχή, I have no wish to molest them and I even admit that they achieve, in this sphere only, results which are inaccessible to those of us adept at the experimental method.

Finally, this question of the intrinsic value of certain doctrines has nothing to do with their social utility. There is no relation between the one and the other.

Since we do not know any concrete phenomenon completely, our theories about these phenomena are only approximations. We only know ideal phenomena, which more or less approximate the concrete phenomena. We are in the position of a person who knows an object only by means of photographs. However perfect they may be, they always differ in some way from the object itself. Hence we should never judge the value of a theory by investigating whether it deviates in some way from reality because no theory withstands or will ever withstand that test.

It must be added that theories are only means for knowing and for studying phenomena. One theory may be good for accomplishing a certain purpose; another for accomplishing another purpose. But in any case they must be in accord with the facts, for otherwise they would have no usefulness.

It is necessary to substitute quantitative study for qualitative study and investigate the extent to which the theory departs from reality. Of two theories we will choose the one which departs from it the least. We will never forget that a theory should only be accepted provisionally. One we hold true today will have to be abandoned tomorrow if another one which comes closer to reality is discovered. Science is in perpetual development.

12. It would be absurd to make the existence of Mont Blanc an objection to the theory that the earth is spherical; i.e. the height of that mountain is negligible relative to the diameter of the terrestial sphere.[6]

13. By representing the earth as a sphere we come closer to reality than by imagining it to be a plane or a cylinder, as certain persons did in antiquity[7]; consequently, the theory of the sphericity of the earth must be preferred to that of a flat or cylindrical earth.

By representing the earth as an ellipsoid of revolution we come closer to reality than by considering it spherical. Hence it is worth while that the ellipsoidal theory has replaced the spherical one.[8]

---

[6] Pliny was mistaken in his estimate of the height of the Alps; accordingly, with reference to the observation of Dicaearchus that the height of the mountains is negligible compared to the size of the earth, he said: *Mihi incerta hàec videtur conjectatio, haud ignaro quosdam Alpium vertices, longo tractu, nec breviore quinquaginta millibus pasuum assurgere. Hist. Mundi*, II, 65. We would thus have a height of about 74,000 meters, whereas in reality Mont Blanc is only 4,810 meters.

[7] Anaximenes believed it a plane; Anaximander believed it a cylinder.

[8] Paul Tannery, *Recherches sur l'histoire de l'astronomie ancienne*, p. 106, speaking of the postulate of the sphericity of the earth, says: "Nevertheless,

But even this ellipsoidal theory must be abandoned today, because modern geodesy teaches us that the shape of the terrestrial spheroid is much more complex. Each day new studies bring us closer to reality.

Nevertheless, for some approximate calculations, we still use the ellipsoidal form. In doing so we commit an error, but we know that it is less than other errors to which these studies are subject, so we may disregard the differences between the ellipsoid and the terrestrial spheroid in order to simplify the calculations.

14. This manner of approaching reality by theories which are ever more in accord with it, and which in consequence generally become more and more complex, is called the method of *successive approximations*. It is used, implicitly or explicitly, in all the sciences (§ 30, note).

15. Another consequence. It is wrong to believe that the exact properties of concrete facts can be discovered by studying our *a priori* ideas about these facts without modifying such concepts by comparing *a posteriori* the results with the facts. This error is analogous to the one which a farmer would make if he imagined that he could judge the benefit of buying a piece of property which he only knew about by means of a photograph.

The notion which we have of a concrete phenomenon agrees with that phenomenon on some points but differs from it on others. An equality which exists between the conceptions of two phenomena does not make the phenomena themselves equal.

It is quite obvious that any phenomenon whatsoever can be known only through the idea which it gives rise to within us; but precisely because we thus get only an imperfect image of the reality, we must always compare the subjective phenomenon, that is, the theory, with the objective phenomenon, that is, with the experimental fact.

16. Moreover, since they exist within us, the ideas we have of phenomena, without other experimental verification, make up the materials most readily at our disposal. Occasionally we can make something out of these materials. As a result, especially in the beginnings of a science, men have an irresistible tendency to reason about

---

considering its objective part, it had the value of a first approximation, just as, for us, the hypothesis of the ellipsoid of revolution constitutes a second approximation. The great difference is that as a consequence of the measures and observations obtained at different points of the globe, we can assign limits to the differences between that approximation and reality, whereas the ancients could not seriously do so."

the ideas which they already have about the facts, without bothering to correct those ideas by means of experimental investigations. Similarly they want to find in etymology the properties of the things expressed by the words. They experiment on the names of things instead of experimenting on the things themselves. Certain truths may indeed be discovered that way, but only when the science is in its beginnings. When it has developed a bit that method becomes absolutely fruitless; and in order to acquire ideas which approach ever closer to the facts, we must study the latter directly and no longer by regarding them through certain *a priori* notions, or through the meaning of the words which are used to designate them.

17. All the natural sciences now have reached the point where the facts are studied directly. Political economy also has reached it, in large part at least. It is only in the other social sciences that people still persist in reasoning about words[9]; but we must get rid of that method if we want these sciences to progress.

---

[9] M. Croce observes: "As if even the *Manuel* of M. Pareto were not a tissue of *conceptions* and of *words!* Man thinks by means of conceptions and expresses them by means of words!"

This is another verbal criticism, such as those we have already noted (§ 7, note; § 10, note). It is quite obvious that we never intended to deny that any work is a tissue of conceptions and words, but that we meant to distinguish words behind which there are only fancies from words behind which lie realities.

Now if any metaphysician is shocked by the term "realities," I can only advise him not to continue reading this book. I warn him — if he has not already perceived it — that we are speaking two different languages such that neither of us understands that of the other. For my part, I believe I am sufficiently clear in saying that we must distinguish a real gold louis from an imaginary gold louis; and if anyone asserts there are no differences, I would propose to him a simple exchange: I will give him some imaginary gold louis, and he will give me some real ones.

Finally, leaving aside all debate about ways of naming things, there are several types of "tissues of conceptions and words." There is a type which is customary with metaphysicians, and which I try to stay as far away from as possible; there is another type which is found in works on the physical sciences, and this is the type I wish to approximate in dealing with the social sciences.

Hegel says: "The typical crystal is the diamond, that product of the earth at the sight of which the eye rejoices because there it sees the first born of light and weight. The light is the abstract identity and completely free. The air is the identity of the elements. The subordinate identity is an identity passive to the light, and that is the transparency of the crystal." (That translation [into French] does not belong to me [Pareto], it is by an eminent Hegelian, A. Vera, *Philosophie de la nature*, II, p. 21).

This explanation of transparency must be excellent, but I humbly avow

18. Another consequence. The method of reasoning, which could be called *by elimination*, and which still is often employed in the social sciences, is incorrect. Here is what it consists of: a concrete phenomenon X has a certain property Z. According to what we already know, this phenomenon is composed of parts A, B, and C. We prove the Z belongs neither to B nor to C, and conclude that it necessarily must belong to A.

The conclusion is incorrect because the enumeration of the parts of X never is and never can be complete. In addition to A, B, and C, which we know — or which the author of the reasoning only knows, or which he only considers — there may be others D, E, F, . . ., which we are unaware of or which the author of the reasoning has omitted.[10]

19. Another consequence. When the results of theory pass into practice, we can be sure that they will always be somewhat modified by other results which depend on phenomena not considered by the theory.

20. From this point of view there are two large classes of sciences: those like physics, chemistry, and mechanics which can resort to experiment, and those like meteorology, astronomy, and political economy which cannot, or can do so only with difficulty, and must be content with observation. The former can physically separate the phenomena which correspond to the uniformity or law which they want to study; the latter can separate them only mentally, theoretically. But in both cases, it is always the concrete phenomenon which determines whether a theory should be accepted or rejected. There is not, and there cannot be, any other criterion of the validity of a

---

[10] *Systèmes*, II, p. 252.

---

that I understand none of it, and it is a model that I am very desirous not to imitate.

Hegel's demonstration of the laws of celestial mechanics (*Systèmes*, II, p. 72) seems to me to be the height of absurdity, whereas I understand perfectly books such as *Les méthodes nouvelles de la mécanique céleste*, by H. Poincaré. When that author says: "The final end of celestial mechanics is to resolve that great question of whether Newton's law explains all the astronomical phenomena by itself alone; the only means of attaining that is to make observations as precise as possible and then compare them to the results of the calculations" (I, p. 1), I find "a tissue of conceptions and words" very different from those I have met with in Hegel, Plato and other similar authors. And my purpose is to make, with regard to the social sciences, "observations as precise as possible and then compare them to the results of theories."

An author owes it to his readers to warn them of the route which he intends to follow; and it is solely for that purpose that I have written this first chapter.

theory than its more or less complete accord with concrete phenomena.

When we speak of the experimental method, we are expressing ourselves in an elliptical manner and we mean the method which makes use either of experiment or of observation, or of the two together if that is possible.

Those sciences which are only able to utilize observation separate certain phenomena from certain others by abstraction. The sciences which can also use experiment achieve this abstraction physically; but abstraction is, for all the sciences, the preliminary and indispensable requirement for all research.

21. This abstraction is the result of subjective necessities; there is nothing objective about it; therefore it is arbitrary, at least within certain limits, because the purpose which the abstraction has to serve must be taken into account. Consequently a certain abstraction or a certain classification does not necessarily exclude another abstraction or another classification. Both can be used depending on the purpose one has in mind.

Rational mechanics, when it reduces bodies to simple physical points, and pure economics, when it reduces real men to the *homo oeconomicus*, make use of completely similar abstractions,[11] imposed by similar necessities.

Chemistry also makes use of an abstraction when it talks about chemically pure substances, but it has the possibility of artificially obtaining real substances which more or less realize that abstraction.

22. An abstraction can assume two exactly equivalent forms. In the first, one considers an abstract entity which possesses only the qualities which one wants to study; in the second, these properties are considered directly and separated from the others.

23. The real man performs economic, moral, religious, esthetic, etc., actions. Exactly the same idea is expressed whether one says: "I study the economic actions, and abstract from the others," or "I study *homo oeconomicus*, who performs only economic actions." Similarly, the following two forms express the same idea: "I study the reactions of concrete sulphur and oxygen, abstracting from the foreign bodies which they may contain," or "I study the relations of chemically pure sulphur and oxygen."

The same substance which I consider as chemically pure in chemistry, I may consider as a physical point in mechanics. I may consider only the shape in geometry, etc. The same man I consider

---

[11] Vito Volterra, *Giornale degli economisti*, November 1901.

as *homo oeconomicus* in economics, I can consider as *homo ethicus* in a work on morality, as *homo religiosus* in a work on religion, etc.

The concrete substance includes the chemical substance, the mechanical substance, the geometric substance, etc.; the real man includes the *homo oeconomicus*, the *homo ethicus*, the *homo religiosus*, etc. In sum, to consider these different substances, these different men, amounts to considering the different properties of this real substance, of this real man, and seeks only to carve the material into pieces for study.

24. One is grossly mistaken then when he accuses a person who studies economic actions — or *homo oeconomicus* — of neglecting, or even of scorning moral, religious, etc., actions — that is the *homo ethicus*, the *homo religiosus*, etc.—; it would be the same as saying that geometry neglects and scorns the chemical properties of substances, their physical properties, etc. The same error is committed when political economy is accused of not taking morality into account. It is like accusing a theory of the game of chess of not taking culinary art into account.

25. In studying A separately from B we implicitly submit to an absolute necessity of the human mind; but because we study A, we do not mean to assert its preeminence over B. In separating the study of political economy from that of morality, we do not intend to assert that the former matters more than the latter. In writing a tract on the game of chess one certainly does not intend to assert thereby the preeminence of the game of chess over the culinary art, or over any science or any art.

26. When we return to the concrete from the abstract, the parts which had been separated in order to study them better must be united again. Science is essentially analytic; practice is essentially synthetic.[12]

Political economy does not have to take morality into account. But one who extols some practical measure ought to take into account not only the economic consequences, but also the moral, religious, political, etc., consequences. Rational mechanics does not have to take into account the chemical properties of substances; but one who wants to foresee what will take place when a given substance is put in contact with another substance should take into account not only the results of mechanics, but also those of chemistry, physics, etc.

---

[12] There will be an example — in which, however, the synthesis is not yet complete — in Chapter IX, where we discuss free trade and protection.

27. For certain concrete phenomena the economic side matters more than all the others. In such a case, one can, without serious error, restrict himself to the results of economic science alone. There are other concrete phenomena in which the economic side is insignificant, and there it would be absurd to restrict oneself to the results of economic science alone. Quite the contrary, they should be disregarded. There are intermediate phenomena between those two types; and economic science will reveal a more or less important aspect of them. In all cases, it is a question of degree, of more or less.

In other words we can say: sometimes the actions of the concrete man are, except for a slight error, those of the *homo oeconomicus;* sometimes they accord almost exactly with those of the *homo ethicus;* sometimes they agree with those of the *homo religiosus*, etc.; at still other times they partake of the actions of all these men.

28. When an author is not mindful of this observation, it is customary to attack him by putting theory and practice into opposition. This is a faulty way of expressing oneself. Practice is not opposed to theory; rather it combines the different theories which apply to the case under consideration and uses them for a real life purpose.

The economist, for example, who in commending a law takes into consideration its economic effects alone, is not very much of a theorist. He is not theoretical enough because he is neglecting other theories which he should combine with his own in order to make a judgment in this practical case. One who praises free trade, restricting himself to its economic effects, is not constructing a faulty theory of international commerce, but rather is making an incorrect application of an intrinsically true theory. His error consists of disregarding other political and social effects, which are the subjects of other theories.[13]

---

[13] G. Sorel is partly right when he says: "The statesman will ordinarily be impressed very little by a demonstration which proves to him that protectionism always destroys wealth, if he believes that protectionism is the least expensive means for acclimatizing industry and the spirit of enterprise in his country. . . ." (*Introduction à l'économie moderne*, p. 26). In place of that qualitative comparison, it is necessary to substitute a quantitative comparison and say "I will lose so many millions per year, and I will gain so many," and then decide. If in this way 500 millions of wealth per year are destroyed in order to gain only 100, it would be a poor bargain. I note again that Sorel poses the problem only from the economic point of view, and that there is a very important social and political side which must also be taken into account.

29. Separating the different parts of a phenomenon in order to study them individually, then putting them together again by a synthesis, is a procedure which is followed, and can be followed, only when a science is already quite advanced. In the beginning all the parts are studied at the same time, analysis and synthesis are intermingled.

That is one of the reasons why sciences first arise in the form of art, and it is also one of the reasons why, as they progress, sciences are separated and subdivided.

30. Sorel, in his *Introduction à l'économie moderne*, proposes returning to that state of the science in which analysis is not distinguished from synthesis, and his endeavor is understandable if we consider the not very advanced state of the social sciences; but that is going up the river toward its source, and not following its course downstream. Moreover, it must be noted that one thereby is implicitly theorizing. Indeed Sorel does not have in mind only describing the past, he wants to know the future as well. But as we have already pointed out, the future can be connected to the past only if certain uniformities are acknowledged, either explicitly or implicitly; and these uniformities can be known only through scientific analysis.[14]

---

[14] Sorel says, *op. cit.*, p. 25: "One could not . . . imagine a method of successive approximations for solving the question of whether it is better to marry a young girl who is intelligent but poor or a rich but feeble-minded heiress."

Let us note first of all that the problem posed is a problem of private concern and ordinarily is solved, not by reason, but by sentiment. If one wants to use reasoning, however, we can devise quite well the method that could be followed.

1st approximation.—We will examine the material and moral conditions of the future husband and wife. If the man, for example, values material goods more than intellectual faculties, it would be right for him to marry the rich heifess.

2nd approximation.— Let us examine the qualities of that wealth more closely. In former times, if the man and the woman had neighboring properties, a marriage which united those properties was considered very advantageous. Let us inquire whether the woman having the fortune does not by chance have the habit of spending more than her income. What is the nature of the intelligence of the one who is poor? If she has business aptitudes, and if the future husband is the head of a commercial or industrial organization which he is unable to direct and which the woman could direct properly, it may be advantageous for him to take the poor but intelligent woman.

3rd approximation.—We have spoken of the wealth and the intelligence; but is no account to be taken of health, beauty, sweetness of character, etc.?

31. Completely negative criticism of a theory is absolutely fruitless and sterile; in order for it to have any usefulness, the negation must be followed by something affirmative; a more accurate theory must be substituted for the false theory. If sometimes this is not done, it is simply because the more exact theory is taken for granted.

If someone denies that the earth is flat, he certainly is not increasing the sum of our knowledge as he would do if he declared that the earth is not flat but round.

Let us note, however, that if we want to be completely rigorous, every theory is false in the sense that it does not agree with and can never agree with reality (§ 11). Hence it is a pleonasm to repeat for one particular theory what is true for all theories. We do not have to choose between one theory which comes fairly close to the concrete and one which corresponds to the concrete in every way, since the latter does not exist, but between two theories one of which comes closer to the concrete than the other.

32. It is not only because of our ignorance that theories deviate more or less from the concrete. We often depart from the concrete in order to attain more simplicity in exchange for that deviation.

The difficulties which we encounter in the study of a phenomenon are of two kinds, objective and subjective. They depend on the nature of the phenomenon and on the difficulties we have in perceiving a rather extensive set of objects or of particular theories.

The economic phenomenon is exceedingly complex, and there are great objective difficulties to knowing the theories of its different parts. Let us assume, for a moment, that we have overcome these difficulties, and that, for example, the laws of the prices of all commodities are contained in certain great folio volumes. We will be far from having an idea of the phenomenon of price. The abundance of information in all these volumes would itself prevent us from having any notion whatsoever of the phenomenon of price. When someone, having perused all these documents, would tell us that *the demand falls when the price rises*, he would be giving us very

---

For many, these qualities will take first place. And an infinite number of circumstances still remain to be considered.

If the problem were social instead of individual, that is to say, if it is asked whether it is useful for society that young men consider the choice of their spouse by pre-occupying themselves with her wealth or her intelligence, one would arrive at some analogous considerations which consist essentially of analysis (separation of the parts), successive approximations and finally synthesis, that is, the rejoining of the elements previously separated.

valuable information, although departing a great deal more, a very great deal more, from the concrete than the documents he studied.

And so the economist, as all those who study very complex phenomena, must in each case solve the problem of deciding how far it is appropriate to go in the study of details. The point at which it is desirable to stop cannot be determined absolutely. That point depends on the purpose one has in mind. The producer of bricks who wants to know at what price he will be able to sell them must take into account elements other than those which are considered by the scholar who is seeking the general law of the prices of building materials. Still other elements must be considered by one who is seeking not the laws of particular prices, but rather the law of prices in general.

33. Studies of the origin of economic phenomena have been carefully made by many modern scholars, and they are certainly useful from the historical point of view; but it would be an error to believe that we could thus arrive at a knowledge of the relations which exist among the phenomena of our own society.

This is the same error committed by the ancient philosophers who always wanted to go back to the origin of things. Instead of astronomy, they studied cosmogonies; instead of trying to learn something in an experimental fashion about the minerals, vegetables, and animals which they had before their eyes, they sought the way those entities had originated. Geology did not become a science and did not progress until someone set out to study the existing phenomena, in order then to go back to past phenomena, instead of going in the opposite direction. In order to know a tree completely we can begin with the roots and go up to the leaves, or begin with the leaves and work down to the roots. Older metaphysical science largely took the first route; modern experimental science has used the second exclusively; and the facts have demonstrated that the latter alone leads to knowledge of the truth.

To know how private property was constituted in prehistoric times is of no help in understanding the economic role of property in our modern societies. It is not that the one of these facts is not intimately connected to the other, but the chain which unites them is so long and is lost in regions so obscure that we cannot reasonably hope to understand it, at least for the time being.

We do not know from what savage plant wheat derives; but even if we did, it would be of no use in learning the best way to cultivate and produce wheat. Study the seeds of the oak, the beech, and the linden as much as you like; for one who needs construction timber, such a study will never be able to replace the direct study of the qualities of the wood produced by these trees. And yet, in this case, we know perfectly the relation between the extremities of the phenomenon, between the origin and the end. It is not to be doubted that the acorn will produce the oak. No one has ever seen an acorn produce a linden, nor a linden seed produce an oak. The relation between the oak wood and its origin is known with a certitude which we will never have regarding the connection between the origin of private property and property in our times, or in general between the origin of any economic phenomenon and that phenomenon in our times. But to know which of two facts is necessarily the consequence of the other is not enough to be able to deduce the properties of the one from those of the other.

34. The study of the evolution of economic phenomena in periods close to our own and in societies which do not differ greatly from our own is much more useful than the study of their origin. And this is so from two points of view. First of all it permits us to substitute for direct experiments which are impossible in the social sciences. When we can make experiments, we try to produce the phenomenon which is the subject of our study in varied circumstances, in order to see how these circumstances act on it, whether they modify it or not. But when we cannot proceed in that way, the only alternative is to see whether we find these experiments, which we cannot realize artificially, occurring naturally in space and time.

The study of the evolution of phenomena can also be useful in that it facilitates discovery of uniformities which that evolution may display; and it puts us in a position to derive a forecast of the future from the past. It is obvious that the longer the chain of deductions between past facts and future facts, the more uncertain and doubtful these deductions become. Thus only from a very recent past can we forecast a very near future and, unhappily, even within these narrow limits, forecasts are very difficult.[15]

35. Disputes about the "method" of political economy are useless. The goal of the science is to know the uniformities of phenomena. Consequently, it is necessary to employ all procedures and utilize all methods which lead us toward that goal. The good and bad methods are discovered by trial. One which leads us to the goal is good—at least as long as a better one has not been found. History is useful in that it extends the experience of the past into the present

[15] *Cours*, § 578. [Vilfredo Pareto, *Cours d'économie politique professé a l'université de Lausanne*, Vol. I, 1896, Vol. II, 1897, reprinted 1964.]

and supplies experiments which we are unable to make; hence the historical method is good. But the deductive method, or the inductive method, which is applied to present facts, is no less worthy. Where ordinary logic is adequate in deductions, we are satisfied with it; where it is not we replace it, without any qualms, by the mathematical method. In short, if an author prefers such or such a method, we will not quibble about it. We will simply ask him to show us the scientific laws, without caring too much about how he came to know them.

36. Certain authors are accustomed to saying that political economy cannot use the same methods as the natural sciences "because it is a moral science." Some thoughts which are worth analyzing lurk beneath this very imperfect way of speaking. First of all, with regard to the *truth* of a theory, there can be no other criterion than its accord with the facts (II, 6), and there is only one way to recognize that accord. From this point of view no differences could be found between political economy and the other sciences.

But certain persons maintain that beyond this experimental truth there is another, which escapes experiment, and which they consider superior to the first. Those who have the time to waste may indeed wrangle about words. Those who aspire to something more substantial will refrain from it. We will not quarrel with the use which anyone wants to make of the word "truth", we will simply say that all propositions can be divided into two categories. Into the first, which, to be brief, we will call X, we will put affirmations which can be verified experimentally; into the second, which we will call Y, we will put those which cannot be verified experimentally. In addition we will subdivide this last category into two. Affirmations which cannot be verified experimentally at the present time but which could be some day will be called Yα. Into that category will go, for example, the claim that some day the sun, with its retinue of planets, will carry us into four dimensional space. Affirmations which neither now nor later, as far as can be foreseen with our limited knowledge, can be subjected to experimental verification, will be called Yβ. Into this category would go the assertion of the immortality of the soul, and other similar assertions.

37. Science only deals with propositions X, which are the only ones amenable to proof; everything which is not included in this category X remains outside of science. We certainly do not propose, however, to exalt one category in order to deprecate the other, we only want to distinguish them. Let the scientific propositions be deprecated as much as one wants, and the others be exalted as much as

the most fervent believer desires, it will still remain true that they are essentially different from each other. They occupy different domains which have nothing in common.

38. One who asserts that Pallas Athena, *invisible and intangible*, inhabits the Acropolis of the city of Athens, asserts something which, since it cannot be verified experimentally, is outside of science. The latter is unable to deal with this assertion, either to accept it or to reject it; and the believer is quite right to disdain the assertions which a psuedo-science would attempt to set in opposition to it. It is the same with the proposition: Apollo inspires the priestess of Delphi; but not for this other proposition, that the oracles of the priestess agree with certain future facts. This last proposition can be verified by observation; consequently it comes within the domain of science, and faith has nothing more to do with it.

39. Anything which has the appearance of a precept is not scientific, unless the form alone has the appearance of a precept and in reality it is an affirmation of facts. These two propositions are essentially different: to obtain the area of a rectangle, *one must* multiply the base by the height;[16] and, *one must* love his neighbor as himself.[17] In the first, we can suppress the words *one must*, and simply say the area of a rectangle is equal to the base multiplied by the height; in the second, the idea of obligation cannot be suppressed. This second proposition is not scientific.

Political economy tells us that bad money drives out the good. That proposition belongs to the scientific order, and it is for science alone to verify whether it is true or false. But if it were said that the

---

[16] From our point of view geometric truths are experimental truths, logic itself being experimental.

Moreover it may be noted, in this case, that the area of a concrete rectangle will approximate the product of the base times the height better than the concrete rectangle will approximate the abstract rectangle considered by geometry.

[17] It has been objected that "all *honest men* think so." First, this is a different proposition from the one in the text. The two propositions "A is equal to B" and "All men—or certain men—think that A is equal to B, or must be equal to B" express completely different things.

Next, it is a known fact that there are some men—such as, for example, the disciples of Nietzsche—who are far from admitting that proposition. If one replies that they are not "honest men," one is precluded from giving a proof—which appears to us to be very difficult if not impossible—which will not, in the final analysis, reduce to asserting that they are not honest men because they do not love their neighbor; if one gives that proof he is simply reasoning in a circle.

state *should not* issue bad money, that would be a proposition which does not belong to the scientific order. Since political economy has up to now contained propositions of that type, we can find an excuse for those who maintain that political economy, being a moral science, is not subject to the rules of the natural sciences.

40. Let us note in addition that this last proposition could be elliptical and, in that case, it could become scientific by removing the ellipsis. For example, if it were said that the state *should not* issue bad money if obtaining maximum utility for society is desired, and if what is meant by this *maximum utility* were defined by means of facts, the proposition would become amenable to experimental verification and consequently would become a scientific proposition (§ 49, note).

41. It is absurd to assert, as some people do, that their belief is *more scientific* than that of others. Science and faith have nothing in common, and the latter cannot contain either more or less of the former. A new faith has sprung up in our day which asserts that every human being *ought* to sacrifice himself to the good "of the small and the humble," and its believers speak with scorn of other creeds which they consider not very scientific. These good people do not perceive that their precept has no more scientific foundation than any other religious precept.

42. From the remotest times to the present day, men have always wanted to mix together and confound propositions X and Y, and that is one of the most serious obstacles to the progress of the social sciences.

Those who believe in propositions Y constantly encroach upon the domain of propositions X. For most people this comes from not distinguishing between the two domains; for many others the weakness of their faith calls for the assistance of facts of experience. The materialists are wrong to ridicule the *credo quia absurdum*, which, in a certain sense, admits this distinction between the propositions. Dante has expressed this very well: [18]

> State contenti, umana gente, al *quia;*
> Chè se potuto aveste veder tutto,
> Mestier non era partorir Maria.

43. We must be on guard against a certain way of confounding propositions X and Y, which rests on an ambiguity similar to the

---

[18] *Purgatorio*, III, 37-39. And *Paradiso*, II, 43-44.
> Li si vedra ció che tenem per fede,
> Non dimostrato, ma fia per se noto,
> A guisa del ver primo che l'uom crede.

one in § 40. Let us assume that the proposition "A is B" is not in the domain of experience, and consequently, of science; some think they are giving a scientific proof of it by showing the utility which men derive from believing that A is B. But these propositions are not at all identical; and even if experience does show that this second proposition is true, we can conclude nothing thereby about the first one. Certain persons assert that only the *truth* is useful, but if the word *truth* is given the meaning of *experimental truth*, that proposition is not in accord with the facts, which contradict it at every turn.

44. Here is another ambiguous procedure. Some people show, or more exactly they think they show, that "evolution" brings A nearer to B, and they think they have thus demonstrated that everyone *should* try to make A be equal to B, or even that A is equal to B. These are three different propositions, and the demonstration of the first does not entail the demonstration of the others. Let us add that ordinarily the demonstration of the first is very imperfect.[19]

45. Confusion between propositions X and Y may also come from the fact that some people try to show that, since they may have a common origin, they have one nature and common characteristics. That is an old procedure, which reappears from time to time. This common origin has sometimes been found in universal consent or something similar; in our day it is found most often in *intuition*.

Logic is useful for proof but almost never for making discoveries (§ 51). A man receives certain impressions; under their influence he states—without being able to say either how or why, and if he attempts to do so he deceives himself—a proposition which can be verified experimentally and, consequently, is the type of proposition which we call X. When that verification has been made, and the fact develops as predicted, the operation we have just described is called INTUITION. If a peasant looking at the evening sky says, "It will rain tomorrow," and if it does rain tomorrow, one says that he had an intuition that it must rain; but one would not say that if the weather had been good. If an individual experienced with sick persons remarks about one of them, "Tomorrow he will be dead", and if indeed the sick person does die, it will be said that this individual had an intuition of that death; this could not be said if the sick person had recovered.

As we have already said so often, and will repeat again, it is completely useless to argue about the names of things. Consequently, if it pleases someone to give the name intuition also to the operation

---

[19] *Systèmes*, I, p. 344; *Cours*, II, 578.

whereby one predicts rain when the weather is then fair, or the death of someone who then recovers, he is free to do so. But in that case false intuitions must be distinguished from true ones; experimental verification does this; the first ones will not be useful, the second will be.

The same process which yields propositions amenable to experimental verification, and which can be identified as true or false, also may lead to propositions not amenable to experimental verification. And, if desired, this process may be called *intuition*.

Thus we will have three kinds of intuition: 1° intuition which leads to propositions X, which experiment then verifies; 2° intuition which leads to propositions X, which experiment then does not verify; 3° intuition which leads to propositions of type Y, and which, consequently, experiment can neither verify nor contradict.

Thus by giving the same name to three quite different things, it becomes easy to confound them. Some people deliberately confound the third and the first by conveniently forgetting the second. They say, "by intuition man achieves a knowledge of the *truth*, whether it be experimental or not", and in this way they have attained the desired goal, which is to confuse propositions X with propositions Y.

If Pericles had been asked the following two questions: "What do you believe the Athenians will do in such and such circumstances?" and "Do you believe that Pallas Athena protects your city?," he would have given, by intuition, two answers having entirely different natures, because the first could be verified experimentally, whereas the second could not be.

The origin of these replies is the same; they are both, without Pericles being conscious of it, the translation of certain of his impressions. But that translation has a quite different value in these two cases. Pericles's opinion about the first question had great value, whereas the opinion of some Scythian who did not know the Athenians would have been worth nothing. But on the second question, the opinion of Pericles and that of the Scythian had the same value for, to tell the truth, neither of them had any contact with Pallas Athena.

Pericles had had many occasions to verify, correct, and revise his predictions on the subject of the Athenians; and the result of his past experience was translated into a new intuition, deriving all its value from this past experience; but it could not be the same with regard to Pallas Athena.

If someone who knows nothing about arboriculture tells us that a tree he has seen is going to die, we will attach no more importance to his words than if he had spoken them by chance. If, on the other hand, it is a judgment given by an experienced arboriculturist, we will consider his intuition to be worth while because it is based on experience. And even if these two men have the same *a priori* knowledge but we know by experience that the latter is rarely mistaken in his predictions or intuitions, and that the former, on the contrary, is very often mistaken, we will place a confidence in the second which we will deny the first. But where experience cannot enter into it, the predictions or intuitions of both of them will have the same value, and that value is experimentally equal to zero.

Intuitions regarding facts of experience can be contradicted by the facts themselves; hence the intuitions must adapt themselves to the facts. Non-experimental intuitions are contradicted only by other intuitions of the same type; for there to be adaptation, it is enough that certain men all have the same opinion. The first adaptation is objective; the second, subjective. If the one is confounded with the other, it comes from that common error by which man considers himself the center of the universe and the measure of all things.

46. The universal consent of men does not have the faculty of making experimental a proposition which is not so, even if this consent stretches through time, and if it includes all men who have existed. Thus the principle that what is not conceivable cannot be real is absolutely worthless, and it is absurd to imagine that what is possible in the universe is limited by the capacity of the human mind.

47. Metaphysicians, who use propositions Y, ordinarily assert that they are necessary in order to draw any conclusions whatsoever from propositions X, because, without a superior principle, the conclusion would not follow *necessarily* from the premises. They thereby set up a vicious circle, precisely because they assume that we want to put propositions X in the category of propositions which have a character of *necessity* and of absolute truth[20]; and, indeed, it is correct that if one wants to give the characteristics of propositions Y to

---

[20] I am using these expressions because they use them, but what they mean by these words is not very clear to me.

M. Croce invites me to learn, and, in order to do so, to read Plato, Aristotle, Descartes, Liebnitz, Kant and other metaphysicians. Alas! I must give up hope that my ignorance can ever be dispelled, for it is precisely after an attentive study of these writers that this term *absolute* has appeared incomprehensible to me . . . and, I fear, to them as well.

In addition I ought to confess that it seems to me that much of Plato's

any consequence of category X, the former must enter into either the premises or the method of drawing the conclusion. But if one maintains that propositions X are closely dependent on experience and are never accepted conclusively but only as long as experience does not contradict them, there is no need to resort to propositions Y. From this point of view, logic itself is looked upon as an experimental science.

48. Furthermore, those who deal with propositions X also often encroach upon the territory of propositions Y, either by giving precepts in the name of "science," which appears to give oracles as if it were a God, or by denying propositions Y, over which science has no authority. It is that encroachment which partially justifies M. Brunetière's claim that "science has failed." Science has never failed as long as it has stayed in its own domain, which is that of propositions X; it has always failed, and it always will fail, when it has encroached, or when it shall encroach, upon the domain of propositions Y.

---

reasoning can be placed into two classes. That which is comprehensible is puerile; that which is not puerile is incomprehensible. If one wants to see how far that writer can be carried away by the mania for purely verbal explanations, he has only to reread the Cratylus. It is hard to imagine anything more absurd than that dialogue. The most dour fellow will break into smiles when he learns that the gods have been called θεοί because they are always running!

One recalls that Diogenes, arguing with Plato about ideas and the latter mentioning the τραπεζότης (essence of the table, quality of being of the table, the table in itself) and the χυαθότης (essence of the glass, quality of being of the glass, the glass in itself), says: "Me—oh Plato—I see the table (τράπεζα) and the glass (χύαθος), but I do not see the τραπεζότης and the χυαθότης at all." To this, Plato: "That is proper, for you have the eyes with which the table and the glass are seen, but you do not have those with which the τραπεζότης and the χυαθότης are seen."

Ηλάτωνος περὶ ἰδεῶν διαλεγομένου, χαὶ ὀνομάζοντος τραπεζότητα χαὶ χυαθότητα, 'Εγώ, εἶπεν, ὦ Ιλάτων, τράπεζαν μὲν χαὶ χύαθον ὁρῶ· τραπεζότητα δὲ χαὶ χυαθότητα, οὐδαμῶς (Diogenes Laertius, VI, 53).

I must confess to the reader that I am nearly as blind as was Diogenes, and that the essence of things escapes me entirely.

Claude Bernard, La science expérimentale, p. 53: "Newton has said that one who devotes himself to the investigation of first causes by that very act provides the proof that he is not a scholar. Indeed, that investigation remains sterile, because it poses problems which cannot be handled by the experimental method."

In the study of political economy and sociology I only intend to use the experimental method; hence I will restrict myself exclusively to those problems which it can solve.

"If one wanted to reply to this question, 'Why does hydrogen, on combining with oxygen, give water?,' he would be obliged to say, 'Because there is in hydrogen a property capable of producing water.' Thus it is only the question 'why' which is absurd, since it entails a reply which appears naive or ridiculous. It is better to recognize the fact that we do not know, and that there our knowledge ends. We may know how, and under what conditions, opium brings sleep, but we will never know why." (Claude Bernard, *La science expéri-mentale*, p. 57, 58.)

49. When we start with a premise which cannot be verified experimentally and logically deduce conclusions, the situation is completely different from the one of which we have just been speaking. The conclusions cannot be verified experimentally either, but they are linked to the premise in such a way that, if the premise is a proposition which may later be verified by experiment, that is, one of the propositions which we called $Y\alpha$ in § 36, the conclusions will also become experimental. If the premise is a $Y\beta$ proposition, the conclusions will always remain outside of experience, all being connected to the premise in such a way that one who accepts the latter must also accept the former.[21]

50. In order that this mode of reasoning be possible, the premises must be clear and precise. For example, the space in which we live is euclidian space, or differs from it only slightly, as innumerable facts of experience demonstrate. Nevertheless, we can imagine non-euclidian spaces, and thus, by starting from precise premises, have been able to construct non-euclidian geometries, which are outside of experience.

When the premises are not precise, as is the case for all those which the moralists would like to introduce into social science and political economy, it is impossible to draw any rigorously logical conclusion. These imprecise premises might not be useless, if we could verify the conclusions and thus little by little correct their imprecision; but where that verification is lacking, the pseudo-reasoning that some are willing to use ends up having no more value than a day dream.

51. Until now we have only talked about proof; discovery is a completely different matter. It is an established fact that the latter

---

[21] This proposition is elliptical—of the same type as those we were speaking about in § 40. "If one wants to reason logically" must be understood. It is obvious that nothing could be proved to a person who would refuse to accept that condition.

may occasionally have its origin in ideas which have nothing to do with reality and which may even be absurd. Chance, poor reasoning, and fanciful analogies can lead to true propositions. But when we want to prove them, there is no alternative to investigating whether, directly or indirectly, they are in accord with experience.[22]

---

[22] *Systèmes*, II, p. 80, note. Paul Tannery, *(Recherches sur l'histoire de l'astronomie ancienne*, p. 260) who, however, has a tendency to go a little beyond the facts in order to defend certain metaphysical ideas, says with regard to theories of the solar system: "There is a notable example, and one on which we could not insist too much, of the capital importance of *a priori* (metaphysical) ideas in the development of science. When the latter is established, it is easy to discard the considerations of simplicity of the laws of nature, etc., which guided the founders. . . . But we forget that that is not the way the great discoveries have been made, or the most important progress realized. . . ."

CHAPTER II

INTRODUCTION TO SOCIAL SCIENCE

1. Clearly psychology is fundamental to political economy and all the social sciences in general. Perhaps a day will come when the laws of social science can be deduced from the principles of psychology, just as some day perhaps the principles of the composition of matter will give us all the laws of physics and chemistry by deduction; but we are still very far from that state of affairs, and we must take a different approach. In order to explain the phenomena of sociology, we must start with certain empirical principles, as is done in physics and chemistry. Later, psychology, by extending the chain of its deductions, and sociology, by going back to still more general principles, will be able to reunite and form a deductive science; but these hopes are still far from the possibility of being fulfilled.

2. In order to introduce some order into the infinite variety of human activities which we have to study, it will be useful to classify them according to certain types.

There are two which present themselves immediately. Here is a well-bred man who enters a room; he takes off his hat, says certain words, and makes certain gestures. If we ask him why, he will only be able to say this: it is the custom. He behaves in the same fashion in connection with certain much more important things. If he is Catholic and attends Mass, he will perform certain actions "because one ought to do so." He will justify another quite large number of his actions by saying that morality requires it.

But let us imagine that this same individual is in his office and is busy purchasing a large quantity of wheat. He will no longer say that he acts in such a way because it is the custom, rather the purchase of the wheat will be the last term in a series of logical

29

reasonings which depend upon certain data of experience. If these data change, the conclusion would change also, and it may happen that he would not buy, or even that he would sell wheat instead of buying it.

3. Hence, by abstraction, we can distinguish: 1° non-logical actions, and 2° logical actions.

We say by abstraction, because in real-life actions the types are almost always mixed together, and an action can be primarily non-logical and only somewhat logical, or conversely.

For example, the actions of a speculator on the Bourse are certainly logical; but they also depend, even if only in small measure, on the character of the individual, and in that way are also non-logical. It is a known fact that certain individuals usually speculate on a rise, and others on a fall.

Let us note, moreover, that non-logical does not mean illogical; a non-logical action may be one which a person could see, after observing the facts and the logic, is the best way to adapt the means to the end; but that adaptation has been obtained by a procedure other than that of logical reasoning.

For example, it is known that the cells in a honey-comb of bees terminate in a pyramid, and that with the minimum of surface, that is to say, with the least use of wax, they have maximum volume, in other words they can hold the largest quantity of honey. No one imagines, however, that this is the case because bees have solved a maximization problem by use of syllogisms and mathematics; obviously it is a non-logical action, even though the means are perfectly adapted to the end, and as a result the action is far from illogical. The same observation can be made about a large number of other actions, either of men or animals, which ordinarily are called instinctive.

4. It must be added that man has a very marked tendency to imagine that non-logical actions are logical. It is because of a tendency of the same type that man animates, personifies, certain material objects and phenomena. These two tendencies are also found in current language which, preserving the imprint of sentiments which existed when it was formed, personifies things and facts, and presents them as results of a logical will.

5. This tendency to regard non-logical actions as logical lessens and becomes the equally erroneous tendency to consider relations between phenomena as having only the form of relations of cause and effect, whereas relations which exist between social phenomena are much more frequently relations of mutual depend-

ence.[1] Let us note in passing that relations of cause and effect are much easier to study than relations of mutual dependence. Ordinary logic usually suffices for the first, whereas for the second it is often necessary to use a special form of logical reasoning, namely mathematical reasoning.[2]

6. Let A be an actual fact and B another actual fact, related by cause and effect, or by mutual dependence. We will call this an *objective* relation.

To this relation there corresponds, in the mind of man, another relation A′B′, which is really a relation between two mental concepts, whereas AB was a relation between two things. To this relation A′B′ we will apply the term *subjective*.

If we find in the minds of men of a given society a certain relation A′B′, we can investigate: α) what is the nature of this subjective relation, whether the terms A′B′ have a precise meaning, whether there is, or is not, a logical link between them; β) what is the objective relation AB which corresponds to the subjective relation A′B′; γ) how did this subjective relation A′B′ originate and how has it been determined; δ) how was the relation AB transformed into the relation A′B′; ϵ) what is the effect on society of the existence of these relations A′B′, whether they correspond to some objective thing, AB, or whether they are completely imaginary.

When A′B′ corresponds to AB the two phenomena develop in a parallel fashion; when the former becomes a bit complex, it takes the name of *theory*. A′B′ is considered *true* (I, 36) when in all its development it corresponds to AB, that is to say when theory and experience agree. There is not, and there cannot be, any other criterion of scientific truth.

Moreover, the same facts may be explained by an infinity of theories, all equally true, because they all reproduce the facts to be explained. It is in this sense that Poincaré could say that from the very fact that a phenomenon allows one mechanical explanation, it allows an infinity of them.

More generally, it can be said that establishing a theory is some-

---

[1] *Cours d'économie politique*, I, § 225.

[2] This is not understood by many economists who speak of the "mathematical method," without having the least notion o what it is. They have conceived of all kinds of reasons to explain, according to them, the use of this unknown monster to which they have given the name "mathematical method," but they have never dreamed of this one, even after it has been explicitly pointed out in Vol. I of the *Cours d'économie politique*, published in Lausanne in 1896.

what like passing a curve through a certain number of fixed points. An infinite number of curves can satisfy this condition.[3]

7. We have already pointed out (I,10) that we cannot know all the details of any natural phenomenon; consequently, the relation A′B′ will always be incomplete when it is compared to the relation AB; these relations can never coincide entirely even in the absence of any other reason. The subjective phenomenon can never be a rigorously faithful copy of the objective phenomenon.

8. These phenomena can diverge from each other for many other reasons. Thus, for the scholar who studies facts of nature experimentally in his laboratory, the subjective phenomenon approaches the objective phenomenon as much as that is possible; for the man who is stirred up by sentiments and passions, the subjective phenomenon can diverge from the objective phenomenon to the point of no longer having any connection with it.

9. It must be noted that the objective phenomenon appears in our mind only in the form of the subjective phenomenon, and as a result it is the latter, not the former, which is the cause of human actions; in order for the objective phenomenon to be able to affect them, it must first be transformed into a subjective phenomenon.[4] From that comes the great importance which the study of subjective phenomena and their relations to objective phenomena has for sociology.

Very rarely are the relations between subjective phenomena a faithful copy of the relations which exist between the corresponding objective phenomena. The following difference is very frequently noted. Under the influence of real-life conditions, one takes certain actions P . . . Q; then, when he thinks about them he discovers, or thinks he has discovered, a principle common to P . . . Q, and so he imagines that he has performed P . . . Q as a logical consequence of that principle. In reality P . . . Q are not the result of the principle, but rather, the principle is the result of P . . . Q. It is true that when the principle has been established, it does lead to the actions R . . . S which have been deduced from it, and in this way the disputed proposition is only partially false.

The laws of language furnish a good example. Grammar did not precede, but followed the formation of words; once established, however, the rules of grammar have given rise to certain forms which have been added to existing forms.

---

[3] *Rivista di scienza*, Bologna, no. 2, 1907, *Les doctrines sociales et économiques considérées comme science.*

[4] *Systèmes socialistes*, I, p. 15.

To summarize, let us consider two groups of actions P . . . Q and R . . . S; the first, P . . . Q, which is the larger and more important, exists prior to the principle which seems to govern these actions; the second, R . . . S, which is incidental and often has little importance, is the consequence of the principle; in other words, it is an indirect consequence of the same causes which produced P . . . Q directly.

10. Phenomena A′ and B′ of § 6 do not always correspond to the actual phenomena A and B; very often it happens that A′ or B′, or even both, correspond to nothing real, and are only imaginary entities. Moreover, the relation between A′ and B′ may be logical only in appearance and not in reality.[5] There are different cases of this which it is desirable to distinguish.

11. Let A be an actual phenomenon, of which another phenomenon, B, also real, is the consequence. There is an objective relation of cause and effect between A and B. If an individual has some ideas more or less roughly approximating A and B, and if he puts these ideas together as cause and effect, he obtains a relation A′B′, which is a more or less faithful image of the objective phenomenon. The relationships which the scholar discovers in his laboratory belong to this type.

12. One can be unaware of the fact that B is the consequence of A, and believe on the contrary that it is the consequence of another real fact, C; or, while knowing that B is the consequence of A, one may even want deliberately to consider it as the consequence of C.

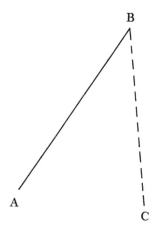

FIG. 1

---

[5] *Systèmes socialistes*, I, p. 22.

Scientific errors belong to the first case; and there will always be examples of this because man is subject to error. Examples of the second case are found in *legal fictions*, in the arguments used by political parties to disparage each other, or in other similar situations; it is the same as the reasoning, in the fable, of the wolf who wants to eat the lamb. The majority of arguments which are made for the establishment of taxes belong to this same type: one declares what one wishes, that taxes B follow from certain principles of justice, or of the common interest; but in reality B is connected, by a relation of cause and effect, to the advantage, A, of the dominant class. Finally, we can, at least in part, connect the origin of casuistry with this type of reasoning.[6]

13. So far we have talked about three actual facts, A, B, and C; but completely imaginary facts very often enter into human specutions.

One of these imaginary facts M can be put into a logical relationship with a real fact B; this error, which is still frequent in the social sciences, was common at one time in the physical sciences. For example, remove the air from a tube which is connected to a container full of water. The pressure of the air on the surface of the water is fact A, the rising of the water in the tube is fact B. Now this

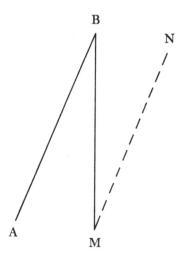

FIG. 2

---

[6] *Systèmes socialistes*, I, p. 178, 27.

fact formerly was explained by another completely imaginary fact, M, that is to say by "nature's abhorrence of a vacuum," which has many logical consequences besides B. At the beginning of the 19th century "life force" explained an infinite number of biological facts. Contemporary sociologists explain and demonstrate an infinity of things by use of the notion "progress." "Natural rights" have had and continue to have great importance in the explanation of social facts. For many people who have learned socialist theories like parrots, "capitalism" explains, and is the cause of, all evil found in human society. Others speak of "free land" which no one has ever seen; and some tell us that all the ills of society were born on the day when "man was separated from the means of production." At what moment? That is not known; perhaps the day when Pandora opened her box, or even at the time when beasts talked.

14. When imaginary facts, M, are brought in, it seems that since one is free in his choice of them they at least should be chosen so as to make the link, MB, logical; that is not always the case however, either because certain men are unaffected by logic, or because it is intended to play upon sentiments. It follows that often the imaginary fact M is related to another imaginary fact N by a logical link, or even by an illogical link. We find numerous examples of the latter type in metaphysics and theology, and in certain philosophical works such as Hegel's *Philosophy of Nature*.[7]

Cicero (*De Natura Deorum*, II, 3) mentions an argument by which, from the existence of divination, M, one deduces the existence of gods, N. In another work he mentions an opposite argument, by which from the existence of gods one deduces that of divination[8]; and he shows that it is false.

Tertullian knew why demons could predict rain: it is because they live in the air, and they feel the effects of the rain before it reaches the earth.[9]

In the Middle Ages, when men wanted to construct a theory, they were almost irresistibly inclined to reason, or rather to disreason, in this fashion; and if by some rare chance someone dared to express

---

[7] *Systèmes socialistes*, II, p. 71 *et seq.*

[8] *De Divinatione*, I, 5: "Ego enim sic existimo: si sint ea genera divinandi vera, de quibus accepimus, quaeque colimus, esse deos; vicissimque, si dii sint, esse, qui divinent."

[9] *Apologeticus adversus gentus*, 22: "Habent de incolatu aëris, et de vicinia siderum, et de conmercio nubium coelestes sapere paraturas, ut et pluvias quas jam sentiunt, repromittant."

any doubts, he was persecuted, as an enemy of God and of men, by those who certainly were completely at variance with good sense and logic. Strange disputes about predestination, about the efficacy of grace, etc., and in our day incoherent ramblings on solidarity show that men have not freed themselves from these daydreams which people have gotten rid of only in the physical sciences, but which still burden the social sciences.

In our time a tendency to justify these types of reasoning has arisen. What there is of truth in this new point of view is the idea of the relativity of all theories and a reaction against the sentiment which attributes an absolute value to modern scientific theories.

The theory of universal gravitation does not have a real absolute content to oppose to "the error" of the theory which assigns to each heavenly body an angel who regulates its movements. Moreover, this second theory may be made as true as the first one by adding that the angels, for reasons unknown to us, make the heavenly bodies move *as if* they were attracted to each other in direct proportion to the masses and inversely to the squares of the distances. But then the intervention of the angels is superfluous, and ought to be elim- inated on the grounds that in science any unnecessary hypothesis is bad. Perhaps, some day, the same reason will eliminate the concept of universal gravitation; but—and this is the important thing—the equations of celestial mechanics will remain.[10]

15. If an objective relation AB coincides approximately with a subjective relation A'B' in someone's mind, that person, by logical reasoning, will be able to derive from A' other consequences C', D', etc., which will not depart too much from the actual facts C, D, etc. On the other hand, if M is an imaginary cause, or even an actual fact different from A, the objective relation AB corresponds to the sub- jective relation MB' in someone's mind, and the latter, still reasoning logically, will derive from it certain consequences N, P, Q, etc., which have no reality. If he then compares his deductions to reality,

---

[10] H. Poincaré, *La science et Phypothèse*, pp. 189-190: "No theory seemed more solid than that of Fresnel who attributed light to movements of the ether. Maxwell's theory, however, is now preferred. Does this mean that the work of Fresnel was in vain? No, because Fresnel's objective was not to know whether there really is ether, whether it is or is not formed of atoms, whether these atoms really move in such and such a way; it was to predict optical phenomena. But Fresnel's theory still permits that, today as well as before Maxwell. The differential equations are still true; one can still integrate them by the same procedures and the results of that integration still retain their value."

with the intention only of seeking truth and without any strong emotion confusing him, he will perceive that M is not the cause of B; and thus little by little, from experience and from comparing his theoretical deductions to reality, he will modify the subjective relation MB' and replace it with another, A'B', which approaches more closely to reality.

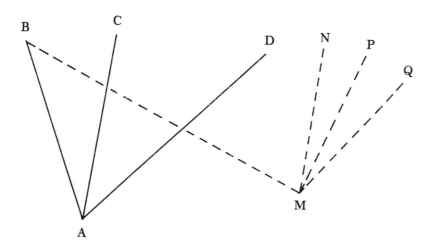

FIG. 3

16. To this type belong the experimental studies of the scholar, and also a large number of man's practical actions, including the ones which political economy studies. These actions are repeated a very great number of times, and the conditions are varied so as to be able to examine a large number of consequences of A, or of M, and arrive at an exact idea of the objective relations.

17. On the other hand, one who rarely acts according to the relation AB, or always is acting under the same circumstances, or allows himself to be dominated by his sentiments, may get from the relation AB a notion MB' which is partly imaginary, and sometimes an entirely imaginary notion MN.

18. The theory of this first kind of action is essentially different from the theory of the second kind. We will give only a few suggestions about the latter since the principal object of our manual is the study of the former.

Let us note that, in social life, this second kind of action is very widespread and of very great importance. What are called morals and mores depend on it entirely. It is evident that so far no people have had a scientific or experimental morality. The attempts of modern philosophers to reduce morality to such a form have not succeeded; but even if they had been successful, it would still be true that they would affect only a very limited number of individuals and that the majority of men, almost all, would ignore them completely. Similarly, from time to time someone points out the anti-scientific, anti-experimental character of such or such a custom; that can give rise to a large amount of literary output, but it cannot have the least influence on these customs, which change for completely different reasons.

There are certain phenomena called ETHICS or MORALS, which everyone believes he understands perfectly, and which no one has been able to define in a rigorous way.

They have almost never been studied from a purely objective point of view. All those who deal with them are maintaining some principle which they would like to impose on others, and which they consider superior to any other. Thus they are not looking for what men of a given time and place have called moral, but for what, according to them, ought to be called by this name; and when they deign to study some other morality, they view it only through their prejudices and are content to compare it to their own morality, which becomes the measure and the standard for all the others. Then a certain number of implicit or explicit theories flow from this comparison. The moral prototype has been viewed as something absolute, revealed or imposed by God according to the majority, derived from the nature of man according to certain philosophers. If there are some peoples who do not follow it, it is because they are unaware of it, and missionaries ought to teach it to them and open the eyes of these unfortunates to the light of truth; or the philosophers will strive to lift the thick veils which prevent feeble mortals from knowing absolute *Truth, Beauty, Good;* these words are in common use although no one has ever known what they mean or to what realities they correspond. Those who subtilize on these matters see in the diverse species of morality—some say also in the diverse species of religion—an attempt by *Humanity* (another abstraction of the same kind as the preceding ones, although a little less unintelligible) to arrive at a knowledge of the *Good* and of the supreme *Truth*.

These ideas have changed in our time, perhaps much more in form than in substance, but in any case have moved a bit closer to reality, and an evolutionist morality has been worked out. The idea of a moral prototype, however, has not been dropped; it has only been put at the end of the evolution of which it is the outcome, either absolutely or temporarily. It is obvious that this moral prototype, formulated by the author who proposes it, is better than all those which have preceded it. This can be proved, if one so desires, with the aid of another very beautiful and, at present, very powerful metaphysical entity, *Progress*, which assures us that each stage of evolution marks a better state than the preceding stage, and which, thanks to certain occult but nevertheless very efficacious qualities, prevents that state from becoming worse.

In reality, and leaving aside all these empty and meaningless discourses, the moral prototype is only a product of the sentiments of the one who constructs it, sentiments which, for the most part, are borrowed from the society in which he lives, and which, in a very small part, are his own; sentiments which are a non-logical product which reasoning changes very little. It has no more value than being the manifestation of these sentiments and of this reasoning.

Such is not, however, the opinion of its author. He has accepted this morality under the influences of sentiment, and he asks himself this question: how can it be demonstrated *via* experience and logic? Thus he necessarily falls into pure logomachies, because this problem is insoluble by its very nature.

19. Men, and probably social animals as well, have certain sentiments which, in certain given circumstances, serve as a norm for their actions. These sentiments of men have been divided into different classes, among which we have to consider those which are called religion, morality, law, custom. Even today, the limits of these different classes cannot be marked off with precision, and there was a time when all these classes were mingled together and formed one nearly homogeneous whole. They do not have any precise objective reality and they are only a product of our mind; that is why it is vain to seek, for example, an objective morality or justice. Men have always reasoned, however, as if morality and justice had an existence of their own, acting under the influence of that very strong propensity which makes them attribute an objective character to subjective facts, and of that pressing need which makes them cover the relations between their sentiments with a logical varnish. Most theological disputes, as well as the truly monstrous idea of a scientific religion, have this origin.

Morality and justice were at first made dependent upon the Divinity; later they acquired an independent existence and some even wished, by a reversal of terms, to subordinate the Almighty

Himself to their laws.[11] This is indeed a manifestation of the changing character of faith in the mind of man. When faith is all powerful,
the concept of a Divinity is preponderant, when faith diminishes, the
concept of a Divinity gives way to metaphysical concepts such as
those we have indicated (§ 18) and still later to experimental notions.
This movement is not always in the same direction; it is subject to
large oscillations. Plato found fault with the gods of Olympus in the
name of metaphysical abstractions; there was then a return to faith,
followed by other oscillations; finally, for certain theologians of our
era, belief in God is no more than a belief in "solidarity," and religion
a nebulous humanitarianism. They think they are reasoning scientifically because they have freed their way of viewing things from every
notion of positive religion, and they do not realize that their point
of view, having no more of an experimental base than do religions,
is expressed only by meaningless words capable only of arousing
in certain men, by the noise they make, indefinite sentiments, as imprecise as those one has when half asleep. If a life of a saint written
in the Middle Ages is compared to these fruitless discourses, one
sees that the latter just as the former does not\rest on any experimental concept; but the former at least is intelligible, whereas the
latter are unintelligible.

20. Useful studies of these sentiments can be initiated on the
subject of their nature, their origin, and their history; the relations
they have with other social facts; and the relations they may have
to the utility of the individual and of the species (§ 6).

But even if one engaged in this kind of research, it is very difficult
to proceed in an entirely serene and scientific manner because the
profound emotion which these kinds of things make men feel stands
in the way. Ordinarily those who reason about these sentiments
distinguish two classes; in the first they put those which they share,

---

[11] In our time this view is common. Montesquieu had already written,
Lettres persanes, LXXXIII: "If there be a God, my dear Rhédi, he is necessarily just; for if he were not, he would be the worst and the most imperfect
of all beings. Justice is a relationship of fitness which exists in reality between
two things. This relationship is always the same, whoever considers it, be it
God, be it an angel, or finally be it a man."

Let us first raise a contradiction. The Almighty has created, along with the
things, this "relationship of fitness" which they have between them; and therefore he finds himself obliged to submit to this "relationship of fitness."

We point out next the current error which gives an objective value to something which has only a subjective value. This relation of fitness exists only
in the mind of man. This error explains, and partially eliminates, the contradiction we raised.

and which they declare are good and true; and in the other, those they do not share, and which they declare are false and bad; and this opinion reacts on their judgments, and dominates all their investigations. In Europe, from the Middle Ages to the 18th century, it was not permissible to speak of religions other than the Christian religion except as of fatal errors. In our day there has arisen a humanitarian-democratic religion, which alone is true and good; all others, including the Christian religion, are false and pernicious. Those who champion these conceptions naively imagine that they are scientifically greatly advanced over those who practiced the same intolerance in the past.[12]

This is a failing from which few of the moderns who study the evolution of sentiments are exempt because ordinarily they have a faith to which they more or less subordinate the facts, and because they wish to show that evolution procedes in the direction they are anxious for. Nevertheless, their works have contributed to the development of science because of all the facts which they have collected, arranged, and illustrated, and also because this kind of study has engendered the habit of considering, at least to some extent, these sentiments in an objective manner. In any case, the evolution or the history of these sentiments is what is more known, or less unknown, in sociology; so given the small space at our disposal, we will not dwell on this subject in order that we may spend more time on the less known parts which themselves cannot be studied in their entirety. We will only enumerate certain particular cases which will illustrate the general theories.

21. The relations between religious sentiments and moral sentiments have been debated for a long time. The two extreme opinions are: 1° that morality is an appendage of religion; 2° that on the contrary morality is autonomous; the theory of "independent morality" comes from the latter.

Let us note first that these arguments are not without ulterior motives. Those who champion the first of these opinions propose to demonstrate the usefulness of religion as the creator of morality; those who champion the second wish to show the uselessness of religion or, more exactly, of a certain religion which does not please them. If we examine the problem intrinsically, we will see that it is

---

[12] Alfred de Musset, *L'Espoir en Dieu:*
  "Under the absolute kings, I find a despotic God;
  they tell us today of a republican God."
Currently they tell us of a socialist God; and there are some Christians who admire Christ only as a precourser of M. Jaurès.

poorly posed because two different problems, which we are going to show may have divergent solutions, are reduced to a single one. Here, as in all similar cases, we must distinguish between logical relations which it may suit us to establish between these sentiments, and the factual relations which exist between them, that is to say, it is necessary, as usual, to distinguish between subjective and objective relations.

22. Let us assume that an individual has certain sentiments A, B, C. If, in order for them to exist at the same time, it were necessary that there be a logical link between them, the two problems we just distinguished would be reduced to a single one. So ordinarily this reduction is made. It is a common view, implicit or explicit, that men are guided solely by reason and that as a result all their sentiments are linked in a logical fashion; but that is a false view contradicted by countless facts, which makes us tend toward another extreme viewpoint, just as false however, namely that man is guided by his sentiments alone and not by reason. These sentiments originate in the nature of man together with the circumstances in which he has lived, and we cannot assert *a priori* that there is a logical link between them. There is a logical link between the shape of a pheasant's beak and the quality of its diet, but there is none, or at least it is unknown to us, between the shape of the beak and the color of the male's plumage.

23. Thus the problem posed in § 21 is divided as follows: 1° if we assume (let us note this premise) that someone wishes to demonstrate logically that man should follow certain moral rules, what is the reasoning which appears most rigorous in form? 2° Are religious sentiments or, to limit somewhat this problem which is perhaps too general, are sentiments determined by a positive religion asserting a personal God, sentiments which we will call A, always, or ordinarily, accompanied by moral sentiments B; that is, do A always, or ordinarily, exist at the same time as B, or are the B found alone, or ordinarily without A?

The first problem belongs to those we have designated by (α) in § 6, the second, to those we have designated by (β).

24. Let us take up the first of these problems. Ordinarily reason has a tendency to lead man to do a certain thing A which is not agreeable in itself, or which is not sufficiently agreeable that man be directly induced to do it. In addition A generally includes not only action but also abstention.

25. Among the countless reasonings which are made in connection with the first problem, it will be necessary to consider the fol-

lowing: (I) A is shown to be, in the final analysis, advantageous to man: (Iα) because a supernatural being, or even simply a natural law or a supernatural one (Buddhism), rewards those who do A, punishes those who do not do A, either (Iα 1) in this life, or (Iα 2) in the other; or (I β) because A in itself is advantageous: (I β 1) to the individual, or (I β 2) to the species. (II) A is shown to be the consequence of a certain principle, usually metaphysical, of a certain precept accepted *a priori*, or of some other moral sentiment. For example: (IIα) A coincides with what *nature* wills; or, for certain modern writers, with evolution, with the theory of "solidarity," etc.; (II β) A is the consequence of the precept that we *ought* to work at bringing ourselves closer to perfection; that we ought "to pursue the happiness of mankind, or better, of all sentient beings"[13]; or that we ought to do everything which may improve and glorify *humanity;* or that "we ought to act so that the guiding principle of our will can become a principle of universal law" (Kant), etc.

26. Reasonings (Iα) are the most logical and among them the best are (Iα 2). When, in order to prove that guests ought to be treated well, Ulysses says that they come from Zeus,[14] he uses an argument which, if one accepts the premise, is perfectly logical. It can be challenged only by those who, like Cyclops, believe themselves to be as strong as Zeus, but those who know themselves to be weaker cannot avoid it; and, let us note, they are beaten by their own weapons: it is because of egoism that they refuse aid to the guest, and it is due to egoism that they have to fear the omnipotence of Zeus.

27. The logical link is very strong; let us examine the premise found in this affirmation that Zeus avenges strangers. In case (Iα 1) this proposition can be verified experimentally (I, 36), and consequently it can be easily demolished by the arguments of some Diagoras,[15] or by those which Cicero put into the mouth of Cotta *(De natura deorum,* III, 34 *et passim);* vut in case (Iα 2) the proposi-

---

[13] John Stuart Mill, *Logic*, VI, 12, § 7.

[14] *Odysseus*, VI, 207-208. πρὸς γὰρ Διός εἰσιν ἅπαντες ξεῖνοί τε πτωχοί τε. "Because from Zeus come all strangers and mendicants."

To Cyclops (IX, 270) he says: Ζεὺς δ᾽ ἐπιτιμήτωρ ἱκετάων τε ξείνων τε, "Zeus avenges suppliants and strangers."

Cyclops replies (IX, 275): Οὐ γὰρ Κύκλωπες Διὸς αἰγιόχου ἀλέγουσιν, "The Cyclopes are not concerned with Zeus."

[15] Some claim that Diagoras became an atheist because an individual who had injured him by perjury remained unpunished. Sextus Empiricus, *Adversus physicos*, p. 562; Scholia in Aristophanes, *Clouds*, 830.

tion, not being experimental, escapes all experimental verification, and the reasoning becomes so forceful that it can only be opposed by a *non liquet;* it is impossible to refute it by proving the opposite.

28. Reasonings of the type (I β), and especially reasonings (I β 1), lead to obvious sophisms. In sum, putting aside the metaphysical veils, to assert that the individual pursues his own advantage by conducting himself according to the moral rules amounts to asserting that virtue is always rewarded and vice punished, which is obviously false. The proof usually employed, ever since Plato,[16] consists in replacing the agreeable or painful sensations which man experiences by some abstractions which are defined so as to make them depend on the fact of having acted morally; then one has a vicious circle: if happiness is the consequence of moral conduct, it is not difficult to conclude that moral conduct produces happiness.

29. These errors follow from not wanting to admit that an agreeable or disagreeable sensation is a primitive fact, which cannot be deduced by reasoning. When a man experiences one sensation, it is absurd to want to demonstrate to him that he is experiencing a different one. If a man feels happy, it is absolutely ridiculous to want to show him that he is unhappy, or *vice versa.*

It is strange that a man such as Spencer could have fallen into an equally gross error; his entire treatise on morality is unworthy of his intelligence. In § 79 of *Morale évolutionniste* he wants to show that "actions taken in the interest of someone else bring us personal pleasure, because they make joy prevail around us." This is begging the question. Either a man does experience pleasure in seeing others content, and in that case it is unnecessary to prove to him that he will feel pleasure in making others content; it is as if one said: "Wine pleases you, therefore to obtain pleasure, drink wine." Or the man doesn't feel any pleasure in seeing others content, and in this case, it is not at all true that rendering service to others will secure pleasure for himself. It is as if one said: "Wine does not

---

[16] *Civitas,* I, 353, 354: "*Socrates:* Is not justice the virtue of the soul, and injustice its defect? *Thrasymachus:* So it would seem. *Socrates:* But one who lives well is content and happy; the contrary prevails for one who does not live well. *Thrasymachus:* Obviously. *Socrates:* The just, then, is happy; the unjust unhappy. Ὁ μὲν δίκαιος ἄρα εὐδαίμων, ὁ δ' ἄδικος ἄθλιος.'' This is rehashed in III, 444, 445. We do not know Socrates's true way of looking at things; but the Socrates of Xenophon almost always considered the good and the useful to be identical and similarly the bad and the useless. When one proceeds thus, he goes against the facts, and in order to prove his assertion he can then only resort to sophisms.

please you; but if it pleased you, and if you drank some, you would be content, therefore drink some and you will be content."

In § 80 Spencer wishes to demonstrate to us that "one who exerts himself obtaining pleasure for others feels his own pleasures much more deeply than one who cares only about himself." Here again is a vicious circle; what must be proved is assumed as a premise. It is a strange pretention for Spencer to want to demonstrate to us logically that we feel what we do not feel! Take a man who is eating a chicken; someone wishes to demonstrate to him that he would experience more pleasure if he ate only half of it and gave the other half to his neighbor. He replies: "Certainly not; I have already tried that and I assure you that I experience more pleasure by eating the whole thing than by giving half of it to my neighbor." You can call him wicked, you can insult him, but you cannot prove to him logically that he does not experience that sensation. The individual is the sole judge of what pleases or displeases him; and if, for example, a man does not like spinach, it is the height of ridiculousness and absurdity to want to show him, in the same way that one proves the Pythagorean theorem, that it does please him. Indeed, one can prove to him that by enduring a certain disagreeable sensation he will obtain another agreeable sensation; that, for example, by eating spinach every day, he will recover from a certain illness, but he still remains the only judge of whether or not there is a compensation between this pleasure and that pain, and no one can demonstrate to him by logic that such a compensation exists if he feels that it does not.

We put aside the phenomena of suggestion, which has nothing to do with logical proof.

30. In reasonings of type (I β 2) a premise is generally implied; the complete reasoning would be: "The individual ought to do everything which is useful for the species; A is useful for the species, therefore the individual ought to do A." The premise is not mentioned because it would not be easy to find unreserved acceptance of the proposition that the individual ought to do everything which is useful for the species; and the introduction of reservations forces us to solve a difficult problem because the utility of the individual and the utility of the species are very heterogeneous quantities which lend themselves badly to a comparison. Selection operates by sacrificing the individual to the species (VII, 99). It happens very often that what is good and useful for the individual is in absolute opposition to certain circumstances which are favorable for the species. Without any doubt the individual cannot exist without the species, and *vice versa*; consequently, if the species is destroyed, the indi-

vidual is destroyed, and conversely; but that is not enough to consider the good of the individual and that of the species to be identical. An individual can live and be happy seeking evil for all the other individuals who make up the species. Reasonings of the type just indicated are generally defective from the logical viewpoint.

31. Reasonings of class (II), like those in class (I), may be considered from two points of view. One could claim that the principle to which one wants to reduce moral sentiments is simply the type of sentiments existing. Similarly there are an infinite number of crystals which can be deduced from the cubic system. But authors of reasonings (II) usually do not intend it in this way; and if they do so intend it, it would be impossible for them to demonstrate that all sentiments now existing and which have existed can be deduced from the principle which they are espousing. It is impossible to see how, from the same principle, could be deduced the following precept, which is found among many peoples: "one ought to take vengeance on his enemy," or even simply the Greek precept: "hate him who hates you, love dearly him who loves you,"[17] and also this one "forgive your enemies, love your neighbor as yourself." In general the authors want to furnish the type, not of sentiments which have existed, but of those which *ought* to exist. Whence the second point of view from which these reasonings appear to us, reasonings which have as their objective not describing what is, but what *ought* to be; and because of that they have no logical value.

Herbert Spencer escaped this difficulty by calling usages and customs which observation proves exist or have existed *pro-morality*; he reserves the name morality for something absolute which *ought* to be. He finds fault with *a priori* morality, such as the Christian morality; but at bottom his morality is just as *a priori* as those which he rejects, and he is himself forced to recognize that observation gives us only *pro-morality*.

For example, he is convinced that war is immoral. This proposition may satisfy his sentiments and those of others, but it cannot be demonstrated scientifically, and no one can say whether war will ever disappear from the earth. Spencer's aversion to war and warlike sentiments is purely subjective; but, in accord with current procedure, he makes it an objective principle which he uses to judge the morality of various peoples. He does not perceive that he is only imitating the religious man for whom all religions other than his own are false. Spencer simply embraces the religion of peace, and

---

[17] Μισοῦντα μίσει, τὸν φιλοῦνθ' ὑπερφίλει.

that religion is worth neither more nor less than Islamism, Buddhism, or any other religion.

Spencer goes along part of the way following the methods of scientific reasoning, then he abandons that path, impelled by the powerful force which makes men attribute an objective value to subjective facts, and he moves onto the terrain of faith where he sinks deeper and deeper.

32. In such cases, the principle used by the authors is no more evident than the conclusions they want to reach; and they end up by proving one dubious thing by deducing it from something else still more dubious. Let us not investigate whether something is in conformity with *nature*,[18] with the end of man, or with some other imaginary entity, or whether it is in conformity with evolution or some analogous abstraction, because even if we could make certain of it, which we cannot, we could not thereby draw the conclusion that some specified individual ought to do that thing. Let us go on to reasonings (II β), in which there seem to be fewer gaps.

33. They have a common flaw, from the logical point of view, in that their premises lack precision and do not have a corresponding real meaning. This is not noticeable at first, because these premises are in accordance with certain of our sentiments, but when we examine them more closely, the more we try to understand what they mean, the less intelligible they become.

34. Let us take as an example one of the least faulty of these theories, that of John Stuart Mill. Leaving aside the last part, concerning sentient beings—which would prevent us from eating meat and fish, and even from walking for fear of crushing some insect— let us consider it in its most reasonable form, that of the pursuit of the happiness of mankind. These terms deceive us, they seem clear but they are not. "Mankind" is not an individual who has simple sensations of happiness or unhappiness, rather it is a totality of individuals who experience these types of sensations. The definition given implicitly assumes: 1° that one knows exactly what is meant by mankind, whether it includes only those who are alive at a given moment, or those who have lived or those who will live; 2° that the conditions for the happiness of each individual of a given collectivity are not contradictory; otherwise the problem of assuring the happiness of this collectivity would be like the problem of constructing a square triangle; 3° that the quantities of happiness enjoyed by each individual are homogeneous so that they can be added;

---

[18] *Systèmes socialistes*, II, p. 21.

otherwise one cannot see how the sum total of happiness enjoyed by a collectivity could be known; and if that sum is unknown, we have no criterion for knowing whether, given certain circumstances, the collectivity is happier than in other circumstances.

35. 1° In reality, those who talk about mankind ordinarily mean thereby their own countrymen, or at most their own race; and very moral civilized peoples have destroyed, and continue to destroy, without the least scruple, savage or barbarian peoples. But suppose that by mankind one means all men; then there are still some very serious questions to be resolved: When the happiness of men now alive clashes with that of men who are to come, which ought to prevail? When, as often happens, the happiness of actual individuals clashes with that of the species, which ought to give way? Let us note that European civilization is the fruit of an infinite number of wars and of much destruction of the weak by the strong; it is with these sufferings that the present prosperity has been acquired; is this good or bad? The principle proposed is not enough by itself to resolve these questions.

36. 2° Assume a collectivity made up of a wolf and a sheep; the happiness of the wolf consists in eating the sheep, that of the sheep in not being eaten. How is this collectivity to be made happy? Mankind is made up of war-like peoples and of peaceful peoples; the happiness of the first lies in conquering the second; and the happiness of the latter lies in not being conquered. We must resort to some other principle to rule out, for example, the happiness of the war-like peoples, to judge it less worthy than that of the peaceful peoples, which alone counts. In this case, this beautiful principle which was meant to permit the solving of moral problems is put aside and is good for nothing.

The happiness of the Romans lay in the destruction of Carthage; the Carthaginians' happiness, perhaps in the destruction of Rome, in any case in the saving of their city. How can the happiness of the Romans and that of the Carthaginians both be realized?

37. 3° It could be replied: the total happiness would be greater if the Romans would not destroy Carthage, nor the Carthaginians Rome, than if one of these cities were destroyed. This is an idle affirmation which cannot be supported by any proof. How can one compare these agreeable, or painful, sensations, and add them? But to push our concessions to the extreme, let us admit that it be possible and try to solve this problem: is slavery moral or not? If the masters are numerous and the slaves few, it is possible that the agreeable sensations of the masters form a larger sum (?) than the painful

sensations of the slaves; and conversely if there are few masters and many slaves. This solution, however, would not be accepted by those who extol the principle of the greatest happiness of mankind. To know whether theft is moral or not, should we compare the painful sentiments of the robbed with the agreeable sentiments of the robbers, and look for those with the greater intensity?

38. In order to use Mill's principle, one is led into combining it implicitly with other principles; for example, with principles of which Kant's furnish us a type. Even then, the difficulties which seem to be overcome in this way reappear as soon as one wants to reason with some rigor. There can be no principle of absolutely universal legislation in a society, such as that of men, composed of individuals who differ according to sex, age, physical and intellectual qualities, etc.; and if this principle must be subjected to restrictions which take into account such or such circumstances, the main problem then consists in knowing which restrictions must be accepted and which rejected; and the premises laid down become entirely useless.

Do the dispositions which one reads in Gaius, *De conditione hominum*, I, §9, 10, 11, [19] have the character of a "principle of universal law" or do they not? If yes, slavery is justified, if no, it is not even licit to decide that certain men, elected by the people for example and in charge of certain services, should command and others obey. From a formal point of view, all these dispositions are identical, and differ only in the nature and kind of restrictions.

39. The great influence sentiment has on men is known; most of them lose the use of sound reason. For example, at this moment in France many men, who in other respects seem reasonable, admire the meaningless words of the celebrated *Declaration of the Rights of Man*. The first paragraph has some resemblance to a principle of universal law. It declares that: "Men are born and remain free and equal in their rights; social distinctions can only be based on the common good." Let us overlook the fact that this liberty and this equality mean only that men are born and remain free, except for those things to which they are subject, and equal in everything except for those things in which they are unequal, which means less

---

[19] § 9. Et quidem summa divisio de iure personarum haec est, quod omnes homines aut liberi sunt aut servi.

§ 10. Rursus liberorum hominum alii ingenui sunt; alii libertini.

§ 11. Ingenui sunt, qui liberi nati sunt; libertini, qui ex iusta servitate manumissi sunt.

than nothing; and let us concentrate solely on the proposition that social distinctions can be based only on the common good. This does not serve us very well in resolving the difficulty which consists now in determining what this common good is. It suffices to read Aristotle to see that slavery can be defended on the basis that it is for the common good[20]; feudalism, so detested by the revolutionaries who wrote that *Declaration*, can be justified similarly. In our day the French Jacobins consider the distinction they make between citizens who belong to Masonic lodges and those who belong to religious orders to be justified by the common good; but the Athenians also considered the distinction which they drew between the barbarian and the citizen of Athens to be based on the common good.

To summarize, all these pseudo-scientific reasonings are less clear and have less value than the Christian maxim: "Love thy neighbor as theyself." Moreover we find this maxim in very different epochs and among totally distinct peoples; one can even find it in the Chinese Lun-Yu.[21]

40. The metaphysical reasonings which we have dealt with have no objective value because they are concerned with things which do not exist. They are of the same type as those which would be used to know whether Eros had preceded Chaos, Earth and Tartarus, or whether he was the son of Aphrodite. It is vain to seek which was the actuality; we can only study how it was conceived by the Greeks; their ways of viewing things are for us the facts from which we can fashion history.

Many are the moral systems which have been in vogue and which are still in vogue today; none of them has secured a marked preference over the others. The question of which system is the best is still undecided, just as that of the three rings Boccaccio tells about in one of his stories; and it cannot be otherwise because there is no experimental or scientific criterion for deciding such a question.

---

[20] *Systèmes socialistes*, II, p. 110.

[21] *Lun-Yu ou colloques philosophiques*, Pauthier translation [into French], I, 4, 15: "Our master's doctrine consists solely in being right minded and in loving his neighbor as himself." The translator adds: "It will be difficult to believe that our translation is correct; nevertheless we do not think that a more faithful one can be produced."

It is likewise said in the *Mahabharata* that we ought to treat others as we would want to be treated. More or less similar maxims are found among many peoples. They come from sentiments of good will toward others, and from the need felt by the weak man to appeal to sentiments of equality to protect himself.

The only experimental or scientific content in all these systems is found in the fact that certain men have experienced certain sentiments and in the way in which they have expressed them.

41. In the preceding paragraphs we have considered what men think regarding certain abstractions from the viewpoint of their similarities; but other more important studies remain to be made. We can study the nature of these sentiments, and the relations which really exist between them, disregarding the imaginary relations which men fancy exist. Then we can seek how and in what way the real relations are transformed into imaginary relations. This leads us to a consideration of problems (β), (γ), and (δ) of § 6.

42. Let us first investigate whether these sentiments have an objective existence independent of the diversity of human intellects, or whether they are dependent upon that diversity. It is easy to see that we can only retain the second hypothesis. Even when sentiments related to religion, morality, patriotism, etc., have expressions literally and specifically common to many men, the latter understand them differently. The Socrates of Plato (§ 65) and the superstitious men of Theophrastes had the same religion, but they certainly understood it in very different ways.[22] Moreover, countless examples can be found all around us without resorting to history. When we speak of love of country, for example, we have in mind an abstract class of sentiments made up of particular sentiments which exist in different individuals, and this class has no more objective existence than does the class "mammals" made up of each of the particular animals which alone actually exist. Nevertheless, for the men who make up one nation, these sentiments, even if they do differ in part, do have something in common.

43. Sentiments which belong to different classes do not seem to be completely independent. This dependence is not generally logical, as most men wrongly imagine, but comes from the fact that these sentiments have remote and common causes; and that is why they appear to us as so many branches which spring from the same trunk.

---

[22] G. Boissier, *La religion romaine* I, p. 179., speaking of the deification of the emperors says: "In general, the common man thought that the Caesars were gods like the others; he attributed to them the same power and supposed that it was revealed in the same way, through apparitions and dreams; enlightened people, on the other hand, saw a certain difference between them and the other divinities; they were for them something like the *heros* or demigods of the ancient Greeks. In sum, they accorded them no more status than the Stoics attributed to their sage after death."

Interdependence appears between actions of the same kind; nonlogical actions are favored or opposed together and the same for logical actions. Those who yield to one kind of sentiments, will yield more readily to other kinds; while those who are in the habit of using reasoning in certain cases, will use it more readily in others.

44. If then, as we will do with respect to wealth (VII, 11), we arrange men into strata according to the qualities of their intelligence and their character, putting into the higher strata those who possess these qualities in the highest degree, and into lower strata those who possess one or both qualities only in a low degree, we will then see that the different sentiments are less interdependent as one goes up to higher levels, and more interdependent as one moves down to lower levels. To continue our comparison, we will say that in the higher strata the branches are distinct and separate, while in the lower strata they are intermixed.

Thus human society displays a form in space analogous (but not identical) to that which it displays in time; indeed, we know that in primitive times different sentiments, now completely distinct, made up a homogeneous mass (§ 81, note).

45. Qualities of intelligence and of character are not the only ones which act in opposite directions; many other circumstances produce this same effect. Those who govern, whether at the bottom or at the top of the scale, whether in private industry or in public affairs, generally have more distinct and more independent sentiments than do those who are governed; and this follows from the fact that the former, more than the latter, must necessarily have broad views; and precisely because they see things from higher up, they acquire through practice notions which those whose occupations keep them in a more restricted sphere lack.[23]

46. This additional classification coincides partially with the preceding óne, and also coincides in part with the classification obtained by arranging men according to their wealth;[24] but these classes also differ in part. First, it can be observed that some elements in the

---

[23] It must be noted that a statesman must not be confused with a politician; moreover the habit acquired by one who has long governed any part, large or small, of human activity, and the habit acquired by the glib speaker, the schemer, the flatterer of the Demos, are essentially different.

[24] Those who have a large fortune and administer it themselves govern a considerable part of human activity, and consequently they ordinarily acquire the habits of the function they perform. One who simply lives on his fortune, and has a manager administer it, does not belong to that class, just as a politician does not belong to the class of those who rule.

upper strata move downward, and in the lower strata some elements rise. Then there are men who belong to the intellectual aristocracy but do not use their talents to secure material goods, rather they occupy themselves with art, literature, and science; there are the idlers and the incompetent who waste their intelligence and energy on sports, etc. Finally, countless circumstances can place men who have the same qualities of intelligence and character in different positions in the social hierarchy.

47. Let us note, and this is an additional analogy with what takes place through time (§ 81, note), that the faculty for abstraction increases from the bottom to the top; it is in the higher strata only that we find general principles summarizing diverse types of actions; and with the appearance of these principles contradictions which may exist between them show up, contradictions which are overlooked more easily in the concrete cases from which these principles are abstracted.

48. The human mind is so constituted that in times of ardent faith it finds no contradiction between its ideas on religion and its other ideas on morality or on the facts of experience; and these different ideas, even though sometimes completely contradictory, can coexist in the same mind. But, when faith vanishes, or even when, going from lower to higher strata in the same society, the diverse types of sentiments become more independent (§ 19), this coexistence becomes unpleasant, painful, and man seeks to get rid of it by suppressing the contradictions which he only discovers at that time.

In the mind of the ancient Greeks were mingled, without clashing, the scandalous adventures of their gods and some rather pure principles of morality. In the same intellect is found the belief that Kronos had cut off the male parts of his father Uranus with a jagged scythe[25] and the belief that the gods would reject a man who had offended his old father.[26] By the time of Plato, on the other hand, the contrast had become sharp, and one of these beliefs was on the point of driving out the other. Plato cannot concede that anyone thinks that Zeus married his sister Hera without the knowledge of their parents, nor that "we believe or would let anyone tell us that Theseus, son of Poseidon, and Piritoos, son of Zeus, had tried to carry off Persephone, or that any other sons of the gods or any heros were guilty of the impiety and the crimes of which the poets speak." The mania for artificially interpreting the ancient beliefs

---

[25] Hesiod, *Theogony*, 180.

[26] Hesiod, *Opera et dies*, 329.

and changing their meaning grew in the course of time; although, as Grote rightly remarks, "the doctrine which is assumed to have been expressed symbolically by the Greek myths, and which subsequently would have become obscure, was really introduced by the incautious speculations of the modern interpreters. This was one of the means which cultivated men used to escape the necessity of accepting the ancient myths literally, to reach some new form of belief which corresponded better to the idea which they had formed of the gods."

Similarly the Christians of the Middle Ages did not see, and could not see, the contrasts between the stories of the Bible and morality, which the 18th century philosophers pointed out so maliciously.[27]

49. The contrast we have just pointed out is only a particular case of a much more general fact. Barbarian peoples and the common people among civilized nations have more to do than study their sentiments. If some philosopher practices the maxim "know yourself", the great majority of men care little about it. Moreover, the man who has certain concepts, who experiences certain sentiments, does not care about relating them to one another, and even when, with the progress of the times, a small number of men, accustomed to reasoning, begin to concern themselves with it, they are easily satisfied with any relationship which their imagination suggests. Thus among certain peoples everything which man ought to do is commanded by God; and this command forms the connection which fixes the relation between completely different facts; those who reason further assume some metaphysical connection; and finally, only when civilization has made a great deal of progress do a very small number of men endeavour to study the experimental connections between these facts.

If one does not ordinarily have a clear idea of this it is because he falls into the error pointed out in § 9. It is assumed that these facts are the logical result of a principle, and then it seems strange that they can be contradictory; it is assumed that man acts under the influence of these logical deductions, and in that case it is not

---

[27] As is well known, Dante, although profoundly Christian, believed that vengeance is just (*Inferno*, XXIX, 31-36).

> O Duca mio, la violenta morte
>   Che non gli è vendicata ancor, diss'io,
>   Per alcun che dell'onta sia consorte,
> Fece lui disdegnoso; onde sen gio
>   Senza parlarmi, si com'io stimo:
>   Ed in ció m'ha e'fatto a se più pio.

perceived that his different acts can, in part, not be connected to each other.

50. Under the influence of these prejudices, man is always seeking to restore the logical relations which he believes must necessarily exist between facts, and which can have become obscure only because of gross error or profound ignorance.

Attempts to reconcile faith with reason, religion with science, experience, and history, furnish notable examples of this approach.

It must be observed that up to now none of these attempts have succeeded; moreover, it could be proposed as a general rule that the more any faith tries to reconcile itself with science, the more rapid is its degeneration[28]; and that is natural; one only has to open his eyes a little to perceive that no one has ever become a believer because of a demonstration similar to that for a geometrical theorem.

Similarly the metaphysical religions have no or almost no practical value, because they do not have the qualities necessary to influence the reason and the feelings of the common man.

The *Salvation Army*, by using means appropriate to the persons it wants to reach, has a social effectiveness much greater than that of the most learned and subtle metaphysical discussions.

Those who wish to introduce historical criticism of the Bible into the Christian religion do not see what absolute divergence there is between science and religion, between reason and faith, and that they correspond to different needs. The sacred books of all religions draw their value not from their historical precision, but from the sentiments they can awaken among those who read them; the man, overwhelmed by sorrow, who calls on the help of religion, does not desire a learned historical dissertation, of which he would comprehend nothing, but words of comfort and hope. What religion has become for certain humanitarian theologians is no more than a simple plaything for the use of the literati and the metaphysicians.

If we consider the societies of the present era, we will see that this need for reconciliation between the religious sentiments and other sentiments exists only among the upper classes; and in order to make their lucubrations acceptable to the people, they are obliged to present them in an altogether different light, that is as a reconciliation of the interests of faith and of the material interests with which the lower classes are principally concerned. It is in this way that we see the doctrine of the *christian-democrats* developing.

---

[28] This has happened to a certain "liberal protestantism," which is no longer even a theism. One theologian defined religion as "a collection of all the solidarities."

The trade-unionists wish to be considered as at least equal to the bourgeois, by virtue of the principle that all men are equal; but then they no longer care about that beautiful principle and regard themselves as greatly superior to the non-union workers and to the "Kroumirs" ["scabs"]. When the sailors of the port of Marseilles went on strike, they figured that the government would have infringed the right to strike if it had replaced them by sailors from the navy; then when the merchant marine officers went on strike in their turn, the sailors demanded that the government send navy officers to command their ships; they had completely forgotten the principle of the right to strike. It is this kind of sentiment which dictated the reply a Bushman made to a traveler: "When someone takes my woman, he does something bad; when I take somebody else's woman, I do something good."

In the lower socialist classes, they do not perceive the contradiction in the reasoning of the union workers and the Marseilles sailors; and if anyone does perceive it somewhat, he does not bother about it. Only the leaders perceive this contradiction, and they immediately resolve it with a subtle casuistry, and it may even be that some of them do so in good faith.

A most obvious and somewhat comical contradiction is that of people who, on the one hand, clamor for the abolition of the military courts in the name of the equality of citizens before the law; and on the other hand demand a special tribunal, an arbitration board, for workers and other employees.

The same persons who approved the fantastic decisions of presiding judge Magnaud, explicitly and deliberately contrary to the law, have been indignant at the timid exceptions made in other decisions on the subject of the law of separation. In the first case they said: "The judge should be guided by his sentiment of equity, without bothering about the law." In the second case, they asserted no less resolutely that, "the judge has only to apply the law strictly, and if his sentiments are contrary to it, he can withdraw." Sentiment having priority over reason prevents seeing so obvious a contradiction, or at least prevents taking it into account.

In Italy the decisions of the courts on a matter of private defamation are null and void when the culprits are socialist deputies; and this is approved by the proponents of a strictly absolute equality of citizens before the law.

The "intellectuals" who have ferociously indicted the proceedings of the military courts in a celebrated case, and filled the world with their lamentations, listen without protest to Attorney-General Bulot assert that there is a *reason of State* before which the judge has to bow under pain of being removed from office.[29] And despite the very clear words of M. Bulot who has even called it explicitly "restraint of princes," there are some people who believe that the Republic is free from the faults which are found in a monarchy.

Other "intellectuals" imagine, in good faith, that the Catholics are a menace to "freedom of thought"; and so, to win that freedom they approve without restriction the persecutions directed against the Catholics, and they are admirers of M. Combes. And even when the latter declares in a very plain way that his intention is to establish a new and uniform faith, as intolerant as the others,[30] they do not perceive the contradiction into which they are falling.

---

[29] An official statement made to the press about the June 24 meeting of the parliamentary Commission of Inquiry on the Chartreux affair.

"*Sembat.*—You too have spoken, Mr. Attorney-General, of a higher interest. There is then a reason of State before which a magistrate is obliged to give way?

"*Bulot.*—Under pain of being dismissed, obviously. (Laughter).

. . . .

"*Berthoulat.*—How is it that the inquiry has continued to go on although you have not had the name which you declared indispensable to the President of the Counsel?

"*Bulot*:—It has not gone on long, and it has ended nowhere because we could go no farther; I have yielded to the reason of State, to the 'restraint of princes,' if you will."

If one accepts the "restraint of princes," one understands why the magistrate was so indulgent with the Humberts and so hard on the victims of those notorious swindlers.

Funck-Bretano, *L'affaire du collier*, Paris, 1901, p. 325: "And such was the absolute power of the monarchy under the old order. . . . The honor of the queen is at stake, the crown can be affected. The king entrusts the care of the judgment to a court none of whose judges are appointed by him; to magistrates over whom he has no power and will never have power at any time in their career in any way; to magistrates who, by disposition and tradition, are hostile to him. Just as Bugnot shows, the attorney of the king himself is not, in the Parliament, freely chosen by the king. But in addition, there is even the controller general, assisted by the king's librarian . . . who directly opposes in such a serious circumstance, the interests of the king and of his authority. No one is astonished. Is there a government today which has the guts to see similar liberties flourishing under its very eyes?"

The government which conceded such liberties was the government of a decaying class, and it has fallen; the government which suppresses them today is the government of an aristocracy which is rising, and which is prospering. And the bourgeoisie, ignorant and craven, helps it with its money.

[30] See the note to § 94.

Anti-alcoholism has become a religion in a certain number of countries, and it has ferocious partisans; some of them also accept the religion of materialism or some other similar religion, which makes them declared adversaries of Catholicism and hence they jeer at the obligation of abstaining from meat! If anyone pointed out to them that, at bottom, to require a man to abstain from meat on certain days is a prescription of the same type, albeit less troublesome, as one which prohibits him from consuming a few alcoholic drinks, they think they resolve the contradiction by saying that their prescriptions are based on true "science," on the sacrosanct democratic and progressive "science." This means only that certain physicians add this to the large number of more or less reasonable things which they assert. And these sectarians forget, or pretend to forget, or they do not perceive, that their "science" in our day supports the Catholic prescriptions, by showing that one avoids certain maladies by abstaining from meat.[31] An infinite number of similar examples could be cited regarding every variety of fanatic sectarians, in all times and in all countries.

Herbert Spencer points out "the absolute contradiction which exists in all Europe between the codes which regulate conduct, and which are sometimes adapted to the needs of amity within a country and sometimes to those of enmity outside,"[32] to reconcile these opposing precepts he follows a circuitous course: he abolishes the latter

---

[31] In 1904, in a long paper read to the Paris Academy of Medicine, Doctor Lucas-Championniere concluded that eating meat promotes intestinal maladies and appendicitis following influenza. He advises eating vegetables occasionally, that is, abstaining from meat from time to time.

At the time of the publication of our *Systèmes socialistes*, Lord Salisbury had just beat back one of the countless absurd laws proposed by messieurs the anti-alcoholics, but their successors have had a similar law approved. *Systèmes socialistes*, I, p. 274.

M. Yves Guyot having asked that it be proved to him that absinthe is a poison, a good humanitarian replied by proposing the following experiment to decide the question: "Each of us in 24 hours will drink two litres, absinthe for him, water for me."

If the humanitarians deigned to reason it could be pointed out that, according to that proposition, the way to decide whether or not a substance is toxic is to compare the effects produced by the ingestion of equal quantities of that substance and of water. M. Yves Guyot could then make a counter-proposition to his adversary, and demand that he consume in 24 hours two litres of salt (sodium chloride) while M. Guyot contented himself with drinking two litres of water. Table salt would thus find itself classified among the toxic substances whose usage ought to be prohibited.

[32] *Morale des divers peuples.*

in the name of *his* morality, and it does not enter his mind that these precepts can be as useful, and even as indispensable as the first ones.

51. Certain circumstances favor the development of sentiments of a certain category; other circumstances inhibit them. In this way one of the main kinds of interdependence of these phenomena shows itself, namely, that they have a common origin. The interdependence which exists between religious sentiments and moral sentiments belongs in large part to this category, as we have already noted in § 43; they are often favored or inhibited at the same time, and this should be said even more explicitly about all analogous sentiments.[33] Similarly rain causes different sorts of grasses to grow in a meadow; a prolonged drought is harmful to them; in this way the sentiments of which we have spoken are tied together, but one type does not depend directly on the others (§ 70).

It is appropriate to add to these general principles the observations of M. S. Reinach, who sees the origin of ethics in *taboos*.

The primitive religion of Rome was only a cult nearly devoid of theological concepts; and that circumstance is not unconnected to the fact of the Romans' spirit of discipline, and consequently also to the fact of their domination over the entire Mediterranean basin.

52. This is not to say that we should find all sentiments among all peoples, nor that all these sentiments increase or decrease equally in intensity. It simply means that those sentiments which, for countless reasons, are found among one people are dependent on certain circumstances which act on them all. For example, one people may have certain sentiments A, B, C. . . , and some other people may have sentiments B, C. . . and not sentiment A. If certain circumstances change, the sentiments of the first of these peoples will become A', B', C'. . . , their intensity having been modified, but not equally; and it will be the same for the sentiments of the other people.

53. Not only do these sentiments differ from people to people, but among the same people they differ according to the individuals; and the circumstances which influence these sentiments have different effects from individual to individual. For persons among whom there is a considerable independence between sentiments, certain categories of these sentiments may be promoted or opposed; for those among whom this independence is less marked, the different categories of sentiments are promoted or opposed at the same time. This

---

[33] Here is a fact which has a remote but not negligible relation to another well known fact, that one who has often been put to sleep by hypnotism loses all faculty of resistance and can be put to sleep by a simple sign.

is why one can easily find in the upper classes of the population some persons among whom certain sentiments are absent whereas certain others are very developed.[34]

54. If men lived completely separated from one another, they could have completely different religious, moral, patriotic, etc., sentiments; but men live in society and, consequently, more or less in a state of communism insofar as sentiments are concerned. Material patrimonies can be entirely distinct; patrimonies of sentiments and intelligence are, in part at least, joint.

55. The changes which take place in the sentiments of one social class operate in such a way that they bring about other changes in the sentiments of other classes. The movement may be more or less rapid, sometimes even very slow. Ordinarily sentiments are vigorously attacked and weakened by reasoning in the upper classes, and it is only indirectly and belatedly that this change spreads to the lower classes. In such case it changes in character and in form; skeptical reasoning in the upper classes may, in the lower classes, be the origin of a new faith. Conversely the sentiments of the lower classes affect the thinking of the upper classes, which transform them into pseudo-scientific reasoning.[35]

56. The ancient Spartans possessed the sentiment of love of country to a high degree; they seem also to have been rather religious, but they were not moral to the same degree.[36] Moreover this could be said about the majority of the Hellenes; it is all the more significant to observe—and this supports our general proposition still better—that, circumstances having changed, all these sentiments grew weaker together, those which were strong as well as those which were weak.

----

[34] Bayle, *Pensées diverses . . . à l'occasion de la comète*, 4th edition, p. 353, ". . . I will remark that the few persons who openly professed atheism among the ancients, one Diagoras, one Theodorus, one Evemerus, and a few others, did not live in a manner which made anyone cry out against the licentiousness of their ways. I do not see that anyone accused them of being noted for the dissoluteness of their lives. . . ."

That argument, very often mentioned and given a general significance (it is also found in Spencer, *Facts and Comments*), has only the very limited significance indicated in the text.

[35] As many examples as anyone would want may be found in antiquity, in the Middle Ages, and in modern times.

[36] Fustel de Coulanges, *Nouvelles recherches sur quelques problèmes d'histoire*, p. 92: "There is no Greek city where history shows as many cases of corruption." And he cites a large number of these cases.

57. Thanks to literary works, we can, for Athens, follow the decaying of religious sentiments within the intellectually superior classes from the time of Aeschylus, through that of Euripides, up to the time of the Cynics, the Epicureans, and the Sceptics. The lower classes resisted irreligion and only slowly followed the example given them from on high. Numerous facts provide proof of this resistance; it will suffice to recall the condemnations of Diagoras, of Socrates, etc. We can observe an analogous phenomenon in Rome in the time of Cicero, when, however, the resistance of the common classes was only passive; but it became active, and it extended to the upper classes when the oriental cults multiplied and when finally Christianity triumphed and persecuted the philosophers. Reactions of the same type are observed at the time when the mendicant orders were founded; later when irreligion in the cultivated classes, especially in the Latin world, was rejected by the great religious reaction of protestantism; and again in France when irreligion in the upper classes ended in the revolution of 1789 which was, as Tocqueville very rightly notes, a *religious* revolution.

58. Let us note that in all these cases, and in other similar ones which could be mentioned, the religious reaction has been accompanied by a moral reaction.[37] The description of these phenomena is always the same; the use of reason weakens religious sentiments among the upper classes and at the same time weakens moral sentiments, and sometimes those of patriotism also, and then the cosmo-

---

[37] G. Boissier, *La Religion romaine*, II, p. 377, points out as an unusual fact something which is, on the contrary, the rule. With respect to the Roman society of the 3rd century of our era, he says: "What makes the changes which took place at that time in religious opinions so remarkable, is that they coincided with those observed in public morality."

Lea, *Histoire de l'Inquisition*, translated [into French from *History of the Inquisition*] by S. Reinach, J, p. 126 (p. 111 of the original), gives an example of the awakening of moral at the same time as religious sentiments: "One afternoon when he (Gervais de Tilbury) was out riding in the company of his archbishop Guillaume, his attention was drawn to a pretty girl who was working alone in a vineyard. He immediately made overtures to her, but she repulsed him saying that if she listened to him she would be irrevocably damned. Such strict virtue was an obvious indication of heresy; the archbishop immediately had the girl put in prison as suspected of Catharism."

Machiavelli, *Discourso sulla prima decade di Tito Livio*, I, 12, speaking of his era, holds the Church of Rome responsible for the misfortunes of Italy, because "due to bad examples of that court this province has lost all devoutness and all religion, which leads to countless disturbances. . . . Hence we are, we other Italians, obliged to the Church and the priests for this, that we have become irreligious and wicked. . . ."

polites appear; generally one can say that many non-logical sentiments diminish equally. Little by little, the movement spreads to the
lower classes; then it provokes a reaction among the latter, which
revives religious and moral sentiments in the lower classes, and often
patriotic sentiments also. This sentiment, thus produced among the
lower classes, extends little by little to the upper classes among
whom religious sentiments acquire a renewed vigor. And then again
these sentiments weaken just as the older ones had weakened. A
cycle similar to the one we have just described begins again. This
is how the rhythmic variations which have long been observed in the
intensity of religious sentiments occur.[38]

59. We must not forget that we are speaking of sentiments,
and we should not confuse them with the form which these sentiments may take. It often happens that the popular reaction, while
reviving and exalting religious sentiments, gives them a new form;
thus it is not the old religious fervor which reappears, but a new
faith. We must not confuse religious sentiments with worship either;
the former can diminish and the latter endure. But some persons do
not believe that religious sentiments necessarily have a personal god
for an object; the example of Buddhism would be enough to prevent
us from falling into so gross an error; besides we have an example
in our own time in socialism, which has become in fact a religion
(§ 85 note).

60. If the upper classes were able and willing to reserve the
result of their reasoning for themselves, this series of actions and
reactions would perhaps be less frequent and less intense. But due
to the very conditions of social life, it is difficult for the upper classes
to be able to do this; they do not even do the little that they could,
because, in addition to those who betray their class in order to obtain
illicit gains, other basically honest individuals belonging to the upper
classes are led by a lack of good sense to share their reasoning with
the lower classes; furthermore they are driven by the envy and aversion they feel for the old doctrines as regards sentiment, which they
wish to judge, through a very serious error, by only taking into
account the intrinsic logic. Not understanding their great social
value, they regard them as vain superstitions, thus displaying a defect in reasoning which they take for wisdom.

61. In so acting, and insofar as they succeed in their project,
which generally consists in weakening certain forms of religious
sentiment in the lower classes, they also attain the further result

---

[38] *Systèmes socialistes*, I, p. 30.

of weakening moral sentiments as well, which they certainly have not intended. Then when they see the reaction of religious sentiments arise, in the old form or in a new form, their reason is shocked and overcome, and, to sum up, they go where they certainly would not have wanted.

62. In Athens the resistance of the lower classes did not change into a reaction which reached the upper classes; and that was probably because the phenomenon was interrupted by the Roman conquest. That coexistence, for a certain time, of an upper class in which reason dominated, and a lower class, in which sentiment dominated, is not one of the least reasons for the extraordinary development of the civilization of Athens at that time.[39]

63. Persons who were outspoken about the popular beliefs were already gathered around Pericles, and their conversations at Aspasia's house remind one of the French salons on the eve of the revolution; in both cases the philosophy blended easily with the loose morals.[40] Perhaps the accusations directed against Aspasia and against Anaxagorus originated in the political hatred which some persons had for Pericles; but the very form of the accusation, which was an accusation of impiety, certainly must have had some basis in the facts; that is evident with respect to Anaxagorus. It is in his conversations with that philosopher, according to Plutarch, *Pericles*, 6, that Pericles learned to recognize the worthlessness of popular superstitions regarding wonders. And already in the works of Anaxagorus love of country as well as religion had become weakened[41];

---

[39] See the example of Scipio and his comrades, which has another but analogous significance. *Systèmes socialistes*, I, p. 303.

[40] Plutarch, *Pericles*, 24, relates that Aspasia did a business in courtisans. Athenaeus, XIII, p. 570: Καὶ ᾽Ασπασία δὲ ἡ Σωκρατικὴ ἐνεπορεύετο πλήθη καλῶν γυναικῶν, καὶ ἐπλήθυνεν ἀπὸ τῶν ταύτης ἑταιρίδων ἡ ῾Ελλάς... "Aspasia, the Socratic, did a good business in beautiful women, and thanks to her Greece was full of prostitutes." The comic authors added their fabrications, but all in all the fact doesn't seem questionable; or at least it is neither more nor less probable than nearly all the facts of Greek history.

Plutarch, *Pericles*, 32, tells how Aspasia was accused of impiety (ἀσέβεια) by Hermippus, and also of being a professional procurer for having obtained loose women for Pericles. Phidias was accused of having plied the same trade of procurer on behalf of Pericles (*Ibid.*, 13).

[41] Diogenes Laertius, II, 6: "To someone who asked him, are you not concerned about the country? he replied, I am much concerned about the country, and he pointed to the sky."

finally Diogenes, the precursor of our *internationalists*, openly declared himself to be a cosmopolite.[42]

64. From the philosophers' discourses and the theatrical productions irreligion spread among the people, but not without resistance. Euripides began his drama about *Melanippus* [sic] as follows, "Zeus, whatever he may be, since I know only the name," but the public was so shocked that he had to change this line.[43] Many passages in his dramas were directed against religion, at least as it was understood by the common people; he even cast doubt on the foundations of morality.[44]

65. The example of Socrates is instructive. He was very respectful of popular religious beliefs, very moral, abided by the laws of his country, even suffering death in order not to elude those laws, and yet his work unwittingly was directed against religion, morality, and love of country. That was because by his dialectic, inducing men to investigate the causes and the nature of these sentiments by means of the use of reason, he destroyed them at their roots. This is a typical example of the general theory set forth in § 43.

66. Thus one ends up with seemingly paradoxical conclusions; although the accusations directed against Socrates are false from the formal point of view and in the details, they are true basically and in general. Of all the accusations made by Aristophanes in his *Clouds* none is literally true, even in part, and yet the general idea that the *Clouds* must have planted in the mind of those who heard it, namely, that the work of Socrates was in the last analysis contrary to religious and to moral sentiments, is completely justified. Similarly, it is false that Socrates "did not consider as gods those whom the city regarded as such," and still more false that he "corrupted

---

[42] Diogenes Laertius, VI, 63: "When someone asked him his nationality, he replied: cosmopolite. ἐρωτηθεὶς πόθεν εἴη; Κοσμοπολίτης, ἔφη." See also Lucian, *Vitar. auctione*. Similarly Epictetus, Arrianus, *Epicteti dissertationes*, III, 24, and Antigonus, *Philo Judaeus*. Some say it about Socrates too, but that is unlikely.

[43] He replaced it by this line: "Zeus, as they call you in truth"; Plutarch, *Amat.*, XIII, 4. See also Lucian, *Iup trag.*, 41; *Iust. Mart.* p. 41.

[44] *The Phoenissae*, 504, 525; *Ion*, 1051, etc. Moreover the words which he put into the mouth of Hippolytus saying that: "the tongue has sworn but not the spirit," and to which contemporaries have often objected as being very immoral, actually mean that the promise obtained by fraud or by a ruse does not need to be kept; within certain limits, this may be granted. We have here an example of casuistry. *Systèmes socialistes*, I, p. 29. Aristotle, *Rhetorica*, I, 15, 29.

youth,"[45] as the accusation which let to his death claimed, in the sense given to the words *to corrupt* by the accusers. It is none the less absolutely true that, debating everything with everybody, he unconsciously attacked belief in the gods of the city and he corrupted the young people in the sense that he weakened in them the faith necessary for them to act in conformance with the good of the city. In addition, not charging for his teaching, a circumstance which does Socrates all the more credit and which, in an abstract fashion, seems to greatly increase his merits, is precisely what made his teaching more dangerous for the city. Indeed, the Sophists, who were highly paid, could have only a small number of listeners, who belonged for the most part to the intellectual aristocracy; consequently they could only shake the national beliefs of a small number of persons, and the Sophists could do more good than harm because their disciples became accustomed to making use of reason. Socrates, on the other hand, addressed himself to the artisan, to the man for whom the cares of daily life made it impossible to follow long, subtle, and abstract arguments profitably, and he destroyed their faith without being at all able to replace it by scientific reasoning.

67. This insidious and pernicious work was quickly perceived by contemporaries, who understood instinctively all the harm it could do; that is why Socrates had enemies among the partisans of the oligarchy as well as among those of the democracy; the Thirty expressly forbade him to speak with young people,[46] the democrats condemned him to death.

68. As Zeller *(Philosophie der Griechen*, vol. III, 2nd ed., p. 193) pointed out, the trouble was general and not limited to the teachings of Socrates: "Had not all cultivated men of that time gone through the school of an independent critic who had undermined the foundations of beliefs and of traditional morality?" Aristophanes himself, who wanted to lead his contemporaries back to the old ideas, "is full of the ideas of his times."

---

[45] Diogenes Laertius, II, 40: ". . . ἀδικεῖ δὲ καὶ τοὺς νέους διαφθειρῶν."

[46] Xenophon, *Memorabilia*, I, 2, 36. The Thirty had summoned Socrates before them, and the latter, acting as though he did not understand, asked if, when he made a purchase from a man under thirty years, he was not supposed to ask the price. Charicles replied that he could do so, "but you have the habit, Socrates, of asking what you know perfectly; give up these interrogations." Critias, another member of the Thirty, said: "It is advisable, Socrates, that you not concern yourself with shoe-makers, carpenters, blacksmiths, because they are tired of your discourses."

69. We must not forget a circumstance which has no great importance for the history of that era, but which is important in that it enables us to discover an analogy with other later phenomena: whereas the ancient beliefs were diminishing, the practices of the *Mysteries* became quite widespread. Here we have an indication of another kind of resistance which was strongly manifested in other phenomena, that is, that we see the religious phenomena persist by appearing in a new form (§ 59).

70. It remains to be seen how the moral and patriotic sentiments diminished in intensity at the same time as the religious sentiments. Note that we are speaking only of the sentiments which are connected with the positive religions and not of those which belong to the metaphysical religions, which, by their very nature, are followed by only a very limited number of persons (§ 50).

If we compare the time of Marathon to that of Socrates, opinions differ. Some people, such as Grote, do not believe that morals had decayed; on the other hand, others, such as Zeller, think that they had become worse; but if we go up to the times of Demetrius Poliorcetes, for example, the decadence of morals is clear, and no one denies it.[47] That is enough to support our general proposition, according to which the religious, ethical, and patriotic sentiments often decrease or increase together; whereas the question of knowing whether the decadence had begun at the time of Socrates is only of importance in order to establish the speed with which the movement spread from the upper classes to the lower classes.

71. If we could rely on the comparisons that contemporaries made between the older mores and those of their era, we would have to conclude that from the time of Socrates, and even before that, morality was in great decadence; but these comparisons, even when made by men such as Thucydides (III, 82, 83), have no value because

---

[47] There is an enormous difference between the Athenians who had refused "the land and water" demanded by Darius, and who had then withstood the onslaught of the powerful Persian fleet at Salamis, and the Athenians who shamefully prostrated themselves at the feet of Demetrius Poliorcetes. They placed the latter and Antigonus among their *gods-saviors*, and designated the year, not by the name of an archon, but by that of a priest of the *gods-saviors*. They consecrated the place where Demetrius descended from his chariot for the first time, and erected a statue there to *Demetrius-savior*. It was decreed that personages sent to Demetrius were not to call themselves ambassadors, but *suppliants*, like those who are sent to the Pythia and to Olympia. They even changed the name of one of their months which they called Demetrius. The rest can be seen in Plutarch, *Demetrius*, 10, 11, 12.

all the early writers shared the prejudice that the present was worse than the past.[48]

Hence we must reject entirely that easy but misleading confirmation of our general proposition, and investigate *via* another means whether it conforms to the facts.

72. We have only to turn to history. The contrast between the heroes of Salamis and the foolish courtesans of Demetrius Poliorcetes is too great, and there are too many other similar facts, for us to have the least doubt on this subject.

73. Let us add that the doubt which attaches to comparisons between the past and the present does not exist when it is a question of facts of the same era, and in that case we have the testimony of Polybius. He remarks[49] that "the excess of religion, which other peoples hold to be a vice, is what maintains the Roman republic. Religion is exalted and it has an extraordinary power in all private affairs. Many will be astonished at this, but I estimate that such is the case with respect to the great majority.[50] If it were possible to have a republic made up entirely of wise men, perhaps that would not be necessary. . . . Consequently it seems to me that the old opinions on the gods and on the penalties of Hades have been introduced into the mind of the common people neither by chance, nor rashly, whereas the moderns have rejected them with much more rashness and lunacy.[51] And so, without talking about the rest, the Greeks who handle public wealth do not respect their pledges, even when there are ten sureties, ten confirming seals, and twice that number of witnesses, even when one only entrusts a single talent to them; whereas among the Romans those who, as magistrates or legates, handle considerable sums, do respect the sworn word, be-

---

[48] Horace, *Carmen Saeculare*, III, VI, summed up a time-honored opinion in these lines:

> Aetas parentum, pejor avis, tulit
> Nos nequiores, mox daturos
> Progeniem vitiosiorem.

"Our fathers were worse than our grandfathers, we are worse than our fathers, and we will leave behind sons worse than ourselves."

In our days the contrary opinion has become an article of faith.

[49] VI, 56, 57, *et seq.*

[50] Ἐμοί γε μὴν δοκοῦσι τοῦ πλήθους χάριν τοῦτο πεποιηκέναι.

[51] Scipio Africanus had a group of friends, one of whom was Polybius, and it is very probable that the latter reproduces the ideas of that group.

Later, Cicero, *De haruspicum responso*, 9, made an idea which was current in Rome his own, declaring that it is because of their religion that the Romans had conquered other peoples: *omnes gentes nationesque superavimus.*

cause of respect for their oath." Shortly, however, in the time of Sallust and Cicero, the Romans became similar to the Greeks of Polybius.

74. We must call attention to two points in what Polybius says: 1° the facts; and there is no good reason not to believe that they are accurate; 2° the interpretation, which shares the current error which consists in establishing a relation of cause and effect between religious and moral sentiment, whereas there is only a relation of dependence via common origins and causes (II, 43).

75. (§ 6, γ) Let us investigate how these sentiments originate and continue, and in order to do so let us consider a more general problem, that of knowing how and why certain facts A, B, C,... exist in a society whether they be sentiments, institutions, customs, etc.

76. A solution of this problem has recently been offered which, if it could be accepted, would be perfect and would, in one stroke, make sociology one of the most advanced sciences. That solution is obtained by extending to social facts the theory which Darwin has given to explain the form of living beings; and there is certainly a resemblance between the two cases. We will say, then, that the sentiments, the institutions, and the customs of a given society are those which best correspond to the circumstances in which that society finds itself, in a word, that there is a perfect adaptation between the one and the other.

77. The facts appear to confirm that solution because it indeed contains an element of truth—the same element of truth which is found in the theory of the forms of living beings as elucidated by the neo-darwinists. Indeed we have to admit that selection only intervenes to destroy the worst forms, the ones which deviate too much from those which are adapted to the circumstances in which the living beings, or the societies, find themselves; hence it does not determine the forms precisely, but it sets certain limits that these forms cannot go beyond.

Thus a war-like people certainly cannot have completely cowardly sentiments, cannot have excessively peaceful institutions, cannot have habits of weakness; but beyond these limits their sentiments, their institutions, their habits may vary considerably, and as a result they are determined by other circumstances unrelated to selection.

78. Somewhat civilized peoples have less harsh institutions regarding debtors insofar as they possess more mobile capital. This fact, considered in a superficial way, seems to confirm the theory of § 76 completely, and it can be said that the less mobile capital a

society possesses, the more precious it is and the more they need to conserve and increase it, consequently the stricter the institutions for this purpose ought to be.

This argument is partly true, but also partly false. It is true in that if peoples who have little wealth do not have institutions which prevent its destruction, they rapidly fall back into barbarism. It is false in that these institutions do not follow the increase in wealth in a precise way, and consequently they do not always become less severe in proportion as wealth increases; it may happen that they remain as they were for a short time, or even that they become more severe, even though wealth has increased. The correspondence between these two phenomena is not perfect, but only roughly approximate.

It is also necessary to note that that correspondence between the two phenomena does not occur solely by the action of selection. In a society where mobile capital is rare, any destruction of it causes serious suffering, and gives rise directly to sentiments which bring about measures designed to prevent that destruction; and this happens not by virtue of logical reasoning, but in a way analogous to that which leads not only men but also animals to avoid everything which causes them pain.

79. A society in which each individual would heartily detest his fellow-man obviously could not survive and would break up. Hence there is a certain minimum of benevolence and mutual understanding necessary in order that the members of that society, through mutual assistance, can resist the violence of other societies. Beyond this minimum, the sentiments of affection can vary.

80. We come to another very simple solution, of the same type as the preceding one, by assuming that the moral sentiments, the religious sentiments, etc., are those which are most favorable to the dominant social class.

That solution is true in part, but has a smaller proportion of truth and a larger proportion of error than the preceding one. Moral precepts often have the purpose of consolidating the power of the dominant class, but also very often of restricting it.[52]

81. The instinct of sociability certainly is the main fact which determines general moral maxims. We will ignore why this instinct exists among certain animals and does not exist among others; therefore we must take it as a primitive fact beyond which we cannot go.

---

[52] *Systèmes socialistes*, II, p. 115.

It seems likely that, for morality as for law,[53] this instinct was first manifested in distinct facts; the latter were then combined and summarized in some maxims of morality which thus appear to be the result of experience. In a certain sense one can also look upon the divine sanction given to these maxims from this point of view, because one who did not observe them showed that he did not have the sentiments requisite to the circumstances of social life in which he found himself. Sooner or later he could suffer for it, so that, for example, Zeus avenging suppliants was not entirely a fiction.

People usually reason as if the maxims of morality originated exclusively in the sentiments of the persons on whom certain rules of action or of abstinence were imposed, whereas in reality they also originated in the interests of the persons who drew some advantage from them. Someone who desires that others do something for him rarely expresses this desire outright; he finds it preferable to give it the form of a general idea or of a maxim of morality. This is seen very clearly in our day when the new morality of solidarity is considered.

82. Social problems are essentially quantitative, even though we give them qualitative solutions; it follows that there are maxims of morality which are literally contrary to each other and which have the aim of restraining excessive deviations in one direction or the other, bringing us back to a point which we estimate is quantitatively the best. Thus it is that the maxim: love thy neighbor as thyself, is in conflict with: charity begins at home.[54] There are, in a society, some maxims favorable to the dominant class, but there are others

---

[53] See Post, *Grundriss der ethnologischen Iurisprudenz*, and principally Sir Henry Sumner Maine, *Ancient Law*. The latter notes that in very early Greek antiquity the Θεμιστες were decisions dictated to the judge by the divinity. "In the simple mechanism of ancient societies, repetition of the same circumstances was probably seen much more frequently than today, and in a succession of similar cases the decisions would naturally follow and resemble each other. Here is the germ or rudiment of a custom, a conception posterior to that of the Themistes or judgments. With our associations of modern ideas, we are strongly inclined to think *a priori* that the notion of a custom must precede that of a judicial decision, and that a judgment must affirm a custom or punish its violation; but it seems quite certain that the historical order of these two ideas is that in which I have placed them." Courcelle-Seneuil translation [into French], p. 5.

[54] Theognis of Megara says, 181-182, that "it is better for man to die than to be poor and live in dire poverty," and a little farther along, 315-318, he remarks that many wicked persons are rich and many poor persons are good and adds: "I would not exchange my virtue for their wealth."

which are opposed to it[55]; in societies where there is the most in-humane usury, one finds morality maxims which are entirely opposed to it. In all these cases what is regarded as a social evil is reme-died by certain facts which are then summed up in the form of maxims or precepts. A similar origin is attached to maxims or precepts which apply to certain social classes, to certain castes, to certain groups, etc.

What is thought, rightly or wrongly, to be detrimental to a more or less restricted group, is prohibited by a precept of morality pecu-liar to that group; and what is thought to be useful is imposed in the same way. And so there occurs the phenomena of interposition be-tween these different moralities, and between them and the general morality.

83. Investigating whether moral sentiments have an *individual* or a *social* origin is useless. The man who does not live in society is a very unusual man, one who is almost, or rather entirely, un-known to us. And a society distinct from individuals is an abstraction which does not correspond to anything real.[56] Consequently, all the sentiments which are observed in a man living in society are indi-vidual from a certain point of view, and social from another. The social metaphysics which serves as a substratum for this type of study is simply the socialist metaphysics, and tends to uphold certain doctrines *a priori*.

84. It would be much more significant to know how sentiments arise, change, and disappear in our own times than to investigate their origins. To know how certain sentiments originated in primi-tive societies simply satisfies our curiosity (I, 33), and has almost no other utility. Similarly the sailor does not need to know the boun-daries of the seas in ancient geological eras, whereas it is very impor-tant to him to know the seas of today. Unhappily, we know very little of the natural history of the sentiments of our times.

85. (§ 6, γ) Under our very eyes, in France, where democracy is farthest advanced, some notable changes took place in the second half of the 19th century. Religious sentiments seem to have increased in intensity; but they have changed form in part and a new jacobin-socialist religion has grown vigorously.[57]

---

[55] *Systèmes socialistes*, II, p. 315.

[56] [V. Pareto,] *L'individuel et le social*. Paper presented to the *Congrès inter-national de philosophie*, Geneva, 1904.

[57] Here is one example, among thousands, of the way in which the majority of people understand the new faith. M. Pidoux, *La jeunesse socialiste*, Lau-sanne, January 15, 1903: "Socialism is itself a religion. It is the religion

The following changes in moral sentiments can be observed: 1° A general increase in morbid pity to which is given the name *humanitarianism*. 2° More especially a sentiment of pity and even of benevolence toward malefactors, whereas there is a growing indifference toward the misfortunes of the honest man who has fallen prey to these malefactors. 3° A notable increase in indulgence and approbation for the loose morals of women.

Facts which are connected with these changes are the following: 1° An increase in the wealth of the country, which permits squandering part of it on *humanitarianism* and on indulgence toward malefactors. 2° A greater participation in government by the poor classes. 3° Decadence of the bourgeoisie. 4° A condition of uninterrupted peace for thirty-four years.

The relationships which follow from the first fact belong to the kind we spoke of in §§ 76-79. Those which follow from the second fact belong to the type cited in § 80.

Finally, the change began in the intellectually superior classes; it manifested itself in literature, then it reached the lower classes, and has taken practical forms.

86. Sentiments of disapproval for malefactors, especially for thieves, clearly have become much weaker; today judges are considered good who, with little learning and no scruples, eager only for an unwholesome popularity, protect the malefactors and are severe and harsh only with honest people. This is an outlook which the majority of Frenchmen living in 1830 for example would not have understood, although it had already penetrated the literature; but it seemed that it was a case of innocent literary exercises.

It is the same with respect to loose morals. It could be possible that, in fact, morals are not worse than they were fifty years ago, but the theory is certainly no longer the same.

---

par excellence, the human religion which no longer believes hypocritically in a better world, but which wants men, solidly together, to unite their efforts to make the earth a paradise where the human species can enjoy the greatest amount of happiness possible. . . . This religion has progressed since twenty years ago it planted its cross upon the earth. . . . Our religion wishes to establish equality between men. . . . It is the religion of man, of science, of reason. . . . Our religion arouses in one's heart love of neighbor and hatred of evil. It also stimulates the revolt which frees and consoles. . . . It stimulates the revolt against the society in which we live, and prepares for its transformation on the basis of collectivism. There are two opposing religions, the one is the religion of egoism and envy, the other is that of solidarity and science. This last one will be the religion of the future."

This change has also taken place in the intellectual part of society; it was first manifested in literary form alone; this was looked upon only as a mental game, and no one believed that one day it would be a part of social morality.

Later all these changes became weapons in the hands of the adversaries of the present social order; they have found support in socialist theories, which they have strengthened, at the same time as they were accepted by a decadent bourgeoisie eager for perverse enjoyment, as is often the case among degenerates.

Positive law has followed this evolution of morality only slowly; so certain judges, avid for the public's praises and desirous of winning favor with the new rulers, openly scorn the code and the laws, and seek the grounds for their decisions in the novels of George Sand and in Victor Hugo's *Les Miserables*.

87. The decline in the disapproval of thieves has some connection perhaps with the progress of theories which attack individual ownership, but that connection is not certain. On the other hand the connection with democracy and universal suffrage is more obvious.[58] It must be remarked here that, even if the upper and the lower classes had the same proportion of wrongdoers, the effects would still be different depending on whether the power is in the hands of the one class or of the other.

In the upper classes they endeavor to maintain the laws and the moral rules, although they are broken; in the lower classes the tendency is to change these laws and these rules, and this is because the strong put themselves above the law and customs, whereas the weak are submissive to them.

In France cases in which the deputies have to intervene in favor of small offenders, their constituents, are so numerous that they have developed into general maxims which form unwritten legislation parallel to, but different from, the written legislation. And judges desirous of not being dismissed by the government, or of gaining its favor, follow the former and not the latter. The history of defrauders continually going unpunished whenever they have a little political influence is particularly edifying. In reality a large number of offenses are no longer prosecuted though they are still punishable by law (IX, § 32 *et seq.*). The magistrates jest about adultery.

---

[58] In Australia thefts of gold from the mines go unpunished because the thieves are very numerous and, through their vote, have an appreciable hand in the government.

The easing of the penal laws in several countries of Europe have considerably increased the number of malefactors who retain their right to vote.

"Why continue with your case"—said one of these judges to the lawyer. "You know this court's rate; it is twenty-five francs, and that's it." It is the charge made by other French judges also; and the one who has won the title *good judge* through his benevolence toward dishonest persons, levies only a one franc fine for adultery, and delights in this new attack on the law, the organization of the family, and good morals.

Some of these prostitutes, so dear to the humanitarians, get paid more. The poor women who, after having belonged to a religious order, are accused of violating the law by pretending to belong to it no longer, are punished much more severely, and the evidence brought against them is primarily that they continue to observe the vow of chastity.

The development of democracy has strengthened the sentiment of equality between the two sexes; but it is likely that the cessation of war has played a still greater role in this since it is there that the superiority of the male is most apparent. This sentiment of equality has given birth to the theory of a single sexual morality for men and women; some dreamers interpret this to mean that men ought to become more chaste, but most people who confine themselves to reality understand it to mean chastity for women is out of date.

There is even a writer who has claimed for women "the right to immorality." The fact that the way of life of young girls has become more and more free certainly does not hinder irregular union of the sexes, although that is denied by many who see only what they want to see and what their faith in "progress" prescribes, and not what takes place in reality, as the gynecologists, for whom the free modern young women are excellent clients, do know.

The ready availability of abortions in certain large modern cities calls to mind the Rome described by Juvenal; and, with neither disapproval nor disgust, the public listens to plays which indirectly justify abortion and lay the responsibility on society.

All these phenomena are related to the decadence of the bourgeoisie. That decadence is only a particular case of a much more general fact, the circulation of the elites.

88. The example of France has an effect on the sentiments of peoples, Italians for example, who have numerous and frequent personal and intellectual relations with it; we have here another cause of changes in sentiments: imitation.

This imitation occurs not only from people to people, but indeed between the different social classes, and between the different individuals who compose them; in this way a change which has arisen at some point in a society is spread by imitation, and it continues to spread where circumstances are favorable to it; it comes to a halt if circumstances are opposed to it.

Imitation has a counterpart in opposition.[59] When a doctrine is generally accepted, an adversary turns up to attack it. By dint of hearing the same thing repeated over and over, the desire comes to certain persons to assert the contrary. A theory leaning too far in one direction necessarily calls forth another which will lean too far in the opposite direction. The theory of *humanitarianism* and of the equality of men has found its counterbalance in the egoistic theories of Nietzsche's *superman*. In the Middle Ages witches were in part a product of religious exaltation.

89. (§ 6, δ). Let us see how the objective relations we have just studied are transformed into subjective relations. In general we observe the following uniformities:

1° A double transformation takes place. Without a man being aware of it, a real objective relation A turns into a subjective relation B. Then, by virtue of the tendency which transforms subjective relations into objective relations, relation B turns into another objective relation C, different from A and usually imaginary. 2° Man always tends to give an absolute value to what is only contingent. This tendency is partially fulfilled by the transformation of the contingent fact B into the imaginary fact C, which is much less contingent, or even absolute. 3° Man always tends to establish a logical relation between the different facts which he feels are dependent on each other, without understanding either how or why. Furthermore, that logical relation is usually one of cause and effect. If mechanics and similar sciences are excepted, relations of mutual dependence are very rarely used. 4° Man is guided by private interests and mainly by sentiments, whereas he imagines and persuades others that he is guided by public interests and by pure reason.

It happens very frequently that A (Figure 4) is a private interest which, without a man being aware of it, turns into B; and then B turns into the public interest C, which is imaginary. It also often happens that the transformation AB is at first conscious, that is to say, the man is aware that he is guided by a private interest, but then little by little he forgets this and he substitutes the relation CB for

---

[59] On imitation and opposition one can read the works of Tarde, *Les lois de l'imitation* and *L'opposition universelle*, which, however, lack scientific precision to an extraordinary degree.

I remind the reader that, for reasons of space, I must indicate by a word theories to which one could devote volumes.

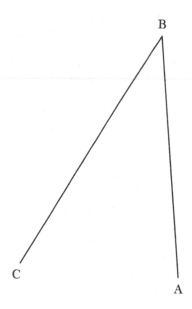

Fig. 4

the relation AB, that is he believes that he is motivated by the public interest.

Let us take an example in order to be more clear. A represents sentiments of sociability and certain relations useful to the individual and the species; B represents sentiments of benevolence with regard to guests; C represents the explanation that is given for these sentiments, by saying that the guest is sent by Zeus. Another example: A represents the poor man's sentiments of cupidity; B is the sentiment that the rich ought to give to the poor; C is the principle of "solidarity" between men.

90. It must be added that the belief in the imaginary cause C is, for its part, a psychological fact, and is thus placed among the real facts of type A which give rise to B. We thus have a series of actions and reactions. The study of language demonstrates this admirably.

The facts of phonetics and syntax certainly did not have their origin in certain preexisting grammatical rules; on the contrary the latter were derived from the former. When that operation had been accomplished, however, the existence of these rules affected the facts of phonetics and syntax in turn. Similarly for the facts of law. Although some people still attribute them to some imaginary cause and give their origin, for example, as a certain "juridical sense," we are beginning now to understand that, quite the contrary, it is the facts of law which have given rise to the abstract rules (§ 80), and also, if one likes, to that "juridical" sense; but when these rules and this sense exist, they become facts in their turn, and they act as such in determining the actions of men. Moreover, in this particular case, that action rapidly becomes most important and decisive because these rules are imposed by force.

91. If by C one means the principle "what is moral is anything which can be taken as a general rule for human actions" (or any other analogous principle), all the uniformities of § 89 can be established. 1° The moral sentiments which one wishes to explain in this way have arisen from certain other objective facts A, as we have already seen. 2° The principle laid down is absolute; there is no restriction, either of time or place; it applies to the lowest Negro and to the most civilized European, to prehistoric man and to modern man. The relation CB is of the same type as a theorem of geometry, which applies always and everywhere. Metaphysicians do not perceive what is absurd about this result. 3° The relation between this beautiful principle of the universal rule for human actions and the consequence, B, which some persons want to draw from it, is logical, at least in appearance and insofar as the nature of the principle, which has no real content (§ 38), allows. Moreover it is a relation between a cause C and an effect B. 4° This reasoning is used principally to ask someone else to make some sacrifice, or to induce the public authority to impose it on him. If someone were to say: "give me such and such a thing because it pleases me," he would not often be successful; he must say, on the contrary, "give me that, because to do so would be good for everyone," and then he finds allies. Note that the person from whom the thing is taken is not generally included in this *everyone;* often what is meant is the greatest number, and that is enough for the unsuitable terms in these pseudo-scientific arguments to go unnoticed.

Workers on strike are contending against the factory owners, but in the name of solidarity they beat up workers who want to work. It is obvious that that solidarity can very well exist among the strikers, but not between the latter, the employers, and the "kroumirs." And yet the theorists talk about solidarity between all men; and then they extend the propositions which they have reached to what would be more correctly called a *coterie.* Solidarity is always invoked to receive, never to give. The worker who makes ten francs a day thinks that, in the name of solidarity, the rich man ought to divide his fortune; but he would think it ridiculous if he were asked, in the name of that solidarity, to divide what he makes with someone who has a wage of twenty sous a day.

The "democracy" of the United States of America has the equality of men for a principle, and it is for that reason that Negroes and Italians are lynched in that country, that Chinese immigration is prohibited, and it would make war on China if the latter refused admittance to Americans. In New York midwives examine female immigrants; those who were not married in a proper ceremony are rejected in order to prevent corruption of American purity. The Australian socialists desire to help "the weak and the humble" and bourgeois cowardice supports them; but in 1894, a missionary having been killed by natives, the Australians undertook an expedition which destroyed without pity a great number of these perfectly innocent unfortunates. The French socialists have a passion for peace, they see war as a crime, but they preach openly the extermination of the bourgeois. In the meantime they injure policemen and kill officers and soldiers whom the government have charged with maintaining order. Pillage of factories goes unpunished. In Russia attacks on factory managers are no longer counted. Near the beginning of the year 1907, some workers put a manager in an iron pipe and heated it on a slow fire causing his death. The European and American humanitarians breathed not a word; but they scream like sea-eagles if the police have the misfortune to mistreat some assassins whom they are arresting. The sympathy of the humanitarians comes to a stop with malefactors, and does not extend to decent people. The decadent bourgeois voluntarily close their eyes and ears so that they neither see nor hear; and while their adversaries are preparing to destroy them, they are filled with tender feelings at the idea of the coming of a "new and better humanity."

92. It must be noted that, with the pseudo-logic which is often used to establish relations CB, the equality of M and N does not imply the equality of N and M, as would be the case with ordinary logic. For example, in the modern democracies, the poor ought to enjoy the same rights as the rich, because all men are equal; but they are no longer equal if someone demands for the rich the same rights as the poor. The workers now have special and privileged tribunals, the arbitration boards, which in certain countries always decide against employers or bourgeois and always side with the worker.[60] If an employer or a bourgeois were to set fire to a worker's house he would certainly be sentenced to the penalty provided by

---

[60] *Systèmes socialistes*, I, 136.

the law; on the other hand, French strikers and their friends can burn and plunder the houses of employers and bourgeois without the government daring to make use of the police to oppose them. In Italy, socialist lawyers and their friends indulge in abuses and insults against magistrates which would be repressed among others. In July 1904 at Cluses there was a strike of watchmakers. One of the employers demanded that the workers pay for the windows they had broken at the beginning of the strike, as a condition for reinstatement. The workers were extremely indignant at that outlandish claim; and that is understandable since everyone looks after his own interests. But the bourgeois humanitarians were also thoroughly indignant about it, and that would be less comprehensible if one did not know what a contemptible and decayed species they form. The proverb: "he who breaks windows pays for them" evidently applies only to the bourgeois, and not to workers, and still less to the sacrosanct workers on strike. The factory was besieged; one of the owners' small child being held by his mother was hit by a stone. In order to defend themselves the owners fired on the aggressors. Then the factory was looted and set on fire, and the police force which was present did nothing to stop it. Only some of the looters, selected from among the least culpable moreover, were pursued. Since a general strike would have been declared if they had been arrested, they were allowed to stay at liberty; on the other hand the employers who had been defending themselves were imprisoned while awaiting trial; the latter were convicted[61] and the looters absolved.

Near the end of 1903 the French Parliament voted an amnesty for all strike and strike-related occurrences. While the amnesty was being debated, some individuals, confident they would not be punished, looted several shops in Paris. Two of them were taken before a court which declared that the amnesty was applicable to them; the others were left alone. If a shop owner had sacked the house of one of those malefactors, he would certainly have been convicted by the courts. And yet there are people who honestly believe that there is a regime of equality between citizens, and who are consumed with joy thinking of its superiority to older regimes under which there were privileged citizens.

93. Those who are anxious to prove that they are guided by the public interest and not by a private interest sometimes may not be sincere. It is necessary to call attention to the following which is one of the most common sophisms which arise when someone desires

---

[61] Even the government of M. Combes became ashamed, and four months later pardoned these unfortunate fellows.

to attack a thing while appearing to establish a measure of general order. The thing E has certain characteristics M, N, P, . . .; one of these is chosen, for example M, which outwardly seems to distinguish that thing from others, and it is asserted that the measure is general and directed against M. The ancient republics often passed laws which seemed general, but which, at bottom, tended to apply to a small number of individuals, or even to only one.

At the beginning of the Peloponnesian War Sparta sent ambassadors to Athens demanding that the "Athenians avenge the sacrilege committed against the goddess."[62] This was a circumlocution for demanding that they banish Pericles, who, through his mother, was a descendant of the Alcmeonides who was considered guilty of that sacrilege.

The sophism is more obvious when M is also found in another thing F to which the measure taken against E—because of M so they say—is not applied. For example, in 1906 in France, in order to prohibit teaching by the religious orders, certain persons claimed that the prohibition was intended only to abolish the possibility of teaching by persons who were unmarried. But it is obvious that if the men, and the women, who belong to the orders are not married, it is likewise true that all single persons are not members of an order; and if it had been desired to reach the latter, it would have been possible to do it directly and not through the intermediary of the orders.

94. The same idea can be expressed in several different languages and, in the same language, in several forms. The same discussion which would have taken the theological form a few centuries ago, would take the socialist form today. When it is said in the modern jargon that a law is "broadly humane," it must be translated like this: it favors idlers and rogues at the expense of energetic and honest men. If one wanted to express the idea that a man appears to deserve censure, one would say in the language of the Middle Ages that he is a heretic or an excommunicated person; in the language of Jacobins of the end of the 18th century, that he is an aristocrat; in the language of the modern Jacobins, that he is a reactionary.[63] These are simply different ways of expressing the same idea.

---

[62] Thucydides, I, 126: ". . . ἐκέλευον τοὺς Ἀθηναίους τὸ ἄγος ἐλαύνειν τῆς θεοῦ."

[63] The Paris correspondent of the *Journal de Gèneve* (January 29, 1905) put it very well: "For the word clerical has lost its correct meaning today just as did the word aristocrat under the Committee of Public Safety."

More generally it can be noted that in a society a phenomenon which remains basically the same takes on various and often quite dissimilar forms in the course of time; in other words, there is persistence of the same phenomenon under diverse forms.[64]

95. The preceding shows us that there is some truth in that observation of G. Sorel to the effect that things which concern the country and tradition have a mythical character[65] and that "myths are necessary in order to set forth in an exact way the conclusions of a social philosophy which does not want to be mistaken. . . ." Indeed whenever we want to try to understand what certain men have thought or do think, we must understand the language and the forms in which they express their thoughts. Grote, for example, has shown that we cannot understand the history of ancient Greece if we do not try to master as much as possible the myths which formed the intellectual milieu in which they lived.[66]

Similarly someone who wants to have a real influence on people should speak their language and adopt the forms which are appealing to them, and consequently, employ the language of myths.

96. But the theory of G. Sorel is incomplete, because in addition to these subjective phenomena there are some which are objective. Other persons cannot be precluded from dealing with them. His error comes from the precept he lays down: "What is necessary for sociology is that it adopt, from the beginning, a frankly subjective procedure, that it know what it wants to do and that it thus direct all its investigations toward the type of solution which it wants to advocate."[67] This is indeed the objective of propaganda, but not

---

[64] Numerous facts to support this theory will be found in our *Systèmes socialistes*, and in the table of contents under *Persistance des mêmes phénomènes sociaux*. We will add only one item which occurred after the publication of that book.

In the June 24, 1904, meeting of the French Senate, the president of the Council, M. Combes, defending the law which excludes the religious orders from teaching, said: "We believe that it is not fantastic to consider it desirable and practical to realize in contemporary France what the old regime had so well established in bygone days. One king, one faith; such was the slogan then. That maxim gave strength to our monarchical governments; an analogous one which corresponds to the exigencies of the present time must be found."

Many people in France think the same way; the persistence of that state of mind is observable from the revocation of the Edict of Nantes, to go back no farther than that, up to the present day. The form changes, the underlying idea remains the same.

[65] *Introduction à l'économie moderne*, p. 377.

[66] *La ruine du monde antique*, p. 213.

[67] *Introduction à l'économie moderne*, p. 368.

of science. But let us not argue about words, let the thing be called whatever anyone likes! How will anyone be prevented from seeking the objective facts which are behind the subjective facts, or even simply seeking the uniformities displayed by these ways of considering subjective facts?

G. Sorel himself furnishes an example of two types of consideration which a subjective fact permits. He says that "it is likely that even then Marx only presented the catastrophic conception [the destruction of the bourgeoisie resulting from the concentration of wealth] as a myth, illustrating class struggle and social revolution in a very clear way."[68]

Marx thought what he wanted, but we are free to inquire whether that catastrophe has or has not occurred within the time limits assigned to it. It is not at all clear how giving attention to that objective fact could be prohibited.

Moreover, if Marx wanted to speak through myths, it would not have been amiss if he had warned us of this before the facts had contradicted his predictions; otherwise the prophet's trade would become too easy. One makes a prophesy; if the facts prove it correct, the wisdom of its author is admired; if it is contradicted by the facts, it is declared that it was a matter of a myth.

97. (§ 6, ε). Up to now our research has been related to facts which have actually taken place, to movements which we can call REAL, in order to distinguish them from other movements which are hypothetical, and which we will call VIRTUAL (III, 22).

We have not exhausted our subject by studying how certain facts occur; a problem of great importance remains to be studied: if one of several facts which have been related to each other is modified by hypothesis, what changes would the others experience? This problem is a necessary preparation for the solution of a second problem which consists in seeking the conditions which provide maximum utility for society, for a part of society, for a social class, and for a given individual—after what is meant by utility has been defined, of course.

98. These problems arise with regard to all of man's actions and, therefore, with regard to those which are the subject matter of POLITICS. Practically, they are more important than all the others. Moreover, still from this practical point of view, they are the only ones which matter, and any other study is useful only insofar as it

---

[68] *Introduction à l'économie moderne*, p. 377. [The insertion in the quotation above was made by Pareto.]

paves the way for their solution. They are also the most difficult; we will meet them again in political economy, and we then will be able to arrive at some at least approximate solutions. On the other hand, these problems as yet have no solutions, even grossly approximate ones, when it is a question of actions which depend on sentiments and politics. This difference provides us with the main reason for the more advanced state of the science of economics compared to the other social sciences.

99. In this matter, the basis of all reasoning lies in the following problem: what effects will certain given measures have on sentiments? Not only are we not able to solve this problem in general theoretically, but we do not even have the practical solutions which usually, in the history of human knowledge, precede the theoretical solutions and which often form the material from which the latter are derived. Even the most eminent statesmen almost always make mistakes when they search for these solutions. It is enough to recall the example of Bismark. He proposed to solve the following problem: what measures can weaken the sentiments which maintain the Catholic party and the socialist party? He believed he had found the solution in the *Kulturkampf* measures and some extraordinary laws against the socialists. The facts have shown that he was grossly mistaken. The effects which followed were precisely contrary to those he had hoped for: the Catholic party has dominated in the Reichstag; the socialist party has grown ever stronger, and each election has seen an increase in the number of votes they received. Not only have Bismark's measures not prevented these consequences, they have greatly contributed to them.[69]

100. The difficulties which stand in the way of working out a theory on this subject are in part objective and in part subjective.

Among the objective difficulties we will note the following:

1° The phenomena take place very slowly, and consequently without the frequency necessary to be able, with proofs and counterproofs, to form a theory. All the sciences have made extraordinary progress, and yet, on the topic we are dealing with, the best we have is still in the works of Aristotle and Machiavelli. Among the numerous reasons for this fact, not the least is the circumstance that these two writers lived in periods when political changes were rapid,

---

[69] The best knowledge we have on this point is to be found in Machiavelli: ". . . men must be either cajoled or exterminated, because they take vengence for small injuries, but cannot do so for serious ones; therefore the injury that one does a man ought to be such that one need not fear his vengeance." *The Prince*, Chap. III.

occurred in many places, and were frequent. Aristotle found very abundant material for his studies in the numerous Greek republics, as did Machiavelli in the many Italian states.

Assume that experiences similar to those we spoke of in connection with Bismark had been numerous and repeated over a short span of years. By comparing them and investigating what they had in common and how they differed, we would have been able to discover perhaps some uniformity which would be the beginning of a theory. We have been forced, on the contrary, to wait until now for a similar experience, the one furnished by the struggle of the French Jacobins against the Catholics. If it results in a situation similar to that which followed the German *Kulturkampf* we will have an indication of a uniformity. But what a feeble indication is one which is based on only two facts!

2° Phenomena connected with sentiment cannot be measured with precision; hence we cannot resort to statistics, so useful in political economy. The assertion that certain sentiments are weakened or strengthened is always a little arbitrary, and always depends somewhat on the writer who is considering the events.

3° Sociological phenomena are sometimes much more rare and more complex than those which are studied by political economy, and they are the result of many more causes, or more exactly, they are mutually related to a much greater number of other phenomena.

4° Since they very often are non-logical (§ 3) we cannot place them into reciprocal relationship by means of logical deductions, as we can do in political economy. The difficulty is increased still more by the fact that people are in the habit of attributing non-real logical motives to their actions.

5° It is very difficult to know another person's, or even one's own, sentiments in a precise way; the material which must serve as the basis of the theory is always a little uncertain. For example, in § 99 we gave as evidence of the power of socialist sentiments in Germany the fact that the number of votes received by the socialist party was growing larger. But that is only an indication, which needs to be supported by other evidence, because many of those voters are not socialists, but radicals, liberals, and simple malcontents.

101. Let us move along to the subjective difficulties:

1° Writers almost never are seeking the truth; they are seeking arguments to defend what they already believe to be the truth and is an article of faith for them. Research of this type is always sterile, at least in part. Writers follow such a procedure not only because they are unwittingly the plaything of their passions; often they do so deliberately, and they violently censure those who refuse to do so. What ridiculous charges have been levied against Machiavelli! This trouble also exists in political economy; and similarly the difficulties we are going to speak of are common to sociology and political economy. The majority of economists study and describe phenomena with the determination of ending up in a certain way.

2° The preconceptions and *a priori* ideas dependent on religion, morality, patriotism, etc. are infinite, and they prevent us from reasoning about social matters in a scientific manner. For example, the Jacobins seriously believe that "kings and priests" are the cause of all the ills of humanity,[70] and they see all history through these distorted glasses. Many of them imagine that Socrates was the victim of the "priests," whereas the priests had absolutely no part at all in the death of Socrates. For many socialists any misfortune, small or large, which can befall man is clearly a result of "capitalism". Mr. Roosevelt is persuaded that the American people are vastly superior to other peoples; and he does not see how ridiculous it is to cite Washington in order to show the world that "the most certain way to have peace is to be prepared for war" *(American Ideals,* Chapter VIII; this chapter is entitled "A Forgotten Precept of Washington").[71] We poor Europeans thought that, quite some time prior to Washington, certain inhabitants of a little country called Latium had already said, in their own idiom: *si vis pacem, et cetera;* but it seems that we have been deceived, the Latins undoubtedly copied Washington and repeated what he first had said.

Examples of other difficulties of the same type will be found in Herbert Spencer's *Introduction to Social Science.*

The same difficulties are encountered in the study of political economy. The "ethical" economists talk with a magnificent conceit about what they do not understand. Another, to hide his ignorance, spreads out his tail like a peacock and announces to the public that he follows the "historical method." Still another speaks of the "mathematical method" and he considers and condemns it, but he understands what he is talking about as much as an Athenian of the time of Pericles could understand Chinese.

---

[70] *Systèmes socialistes,* II, p. 491.

[71] French translation by de Rousiers, p. 130: "A forgotten maxim of Washington.—A century ago Washington wrote: 'The surest way of obtaining peace is to be ready for war'. We give lip-service to this maxim as we so often do to the words of Washington; but it has never been deeply engraved in our hearts."

3° The objective difficulty indicated in item 5 of § 100 is related to an analogous subjective difficulty, that is, that it is very difficult for us not to judge the actions of others according to our own sentiments. It has not been long since we have finally understood that to have a clear idea of the facts about a given people and a given period, it was necessary to endeavor, as much as possible, to look at them with the sentiments and the ideas of a person belonging to that people and that period. It has also been discovered that there are many things which, though having the same name, are essentially different in the places and in the times in which they have been observed. The French Jacobins of the first revolution believed, and some of their successors today still believe, that the French republic is the same or almost the same as the Roman republic or the Athenian republic.

4° Faith alone strongly moves men to act; and so it is not desirable for the good of society that the bulk of men, or even many of them, deal with social matters scientifically. There is an antagonism between the conditions for *action* and those for *knowledge*.[72] Here we have an additional argument (§ 60) which shows us how little wisdom is displayed by those who want to make everyone, indiscriminately and without distinction, participate in knowledge. It is true that the evil which that could entail is partially offset by the fact that what they call *knowledge* is simply a particular form of sectarian faith; and we would have to be concerned less with the evils which scepticism entails than with those which result from faith.

5° The contrast between the conditions for action and those for knowledge also appears in the fact that so far as actions are concerned we abide by certain rules of custom and morality; indeed it would not be possible to do otherwise if only because we have neither the time nor the means to go back to the beginning, in each particular case, and make a complete theory for it. On the other hand, in order to understand the relations between things, for

---

[72] For example Mr. Roosevelt's book, *American Ideals*, can perhaps serve to move the citizens of the United States to action, but certainly it adds nothing to our knowledge, and its scientific value is very close to zero.

The writer believes that his country is the foremost in the world; "to have the name American is to have the most honorable of all titles"; an Englishman may think the same thing about England, a German about Germany, etc. Logically the following two propositions, A outweighs B, and B outweighs A, are contradictory and cannot both hold good at the same time; but they can very well hold good at the same time if they have as an objective only moving men to action.

knowledge, to question these principles themselves is precisely what is necessary.

For example, among a warlike people mores are favorable to warlike sentiments. If it is accepted that this people should remain warlike, then it is useful for individual activity to be in accord with these sentiments, at least within certain limits. Thus it is right, always within these limits, to judge a given activity to be harmful solely because it is in opposition to these sentiments. But that conclusion is no longer valid if the inquiry is concerned with whether it is good for this people to be warlike or peaceful.

Similarly where private property exists, there also exist sentiments which are shocked by every infringement of this right; and as long as it is believed useful to maintain it, it is logical to condemn actions which are opposed to such sentiments. The latter thus become an appropriate criterion for deciding what is good or bad in that society. But they can no longer fulfill that role when the question is whether private property should be maintained or abolished. To oppose socialists, as some writers of the first half of the 19th century did, by saying they are criminals because they want to abolish private property, actually creates a vicious circle, allows the accused to be judge. The same error would be committed by wanting to pass judgment upon free love by invoking sentiments of chastity, decency and modesty.

In a society organized in a certain way, and where certain sentiments A exist, it is reasonable to think that a thing B which is contrary to those sentiments may be harmful. But experience tells us that there are societies organized in a different way; so the latter may contain sentiments C favorable to B, and B may be useful in that society Consequently when it is proposed to establish B in order to move from the first type of organization to the second, it can no longer be objected that B is contrary to the sentiments A which exist in the first type of organization.

Let us note again that the universal consent of men, assuming that it could be known, would not change that conclusion at all, even if one ignored the fact that yesterday's universal consent may well not be tomorrow's.

6° To convince someone about a scientific matter it is essential to set forth facts which are as definite as possible, and to put them into a logical relationship with the consequences one wants to draw from them. To convince someone about a matter of sentiments, and almost all reasonings about society and human institutions belong to that category, facts capable of rousing those sentiments must be presented so that they suggest the conclusion desired. It is obvious that these two ways of reasoning are completely different.

Here is an example. Brunetière, replying to M. René Bazin in the April 29, 1904, session of the French Academy, began by demonstrating that art ought to be *human*: "We can believe, everything calls on us to believe, that if we did not exist, the planets would no less describe their orbits through space; and it does not seem likely that if some day we disappeared from the face of the earth, nature and life must necessarily be destroyed and disappear with us. But what is art without man? To what would it relate? And what would its material be? Art has in fact no existence or reality other than for man and through man. . . . That is why the first requirement for art is to be human, even before that of being art." Let us note that here *human* means simply that which pertains to man; and in this sense the proposition stated is incontestable. But scarcely has Brunetière demonstrated his proposition in a certain sense, when he uses it in another; and by a sleight-of-hand trick *human* is changed into *humanitarian*, and that is not the same thing at all. "The naturalists have come to understand this [the proposition in the sense indicated above] . . . they have realized that the naturalistic novel, freed from its old contraints, could not fail to lead to the social novel sooner or later." Thus the new meaning reveals itself. "*By immersing itself in the masses*, in the words of La Bruyère, "it was then inevitable that naturalism made some discoveries. . . ." And thus *social* takes on a particular meaning and signifies that which pertain to certain classes; farther along this meaning becomes still more particular, and *human* art becomes not only *humanitarian* art, but even *humanitarian* in a sense which suits Brunetière: "You have realized that curiosity about the pleasure or the suffering of others is only from tactlessness or even perversity if we are not looking for reasons and means for establishing or tightening the bonds of solidarity which link us to them." It seems that the unhappy bourgeois are not men, and what relates to them is not *human*. Brunetière asks whether it has been noticed that in the novels of M. Bazin "one rarely saw any bourgeois heroes, in the background or barely outlined. But the real people, the ones you love, the favorites of your heart and your talent . . . are all of the people, of the true people, those who work with their hands, farmers, factory workers. . . . Within the narrow sphere of their work you have confined the drama of their existence. In *La terre qui meurt* the owner of the land which the Lumineau family farms does not even appear. . . ." If he had appeared, the novel would no longer have been *human*, a landowner is not a man.

Finally, in a burst of lyricism our writer, addressing himself to M. Bazin, declares: "I hardly know of a work in contemporary literature which is less aristocratic and less bourgeois, and more of the common people than yours. Not one of the masters of the theatre or of the contemporary novel is more obligingly inclined toward the humble or has a more anxious or more passionate interest in their misfortunes".[73]

To sum up, our writer's reasoning boils down to this: art ought to deal with things which concern man, to be human; thus it only ought to deal with the people, with workers, to have solidarity as an objective, to be humanitarian.

Logically this reasoning is absurd; yet it has been favorably received and applauded by the good bourgeois who listened to it, because they are not interested in reasoning but in words which gratify certain of their sentiments. These worthy people believe that by prostrating themselves before the people and humbly flattering them they will return to power. Moreover they are completely lacking in civic vigor; to experience agreeable sensations it is enough for them to contemplate some slick production where the words people, workers, the small and humble, human, solidarity, etc., appear again and again.

Among many peoples, reasoning on social matters stops where it appears that certain facts are, or are not, in agreement with religious sentiments. At the present time among civilized peoples, this point is found where the facts do, or do not, accord with humanitarian sentiments; and no one would dream of examining these sentiments themselves, as he would have to do to be scientific.

For example, Herbert Spencer has sentiments absolutely opposed to war; consequently when he has pushed his reasoning up to the

---

[73] In order to understand the meaning of this discourse, it is essential not to forget that there is a strong rivalry between the Catholic socialism of Brunetière and the other socialisms. The partisans of any one of these doctrines always go to great lengths to demonstrate that they are more concerned with the good of the people than are the partisans of the other doctrines. Each seeks to lead the water to his mill by flattering and beguiling the Demos.

Brunetière reserves the name social novel for novels which he likes, and denies that name to the novels of his adversaries: "for I call neither the Mystères de Paris, nor the Compagnon du Tour de France, nor Les Misérables a 'social novel'." For their part, the socialists do not permit Brunetière to call himself a socialist.

Someone who could call himself a "true socialist" without anyone contesting that title would have solved the most insoluble of problems. [The brackets in the paragraph in the text are Pareto's.]

point where it turns out that certain facts collide with these sentiments, there is nothing more to say as far as he is concerned, and these facts are condemned.[74] Other writers stop at the point where they can demonstrate that a certain thing is contrary to "the equality of men," and it does not enter their minds that this equality may very well be challenged.

102. Human society is not homogenous; it is made up of elements which differ more or less, not only according to the very obvious characteristics such as sex, age, physical strength, health, etc., but also according to less observable, but no less important, characteristics such as intellectual qualities, morals, diligence, courage, etc.

The assertion that men are objectively equal is so absurd that it does not even merit being refuted. On the other hand, the subjective idea of the equality of men is a fact of great importance, and one which operates powerfully to determine the changes which society undergoes.

103. Just as one distinguishes the rich and the poor in a society even though income increases gradually from the lowest to the highest, one can distinguish the elite in a society, the part which is *aristocratic*, in the etymological sense ($\alpha\rho\iota\sigma\tau\sigma\varsigma =$ best), and a common part. But we must always remember that one moves imperceptibly from the one to the other.

The notion of this elite is dependent on the qualities which one seeks in it. There can be an aristocracy of saints, an aristocracy of brigands, an aristocracy of scholars, an aristocracy of thieves, etc. If we consider a set of qualities which favor the prosperity of and domination by one class in the society, we have what we will call simply *the elite*.

---

[74] In the *Morale des divers peuples*, § 127, our writer says: "the name great is given to the Czar Peter, to Frederick [of Prussia], to Charlemagne, to Napoleon, despite the most cruel acts committed by them." And it does not enter his mind that many of these acts may have contributed considerably to human civilization. There is more: he condemns the Duke of Wellington, general of the English army, for having said to his soldiers that they "ought to believe that the obligations of their position are the most noble that a man can fulfill." But how could a general say anything else? Should he say to his soldiers: "You are malefactors because you fight; you ought to run away"? [The brackets in the quotation above are Pareto's.]

Spencer himself recognized, in his *Principles of Sociology*, that in former times war has been useful for civilization. We should now have arrived at a period when it is no longer useful, but harmful. That proposition may be true —it may also be false—but certainly is not so obvious that it can become an axiom suitable for judging all the actions of men of our times.

This elite exists in all societies and rules them, even when the regime is seemingly one with the most widespread democracy.

According to a very important law and one which is the principal explanation of many social and historical facts, these aristocracies do not endure, and are continually being reconstituted; thus we have a phenomenon which could be called the *circulation of the elites*.

We will have to come back to this when discussing population; here it is sufficient to have mentioned these facts briefly since we need them in the considerations which follow.

104. Let us assume a society composed of a dominant collectivity A and a subject collectivity B, which are clearly hostile to each other.

Both groups could appear as they really are. But it will more often happen that the dominant part A will want to appear to be acting for the common good because it hopes thereby to decrease the opposition of B, whereas the subject part B will frankly lay claim to the advantages it wants to obtain.

Similar facts are observed when the two parts are of different nationalities, for example, the English and the Irish, the Russians and the Poles.

The phenomenon becomes much more complex in a society of homogeneous nationality or, what comes to the same thing, a society considered to be such by those who comprise it.

At first, in this society, a part C, which partakes of both of the two adverse parts A and B, comes between them, and may be now on the one side and now on the other. Later part A divides into two: one part, which we will call Aα, still has enough strength and energy to defend its share of authority; the other part, which we will call Aβ, is made up of degenerated individuals, with feeble intelligence and will, *humanitarians*, as is said today. Similarly part B divides into two: the one part, which we will call Bα, constitutes the new aristocracy which is arising. It also acquires elements of A who, through cupidity and ambition, betray their own class and assume leadership of the opposition. The other part, which we will call Bβ, is composed of the common herd which forms the largest portion of human society.[75]

105. Objectively the struggle consists solely in the Bα trying to take the place of the Aα; everything else is subordinate and incidental.

In this war the leaders, that is the Aα and the Bα, need soldiers, and each side seeks to find them where it can.

---

[75] In reality we pass from one to the other of these classes by imperceptible degrees. We must remember the observation made in § 103.

The Aα try to make people believe that they are working for the common good, but in the actual case this is a two-edged sword. Indeed if, on the one hand, this serves to decrease the resistance of the Bβ, on the other hand it also decreases the energy of the Aβ, who take as true what is only a pure fiction and can only be useful as such. Eventually it can happen that the Bβ believe less and less in this slogan of the Aα, while the Aβ accept it more and more as the rule for their actual conduct, and in this case the artifice employed by the Aα turns back against them and ends up by doing them more harm than good. This can be observed today in certain countries in the relations between the bourgeoisie and the masses.[76]

106. As for the Bα, they appear as the champions of the Bβ and, better still, as the champions of measures useful to all citizens. In this way the dispute which, objectively, is a strugle for domination between the Aα and the Bα, assumes subjectively the form of a struggle for liberty, justice, rights, equality, and other similar things; and this is the form which history records.

For the Bα the advantages of operating in this way are especially that the Bα attract not only the Bβ, but part of the C, and also the majority of the Aβ.

Assume that the new elite were clearly and simply to proclaim its intentions which are to supplant the old elite; no one would come to its assistance, it would be defeated before having fought a battle. On the contrary, it appears to be asking nothing for itself, well knowing that without asking anything in advance it will obtain what it wants as a consequence of its victory; it asserts that it is fighting solely to obtain equality between the B and the A in general. Thanks to this fiction it wins the favor, or at least the benevolent neutrality, of the intermediate part C, which would not have consented to promote the particular objectives of the new aristocracy. Next, it not only is supported by the largest part of the masses, but it also wins the favor of the degenerate part of the old elite. It must be observed that this part, although degenerate, is still superior to the common herd; the Aβ are superior to the Bβ; furthermore they have the money necessary for the expenses of the war. It is a known fact that almost all revolutions have been the work, not of the common people, but of the aristocracy, and especially of the decayed part of the aristocracy; this is seen in history from the time of Pericles up to the time of the first French revolution; and even today we see that a part of the bourgeoisie strongly supports socialism, whose leaders, moreover, are all bourgeois. Elites usually end up committing suicide.

[76] *Systèmes socialistes*, p. 396.

What we have just said is only a *resumé* of numerous facts, and has no other value than that of facts. For lack of space, we refer the reader to the *Systèmes*, where they are partially explained.[77]

We now see the great subjective importance of the concept of the equality of men, an importance which does not exist from the objective point of view. This concept is the means commonly used, especially today, to get rid of one aristocracy and replace it with another.

107. We ought to observe that the degenerate part of the elite, that is the Aβ, is the part which is genuinely deceived and goes where it did not intend to go. The common people, that is the Bβ, often end up by gaining something, either during the struggle, or after a change of masters has taken place. The elite of the old aristocracy, that is the Aα, is not fooled, it succumbs to force; the new aristocracy obtains victory.

The work of the humanitarians of the 18th century in France paved the way for the murders of the *Terror*; the work of the liberals of the first half of the 19th century have paved the way for the demogogical oppression which is now dawning.

Those who demanded equality of citizens before the law certainly did not foresee the privileges which the masses now enjoy; the old special jurisdictions have been abolished, and a new one instituted, the arbitration boards favoring the workers.[78] Those who demanded freedom to strike did not imagine that this freedom, for the strikers, would consist of beating workers who wanted to continue to work and setting fire to factories with impunity. Those who demanded equality of taxes to aid the poor did not imagine that there would be a progressive tax at the expense of the rich, and a system in which the taxes are voted by those who do not pay them, so that one sometimes hears the following reasoning shamelessly made: "Tax A falls only on wealthy persons and it will be used for expeditures which will be useful only to the less fortunate; thus it will surely be approved by the majority of the voters."

Those naive persons who, in several countries, have disrupted the army by allowing themselves to be carried away by declamations on justice and equality, are then astonished and indignant at the rise of the anti-militarism of which they are the authors. They are not even intelligent enough to understand that one reaps what one sows.

---

[77] Many other facts will be found in our *Sociologie*.

[78] *Systèmes socialistes*, I, p. 136.

107b. The great error of the present time is believing that men can be governed by pure reason without making use of force, which is, on the contrary, the foundation of all social organization. It is also curious to observe that the antipathy of the contemporary bourgeoisie toward force ends up leaving the field free for violence. Criminals and rioters, being assured of impunity, do almost anything they want. The most peaceful people are forced, by the governments which have left only that way open to them, to band together and to resort to threats and violence to defend their interests.

The humanitarian religion will very probably disappear when it has accomplished its work of social dissolution and when a new elite has arisen on the ruins of the old one. The naive ignorance of a decadent bourgeoisie provides all the strength for that religion, which will have no more usefulness when the adversaries of the bourgeoisie have become so strong that they no longer hide their cards.

This is already the case with the foremost among them; and *syndicalism* already provides us with a preview of what the strength and dignity of the new elite will be.

One of the most remarkable works of our time is the one which G. Sorel has published under the title *Reflexions sur la violence*.[79] It anticipates the future by departing completely from the meaningless declamations of humanitarianism, and returning to scientific reality.

108. The economic and social theories used by those who take part in the social struggle ought to be judged not for their objective value but primarily for their effectiveness in arousing emotions. The scientific refutation of them which can be made is useless, however correct it may be objectively.

That is not all. When it is useful to them, men can believe a theory of which they know nothing more than its name. This is a phenomenon common to all religions. The majority of Marxian socialists have not read the works of Marx. In some particular cases there is definite proof of this. For example, before these works had been translated into French and Italian, the French and Italian socialists who did not know German certainly could not have read them. The last parts of Marx's *Capital* were translated into French at the time when Marxism began to decline in France.

All the scientific debates for or against free trade have had no, or only a trivial, influence on the practice of free trade or protection.

[79] *Le Mouvement socialiste* since January 1906, and mainly during May-June 1906.

Men follow their sentiment and their self-interest, but it pleases them to imagine that they follow reason. And so they look for, and always find, some theory which, *a posteriori*, makes their actions appear to be logical. If that theory could be demolished scientifically, the only result would be that another theory would be substituted for the first one, and for the same purpose; a new form would be used, but the actions would remain the same.

Thus one can appeal mainly to sentiment and interests in order to induce men to act and to make them follow the path one wants. There is still very little known about the theory of these phenomena, and we cannot go into it further here.

109. The equality of citizens before the law is a dogma for many people, and in this sense it escapes experimental criticism. If we want to discuss this in a scientific manner, we will see immediately that it is not at all evident *a priori* that such equality is advantageous to society; moreover, given the heterogeneity of society itself, the contrary appears more probable.

If, in modern societies, this equality has replaced the personal statutes of former societies, it is perhaps because the evils produced by equality are less than those caused by the contradiction found between the personal statutes and the sentiment of equality which exists among the moderns.

In addition that equality is often a fiction. Every day new privileges are granted to workers, who thus obtain a personal statute which is not without utility for them. We have already noted that, thanks to the logic of sentiment, it does not follow from the notion that the worker is equal to the bourgeois that the bourgeois is equal to the worker.[80]

110. A consequence of the heterogeneity of society is that rules

---

[80] In order to find out just what *equality* is in the most advanced of modern democracies, one has only to read the speech of M. Deschanel in the French Chamber on May 8, 1907.

In this connection M. G. de Lamarzelle writes: "And so, under the so-called democratic regimes it is never the masses, but always a minority, which directs everything, which is master of everything."

"That minority . . . has succeeded in dominating everything in France, and it makes use of that domination—M. Steeg's speech demonstrates this superabundantly—especially to gratify the self-interest, the appetites, of its members."

What these statesmen now conclude from contemporary facts, we had deduced in general from the facts of all history in the *Systèmes socialistes* published in 1902, well before Sir Henry Sumner Maine had pointed out this uniformity of history.

of conduct, beliefs, morals, should be, in part at least, different for the different parts of the society in order to obtain maximum utility for the society. Indeed, this is more or less the case in our societies, and it is only a fiction to speak of a single morality. Governments, for example, have quite different ideas about honesty than private individuals have. It is enough to mention the espionage to which they resort in order to obtain secrets of national defense,[81] the coining of false money, replaced nowadays by issues of paper money, etc.

Among private individuals we can observe various "professional morals" which more or less differ from each other.

These differences do not prevent the different moral codes from having something in common. The problem, as are all problems in sociology, is essentially quantitative.

111. If the different classes of human societies were physically separated, as are those of some insects (termites), these different moralities could exist without clashing too much. But the classes of human societies are intermingled, and in addition, among people nowadays there is a very strong sentiment of equality which could not be offended without serious trouble. And so it is necessary that these essentially different moralities have the appearance of not being so.

Add to this that it is difficult for a given class of people to go on indefinitely appearing to have sentiments which it does not have; thus it is necessary that these different moralities be considered to be equal by those who hold to them. Casuistry, which is to be found at all times and among all peoples, takes care of that in part. A general principle, which everyone accepts, is laid down; then all the necessary exceptions are made, thanks to which the principle is no longer general except in appearance. All Christians of the Middle Ages fully accepted the divine precept of forgiveness of offenses, but the feudal nobility did their best to avenge injuries received. In our day everyone declares himself in favor of the equality of men, but that does not prevent the workers from obtaining new privileges every day.

112. The means which serve to separate moralities are very imperfect, and so moral codes are mixed together in actuality, and in this way we move away from conditions which can make society prosper.

---

[81] In 1904 many French newspapers talked, eulogistically and as if she were a heroine, of a certain woman in the service of the German ambassador to Paris, who betrayed him and turned over to the agents of the French government papers which she had stolen from the Embassy.

113. The lower classes need a humanitarian morality which also serves to alleviate their suffering. If the upper classes subscribe to it only so far as the form is concerned, the evil is not great; but on the other hand, if they actually follow it, serious evils for society result. In former times it was often pointed out that the people needed to be governed with an iron hand in a velvet glove. Justice ought to be strict and appear lenient. The surgeon reassures his patient with kind words while with a sure hand and without pity he cuts the flesh.

114. In a more restricted society, that is to say, that of today's socialists, we see that the leaders, and, in general, the more cultivated socialists, have beliefs rather different from those of the masses. While the latter dream of a future golden age which will come with "collectivism," the former, having learned from experience in the governance of their organization, or in public administration, have less faith in the panacea of collectivism, and prefer to concern themselves with more immediate reforms.[82] This diversity in faith is very useful to the socialists because in this way each one has the faith which corresponds best to the effort which he must put forth.

115. The diverse natures of men, combined with the necessity to satisfy in some manner the sentiment which desires them to be equal, has had the result that in the democracies they have endeavored to provide the appearance of power in the people and the reality of power in an elite. Up to now only the democracies where that could be done have prospered, but this equilibrium is unstable and after many mutations some radical disorders result.

116. The story told by Dionysius of Halicarnassus is typical of many later historical phenomena. Servius Tullius beguiled the common people with centurial meetings, but made himself the government of the state. "They thought that every one had an equal part in the government of the city because each man, in his century, was

---

[82] Toward the end of the year 1906 Jaurès was called upon in the Chamber to state precisely the legislation needed to establish the collectivism which he had been demanding for so long. He asked for three months in order to do so. This is astounding enough, if one takes only the logical point of view, because one would have expected a leader of a party to know exactly what he wanted to obtain. But there is even more; the three months have long since passed and the end of 1907 has come without Jaurès having revealed his plan which still remains hidden in deep clouds.

Behaving like this may seem absurd from an objectively logical point of view; on the other hand it is perfectly sensible and reasonable from the subjective point of view of the effect on sentiments; and this is for the reasons which have just been given in the text.

called on to give his opinion, but they were deceived because each century had only one vote whether it was made up of a great many citizens or of only a few"[83] and because in addition to that the poor people were called on last and only if the vote of the first centuries had not been decisive.

Cicero tells us that liberty consists in giving to the people the right to put their trust in good citizens;[84] and this is in fact the principle which the modern representative regime intended to implement. But in neither Rome nor in the modern states has it been achieved; and the people have wanted more and better than the simple right of electing the best ones to govern.

117. History teaches us that the governing classes have always tried to speak to the people not in words they believe are the most true, but in those which best suit the objectives they have in mind.[85] And this occurs even in the most advanced democracies, such as the French democracy. There we have another notable example of the continuation of the same social phenomena under different forms.

118. For reasons which it is unnecessary to go into here, the governing class in France is made up of two parts, which we will call A and B. The A, in order to rid themselves of the B, called upon the socialists for assistance, but determined to concede little or nothing to the people, feeding them empty words and paying liberally only the leaders whom they desired to have in their service. In order that this behavior not be too obvious and to divert attention from it, they engineered the anticlerical campaign; and with that bait they won over some naive persons, to whom were added without much trouble the humanitarians of feeble intelligence and energy. In a

---

[83] *Antiquitates Romanae*, IV, 21: Ὑπελάμβανον μὲν γὰρ ἅπαντες ἴσον ἔχειν τῆς πολιτείας μέρος, κατ' ἄνδρα διερωτώμενοι τὰς γνώμας ἐν τοῖς ἰδίοις ἕκαστοι λόχοις· ἐξηπατῶντο δὲ τῷ μίαν εἶναι ψῆφον ὅλου τοῦ λόχου, τοῦ τε ὀλίγους ἔχοντος ἐν αὐτῷ πολίτας καὶ τοῦ πάνυ πολλούς.

[84] It was for this reason that he wanted the people to show their ballots and give them to the best citizen. *De Lege Manilia*, III, 17: "habeat sane populus tabellam, quasi vindicem libertatis, dummodo haec optimo cuique et gravissimo civi ostendatur, ultroque offeratur; uti in eo sit ipso libertas, in quo populo potestas honeste bonis gratificandi datur."

[85] Aristotle describes the artifices employed by the oligarchies, *Politics*, IV, 10, 6: Ἔστι δ' ὅσα προφάσεως χάριν ἐν ταῖς πολιτείαις σοφίζονται πρὸς τὸν δῆμον πέντε τὸν ἀριθμόν. "In republics the people are deceived in five ways by these pretenses." And he adds that in democracies similar artifices are employed.

word, there are in France today some "capitalists" who are becoming rich and powerful by making use of the socialists.[86]

---

[86] See an excellent article by G. Sorel in Colajanni's *Rivista popolare*: "The experience with the anticlerical policy which the French government has followed with such obstinancy for the last two years constitutes one of the most significant social phenomena the philosopher can study." The writer points out of cowardice of M. Combes's adversaries, which is, moreover, only one particular case of the general law of the decadence of aristocracies. "When they began to expel the monks, it was announced that there would be vigorous opposition . . . but after a few attempts in Brittany everything calmed down. . . . The courage of the opponents did not extend to legal opposition. . . . The *Libre Parole* has noted several times that the Catholic world has not cut down its feast days and has changed nothing at all in its worldly relationships. . . . Urbain Gohier has revealed in vigorous articles all sorts of traffic which was engaged in by the *Petite République*, and if many young people have become socialists there is no doubt but that it is because they were sure of making a good bargain. They would be really interested in knowing the names of the capitalists who have recently given large enough sums to enable *La Petite République* to be transformed and *Humanité* to be established. No one imagines, I assume, that the capitalists provide money to socialist newspapers out of love for collectivism! Millions are not given to businesses of this type if those who are providing them are not sure of getting some benefit from it. Parliamentary socialism has become an excellent enterprise whose shares are highly regarded in the world of the Bourse."

The writer has a clear notion of the way in which political evolution takes place: "Thus practical questions are hidden under a double layer of sentiments, which prevent people from perceiving that there is more egoism and evil passion in their political leadership than they think. . . . In general, politics is especially dominated by the interests of those who practice it and who plan to derive some advantage from it. These interests combine easily, and this is how liberal governments almost everywhere rely on people who want something for themselves or for their electoral councils or for the social groups whose votes they seek."

As long ago as 1883 M. Germain, who was manager of the *Crédit Lyonnais*, described politicians very precisely: "those men who hold to only one thing: having the majority and administering the budget of France on behalf of their clients."

We can add certain facts brought to light during the inquiry about the Chartreux affair. The first is about someone who disclosed that he, with his friends, had given one hundred thousand francs for the elections, and added that otherwise "he didn't concern himself with politics." The other fact M. Aynard spoke about in the Chamber of Deputies on July 12, 1904: ". . . it is a question of knowing also about the money of the Mascuraud Committee, that auxiliary of the Government. It is a question of knowing who is this strange person who keeps admirable accounts of his banquets, especially his banquets, and of his comings and goings, but keeps no accounts at all of money."

But that is nothing beside what goes on in the United States at election time.

119. The lower one descends in the social classes, the more misoneism dominates, and the more men refuse to act upon any consideration other than those of their direct and immediate interests. In Rome, just as they have among modern peoples, the upper classes relied on that in order to govern. But it cannot last, because the lower classes eventually understand their self-interests better and turn against those who have exploited their ignorance.

120. This phenomenon can be clearly observed in England. The Tory party has played a role in extending the suffrage more and more in order to draw on the classes which were useful to it in controlling the government, repaying their allies with measures which have been justly called "Tory Socialism." Now the Whigs, who formerly championed liberal principles, compete with the Tories for the favor of the common people. They are seeking an alliance with the socialists, and they go much farther than the mealy-mouthed and humanitarian socialism of the Tories. The two parties fight to see which will prostrate itself more humbly at the feet of the common man, and each of them is trying to take the place of the other through its adulation. This appears even in the smallest details. During election campaigns the candidates are not ashamed to send their wives and daughters out to beg votes. The unexpected novelty of such actions captivates the common man, amazed at so much love and goodwill. But in the long run they end up by nauseating those who understand the self-interested flattery only too well.

121. When a social class realizes that the upper classes simply want to exploit it, the latter go to a lower one to find other supporters; but it is obvious that there will come a day when they can no longer do this, because there is no lower one. When the suffrage has been given to all men, including madmen and criminals, when it has been extended to women, and, if you like, to children, it will have to stop. One cannot go any lower, unless the suffrage is extended to animals, which would be easier than making them exercise it.

122. In Germany universal suffrage was established in part as a weapon against the liberal bourgeoisie; thus the phenomenon is similar to what took place in England. Similarly many social laws have been introduced with the hope of winning away supporters of the socialist party. But this result has not been attained, and the people are well aware of the artifices employed to inveigle them. Now the upper classes are beginning to complain about universal suffrage and are looking for a way to turn back.[87]

[87] Professor von Jagemann, who was a member, for the government of Baden, of the Federal Council of the Empire for ten years, and who is now

123. When the democratic evolution, which developed in the course of the 19th century and which seems likely to end in the 20th, first began, several thinkers saw quite clearly what the outcome would have to be. But their predictions are forgotten now when they are coming true, and when at last the man belonging to the lowest social classes will comprehend and make a reality of the logical observation that "if the arbitrary expression of my will is the principle for the legal order, my enjoyment can also be the principle for the distribution of wealth."[88]

But history will not stop at the end of the present evolution, and unless the future is completely different from the past, the present evolution will be succeeded by an evolution in the opposite direction.

[88] Stahl, *Rechtsphilosophie*, II, 2, p. 72.

professor of public law at the University of Heidelberg, has writen an interesting work in which he examines the legal means which could be used to replace the universal suffrage in Germany with a limited suffrage.

CHAPTER III

GENERAL NOTION OF ECONOMIC EQUILIBRIUM

1. The purpose of all the preceding was not to expound theory, but to give some examples of a very extensive class of phenomena which can be abstracted from in practical questions only very rarely. Now we are going to study an entirely different class of phenomena from which we propose to construct our theory.

We will study the many logical, repeated actions which men perform to procure the things which satisfy their tastes.

Let us examine a relation of the type we have indicated by AB in § 89 of Chapter II. We will not have to deal with relations of type BC, at least not in pure economics, nor with the reactions of the latter on B. In other words, we are concerned only with certain relations between objective facts and subjective facts, principally the tastes of men. Moreover, we will simplify the problem still more by assuming that the subjective fact conforms perfectly to the objective fact. This can be done because we will consider only repeated actions to be a basis for claiming that there is a logical connection uniting such actions. A man who buys a certain food for the first time may buy more of it than is necessary to satisfy his tastes, price taken into account. But in a second purchase he will correct his error, in part at least, and thus, little by little, will end up by procuring exactly what he needs. We will examine this action at the time when he has reached this state. Similarly, if at first he makes a mistake in his reasoning about what he desires, he will rectify it in repeating the reasoning and will end up by making it completely logical.

2. Thus by considering only one part of man's actions and, in addition, by assigning certain characteristics to them, we have simplified the problem enormously. The study of these actions makes up the subject of political economy.

3. But on the other hand, the problem is very complex, because the objective facts are very numerous and partly depend upon each other. This mutual dependence makes ordinary logic soon become impotent when we go beyond the first elements of our study. We must then resort to a special logic appropriate to this type of study, that is, to mathematical logic. Hence there is no reason to speak of a "mathematical method" which is *opposed* to other methods. It is a matter of a research procedure and proofs ADDED to the other methods.

4. Moreover, still due to the difficulties inherent in the problem itself, we must subdivide the subject. We must begin by eliminating everything which is not essential and consider the problem reduced to its principal and essential elements. Hence we distinguish pure economics from applied economics. The first is represented by a figure which contains only the principal lines; by adding details the second is obtained. These two parts of economics are analogous to the two parts of mechanics: rational mechanics and applied mechanics.

5. A similar approach is utilized in nearly all branches of human knowledge. Even in grammar one begins by giving the principal phonetic rules, to which particular rules are then added. In Greek grammar, when it is said that the augment is the sign of the past tense of the indicative of historical time, we have a rule of what could be called "pure grammar." But by itself it is not sufficient for knowing what these past tenses actually are; for that, a large number of particular rules must be added.

6. Hence the problem which we propose to study is a very particular problem and we seek the solution so that we may then go on to further investigations.

7. The study of pure economics is composed of three parts: a static part, a dynamic part which studies successive equilibria, and a dynamic part which studies the movement of an economic phenomenon.

This division corresponds to reality. What will the average price of 3 percent French government bonds be on the Paris exchange today? This is a problem of statics. Some others of the same type are: What will the average price be tomorrow, the day after tomorrow, etc.? According to what law do these average prices vary; will they go higher, lower? These are problems of successive equilibria. What laws rule the price movements of 3 percent French government bonds; that is, how does a movement in the upward direction go beyond the point of equilibrium to become itself the cause of a movement in the opposite direction? How do these prices vary, rapidly or slowly, with a movement sometimes accelerated, sometimes retarded? These are problems of dynamic economics.

8. The theory of statics is the most advanced; we have only a very few notions about the theory of successive equilibria; and, except for a special theory, that of economic crises, nothing is known about dynamic theory.

9. At first we will be concerned with static theory exclusively. We may consider an isolated economic phenomenon, for example, the production and consumption of a certain quantity of a good; or we may study a continuing economic phenomenon, that is, the production and consumption of a certain quantity of a good per unit of time. As we have already seen, political economy studies phenomena which are repeated (§ 1), not accidental, exceptional phenomena, but average phenomena. Consequently, we will come closer to reality by studying continuing economic phenomena. Will such and such a person buy, or will she not buy, today, such and such a genuine pearl? This may be a psychological problem, but it certainly is not an economic problem. How many pearls are sold, on the average, per month, per year, in England? That is an economic problem.

10. When it is clearly understood that the phenomenon studied is a continuing phenomenon, no harm is done in simplifying the exposition of the theory by not repeating "per unit of time" each time it is appropriate. For example, when we speak of the exchange of 10 kilograms of iron for 1 kilogram of silver, the words "which takes place per unit of time" must be understood, as well as the fact that we are not speaking of an isolated exchange but of an exchange which is repeated.

11. There are two large classes of theories. The object of the first is to compare the sensations of one man in different situations, and to determine which of these he would chose. Political economy deals with this class of theories primarily; and, since it is customary to assume that man will be guided in his choice exclusively by consideration of his own advantage, of his self-interest, we say that this class is made up of theories of egotism. But it could be made up of theories of *altruism* (if the meaning of that term could be defined rigorously), or, in general, of theories which rest on any rule which man follows in comparing his sensations. It is not an essential characteristic of this class of theories that a man choosing between two sensations choose the most agreeable; he could choose a different one, following a rule which could be fixed arbitrarily. What does constitute the essential characteristic of this class of

theories is that we compare the different sensations of one man, and not those of different men.

12. The second class of theories compares the sensations of one man with those of another man, and determines the conditions in which the men must be placed relative to each other if we want to attain certain ends. This study is one of the most unsatisfactory in social science.[1]

13. Two routes, each of which has advantages and disadvantages, are available to us for the study we want to make. We can study each subject thoroughly in turn. Or we can begin by getting a general, and necessarily superficial, notion about a phenomenon, and then return later to study in detail the things already considered in a general way, completing our study by moving ever closer to the phenomenon under consideration. If the first method is followed the material will be more orderly and there will be no repetitions; but this way it is difficult to acquire a clear view of the complex whole of a phenomenon. By following the second method we obtain this view of the whole, but must then resign ourselves to indicating certain details in passing and must return to them for study later. Despite its drawbacks we believe it is advantageous not to disregard this method, chiefly because it is a good one to use when, as is precisely true of economic science, there has been up to now more study of the details than of the general phenomenon, which has been completely or almost completely neglected. It may be that some day, in a few years or much later, this reason will no longer exist; in that case, it will be better to proceed differently and stick to the first method.

14. The principal subject of our study is economic equilibrium. We will see shortly that this equilibrium results from the opposition between men's tastes and the obstacles to satisfying them. Our study includes, then, three very distinct parts: 1° the study of tastes; 2° the study of obstacles; 3° the study of the way in which these two elements combine to reach equilibrium.

15. The best order to follow would consist of beginning with the study of tastes and exhausting that subject; to go then to the study of obstacles and exhaust it too; and finally to study equilibrium, without returning to the study of tastes or of obstacles.

But it would be difficult for the author, as well as for the reader, to proceed in that way. It is impossible to exhaust one of these subjects without frequently bringing in notions which pertain to the

---

[1] *Cours d'économie politique*, II, § 654.

other two. If these notions are not thoroughly explained, the reader cannot follow the exposition; if they are explained, we are mixing together the subjects which it was proposed to separate. Moreover, the reader easily tires of a long study the purpose of which he does not see. The writer realizes this and will treat tastes and obstacles, not haphazardly, but only insofar as may be necessary to determine equilibrium. The reader also has the justifiable desire to know where the long road which we want him to travel is leading.

To point out where we are going and to acquire certain notions which will be of use in our studies, we will give a general idea of the three parts of the phenomenon in this chapter. We will study tastes and obstacles only insofar as is necessary in order to get some rough ideas of economic equilibrium. Then we will go back to each of the parts of this whole about which we have thus gained a partial understanding. We will study tastes in Chapter IV, obstacles in Chapter V; and finally in Chapter VI we will see how these elements behave when there is equilibrium.

16. Let us assume that certain things capable of satisfying men's tastes exist. We will call these things economic goods. If we pose this problem—how to divide one of these goods among these individuals?—we are faced with a question which involves the second class of theories (§ 12). In fact, each man experiences only one sensation, the one which corresponds to the quantity of the economic good which is assigned to him. We are not dealing with different sensations of the same individual which we could compare with each other, hence we may only compare the sensation experienced by one individual with that which another individual experiences.

17. If there are two or more things, each individual experiences two or more different sensations, depending on the quantity of the things at his disposal. In that case we can compare these sensations and determine which of the different possible combinations will be chosen by that individual. This is a question which belongs to the first class of theories (§ 11).

18. If all the quantities of goods which an individual has at his disposal increase (or decrease), we will see immediately that, with the exception of one case which we will discuss later (IV, 34), the new position will be more advantageous (or less advantageous) for that individual than the old one. Hence in this case there is no problem to solve. But if, on the other hand, certain quantities increase while others decrease, there is occasion for investigating whether the new combination is, or is not, advantageous to the individual. It is to this category that economic problems belong. In real life we

see them arise in connection with the exchange contract, in which one thing is given up in order to receive another, and in connection with production, in which certain things are transformed into certain others. We will deal with these problems first.

19. The elements which we must combine are, on the one hand, man's tastes, and on the other, the obstacles to satisfying them. If, instead of having to deal with men, we had to study ethereal beings with neither tastes nor needs, not even experiencing the material needs of eating and drinking, there would be no economic problem to solve at all. Going to the opposite extreme, it would be the same if we were to assume that no obstacles prevented men from satisfying all their tastes and all their desires. There is no economic problem for one who has everything without limit.

The problem arises because tastes encounter certain obstacles, and it is so much the more difficult to solve if there are several ways of satisfying these tastes and overcoming these obstacles. Thus there is occasion for investigating how and why such and such a means may be preferred by the individuals.

Let us examine the problem more closely.

20. If one only had to choose between two or a few things, the problem to solve would be qualitative and its solution would be easy. Which do you prefer, a cask of wine or a watch? The answer is easy. But in actual fact there is a very great number of things from which choice may be made; and even for two things, the combinations of quantities among which one may choose are innumerable. In one year a man can drink 100, 101, 102, . . . litres of wine; if his watch does not run perfectly, he can get another one immediately, or wait one month, two months, . . . , one year, two years, . . . before making that purchase, and keep his watch while waiting. In other words, the variations in the quantity of things among which one must choose are infinite, and these variations can be very slight, almost imperceptible. We must construct a theory which enables us to solve this type of problem.

21. Consider a series of these combinations of different quantities of goods. A man can pass from one to another of these combinations finally settling upon one of them. It is very important to know which is this final one, and we achieve that by the theory of economic equilibrium.

22. **Economic equilibrium.** It can be defined in different ways which come to the same thing in the end. We may say that economic equilibrium is the state which would maintain itself indefinitely if there were no changes in the conditions under which it is observed.

If, for the moment, we consider only stable equilibrium, we may say that it is determined in such a way that, if it is but slightly modified, it immediately tends to reestablish itself, to return to its original position. The two definitions are equivalent.

For example, certain circumstances or conditions being given, an individual buys 1 kilogram of bread every day. If one day he is obliged to buy 900 grams, and if the next day he again becomes free to do so, he will again buy 1 kilogram of bread. If nothing is changed in the existing conditions, he will continue to buy 1 kilogram of bread indefinitely. This is what is called the state of equilibrium.

It will be necessary to express mathematically that, this state of equilibrium being attained, these variations, or, if you will, these movements, do not occur, which comes down to saying that the system maintains itself indefinitely in the state we have considered.

The movements necessary actually to reach equilibrium can be called *real*. Those which we assume could occur to move us away from the state of equilibrium, but which do not appear in reality because the equilibrium continues, can be called *virtual*.

Political economy studies real movements in order to know how things take place; and it studies virtual movements to understand the properties of certain economic states.

23. Given an economic state, if we were able to move away from it by any kind of movement whatsoever, we could continue indefinitely movements which increase the quantities of all the goods which man may desire; in this way we would reach a state in which man would have everything to satiety. Obviously this would be a position of equilibrium; but it is also obvious that things do not happen that way in real life, and that we will have to determine other positions of equilibrium at which one must stop, because only certain movements are possible. In other words, there are obstacles which limit movements, which do not allow man to follow certain paths, which prevent certain variations from taking place. Equilibrium results precisely from this opposition of tastes and obstacles. The two extreme cases which we have just considered, and which are not encountered in reality, are the one in which there are no tastes and the one in which there are no obstacles.

24. If the obstacles or the constraints were such that they determined each movement in a precise way, we would not have to be concerned with tastes; and consideration of the obstacles would be enough to determine equilibrium. In reality things are not like that, at least in general. The obstacles do not determine all movements in an absolute fashion. They simply establish certain limits; they

impose certain restrictions; but they do allow the individual to move according to his own tastes within a more or less restricted domain. And among all the admissable movements we must look for those which will occur in real life.

25. Tastes and obstacles refer to each of the individuals considered. For one individual the tastes of other men with whom he has relationships appear among the obstacles.

26. In order to have all the data for the problem of equilibrium, it is necessary to add to the tastes and obstacles the factual conditions which determine the state of the individuals and of the transformations of goods. For example, the quantities of goods possessed by the individuals, the means for transforming goods, etc. We will understand this better as our study advances.

27. To determine equilibrium we will set up the condition that at the moment when it occurs, movements permitted by the obstacles are prevented by the tastes; or conversely, what comes to the same thing, that at this moment, movements permitted by the tastes are prevented by the obstacles. Indeed, it is obvious that in these two ways we express the condition that no movement occurs, and this is, by definition, the equilibrium characteristic.

Thus we must investigate, at the equilibrium point, what movements are prevented and what movements are permitted by tastes; and similarly what movements are prevented and what ones are permitted by the obstacles.

28. **Men's tastes.** Means must be found for subjecting them to calculation. Some writers have had the idea of deducing them from the pleasure which certain things cause men to experience. If a thing satisfies the needs or desires of a man, they would say that it had *value in use, utility*.

29. This notion was imperfect and ambiguous on several points. 1° It was not sufficiently demonstrated that this *value in use*, this *utility*, was exclusively a relation between a man and a thing. Moreover, they spoke of it, perhaps unconsciously, as an objective property of the things. Others, who came closer but yet not close enough to the truth, spoke of it as a relation between men in general and a thing. 2° It was not seen that this *value in use* depended on (was a function of, as the mathematicians say) the quantities consumed. For example, to speak of the *value in use* of water does not make sense unless something more is said; and it does not suffice to add, as we have just seen, that this *value in use* is relative to a certain man. It is very different depending on whether that man is dying of thirst or has already drunk as much as he desires. To be precise,

it is necessary to speak of the value in use of a certain quantity of water added to a known quantity already consumed.

30. It was principally through the correction of this error in earlier economics that pure economics arose. It appeared with Jevons as a rectification of the then current theories on *value;* with Walras it became, and this was very great progress, the theory of a special case of economic equilibrium, that is, that of free competition; another case, the case of monopoly, had already been studied, but in a completely different manner, by Cournot. Marshall, Edgeworth and Irving Fisher studied the economic phenomenon in a still more extensive and more general way. In our *Cours* it became the general theory of economic equilibrium, and we are going still farther along this path in the present work.[2] 3° In political economy the word *utility* has come to mean something quite different from what it can mean in everyday language. Thus morphine is not useful, in the ordinary sense of the word, since it is harmful to the morphine addict; on the other hand it is economically *useful* to him, even though it is unhealthful, because it satisfies one of his wants. Although the older economists had mentioned this ambiguity, it is still forgotten occasionally; also, it is essential not to use the same word to mean such different things. In our *Cours* we proposed to designate economic *utility* by the word *ophelimity*, which some other authors have since adopted.

31. Here we must make a general observation which applies to the present case as well as to many others we will discuss later. Our criticisms of the old theories are valid today but do not apply to the time at which they were being developed. It would be a serious error to think that it would have been a good thing had these erroneous theories never seen the light of day. These or other similar ones were indispensable in order to arrive at better theories. Scientific conceptions are modified little by little so as to come closer to the truth; theories are continually being improved. At first one accepts certain imperfect propositions and goes ahead with the study of the science; then he goes back and refines these propositions. It is only in our day that examination of the postulate of Euclid has been resumed. What would have happened to geometry if the ancients had stubbornly and obstinately stopped to examine that postulate and had completely neglected moving forward in the study of the science? There is a great difference between the astronomical theories of

[2] A greater number of details on the history of theories of pure economics will be found in our article: *Anwendungen der Mathematik auf Nationalökonomie,* in *Encyclopädie der mathematischen Wissenschaften.*

Newton, those of Laplace, and other more modern theories; but the first ones were a necessary step for reaching the second, and these latter for reaching the third. The theories of early economics were necessary to reach new theories; and these, still very imperfect, will enable us to reach other theories which will be less so; and so on. Perfecting a theory is completely different from seeking to destroy it by foolish and pedantic subtleties. The first task is sensible and useful, the second is not very reasonable as well as fruitless, and someone who has no time to waste does better not to bother with it.

32. For an individual, the ophelimity of a certain quantity of a thing, added to another known quantity (it can be equal to zero) which he already possesses, is the pleasure which this quantity affords him.

33. If this quantity is very small (infinitely small) and if the pleasure which it gives is divided by the quantity itself, we have ELEMENTARY OPHELIMITY.

34. Finally, if we divide the elementary ophelimity by the price, we have WEIGHTED ELEMENTARY OPHELIMITY.

35. The theory of ophelimity has been improved. There is a weak point, pointed out principally by Professor Irving Fisher, in all the reasoning used to establish it. We have taken this thing called *pleasure, value in use, economic utility, ophelimity,* to be a quantity; but a demonstration of this has not been given. Assuming this demonstration accomplished, how would this quantity be measured? It is an error to believe that we could in general deduce the value of ophelimity from the law of supply and demand. We can do so only in one particular case, the unit of measure of ophelimity alone remaining arbitrary; this is when it is a case of goods of a kind such that the ophelimity of each of them depends only on the quantity of that good, and remains independent of the quantities of other goods consumed (Appendix). But in general, that is, when the ophelimity of a good A, consumed at the same time as goods B, C, . . ., depends not only on the consumption of A, but also on the consumption of B, C, . . ., the ophelimity remains indeterminate, even after the unit which serves to measure it has been fixed (Appendix).

36. Hereafter, when we speak of ophelimity it must always be understood that we simply mean one of the systems of indices of ophelimity (§ 55).

36b. The notions of *value in use, utility,* ophelimity, indices of ophelimity, etc., greatly facilitate the exposition of the theory of economic equilibrium, but they are not necessary to construct this theory.

Thanks to the use of mathematics, this entire theory, as we develop it in the Appendix, rests on no more than a fact of experience, that is, on the determination of the quantities of goods which constitute combinations between which the individual is indifferent[3] (§ 52). The theory of economic science thus acquires the rigor of rational mechanics; it deduces its results from experience, without bringing in any metaphysical entity.

37. As we have already observed there can be certain constraints which prevent phenomena being altered to fit tastes. For example, in former times there were governments which obliged their subjects to buy a certain quantity of salt each year. In this case it is obvious that tastes would not be taken into account. They would not have to be taken into account for anything where the quantity which each person must buy each year were fixed for everyone. If this were so in practice, it would be unnecessary to waste our time investigating the theory of tastes. But the most ordinary observation is sufficient to see that things do not happen that way in reality. Even when there are certain constraints, as, for example, when the State, having a monopoly of a good, fixes the price or imposes certain obstacles to its production, sale, free trade, etc., that does not absolutely prevent the individual from acting according to his tastes within certain limits. Consequently, everyone must solve certain problems in order to determine his consumption according to his tastes. The poor man will ask himself whether it would be better to buy a little sausage or a little wine; the rich man will consider whether he prefers to buy an automobile or a jewel; but everyone more or less solves problems of this type. Hence the necessity of considering the abstract theory which corresponds to these concrete facts.

38. We will try to explain, without making use of algebraic symbols, the results which mathematical economics reaches. We will use the symbols only in the appendix. It will be sufficient here to recall certain principles, of which the main one is, for the moment, the following. The conditions of a problem are interpreted algebraically by equations. The latter contain known quantities and unknown quantities. To determine a certain number of unknowns there must be an equal number of distinct conditions (equations), that is, conditions such that no one of them is a consequence of the others.

---

[3] This cannot be understood by literary economists and metaphysicians. Nevertheless, they will want to interfere by giving their opinions; and the reader who has some knowledge of mathematics can amuse himself by perusing the foolish trash they will put out on the subject of this paragraph and of § 8 *et seq.* in the Appendix.

Moreover, they must not be contradictory. For example, if we are looking for two unknown numbers and have given for conditions (equations) that the sum of those two numbers must be equal to a given number, and the difference to another given number, the problem is completely determined, because there are two unknowns and two conditions (equations). But if, on the other hand, we were given, in addition to the sum of the two numbers, the sum of twice each of those numbers, the second condition would be a consequence of the first, because if 4, for example, is the sum of two unknown numbers, 8 will be the sum of twice each of those numbers. In this case we do not have two distinct conditions (equations), and the problem remains undetermined. In economic problems it is very important to know whether certain conditions completely determine the problem, or leave it undetermined.

39. **Direct and indirect effects of tastes.** Numerous hypotheses about the way in which man is guided by his tastes could be made, and each of them would serve as a basis for an abstract theory. To avoid wasting our time in studying useless theories, we must examine the concrete facts and inquire into what types of abstract theories are appropriate to them.

Assume an individual who buys a 3 percent French government bond at 99.35. Ask him why he made that transaction. It is, he will say, because he considers that at that price it suits him to buy that bond. Having balanced on the one side the expenditure of 99.35 and on the other the income of 3 francs per year, he estimates that, for him, the purchase of that annuity is worth that expenditure. If it could be purchased for 98, he would buy 6 francs of annuity instead of 3 francs. He does not raise the problem of deciding whether he would prefer to buy 3 francs at 99.35 or 6 francs at 98; that would be a useless investigation since the determination of the price does not depend on him. He investigates, because this alone depends on him, what amount of annual income it suits him to buy at a given price. Let us interrogate the seller. It is possible that his decision is made for exactly the same reasons. In that case, we still have the same type of contract. But towards the end of the year 1902 we would have been able to find someone who would have told us: "I am selling in order to lower the price of the annuity, and thus annoy the French government." At every turn we can find someone who will tell us: "I am selling (or I am buying) in order to lower (or raise) the price of the annuity, so as then to make use of it and obtain certain advantages." Someone who acts in this way is motivated by reasons very different from those we have previously considered;

he intends to modify the price and he compares mainly the positions which he reaches *via* different prices. We have here another type of contract.

40. **Types of phenomena in connection with the effects of tastes.** The two types of phenomena which we have just pointed out are very important in the study of political economy; let us investigate their characteristics, denoting the first type by I and the second by II. We begin by considering the case where one who transforms economic goods just has in mind seeking his own advantage; later (§ 49) we will look at cases where this is not so.

We will say that one who buys or who sells a good can be guided by two quite distinct types of considerations.

41. He may be seeking only the satisfaction of his tastes, given a certain state or condition of the market. He certainly contributes, but without directly seeking it, toward modifying that state since, depending on the different states of the market, he is inclined to transform a larger or smaller quantity of one good into another. He compares successive transformations, in a given state of the market, and looks for a state such that these successive transformations lead to a point where his tastes are satisfied. Here we have Type I.

42. On the other hand, the individual considered may seek to modify the conditions of the market in order to gain an advantage therefrom or for any other purpose whatsoever. A certain state of the market being given, exchange causes equilibrium to take place at one point; in another state, equilibrium takes place at another point. He compares these two positions and seeks the one which best attains the end he has in view. After having chosen, he devotes his attention to changing the conditions of the market in such a way as to correspond to that choice. In this case we have Type II.

43. Obviously, although the transactions of any individual who appears on the market can be of Type I, Type II, on the contrary, can include only those who are aware of and who are able to modify the conditions of the market, which certainly is not the case for everyone.

44. Let us pursue our investigations. We will see that Type I includes a very large number of transactions among which are the majority or even all the transactions relating to household consumption. When has anyone ever seen a housewife, buying chicory or coffee, concern herself with anything other than the price of these items, and say: "if I buy some chicory today that may cause the price of this good to rise in the future, and I must consider the harm which the purchase I make today will inflict on me in the future?" Who has

ever abstained from ordering a suit, not in order to avoid the expenditure, but to lower, in that way, the price of suits in general? If someone appeared on the market saying: "It would please me if strawberries sold for only 30 centimes a kilogram, therefore I stick to that price," he would expose himself to ridicule. On the other hand he does say: "at 30 centimes a kilogram I would buy 10 kilograms, at 60 centimes I would buy only 4 kilograms, at one franc I would not buy any"; and he sees whether he can in that way come to an agreement with those who sell. Hence this Type I corresponds to very numerous concrete facts, and it will not be a waste of time to build a theory on it.

45. We also find numerous examples of Type II. On the stock exchange some powerful banking companies and syndicates follow this type. Those who, thanks to great resources, seek to monopolize some goods, obviously wish to modify market conditions in order to make a profit thereby. When the French government sets the price of the tobacco it sells to the public, it operates according to type II. All those who enjoy a monopoly, and who know how to benefit from it, behave according to this type.

46. If we look at real life, we see that Type I is found where there is competition among those who act according to it. The persons with whom they deal may not be in competition and consequently not follow Type I. Moreover, Type I is the more pure as competition is the more widespread and the more perfect. It is precisely because there are many people who buy and sell French rentes each day on the Paris Bourse, that it would be foolish to try to modify the conditions of that market by buying or selling a few francs of rentes. Obviously, if all those who are selling (or buying) were to enter into an agreement, they could actually modify these conditions to their profit; but they do not know one another, and each acts on his own behalf. Amid this confusion and this competition, each individual can do no more than handle his own affairs and seek to satisfy his own tastes, in accordance with the different conditions which may appear on the market. All the sellers (or buyers) of rentes clearly modify the prices, but they modify them without previous design; it is not the purpose, but the effect of their actions.

47. Type II is observed where competition does not exist and where there is engrossment, monopoly, etc. While an individual is acting to modify the market conditions for his profit, he must, if he does not want to work in vain, be sure that others will not come in to disturb his operations. And for that he somehow must rid himself

of his competitors. This can be done either with the assistance of the law, or because he alone possesses certain goods, or because by intrigue, trickery, by his influence or his intelligence, he wards off his competitors. It is also possible that he does not have to bother about his competitors because they are of little importance, or for some other reason.

Finally it must be noted that it often happens that a certain number of individuals join together precisely so that they can dominate the market; in this case we still have Type II, since, from certain points of view, the association can be considered as comprising only one individual.

48. We encounter a similar, but not identical, case when a certain number of persons or associations agree to modify certain conditions of the market, but allow the members complete freedom of action with regard to other conditions. Often the selling price is fixed, each member remaining free to sell as much as he can. Sometimes the quantity that each may sell is fixed, either absolutely, or in such a way that this limit may not be exceeded without paying a certain sum to the association; it may also be stipulated that a premium will be paid to anyone who stays below the quantity fixed; as for price, it is set freely by each seller; only rarely are conditions of sale fixed.

For example, labor unions sometimes impose uniform wages; a firm which purchases the labor of ten workmen at a certain price cannot purchase the labor of an eleventh workman at a lower price. Moreover, the unions ordinarily also fix the price in such a way that not only is the going wage fixed, but also the conditions, and we come back to one of the preceding cases.

The law sometimes requires that all portions of a good be sold at the same price. This is true in nearly all countries with regard to railroads which cannot charge the tenth passenger either more or less than what, under identical conditions, they charge the first. A philanthropist may sell below cost in order to aid consumers or a certain class of consumers. We shall see other cases when we discuss production. It is clear that they can be quite numerous since they are related to the many different conditions in the economic phenomenon.

49. Hence we should examine the different species of Type II. From now on we must distinguish one of these species which we will call Type III. It is the one which occurs when one wishes to arrange the entire economic phenomenon in such a way that maximum welfare is obtained for all those who participate. It will be

necessary, moreover, to define in a precise fashion what this welfare consists of (VI, 33, 52). Type III corresponds to the collectivist organization of society.

50. Note that Types I and II have reference to individuals; hence it can, and ordinarily does happen, that when two persons make a bargain, one follows Type I and the other Type II; or, if a large number of persons are involved, some follow Type I and others Type II. It is the same for Type III, if the collectivist state allows any freedom to its members.

51. One who follows Type II stops, according to the definition given for this type, at a point where his tastes are not *directly* satisfied. Consequently, in comparing the condition which the individual would reach in following Type I and that which he would reach in following Type II, we will see that the second differs from the first by certain quantities, plus or minus, of goods. Hence we could also define Type I in the following way: it is one in which the quantities of goods satisfy the tastes directly, and Type II is one in which the quantities of goods are such that, the tastes being directly satisfied, there is a positive or negative remainder.

52. **Indifference lines of tastes.** Take a man who allows himself to be governed only by his tastes and who possesses 1 kilogram of bread and 1 kilogram of wine. His tastes being given, he is willing to obtain a little less bread and a little more wine, or *vice versa*. For example, he consents to having only 0.9 kilogram of bread provided he have 1.2 of wine. In other terms, this signifies that these two combinations, 1 kilogram of bread and 1 kilogram of wine or 0.9 kilogram of bread and 1.2 kilograms of wine, are equal for him; he does not prefer the second to the first, nor the first to the second; he would not know which to choose; possessing the one or the other of these combinations is *indifferent* to him.

Starting from that combination, 1 kilogram of bread and 1 kilogram of wine, we find a great number of others among which the choice is indifferent, and we have for example

| Bread | 1.6 | 1.4 | 1.2 | 1.0 | 0.8 | 0.6 |
| Wine | 0.7 | 0.8 | 0.9 | 1.0 | 1.4 | 1.8 |

We call this series, which could be extended indefinitely, an *indifference series*.

53. The use of graphs greatly facilitates understanding this point.

Draw two perpendicular axes, OA and OB [Figure 5]; let OA express quantities of bread and OB quantities of wine. For example, Oa represents one of bread, Ob one of wine; the point m, where these two ordinates intersect, denotes the combination 1 kilogram of bread and 1 kilogram of wine.

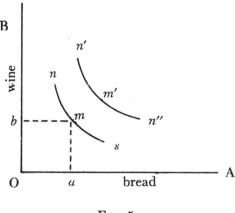

FIG. 5

54. We can represent all of the preceding series in this way, and joining all the points of that series by a continuous line, we will have the line *nms* which is called an INDIFFERENCE LINE or INDIFFERENCE CURVE.[4]

55. Let us give each of these combinations an index which must satisfy the following two conditions, and which is arbitrary in other respects: 1° Two combinations between which the choice is indifferent must have the same index; 2° of two combinations, the one which is preferred to the other must have a larger index.[5]

Thus we have the INDICES OF OPHELIMITY, or of the pleasure which an individual feels when he enjoys a combination which corresponds to a given index.

56. It follows from the above that all the combinations in one indifference series have the same index; that is, all the points on an indifference line have the same index.

Let 1 be the index of line *nms* of Figure 5; let *m'* (for example 1.1 of bread and 1.1 of wine) be another combination which the

---

[4] This expression is due to Professor F. Y. Edgeworth. He assumed the existence of *utility* (ophelimity) and deduced the indifference curves from it. On the other hand, I consider the indifference curves as given, and deduce from them all that is necessary for the theory of equilibrium, without resorting to ophelimity.

[5] See IV, 32, for another condition which it is useful to add, but which it is not necessary to bring in here.

individual prefers to combination m, and give it the index 1.1. Starting from this combination m' we find another indifference series; that is, we describe another curve $n'm'n''$. We can continue in this fashion, of course considering not only combinations which are, for the individual, better than combination m, but also those which are worse. We will thus have several indifference series, each one having its index; in other words, we will cover the part of the plane OAB which we want to consider with an infinite number of indifference curves each of which has its index.

57. This gives us a complete representation of the tastes of the individual with regard to bread and wine, and that is enough to determine economic equilibrium. The individual can disappear, provided he leaves us this photograph of his tastes.

Clearly what we have said about bread and wine can be repeated for all goods.

58. The reader who has used topographical maps knows that it is customary to draw certain curves which represent the points which have, for the given curve, the same height above sea level, or above any other level.

The curves in Figure 5 are contour lines if we consider the indices of ophelimity to represent the height of the points of a hill above the plane OAB which is assumed horizontal. It can be called the hill of the indices of pleasure. There are other similar ones, infinite in number, depending on the arbitrary system of indices chosen.

If pleasure can be measured, if ophelimity exists, one of these index systems will be precisely that of the values of ophelimity (Appendix, 3), and the corresponding hill will be the hill of pleasure or of ophelimity.

59. An individual who possesses a certain combination of bread and wine can be represented by a point on that hill. The pleasure which this individual will experience will be represented by the height of this point above the plane OAB. The individual will experience a greater pleasure insofar as he is at a greater height; of two combinations he will always prefer the one which is represented by a higher point on the hill.

60. **The paths.** Assume an individual who possesses the quantity of bread represented by oa and the quantity of wine represented by ab [Figure 6]. We say that the individual finds himself at the point on the hill which is projected into b on the horizontal plane xy, or in an elliptical fashion, that he is at b. Assume that at another time the individual has oa' of bread and $a'b'$ of wine; leaving b he

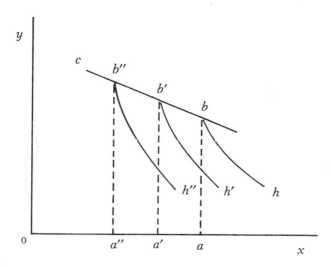

FIG. 6

will be at b'. Next if he has oa'' of bread and $a''b''$ of wine, he will have gone from b' to b'', and so on up to c. Assume that the points b, b', b'', are very close together, and join them by a line; we will say that the individual who has successively the quantity oa of bread and ab of wine, oa' of bread and $a'b'$ of wine, etc., has traveled, on the hill, along a *path*, or route, or road, which is projected into the line $bb'b''\ldots c$ on the horizontal plane oxy, or, in an elliptical fashion, that he *has traveled along* the path bc.

61. Note that if an individual traveled along an infinite number of paths hb, $h'b'$, $h''b''$, $\ldots$, and if he stopped at the points b, b', b'', $\ldots$, we would have to consider him as in fact traveling along the path b, b', b'', $\ldots$, c.

62. Consider [Figure 7] a path mn which is tangent to an indifference curve t'' at c; and assume that the indices of ophelimity increase from t toward t'', and that the path rises from m up to c and then descends from c to n. A point a which, starting from m, precedes point c, and beyond which the obstacles do not permit the individual to go, will be called a TERMINAL POINT. It is only encountered in ascending from m toward c, and not in descending from c to n. Consequently, b would not be a terminal point for one who would travel along the path mn, but it would be for one who would travel along the path nm, that is, for one who, starting from n, would go toward m.

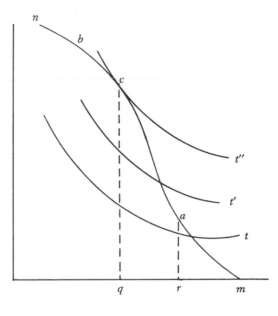

FIG. 7

63. The terminal point and the point of tangency have a common property, namely, that of being the highest point which the individual can reach in traveling along the path mn. Point c is the highest point of the entire path; point a is the highest point of the portion of the path ma which the individual is able to travel.

64. It will be seen below how this way of representing phenomena by indifference curves and paths is convenient for expounding the theories of economics.

65. **Continuous variations and discontinuous variations.** The indifference curves and the paths could be discontinuous, and they are in reality. That is, the variations in the quantities occur in a discontinuous fashion. An individual passes from a state in which he has 10 handkerchiefs to a state in which he has 11, and not through intermediate states in which he would have, for example, 10 and 1/100 handkerchiefs, 10 and 2/100 handkerchiefs, etc.

In order to come closer to reality, we would have to consider finite variations, but there is a technical difficulty in doing so.

Problems concerning quantities which vary by infinitely small degrees are much easier to solve than problems in which the quantities undergo finite variations. Hence, every time it is possible, we must replace the latter by the former; this is done in all the physiconatural sciences. We know that an error is thereby committed; but it can be neglected either when it is small absolutely, or when it is smaller than other inevitable errors which make it useless to seek a precision which eludes us in other ways. This is precisely so in political economy, for there we consider only average phenomena and those involving large numbers. We speak of the individual, not in order actually to investigate what one individual consumes or produces, but only to consider one of the elements of a collectivity and then add up the consumption and the production of a large number of individuals.

66. When we say that an individual consumes one and one-tenth watches, it would be ridiculous to take those words literally. A tenth of a watch is an unknown object for which we have no use. Rather these words simply signify that, for example, one hundred individuals consume 110 watches.

When we say that equilibrium takes place when an individual consumes one and one-tenth watches, we simply mean that equilibrium takes place when 100 individuals consume—some one, others two or more watches and some even none at all—in such a way that all together they consume about 110, and the average is 1.1 for each.

This manner of expression is not peculiar to political economy; it is found in a great number of sciences.

In insurance one speaks of fractions of living persons, for example, twenty-seven and thirty-seven hundredths living persons. It is quite obvious there is no such thing as thirty-seven hundredths of a living person!

If we did not agree to replace discontinuous variations by continuous variations, the theory of the lever could not be derived. We say that, a lever having equal arms, a balance, for example, is in equilibrium when it is supporting equal weights. But I might take a balance which is sensitive to a centigram, put in one of the trays a milligram more than in the other, and state that, contrary to the theory, it remains in equilibrium.

The balance in which we weigh men's tastes is such that, for certain goods, it is sensitive to the gram, for others only to the hectogram, for others to the kilogram, etc.

The only conclusion that can be drawn is that we must not demand from these balances more precision than they can give.

67. Moreover, since it is only a matter of a technical difficulty, those who have time to spare can amuse themselves by considering finite variations; and, after dogged and extremely long labor, they

will arrive at results which, within the limit of allowable errors, do not differ from those at which we arrive easily and quickly by considering infinitesimal variations—at least in ordinary cases. We are writing in order to investigate in an objective fashion the relations between phenomena and not to please the pedantic.

68. **The obstacles.** They are of two kinds: some are self evident, others are less so.

69. The tastes of persons with whom the individual has dealings belong to the first kind. If a given quantity of goods must be divided among different individuals, the fact that this quantity is fixed constitutes an obstacle. If we must produce the goods to be divided, the fact that we can do so only by employing other goods also constitutes an obstacle. Similarly the fact that the goods are not available at the place and at the time when they are needed is an obstacle. Finally there are the obstacles which arise from the social organization.

70. In a general way, when an individual gives up a certain quantity of a good in order to procure another one, we will say that he TRANSFORMS the first good into the second. He can proceed by exchange, giving up to others the first good and receiving from them the second; he can accomplish it by production, actually transforming the first good into the second himself. In addition he can, for this operation, turn to a person who transforms goods, a producer.

71. We will reserve the name PRODUCTION or TRANSFORMATION for this last operation; and production, abstracting from the one who does it as, for example, when it is done on his own account by the individual who owns the good transformed, we will call OBJECTIVE PRODUCTION or OBJECTIVE TRANSFORMATION.

72. With regard to objective transformation, we must distinguish, at least by abstraction, three categories of transformations; namely:

1° Physical transformation: for example, the transformation of wheat into bread, meadow grass (and we must also add the use of ground surface and buildings) into sheep's wool, etc.

2° Transformation in space: for example, coffee in Brazil transformed into coffee in Europe.

3° Transformation in time: for example, the present harvest of wheat saved and transformed into wheat available in a few months; and, inversely, the wheat of the future harvest into wheat consumed now, which one obtains by later replacing the quantity of wheat presently consumed with the product of the future harvest, a means by which we have transformed economically that future harvest into a present good (V, 48).

73. But that is not enough. The subject is not thereby exhausted; there are other impediments or obstacles which constitute the SECOND KIND OF OBSTACLES. For example, an individual has 20 kilograms of wheat; he exchanges 10 of them for 15 kilograms of wine, and then again the 10 others for 15 kilograms of wine. In all, he has exchanged his 20 kilograms of wheat for 30 kilograms of wine. Or he begins by exchanging 10 kilograms of wheat for 10 kilograms of wine, and then 10 kilograms of wheat for 20 kilograms of wine. In all, he again has exchanged 20 kilograms of wheat for 30 kilograms of wine.

The final result is the same, but the individual reaches it in two different ways. It is possible that he is free to choose the way which suits him best; it is also possible that he is not. This last case is the most general. Anything standing in the way of the individual having this freedom of choice is an obstacle of the second kind.[6]

74. There is an infinite number of paths which, starting from point m lead us to point n, namely msn, $ms'n$, $ms''n$, etc. [Figure 8].

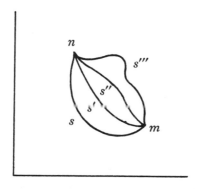

Fig. 8

These paths can take the form of a straight line or of any curve whatsoever. Sometimes the second type of obstacles has the effect of determining the only path which can be followed starting from m, and sometimes the only kind of path which can be followed. For example, we will see a case (§ 172) in which the individual can leave m only by following a single line. We will see another case (§ 172) in which this line can be any straight line whatsoever; that is, the individual has a choice among an infinite number of paths

---

[6] Most of the literary economists have only a very imperfect idea of this type of phenomena.

which pass through m, provided they are all rectilinear. We will see other cases in which the individual follows a bent line (VI, 7).

75. **Indifference lines of obstacles in objective transformations.** For obstacles of the first type there are certain lines which are analogous to the indifference lines of tastes.

Assume that a good A is transformed into another good B, and that we know the quantities of B which would be obtained with 1, 2, 3, ... of A.

Draw two coordinate axes [Figure 9], and for each quantity oa of A indicate the quantity ab of B produced. We thus obtain a curve $bb'b''$. . . , which we will call an INDIFFERENCE LINE OF OB-STACLES. We will give it the index zero because on that line the transformations take place without leaving any residue.

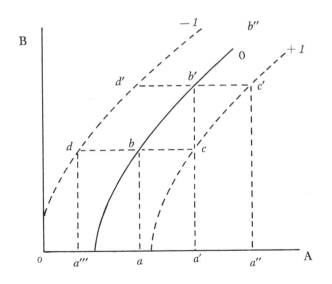

FIG. 9

Set the straight line segments bc, $b'c'$, . . . parallel to the oA axis equal to unity; we will get another indifference line cc'. . . . to which we will give the index 1. If we have the quantity oa'' of A and if we make a transformation which gives $a''c'$ of B, $a'a''$ is left over, that is, a residue of A equal to 1; and it is because of this that the index 1 is given to the line cc'. . . .

In the same way set bd, $b'd'$, . . . equal to unity and join the points dd'. . . . We will get another indifference line to which we will give the index minus 1 because it lacks precisely one unit in the transformation *oa* of A into *ab* of B; only *oa'''* of A is obtained.

Proceeding in this way we will cover the entire plane with indifference curves, some with positive indices and others with negative indices, separated by the line with index zero. This line ought to attract our attention. We will call it the line of COMPLETE TRANSFORMATIONS, since on it transformations take place without leaving any residue, positive or negative.

76. **The producer's indifference lines.** If we consider a single producer, the lines which we have just indicated are also indifference lines for the producer, because on each of them he obtains the same profit if the index is positive, or the same loss if the index is negative; and he neither gains nor loses if the index is zero, that is, on the line of complete transformations. But when there is a larger number of producers, the number of producers itself can constitute a part of the obstacles, and in this case the indifference lines vary.

77. **Analogies between indifference lines of tastes and indifference lines of obstacles.** These lines correspond to each other in part, and differ in other respects. There is an analogy in that the individual strives to move from one indifference line to another having a higher index, as far as that is permitted him, and the producer does the same.

78. Note, however, that the individual who is satisfying his own tastes is governed by considerations of ophelimity; the producer, by considerations of quantities of goods (§ 76).

79. So far as the producer is concerned, certain circumstances often intervene and prevent him from moving above the line of complete transformations. He cannot remain below that line for long because he has losses; consequently, he finds himself obliged to stay on that line. Hence there is an essential difference from the phenomena which relate to tastes.

80. Finally, the shapes of indifference lines of tastes ordinarily are different from those of indifference lines of obstacles. This can be seen in a rough way by comparing Figure 5 and Figure 9.

81. If we consider the indifference lines of the producer as projections of contour lines of a surface each point of which has a height above the plane indicated by the index of that point, we obtain a HILL OF PROFIT, analogous in part to the hill of pleasure (§ 58), but differing from it in that it is partly above and partly below the plane to which it is referred. It resembles a hill which is surrounded by water; the surface of the hill partly emerges above the level of the water, it also extends below.

82. **Competition.** We have alluded to this in § 46; we must now frame a precise idea of it.

Competition between those who exchange must be distinguished from competition between those who produce, and the latter itself is composed of several kinds.

83. One who exchanges strives to ascend as far as possible on the hill of pleasure. If he has an excess of A, he seeks to get a greater quantity of B, and in order to do so he gives up a greater quantity of A for the same quantity of B. That is, if [Figure 10] he finds himself at *l*, he decreases the slope of *ml* with respect to the *o*A axis. If he has an excess of B, that is, if he finds himself at *r*, he gives up less of A for the same quantity of B; that is, he increases the slope of *mr* with respect to the *o*A axis. In a word, the individual moves in the direction of the arrows. This is true whether he is alone or in competition with others.[1]

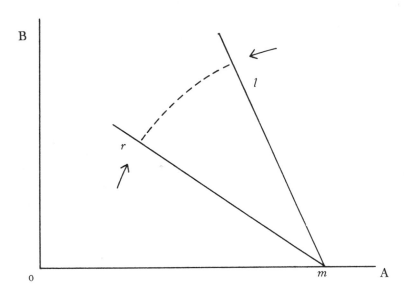

FIG. 10

Competition has the effect of preventing him from comparing positions on two different paths, and of limiting his choice to positions on the given path or to positions very nearby. Moreover, the individuals who are in competition move until all are satisfied; and a single one who is not satisfied is enough to oblige the others to move.

84. A producer endeavors to ascend as far as he can on the hill of profit (§ 81). That is, he strives to have the greatest possible residue of A; he never has an excess of A. Consequently he always moves in the same direction and not sometimes in one direction and sometimes in another, as in Figure 10. To change the direction of his movement, there must be a change in the direction in which there is a greater quantity of A.

85. One generally begins with the study of an isolated collectivity having no communication with others. In such a collectivity the number of those who exchange does not vary. The number of producers, on the other hand, is essentially variable since those who operate their business poorly end up by ceasing to produce; whereas, if there are any who are making money, other producers immediately appear to share the profits. Something analogous takes place for consumers, and we will have to take account of it when we talk about population; but the production of men does not follow the same laws as that of goods, and more particularly, it is spread over a much greater period of time. Furthermore, we ought to devote a separate study to that.

86. Whether there is competition or not, the producer cannot remain on the side of the negative indices, where he has losses. If there is no competition, however, he can remain on the side of the positive indices, where he makes a profit, with a tendency moreover to move toward the part where he would obtain greater profits. Competition tends to diminish this profit, pushing him toward the negative indices.

This competition can occur whether we assume the technical conditions of production constant, or whether we assume them variable. In this chapter we will restrict ourselves to the first type of competition.

87. Assume two consumers. The first possesses oa of A, the second has oa'; together then they have oA, which is equal to the sum of these two quantities [Figure 11]. Assume that these two consumers can only move along the parallel lines ad and $a'd'$. They will stop at certain points, d and d'; that is, the first will transform ab of A or bd of B, and the second $a'b'$ of A or $b'd'$ of B. Add together the quantities transformed and we see that, in total, the consumers transform AB of A into BD of B, moving along a path parallel to ad and $a'd'$. Therefore in place of these two consumers we can consider instead just one who moves along the path AD. The same

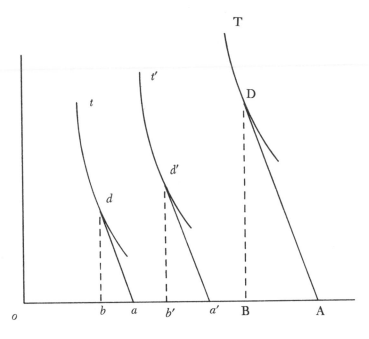

FIG. 11

reasoning applies to any number of consumers which may, consequently, be replaced by a single fictitious consumer who represents them all taken together.

88. We could do the same for producers, but only in the case where we disregard the changes which their number may bring about in the obstacles.

89. **Types of phenomena in connection with producers.** As with consumers we must consider Types I and II, to which may be added Type III. The characteristics are the same. Type I is always that of competition; but competition between consumers differs from that between producers.

90. **Equilibrium.** As we have seen before (§ 27), equilibrium occurs when the movements which tastes would induce are prevented by the obstacles, and *vice versa*. Consequently the general problem of equilibrium is divided into three others consisting of: 1° determining equilibrium with respect to tastes; 2° determining equilibrium with respect to obstacles, or with respect to producers; 3° finding a point common to both these equilibria which will constitute a point of general equilibrium.

91. As for the paths, we must: 1° consider equilibrium on one fixed path; 2° consider it on a class of paths and see how the one which will be followed is chosen.

92. So far as the types of phenomena are concerned we must first of all study Type I for those who exchange and for those who produce. We will next study Type II which can generally occur only for those individuals who deal with others who act according to Type I.

93. **Equilibrium with respect to tastes.** Let us begin by considering an individual who follows a fixed path and who endeavors to reach the point on this path where his tastes will be best satisfied.

94. If obstacles of the first kind place upon this path a point beyond which he cannot go, and if the positions which precede that point are less advantageous for the individual, he obviously will go up to that point and stop there.

At that point there is equilibrium with respect to tastes. That point may be a point of tangency of the path and an indifference curve, or a terminal point (§ 62); in any event, it is the highest point on the segment of the path along which the individual can travel.

95. The point of tangency could also be the lowest point on the path, and at that point the equilibrium would be unstable. We are not concerned with this case for the time being.

96. Henceforth we will consider only rectilinear paths because they occur most often in reality; but our reasoning is general and, by means of slight modifications or restrictions, can be applied to other types of paths.

97. Consider an individual for whom t, t', t'', . . . represent indifference curves of tastes, the indices of ophelimity increasing from t to t''' [Figure 12]. Each week this individual has om of A. Assume that to transform A into B he follows the rectilinear path mn. At the point a, where the path meets indifference curve t, there is no equilibrium because it is better for the individual to go from a to b, on curve t', where he will have a larger index of ophelimity. We can say the same for all the points where the path intersects the indifference curves, but not for the point c'' where the path is tangent to an indifference curve. Indeed, the individual may move from c'' only toward b or toward b', and in both of these cases the index of ophelimity decreases. Hence, if the individual has reached c'' via the path mn, any further movement is opposed by tastes. Consequently c'' is an equilibrium point. Similarly for the analogous points c, c', c'', c''' located on other paths which we assume can be taken by the

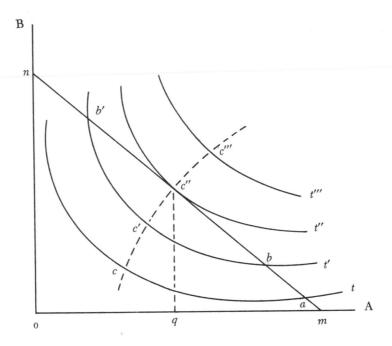

FIG. 12

individual. If we join these points by a line, we will obtain the line of equilibrium with respect to tastes; it is also called the LINE OF EXCHANGES[7, [2]]

Terminal points which, in starting from m, precede the points of the line of exchanges may also be points of equilibrium.

98. It could happen that a path leads to having zero of A without being tangent to any indifference line. In this case we would have a terminal point where the path cuts the oB axis, and that would signify that on this path the individual is disposed to give not only the whole quantity of A which he possesses in order to have some B, but that even if he had a larger quantity of A, he would give it to have more B.

99. By adding the quantities of goods transformed by each individual the line of exchanges for the collectivity made up of these

---

[7] We could cover the plane with a large number of lines of exchanges. In this way we would have a representation of the hill of indices of ophelimity, which would be analogous to that which is obtained by covering the plane with indifference lines (Appendix, 42).

individuals is obtained. And if desired, the indifference curves for that collectivity can be depicted in the same way; they will follow from the indifference curves of the individuals.

100. **Equilibrium of the producer.** The producer seeks to obtain maximum profit and if nothing stands in the way he will ascend as high as possible on the hill of profit. Following a path *ol* [Figure 13] the producer can reach a point *c* where this path is tangent to an indifference curve of obstacles, and this point can have a greater index of profit than the neighboring points on the path. In this case equilibrium of the producer is realized at point *c*, on the path *ol*, just as occurs for the consumer. We will say in this case that competition is incomplete.

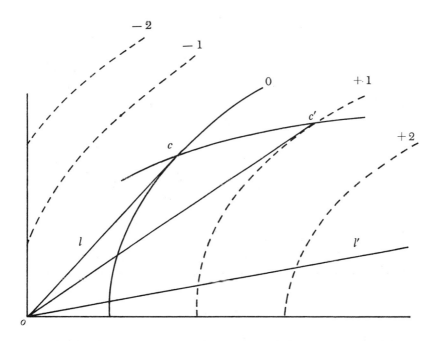

FIG. 13

101. On the other hand, it can happen either that the path *ol'* is not tangent to any indifference curve of obstacles, or that *ol* being tangent at *c* to one of these curves, the index at *c* is less than those of neighboring points on the path [*Cf.* Figure 14]. In this case competition is complete.

The producer will endeavor to continue his course along the path *ol* up to the terminal point which the other conditions of the problem impose on him.

102. Consider two categories of goods: 1° there are certain goods such that the quantity of B obtained per unit of A increases when the total quantity of A transformed increases; 2° there are other goods for which, on the contrary, this quantity of B diminishes.[8]

103. In the first case we have lines similar to the lines *t*, *t'*, . . . of Figure 14, on which we have marked the corresponding index. It is evident that no path of the type *ol* can be tangent to an indifference curve with a positive index.

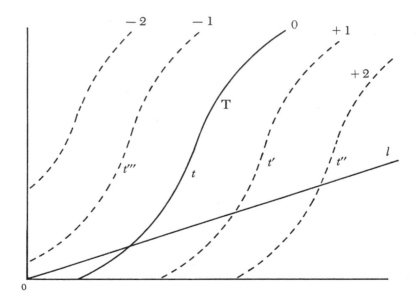

FIG. 14

The line *t* with index zero, that is, the line of complete transformations, divides the plane into two parts or regions; on the one side are found the lines of negative index, on the other the lines of positive index. The producer cannot stay in the first region, or at least he cannot stay long because he has losses there; and it is obvious

---

[8] The first category includes the goods B whose cost of production decreases with an increase in the quantity of goods produced; the second category includes goods whose cost of production increases.

that he does not want, and moreover, in general he is not able, to lose indefinitely. Hence equilibrium is not possible in that region. It is possible in the second, which we will call the REGION OF POSSIBLE EQUILIBRIUM. Indeed, the producer can stop at any point whatsoever where he has a profit. He seeks, however, to increase this profit as much as possible; that is, he seeks to move as far as possible along the path *ol*; equilibrium takes place here at terminal points (§ 62) and no longer at points of tangency. For these goods competition is complete.

104. It is rare, however, for the indifference lines to extend indefinitely in the form which we have specified. Ordinarily, beyond a certain more or less remote point T, the phenomenon changes and the first category turns into the second. The point T and other similar points may be beyond the boundaries which are considered relevant, and in that case it is as if they did not exist.

105. The second category of goods pointed out in § 102 has indifference lines whose shape is similar to those we have depicted in Figure 13. There are some paths such as *oc* which are tangent to an indifference curve; there are others such as *ol'* which can be tangent to none of these curves. Joining the points of tangency *c*, *c'*,. . . , we get a line which we will call LINE OF GREATEST PROFIT. It corresponds to the line of exchanges obtained from the indifference curves of tastes. The region of indifference curves of positive index is, ordinarily, the region of possible equilibrium; but it is obvious that, if he can, the producer will stay on the line of maximum profit. For these goods competition is incomplete (V, 96).

When there is competition, the paths which do not intersect the line of maximum profit and which lead to some point with negative index cannot be followed (§ 137).

106. **Equilibrium of tastes and obstacles.** Consider a certain number of consumers and a single producer, or a certain number of producers but with the condition that their number have no influence on the obstacles. Let us draw [Figure 15] for the consumers the line of exchanges *mcc'* for the total quantities of the goods. That is, we will consider the collectivity as if it were a single individual (§ 87).

For the producers we draw the line *hk*, which will be that of complete transformations for goods of the first category (§ 102), that is, complete competition, and which will be the line of maximum profit for goods of the second category (§ 102), incomplete competition. Let us consider phenomena of Type I.

107. If there is a line of maximum profit and if it intersects the line of exchanges of the consumers, the producers stop on that line

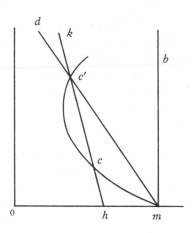

Fig. 15

of maximum profit because they find it to their advantage to do so.
Otherwise we will see (§ 141) that they are driven onto the line of
complete transformations. The line hk is thus the one on which the
producers stop; and there will be equilibrium points, that is, points c
and c', where that line intersects the line of exchanges of the
consumers.

108. All this is true in the case where the paths traveled are
straight lines starting from m, because it is precisely to these paths
that the line of exchanges and that of maximum profit correspond.
If the paths change, the lines also change. For example, if the producers were forced to follow the line of complete transformations,
equilibrium would be at the point where that line is tangent to an
indifference curve of tastes.

109. If two individuals exchange goods between themselves, the
points of equilibrium are at the intersections of the lines of exchange
of the two individuals—the coordinate axes being laid out in such
a way that the path traveled by the one coincides with the path
traveled by the other (§ 116).

It will be the same if, instead of two individuals, a collectivity is
considered.

110. The abstract case of two individuals acting according to
Type I phenomena, a case which we have often considered, does not
correspond to reality. Two individuals who would have to contract
together would probably be governed by motives quite different from
those which we have assumed. In order to be correct we ought to

assume that the pair considered is not a solitary pair, but is one of many such pairs. We study one pair at first in order to be able later to see how things take place when there are many of them. We assume, then, that the pair considered behave, not as if they were isolated, but as if they were part of a collectivity.

The same restriction must be made when we consider a single producer and a single consumer.

111. When an individual operates according to Type II phenomena, he imposes on others the path which is the most advantageous to him personally, and the point of equilibrium is at the intersection of this path and the line of equilibrium of the other individuals.

112. From all the above we can deduce the following general theorem:

For phenomena I, if there is a point where a path traveled by the contracting individuals is tangent to the indifference curves of these individuals, it is a point of equilibrium.

Indeed, if two individuals contract with each other, the points where the lines of exchanges of these individuals intersect constitute equilibrium points; but at these points the paths are tangent to the indifference lines of tastes, since that is precisely the condition which determines these lines (§ 97). Naturally, the axes must be laid out in such a way that the individuals take the same path (§ 116). The same reasoning applies to two collectivities.

113. If some consumers contract with some producers having a line of maximum profit (§ 105), the intersections of that line with the line of exchanges of the consumers will give the equilibrium points; but at these points the paths are tangent to the indifference curves of tastes and to the indifference curves of obstacles since it is precisely this last condition which determines maximum profit. Hence the theorem is proved.

114. If points of tangency do not exist, the theorem is no longer applicable, and it is replaced by the following theorem, which is more general and which includes the first one.

Equilibrium takes place at the points of intersection of the line of equilibrium of tastes and the line of equilibrium of obstacles. These lines are the loci of the points of tangency of the paths to the indifference lines, or the loci of the terminal points of these paths.

115. For phenomena of Type II we have the following theorem:

If an individual acts according to phenomena of Type II with others who act according to phenomena of Type I, equilibrium takes place at the point most advantageous for the first of these individuals,

this point being one of those where the paths intersect the curve
which marks the locus of the points of possible equilibrium.

116. **Modes and forms of equilibrium in exchange.** Now let
us study in detail the phenomena we have just studied in general.

Assume that the obstacles consist solely of the fact that the total
quantity of each good is fixed and that there is variation only in the
division between two individuals. This is the case of exchange.

Assume that the first individual, whose conditions are represented
in Figure 16, possesses *om* of A; while the other individual has a
certain quantity of B and none of A. The coordinate axes for the
first individual are *o*A and *o*B; those for the second *ωa* and *ωβ*, the
distance *ωm* being equal to the quantity of B which the second individual possesses. The indifference curves are *t*, *t'*, *t''*, . . . for the
first, and *s*, *s'*, *s''*, . . . for the second individual. Given the way the

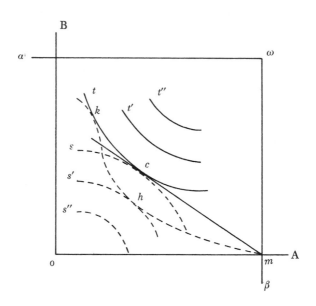

FIG. 16

figure is laid out, a single line is enough to designate the path followed by the two individuals. The indices of ophelimity increase
from *t* to *t''*, and from *s* to *s''*.

117. Let us study the phenomenon of Type I. If a path *mc* is
tangent at *c* to a curve *t* and to a curve *s*, *c* is a point of equilibrium.

If obstacles of the second kind impose, not one path, but only the type of path, the two individuals will try different paths of that type, until they find one similar to mc.

In order to determine the point c, we can proceed in the following manner. We specify, for each individual, the curve of exchanges (§ 97), and we thus have, for each individual, the *locus* of the points where equilibrium has to take place. The point where the curve of exchanges of the first individual intersects the curve of exchanges of the second obviously is the equilibrium point sought since it is a point of equilibrium for both the individuals.

118. If the obstacles were to impose a fixed path mhk, tangent at h to one of the curves $s, s', \ldots$, and at k to one of the curves $t, t', \ldots$, the equilibrium points would be different for the two individuals. Consequently, if neither of them can impose his will on the other, that is, if it is a question of Type I phenomena, the problem we have posed is insolvable. If the first individual can impose his conditions on the second, he will force him to go as far as point k, where equilibrium will occur.

119. It must be noted that that case is not to be confused with the one where one individual can require another individual to follow a certain path (§ 128). In the former the route is determined, and one individual is able to force another to move a considerable distance along it. In the latter the route is undermined, and one individual can fix it to his liking; but then he cannot force another to move far along that route.

120. We said that they try several paths before finding the one which leads to the point of equilibrium; let us look into this more closely.

If we draw the curves of exchanges for two individuals we will see, in numerous cases, that they have shapes similar to those of Figure 17, and they intersect approximately as is shown in these figures; the one gives three points of intersection, the other, one. They are of three types which we will denote by letters a, β, γ. They are shown with more details in Figure 18.

The line of exchange for the first individual, for whom the axes are oA and oB in Figure 17, will always be designated by cd in Figure 18. This line, for the second individual, for whom the axes are ωa and $\omega \beta$ in Figure 17, will always be designated by hk in Figure 18. The point of intersection of these two contract lines, that is, the point of equilibrium, is marked by the point l.

121. Consider the equilibrium for the first individual. In the case of examples (a) and (γ) the points of the line lh come before those

of the line *cd*, and consequently are terminal points (§ 62) for the first individual; hence the line on which he can be in equilibrium

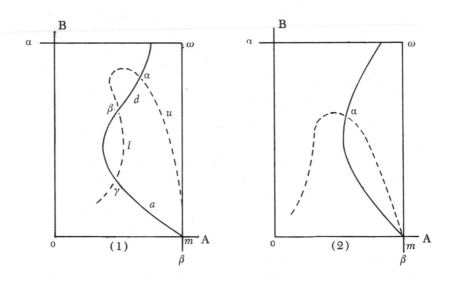

FIG. 17

is *clh*. By analogous reasoning, the line on which the second individual can be in equilibrium, still in the case of examples (*a*) and (*γ*), is also *clh*. In the case of example (*β*), this line of equilibrium for the first, as well as for the second, is *hld*. Hence we only have to consider what takes place on these lines.

122. Let us take up examples (*a*) and (*γ*). The first individual finds himself in a position of equilibrium at *h*. Since we are assuming conditions of Type I, he compares only the condition in which he would be at the different points of the path *mhd*, and he sees that he would be better off at *d* than at *h;* but he cannot move to *d* because that is prevented by the tastes of the second individual. If a large number of individuals are in competition with a large number of other individuals, if our pair is not the only one, the first individual can move, if not to *d*, at least to a point close to it. He follows a path *md′* whose inclination with respect to *ox* is a little less than that of *md;* that is, he gives a larger quantity of A for the same quantity of B. In this way he attracts the customers of the second individual, he obtains B from other individuals, and he is able to move to *d′*, which is the highest point on the path and where he is in equilibrium.[3]

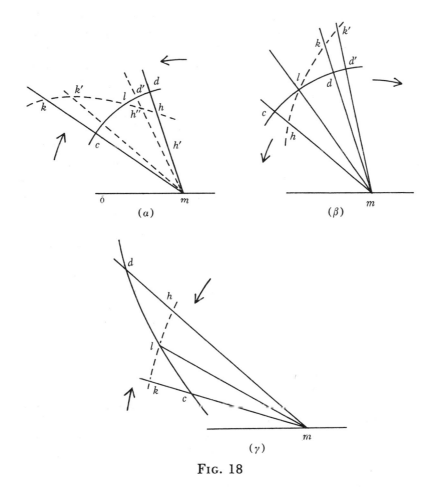

FIG. 18

Let us see what happens to the second individual. He was at h, which is for him the highest point on the path. The loss of customers drives him backward; they bring him less of A because the first individual is receiving more of it; thus this second individual finds himself driven back, for example, to h'. Still comparing only the state in which he would be at different points of the path mhd, he perceives that his condition has grown worse, that he would gain by trying to return to h, or at least to a point close to it. To do so he will follow the example of the first individual and will pay him back in his own coin. He will follow a path very close to but slightly less inclined than md', and he will thus arrive, for example, at the point h'' on the line kh.

Now the first individual must keep alert and be on his guard. He will move along a path still less steep. In such a way the two individuals will approach point l, going in the direction of the arrow.

The phenomena are analogous starting from point c. The second individual who finds himself at c—for him c is a terminal point—wants to move closer to k, which is the highest point of the path mck; consequently he agrees to take a little less A for the same quantity of B; accordingly he follows a path mk', steeper than mk with respect to the ox axis. The first individual is obliged to imitate this behavior and thus, little by little, the two individuals approach l, in the direction of the arrow.

123. Hence the point of equilibrium is at l and we will call it a point of STABLE EQUILIBRIUM, because if the two individuals move away from l, they tend to return to it.

124. Let us take up example (β). As we have seen, the line of equilibrium is the line hld. Assume that the two individuals are at d. At this point, which is for him a terminal point, the second individual would want to move closer to k. In order to get there he can only agree to take less of A for the same quantity of B; that is, he moves along a path $md'k'$, steeper than mk with respect to the ox axis, and he will move away from l. The first individual is forced to follow his example; they will then go in the direction of the arrow. It is the same on the other side of l. If the two individuals find themselves at h, the first will want to move closer to c; to do so he will give a greater quantity of A for the same quantity of B; he will thus follow a path less steep than mc and will move away from l. The second individual must follow his example, and so on. Hence both individuals move away from l. The point l is a point of UNSTABLE EQUILIBRIUM.

125. Let us return to Figure 17. In case (2), there is only a single point of equilibrium, and it is a point of stable equilibrium. In case (1) there are two points of stable equilibrium, that is, (α) and (γ), and one point of unstable equilibrium, that is, (β). In general, between two points of stable equilibrium there is a point of unstable equilibrium, which marks the boundary between the positions from which one approaches the one or the other of the two points of stable equilibrium.

The line of equilibrium is the line $muad\beta lyam$.

126. In the accompanying figure [19], the arrow indicates a direction of rotation which increases the angle α, and which we will call positive. If, moving in the negative direction, and prior to reaching the intersection of the two equilibrium lines, the line of the

individual who is exchanging A for B *precedes* the line of the individual who is exchanging B for A, the equilibrium is stable. In the opposite case it is unstable.

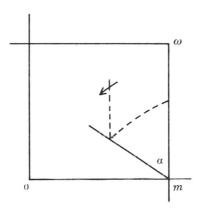

FIG. 19

127. From Figure 18 it follows that each individual always seeks to climb the hill of pleasure, to increase his ophelimity, by continuing to follow the path taken; but competition causes him to deviate, to slip, in moving toward l in the case of stable equilibrium, and away from l in the case of unstable equilibrium.

In between these two equilibria it is a matter of determining whether, on leaving the point of equilibrium in the positive direction of rotation, the first individual can stay on his contract line [i.e., the line of exchanges], or whether he must move onto that of the second individual, the points of which become for him terminal points. In the first case we have examples (α) and (γ) of Figure 18, in the second, example (β). This can be restated as follows: in the case of a negative rotation, if the first individual cannot keep himself on the line of exchanges, and if he must move onto that of the second individual (examples (α) and (γ)), the equilibrium is stable. On the other hand, if he can stay on his own line of exchanges (example (β)), the equilibrium is unstable.

128. Now let us consider phenomena of Type II. Assume that the second individual behaves according to this type, while the first individual continues to follow Type I.

For this first individual, the curve of equilibrium [Figure 20] is again *matsb* which joins the points of tangency of the indifference curves and the various paths which start from m. The second indi-

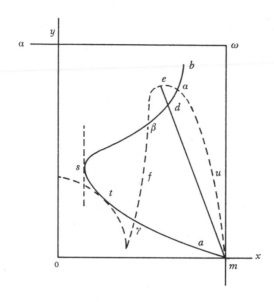

FIG. 20

vidual can indeed choose the path *mde*, but he cannot force the first to go beyond point *d* so as to get to *e*. In addition, he could stop before reaching *d* and thus force the first individual to stop. To sum up, equilibrium is possible within the entire region contained between *mω* and *mαγtsβdb*. The manner in which the point of equilibrium is reached is different in these two cases. For phenomena of Type I the individuals were led to this point by competition; for phenomena of Type II one of the individuals chooses the point which suits him best among those at which equilibrium is possible.

129. The second individual, finding himself at *d*, no longer tries, as before, to go toward *e*, or at least toward a point close to it. He compares his situation at *d* with that in which he would be at any other point whatsoever where equilibrium is possible, and he chooses the point which suits him by imposing on the other individual the path which necessarily leads to that point.

130. The point at which the situation of the second individual is the best obviously is the point which has the greatest index of ophelimity, the highest point of all those which he can choose, that is, the highest point on the hill of pleasure of the second individual. But it is obvious that the points included between *ωm* and *mαγts* are lower than those which are on the other side of *mαγts*. We can

consider this line as a path; its highest point on the hill of pleasure of the second individual will be the point t at which it is tangent to an indifference curve. That, then, is the point at which it is appropriate for the second individual to stop.

131. The determination of this point in practice is very difficult. Also, one who operates according to Type II often has another purpose in mind, namely, to obtain the greatest possible quantity of A. The point which satisfies that condition is the point of tangency, s, of the ordinary equilibrium line and one parallel to the oy axis. This point is easily found experimentally since the individual's budget itself shows how much of A he has received.

132. When, for the second individual, good A has much more ophelimity than good B, point s almost coincides with point t; it coincides completely if A alone has ophelimity for the second individual because in that case the indifference lines are parallel to the oy axis (IV, 54).

Other conditions could be chosen, and then other equilibrium points would be obtained.

133. If, instead of moving along the rectilinear paths given by the prices, the individual moves along the line of transformation imposed by the obstacles, or in general some other fixed path, the equilibrium can be stable or unstable. Let acb [Figure 21] be a line

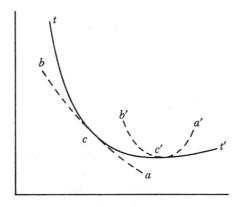

FIG. 21

of transformation and c the point at which it is tangent to an indifference line of tastes; c is the point at which equilibrium takes place. If, as happens ordinarily, the transformation line ab is such that the index of ophelimity at c is greater than the indices at the neighboring points a and b, the equilibrium is stable. Indeed, the individual who moves away from c by chance seeks to return there because he always seeks to move, as far as is possible, from one point to another point having a greater index of ophelimity. For the same reason, if the line of transformations had the form $a'b'$, such that the indices of ophelimity at the points a' and b', near the point of equilibrium c', were greater than the index of ophelimity at c', the equilibrium would be unstable.

134. **Ophelimity maxima.** We must review the various maxima among the equilibrium points. First of all we have an absolute maximum at the highest point of the hill of pleasure, at its peak. At this point the individual experiences satiety of everything; we need not pause here.

Then come a great number of relative maxima. The point c'', Figure 12, is the highest on the path mn; it is a maximum subject to the condition that the individual move only on the path mn. The other points of tangency c', c''', . . . , are also maxima of the same type. One of them may be much higher than the others; it is a *maximum maximorum*. There is a terminal point which also marks a maximum; it is the highest point of a segment of a path, but it is lower than the point of tangency which follows it.

The point t, Figure 20, is for the second individual, the highest point on the ordinary equilibrium line.

As for the point s, it indicates a maximum of a type different from the preceding ones because it is not a maximum of ophelimity, but a maximum of quantity of good A.

135. **Modes and forms of equilibrium in production.** If we assume that the line hk in Figure 18 is the maximum profit line of the producer, or producers, we need only repeat the reasoning which we have just applied to exchange. The producer tends to stay on that line, just as the consumer stays on the line of exchanges.

136. There is a difference, however. It concerns the paths which do not intersect this maximum profit line hk (Figure 22). If the producer follows the path mk, we see that he stops at k, because his condition would be less favorable on both sides of it. But if he follows the path mc, which is not tangent to any indifference curve of obstacles, why would he not go along that path up to the point which the tastes of his customers allow?

137. Competition comes in here. The line hk divides the plane into two regions: on the m side of hk the producer benefits by increasing, along a rectilinear path mc, the quantity ma of good A transformed; on the other side of hk the producer benefits by decreas-

ing, along a rectilinear path mc', the quantity ma' of good A transformed. Also things are not the same for producers who are at c and those who are at c'.

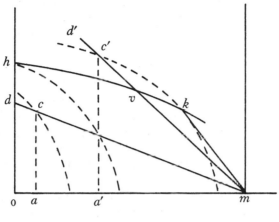

FIG. 22

138. One who is at c may be tempted, even if he is the sole producer, to increase the transformation, and that will be the case if we assume that he follows the principles of Type I phenomena strictly. He will compare the state in which he would be at various points on the path mcd, and he will see that he would be better off beyond c; consequently, if the consumer does not want to go beyond c on this path, the producer will agree to give a greater quantity of B for one unit of A; that is, he will increase slightly the slope of the path mc with respect to mo. If he is the only producer, however, he will end up by perceiving that though he hopes thereby to gain, in reality he loses; and then he will cease acting according to Type I and will, on the contrary, act according to Type II.

If there are several competitors, one who increases the slope of the path mc benefits for a short time. Moreover, if he did not do it, others would; thus little by little the slope of mc with respect to mo increases, and we approach the line hk. After reaching it, there is no longer any advantage in increasing the quantity of A transformed; if the cause disappears, the effect ceases also.

139. If the producer finds himself at c', he very quickly perceives that he benefits by decreasing the quantity ma' of A transformed. To increase this quantity he must contend with his competitors; but to decrease it he acts on his own and without worrying about the others. Hence, he decreases the slope of mc' with respect to mo and

approaches the maximum profit line hk, without being concerned about whether the other competitors follow him or not. Note also that his movement may take place entirely on the path mc'; consequently, operating exactly according to the principles of Type I, he moves to v because he is better off there than at c'. He will not go beyond v toward m because the situation would grow worse if he did so.

140. To sum up then, the producer who finds himself on the side of hk opposite to m is led back to hk by his self-interest. The producer who finds himself on the same side of hk as m is led back to hk, perhaps on his own, but certainly by competition. He would certainly go there of his own accord if it could be assumed that he behaves exactly according to Type I.

141. The case where this line of maximum profit does not exist remains to be examined.

Let cd be the line of exchanges, and hk be the line of complete transformations of the producer [Figure 23]. The region of positive indices is on the side of hk opposite to m. Two cases, indicated by (μ) and by (π), occur.

142. Let us examine case (μ) first. At c the consumer is in equilibrium since he is on the line of exchanges. The producer is satisfied since he is in the region of positive indices. Accordingly, this state of things could last a long time.

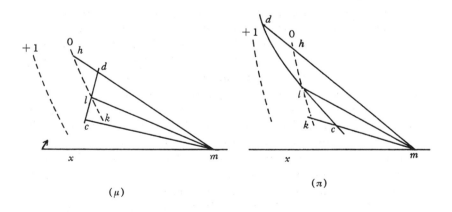

(μ)

(π)

FIG. 23

But if the producer desires to be still better off, and, furthermore, if he conducts himself strictly according to the principle of phenomena of Type I, he will continue to move along the path mc. He is prevented from doing so by the tastes of the consumers, and so he will try giving the consumer a greater quantity of B for the same quantity of A, that is, increasing the path's slope with respect to the A axis, and thus he approaches the line hk.

If he were the only producer, however, he would quickly perceive that it is folly to act in that way because he achieves a result opposite to that which he is seeking. Hence, he would cease to act according to the principles of phenomena of Type I, and would apply those of phenomena of Type II.

143. When there are a certain number of producers in competition, the one who slightly increases the slope of the path mc achieves the desired results, for a short space of time at least. He carries off his competitors' customers and advances more or less into the region of positive indices. He would even be able to remain there if his competitors did not proceed to imitate him. If they do imitate him, if the competition is genuine, they themselves will increase the slope of the path with respect to mx, and thus little by little, going in the direction of the arrow, producers and consumers will approach the point l where the line of complete transformations hk intersects the line of exchanges cd. The producers cannot go beyond that line because, in following the line of exchanges cd, they would enter the region of negative indices, and they cannot go on to lh because the consumers refuse to follow them. Hence, they must stop at l, which is a point of equilibrium, and a point of stable equilibrium.

144. Alternatively, we can note that lc alone is a line of possible equilibrium, not ld, because it is in the region of negative indices. On the line lc the competition of the producers operates in such a way that the point of equilibrium approaches l.

145. Now let us examine case (π). We will see, as above, that ld is the only line of possible equilibrium because lc is in the region of negative indices. If the producers are at d, they are well off because they are in the region of positive indices; but the competition which takes place between them causes the slope of md with respect to mx to increase, and thus we move away from l. It is precisely at l that there could be equilibrium because there both consumers and producers are satisfied; but when we move away from l in the direction of h, instead of being brought back to it, we move away still more. In the direction of k we are brought back to l. We have here a special type of equilibrium, stable on one side and unstable on the other.

We do not have an example of this equilibrium in Figure 18. If

we compare case (β) of Figure 18 with case (μ) of Figure 23, we
see that the stability conditions of the equilibrium are precisely
inverse for (β), that is, for exchange and production with incomplete competition, and for (μ), that is, for complete competition.
This is so because in case (β) the line hk being the line of exchanges
(or of maximum profit), the individuals to which it refers stay there
by deliberate design, whereas in the (μ) and (π) cases the line hk
being a line of complete transformations, the individuals to which
it refers are driven there solely by competition.

146. In the (β) case those who found themselves at h would
stay there because the position was advantageous to them; there
was movement only as a consequence of the consumer, who had cd
for a line of exchanges and who wanted to move toward c. In case
(μ), on the other hand, this movement occurs because those who
are at k want to be better off and they seek to proceed along the path
kc. In case (β) equilibrium is possible at d, but we move away from
it because of those who would want to move toward k; in case (μ),
it is not possible to remain at d because the producers have losses,
are ruined and disappear; and we are thus brought back to l.

We have described the phenomenon as it occurs in the long run.
It is always possible for producers to bear a loss for a short period
of time.

147. Let us see what happens when the number of producers has
an influence on the obstacles.

Let mo and mn [Figure 24] be the axes of the producers, $s, s', \ldots$
the indifference lines, and cd the line of exchanges of the consumers.

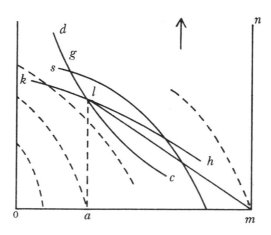

FIG. 24

If there is only one producer he will stop at the intersection, l, of the line of exchanges and the maximum profit line hk. It is the same if there are several producers but with the condition that their number have no influence on the obstacles; consequently—whether there be a few or a large number—they all obtain the maximum profit when the quantity am of A is transformed into al of B.

148. Let us suppose, on the other hand, that the line hk refers to the case of a single producer, and that others can spring up with the same conditions. If there are two of them, all the quantities must be doubled in order that each have the maximum profit; if there are three, they must be tripled, etc. Thus the line hk is shifted, depending on the number of producers, when it refers to a sum-total of production. It would be shifted similarly if, in general, instead of the production doubling, tripling, etc., it would simply increase in certain proportions. The line of complete transformations, s, is also shifted.

If, by a singular chance, the lines thus shifted when there are, for example, two producers, intersect precisely at a point g on the line of exchanges, cd, equilibrium will take place at g. Indeed, one of the producers cannot remain at l because the other, in order to attract customers, changes the slope of the path ml until it coincides with the path mg. He cannot go farther because then he would enter the region of negative indices, and there is no third producer.

149. It will not very readily occur that the shifted lines of maximum profit and of complete transformations intersect precisely on the line of exchanges. As long as the latter intersects the line of maximum profit at a different point from that where it is intersected by the line of complete transformations, equilibrium could take place at the point of intersection of the line of exchanges and the line of maximum profit. But, the producers having a profit at this point, others will spring up, if it is possible of course, until the line of maximum profit no longer intersects the line of exchanges. When this is so, we will have the case already treated (§ 141) and equilibrium will be at the point of intersection of the line of exchanges and the line of complete transformations.

We can use the same reasoning for goods of the second category (§ 102).

150. To sum up, equilibrium takes place at the point where the line of maximum profit and the line of exchanges intersect; but, when it is possible for new producers to appear and the maximum profit line thus is shifted in such a way that it no longer intersects the line of exchanges, equilibrium occurs at the point where the

line of exchanges intersects the line of complete transformations. The first case occurs when competition is incomplete (§ 105), the second when it is complete.

151. For phenomena of Type II, if the producer operates according to this type he will advance as far as he can into the region of positive indices, and as a result the point of equilibrium will be at the point of tangency of the line of exchanges and an indifference line, in the case of complete competition, Figure 14. It will be at the point of tangency of the lines of exchanges and of maximum profit in the case of incomplete competition, Figure 13. Of course all this occurs when these points are within the limits of the phenomenon considered.

If the consumer operates according to Type II he will compel the producers to stop on the line of complete transformations. If the paths must be straight lines from m, equilibrium, in the case of complete competition, will not differ from that which occurs for phenomena of Type I; but it could be different if the consumer were, in some measure, to change the shape of the paths (VI, 17, 18).

152. **Prices.** Up to now we have reasoned in general, making an effort not to make use of prices; but nevertheless we have had to speak of them when we made up concrete examples, and even in the general theories we have had to make use of them more or less implicitly; we have used them without speaking of them specifically. Now it is desirable to resort to them; but it was useful to show that the theories of economics do not proceed directly from the consideration of a market where certain prices exist, but rather from the consideration of the equilibrium which arises from the opposition of tastes and obstacles. Prices appeared as auxiliary unknowns, very useful for solving economic problems, but which must in the end be eliminated so that only the tastes and the obstacles remain.

153. The quantity of X which must be given to obtain one unit of Y is called the PRICE of Y in terms of X.

When the price is constant, any quantity whatsoever of X and Y may be compared to find the ratio between the quantity of X which is given and the quantity of Y which is received, and thus obtain the price. When prices are variables, infinitesimal quantities must be compared.

154. It follows from our definition of price that we move from point c to point d [Figure 25] by exchanging ac of A for ad of B; the price of B in terms of A is equal to the slope of the straight line dcm with respect to the oB axis, and the price of A in terms of B

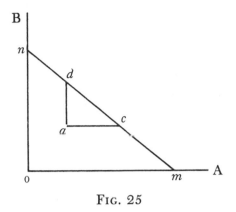

FIG. 25

is expressed by the slope of that same straight line with respect to
the oA axis.[4]

155. In the preceding paragraphs we have often spoken of increasing or decreasing the slope of mm with respect to one of the
axes, for example with respect to oB; it is as though we had spoken
of increasing or decreasing the price of B in terms of A.

156. The VALUE IN EXCHANGE of some economists — if one
wants to examine the nebulous conceptions with which the literary
economists surround it (§ 226) —corresponds closely to price such
as we have just defined it; but the writers who employ this term
value rarely have a clear idea of the thing which it represents.

Furthermore, there have been some economists who distinguished
between *value*, any fraction whatsoever, for example 6/3, and price,
a fraction with a denominator of one, for example 2/1. If 6 of wine
are exchanged for 3 of bread, the *value in exchange* of bread in terms
of wine would be 6/3, and since in this case it is necessary to give
2 of wine to get 1 of bread, the price of bread in terms of wine
would be 2. It is unnecessary to have two names for things which
differ as little as do 6/3 and 2/1, expecially since political economy
has ceased to be a form of literature and is becoming a positive
science.

157. Economists used this notion of *value in exchange* to establish the theorem that a general increase in values is impossible
whereas a general increase in prices is possible. In the preceding
example the value of bread in terms of wine was 6/3, and that of
wine in terms of bread 3/6. The most elementary notions of arithmetic are enough to understand that when one of these fractions increases, the other decreases, their product always being equal to

unity. Thus if 12 of wine are exchanged for 3 of bread, the value of bread in terms of wine increases and becomes 12/3, but the value of wine in terms of bread decreases and becomes 3/12. As for the price of bread in terms of wine, it increases and becomes 4 instead of 2.

158. The general notion of the price of one good in terms of another is useful in economic science because it abstracts from money. In practice, among civilized peoples, the price of all goods is related to a single one of them, which we call money; and in discussing concrete phenomena it is very difficult to avoid speaking of price in this sense. Even in theory it is very useful to introduce this notion in the beginning. It is true that in this way we encroach upon the theory of money which ought to come after the general theory of economic equilibrium; but there is no great evil in that, especially if we consider the greater clarity which the use of this notion gives to the exposition.

159. Let us review, using the general notion of price, the results already reached.

160. Type I is provided by those phenomena in which the individual accepts the prices which he finds on the market and seeks to satisfy his tastes at those prices. In doing so, he contributes unintentionally toward modifying those prices; but he does not act directly with the intention of modifying them. At a certain price he buys (or sells) a certain quantity of a good; if the person with whom he is dealing accepted another price, he would buy (or would sell) another quantity of the good. In other words, in order to make him buy (or sell) a certain quantity of the good, a certain price must prevail.

161. Type II, on the other hand, is formed by phenomena in which the principal objective of the individual is to modify prices so that he can then derive a certain advantage. He does not leave the choice of the different prices to the person with whom he is dealing; he imposes one, and just allows the other person the choice of the quantity to buy (or sell) at that price. The determination of the price is no longer bilateral as in Type I; it becomes unilateral.

162. We have already seen that in real life Type I corresponds to free competition (§ 46), and Type II corresponds to monopoly.

163. Where there is free competition, no one having a special status, the determination of price is bilateral. Individual one cannot impose his price on two, nor individual two his price on one. In this case one who is buying (or selling) asks himself this question: "Given such a price, what quantity shall I buy (or sell)?" Or in

other words: "For me to buy (or sell) such a quantity of the good, what must the price be?"

164. Where there is monopoly, in any form whatsoever, there is someone with a special status. The latter uses his position to set the price, the determination of which becomes unilateral. He asks himself, then, the following question: "What price should I impose on the market to attain the objective I have in mind?"

165. Type III also corresponds to a monopoly; but it is distinguished from Type II by its goal. The question which the socialist State must ask itself is the following: "What prices must be set in order that my members enjoy the maximum welfare compatible with the conditions in which they find themselves, or which I think good to impose on them?"

166. Note that even if the socialist State abolished all right of exchange and prohibited all buying and selling, prices would not disappear on that account; they would remain at the very least as an accounting device in connection with the distribution of goods and their transformation. The use of prices is the simplest and easiest means for solving the equations of equilibrium; if one insisted on not using them, he would probably end up by using them under another name, and there would then be only a change of language, and not of things.

167. **Prices and the second kind of obstacles.** We have seen that among the data of the problem we must have the ratios according to which successive portions of the goods are transformed. When prices are introduced, that is expressed by saying that we must specify the manner in which the prices of the successive portions vary; we must determine, for example, whether these portions all have the same price, which moreover may be unknown, or whether their prices increase (or decrease) according to a certain law.

168. This is a point on which some writers have been mistaken and which therefore deserves to be studied more closely. A fundamental distinction must be made with regard to variations in prices. The prices of successive portions which one buys in order to get to the equilibrium position may vary, or the prices may differ between two entire operations leading to the position of equilibrium.

(*a*) For example, an individual buys 100 grams of bread at 60 centimes a kilogram, then 100 grams at 50 centimes a kilogram, then still another 100 grams at 40 centimes a kilogram, and in this way reaches a position of equilibrium after having purchased 300 grams of bread at different prices. Tomorrow he begins the same operation all over. In this case the prices for the successive portions which are purchased in order to reach the position of equilibrium are variable, but they do not differ when the operation is started again.

(β) On the other hand, tomorrow the same individual buys 100 kilograms of bread at 70 centimes a kilogram, then 100 kilograms at 65 centimes, then 100 kilograms at 58 centimes. The prices vary, not only for the successive portions, but also from one operation leading to equilibrium to another.

(γ) The individual under consideration buys 300 grams of bread at the constant price of 60 centimes a kilogram, and thus reaches the equilibrium position. Tomorrow he repeats the same operation. In this case the prices of the successive portions are constant, and the price does not differ from one operation leading to equilibrium to another operation.

(δ) Finally, today this individual buys 300 grams of bread at the constant price of 60 centimes a kilogram, and thereby reaches the equilibrium position. To reach that position tomorrow he buys 400 grams of bread, paying the constant price of 50 centimes for each of the successive portions. The prices of the successive portions are constant in this case also; what differs is the price per portion as between two operations leading to equilibrium.

169. This will be understood better by means of diagrams [Figure 26].

In all the figures, *ab* and *ac* indicate the routes followed in the different purchases, that is, the prices paid for the various portions. In (α) and in (β) *ab* and *ac* are curves; that is, the prices vary from one portion to another; in (γ) and in (δ) *ab* and *ac* are straight lines; that is, the prices are constant for the various portions. In (α) and in (γ) the individual moves along the route *ab* each day;

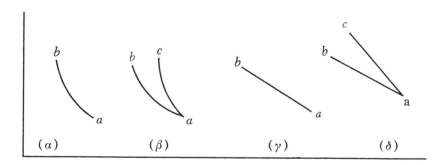

FIG. 26

in (β) and in (δ) he moves along the route *ab* today and *ac* tomorrow. Hence the figures represent the following cases:

(α) Prices variable for the successive portions, but repeat in the same way for the successive operations leading to equilibrium.

(β) Prices variable for the successive portions and for the successive operations leading to equilibrium.

(γ) Prices constant for the successive portions and for the successive operations leading to equilibrium.

(δ) Prices constant for the successive portions but variable as between successive operations leading to equilibrium.

In the present state of the science, the general cases to consider are (γ) and (δ), but there is nothing to prevent a day from coming when it will be profitable to take (α) and (β) into consideration also.

170. When a large number of persons appear on a market and act independently of each other, engaging in competition, it is obvious that at a given time some will buy the initial portions, others the second ones, etc., in order to reach a state of equilibrium; and since on a certain market at a given time, it is assumed that there is only one price, it is seen that the price of these different portions should be the same. Strictly speaking, this would not prevent the price from varying from one portion to another for the same individual, but this hypothesis entails strange and highly unrealistic consequences. Also the hypothesis which conforms best to reality is the one of equal prices for successive portions. Naturally, this does not prevent there being a succession of different prices as in (δ), Figure 26.

This is especially true of consumption. If an individual buys 10 kilograms of sugar, coffee, bread, meat, cotton, wool, nails, lead, paint, etc., he does not buy the first kilogram at a certain price, the second at another, etc. It is not that this is impossible, but ordinarily things do not happen that way. Note, however, that it is perfectly possible that this individual buys 10 kilograms of onions at a certain price today and 10 kilograms at another price tomorrow which brings us to case (δ), Figure 26. In the large cities, it often happens that in the market fish cost more in the early morning than near noon when the market closes. The *chef* of a first class restaurant may come early in order to have more choice, and buy 20 kilograms of fish at a certain price. The *chef* of a second class restaurant will come later and buy what remains at a lower price. We still have case (δ), Figure 26. Furthermore, in the case we are considering, an average price could be used without serious error. Let us never forget that our purpose is simply to arrive at a general idea of the phenomenon.

171. When it is a question of speculation, it is almost always necessary to consider that the different portions are purchased at different prices. If certain brokers, for example, want to monopolize copper, they should not forget that they must buy this metal at increasing prices; thinking about an average price could make them fall into very serious errors.[9] Similarly, if we wished to make a study of the various methods of sale at public auction of certain goods, fish, for example, variations in the prices would have to be taken into account. But all this constitutes a special study of secondary phenomena. They modify the principal phenomenon which, in the final analysis, adjusts consumption to production.

In addition, the case of which we have been speaking, that of speculation, pertains more to dynamics than to statics. In that case there are a very great number of successive positions of equilibrium to consider. Save for certain exceptional cases, prices on the big markets vary only from one day to another, at least in an important way, and ordinarily the different actual prices can be replaced by the average price without gross error.[10]

172. When the price of the successive portions exchanged is constant, the ratio between these quantities is itself constant; that is, if the first unit of bread exchanges for two of wine, the second unit of bread will also exchange for two of wine, and so on. This phenomenon is represented graphically by a straight line whose slope with respect to one of the axes is the price (§ 153). Hence when one prescribes the condition that the price is constant, the only thing determined is that the path followed by the individual must be a straight line, and not which straight line it must be. An individual has 20 kilograms of bread and he wants to exchange them for wine; if the price of the successive portions exchanged is taken to be constant, it is assumed simply that the route to follow is a straight line. If the length *om* on the axis measuring the quantity of bread is taken to be 20, the individual can follow any route chosen from the straight lines *ma, ma′, ma″*, etc. [Figure 27]. If in addition the price of bread in terms of wine is set at 2, that is, if 2 of wine must be given for one of bread, the straight line would then be completely determined. If we take *oc* equal to 40, *mc* will represent that line;

---

[9] This was the reef on which the operation for monopolizing copper attempted in 1887-1888 went aground.

[10] Note 2 of § 928 of the *Cours* rests on some erroneous considerations, and ought to be entirely changed.

it is only on that straight line, starting from m, that one of bread exchanges for 2 of wine.

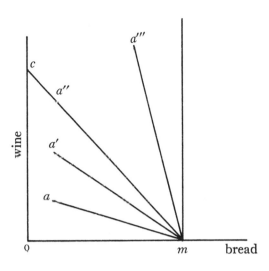

FIG. 27

173. All the angles oma, oma', oma'', . . . , must be acute because price is essentially positive; that is, in exchange, in order that an individual receive something, he must give up something else; consequently, in order to increase the quantity of one good he possesses, the quantity of another good he also possesses must decrease. If one of the angles oma, oma', . . . , were obtuse, the two quantities would increase at the same time. If the angle oma were equal to zero, the price would be zero; one would receive no wine at all for no matter what quantity of bread. If the angle oma were a right angle, the price would be infinite. For an angle just a little smaller we would have a price such that a very small quantity of bread would exchange for a very great quantity of wine. The angles oma, oma', . . . in the figure represent some prices included between these two extremes.

174. When the path followed is not given directly, but only by the designation of the prices of successive portions, we must make a calculation in order to know the quantities of goods transformed.

Assume that there are only two goods A and B, that the price of B is expressed in terms of A, and that, for example, 1 kilogram of A is exchanged for a certain quantity of B at a price of 1/2, then 2 kilograms of A for another quantity of B at a price of 1/3, then 1 kilogram of A for another quantity of B at a price of 1/4. The quantities of B successively obtained in this way will be 2, 6, 4; thus, in the end, 12 kilograms of B will have been obtained at different prices by the exchange of 4 kilograms of A.

If there are more than two goods, and if the prices of B, C, D, . . . are expressed in terms of A, it is obvious that the total quantity of A transformed must be equal to that which is obtained by multiplying each portion of B, C, D, . . . by its price and adding up the total. These quantities give the point at which we arrive by following a certain path.

175. **The budget of the individual.** Through the sale of things which he possesses, the individual obtains a certain sum of money; this we will call his *receipts*. For the purchase of things which he uses, he spends a certain sum of money; this we will call his *expenditure*.

If we consider the transformation of 8 of A into 4 of B, for example, and if A represents money, the price of B in terms of A is 2. The receipts are 8 of A. The expenditure is, in money, 4 of B multiplied by the price of B, 2, which comes to 8. The receipts are equal to the expenditure, and this signifies that 8 of A is transformed into 4 of B.

If there are more than two goods it is easy to see that the receipts must still be equal to the expenditure, because if this were not so, it would mean that the individual had received, or spent, some money in another way than the transformation of goods. This equality of receipts and expenditures is what is called the BUDGET OF THE INDIVIDUAL.

176. **The budget of the producer.** The producer also has his budget; and we have already referred to it without mentioning it expressly when we studied the transformation of one good into another. We have seen that this transformation could leave a positive or negative residue, which is really an element, credit or debit, which is entered in the "profit and loss" account.

This is true of all transformations. The producer buys certain goods, makes certain expenditures, this is the outgo of his budget. He sells the goods produced and this gives the receipts of his budget. The case of complete transformations is one in which the budget balances with neither profit nor loss.

177. **The cost of production.** If we take into account all the expenses necessary to obtain a good, and if we divide that total by the quantity of the good produced, we have the COST OF PRODUCTION of that good.

178. This cost of production is expressed in *numéraire*. Some

writers have considered a cost of production expressed in ophelimity. That is pointless and only gives rise to ambiguities; hence we will never give that meaning to the expression cost of production.

If a certain thing A can be consumed directly and if we transform it into another thing B, the sacrifice made in giving up the direct consumption of A can be considered as the cost, in ophelimity, of B. But there are extremely numerous cases where A cannot be consumed directly; in such a case it is not proper to speak of direct sacrifices when A is transformed into B. In order to find a cost in ophelimity, one is obliged to change the meaning of this expression and say that if A can be transformed into B or into C, the cost of production of B in ophelimity is the satisfaction which is given up in transforming A into B instead of transforming it into C, and *vice versa*.

We must never wrangle over words, and anyone can give what meaning he wants to the expression cost of production in ophelimity. But it must be observed that the first meaning which we have just noted is essentially different from the second. The first separates production from exchange, the second confounds them. The first actually reveals a certain cost in ophelimity, the second only gives one of the conditions which, with others, could determine that cost.[11]

For example, an individual has some meal and he transforms it into bread. He can, by disregarding the expenses of this transformation, consider the cost of the bread in terms of ophelimity as equal to the pleasure he gives up in not eating his meal in the form of porridge. But if he must take into account all the indirect uses that this meal can have, it is impossible for him to have one unique thing to which he can give this name of cost of production. This meal can be transformed into rabbit meat, turkey, or capon, by feeding it to these animals; it can be fed to workers who produce a house, a hat, gloves, and so on, indefinitely. Consideration of this pseudo cost of production leads, then, simply to recognizing the equality of the weighted ophelimities of the goods which the individual consumes (§ 198).

179. Each good does not necessarily have a cost of production of its own. There are some goods which must be produced jointly,

---

[11] This again is one of the innumerable vain attempts to escape the necessity of solving a system of simultaneous equations (§ 219 *et seq.*), to take account in a vague way of the interdependence of economic phenomena, to conceal ignorance of the solutions of the problems by making use of terms lacking precision.

for example wheat and straw, and consequently have only a joint cost of production.

180. **Supply and demand.** In political economy it is customary to distinguish between the quantity of goods which an individual, having arrived at a point of equilibrium, has given up, and what he has received; the first is called his SUPPLY, the second his DEMAND.

181. These two terms have been used, as all the terms of non-mathematical economics, in a way which is equivocal, ambiguous and not very rigorous; and the many vain, purposeless and jumbled discussions of which they have been the subject is truly incredible. Even today it is not difficult to find among the non-mathematician economists some writers who do not know the meaning of these terms which they use, nevertheless, at every turn.

182. Returning to Figure 12, let us begin by considering two goods. An individual has the quantity om of A and nothing of B; by following a certain path mn, he reaches a point of equilibrium c'', exchanging qm of A for qc'' of B. We will say that, on this path and at the point of equilibrium c'', the individual under consideration supplies qm of A and demands qc'' of B.

183. It must be observed immediately that these quantities would be different if the shape of the path were to change; that is, they depend on obstacles of the second type. Even when the shape of the path remains the same, for example when the path is a straight line, these quantities change with the slope of the line, that is, with the price.

184. Let us go back again to Figure 12. Given some price of A in terms of B, that is, given the slope of mn with respect to om, the intersection of this straight line with the line of exchanges cc''' gives us the demand qc'' for B, and the supply qm of A. The curve of exchanges can thus be called the SUPPLY CURVE and the DEMAND CURVE. In Figure 20 the curve $masb$ is, for the first individual, the *demand* curve for B; and this demand is ordinarily related to the price of B in terms of A, expressed by the slope of a path (for example me) with respect to the oy axis. It is also, still for the first individual, the *supply* curve of A; and this supply is ordinarily related to the price of A in terms of B (no longer to the price of B in terms of A), that is, to the slope of a path (for example me) with respect to the mo axis.

185. In the case of two goods, if a rectilinear path is *assumed*, the demand for B then depends only on the price of B; the supply of A, only on the price of A.

186. We must take care not to extend this conclusion to the case of several goods. The supply of a good depends on the prices of all the other goods exchanged, and similarily for the demand for a good.

187. That is not all. We have assumed that the equilibrium was at c in Figure 7; it could happen that it would be at the terminal point a; in this case, the quantity of A supplied would be rm, the quantity of B demanded would be ra; these quantities would depend on the position of the point a, that is, on the obstacles.

In general, supply and demand depend on all the circumstances surrounding economic equilibrium.

188. When we consider only two individuals who are exchanging, the one supplies A and demands B; the other supplies B and demands A. We have seen (§ 117) that there is a point of equilibrium of exchange for the two individuals at the point of intersection of the two individuals' curves of exchanges. Using the new names we have just given these curves, we can say that the point of equilibrium is one of those where the first individual's demand curve for B, intersects the second individual's supply curve of B; or, what comes to the same thing, the point of equilibrium is one of those where the first individual's supply curve of A intersects the second individual's demand curve for A; or again, the point of equilibrium is one of those where for one of the goods the demand is equal to the supply.

189. Non-mathematical political economy had formulated this proposition, but did not have a precise notion of it, and more particularly, it was not aware of the conditions which alone justify the theorem and the restrictions which it requires. Even today the majority of those who call themselves economists are ignorant of them.

There are, incidentally, some people who claim that "the mathematical method has not yet formulated any new truth," and that is true in a certain sense because, for the ignorant person, something he has not the least idea about can be neither true nor new. When one is not even aware of the existence of certain problems, he certainly does not feel the need of having the solution to them.

190. For the producer supply and demand have no meaning at all if one does not add a condition which determines in what part of the region of possible equilibrium we wish to stop. In order to apply the preceding theorem in the case of production, namely, for phenomena of Type I with complete competition, we can add the condition that the supply and the demand are those which occur on the line of complete transformations.

191. Then if we wanted the theorem of equilibrium based on the

equality of supply and demand to be applied also to goods for which there exists a line of maximum profit, as in § 105, we would have to give another meaning to supply and demand and relate them to that line.

192. In the case of several individuals and several goods, we see that by adding, for each good, the demands of the different individuals, we obtain the total demand for each good; and similarly for the supply.

193. The character of the variation in the supply and in the demand has been called the law of supply and the law of demand. We will discuss it in another chapter; at present all we require is a realization that in the case of two goods, when the price of a good increases, the demand decreases, whereas the supply increases at first but may then decrease.

194. If we consider in Figure 15 a path mc' leading to a point c' of the line of complete transformations, the slope of the straight line mc' with respect to the mb axis, on which is measured quantities of good B, is equal to the cost of production of good B obtained by the complete transformation at c'. And if c' is also on the line of exchanges, this slope measures the selling price. It follows from this that at the points of intersection, c and c', of the curve of exchanges and the curve of complete transformations, that is, at the points of equilibrium, the cost of production is equal to the selling price.

195. We have seen that equilibrium may be stable or unstable; an explanation based upon the notions of price, and of supply and demand follows.

Two individuals who are exchanging are at a point of equilibrium; let us assume that the price of B increases and see what takes place.

The first individual, who sells A and buys B, decreases his demand for B; the second individual may increase, or may decrease, his supply of B. Two cases must be distinguished: 1° the supply of B increases, or else decreases, but in a way such that it remains above the demand for B. Things take place as in the two examples (α) and (γ) of Figure 18. 2° The supply decreases in a way such that it becomes lower than the demand. This is the case of example (β) of Figure 18. To sum up, it is only necessary to check whether, with the new price, supply is above or below demand. In the first case the equilibrium is stable; indeed, the one who supplies is induced to reduce his price in order to bring his supply nearer to the demand. In the second case the equilibrium is unstable because the one who demands is not satisfied since he must be content with the smaller supply which is offered him; and as a result he increases his price in order to obtain a larger quantity of the good, but he is mistaken and in the end obtains less of it.

Analogous observations can be made in the case of production; it is very easy to translate into the new language what we have already set forth in §§ 140, 141, 142.

196. **Equilibrium in the general case.** Up to now we have studied primarily the case of two individuals and two goods; we now must deal with the equilibrium of any number of individuals and any number of goods.

In this chapter we will restrict ourselves to examining the general case of equilibrium for phenomena of Type I with complete competition.

Assume that we have arrived at the state of equilibrium, that is, at the point where certain quantities of goods, having certain prices, are being transformed, by exchange or otherwise, indefinitely; and let us try to determine these quantities and these prices. This is the case represented graphically by (γ) in Figure 26 and we are assuming that the operation indicated by (γ) repeats itself indefinitely. Some individual, for example, exchanges 10 kilograms of bread for 5 kilograms of wine, thereby reaching a position of equilibrium, and he repeats this operation indefinitely.

In Type I the individual is guided solely by his own tastes, accepting the market prices as he finds them. In order that his tastes be satisfied by the above exchange, it must be that it suits him neither to go beyond nor to stop short of [the equilibrium point]. The price of wine in terms of bread is 2. If the individual continues the exchange and again gives 10 grams of bread, he will receive 5 grams of wine. If the ophelimity (or index of ophelimity) of this 10 grams of bread were less than the ophelimity of this 5 grams of wine, it would be advisable for this individual to add this exchange to the exchange already made. If the ophelimity of the 10 grams of bread were greater than the ophelimity of the 5 grams of wine, it would be advisable for him not to exchange the entire 10 kilograms of bread for the 5 kilograms of wine, but to exchange only 9.990 kilograms for 4.995 kilograms of wine. Accordingly, if at the point of equilibrium the ophelimity of the 10 grams of bread must be neither greater nor smaller than the ophelimity of the 5 grams of wine, it can only be equal to it.

197. For this reasoning to be rigorous, however, the quantities must be infinitesimal. When they are finite, we cannot say that the ophelimity of 10 grams of bread added to 10 kilograms of bread

is equal to the ophelimity of 10 grams of bread. We could, however, reason simply by approximation and consider an average. But we need not dwell on this; in one way or another, we have a notion of the phenomenon.

198. For very small quantities it can be assumed that the ophelimity is proportional to the quantities. In that case the ophelimity of 5 grams of wine will be in the neighborhood of half the ophelimity of 10 grams of wine (it would be precisely one-half if we were considering infinitesimal quantities). We can say, then, that for equilibrium the ophelimity of a very small quantity of bread must be equal to half the ophelimity of the same very small quantity of wine. The elementary ophelimity (§ 33) of the bread must be equal to one-half the elementary ophelimity of the wine. Or, recalling that the price of wine is two, we can say that the weighted elementary ophelimity (§ 34) of the bread and of the wine must be equal.

In this form the proposition is general for Type I, and applies to any number of individuals who are guided directly by their individual tastes (§ 41), and to any number of goods, provided that we assume that the satisfaction yielded by the consumption of each good is independent of the consumption of the others (IV, 10, 11). In that case each individual compares one of the goods, A for example, to the others B, C, D, . . . ; and he stops his transformations when for him the weighted ophelimities of all the goods are equal. Thus we have, for each individual, as many conditions as there are goods minus one. If, for example, there are three of them, A, B, and C, we should say that the weighted elementary ophelimity of A is equal to that of B, and also to that of C, which gives us precisely two conditions.

199. This category of conditions states that each individual satisfies his tastes DIRECTLY (§ 41), as far as that is permitted by the obstacles. We will call them category (A) conditions in order to distinguish them from others.

200. We get another category of conditions, which we will denote by (B), in making up the budget of each individual (§ 175). Therefore the number of conditions in this category is equal to the number of individuals.

If we add all the individual budgets, we have the budget of the collectivity, which is made up of the residues left after offsetting the sales and the purchases of each good. If some of the individuals have sold a total of 100 kilograms of oil, and the other individuals have purchased 60 of it, the collectivity as a whole has sold 40 kilograms of oil. All these residues, multiplied by the respective prices, must balance. For example, if the collectivity has sold 20 kilograms of wine at 1 franc 20 a kilogram and 60 kilograms of wheat at 0 franc 20 a kilogram, it will have received 36 francs from its sales. And if it has purchased only oil, it must have spent 36 francs for the oil since the receipts balance the expenditures. Consequently, if we know the prices and the quantities bought or sold by the collectivity for all the goods less one, conditions (B) tell us this quantity for the good omitted.

201. Let us count the conditions which we have just enumerated. If there are, for example, 100 individuals and 700 goods, category (A) will give us, for each individual, 699 conditions, and for 100 individuals 69,900 conditions. Category (B) will give us 100 other conditions; we will have 70,000 conditions in all. In general, this total is equal to the number of individuals multiplied by the number of goods.

Let us count the unknowns. One of the goods serving as money, there are 699 prices of the other goods. For each individual there are the quantities of each good which he receives (or which he gives up); we have then, in total, 70,000 quantities. Adding the prices, we have 70,699 unknowns.

Comparing the number of conditions, 70,000, to the number of unknowns, 70,699, we soon see that, for the problem to be completely determined (§ 38), we are lacking 699 conditions, that is, in general, the number of goods minus one.

202. They must be furnished by consideration of the obstacles. In exchange, in addition to the opposition of the tastes of the individuals which we have already taken into account in conditions (A), the obstacles consist simply in the fact that the total quantities of goods are constant because what one of the individuals gives up is received by others; and, in total, for each good, the sales of the collectivity exactly offset the purchases. But conditions (B) give us the total quantity of one good sold, or purchased, by the collectivity when the analogous quantities for the other goods are known (§ 200). Hence it will suffice to set as a condition for all the goods minus one, that is, for 699 goods, that the residue of the purchases or of the sales of the collectivity be equal to zero, because conditions (B) tell us that this residue is also zero for the last good.

Thus we have an additional category of conditions, which we will designate by (C), and which refers to the obstacles.

203. We were lacking 699 conditions, and category (C) is made up of precisely 699 conditions. The number of the conditions is now

equal to that of the unknowns, and the problem is completely de-. termined.

204. We could have said for the 700 goods, that, for the collectivity, the quantities sold were equal to the quantities purchased, hence a zero residue for all the 700 goods. That way we would have had one more condition in category (C); but, offsetting this, we would have had one less in category (B). Indeed, when all the quantities of the goods are known, it is enough to have the budget of all the individuals minus one in order to get the budget of this last one as well. What he receives is obviously equal to what the others give up, and what he gives up is equal to what they receive.

205. Let us consider production. Assume that 200 of the 700 goods are transformed into 500 others, whose cost of production we are going to calculate. If competition is complete, equilibrium can take place only where this cost of production is equal to the selling price. Indeed, if it is higher, the producer has a loss and must abandon the struggle; if it is lower, the producer has profits and others will come in to share in this profit. Thus we have a category of conditions which we shall designate by (D) and which state that for each of the 500 goods produced the cost of production is equal to the selling price.

206. In the case of exchange it was necessary to specify that the total quantities of all the 700 goods, less one, would remain constant. In the case of production this is no longer so, and we have to specify that 200 goods have been transformed into 500 others, that is, that the quantity of the first ones which have disappeared has been replaced by the quantity of those which have been produced. For reasons analogous to those we have already indicated, it is sufficient to express this fact for 200 goods minus one. We thus have another category of conditions, (E).

The conditions of this category state that equilibrium takes place on the line of complete transformations.

207. Toting up the number of conditions (D) and (E), we get 699 conditions, which is what we were short; and thus the problem is completely determined.

208. In the case of phenomena of Type I, with complete competition and constant prices for the successive portions of a given operation, we can state the following theorem:

We have a point of equilibrium where the following conditions are realized: (A) Equality, for each individual, of the weighted ophelimities; (B) Equality, for each individual, of receipts and expenditures. In addition, in the case of exchange: (C) Equality, for all the goods, of the quantities existing before and after the exchange. Then, in the case of production, the following are substituted for the last conditions: (D) Equality of the cost of production and the selling price, for all the goods produced; (E) Equality of the quantities of goods demanded for transformation, and of the quantities of these goods actually transformed (Appendix, 24, 63, 80, 83).

209. In addition, among conditions (B) and (C) there is one superfluous one, and similarly among conditions (B), (D) and (E).

210. Let us choose, at random, a good A which will serve as money; hence the prices of all the goods will be expressed in A. Moreover, as we have done before (§ 198), let us compare the other goods to A one by one, and assume that we have each individual's indifference lines for A and B, the indifference lines for A and C, etc. The points of possible equilibrium are those where the indifference curve of A and B has a tangent whose slope with respect to the oB axis is equal to the price of B in terms of A; similarly, for the indifference lines for C and A, the slope of the tangent with respect to the oC axis must be equal to the price of C in terms of A, etc.

211. We thus have conditions analogous to those which we established for the case of two goods. But, whereas then we knew *a priori* the distance om, Figure 12, which is the quantity of A originally possessed by the individual, in the case of several goods, om, on the contrary, is an unknown; it is that part of A which the individual transforms into another good, for example into B. Hence the conditions of category (A) simply state that equilibrium is possible at the points where the tangent to the indifference curve for good A and any other good has a slope, with respect to the axis of that other good, equal to its price.

212. Category (B), in the case of two goods, shows us the path traveled by each individual. If there are three goods we can still have a graphical representation of conditions (B) by putting the quantity of these goods on three orthogonal axes. One of the budgets (B) represents a plane on which the exchange or the transformation takes place. Similarly, we can say, in the case of more than three goods, that each budget (B) indicates the *locus* of the transformations by the individual to which that budget refers.

213. Conditions (C), in the case of two goods and two individuals, comes down to a single one, namely, that the quantity of A given up by one individual is received by the other. And it is by virtue of this condition that, if we lay out the indifference curves of the two individuals as they are in Figure 16, the path followed by each of the individuals is represented by a single straight line.

214. Let us see what correspondence there is between the conditions referring to the obstacles and those referring to the producers. In the case of two goods, conditions (D) come down to just one which states that the price of the good is equal to its cost of production. Conditions (E) also reduce to a single one, namely, that there is no residue of A; that is, that equilibrium takes place on a line of complete transformations.

215. The equilibrium can be stable or unstable. As a supposition, let us suppress the equations of category (A) which refer to the first individual; that is, we no longer bother to consider whether the tastes of this individual are satisfied; his budget continues to be in equilibrium since all conditions (B) still hold. The equations which we have suppressed in category (A) are equal to the number of goods minus one (§ 198); this is also the number of prices. It follows from this that, if we allow the possibility that the tastes of one of the individuals of the collectivity may not be satisfied, we can arbitrarily choose the prices.

216. That demonstration was necessary in order to show that the analysis we are going to make is possible. Assume that all the members of a collectivity are in an equilibrium position; modify the prices slightly and reestablish equilibrium for all the individuals of the collectivity except the first one; that is possible thanks to the preceding demonstration.

After this operation all the individuals except the first one are satisfied. We must note now that the latter compares successively all the goods to one of them, to A in our case, and, given that we are considering phenomena of Type I, he compares only the ophelimity which he enjoys at the different points of each path. For A and B, for A and C, etc., we will thus have phenomena such as those, so often mentioned, of examples (α), (β), and (γ) of Figure 18, and the analogous cases of stable and unstable equilibrium. In other words, the individual under consideration receives and gives up, at the new prices, certain quantities of the goods which are greater or less than those which, for him, correspond to equilibrium. Consequently he will endeavor to return to the position of equilibrium, which he can do only by modifying the prices at which he buys, and those at which he sells. In doing this, it may happen that he approaches the position of equilibrium from which we assumed he had been driven, or it may be that he moves away from it. In the first, it is a case of stable equilibrium; in the second, a case of unstable equilibrium. In order that the equilibrium be stable for the collectivity, it obviously must be so for all the individuals who make it up.

217. The conditions we have enumerated for economic equilibrium give us a general notion of that equilibrium. In order to understand what certain phenomena are, we had to study their manifestation; in order to understand what economic equilibrium is, we had to investigate how it is determined. Note, however, that this determination certainly is not for the purpose of arriving at a numerical calculation of the prices. Let us make the hypothesis most favorable to such a calculation; assume that we have overcome all the difficulties in the way of acquiring knowledge of the data of the problem, and that we know the ophelimities of all the goods for each individual, all the particulars pertaining to the production of the goods, etc. This is already an absurd hypothesis, and yet it still does not provide us with the practical possibility of solving the problem. We have seen that in the case of 100 individuals and 700 goods there would be 70,699 conditions (in reality a great number of particular details, which we have disregarded so far, would increase this number further); then we would have to solve a system of 70,699 equations. As a practical matter, that is beyond the power of algebraic analysis, and it would be still further beyond it if we considered the fabulous number of equations which a population of forty million individuals, and several thousand goods would entail. In that case the roles would be changed; and it would no longer be mathematics which would come to the aid of political economy, but political economy which would come to the aid of mathematics. In other words, if all these equations were actually known, the only means of solving them would be to observe the actual solution which the market gives.

218. Even if the conditions which we have just enumerated cannot be of practical use to us for numerical calculations of quantity and price, they are the only means as yet known for arriving at a notion of the way in which these quantities and these prices vary, or, more exactly, for understanding in a general way how economic equilibrium takes place.

219. Under the pressure of the facts, even the economists to whom these conditions were unknown have had to take them into account. We can say that they came to this: they searched for the solution of a system of equations without making use of mathematics, and since that is not possible, they had no other means of escaping the difficulty than by recourse to subterfuges, some, in truth, very ingenious. In general, they proceeded in the following fashion: they assumed, more or less implicitly, that all the conditions (equations) minus one were satisfied, and they then had only

a single unknown to determine by means of known quantities. That was a problem which was not beyond the power of ordinary logic.[12]

Instead of a single condition one can also consider only one of the categories of conditions (equations) which determine equilibrium, because, since these conditions are similar, ordinary logic can deal with them, though without great precision, as with a single equation.

Here is an example of the nonsensical talk such as is still employed in literary economics: "If one assumes a condition of full and free competition, the degree of limitation—as also the cost of substitution and the degree of marginal utility—will be identified with the degree of quantitative limitation, that is, with the cost of production."

That looks as if it means something but it does not mean anything at all. The writer was quite careful not to define exactly what *the degree of limitation* is; he has a very vague idea of a certain thing which he calls *cost of production*, and which is certainly not the cost in *numéraire*. He has a glimpse of another thing, *marginal utility;* and by association of ideas he establishes an identity which exists only in his imagination.

Naturally, such a mode of reasoning can lead only to errors. In fact, we are told: "If one considers the value of a good in a single exchange, one can say only that the price of this good is determined by its degree of quantitative limitation."

Let us apply this theory to an example. A traveler is in the middle of Africa. He has a score of *Traviata*. It is the only one in that locality; hence its "degree of quantitative limitation," if that term means anything, must be very high; nevertheless its price is zero. The Negroes with whom our traveler is in contact do not appreciate this good at all.

We have retrogressed. Phaedrus and La Fontaine were better economists. The cock which had found the pearl already understood the outlandishness of considering it a matter "of quantitative limitation"; it is a matter of taste:

Ego quod te inveni, potior cui multo est cibus,
Nec tibi prodesse, nec mihi quidquam potest.

As for La Fontaine's ignoramus, it is possible that the manuscript which he had inherited had a high degree of "quantitative limitation," that it was even one of a kind; but if no connoisseur wanted this manuscript, our ignoramus would not have had his *ducatoon*.

---

[12] I pointed this out for the first time in the *Giornale degli economisti*, September 1901. See also *Systèmes*, II, p. 288 *et seq.*

They have wanted to find at least one limit for prices, and they have declared that "no one would consent to pay more for a good than it would cost him if he produced it himself".

If that proposition is understood strictly, it can only be a question of a cost in *numéraire*, for one cannot compare two heterogeneous quantities: a price and sacrifice. Let us leave aside the error of assuming a cost of production independent of prices, an error which will be considered later (§ 224), and restrict ourselves to remarking that this proposition, even if it were true, would be useless most of the time because among the goods which we consume there are almost none we can produce ourselves, and those few which we could produce ourselves would cost us a price enormously greater than the one at which we buy them. How would you go about producing yourself, directly, the coffee you drink, the cloth with which you are clothed, the newspaper you read? And what would be the price of one of these goods if—even assuming the impossible—you could produce it directly?

Wishing to avoid, at all costs, studying the totality of the conditions of economic equilibrium, the literary economists have tried to simplify the problem by changing the meaning of the term "cost of production" and substituting for cost of production in *numéraire* a cost of production expressed in sacrifices, which has no more than a vague and unspecified meaning, lending itself to any sort of interpretation.

An individual has a garden where he can raise strawberries; they say that it is obvious that he will not pay for strawberries a price which represents a greater sacrifice for him than what he would make in producing them directly. This proposition, which is intended to avoid the complications in the economic phenomenon, is simple only in appearance; if one wants to state it precisely the complications which are thought to be avoided appear anew. How do we evaluate the "sacrifice" of the individual who raises his own strawberries? Is it the pain which he will endure, in addition to the expenditures he will make? We are ignoring how we will go about summing these heterogeneous quantities, but let us pass on and assume that in some manner this sum has been constructed. With this approach, we have in fact isolated our individual's production of strawberries from the rest of the economic phenomenon. But in this sense, the proposition is false. The owner of the garden is a talented painter; by one day of work he earns enough to buy more strawberries than he would produce by working six months in his garden; he has, therefore, an advantage in painting and buying strawberries for more than they would "cost" him (IX, 42 *et seq.*).

In order to make our proposition true, it is necessary to change the meaning of the term *to cost* and say that our individual must consider not the *pain* which he endures directly in producing the strawberries, but the benefits which he gives up by employing his time in cultivating strawberries instead of employing it otherwise. But in this case the phenomenon of the production of strawberries is no longer isolated from the rest of the economic phenomenon; the proposition which we have stated is no longer sufficient to determine the price of strawberries; it says only that every individual tries to make the most advantageous use of his labor and of the other factors of production at his disposal, which, in this case, simply leads to part of the conditions (equations) of economic equilibrium, and specifically to part of the conditions which we have designated by A (§ 199).

We can continue in this way and try to remove the difficulties which we pointed out in beginning. The objection is that a man finds it impossible to produce the majority of the goods which he consumes. Well! let us make the same analysis for the goods which the individual consumes which we made for the factors of production at his disposal. Let us not ask him to produce his watch directly; the poor man would never get that done; and let us call "cost of production" the satisfaction which he gives up elsewhere when he uses his money to buy himself a watch instead of buying something else. Provided that one has the integrity to warn the reader clearly that this strange meaning is being given to the term "cost of production," one can then say that the price which is paid for a watch is such that it represents a satisfaction equal to the "cost of production" of the watch. But in this way one will only obtain the equations which were lacking to make up the total of equations A, part of which we have already obtained in considering the factors of production. A theory of exchange will have been constructed while one appeared to be constructing a theory of production; and it puts this subject on the wrong track when, without realizing it, the meaning of the term cost of production has been distorted in such a strange way.

If we have been a bit prolix on this proposition of literary economics, it is not because it is worse than others, it is only to give an example, chosen at random, of the deplorably vague and erroneous fashion in which these questions are still treated and of the absurdities which are glibly taught under the name of economic science.

220. Consider only category (A) of § 208 and assume that all the other categories of conditions are satisfied. In this case we can say that the prices are determined by ophelimity since it is precisely category (A) which establishes the equality of the weighted ophelimities. Or, using the phraseology of economists who consider the problem in this fashion, we will say that the *values* are determined by the *utilities*, or again, that utility is the *cause* of value.

221. On the other hand consider only category (D) of § 208, and assume that all the other categories of conditions are satisfied. In this case we can say that prices are determined by the equality of the cost of production of each good and its selling price.[13]

If we wish to take into account the fact that the goods under consideration are those which can be produced at this cost in equilibrium, we will speak of the cost of *reproduction*, and not of the cost of production.

Ferrara has gone further; he has considered the cost to produce, not a good, but a sensation,[14] and thus he was led to take into account, in an imperfect fashion to be sure, not only conditions (D), but also conditions (A). When we consider that he arrived at that without recourse to the mathematical considerations which make the problem so simple, we must admire the truly extraordinary power of his intellect. None of the non-mathematician economists have gone farther.

222. Consider categories (A) and (B); they allow us to deduce the quantities of the goods determined by the prices (the quantities as functions of the prices, that is, what economists have called the *laws of supply and of demand*). And if, as above, we assume that the other categories of conditions are satisfied, we can say that the quantities are determined by the prices, by means of the laws of supply and of demand.

The non-mathematician economists have never had a clear idea of these laws. Often they spoke about the supply of and the demand for a good as if they depended only on the price of that good.[15] When they realized their error, they corrected it by talking about the *purchasing power* of money, but without ever knowing exactly what that entity was.

---

[13] *Cours*, I, § 80.

[14] *Cours*, I, § 80.

[15] Cairnes, *Some Leading Principles of Political Economy*, Ch. II. "Supply and Demand, when spoken of with reference to particular commodities, must . . . be understood to mean Supply and Demand at a given price. . . ."

223. Moreover, since they did not see clearly that demand and supply followed precisely from conditions (A) and (B), they spoke of demand and supply as quantities having an existence independent of those conditions; and then they propounded problems such as that of determining whether the desire which an individual has for an object which he does not have the means to buy can be considered as making up part of the demand, and whether or not a quantity of goods which exists on a market, but which the owner does not want to sell, makes up part of the supply.

Thornton[16] assumes that there are a certain number of gloves for sale and that they are sold at successively decreasing prices until they all are sold. He accepts as true that the quantity *supplied* is the total number of gloves, and he notes that the last portion alone is sold at the price which makes the supply and the demand equal, "the greatest part being sold at prices at which the supply and the demand were unequal." He confuses here the equilibrium point, at which the supply and the demand are equal, and the path followed to reach that point, a path on which supply and demand are not equal (§ 182).

224. The literary economists have conceived the cost of production to be a *normal* price which the prices determined by demand and supply revolve around, and thus they came to take into account, although in a very imperfect fashion, the three categories of conditions, (A), (B), and (D). But they considered them independently of each other, and it appeared that the cost of production of one good was independent of the prices of that good and of others. It is easy to see how gross was the error. For example, the cost of production of coal depends on the price of machinery, and the cost of production of the machinery depends on the price of coal; consequently, the cost of production of the coal depends on the price of that same coal. And it depends on it still more directly if we consider the coal consumption of the machinery employed in the mine.

225. Price or *value in exchange* is determined at the same time as economic equilibrium, and the latter arises from the opposition between tastes and obstacles. The person who looks at only one side and considers only tastes believes that they alone determine price and finds the *cause* of value in *utility* (ophelimity). The person who looks at the other side and considers only obstacles believes that they alone are what determines price, and he finds the *cause* of value in the cost of production. And if among the obstacles he considers only

---

[16] *On Labour.*

labor, he finds the *cause* of value exclusively in labor. If in the system of conditions (equations) which we have seen determine equilibrium, we assume that all the conditions are satisfied with the exception of those which refer to labor, we can say that value (price) depends only on labor, and that theory will not be false, but simply incomplete. It will be true provided that the hypotheses made are fulfilled.

226. The conditions which, often unconsciously, were neglected, which were disregarded, reappeared of their own accord; because, having arrived at the solution of the problem it was sensed, often by intuition, that it was necessary to take them into account. This is why Marx, in his theory of value, was obliged to try to eliminate by some means or other the conditions which he had had to omit in order to make value depend on labor alone.[17] Thus among many economists the term *value in exchange* does not signify only a proportion, the rate of exchange of two goods, but there is added, in a somewhat indistinct way, certain notions of purchasing power, of equivalence of goods, and of obstacles to overcome; and the result of this is a certain poorly defined entity, and one which, precisely for that reason, can include a certain notion of the conditions which have been omitted, but which, however, they sense must be taken into account.

All that is concealed by the vagueness and the lack of precision in the definitions, by a jingle of words which look like they mean something but other than that have no significance.[18]

Thus so many vague and occasionally even contradictory meanings have been given to the term *value* that it is better not to use it in the study of political economy.[19] This is what Jevons was doing by using the expression *rate of exchange*; and it is still better to use the notion of the price of a good B in terms of a good A as does M. Walras (§ 153).

---

[17] In a recently published book, it is said that "price is the concrete manifestation of value." We have had incarnations of Buddha, here we have incarnations of *value!*

What indeed can this mysterious entity be? It is, it appears, "the capacity which a good has to be exchanged with other goods." This is to define one unknown thing by another still less known; for what indeed can this "capacity" be? And, what is still more important, how is it measured? Of this "capacity" or its homonym "value" we know only the "concrete manifestation" which is the price; truly then it is useless to entangle ourselves with these metaphysical entities, and we can stick to the prices.

[18] *Systèmes*, I, pp. 338 *et seq.*; II, pp. 121 *et seq.*

[19] *Systèmes*, II, Ch. XIII.

A certain exchange has taken place: 1 of A has been exchanged for 2 of B; in this exchange the price of A in terms of B is 2. That is a fact; and it is from these facts that economic science proposes to construct theory.

Many writers insert into the notion of what they call *value* something more than there is in this notion of price; that is, to the facts of the past, they add a forecast of the future. They say that the value is 2 if 2 of B can be *currently* exchanged for 1 of A.

They do not express themselves too clearly because all these theories need to remain vague in order to hide the errors in them; but such indeed is the character of their thought.

First of all we must observe that in this sense goods which are sold at wholesale would almost never have "value" for their price varies from one purchase to another; very often the opening market price is different from the closing price.

They try to cover up this difficulty by distinguishing between *value* and its magnitude! As if a quantity could exist independently of its size! Moreover, even if that were accepted, consideration of this metaphysical entity would be completely useless. In reality, they thus bury in the vagueness of a definition the conditions which they are incapable of taking into account in determining economic equilibrium.

Furthermore, when building up a theory, the facts which that theory must explain must never be confused with the forecasts which may be drawn from it. The wholesale copper prices on the London exchange are facts; a theory about them must be constructed before there is the least hope of knowing what they will be in the future; and, for the time-being, that forecast is absolutely impossible. Outside of these prices there is nothing real which is the "value" of copper. If persons who do not have scientific ideas about political economy think otherwise, it is because they see vaguely that if certain prices for copper have been realized in London, and if it is probable that other prices, which would not be known exactly, will be realized in the future, it is because copper indirectly serves to satisfy men's tastes, and there are obstacles to obtaining it. These conceptions, which science states precisely, have for these persons only a vague and indeterminate meaning, and they attach them to the term *value* in order to give them a name.

There exists no entity resembling what the literary economists call *value*, and which is objectively dependent on a thing, as would be the density or any other such physical property of that thing. Neither does that entity exist in the form of "the estimation" which one or several individuals make of that thing. Nor is the consideration of certain obstacles to production enough to give it existence.

If this vague and indeterminate thing which the literary economists call *value* has any relation to prices, we can assert that it depends on *all* the circumstances, none excepted, which have an influence on the determination of economic equilibrium.

What is the *value* of diamonds? You can resolve this question neither by considering the desires which they awaken in men and women, nor by considering the obstacles which their production encounters, nor the evaluations into which these desires and these obstacles are translated, nor the "limitations of quantity," nor the cost of production, nor the cost of reproduction, etc.. All these circumstances have an influence on the price of diamonds, but singly or even as a group they are not enough to determine it.

For example, towards the end of the year 1907 no notable change had taken place in the circumstances we have just enumerated; the price of diamonds fell and it would have fallen still more if it had not been supported by a syndicate. The crisis was so great that the principal producers of diamonds, the Compagnie De Beer and the Premier Company, suspended payment of dividends. What circumstances arose to change the *value* of diamonds so abruptly? Simply the financial crisis in the United States of America and in Germany. These countries, large buyers of diamonds, suspended their purchases almost entirely.

In order to explain and foresee similar phenomena the metaphysical theories of the literary economists are worthless, whereas the theories of scientific economics fit these facts perfectly.

227. The thing indicated by the words value in exchange, rate of exchange, price, does not have *one* cause; and it can be declared henceforth that any economist who looks for *the cause* of value shows thereby that he has understood nothing about the synthetic phenomenon of economic equilibrium.

Heretofore it was generally believed that there had to be *one* cause of value; there was debate simply as to what it was.

It is worth noting that the power of the opinion according to which there had to be one cause of value was so great that even M. Walras has not been able to escape it entirely, he who, by giving us the conditions of equilibrium in a particular case, has contributed toward pointing out the error of that opinion. He expresses two contradictory notions. On the one hand, he tells us that "all the unknowns of the economic problem depend on all the equations of economic equilibrium," and that is a good theory; on the other hand, he asserts that it "is certain that *rareté* (ophelimity) is the cause of value in exchange," and that is reminiscent of outmoded theories which do not correspond to reality.[20]

These errors are excusable, and even natural, at the time when we are passing from inexact theories to new and better theories; but they should be inexcusable now that these theories have been developed and have progressed.

228. To sum up, the theories which connect only value (price) and *final degree of utility* (ophelimity) do not have much usefulness in political economy. The more useful theories are those which consider economic equilibrium in general and which investigate how it originates in the opposition of tastes and obstacles.

It is the mutual dependence of economic phenomena which makes the use of mathematics indispensable for studying these phenomena; ordinary logic can serve well enough for studying the relations of cause and effect, but soon becomes impotent when it is a matter of relations of mutual dependence. The latter, in rational mechanics and in pure economics, necessitate the use of mathematics.

The principal utility which is derived from the theories of pure economics is that it gives us a synthetic notion of economic equilibrium, and for the moment we have no other way to reach that goal. But the phenomenon which pure economics studies differs, sometimes a little, sometimes a great deal, from the concrete phenomenon. It is for applied economics to study these divergences. It would not be very reasonable to claim to organize economic phenomena by the theories of pure economics alone.

---

[20] *Eléments d'économie politique pure*, Lausanne, 1900. "Theoretically, all the unknowns of the economic problem depend on all the equations of economic equilibrium," p. 289. "It is certain that *rareté* is the cause of value in exchange," p. 102.

It is probable that M. Walras allowed himself to be deceived by the connotations of the word *rareté*. In his formulas, as he himself concedes, it is the *Grenznutzen* of the Germans, the *final degree of utility* of the English, or even our elementary ophelimity; but here and there in the text there is added in a not very precise way this idea that a good is scarce [*rare*] relative to the wants to be satisfied because of the obstacles to overcome in order to obtain it. One also vaguely catches a glimpse of a notion of the obstacles, and that proposition that "*rareté* is the cause of value in exchange" becomes thereby less incorrect. The error in these conclusions does not belong to this eminent scholar; it belongs entirely to the mode of reasoning in use in economic science, a mode of reasoning which the labors of M. Walras have precisely contributed toward rectifying.

CHAPTER IV

TASTES

1. In the preceding chapter we endeavored to arrive at a very general, and consequently a somewhat superficial, notion of the economic phenomenon; we set aside, instead of solving, a great number of the difficulties which we encountered. We now must study more closely the phenomena and the details which we omitted and complete the theories which we have only sketched.

2. **Tastes and ophelimity.** We tried to reduce the phenomenon of tastes to the pleasure which man experiences when he consumes certain things, or when he uses them in any way whatsoever.

A difficulty appears here immediately. Should we consider use, consumption, simply as optional, or as obligatory? In other words, should the quantities of goods which appear in the formulas of pure economics be understood as being consumed only as long as they please the individual, or as necessarily consumed, even if instead of pleasure they cause him pain? In the first case the ophelimities are always positive; they cannot fall below zero since, when the individual is satisfied, he stops. In the second case, the ophelimities can be negative and represent pain instead of pleasure.

Both cases are theoretically possible; to resolve the question we have just posed, we must turn to reality to see which one political economy ought to deal with.

3. It is not difficult to see that it ought to build theory on the first category. If a man has more water than he needs to quench his thirst he certainly is not obliged to drink it all; he drinks what he wants and throws away the rest. If a woman has ten dresses, she need not wear them all at once; also it is not customary to wear all the gowns one possesses. In short, everyone uses the goods he possesses only to the extent that it suits him.

181

4. But granted that, the meaning of the quantities regarding goods which enter into the formulas of pure economics changes somewhat. They are no longer quantities consumed, but quantities which are at the individual's disposal. For this reason the concrete phenomenon diverges somewhat from the theoretical phenomenon. For the sensation of present consumption we substitute, as the cause of the actions of the individual, the present sensation of the future consumption of the goods which are at his disposal.

5. Moreover, in the case where the individual possesses a quantity of goods such that he has reached satiety, we neglect the trouble which he may have in getting rid of the superfluous amount. True, this is ordinarily insignificant; and as the proverb says, abundance of goods never hurts; but there are certain exceptional cases in which it may be rather important and where we ought to take it into account.

6. As for the substitution of the sensation of possible consumption for the sensation of actual consumption, if we consider repeated actions, and this is what political economy does, both sensations, when all is said and done, are found in such a constant relationship that the first can replace the second without serious error. In exceptional cases, for example, for very improvident and thoughtless individuals, it may be useful to take account of the difference which exists between the two sensations, but for the time being we will not bother with it.

7. Consideration of the quantities which are at the individual's disposal has another advantage also; it enables us to disregard the order of consumption, and to assume that the order is the one which suits the individual the best. Obviously, one does not experience the same enjoyment if he eats the soup at the beginning of a meal and the dessert at the end, or begins with the dessert and ends with the soup. Hence we ought to take account of the order, but that would increase the difficulties of the theory considerably, and it is not amiss to avoid that problem.

8. That is not all. The consumption of goods can be independent; the ophelimity procured from the consumption of a good may be the same whatever be the other goods consumed; it can be independent of them. But generally this is not so, and often it happens that consumption is dependent; that is to say, the ophelimity obtained from the consumption of one good depends on the consumption of other goods.

Two species of dependence must be distinguished: 1° one which arises from the fact that the pleasure from one consumption is connected with the pleasure from other consumption; 2° one which manifests itself in the fact that one thing may be substituted for another to produce sensations, if not identical, at least approximately equal.

9. First let us examine the first type of dependence. In reality, the pleasure which one consumption yields us depends on our other consumption; and moreover, in order for certain things to yield us pleasure they must be joined with others: for example, soup without salt is not very agreeable, and clothes without buttons are most inconvenient.

At bottom, the cases we have just considered differ only quantitatively; the first has, though less pronounced, the same character as the second, and we pass from the one to the other by imperceptible degrees. It may be useful, however, to distinguish the extreme cases, which are as follows: (a) Dependence can result from the fact that we appreciate the use and consumption of a thing more or less according to the circumstances in which we find ourselves. (β) This dependence can arise from the fact that certain things must be used jointly in order to yield us pleasure; these are called COMPLEMENTARY GOODS.

10. (α) The first type of dependence is very general, and we can not neglect it when considering substantial variations in the quantities of things; it is only when these variations are trifling that we can assume as an approximation that some consumption is independent. It is certain that someone who is suffering severely from the cold holds a delicate drink in low esteem; one who is starving does not experience great pleasure in looking at a painting or in listening to a good speech; and if he were given something to eat it would matter little to him whether he were served with crude pottery or fine porcelain. Besides, in this type of dependence, and for small variations in quantity, the principal part of the variations in ophelimity comes from the variation in the quantity of the goods. It is preferable to eat chicken from a nice plate, but, to be brief, if the plate is simply more or less beautiful, the pleasure is not very different. Conversely, the pleasure which one feels in using a beautiful plate depends principally on the plate and does not vary much if the chicken is larger or smaller or of a better or poorer quality.

11. Some of the writers who have built up pure economics have been led, in order to simplify the problems they wanted to study, to assume that the ophelimity of a good depended only on the quantity of the good at the individual's disposal. We cannot blame them, because, briefly, questions must be resolved one after the other, and

it is always better not to hurry. But it is time now to take a step forward and also consider the case in which the ophelimity of a good depends on the consumption of all other goods.

With regard to the type of dependence we are studying at the moment, we will be able, but always approximately and provided that it is a matter of small variations, to consider the ophelimity of a good as depending exclusively on the quantities of that good. But we must take the other types of dependence into account.

12. (β) The notion of complementary goods can be more or less extended. To have a light, one must have a lamp and also some oil. But it is not necessary to have a glass to drink wine; one can drink from the bottle.

By extending the notion of complementary goods we could take this dependence into account by considering as distinct goods all the combinations of goods which the individual uses or consumes directly. For example, we would not take account of the coffee, the sugar, the cup, the spoon separately, but would consider only one good composed of these four goods necessary to have a cup of coffee. But in this way we dispose of one difficulty only to fall into greater ones. First, in constructing this imaginary good, why stop at the spoon? We also would have to take into account the table, the chair, the table cloth, the building where all these things are located, and so on *ad infinitum*. We thereby multiply the number of goods without bound inasmuch as every possible combination of real goods gives us one of these imaginary goods.

Hence we must choose the lesser of two evils, and take these composite goods into consideration only in the cases where they are so closely dependent on each other that it would be very difficult to consider them separately. In the other cases it is better to consider them separately, and we revert to the preceding case. But when we proceed in this way, it must never be forgotten that the ophelimity of one of these goods depends not only on the quantity of that good, but also on the quantities of the other goods it is accompanied by in order for it to be used or consumed, and that we certainly commit an error in considering it as depending only on the quantity of the given good. This error may be negligible when there are only small variations in the quantities of the goods because in that case we can assume approximately that the consumption of the good under consideration takes place under certain average conditions with respect to the accessory goods.

Returning to the preceding example, if we had to consider the extreme case in which there is no cup for the coffee, we could not,

without serious error, assume the ophelimity of the coffee to be
independent of the cup; but if on the other hand we are considering
a situation which deviates only slightly from the existing situation,
that is, a situation in which the variations consist simply in having
a cup of a little better or a little poorer quality, we can, without
serious error, consider the ophelimity of the coffee to be independent
of the cup. Strictly speaking, the ophelimity of the coffee for an
individual varies with the sugar, the cup, the spoon, etc., which he
has at his disposal; but if we assume a certain average situation for
all these things, we can, as a rough approximation, assume that the
ophelimity of the coffee depends solely on the quantity of coffee
which a given individual has at his disposal. Similarly the ophelimity
of the sugar will depend solely on the quantity of sugar, etc. That
would no longer be true if we were considering large variations in
quantities, or in prices. Whether sugar costs 40 or 50 centimes a
kilogram changes the ophelimity of the coffee very little; but if we
could no longer have any sugar, that would change the ophelimity
of the coffee very much; even a rise in the price of sugar from 50
centimes to 2 francs a kilogram would bring about a change in the
ophelimity of the coffee which should not be neglected.

13. We conclude then that if we are dealing with very wide
variations, it is necessary, at least for the majority of goods, to consider the ophelimity of a good as dependent, not only on the quantity
of that good used or held, but also on the quantity of the many other
goods used or consumed at the same time. If we do not do so and
if we are content to consider the ophelimity of a good as dependent
solely on the quantity of that good, it becomes necessary to reason
only about very small variations, and consequently to study the phenomenon only in the neighborhood of a given position of equilibrium.

14. Let us go on now to a second type of dependence. A man
can satisfy his hunger with bread or with potatoes, he can drink
wine or beer, he can dress in wool or cotton, he can burn oil or
candles. We perceive that a certain equivalence can be established
between the goods which correspond to a certain need. But we
must make a distinction depending on whether this equivalence is
relative to the man's tastes, or to his needs.

15. If the relation of equivalence refers strictly to the tastes of
the individual, it is nothing else but the relation which gives the
indifference curve for equivalent goods; hence it is unnecessary to
make a separate study of it. To say that a man considers two kilograms of potatoes equivalent to one kilogram of kidney beans as far
as his tastes are concerned is to say that the indifference curve

between kidney beans and potatoes passes through the point 1 kilo-gram of kidney beans and 0 of potatoes, and through the point 2 kilograms of potatoes and 0 kilograms of kidney beans.

16. Sometimes the equivalence does not refer to tastes, but to needs. In this case there would no longer be an identity between the equivalence relationship and the indifference curve. For example, a man can satisfy his hunger by eating 2 kilograms of corn meal or 1 kilogram of bread; a woman can adorn herself with a necklace of imitation pearls or with a necklace of real pearls. So far as tastes are concerned, no equivalence exists between these things; the man prefers the bread, the woman the real pearls, and it is only under the pressure of necessity that they replace them by the corn meal and the imitation pearls.

17. When the man consumes some bread and corn meal at the same time, when the woman adorns herself with imitation pearls and real pearls, we can no longer assume that the ophelimity of the corn meal is independent of that of the bread, nor that the ophelimity of the imitation pearls is independent of that of the real pearls. In such a case we must consider the ophelimity of a certain combination of imitation pearls and real pearls, of bread and corn meal, or in some other fashion take account of the dependence in the consumption.

18. The phenomenon of this dependence is very widespread. A large number of goods are available with important quality dif-ferences, and these qualities are substituted, one for the other, when the resources of the individual increase. Under the name chemise we include many very different objects, from the rough dress of the peasant woman to the fine batiste of an elegant lady. There are very many grades of wine, of cheese, of meat, etc. One who has nothing else eats a lot of corn meal; if he has some bread, he will eat less corn; if he has some meat, he will also decrease his consumption of bread. We cannot say what pleasure someone gets from a certain quantity of corn meal if we do not know what other foods he posses-ses. What pleasure does a cloak of rough wool provide to a given individual? In order to answer, we must know what clothing he has at his disposal.

19. These phenomena reveal a certain hierarchy of goods. If, for example, the goods A, B, C . . . are capable of satisfying a certain need, an individual will make use of good A because he cannot obtain the others, which are too expensive. If his affluence increases, he will use A and B at the same time; if it increases still further, he will use only B; then B and C, then only C; then C and D, etc. It is

clear that in the foregoing we have only a small part of the phenomenon, and that one who uses D may still occasionally, perhaps,
consume small quantities of A, B, C, etc.

We will say that any one of the goods in a series of similar goods
is *superior* to those preceding and *inferior* to those following it. We
have, for example, the series: corn meal, bread, second-grade meat,
first-grade meat. One who is very poor eats a lot of corn meal, a little
bread, and very rarely any meat. His resources increasing, he will eat
more bread and less corn meal; if his situation improves again, he
will eat bread and second-grade meat, and corn meal only occasionally; his affluence increasing, he will eat first-grade meat and other
good quality foods, very little corn, little bread, and bread of a better
grade than that which he had eaten before.

We see how widespread is the type of dependence of which we
are speaking, and that we must necessarily take it into account. As
before, two avenues are open to us.

20. One may only bother with this type of dependence in cases
where it is very marked and the individual's preference is not trivial,
considering other such consumption as independent.

21. But at this level of approximation, we could proceed in a
different way and extend rather than restrict the consideration of
this type of dependence. For example, we could consider a fairly
large number of tastes and needs of a man, and with regard to them
assume equivalent certain quantities of goods which are substitutable
for each other. With regard to nourishment, for example, establish
certain equivalences between quantities of bread, potatoes, kidney
beans, meat, etc. In this case, we would only need to take account of
the total ophelimity of these equivalent quantities.

22. Since these equivalences based on substitution are only
approximations, they ought not, even for the second type of dependence, divert us from a certain average situation for which these
equivalences have been established approximately.

23. The difficulties which we encounter here are not peculiar to
this question. We have already seen (§ 18) that they generally are
found in connection with very complex phenomena. Among civilized
peoples there is an enormous number of diverse goods capable of
satisfying innumerable tastes. To get a general idea of the phenomenon we must necessarily omit numerous details, and we can
do this in various ways.

24. We have considered the principal types of dependence; there
are others, and the phenomenon is quite varied and very complex.
To sum up, the ophelimity of any consumption depends on all the cir-

cumstances in which the consumption takes place. But if we wish to consider the phenomenon in all its aspects, theory will no longer be possible for reasons set forth many times already. Hence it is absolutely necessary to separate the main parts of it and to disentangle, from the complete and complex phenomenon, the ideal and simple elements which can provide the subject matter of theories.

We can attain this end in many ways; we have indicated two; but there are other possibilities. Each of these procedures has its advantages, and, depending on the circumstances, one may be preferred to the others.

25. As in all the concrete sciences in which we substitute one phenomenon as an approximation to another, a theory should not be stretched beyond the limits for which it was constructed; and whatever be the route followed, the conclusions cannot be extended, at least not without further investigations, beyond the limited region in the neighborhood of the equilibrium point under consideration.

26. Other facts of great importance also oblige us to proceed in that way. When conditions change, men's tastes change too. We can, with the hope of getting a reasonable reply, ask a woman who already possesses some diamonds, "if diamonds were to cost a little more, how many less would you buy?" But if we were to ask a peasant woman who has never had any diamonds, "if you were a millionaire, how many diamonds would you buy at such and such a given price?", we would get a reply made at random and without any value. Martial tells us in one of his epigrams: "You often ask me, Priscus, what I would be like if I should become rich and powerful. Do you think anyone can know his future feelings? Tell me, if you should become a lion, what would you be like?"[1]

If we want to be exact, we must say that it is not even necessary that the conditions surrounding the phenomenon change radically in order for tastes to change; they can also change with slight changes in external conditions. Let us add that an individual is not exactly the same from day to day.

27. That observation puts us on the track of a proposition which is of very great importance. Let us begin by citing an example. In Italy, the people drink coffee, but not tea. If coffee were to increase considerably in price, while the price of tea decreased considerably, the immediate effect would be a decrease in the consumption of coffee, whereas the consumption of tea would not increase or would increase only imperceptibly. But little by little, after a time which

---

[1] XII, 93. [The correct reference is XII, 92.]

would certainly be quite long because men's tastes are very tenacious, the Italian people would be able to replace coffee by tea; the final effect of the great decrease in the price of tea would be to increase its consumption greatly.

In general, we should always distinguish between changes which take place in short periods and those which come about in long periods. In economic statistics we must, save in exceptional cases, study the first exclusively. Assume that today the indifference curves for a good B and another good A (which could be money) are those indicated by the solid lines *s* of Figure 28, and that after a hundred years they become the dotted lines *t*. Assume further that the individual has the quantity *oa* of money. Today, this individual will spend about the same amount, *ah*, of A whatever be the price of B (within certain limits); after a hundred years he will spend the amount *ak*, which will remain nearly the same as the price varies but which will be different from *ah*.

28. Much time must pass before the indifference curves *s* change into indifference curves *t;* hence we can assume, without perceptible

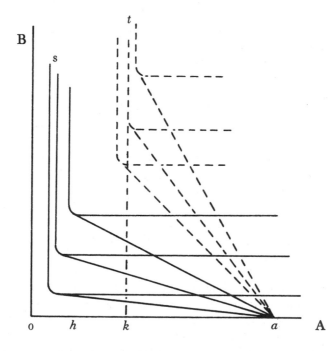

error, that in a short space of time, for example one, two, or even four or five years, they remain equal to s.

29. We have assumed that a man can compare two sensations; but, when they are not simultaneous, and in truth it does not seem possible that they can be, he can only compare one sensation with the idea he has of another sensation. For this reason too, the real phenomenon differs from the theoretical phenomenon; and it may be useful, in some cases, to keep this divergence in mind for a further approximation. Frequently, on the other hand, we can concede that the conception of a future sensation does not deceive us too much, especially since economics is concerned only with average and repeated phenomena. If the conception based on former experiences diverges too much from the future sensation, it is rectified by the experiences which follow.

30. We see then that though the theoretical phenomenon which we study differs considerably from the concrete phenomenon in certain cases, for the majority of common concrete phenomena it represents it as a more or less rough approximation provided the following conditions are always realized: 1° We only study what occurs in a small region surrounding the concrete phenomenon which provides the factual data necessary to construct the theory. In real life we are observing a position near the equilibrium position of the economic system; we can know how the system behaves in the neighborhood of that position, but we lack the data to know how things would work out if the factual conditions of the system were considerably altered. 2° We only consider average phenomena, those which repeat, so as to eliminate the greatest number of accidental variations.

If anyone thinks that this is too little, he has only to show us how to do better. The road is open and the progress of science is continuous. But meanwhile this little is better than nothing, the more so since experience teaches us that in all the sciences the little is always necessary in order to arrive at the more.

31. Certain persons believed that, simply because it employs mathematics, the deductions of political economy should have acquired the rigor and certitude of the deductions of celestial mechanics. This is a serious error. In celestial mechanics, all the results which are drawn from an hypothesis have been verified by the facts and from that it was concluded that it is very probable that such hypothesis suffices to give us a precise idea of the concrete phenomenon. In political economy we cannot hope for a similar result because we know, without any doubt, that our hypotheses

deviate in part from reality; and consequently the results we can deduce from them will be able to correspond to the facts only within certain limits. Moreover, it is that way in most of the concrete arts and sciences, for example in the engineer's art. Theory of such sort is more often a mode of research than of proof, and we should never neglect to check whether the deductions correspond to reality.

32. **Ophelimity and its indices.** In speaking of ophelimity we must not forget to distinguish between TOTAL OPHELIMITY (or its index) and elementary ophelimity (or its index). The first consists of the pleasure (or the index of the pleasure) which is provided by the total quantity of good A possessed; the second is the quotient of the pleasure (or the index of the pleasure) from an additional very small quantity of A, divided by the quantity (III, 33).

An individual who finds himself at a point on the hill of pleasure (III, 58) enjoys total ophelimity represented by the height of that point above the horizontal plane. If the hill of pleasure is cut by a vertical plane parallel to the axis oA on which is measured the quantities of good A, we have a certain curve; the slope, with respect to a horizontal straight line, of the tangent to this curve at the point where the individual finds himself is equal to the elementary ophelimity (§§ 60, 69).

A man can know whether the pleasure which a certain combination I of goods provides him is equal to the pleasure he gets from another combination II, or whether it is greater or smaller. We have taken account of this fact (III, 55) in order to determine the indices of ophelimity, that is, the indices which denote the pleasure provided by any other combination, or whether it is neither greater nor smaller.

Moreover, a man can tell fairly well whether in passing from combination I to combination II, he experiences a greater pleasure than in passing from combination II to another combination III. If this judgment could be of a sufficient precision, we would be able, at the limit, to know whether in passing from I to II this man experiences a pleasure equal to that which he experiences in passing from II to III. And consequently, in passing from I to III he would experience a pleasure double that which he gets in passing from I to II. That would be enough to permit us to consider the pleasure or ophelimity as a quantity.

But it is not possible for us to attain that precision. A man can know that the third glass of wine gives him less pleasure than the second; but he can in no way tell what quantity of wine he must drink after the second glass in order to get pleasure equal to that which the second glass of wine provided him. From that comes the difficulty of considering ophelimity as a quantity, unless it is no more than a mere hypothesis.

Among the infinite number of systems of indices which we can have, we must retain only those which have the following property, namely, that if in passing from I to II the man experiences more pleasure than in passing from II to III, the difference between the indices of I and of II is greater than the difference between the indices of II and of III. In this way the indices always represent the ophelimity correctly.

The ophelimity, or its index, for one individual, and the ophelimity, or its index, for another individual, are heterogeneous quantities. We can neither add them together nor compare them. *No bridge*, as the English say. A sum of ophelimity enjoyed by different individuals does not exist; it is an expression which has no meaning.

33. **Characteristics of ophelimity.** In all that follows, we will assume that the ophelimity for an individual is a quantity; it would be easy, however, to modify the reasoning simply by making use of the concept of indices of ophelimity.

By virtue of the hypothesis made about the quantities of goods—and by these quantities we understand only those which are at the disposal of the individual (§ 3)—ophelimity is always positive; and that is its first characteristic.

The second characteristic, which was recognized by the first economists who studied the subject, consists of this: that if the ophelimity of a good is considered as depending only on the quantity of that good, the elementary ophelimity (III, 33) decreases when the quantity consumed increases. Some have wanted to make this property depend on Fechner's Law,[2] but that necessarily assumes consumption, and we have already seen (§ 3) that that would entail many difficulties. Furthermore, in the great variety of economic uses, there are many which are too far removed from the phenomena to which Fechner's Law applies.

It is better to resort directly to experience, and the latter shows us that for a great many uses or consumptions the elementary ophelimity does indeed diminish with an increase in the quantities consumed.

34. Finally, it is a very general fact that the more we have of

---

[2] Fechner, *Revision der Hauptpunken der Psychophysik*, Leipzig, 1888; Wundt, *Gründzuge der Physiologischen Psychologie.*

a thing, the less precious to us is each unit of that thing. There are exceptions. For example, if one is making a collection, he is the more attached to it according as the collection is the more complete; it is a well known fact that certain peasant proprietors become more desirous of extending their property the more it is increased. Finally, everyone knows that the more a miser's patrimony increases, the more he desires to increase it. In general, savings have a certain ophelimity of their own, independent of the gain which one derives from the interest, and this ophelimity increases with the amount of the savings up to a certain limit, then, except for the miser, it diminishes.

35. Then there are goods for which the ophelimities are not independent (§ 9). For dependence (α) we can consider, at least in general, that elementary ophelimity diminishes as the quantity increases; often it diminishes even more rapidly than if the ophelimity were independent. For dependence (β), the elementary ophelimity may increase, and then diminish as the quantity increases. For example, if one has a shirt which lacks one button, the ophelimity of this button is greater than that of the others; and that of yet another button is very small. But this phenomenon is analogous, in part, to those of discontinuous variations which we have already studied (III, 65). We must remember that we are not studying individual phenomena, but collective and average phenomena. Shirts are not sold with one button missing, the abstract case we just spoke of is not encountered in practice. We must consider the consumption of thousands of goods and thousands of buttons, and in that case we can without gross error take it to be true that elementary ophelimity diminishes with increase in the quantities.

36. As for dependence of the second type (§ 8), we can note, in general, that the elementary ophelimity of a good diminishes to zero when the quantity of the good increases. This elementary ophelimity remains at zero until the good to which it refers is eliminated from consumption, or remains only in an insignificant quantity, and is replaced by another, superior, good.

37. To sum up, except for a part of the phenomenon in the case of complementary goods, for the majority of goods elementary ophelimity diminishes when quantity consumed increases. The first glass of water gives more pleasure than the second to one who is thirsty, the first portion of food gives more pleasure than the second to one who is hungry, and so on.

38. We can go further along this line and find a third characteristic of the ophelimity of a very large number of goods. Not

only does the second glass of wine give less satisfaction than the first, and the third less than the second, but the difference between the pleasure provided by the third and that provided by the second is less that the difference between the pleasure provided by the first and that provided by the second. In other words, as the quantity consumed increases, not only does the pleasure provided by additional small equal quantities added to consumption diminish, but the more the pleasures provided by these small quantities tend to become equal. For a person who has 100 handkerchiefs, not only is the pleasure which the 101st handkerchief provides him very small, but it is also practically equal to the pleasure which the 102nd handkerchief provides him.

39. We must now see what happens when what varies is no longer the quantity of the good whose elementary ophelimity is being considered, but the quantity of other goods with which it has dependence relationships.

In the case of dependence (α) (§ 9) the pleasure provided us by a small quantity of good A, added to the quantity consumed, is ordinarily greater the less we suffer from the absence of other goods; consequently, the elementary ophelimity of A increases when the quantities of B, C . . . increase. That happens also in the case of dependence (β), at least within certain limits. The pleasure given by one lamp, added to some others, is greater if one has plenty of oil of a type which can also be used in the new lamp; and, conversely, of what use is it to have plenty of oil if one doesn't have lamps in which to burn it? We conclude, then, that in general, for the first type of dependence, the elementary ophelimity of A increases when the quantities of certain other goods B, C, . . . increase.

40. It is completely different for the second type of dependence. If A can replace a good B, the elementary ophelimity of A will be smaller insofar as one has a larger amount of its substitute B.

41. In order to understand all this better, let us set up a table, with numbers chosen arbitrarily, however, and which has no purpose other than to give a tangible form to the preceding ideas.

Notice that the difference between the pleasures provided by 1 of A is positive for dependence of the first type; negative for dependence of the second type. This difference is always equal to that which would be obtained by comparing the pleasure provided by 1 of B. This is so because we have implicitly assumed that the pleasure from the combination AB is independent of the order of consumption.

Quantity of A	B	Pleasure provided by AB	Quantity of A	B	Pleasure provided by AB
Dependence of the first type (α) (§9)					
10	10	5.0	10	11	5.2
11	10	5.4	11	11	6.1
Pleasure provided by 1 of A . .		0.4			0.9
Difference between these pleasures					ǀ 0:5
Dependence of the first type (β) (§9)					
10	10	5.0	10	11	5.15
11	10	5.1	11	11	7.00
Pleasure provided by 1 of A . .		0.1			1.85
Difference between these pleasures					+1.75
Dependence of the second type (§14)					
10	10	5.0	10	11	6.0
11	10	5.9	11	11	6.1
Pleasure provided by 1 of A . .		0.9			0.1
Difference between these pleasures					−0.8

42. Let us make up a good A with proportional parts of two other goods B and C, for example with 1 of bread and 2 of wine. If B and C are independent, or if they are connected by the first type of dependence, we can repeat the reasoning above and see that in general the ophelimity of A diminishes when the quantity of A increases. The exceptions can be neglected for reasons indicated in § 35.

43. **The characteristics of indifference lines.** Economists began by appealing to experience for the characteristics of ophelimity; they then deduced indifference lines from those characteristics.

The reverse route may be followed. In the case where the elementary ophelimity of a good depends only on the quantity of that good, the two procedures are equivalent. But it is well to note that in the general case, namely, in the case where consumption is dependent, the study of indifference lines gives us results which we would achieve less easily, for the moment at least, by recourse to experience alone in determining the characteristics of ophelimity.

44. A first characteristic of indifference lines comes from the fact that the quantity of one good must be increased in order to compensate for the decrease in the quantity of another. From this it follows that the angle α [Figure 29] is always acute. This property corresponds precisely to a property of elementary ophelimity, that of always being positive.

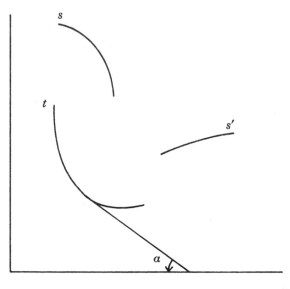

FIGURE 29

45. Furthermore, if the few cases pointed out in § 34 are excluded, it can be established that the more one possesses of a given good the less of another is necessary in order to compensate for giving up a small quantity, always the same, of the first. From this it follows that indifference lines are always convex to the axes, that they have shapes similar to *t* and never like *s* and *s′* (Figure 29). To have these latter shapes, it would be necessary that they pertain to a good each unit of which becomes more precious as the quantity of that good at the individual's disposal increases. It is obvious that this case is quite exceptional.

46. When several goods, A, B, C, . . . are considered we can no longer properly speak of indifference lines; but there are then some

properties analogous to those which we have just indicated, and which are very useful for theory.

Any one of these goods whatsoever, A for example, can be chosen as money. As for the others, certain ones will be sold, certain ones bought; the quantities of money necessary for these purchases or received from these sales can be considered separately. Subtracting the total paid out from the total provided by the sales, we will have the quantity of A which is realized altogether from these operations, or conversely.

If we successively compare A to each of the goods B, C, . . ., we will have indifference lines possessing properties identical to those which we have already mentioned.

47. Moreover: 1° if on the whole we have a positive expenditure, that signifies that the purchases have more than offset the sales; that is to say, the decrease in A has been offset by an increase in one or more of the goods B, C, . . .; 2° whatever may be the dependence involved, let us assume that to compensate for the expenditure of one franc requires a certain fraction of a certain combination of B, C, D, . . .; as the income of the individual decreases this fraction will increase, and conversely.

If an individual makes a certain expenditure for a lamp, a wick, and oil (dependence of the first type, β subgroup), and for lodging, clothing, food (dependence, with the lamp, of the first type, α subgroup); and if there is, for him, an exact balance between the expenditure and the enjoyment he obtains, it is obvious that this balance would no longer exist if all these expenditures were exactly doubled, because, on the one hand, the money becomes more precious to him since he would have less of it, and the lamps, etc., would become less precious since he would have more of them.

Ordinarily, in considering a large number of individuals, discontinuous variations are converted into continuous variations with very little error.

48. **Relation between ophelimity or indifference lines and supply and demand.** The properties of ophelimity and of indifference lines are closely connected to certain characteristics of the laws of supply and of demand. We are going to set forth some of these relations; their proof must be relegated to the appendix.

49. Let us consider supply and demand with reference to one individual who has two or more goods at his disposal. If the consumption of these goods is independent, or if there is a dependence of the first type between them, the demand for a good always decreases with an increase in the price of that good; the supply in-

creases at first, then it may decrease even though the price increases.

For goods having a dependence of the second type, when the price rises, the demand may increase and then decrease; the supply may decrease, then increase.

This difference occurs in real life particularly for demand. It is most striking in certain circumstances. Let us assume an individual who disposes of a certain income which he divides among the purchases of various goods. If the consumption of these goods is independent or if there is a dependence of the first type between them, the demand for each of these goods always increases when income increases. On the other hand, if it is a case of a dependence of the second type, demand may increase, and then decrease, when income increases.

50. This relationship is enough to demonstrate the necessity for studying dependence of the second type. Indeed, let us see what correspondence there is between the theoretical deductions and the concrete facts. If we assume that the ophelimity of a good depends only on the quantity of that good which the individual consumes or has at his disposal, the theoretical conclusion is that, for these goods, consumption increases when income increases, or, in the limit, that it is constant above a certain income. Consequently, if a peasant sustains himself on corn alone, and if he becomes rich, he will eat more corn, or at least as much as when he was poor. Someone who gets only one pair of wooden shoes each year, because they are so expensive, may use a hundred pairs when he becomes rich, but in any case he will use at least one pair. All this is in obvious contradiction to the facts: accordingly our hypothesis ought to be rejected unless we can assert that these are insignificant facts.

51. Such is not the case; rather, as we have already seen (§ 19), we are faced with a very general phenomenon since for a very large number of goods there are a certain number of grades of each. And, as income increases, the superior grades replace the inferior grades; consequently the demand for these latter increases at first with the increase in income, but then decreases until it becomes insignificant or even nil.

52. This conclusion would no longer be true if, instead of considering actual goods, we had been considering large classes of ideal goods (§ 21); for example, if we considered food, lodging, clothing, ornamentation, amusement. In this case it is not absurd to say that with an increase in income the expenditure for each class of goods increases; and we could assume, without gross error, that the opheli-

mities are independent, or better, that there is a dependence of the first type between the ophelimities.

53. In real life an individual generally demands a great variety of goods and supplies only one or a few. A very great number supply only labor; others, the use of savings; others, certain goods which they produce. The case of simple exchange of two goods between which there is a dependence of the second type is definitely the exception; a workman sells his labor and buys some corn and bread, but we do not observe the exchange of bread for corn. Hence the deductions of the theory could not be directly verified in this case, and we would need to have another procedure for verification, which we can get by considering the allocation of income.

54. **Variation in the shapes of indifference lines and lines of exchange.** It is useful to represent the properties of ophelimity graphically. Assume that an individual has two goods A and B, only one of which, A, has ophelimity for him. In this case the indifference lines are straight lines parallel to the oB axis [Figure 30]. The hill of ophelimity is a cylindrical surface any section of which, taken parallel to oA, is indicated by bgh. If the quantity oa of A is sufficient to satisfy him, the cylindrical surface tends toward a high plateau represented by gh on the section. The property which elementary

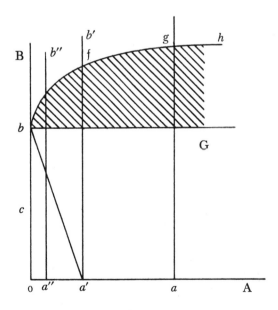

FIGURE 30

ophelimity has of decreasing when the quantity of A increases causes the slope of the hill to decrease from oB to g, that is to say, on the section, from b to f and to g (§ 32).

The individual never has a demand for B since, for him, that good has no ophelimity; but he may offer it if he has a certain quantity, for example ob. We have here the case indicated in III, 98. There is no rectilinear path which, starting from b, can be tangent to an indifference line, and at $a, a', a'', \ldots$ we have so many terminal points. The oA axis, then, makes up a portion of the contract line. It is obvious that bo similarly makes up part of it. If the contract line of another individual intersects bo at c, the quantity of B transferred is bc, and the price is zero. If this contract curve intersects oA at a, or at another similar point, the quantity transferred is always the entire quantity bo; the price varies with the position of the points a; it is equal to the slope of the straight line ba with respect to oB. In the case of Figure 30, we say that *one offers all the existing quantity of B*.

55. If A and B are two complementary goods, which can be used only by combining them in strictly defined proportions, the indifference lines are the straight lines $ac\beta$, $a'c'\beta'$, which intersect at right angles [Figure 31]. The hill of ophelimity is formed by two

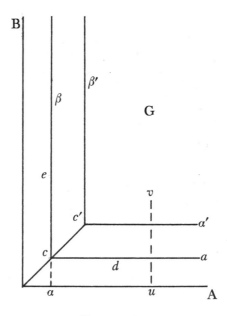

FIGURE 31

cylindrical surfaces, and at G may have a plateau which indicates satiety. The pleasure which an individual experiences at *c* is the same as that which he feels at *d* or at *e* because the goods being combined in strictly defined proportions, the quantities *cd* of A, or *ce* of B, are superfluous.

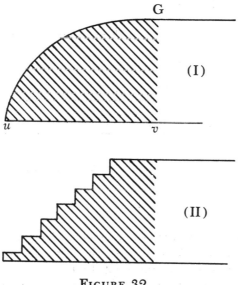

FIGURE 32

56. When the hill of ophelimity has a continuous surface, a section taken along *uv* (Figure 32) has a shape similar to (I). In reality, for a great many complementary goods, we have, on the other hand, a stairway, as in (II). For example, the handle of a knife has one blade for a complement, and it is not possible to use one handle and one-tenth of a blade; consequently we shall have many steps of a width exactly equal to unity. As we have often repeated, for large numbers this stairway can be replaced, with negligible error, by a continuous surface resembling that in section (I) and which will be bounded by a continuous curve (III, 65).

57. If the goods are only approximately complementary, the angles *c*, *c'*, . . . are more or less rounded [Figure 33]. Consider an individual who only has bread A and water B, or, if you like, food and drink. Without bread he dies of hunger, whatever be the quantity of water at his disposal; and hence along *o*B total ophelimity is equal to zero, and the elementary ophelimity of a small portion is infinite, that is to say the hill rises perpendicularly. Without water

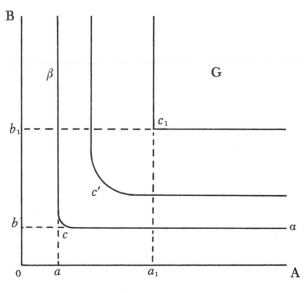

Figure 33

he dies of thirst, whatever be the amount of bread at his disposal; and consequently on oA total ophelimity or the pleasure experienced is also zero, and the elementary ophelimity is again infinite. Let oa be the smallest quantity of bread he needs in order not to die of hunger, and ob the smallest quantity of water he needs in order not to die of thirst. It is obvious that he would not give up a small quantity of bread even for a great deal of water, or conversely; consequently, the indifference lines will be ca, $c\beta$ with a very slightly rounded angle at c. For large quantities of bread and of water the angle may be more rounded, but it will not be nearly as much so or not at all at c_1 where the individual will have the quantity oa_1 of bread and ob_1 of water which would satiate him completely. Beyond is the plateau G.

58. The reader should never forget that political economy, as every other concrete science, proceeds only by approximations. For reasons of simplicity, theory studies the extreme cases; but concrete cases only approach them. Thus, when the architect considers a wall as a parallelopiped rectangle in order to figure how many cubic meters of masonry he must pay the builder for, it would be truly ridiculous to point out to him that the wall is not a perfect geometric parallelopiped, and then to talk foolishly about the rigor of mathematics. This is what often happens in political economy.

59. We get the line of exchanges by joining the points c, c', ...
of Figure 31, or the points c, c', c_1, ... , Figure 33, at which the
rectilinear paths starting from a point analogous to point a of Figure
28 are tangent to the slight curves which replace the angles, or by
joining the analogous points which would be obtained if the paths
started from a point situated on the oB axis.

60. Let us assume that the elementary ophelimities of A and of B
are independent, that is to say, that the elementary ophelimity of A
depends only on the quantity of A, and the elementary ophelimity of
B solely on the quantity of B. This property is expressed graphically
in the following manner [Figure 34]. Draw any straight line uv
parallel to oB, and insert the lines bh, $b'h'$, ... parallel to oA. The
hill of ophelimity will be divided into sections by as many curves
bc, $b'c'$, ...; the slope, with respect to the horizontal lines bh, $b'h'$, ...,
of the tangents bt, $b't'$, ... to these curves at the points b, b', ... is
equal to the elementary ophelimity of A corresponding to the quantity
ou of A (§ 32). Since this elementary quantity [ophelimity] does
not vary with the quantity of B, the slopes of the tangents bt, $b't'$, ...
are all equal. We would have analogous properties for a straight line
parallel to oA.

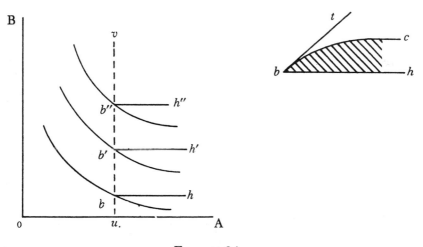

FIGURE 34

61. Hence it follows that the lines of Figure 31 cannot represent
the indifference lines of two goods whose ophelimities are independent; it is true that the slopes which we have just mentioned are
constant from β to c, but then they diminish all at once, or rapidly, at

c and become equal to zero from c to a. Thus we find confirmation of the necessity for considering the consumption of certain goods to be dependent.

62. To get an idea of indifference curves when it is a case of dependence of the second type, let us consider two goods A and B, where A is inferior to B (§ 19) and where they can be substituted for one another. This will be, for example, the bread and the corn meal. An individual can satisfy his hunger eating only "polenta" or eating only bread, or he can live on both of those foods; he prefers the bread to the "polenta", at least within certain proportions.

Assume, for simplicity, that 3 of A can replace 2 of B. The reasoning would be the same, however, whatever be the law of substitution. Take om [Figure 35] equal to 3 and on equal to 2, and draw the line mn. Along this line the material need of the individual is satisfied. For example, at m he satisfies his hunger with 3

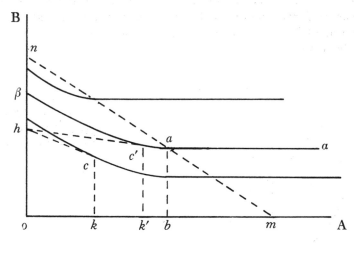

FIGURE 35

of polenta; at n, with 2 of bread; at a, with ba of bread and ob of polenta; but his satisfaction is not the same. When he is at a, any additional quantity of A is superfluous; consequently $a\alpha$, parallel to om, is an indifference line. The rest of this line is $a\beta$. At n the individual would have B to satiety; at β he has a little less of it. This difference in pleasure between the use of on and that of $o\beta$ is the same as that which the individual experiences when he is able to use only B and when he must content himself with ab of B and ob of A.

If the individual has *oh* of B, which he exchanges for A at a price of A in terms of B given by the slope of *hc* with respect to *oA*, he demands *ok* of A; and at a lesser price, given by the slope of *hc'*, he demands a greater quantity, *ok'*.

63. In the extreme case of two goods A and B, one of which can replace the other always in the same proportion, for example, if 4 of A are always equivalent to 3 of B, the indifference lines are straight lines having a [common] slope such that *oa* is to *ob* as 4 is to 3, Figure 36. Starting from *a*, the contract line is that same straight line *ab*.

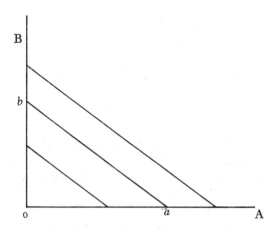

FIGURE 36

64. If we have a certain number of goods A, B, C, . . ., we can assume, for the moment, that the prices of B, C, . . . are fixed and allocate a certain sum of money among these goods. In this case that sum of money becomes a good which we can compare to A; in this way we can extend the use of graphs to a large number of goods.

65. The indifference curves between this sum of money and good A very often will be of a form analogous to that of Figure 37. We measure the quantities of money on *oQ*; the quantities of good A on *oA*. From the points *q*, *q'*, *q''*, we draw the tangents *q'm'*, *qm*, *q''m''*, to the indifference curves. These latter are such that the slopes of the tangents, with respect to *oA*, increase as we move away from *o* along Q.

The slope of *qm* with respect to *oA* gives us the price of good A. Note that for someone who is at *q*, equilibrium is not possible with a straight line with a slope with respect to *oA* greater than that of

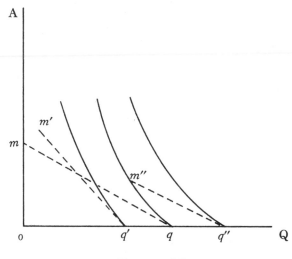

FIGURE 37

qm; that is, with a higher price. If, then, the minimum price of A is given by the slope of qm with respect to oA, someone who has oq of resources can hardly begin to buy any A; someone who has only oq' of resources could buy none since the tangent $q'm'$ is inclined less with respect to oA than is qm. Someone who finds himself at q'' can, on the other hand, buy a certain quantity of good A because $q''m''$ is steeper, with respect to oA, than qm. Consequently, when a good has a minimum price below which it cannot be obtained, only someone who has an income exceeding a certain limit can buy it. And, as everyone knows, this is indeed the way things are.

66. In this way, and taking the hierarchy of goods into account, we have a model much like the concrete phenomenon. Let us assume that we have different series A, B, . . . of those goods which substitute for one another.

A	B	C	D	E	F	G
A′	B′	C′	D′	E′	F′	G′
A″	B″	C″	D″	E″	F″	G″
A‴	B‴	C‴	D‴	E‴	F‴	G‴

When the individual has a certain income, he uses the goods enclosed in the rectangle indicated by the solid lines; if his income increases, he uses the goods enclosed in the rectangle indicated by the broken lines; with the increase in his income he omits certain goods of lower price and inferior quality, and uses goods which are more expensive and of better quality.

67. Indifference curves which have the form of those in Figure 38 do not correspond to the majority of common goods because, according to these curves, even an individual who had a very low income would buy some of these goods, a small amount without doubt, at a very high price.

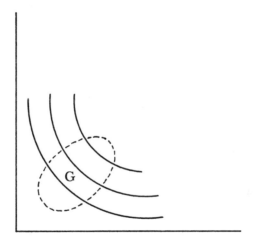

FIGURE 38

If we wanted to consider, however, the indifference curves in a small region G, we could adopt them, as others, according to convenience. The real curves are certainly very complicated; it is sufficient that the theoretical curves agree approximately with the real curves for that small part which one is considering. Moreover, it can happen that curves which approach the real curves more closely than others within this small region, diverge from them considerably outside it, and *vice versa*.

68. The case in which we have many goods is very complex; hence it is useful to have available several means for simplifying it. In order to move from a certain combination of goods A, B, C, . . . to another A, B', C', . . . we can divide the operation in two: 1° We keep the proportions in the combination intact and increase (or de-

crease) all the quantities proportionally; 2° we change the proportions, and thus finally arrive at the combination A', B', . . . For example, let us assume an individual who has 1,200 francs annual income; this income increases to 2,400. The allocation will be as follows:

Expenditures for	First real situation		Intermediate theoretical situation		Second real situation	
	francs	% of income	francs	% of income	francs	% of income
Food	720	60	1,440	60	1,200	50
Housing	360	30	720	30	600	25
Clothing	120	10	240	10	600	25
Income	1,200	100	2,400	100	2,400	100

It should be noted that the first operation is much more important than the second, especially for increases in income which are not very substantial. When income increases, it is true that the proportions spent on the large categories, food, housing, clothing, amusement, change, but that is a secondary phenomenon compared to the principal phenomenon, which is the increase in all these expenditures.

69. **The hill of ophelimity.** From elementary ophelimity's property of decreasing when the quantity of a good at the disposal of an individual increases, it follows that the slope of the hill of ophelimity is steeper at the base and more gentle as the height increases (§ 32).

70. The following property has great importance for theory. In moving along a rectilinear path in a certain direction, when one starts to descend, he will continue to descend as long as he moves in the same direction. On the other hand, if one begins to ascend, it may happen that he later descends.

We will give a proof of this in the Appendix; here we can give only an intuitive sketch.

For paths of the type ab [Figure 39] it is obvious that one always ascends in the direction of the arrow, one descends in the opposite direction. For paths such as mc one ascends in the direction of the arrow up to c, and then descends. From c to m, going in a direction opposite to that of the arrow, one always descends. In order to be able to ascend at some point such as c'', it would be necessary that

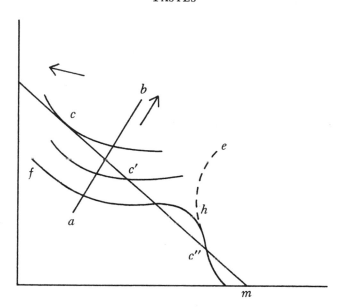

FIGURE 39

one pass from below to above, instead of passing from above to below the indifference line as at c'. But if this is so, the curve which passes through c'', since its tangent must always form an acute angle a as indicated in Figure 29, cannot go from c'' toward e, but must necessarily bend around to go toward f. But this concavity at h is contrary to the property of indifference lines which we have pointed out in § 45; hence our hypothesis cannot be maintained.

CHAPTER V

THE OBSTACLES

1. The study of the way in which the obstacles are overcome, that is to say, the study of production, is longer than that of the way tastes operate. This is because of the great complexity of production among civilized peoples.

2. **Division of labor and the enterprise.** Among all peoples we find a phenomenon known by the classic name of DIVISION OF LABOR. It depends essentially on the fact that production necessitates the assembly and use of a large number of elements. As Ferrara has quite well observed, if we consider each of these elements and the role that it plays in production, we have the *division of labor;* if we consider these elements as a whole and envisage the purpose for which they are brought together, we have *cooperation.*[1] The same phenomenon has two different names, depending on the point of view taken.

3. When the division of labor is given its narrowest, and etymologically best meaning, that of the partitioning of a job among several individuals, we assert that, on the one hand, it leads to separating functions, and on the other to making individuals mutually dependent upon each other. With the expansion of the division of labor, there is an increase in the number of parts which together make up production; and since these parts depend upon each other, cooperation between individuals becomes more extensive.

---

[1] Ferrara uses the word *association.* In the Preface entitled *L'agricoltura e la divisione del lavoro,* xiv, after having recalled the fact that many individuals, rather than just one, unite in the work of production, he adds: "When we envisage this fact, this uniting, from the point of view of the purpose and the common result, we see that there is *association;* when we look at it from the point of view of the individuals, we see that there is a *division.*"

4. The *enterprise* is the organization which assembles the elements of production and directs them so as to accomplish the objective. It is an abstraction, as is *homo oeconomicus*, and it has the same relation to real enterprises as *homo oeconomicus* has to the real man, the concrete man. Consideration of the enterprise is only a means for studying separately the different functions performed by the producer. The enterprise can assume different forms: it may be entrusted to private individuals, or it may be exercised by the State, the communes, etc.; but that changes nothing about its nature.

5. We can make a rough model of the enterprise by considering a reservoir where numerous streams which represent the elements of production come together, and from which flows a single stream which represents the product.

6. Some of these elements of production come from individuals, for example, labor and certain products; some come from other enterprises, for example, certain products which must be used to obtain other products.

Economic circulation can be represented roughly in the following way [Figure 40]. A, A′, A″, . . . are enterprises; m, m', m'', . . ., n, n', n'', . . . are individuals. Some of these individuals, for example m, m', m'', n, n', n'', furnish certain things to enterprise A (for example labor, savings, etc.); and we can imagine a certain number of streams which, starting from these individuals, empty into A, to which come also the products of other enterprises. It may happen

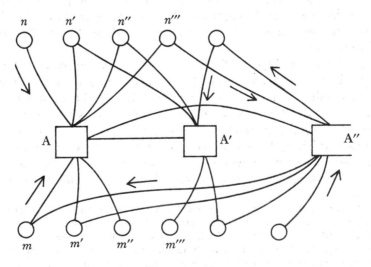

FIGURE 40

that the products of A are not appropriate for consumption directly; in this case a stream of output, which is divided among the other enterprises A', A'', flows from A. Individuals $m, m', \ldots, n, n', \ldots$ receive the products they consume either from enterprises A', A'', or solely from other enterprises A'''. . . . These flows cross each other in an almost inconceivable fashion, so great is their variety. Ordinarily a workman furnishes his labor to just one enterprise, and he receives products from a very great number of other enterprises which may not be related to the first in any way at all. We must find the thread of this extremely intricate skein, and try to unravel the phenomenon into its elements.

7. To do so, let us consider one enterprise separately; we will see what it receives and what it supplies; we will calculate the receipts and expenditures and study the way in which it regulates production.

8. **The objective of the enterprise.** We must make a distinction similar to the one made for the individual (III, 40). We have two types of phenomena: (I) The enterprise accepts the market prices without trying to modify them directly, although it contributes, without knowledge or volition, toward modifying them indirectly.[2] It has no other guide than the objective which it wants to attain. For the individual, this was the satisfaction of his own tastes; later on we will speak about the objective which the enterprise has in mind. (II) On the other hand the goal of the enterprise may be to modify market prices directly, in order to benefit from it later, or for any other purpose.

9. What we have said about Types I and II regarding the individual applies to the enterprise as well, and the reader may refer to that. For the enterprise, as for the individual, Type I is free competition, Type II is monopoly.

We can conceive of numerous goals for the enterprise, but obviously we must take those which real life provides us.

10. Very frequently the enterprise endeavors to secure the greatest gain; and this gain is almost always, we could even say always, measured in money. The other cases can be considered as exceptions.

---

[2] This condition is essential. If it is omitted, it turns a proposition which was true into a false one.

It is untrue that market prices exist independently of the enterprise. It is true that it makes its calculations as if they did; and that it modifies them without volition and even often without knowing it does so. The phenomenon is the kind represented by pursuit curves, § 11.

[In the French text these two paragraphs appear in the footnote at the end of § 15 where they are quite inappropriate.]

In order to obtain the greatest money profit, direct and indirect means are used. Directly, each enterprise strives to pay as little as possible for what it buys, and to be paid as much as possible for what it sells. Moreover, when there are several ways of obtaining a good, it chooses the one which costs the least. This is true for Type I as well as for Type II; the difference between the two types consists solely in that in Type I the enterprise accepts market conditions as they are, while in Type II it seeks to modify them.

Indirectly, the enterprise, when it can, that is to say when it is Type II, endeavors to make all the modifications in the conditions of the market and in production which can, or which this enterprise believes can, secure some pecuniary profit. In discussing exchange (III, 47), we pointed out several methods which are used; we will examine some others now.

11. Note that the objective which the enterprise pursues may not be attained, and this occurs in different ways. First, it may be completely mistaken and, expecting to make a pecuniary profit, employ means which, on the contrary, cause a loss. Also, it may happen that this money profit corresponds to a loss in ophelimity for the persons who receive it. Finally, and this is a less obvious and more subtle case, the objective itself may change as a consequence of the means used to attain it, and the enterprise may travel along one of those curves known as pursuit curves. For example [Figure 41], suppose the enterprise is at a, and wants to go to m following the route am; but in doing so it displaces m, and when it is at b, m is at m'. Again,

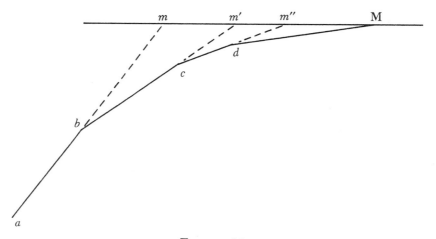

FIGURE 41

the enterprise moves toward m' and to do so follows the route bm'; but on arriving at c, the goal has shifted and is at m''; it then will follow the path cm'', and so on. In such a way, leaving a to go to m, it finally goes to M, which represents an objective which it was not seeking in the beginning. Later we will see how things take place in a very important case, that of free competition (§ 74).

12. Just as for exchange (III, 49), we must, for production, remove from Type II a class of phenomena which are characterized by this fact: that the goal of the enterprise is to obtain the maximum welfare for all those who participate in the economic phenomenon. And thus we have the same Type III which we have already mentioned in connection with exchange.

13. **The various methods of the enterprise.** First of all, when the enterprise goes to the market to buy or to sell, it can follow the different paths which we studied in connection with exchange (III, 97, 98); also, it ordinarily has several ways of producing the commodity it desires to produce. Certain elements of production are fixed; but others are variable. In order to get wheat flour, wheat obviously is necessary, but the wheat can be ground in a mill whose power is provided by a man, or by an animal, by the wind, by water, by steam. Millstones of stone or cylinders of hardened castings may be used. More, or less, effective methods for separating the bran from the flour can be employed, etc.

14. Moreover, the quantities of these elements are themselves variable within certain more or less narrow limits. The classic example of this is extensive versus intensive cultivation of the soil. The same quantity of grain can be obtained from a large or a small area of cultivated soil by varying the other elements of cultivation. But the same phenomenon appears in all production. Certain elements vary only slightly; for example, one can obtain a little more or a little less flour from the same quantity of grain. Other elements vary considerably; there is an enormous difference between a mill powered by a mule and one of those great steam mills which are now used to transform wheat into flour. There is also an enormous difference between the crew of an ancient galley and the crew of a transatlantic liner; and consequently also a great difference between the ratios, for the two types of transport, between labor and the value of the vessel. We could multiply these examples at will.

The enterprise must choose among these various methods, and must do so in the case of Type I just as in that of Type II.

15. Here we encounter one of the most serious errors in political economy. It has been assumed that this choice is imposed by the

technical state of production; that is to say, that it is determined exclusively by the state of technical progress. That is not correct. Technical progress is only one of the elements in the choice. Naturally, when railroads had not been invented, no one could use them to transport goods; but they have not replaced all other means of transportation now. In certain circumstances goods are transported by hand cart, in others by wagons, or by still other means. Since the invention of the sewing machine, sewing indeed is done by machine, but hand sewing has not disappeared. Candles, oil, petrol, gas, electricity are all used for illumination.[3]

16. In each case it is necessary to investigate which means is the best. Consider an entrepreneur who must transport gravel from the quarry to some other place. Depending on the situation, he will find it expedient to transport it by carts drawn by horses, or by constructing a small railroad. Another has timber to saw; depending on the situation, he will have it sawed by hand, or he will install a mechanized sawmill. In these cases, and in all analogous cases, the entrepreneur's decision will be determined not by technical considerations alone, but also by economic considerations.

In order to be able to choose among the different methods they must be known. Let us select one of them for study.

17. **Capital.**[4] Let us assume that we wish to set up the accounts of a small mill powered by a water-wheel.

It produces flour and bran. The principal elements of production are: the stream of water—the mill building—the water-wheel, the transmissions, the machines, etc.,—the tools, the lighting apparatus, etc.,—the oil used on the machines, and other materials for illumination, cleaning, and for many other purposes—the labor of the miller, and of his assistants—the circulating funds to meet expenses—and the wheat to be ground.

18. We must put a little order into all these quite varied elements, and set up a classification which will, however, be partly arbitrary as are all classifications.

In reality, it is the energy, the mechanical force of the stream of water which is transformed in production; but in the economic phe-

---

[3] *Systèmes*, II, p. 372 *et seq.* See another similar error, § 70.

[4] On the diverse meanings which this word can have, see Irving Fisher, "What is Capital," *Economic Journal*, Dec. 1896; "Senses of Capital," *ibid.*, June 1897; "Precedents for Defining Capital," *Quarterly Journal of Economics*, May 1904; *The Nature of Capital and Income; The Rate of Interest.* These last two books are of capital importance.

See also my *Systèmes*, I, pp. 138, 357-362.

nomenon this element of production appears in diverse forms, that is to say, in the form of the possession, or of the use, of the water course.

Similarly the building is also transformed in production, little by little. This building necessarily rests on the surface of the ground. In this case, the latter is not consumed in any way, we have here an element which is used without being consumed.

19. We can extend this notion in a rough way to the other objects, and divide the elements of production into two large classes: the first contains the things which are not consumed, or which are consumed slowly; the second contains the things which are consumed rapidly.

20. This classification is arbitrary and not very rigorous, just as the words *slowly* and *rapidly* are arbitrary and not very rigorous; but experience tells us that it is very useful in political economy. Similarly it would be very difficult to speak about men without using the words *young* and *old*, although no one can say at what precise moment youth ends and age begins. Ordinary language is obliged to replace real quantitative differences by arbitrary qualitative differences.

21. Things which are not consumed, or which are consumed slowly, in the act of production have been given a name; they are called CAPITAL.

The precise point at which the class capital stops and the other class of the elements of production begins is no better determined than the one at which youth ends and middle age begins.

Moreover, depending on the point of view, the same thing can be classified either as among the objects used up or as capital. In the preceding example the mechanical energy of the water which runs the mill is consumed, so that, from this point of view, we can say that in order to produce the flour the energy is consumed, and in the budget of the enterprise we can enter so much horsepower consumed at such and such a price. But this same thing can be expressed in a quite different way. In order to produce the flour we use the water course, which is not consumed, but remains; and, in the budget of the enterprise, we can write down so much expense, no longer for the consumption of the energy, but for the use of the water course. In the last analysis, nothing is changed in the budget.

22. If we wish to utilize the notion of capital, we will include, without difficulty, the stream of water the use of which runs the mill, and the mill building as well. The water-wheel may also be included. But what shall we say about the millstones? If we consider them as consumed slowly, we include them in capital; but if

we note that they are consumed much faster than the building or the water-wheel, we can classify them with the objects which are used up.

23. If used without caution, so uncertain a classification can easily lead to meaningless conclusions, and, in fact, economists who have used these qualitative classifications without modification have often ended up in real wars of words.

Despite the usefulness of using ordinary language, we will not hesitate to abandon it if we cannot rectify it and bring it back to quantitative reality.

24. But that is possible. All we need is to put into the budget of the enterprise certain expenses which will serve to replace the things which are considered as capital. We can then agree, on a rigorous basis, that they are used without being consumed.

Let us assume that our miller uses up exactly two sets of millstones per year. He begins the year with a set of new millstones and he ends it having used up a second set of millstones. If he wishes to classify the millstones with the objects consumed he will record as expenses: on January 1st, the purchase of the first set of millstones; on July 1st, the purchase of the second set. If he wants to consider them as capital, he will enter in the expenses on July 1st the expense of the first set of millstones, in order to restore the capital; on December 31st he will enter the expense of a second set of millstones, in order to restore the capital again.

The expenses are identical whichever way one views the millstones. There is indeed a difference in the time at which they are incurred, but we will discuss that when we deal with transformations in time; for the moment, we see that in whichever way we classify the millstones, the result in the budget is the same (and it will be seen that it is still the same when we consider transformations in time, § 47). Since what matters is the effect on the balance sheet, we can retain the qualitative classification of capital; and we can put certain objects into it and exclude certain others as we please.

Similarly, it matters little to an insurance company which has precise mortality tables whether a man of thirty be classified among the young men or among the middle aged men; either way, the coefficient of mortality is the same for him.

25. **The theory of economic equilibrium with and without the concept of capital.** Given that economic equilibrium results from the opposition between the tastes of man and the difficulties he encounters in obtaining things which are able to satisfy them, we may consider only things which will be consumed directly or the use of which will be consumed. In the production of these things, we may

think of the using up processes exclusively and in this case we abstract from the notion of capital; or else we can think of the using up of certain commodities and the use of certain capital goods. In the end, we will reach the same result. In the one case as in the other we must take into account transformations in time (§ 47).

These two ways of considering the phenomenon more or less coincide in real life. So far as obtaining some bread and satisfying one's hunger is concerned, an obstacle exists in the fact that it is necessary to have an oven in order to bake the bread. The oven appears here as a capital good; by means of certain expenditures it will last indefinitely and will always produce bread. Or else the obstacle consists in procuring the things (bricks, lime, etc.) which will become the oven when consumed and transformed. In this form it is no longer a case of capital. There is no longer a using up process which is spread over a more or less large quantity of bread produced. In addition there will be the expenses of transformations in time, which we are not dealing with at this moment.

In civilized countries, the oven, and all the things necessary to build the oven, are taken as equivalent to their prices in *numéraire*; that is to say, capital goods like consumption goods can be replaced by their prices in *numéraire*. Here the obstacle appears to us in a third form, namely, in the form of a certain expenditure which must be made.

26. Consequently, one of the obstacles to getting bread appears in one of the following three forms: having an oven—having the ground, the labor, the bricks, the lime, etc., necessary to build the oven—having disposition of the amount which an oven costs, or the amount which the things necessary for its construction cost.

27. We said it was necessary to have disposition of this amount, and not that it would be necessary to possess it physically in the form of money. Indeed, thanks to certain arrangements in use among civilized peoples, a considerable expenditure can be made with a small sum of circulating money.

Some writers have occasionally failed to make this observation, most obvious in itself, and have fallen into a strange error. They have thought that the obstacle, in this third form, consisted of the physical possession of the entire sum of money equal to the price of the object, in our example the oven. Then, reverting to the notion of capital in the first form, they concluded that capital consisted of money exclusively.

There is some truth in this observation; it is that all capital can be evaluated in *numéraire* or in money. Likewise all consumption can be evaluated in *numéraire* or in money. When we say that an individual has dined on five francs, we are not saying that he has eaten a five franc piece; when we say that to produce bread a thing worth a thousand francs is necessary, we are not saying that it is necessary to use physically two hundred crowns or fifty louis to produce the bread. In the one case as in the other, in order to make a total expenditure of one thousand francs, the physical use of ten louis can suffice; and it is then these ten louis, that is, 200 francs, which can be regarded as capital.

The study of economic equilibrium, in considering only consumption, gives us an idea of the phenomenon as a whole, and causes us to overlook the different parts. That can be useful in certain cases, but in general we cannot neglect these parts. It is certain that, in the final analysis and without speaking of transformations in time which we will treat later, the obstacles to traveling on a railroad reduce to the labor and materials necessary to build the railroad and the transportation equipment, and operate it. Thus there is no doubt that equilibrium finally must result from the opposition which exists between the obstacles and man's tastes for traveling. But the jump from the latter to the former is too great, so we must place some emphasis on the intermediate links in so long a chain. We must at least examine separately the structure and the management of the enterprise; thus we study the phenomenon under the first form, and, if one so pleases, under the third.

28. Similar remarks could be made on the subject of the goods which are consumed in production. Some people do not see why, earlier, we stopped at the bricks, the lime, etc., necessary for the construction of the oven, and why we did not go back to the clay for the bricks, to the consumption necessary to build the kiln which baked them, and so on; but by so doing we would arrive at an idea of the phenomenon which is too general and too far removed from reality. As a matter of fact there are various enterprises, and one which produces bread generally does not produce bricks. Therefore we should consider them separately.

Certain economists have wanted to reduce production, in the final analysis, to sacrifices of ophelimity. It is true that if production only transforms goods which could be consumed directly, or the use of which at least could be so consumed, this reduction is possible. But then there is no longer a place for the large number of things which have ophelimity only after having been transformed. For example, a copper mine has no other use than that of producing copper. The high cost of gold production does not come from the fact that by working the gold mines a sacrifice is made in giving up the pleasure which direct use of the mines would provide, since such pleasure does not exist. It is true that by giving up one's savings, the pleasure provided by the contemplation of it in the form of gold coins is renounced, but that has only a very remote connection with the rate of interest.

Hence some people get themselves on a wrong road which cannot lead to any satisfactory result. Rather, all the things which are available for production must be considered and the results which would be obtained by utilizing these things in different ways must be compared. These results may be described by valuations in *numéraire*, or by the different pleasures and the different sacrifices they entail. There will be agreements and differences which must be studied.

29. The budget of the enterprise will be set up in the following manner. One enterprise receives from other enterprises certain goods which it consumes; it has certain things called capital which, thanks to the ingenuity of bookkeeping, will be considered as always remaining the same. In the budget this capital will appear as the expenditures necessary to renew it plus a certain sum which is paid for its use. In the example of the millstones, this sum will serve precisely to cover the difference between the two phenomena of which we spoke in § 24. For the first, that is, when the millstones are considered as objects consumed, expenditures for purchasing one set of millstones are found in the January 1st and July 1st records; in the second, that is, when we consider the millstones as capital, these expenditures appear on July 1st and on December 31st.

We will return to all this when we study transformations in time; we must now study expenditures made to replace objects considered as capital a little more closely.

30. **Amortization and insurance.** Things may deteriorate slowly, because they wear out, or they may be destroyed, completely or partly, by a chance occurrence.

In the first case repairs and amortization provide the means for restoring the capital; insurance does this in the second case.

Repairs keep a machine in good condition, nevertheless it gets old, and the day comes when it is better to buy another one than to continue making expenditures to keep it in condition. A ship can be kept in good condition by means of repairs, but not indefinitely. Amortization must provide not only for physical deterioration, but also for what could be called economic deterioration. There comes a day, in fact, when the machine, the ship, etc., may still be in good physical condition, but are obsolete; and then they must be replaced by another machine, another ship, etc., of a more modern and improved type. In the budget, expenditures for repairs generally appear among the operating expenses, amortization serves to reconstitute the capital.

Insurance premium is the name given to the sum which must be saved each year and accumulated in order to be prepared for chance occurrences. An enterprise may itself insure the objects it possesses which are subject to chance occurrences. In fact, this occasionally occurs in the case of certain large shipping companies which insure their own ships. In this case the insurance appears in the balance sheet as amortization, and is a sum which constitutes a special fund administered by the company. More often it is another enterprise which provides the insurance, and engages in this type of business exclusively. In this case the enterprise which has objects to insure pays an *insurance premium* to one of those companies, which returns the price of the object to the former if the object is destroyed in whole or in part by one of the chance events specified in the contract. There is an infinity of possible contracts; but the main point is always the same; it is always a matter of restoring the capital.

31. Industrial companies customarily have a third special fund, called reserve fund, which serves a variety of purposes the most important of which is to insure the invested capital of the firm and to restore it in case of need. In real life, the chance event does not appear only in the loss of material objects. A war, an epidemic, a commercial crisis, by changing the conditions under which an industry operates, can cause it brief and transitory losses. A part of the capital of the firm is then lost, and is reconstituted by means of the reserve fund.

By these brief remarks we simply wanted to point out the processes by which the restoration of capital is provided for, and in no way intended to exhaust the subject (§ 68; VIII, 12 *et seq.*). It is sufficient to know that, in one way or another, it is necessary to provide for the restoration of capital and to take account of its variations.

32. Suppose a house is located in a city of declining population where building values are falling. This fact must be taken into account in amortization. Consider another house in a city which is prospering and where building values are increasing. In that case we have a phenomenon which is the inverse of the preceding one; and, in order to avoid a proliferation of terms, we will consider as negative amortization the sum needed to maintain the capital always at the same value. Similarly there can be a negative insurance

premium when the chance event is advantageous rather than detrimental to the owner of the object.

Securities on the exchange furnish a good example of these phenomena. Assume that an individual buys at a price of 120 francs securities having a face value of 100 francs and which in ten years will be redeemed by the company by the payment of 100 francs to the holder of the security. The owner of this security has an object which, costing 120 francs today, will cost only 100 francs in ten years. If these securities are regarded as capital, it is necessary to resort to amortization to cover the difference.

If these securities cost 80 francs today instead of 120 francs, there still would be a difference from their price in ten years, but this difference would be to the advantage of the present owner, and we would take it into account by a negative amortization.

If, instead of all these securities being redeemed after ten years, they are redeemed according to annual drawings, someone who holds a certificate purchased for 120 francs loses 20 francs this year if its number is called for redemption. He would gain 20 if he had purchased it for 80 francs. A positive insurance premium corresponds to the first case, a negative insurance premium to the second.

There would also be occasion to take account of dynamic variations, of the *appreciation* or *depreciation* of gold; but we will abstract from that type of phenomena here.

33. **The services of capital.** Since, by a fiction which brings us more or less close to reality and even becomes reality if we bring in amortization and insurance, capital goods are deemed to remain always in their original condition, we cannot say that they are transformed into the product. It is their use alone which contributes toward obtaining this product, and we will say that it is the SERVICE of the capital which is transformed.

Note that this is only a question of form. In reality it is the energy, the mechanical power of the stream of water, which breaks up the wheat and produces the flour; correctly then, it is the energy from the water course which, with the grain, is transformed into flour. At bottom we express the same thing, but in another form, when we say that the use of the water course enables us to obtain the flour, or that it is the SERVICE of the water course which, with the wheat, is transformed into flour.

34. **Material goods and immaterial goods.** From the beginning of the nineteenth century economists have argued at great length the question of whether all economic goods are material, or whether there are also immaterial goods; and the debate has ended in a pure

war of words. In our opinion the question has been definitively settled by Ferrara, who showed very clearly that "all products are material if the means by which they are manifested are considered; and all are immaterial if we consider the effect that they are destined to produce." It must be added immediately, however, that the physical identity of two things does not entail their economic identity; this observation will be utilized later.

35. **The coefficients of production.** To obtain one unit of a product, certain quantities of other products and of services of capital are used. These are the quantities which are called the COEFFICIENTS OF PRODUCTION.

36. If, instead of considering one unit of the product, we consider any quantity whatsoever of the product, the quantities of other products and of the services of capital used to obtain that quantity of product constitute the FACTORS OF PRODUCTION.

It is really useless to have two expressions for things differing only by a simple proportion and we will generally employ the term coefficient of production. We have mentioned the other only because it is used by certain writers.

37. The coefficients of production can vary in several ways (§ § 15, 76), and they are determined by firms in different ways according as the economic phenomena correspond to Type I or to Type II.

38. **Transformations in space** (III, 72). We do not have to deal with these transformations at length. We need simply remark that they give us a prime example of things which, while physically identical, are economically different. A ton of wheat at New York, and a ton of the same quality wheat at Genoa, are physically identical things, but economically different. The difference in price is not necessarily equal to the cost of transport from one of these locations to the other. That method of evaluation of the difference between prices rests on an incorrect theory of economic equilibrium (III, 224).

There are always transformations in space; they are sometimes insignificant, sometimes of the foremost importance. There are some enterprises which make them their sole business; these are the transport companies. Ease of transformations in space enlarges the extent of markets and makes competition more vigorous. Consequently these transformations have great social importance. The nineteenth century will remain one of those in which there has been a great deal of improvement in this kind of transformation, which has brought about very important social changes.

39. **Transformations in time** (III, 72). These are entirely

analogous to the preceding ones; but although transformations in space have always been taken into account, transformations in time have very often been neglected, and are still very often neglected. The reasons for this are many; we will point out only two.

Transformations in space necessitate labor and a cost which are very obvious; and when one speaks of them he does not shock the prejudices of those who believe that the difference in price between two goods can depend only on the difference in the labor necessary for the production of those goods or, more generally, on the difference in cost of production. In transformations in time, the false theories which we have just mentioned do not show the physical interdependence in these transformations.

But there is another, more important, reason which causes the role of these transformations in time to be unappreciated. It is that this is a matter which is studied more with sentiment than with reason, and these sentiments themselves rest on certain prejudices. No one, or almost no one, studies the question of transformations in time with an open mind. Everyone knows, even before having studied the question, how it ought to be decided, and he talks about it the way a lawyer talks about a case he is entrusted with defending.

40. If we take an exclusively scientific point of view, we will see immediately that, just as two physically identical objects are economically different depending on the place where they are available, they likewise are different from the economic viewpoint, depending on the time when they are available. A meal today and a meal tomorrow are not the same thing at all; if an individual is suffering from the cold, he has an immediate need for a cloak, and the same cloak available in a day, in a month, in a year, most certainly does not render him the same service. Hence it is obvious that two economic goods which are physically identical, but are available at different moments, can have different prices. It is incomprehensible why people find it completely natural that the price of wine is different from that of bread, or that the price of wine in one place is not the same as that of wine in another place, and then are astonished by the fact that the price of wine available today is not the same as the price of the same wine available in a year.

41. But, due to that irresistible tendency to think immediately about practical applications, they scarcely pause at the scientific problem we have just posed and immediately set out to investigate whether it is not possible to find means which allow the price of wine available today to be made precisely equal to that of wine available next year.

That is not the question which we want to study at the moment, just as we are not investigating whether there are technical means for making the price of wine equal to the price of bread, or the price of wheat in New York equal to the price of wheat in Genoa. It is enough for us to have shown that goods available at different moments are economically different goods and consequently can have different prices.

42. The theory of economic equilibrium will tell us how these prices are determined. Hence it is necessary to be careful not to commit the error which consists of saying that *the cause* of the difference between these prices is the difference in the times at which these goods are available. For there is not *one* cause of that difference; there are very many of them; they are all the circumstances, without a single exception, which determine economic equilibrium. The consideration of time serves only to distinguish between two goods which are not available at the same moment. Similarly the chemical composition distinguishes copper ore from copper metal, but is not the CAUSE of the difference in the price of copper ore and the price of copper metal. This difference does not have ONE cause; it has a large number of them; or, to express ourselves more rigorously, it is related to many other facts, which are precisely those which determine economic equilibrium.

43. **The balance sheet of the enterprise and transformations in time.** We have seen in § 26 that production can be considered in three different ways, which, in the end, come to the same result.

44. I. *The using up process is considered without making use of the concept of capital.* In this case transformation in time consists of replacing a good available at a certain moment by a good available at another moment. To produce wheat it is necessary to use seed. It can be thought of as a using up taking place at the moment of sowing. This quantity of wheat is not economically identical with another equal quantity of wheat which would be available only at the time of the next harvest. The two economic combinations for production, (A) 100 kilograms of wheat to be used at the time of planting, and (B) 100 kilograms of wheat to be used at the time of the next harvest, are not identical; they are different *goods*. Consequently the price of A can be different from the price of B. Generally this price is greater (in exceptional cases it could be smaller). The difference between the price of A and the price of B is the price of a transformation in time and appears in the expenses of the enterprise. For example, one who is sowing wheat for the first time most certainly cannot use wheat from his *last harvest* since the latter does

not exist; he will have available, at this time, only the wheat from the *future harvest*. Hence a certain expenditure for this transformation should be carried as a debit in his budget.

45. II. *The concept of capital is used.* In this case the transformation in time results from the necessity of having, or producing, the capital *before* the good can be produced. The price of the transformation in time will be part of the cost of the use of the capital.

The seed necessary to produce the wheat can be regarded as a capital good. It is used up at the moment of sowing; it is restored at the time of the harvest, so that as far as the agricultural enterprise is concerned it always remains the same; and it is only its use for a certain time which is employed in the production of wheat. In 1895, an agricultural enterprise had 100 kilograms of wheat; they were used as seed; from the 1896 harvest 100 kilograms of wheat were put aside; they were used again that same year as seed; from the harvest of 1897 100 kilograms of wheat were put aside. Let us stop here and set up the balance sheet for the operation. The enterprise began with 100 kilograms of wheat at its disposal; at the end of the operation it still has 100 kilograms of wheat. In reality, it has not consumed it; it has simply enjoyed the *use* of this quantity. The transformation in time consists in this use, and the price of this transformation is part of the price of the use. If there is just the one enterprise, the price of this use will be paid to itself, and will be in keeping with the sacrifices necessary to produce the object which the enterprise uses. If the enterprise buys this object from another enterprise, it will have to take into account, on the one hand, the sacrifice it makes by advancing the price paid for the object, and, on the other hand, the advantage it reaps from its use, and then see if there is a balance between them. Finally, instead of producing the object or buying it, the enterprise can simply buy the use of it, and the price of this use will appear among the expenditures in its budget.

46. III. *The money value of the factors of production is considered.* In this case the transformation in time involves money, and consists in exchanging a sum available at a certain moment for an identical sum available at another moment.

Let us assume that the 100 kilograms of wheat are worth 20 francs. For the agricultural enterprise, having these 20 francs available means having available the 100 kilograms of wheat needed to sow a field. It is not necessary for it actually to have a louis; it may be sufficient, for example, to have a half-louis. With that money it buys 50 kilograms of wheat; then it sells some cheese and has another half-louis with which it buys another 50 kilograms of wheat. It thus has 100 kilograms of wheat. Accordingly the transformation in time consists in this: that in 1895 the enterprise needs to have twenty francs available, which it will not return until 1897. The expense necessary to have this sum available for use must go into its budget whether this expense is paid to the enterprise itself or is paid to others.

47. Let us return to the example in § 24. If the miller considers his millstones as objects consumed, we have these expenses in his budget:

(A)

January 1st............	100 francs
July 1st..............	100 "
Total for the year......	200 francs

If they are considered as capital, the expenses are:

(B)

July 1st..............	100 francs
December 31st..........	100 "
Total	200 francs

Plan A gives the same expense as plan B, but at a different time.

The millstones must be paid for with the flour produced. In plan A, it is necessary to buy on January 1st millstones which will be paid for with the flour produced from January 1st to June 30th; hence it is necessary to effect a transformation in time in order to have available on January 1st what would not be available until June 30th of the same year. If we use the notion of money, it is necessary to have available on January 1st a sum of 100 francs, which would only become available on June 30th. Assume that 2 francs is paid for that. The same operation must be repeated from July 1st to December 31st. In all 4 francs will be spent, and the total expense of plan A will be 204 francs.

In plan B the millstones are not paid for until July 1st—at the end of the period, January 1st to June 31st, during which a quantity of flour sufficient to cover this expenditure has been produced. But, on the other hand, in order to be able to use plan B it is necessary to have the use of this capital. Consequently, exactly as in plan A, it is necessary to have the use of the millstones from January 1st. If this capital is evaluated in money, it is necessary to have the use of 100 francs during the year, and if 4 francs is spent for this use, the total expense of plan B will be 204 francs, and will be equal to that of plan A.

48. **The income from capital.** The obstacle which manifests itself by the cost of the use of capital is partially independent of the social organization and has its origin in transformation in time. Whatever be the organization of society, it is obvious that a meal one can have today is not identical to a meal one can have tomorrow, and 10 kilograms of strawberries available in January are not identical to 10 kilograms of strawberries available in June. The organization of society determines the form in which this obstacle manifests itself and it partially modifies the substance of it. It is exactly the same as regards physical transformations and transformations in space (VIII, 18 *et seq.*).

The same object may be produced by any one of these three transformations. For example, during the month of July, in Geneva, an individual uses a piece of ice to cool his drink. This piece of ice may have been produced by an artificial ice plant (physical transformation); it may have been brought from a glacier (transformation in space); it may have been cut during the winter and preserved until summer (transformation in time).[5] These transformations are purchased at the price of certain sacrifices or costs, which depend in part on the social organization and are in part independent of it. For example, if the members of a collectivity gather ice in January and wood in July of the same year, they will have cool drinks in July, but will suffer from the cold in January. If they could have gathered the wood in the month of January and the ice in the following July, the labor would have been the same, and they would have been warm in winter and cool in summer. The fact of having had to furnish the labor necessary to gather the ice first, cost them the cold which they suffered during the month of January and obviously that is independent of the social organization.

If there is a second collectivity which in January *lends* to the first one wood which will be returned in July, the first collectivity will no

---

[5] These are the principal transformations in the three cases considered; but, in each of these cases, the principal transformation is accompanied by the other two, which are secondary. The artificial ice plant does not produce the ice at the precise moment that it is consumed; a certain time is required to bring the ice from the glacier to the place where it is consumed. Hence transformation in time is not absent from these two cases, although it is secondary. Similarly transformation in space is not absent from the first and third cases. Finally, physical transformation, be it only to break up the ice into pieces, is not absent from the second and third cases.

longer suffer from the cold; thanks to that loan, in January it will consume, not physically but economically, the wood which will only be gathered six months later, and it will have the enjoyment of this transformation in time. The second collectivity makes a precisely inverse transformation in time.

49. When capital goods are private property, the one who lends them, that is, allows their use by others, ordinarily receives a certain sum which we will call the GROSS INTEREST of these capital goods.

50. This interest is the price of the *use* of the capital goods; it pays for their *services* (§ 33). This is still a question of form and not of substance. If an individual pays 10 francs to get a certain quantity of cherries, he buys a good. Assume that this quantity is precisely the amount produced by one cherry tree in one year; if this individual purchases, with the 10 francs, the use of this cherry tree for one year, he will have, at bottom, for the same price, the same quantity of cherries as before. Only the form of the operation differs; he has now purchased the *services* of a capital good (§ 33).

51. Note that if the person who eats the cherries is the same as the one who owns the cherry tree, there is no longer anyone to pay the 10 francs to, but the fact still remains that this person has the enjoyment of the cherries; and this fact may be viewed in two ways: 1° directly, as the enjoyment of a good; 2° indirectly, as the enjoyment of the *service* of a capital good.

52. When the phenomenon is studied in the form of the services of capital, it is necessary to investigate how the price is established, that is, what is the amount of the gross interest. It should readily be seen that it would be equal to all the expenses necessary to maintain the capital intact, that is, expenditures on repairs, along with amortization and insurance; but ordinarily this gross interest is greater than that sum, and the difference, which we call NET INTEREST, shows up as an entity whose origin is not so obvious.

53. When one says that this net interest pays for the transformation in time, the difficulty is set aside without being solved, because in that case we will ask why the transformation in time has a price, and how this price is determined.

54. A first reaction is to join together the fact of the appropriation of capital and that of the existence of this net interest as a relation of cause and effect. Indeed, these are concomitant facts; and besides, it is plain that if there were no owners of capital there would be no one to whom the net interest could be paid; only the expenses of maintaining the capital intact would remain, expenditures which must be made in any case. In other words, the obstacles

which manifest themselves through the existence of net interest have their origin exclusively in this fact that capital has been appropriated.

55. This claim is far from being absurd *a priori* and it very well could be true. Hence it is necessary to examine the facts and see whether they do or do not confirm this claim.

The obstacles encountered in procuring sea water in Italy, if we disregard the labor and other expenditures necessary to obtain it, arise exclusively from the fact that the government, having a monopoly of the sale of salt, prohibits private individuals from taking water from the sea. Thus these obstacles depend solely on the social organization. If the government would leave everyone free to take the water, all the obstacles which prevent the Italians from procuring it would disappear, except, of course, those which we have mentioned, the labor and the other expenditures needed to transport this sea water to the place where one wants to use it. Here we have an example favorable to the thesis that net interest on capital has its origin in the social organization.

Obstacles encountered in obtaining cherries appear in the form of the price asked by the cherry merchant. This new example seems similar to the preceding one; and we are thus led to think that the elimination of cherry merchants would suffice to remove the obstacles which impede us in obtaining them. But a little reflection is enough to see that this is not so. Behind the merchant there is the producer; behind the producer is the fact that cherries do not exist in a quantity exceeding the quantity necessary to satisfy our tastes, as is the case with sea water. Shall we say, then, that the social organization, by virtue of which the cherry merchant exists, has no place at all among the obstacles to obtaining cherries? Certainly not; but we will say that it is only a part of the obstacles; and careful observation of the facts will make us add that it is often only a very small part compared to the other obstacles.

The obstacle which we encounter in obtaining cherries—or, what comes to the same thing, in having the use of a cherry tree—comes from the fact that the amount of cherries available is smaller than the amount necessary to satisfy our tastes completely. And the phenomenon of the price of the use of a cherry tree arises from the opposition between this obstacle and our tastes.

56. In general, the obstacle which is encountered in the use of capital—or with regard to the corresponding transformation in time—comes from the fact that the quantity of capital—or the means to carry out this transformation in time—is less than we need in order to satisfy our tastes. And the phenomenon of a net return on the

capital—or the price of the transformation in time—comes from this opposition between the obstacle and our tastes.

Thus we are led back to the general theory of the price of anything whatsoever, which always results from the opposition between tastes and obstacles, an opposition which can never exist except when the thing considered is available in a smaller quantity than what would be necessary to satisfy our tastes completely (III, 19).

57. Hence net interest is ruled by the same laws which rule any price whatsoever; and the cost of transformation in time follows the same laws as the cost of transformation in space, or the cost of any transformation.

This cost of transformation in time cannot be determined separately from other prices and all the other circumstances on which economic equilibrium depends. It is determined at the same time as all the other unknowns, by the conditions of economic equilibrium.[6]

58. **Net interest on diverse capital.** From the foregoing it by no means follows that there is only a single net interest for all capital, that is, that the price of the transformation in time does not vary according to the circumstances under which it occurs. Indeed, different net interest is yielded by different capital. Very different interest is paid for the use of a horse, for the sum which the horse is worth, for that same sum lent on a mortgage, or lent on a bill of exchange, or based only on a simple promise, etc.

The theory of economic equilibrium will tell us that different classes of capital can be established approximately, and that within most of these classes the net interest tends to become equal; and it will show us under what conditions this happens; but it is essential not to confuse the characteristics peculiar to certain phenomena and the characteristics which these phenomena assume only in the case of economic equilibrium.

59. **The balance sheet of the enterprise and interest on capital.** The balance sheet of an enterprise should be made up for a specified period; and all the sums acquired or expended by the enterprise should be entered for that period; a certain sum which depends on net interest is added or subtracted. For short periods of time simple interest is generally used; for longer periods, compound interest.

In insurance calculations the *present* value of a *future* sum is often taken into account. Let us assume, for example, that a company must pay 100 francs at the end of each year to an individual 30 years old, and must do so until his death. Let us take the experimental data gathered by the English insurance companies. By various proce-

---

6 *Systèmes, II,* pp. 288 *et seq.*

dures, which need not be considered here, these data have been modified so as to eliminate certain irregularities which are assumed to be accidental. Thus we know that of 89,865 individuals alive at 30 years of age, 89,171 remain at 31 years; 88,465 at 32 years, etc. Consequently, if 100 francs had to be paid to each of these individuals, 8,917,100 francs would have to be paid at the end of the first year; 8,846,500 francs at the end of the second year, etc. It is assumed, and this is hypothetical, that the future will be similar to the past; moreover, for each individual, numbers proportional to those we have just reported are used; that is to say, we assume that, on the average, each individual will have to be paid 8,917,100/89,865 = 99.228 at the end of the first year; 8,846,500/89,865 = 98.442 at the end of the second year, and so on.

We then look for the sums which, with interest compounded annually, produce the sums above. Here it is necessary to make a hypothesis about the interest. Let us assume that it is 5 percent. We find that a sum of 94.503 at 5 percent becomes 99.228 after a year; 89.290 becomes 93.7545 after one year and 98.442 after two years. Accordingly we will say that the *present* value of the sum of 99.228 payable in one year is 94.503; and the present value of 98.442, payable in two years, is 89.290.

60. Industrial balance sheets are set up more simply. The greatest part of the interest is simple, and is taken into account in an approximative way.

In short, each balance sheet, to be correct, should be set up for a specified period, and all the expenses and all the receipts should be computed for that period. Let us assume that the balance sheet is set up on January 1st, 1903, and that interest on capital is 5 percent. An expenditure of 1,000 francs made on June 30, 1902, should appear as 1,025 francs in the balance sheet. Similarly for receipts. On a cash basis, this expenditure or this receipt appears as 1,000 francs on June 30; but, in the case of the expenditure, we find an expense of 25 francs spent as interest, and in the case of the receipt, we find an equal sum collected as interest. It comes to the same thing in the end.

61. **The balance sheet of the enterprise, the labor and the capital of the entrepreneur.** The balance sheet of the enterprise must take account of all expenses; and if the entrepreneur renders any service to the enterprise, he should evaluate it and enter the amount among the expenses.

An individual may be manager of a business on behalf of a joint stock company, or some other individual, and in that case he receives a salary; or he may be manager of his own business, in which case his salary is mingled with the profit withdrawn from the business. But we must avoid this commingling if we want to know the exact cost of the products and the results of the undertaking. Similarly, the capital which this individual uses in his business should be considered as borrowed, and the interest entered among the expenses. Take an individual who earns 8,000 francs a year by managing a business for another person; suppose he sets up on his own account, and spends 100,000 francs for the business, which he directs himself. Suppose the profit of this enterprise, not counting the labor and capital of its proprietor, is 10,000 francs. In reality, there is a loss of 2,000 francs since 8,000 francs for the salary of the manager and 4,000 francs for the interest on the capital must be recorded in the accounts as expenses. If this individual had continued to be a manager in the service of others and if he had purchased annuities yielding 4 percent, he would have had 12,000 francs per year; he has only 10,000; he thus loses 2,000 francs.

This is only one way of calculating the profit or the loss, under certain hypotheses. Any other way of making these calculations may be satisfactory, provided it gives a correct accounting of the facts. Suppose an individual is receiving a salary for managing an undertaking and wants to know whether or not he will blunder by resigning and going into business for himself. If his accounting is done properly, it ought to give him all the relevant facts.

62. **The enterprise and the owner of economic goods.** As we have already said in § 4, the enterprise is only an abstraction by which one of the parts in the production process is isolated.

The producer is a complex being in which are blended the entrepreneur, the manager of the business and the capitalist; we have separated them, but that is not enough; we must still consider the owner of certain economic goods which the enterprise uses.

Let us imagine a landowner who produces wheat on his land; he can be depicted by the producer considered in III, 102, who produces a good at a cost which increases with the quantity produced. But there are two aspects of this individual to consider: 1° the owner of the land; 2° the entrepreneur who uses the land and other economic goods in order to produce wheat. To use a concrete example, let us consider an entrepreneur who rents this land and produces wheat.

63. If the producer finds himself on the side of positive indices, he makes a profit; to whom does this profit go now that we have a landowner and an entrepreneur?

This problem can be resolved by appealing to the general principles already laid down. The quantity of land which the landowner has is represented by *oh* [in Figure 42]; assume that it has no direct ophelimity for him. On the *oa* axis measure, in *numéraire*, the amount

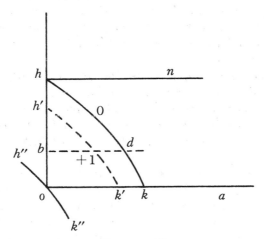

FIGURE 42

which the owner derives from his land. We have the case of IV, 54; the line of exchanges for the landowner is *hoa*. For the entrepreneur, the axes will be *hn* and *ho*. Let *hk* be a line such that, if for any quantity *hb* of land the entrepreneur pays *bd*, he makes no profit at all; *hk* will be an indifference line for him, and is precisely the line of zero index, that is, that of complete transformations. If we set *kk'* equal to unity, the curve *k'h'*, parallel to *kh*, will be another indifference curve, the curve of index one, and along it the entrepreneur will make a profit of one. The curves of negative index are on the other side of *hk*.

64. If the entrepreneur has a monopoly, he will obtain the maximum profit for himself by moving on to the indifference curve *h"k"* which passes through the origin. He will keep all the profit from the production, and the landowner will get none. If there is competition between entrepreneurs, he will have to end up on the line *hk* for reasons already developed many times. The equilibrium point is at *k*, at the intersection of *hk* and the landowner's line of exchanges *oa*. The latter will take all the profit of the production, and the entrepreneur none. Plainly it would be the same if the land, or any other good of this type, did have ophelimity for the owner.

65. We conclude from this that when there is competition between firms, they must stay on the line of complete transformations; they then have neither profit nor loss.

The indifference curves of obstacles do not change, nor can they change; but the curve of maximum profit for the landowner becomes the curve of complete transformations for the enterprise.

We must now see how and to what extent this theoretical proposition may be true for real enterprises, which differ more or less from the theoretical ones.

66. **Real enterprises, their profits and their losses.** First of all it is obvious that the theoretical proposition can be true only on the average for real enterprises. Indeed, the latter differ from abstract enterprises in that they have a certain organization, a certain reputation which attracts customers, certain lands, mines, and factories which they have purchased, etc. The abstract character of the enterprise is always more or less merged with that of the ownership.

67. For real enterprises, it is easy to see, if we reason in an objective fashion, that there may be, at least for a very wide class and on the average, neither profit nor loss, where, of course, all the expenses are taken into account including the income on the capital of the enterprise. At present a great number of these enterprises take the form of joint stock companies, and their securities are sold on the exchange; moreover there are new ones every day.

Any individual who has some money, even a small amount, can participate in these enterprises by buying one or more shares. It would be hard to understand, then, how the latter could have any advantage over government issues or other securities which pay a fixed income. If such an advantage did exist, everyone would buy the shares of joint stock companies. We have said that it was necessary to take all the circumstances into account; hence it is necessary to make allowance for the uncertain character of dividends, the fact that these companies have a shorter or longer lifetime, etc. It may seem that their shares yield more; but if these allowances are made, the return, on the average, becomes equal to that from fixed interest government bonds. For example, in Germany, coal mine stocks which yield in the neighborhood of 6 percent are approximately equivalent to Prussian debt securities which return 3⅓ percent.

68. In addition it may be noted that this equivalence is in part subjective, that is, the Germans in fact believe this equivalence to be so—otherwise they would sell their Prussian consols in order to buy mining or other shares—but reality could, in part at least, be at variance with what men think it is.

Thus the concrete phenomenon does differ from the theoretical phenomenon. For frequently repeated short-term commitments where there can be numerous adaptations and readaptations, it seems that this divergence ought to be slight; but we cannot assert, *a priori*, that it is equal to zero; it seems more likely that, however slight, it must always exist.

For example, let us assume two uses of savings which provide an equal net revenue when allowance is made for insurance premiums and amortization and that, for the first, there are probabilities of great profits and of great losses which do not exist for the second (VIII, 12).

A venturesome population will prefer the first, a cautious population, the second; consequently, because of the difference in the demand for these two uses of capital, the net revenues can cease to be equal. A venturesome people will more readily buy shares of industrial companies than government bonds; and a frugal-minded and economically timid people will do the opposite. Thus it can happen that in real life industrial enterprises will have a small advantage, or a slight disadvantage.

69. Experience alone can enlighten us. Very fortunately the statistics worked out with great care by the *Moniteur des intérêts matériels* enable us to get an empirical notion of the phenomenon.

Using official documents, this excellent publication has patiently investigated the fate of Belgian joint stock companies created between 1873 and 1887. There are 1,088 of them with a total capital of 1,605.7 million. We must deduct 112.6 million not paid in; thus a total initial capital of 1,493.1 million remains.

Of these companies, 251, with a capital of 256.2 million, have disappeared, and it is no longer possible to find a trace of them; it is probable that all their capital has been lost. Ninety-four, with a capital of 376.5 million, have been liquidated, after having lost, it seems, all their capital. The following companies have also liquidated: 340, with a capital of 462.4 million, have repaid in the neighborhood of 337.0 million; 132, with a capital of 166.8 million, have liquidated with a profit, and paid back 177.5 million. The total of reimbursements is 514.5 million. Of the capital put into the companies, 978.6 million, part of which has been lost and part of which still existed in 1901, has not been repaid. This totals to the original, as above, 1,493.1 million.

The total income obtained by the surviving companies is 55.9 million per year; comparing this to the original capital, we see that in the final analysis the latter has yielded 5.7 percent.

We are not far from the income which can be obtained from a simple money loan.

The net income must be less than what we have found, because it is necessary to deduct from these receipts of 55.9 million, amortization charges and insurance premiums, the precise value of which is unknown. But counting the return at 5.7 percent, we know that from 1873 to 1886 there have been numerous opportunities for purchasing securities issued by perfectly solvent nations so as to obtain an income of 4 to 5 percent. We see, then, that in Belgium the income from savings put into joint stock companies is about equal to that which would have been obtained by purchasing government bonds of countries with good credit standing.

We must note also that the income of some of these companies, for example the mining companies, includes the income of the landowner [*propriétaire*].

Even if, in order to make allowance for the uncertain character of the statistics, we assume that the 251 companies which have disappeared without leaving any trace have paid back half of their capital—and anyone who has had any experience on the exchange knows how improbable is this hypothesis—the net income is less than 6.6 percent; consequently the difference from the average income from a simple loan is not great, if anything.

These results are confirmed by other statistics published by the same journal on January 31, 1904.

From 1888 to 1892, 522 joint stock companies were established in Belgium, with a capital, from the last balance sheet, of 631.0 million francs. 37.3 million remain to be paid in; the paid-up capital is, then, 593.8 million.

There is no more information about 98 companies having a capital of 114.3 million. Let us assume that they have paid back half of their capital, that is, 57.6 million; 38 companies, with a capital of 51.7 million, of which 4.0 million remained to be paid in, have been liquidated, with a gain of 3.6; they have thus paid back 51.3. Ninety-five companies, with a capital of 94.7, of which 3.1 remained to be paid in, have been liquidated with a loss of 18.6; hence they have paid back 73.0. Five other companies have liquidated with a trifling loss, and have paid back 35.5. The total reimbursements are 216.4. Hence a capital of 377.4 million remains.

The annual profit was 12.5 million, hence the return was 5.9 percent.

Naturally, if the enterprises which are experiencing losses and disappearing are not taken into account, the return is larger; and this fact is the reason for the preconceived opinion according to which, where there is competition, enterprises obtain a profit considerably greater than the current net return of capital. This preconception is further reinforced because of confusing the profit of the enterprise with the income of the owner [*propriétaire*], or with the income from certain monopolies, or from patents for inventions, etc.

The average of the returns is obtained from the total of high returns and low ones. In its issue of March 31, 1901, the publication which we have cited calculated these returns for diverse enterprises. For banks they vary between 10.7 and 1.8 percent; for railroads, between 20.4 and 1.6 percent; for tramways between 9.6 and 0.8 percent; for coal mines between 17.8 (leaving out an exceptional case in which it was 38.3 percent) and 0.86 percent; for iron works and machinery between 12.9 and 2.1 percent; for zinc products, between 30.9 (Vieille Montagne) and 11.8; for linen factories, between 16.5 and 0.66 percent; for glass works, between 13 and 3.1 percent. All these returns have been calculated with reference to the authorized capital.

To sum up, abstracting from all theory and making the greatest allowance for the imperfections and lack of certainty in the statistics, the facts show that, at least in Belgium, enterprises, where there is free competition, obtain on their capital, on the average, a net return which does not differ much from the current return from loans, if for that matter, these two types of return are not almost equal.

The facts, then, correspond fairly well to the logical deductions.

70. **Variability of the coefficients of production.** We have already noted (§ 15) the error in thinking that the coefficients of production depend solely on the technical conditions of production.

Another completely erroneous theory is that called *definite proportions*. This name is singularly ill chosen, for it is borrowed from chemistry, which indeed has recognized that elements combine in strictly defined proportions. But, much to the contrary, the factors of production of political economy can, within certain limits, combine in any proportions whatsoever. Two units of hydrogen combine with one unit of oxygen to give water, but it is impossible to obtain combinations containing two and one-tenth units, two and two-tenths units, etc., of hydrogen for one unit of oxygen. On the other hand, if within a given industry 20 of labor are combined with 10 of mobile capital, you will find in the same industry slightly different proportions, such as 21, 22, etc., of labor for 10 of mobile capital.

But let us not dwell on that. The names of things are not of importance; the things themselves are what we must study.

The majority of economists who make use of the theory of *definite proportions* appear to believe that there are certain proportions in which it is proper to combine the factors of production, independently of the prices of these factors. That is false. Where labor is cheap and mobile capital is dear, labor will replace machines, and *vice versa*. There is no objective property of the factors of production corresponding to fixed proportions in which it is appropriate to combine these factors; there are only proportions, varying with the prices, which give certain profit maxima, either in *numéraire* or in ophelimity.

That is not all. These proportions vary not only with the prices of the factors of production, they also vary with all the circumstances of economic equilibrium.

Ask a chemist in what proportions hydrogen combines with chlorine; he will answer you without hesitation. Ask an entrepreneur in what proportions labor and mobile capital must be combined to transport some freight; he will not be able to answer you if you do not proceed to tell him the price of the labor and the price of the mobile capital. That will not be enough. He will also want to know the quantity of goods to be transported, the distance which it must be moved, and a multitude of other similar circumstances.

These considerations are general for all kinds of production. Save for exceptional cases, there are no fixed proportions which must be assigned to the coefficients of production to obtain maximum profits in *numéraire*, rather these proportions vary not only with the prices but also with all the other circumstances of production and consumption.

Naturally, there are limits beyond which the variability of the coefficients of production can not extend. For example, however improved the extraction process used, it is certain that there can never be extracted from an ore more metal than it contains. By improved processes of cultivation, 40 hectolitres of wheat may be obtained from one hectare of ploughed land which had been yielding only 10; but, at least in the present state of things, one certainly cannot obtain 100.

Technical conditions establish limits within which the determination of the coefficients of production is an economic problem.

In sum, these coefficients cannot be determined independently of the other unknowns of economic equilibrium; they are in a relation of mutual dependence with the other quantities which determine economic equilibrium.[7]

In matters of production the principal object of the enterprise is to determine the coefficients of production in keeping with all the other technical and economic conditions.

71. We must distinguish here two types of phenomena, just as we did for the consumer and for the producer (III, 40). Type I is the one which enterprises generally follow at present. They make their calculations according to the prices which prevail in the market, with no other objective; it would be impossible for them to act otherwise. Assume that an enterprise sees that, at market prices, it would obtain a lower cost of production by decreasing the quantity of labor and increasing the quantity of mobile capital (machines, etc.). It sets out on this path without further ado. In reality, the increase in demand for savings may raise its price; the decrease in demand for labor may lower its price. But the enterprise has no criterion for assessing these effects, even by a rough approximation, and it refrains from all conjecture about them. Moreover, whatever be the reasons for the phenomenon, it is enough to observe how any enterprise whatsoever operates in order to see that such is indeed the case. If some day the trusts invade a large part of production, this state of things will be able to change, and many industries will follow Type II in the determination of production coefficients. Matters are not at such a point as to permit many enterprises to follow Type II in the sale of their products.

---

[7] The literary economists—being not only incapable of solving the system of simultaneous equations which alone allows one to acquire an idea of the mutual dependence of economic phenomena, but even of merely comprehending what it is—make superhuman efforts to treat separately phenomena which they do not know how to consider in their state of mutual dependence. This is the reason why they have conceived vaguely metaphysical theories of *value*; this is the reason why they have attempted to *determine* selling price by cost of production; this is the reason why they have created the theory of *definite proportions*; and again this is the reason why they continue to propound a mass of erroneous propositions.

Here we are only speaking of persons who wish to deal with questions of pure economics without having the knowledge which is indispensable for doing so. Nothing is farther from our thought than to deprecate the work of economists who deal with questions of applied economics in non-theoretical studies. One can be an eminent engineer and have only very superficial notions about integral calculus; but in that case he will be wise to refrain from writing a treatise on the calculus.

It must be added that there are mathematicians, wishing to deal with questions of pure economics without having the necessary economic knowledge, who fall into errors comparable to those of the literary economists.

72. It is very important to understand the operations performed by the enterprise. It bases its calculations on market prices, and it alters its demands for economic goods and for labor accordingly. But these changes in demand modify the prices; the calculations made are no longer correct; the enterprise redoes them on the basis of the new prices; again, the changes in the enterprise's demands, and in those of others which are doing the same thing, modify the prices; the enterprise must again redo its calculations of costs, and so on, until, after successive attempts, it finds the position where its cost of production is a minimum.[8]

73. As we have seen in similar cases (III, 122), even the producer who would not want to follow Type I is obliged to do so by competition. For example it could happen that an enterprise refrains from increasing the labor which it employs for fear of causing its price to increase; but what that enterprise does not do, a competing enterprise will do, and the first will finally have to do the same if it does not want to find itself worse off and ruined.

74. It must be noted then, that with competition pushing enterprises onto the line of complete transformations, the result actually is (if the phenomenon is considered on the average and for a very long period) that it is the consumers who end up by gaining the largest part of the benefit resulting from all this effort of business.

In this way competing enterprises end up where they certainly had not intended to go (§ 11). Each of them seeks only its own advantage, and cares about consumers only insofar as it can exploit them; but, nevertheless, as a result of all of these successive adaptations and readaptations forced on them by competition, all this activity of the enterprises redounds to the profit of the consumers.

75. If any one of these enterprises were to gain nothing from these operations it would not behave that way for very long. But in real life the most shrewd and most diligent do make a profit, for a certain time and until the point of equilibrium is reached, while those which are more lackadaisical and less qualified have losses and are ruined.

76. There are certain relationships between the coefficients of production which permit compensating a decrease in some by an increase in others; but that is not true for all the coefficients. For example, in agriculture one can offset, within certain limits, a decrease in the cultivated area by an increase in mobile capital and labor, and still obtain the same product. But it is quite obvious that the same wheat production could not be maintained by increasing

---

[8] *Cours*, § 718.

the granaries and decreasing the area cultivated. A jeweler may increase his labor as he will, but he will never be able to recover more than one kilogram of gold from one kilogram of gold jewelry of the same fineness.

77. There are also cases where such compensation is theoretically, but not economically, possible; but it is quite useless to consider all the relationships between the coefficients of production which do not appear among practical possibilities. For example, it is useless to investigate whether the labor necessary to tin copper saucepans can be decreased by using gold ones. But if silver continues to fall in price, one could visualize the substitution of silver saucepans, or silver plated copper saucepans, for copper ones.

78. **Division of production among enterprises.** The cost of production does not depend only on the quantities transformed, it also depends on the number of producers or enterprises. For each of the latter there are fixed expenses [*frais généraux*] which must be distributed over its output; furthermore, the size of the enterprise alters the technical and economic conditions of production.

79. Some have assumed that the greater their output the better off enterprises would be, and this notion has given rise to a theory according to which competition must end up with the establishment of a small number of large monopolies.

The facts are not in accord with this theory. It has long been known that in agriculture there are, for each type of production, certain limits to the size of the enterprise which it is not appropriate to exceed. For example, the cultivation of the olive tree in Tuscany and raising cattle in Lombardy are two completely different types of enterprise. The large Lombard farmers would have nothing to gain by leasing the olive land of Tuscany, where *metayage* continues to flourish.

Numerous facts have shown, for industry and commerce, that consolidation of enterprises beyond certain limits is more detrimental than useful. Some said that in Paris the large stores would end by combining into only one; they have, on the contrary, multiplied and their number continues to grow. As for the American trusts, some have prospered, other have foundered with great losses.

80. We can accept it that, in general, for each type of production, there is a certain size of enterprise which corresponds to the minimum cost of production; consequently, production left to itself tends to be divided among firms of this size.

81. **General equilibrium of production.** For phenomena of Type I, we have already seen (III, 208) that equilibrium would

be determined by certain categories of conditions[9] which we designated by (D) and (E). The first, category (D), asserts that the costs of production are equal to the selling prices; the second asserts that the quantities demanded for transformation are the quantities actually transformed.

At bottom, the consideration of capital changes nothing in these conditions; the form alone is different, in that instead of only taking into account goods transformed, both goods and the services of capital are taken into account.

Note that it is not necessary that each good have its own cost of production. For example, wheat and straw are obtained at the same time, and we have a total cost of production. In this case certain relations exist which tell us the connections between goods linked in that way; for example, the quantity of straw obtained per unit of wheat is known. These relations are part of category (D) conditions.

82. We must now take the variability of the coefficients of production into account. Let us begin by assuming that the entire quantity of a good Y is produced by a single enterprise. In Type I phenomena, which we are studying at the moment, the enterprise accepts the prices in the market, and is governed by them in choosing the coefficients of production.

Assume that to produce that same quantity of Y, the enterprise is able—at the market prices, for example at a price of 5 francs a day for a workman—to decrease labor by 50 francs a day, provided it increases expenditures on machines by 40 francs a day; it is obvious that this entrepreneur will be interested in doing so.

But when, as a result of this choice, the demand for labor has decreased and that for machines has increased, the prices will change; the total quantity of good Y produced by the enterprise will likewise change because at the new price of Y a different quantity will be sold.

Again, given the new prices and the new total quantity of the good produced, the enterprise will redo its calculations. And this will continue until for certain prices and for certain quantities, the saving on labor will be equal to the increased expenditure on machines; at that time it will stop.

83. For Type II phenomena the procedure will be different. When it is a practical possibility, which is, however, not often, the

---

[9] There are some writers who confuse these conditions with theorems. They must certainly be very ignorant not to be able to distinguish between such different things.

changes in the prices and in the quantities are taken into account immediately. Consequently, in the preceding example, the enterprise will not base its computations on the assumption that the daily pay of the laborer will be 5 francs, but it will figure it, for example, at 4 francs 80, in order to make allowance for the fall in the price of a day's work which should follow the fall in the demand for labor; it will do the same for the machines, and also with regard to the quantity produced.

It is obvious that to be able to operate in this way, it is necessary to be able to calculate the variations in prices and in quantities; in real life one rarely can; moreover, this is just barely possible only in cases of monopoly. A farmer can easily calculate, at the market prices, whether it is more advantageous for him to use the power of a horse or that of a steam engine to run a pump; but neither he, nor anyone in the world, is capable of knowing either the effect the substitution of a steam engine for a horse will have on the prices of horses and steam engines, or the greater quantity of vegetables which will be consumed when consumers enjoy the savings resulting from that substitution.

84. Let us return to the case of phenomena of Type I. In general, there are many producers. Production is divided among them as we said in §§ 78 to 80, and then each of them determines the coefficients of production as if he were the only producer. If the division is changed, the calculations are redone with the new division, and so on.

85. The conditions thus obtained for the division, and the conditions for the determination of the coefficients of production, will form a category which we will call (F).

With regard to the determination of the coefficients of production, there will be the relations which exist between these coefficients, and then the designation of the coefficients which are constant; next come the conditions by virtue of which the values of these coefficients are determined so as to obtain the least possible cost of production (§ 82).

That the number of conditions (F) is equal to the number of unknowns to be determined is demonstrated in a manner similar to that which we used before.

86. For phenomena of Type II, conditions (D) are replaced, in part, namely, for enterprises which follow Type II, by other conditions which state that these enterprises extract the maximum profit from their monopolies. Generally this profit is expressed in *numéraire*. Conditions (E) do not change. Conditions (F) change, either because, as has been seen in § 83, the path followed is different,

or because there may be monopoly affecting certain factors of production or by certain enterprises.

87. In general, when we consider an entire economy and limit ourselves to the study of economic phenomena, without taking other social phenomena into account, we can say that the sum in *numéraire* of what enterprises sell is equal to the sum spent on consumption (savings being considered as a good), and that the sum of what enterprises purchase is equal to the sum of the incomes of the individuals in that economy.

88. **Production of capital.** The principles which we have just laid down are general and apply to all types of production, but one of the latter deserves separate consideration.

Capital goods are often produced by the enterprises which use them, but often also by other enterprises. These are goods which yield a profit only *via* the interest which they bring in; hence one who produces or buys them must pay a price equivalent to the interest, once equilibrium is established and if they operate according to Type I.

But under these conditions the selling price is equal to the cost of production, and in addition, there is only one price on the market for a given good. It follows from this that, under the above conditions, the net interest (§ 52) on all capital goods should be equal.

This conclusion is closely dependent upon the hypothesis that all these capital goods are produced at the same time.

We thus have, however, only the main part of the phenomena, in general, as when we say that the earth has a spherical form.

As a second approximation, it is necessary to set up large classes of capital keeping in mind qualifications of the type we have mentioned previously (§ 58 *et seq.*).

89. **Successive positions of equilibrium.** Let us consider a certain number of equal and successive periods of time. In general, the equilibrium position changes from one of these periods to another. Assume that a certain good A had a price of 100 in the first time period and that it had a price of 120 in the second. If in each time period the quantity of A consumed in that period is identical to the quantity produced, there would be nothing to say but this: the first portion of A is consumed at a price of 100 and the second at a price of 120. But if, at the end of the first time period, a certain amount of A (or all of A) is left over, the phenomenon becomes much more complex and gives rise to considerations of great importance.

The A which was left over had the price of 100; but it is now mingled with the new batch of A which has a price of 120, and as a result it also will have this price. Thus the owner of this left over quantity of A, whether it be a private individual or the collectivity, makes a profit equal to the difference in the prices, 20 that is, multiplied by the quantity left over. On the other hand, if the second price were lower than the first, there would be an analogous loss.

This profit, however, would be only nominal if all the prices of other goods had increased at the same rate; in order that the possession of A yield an advantage, compared to the possession of B, C, . . ., these rates must be different.

90. **Rent.** This phenomenon, while remaining basically the same, changes in form when the concept of capital is introduced.

Let A be a capital good. As we have seen in § 24, the accounts are set up so that it can be assumed that A is used without being consumed, that it is simply utilized. Consequently, the entire quantity of A remains after the first time period, not just part of it.

Let us begin by assuming that the net interest on capital is the same in the first time period and in the second, and that it is 5 percent, for example. This means that A, the price of which was 100 in the first time period, yielded 5 net; and that in the second time period, having a price of 120, it yields a net interest of 6.

Conversely, the prices can be deduced from the incomes. Let A be capital that is not produced, ground surface for example. In the first time period it yielded a net income of 5; we deduce from this that its price must have been 100. In the second time period it gives a net income of 6; we deduce from this that its price has become 120.

That is advantageous to one who possesses A; but if all the other capital goods have increased in price at the same rate there is no advantage in having A rather than B, C, . . . If, on the other hand, the prices of all capital goods have not increased at the same rate, the possession of one of them can be more or less advantageous than the possession of another one.

91. Let us assume that, on the average, all the prices of capital goods have increased by 10 percent; the price of A would be 110 instead of 100, and at 5 percent it ought to yield a net income of 5.5; consequently, compared to other capital, A yields 0.50 more net income. We will call this quantity the *rent acquired* in moving from one position to another.[10]

92. Let us assume next that the change also affects the rate of net interest; it was 5 percent in the first position, it becomes 6 percent

10 *Cours,* § 746 *et seq.*

in the second. In this case, A, which was worth 100 in the first position, yielded a net income of 5; being worth 120 in the second, it will yield 7.20 net interest. But let us assume that, on the average, the prices of all capital goods had increased by 10 percent. If A had been average it would have a price of 110 and would yield, at 6 percent, a net income of 6.6; however, it yields a net income of 7.20; the difference, that is, 0.60, indicates the profit of someone who possesses A, and it is the *rent acquired* in moving from the first position to the second.[11]

93. The *rent* of land, or Ricardian rent, is a particular case of the general phenomenon we have just studied.[12] It has given rise to endless unnecessary arguments. Whether landownership alone enjoyed this privilege has been investigated, and some have recognized that the phenomenon was more general; others have denied the existence of rent, with a view to defending the landowners; others, on the other hand, in order to attack them, have seen in rent the origin of all social evils.

94. Ricardo claimed that *rent* is not a part of the cost of production. First of all, this is an example of the current error which imagines that the cost of production of a good is independent of the totality of the economic phenomenon. If we overlook this point and examine the reasoning which is used to prove that rent is not part of the cost of production, we see that it comes down to the following propositions: 1° it is assumed that a good, wheat for example, is produced on lands of decreasing fertility; 2° it is assumed that the last portion of the good is produced on land which yields a zero rent. Since the good has only one price, it is determined by the equality of the cost of production and the selling price of this last portion, and this price obviously will not vary if, for the first portions, the rent, instead of being collected by the landowner, is collected by the entrepreneur; it simply will be a gift made to the latter.

95. It should be observed that often the second hypothesis is not correct, and that there can be a rent for all the landowners. Moreover, assuming that these hypotheses are correct, let us note that if the landowner were at the same time entrepreneur and consumer, the rent necessarily should be deducted from the cost of production. We have, for example, two plots of ground the first of which, with an expenditure of 100, produces 6 wheat, the second, 5; the price of wheat is 20 francs. The first plot has a rent of 20, the second

---

[11] The general notion, with algebraic symbols, is set forth in my *Cours*, § 747, note.

[12] *Cours*, § 753.

of zero. In an organization where there is an owner, an entrepreneur, and a consumer, the consumer pays 220 for 11 of wheat; of this amount 20 goes to the landowner as *rent*, 200 francs are expenses. The cost of production, for the entrepreneur, is equal to the selling price, it is 20.

If there is only a single person who is landowner, entrepreneur, and consumer, this quantity of 11 wheat is produced with an expense of 200, and each unit costs 18.18. The cost of production is no longer the same as before.

96. We must examine the relation between these particular cases and the general theory of production (III, 100).

Let us measure on *oy* [Figure 43] the values of different amounts of wheat, on *ox* the amounts of money which represent the expenses. Construct *oa* equal to *ab* equal to 100; *ah*, equal to 120, is the value of the wheat produced on the first piece of ground; *lk*, equal to 100, is the value of the wheat produced on the second piece of

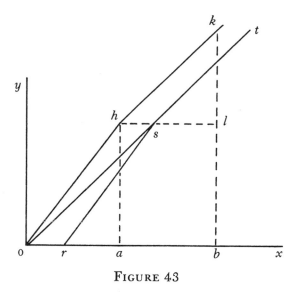

FIGURE 43

ground; *ohk* is the line of complete transformations. If we draw the line *ost* parallel to *hk*, *hs* will be equal to 20, the line *rst* is the indifference line of obstacles of index 20. It is the only one such that a rectilinear path from *o* can be tangent to an indifference line above *hl* (it merges with this line from *s* to *t*). There is a line of maximum profit, which is precisely *st*. Equilibrium will have to take place on this line. This is only repeating what we said in the preceding paragraphs.

97. When the landowner is also the entrepreneur and the consumer, he no longer consumes his wheat at the same price for all portions; he follows the line of complete transformations *ohk*, instead of following the line of constant prices *ost;* equilibrium takes place at a point on *hk*, instead of occurring at a point on *st*.

This phenomenon appears in much more general cases than the one which we have just treated, and we will study it in the following chapter.

CHAPTER VI

ECONOMIC EQUILIBRIUM

1. **Examples of equilibrium.** Let us begin by studying some
cases which are specific and as simple as possible.

Assume an individual who transforms wine into vinegar in the
ratio of one of wine for one of vinegar. We disregard all the other
expenses of production. Let $t, t', t'', \ldots$ [Figure 44] be indifference
curves of the individual's tastes for wine and vinegar, and let om
be the quantity of wine which he has at his disposal every month; we
will assume that it is 40 liters. We want to know where the point
of equilibrium is.

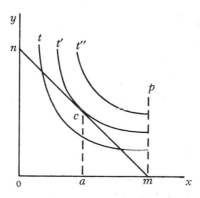

FIG. 44

The problem is extremely simple and is solved immediately.
From m draw the straight line mn inclined 45° with respect to the
ox axis; the point c where it is tangent to an indifference curve is the

251

point of equilibrium. The quantity of wine transformed is indicated by *am*, which is equal to *ac*, which indicates the quantity of vinegar obtained.

The cost of production of the vinegar, expressed in wine, is 1; and, when we draw the straight line *mn* inclined 45° with respect to the *ox* axis, we are assuming that the price of vinegar, expressed in wine, is 1.

2. We must see what becomes of the general theories in the different specific cases which we study.

The indifference lines of obstacles are parallel straight lines inclined 45° with respect to the *ox* axis [Figure 45]. In effect, whatever be the quantity of wine which one has at his disposal, a large or a small part of it can always be transformed into vinegar in the ratio of one of wine to one of vinegar. The indifference line *oh* has an index of zero; it is the line of complete transformations. If we set

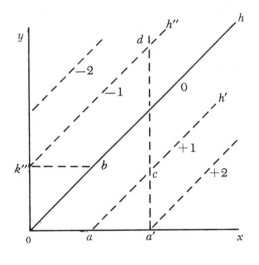

Fig. 45

oa equal to 1, the straight line *ah'* parallel to *oh* will be the indifference line with a positive index of one. Specifically, if one has the quantity of wine *oa'*, equal to 2, and if in the transformation we stop at *c*, on the straight line *ah'*, we will have transformed one of wine into one of vinegar, and we will have a positive residue equal to one of wine. If *k"b*, parallel to *ox*, is equal to one, the straight line *k"h"*, parallel to *oh*, will be an indifference line of index minus one. Specifically, if having 2 of wine, we stop at *d* on that line, we ought to have 3 of vinegar, but we lack 1 of wine in order to get that quantity.

3. The case which we are examining is a limiting case. If the straight line *oh* were moved to the left, it would be a case of goods with increasing cost of production (III, 102); if it were moved to the right, it would be a case of goods with decreasing cost of production. In our case, the cost of production is constant, neither increasing nor decreasing. The straight line *oh* is not only the line of complete transformations, it is also its own tangent. Moreover, if we superimpose Figure 44 onto Figure 45 making point *o* of Figure 45 coincide with point *m* of Figure 44 and the *ox* and *oy* axes of Figure 45 coincide with *mp* and *mo* of Figure 44, the straight line *oh* of Figure 45 will coincide with the straight line *mn* of Figure 44, and it will designate the sole path travelled in the production and consumption.

4. Let us modify the conditions of the problem a little. Assume that the ratio of the quantity of wine to the quantity of vinegar obtained (the price of vinegar in terms of wine) is not constant. For example, the transformation expenses which we had disregarded are taken into account. Each week 14 litres of wine are given to a man who furnishes the cask and tools and labor to obtain this output. In this way, up to 60 litres can be transformed into vinegar. Furthermore, let us separate the producer from the consumer. There will be a man who produces the vinegar and sells it to the consumer and who gets paid in wine.

Graphically, in superimposing the figure for production onto that for consumption [Figure 46], we will make *om* equal to 40 litres of wine, *mh* equal to 14, and we will draw the straight line *hk* inclined 45° with respect to *mo*;[1] this will be the indifference line of zero index, that is, the line of complete transformations. If the line of exchanges of the individual under consideration is *acdc'*, its intersections *c* and *c'* with the line of complete transformations will be points of equilibrium.

5. If there is only one producer and if he can act according to Type II, he will try to obtain the maximum profit, and the equilibrium point will be the point *d*, where the line of exchanges is tangent to the straight line *h'k'* parallel to *hk*.

6. If there is competition, the producer will not be able to stay at *d* and he will be pushed back onto the line *hk*.

---

[1] Due to lack of space, the point *e* has been placed on the figure between *c* and *c'*; in reality, it ought to be found beyond *c'*, going from *c* toward *c'* on the straight line *hk*. [But see § § 7 and 9 below.]

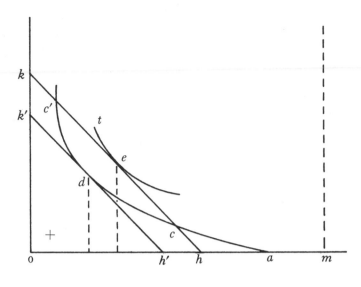

FIG. 46

7. If the consumer is the same person as the producer and if he has not decided *a priori* on the route to follow (Appendix), he follows the line of complete transformations, without being concerned about anything else, and he stops at the point *e*, Figure 46, where this line is tangent to an indifference curve of tastes, *t*. The point *e* differs from points *c* and *c'* because the types of paths followed are different.

In exchange at constant prices, the paths followed are *mc*, *mc'*. When the producer is also the consumer, the path followed is the bent line *mhe* (V, 97).

8. This route could also be followed in exchange. For example, an innkeeper is paid by his customers: 1° a fixed sum for his overhead expenses and his profit, and 2° the direct [*simple*] cost of the food which he furnishes them.[1] In this case the buyer follows a route similar to *mhk*.

9. Let us note that the point *e* is higher than the points *c* and *c'*, that is to say, the customer enjoys more ophelimity at *e* than at *c* and *c'*.

This may be verified in practice, without any theorizing. An innkeeper gets paid 4 francs for a bottle of wine, 2 francs of this for his overhead expenses and his profit, and 2 francs for the wine. A customer drinks only one bottle because he would be willing to spend

2 francs for a second bottle but not 4. But suppose the innkeeper changes his way of doing business. First of all he gets paid 2 francs by each customer; then he gives them as many bottles as they desire at a price of 2 francs. The customer we are considering will drink two bottles. Consequently, he will get more pleasure, while the innkeeper will make as much as before.

10. Let us return to the case of the producer who has the power to compel the consumers to descend as far as d. Assume that there is a syndicate which prohibits the producers from accepting a price below that which corresponds to the point d, or to another point between d and c. Competition can no longer operate as above. The profit which the producers obtain at d induces other producers to share in it; the number of producers increases, and since each of them must get his own livelihood out of the production, the cost of production necessarily increases. In other words, the line of complete transformations hk is displaced and ends up by passing through the point to which the producers restrict themselves. This phenomenon has become common in certain countries, where a large number of people, thanks to the syndicates, are living as parasites on production.

11. The case which we have just considered is a simplified version of very common phenomena which occur when the overhead expenses are distributed over the output in such a way that the cost of one unit of output falls as production increases, within certain limits of course.

12. Let us see how things take place for another class of goods whose cost of production increases when the quantity produced increases.

For example, let us assume that with 1 of A we at first obtain 2 of B, and then, for each unit of A, one unit of B. The costs will be the following:

A transformed	B produced	Cost of B in A
1	2	0.500
2	3	0.667
3	4	0.750
4	5	0.800

Graphically [Figure 47], if we set mh equal to one, hl equal to two, and draw the straight line lk, inclined 45° with respect to mo, the bent line hlk will be the line of complete transformations; the other indifference lines will be given by lines parallel to hlk. If the angle at l is rounded off a little, we will have at the same point l the

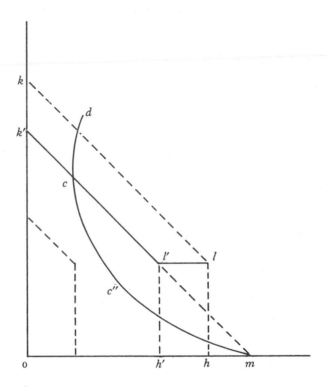

Fig. 47

point of tangency of the path ml and an indifference line. Joining these points of tangency, we will get the line ll'. Then if $k'l'$ passes through m, the rectilinear path starting from m and tangent to the indifference curve $h'l'k'$ will coincide with the same straight line $l'k'$. Consequently, the *locus* of the points of tangency, that is, the line of maximum profit (III, 105), will be the bent line $ll'k'$. Its point of intersection c with the line of exchanges mcd will give a point of equilibrium.

The producer naturally would like to go a little farther on the side of the positive indices. For example, he would be better off at the point c''; but he is driven along by competition, as we have already seen (III, 137).

13. In this case competition may also have another effect, as we have already shown for goods with a decreasing cost of production (§ 10). It may, without changing the prices, increase the number

of competitors, and consequently, increase the cost of production. Thus the line of maximum profit shifts and ends up by passing through the point where the producers stand firm at a price fixed by their syndicate, or determined some other way.

Equilibrium will again take place on this line. The producers approach this line if competition affects the prices; it moves toward the producers if competition operates so as to increase the number of producers and the expenses of production.

14. All this corresponds to reality. Given the economic circumstances of a country, there is a certain output of wheat per hectare which, for a fixed amount of land, corresponds to the maximum profit; the producer stops at that output. The price is determined by the equality of the cost of production, profit included, and the price which the consumer is willing to pay for the quantity produced in these circumstances. Naturally, the producer would want to obtain a higher price, but competition prevents that.

15. Current economics has been aware of the differences between the cases we have examined, but it has never arrived at a precise notion of them; and it would not even know how to explain the different ways in which competition operates.

16. If in the hypothetical case which we have just considered some persons act according to Type II, the equilibrium point will be l'' where the line of exchanges mcd is tangent to a producer's indifference curve, because that is the point where there is maximum profit. If the shape of mcd were a little different, this point could be in the vicinity of l'.

17. If the consumer is also the producer, he will follow the line of complete transformations hlk, and the equilibrium point will be given by the point of tangency of this line and an indifference line of tastes.

18. There could also be consumers able and willing to force the producers to follow rectilinear paths which, starting from m, meet the line of complete transformations. In this case the equilibrium point would be at l (§ § 43-47).

19. **The usual shapes of curves in exchange and production.** We can conceive of very strange shapes for the indifference curves of tastes and of obstacles; and it would be difficult to prove that they never have existed or that they never will exist. Obviously we must limit ourselves to considering those which are the most common.

20. Among widely used commodities, only for labor is it observed, in practice, that, beyond a certain limit, supply decreases instead of increasing with price. In all the civilized countries, the

increase in wages has resulted in a decrease in the hours of labor. For other goods, we almost always observe that the supply increases at the same time as the price; perhaps such is the case because we look at the law of supply in production rather than the law of supply in simple exchange.

21. At any rate, save for labor, we cannot claim that in real life we will find exchange curves with shapes such as those of Figure 17 (III, 120). On the contrary, they appear to have shapes similar

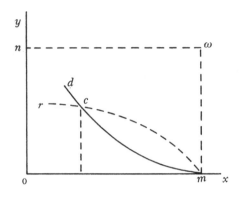

FIG. 48

to those of Figure 48. The exchange curve relative to the ox and oy axes is mcd; similarly this curve, for another individual, referred to the ωm and ωn axes is mcr. This is true within the limits of observations, which are, moreover, narrow. We do not know what becomes of these curves beyond d and r.

22. In these circumstances there is only one point of equilibrium, at c; and it is a point of stable equilibrium.

23. In production, we observe many examples of goods of decreasing cost and others of increasing cost; but it seems that beyond certain limits the cost, which at first decreases, always ends up by increasing. For these goods there are points of tangency of rectilinear paths starting from m, and consequently there is a line $l'll''$ of maximum profit [Figure 49]. If we only observed the phenomena in the hatched part of the figure, where the costs are always decreasing with the increase of the quantity transformed, this line $l'll''$ would not exist.

24. For goods of decreasing cost, we observe, in real life, the two equilibrium points given by the theory, Figure 46 (§ 4), but there

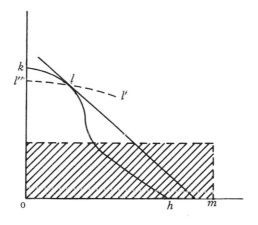

FIG. 49

are powerful frictions which occasionally permit an unstable equilibrium to last a fairly long time.

A railroad can offset its expenses with high rates and little traffic, or with low rates and much traffic. In that way we get the two points c and c' of Figure 46 (§ 4). Small shopkeepers stick to the point c, selling at high prices; the larger stores have carried the point of equilibrium to c', by selling at low prices; and now the small shopkeepers demand the intervention of law to bring the point of equilibrium back to c.

25. There are also numerous examples of the line of maximum profit for goods of increasing cost. Extensive cultivation in the vicinity of Rome cannot be explained otherwise. In England, due to the competition of foreign grain after the removal of the corn duties, the shapes of the indifference curves of obstacles with reference to the cultivation of grain changed, and, within certain limits, the cost of production of grain has fallen, instead of increasing, with the quantity produced. Hence the change in the cultivation of grain, which then became more intensive.

26. **The equilibrium of tastes and production.** Let us consider a closed economy [*collectivité isolée*] and assume that the individual's expenditures are all made on goods which he purchases, and that his receipts all come from the sales of his labor, services of capital, or other goods.

In these circumstances economic equilibrium is determined by the conditions which we have already set forth (III, 196 *et seq.*)

with regard to tastes and obstacles. We have seen that tastes, and the consideration of the existing quantities of certain goods, determine the relationships between prices and the quantities sold or purchased. Furthermore, the theory of production tells us that, given these relationships, the quantities and the prices are determined. The problem of equilibrium is thus completely solved.

27. **Equilibrium in general.** The theoretical case above differs greatly from reality in one respect. Actually, the receipts of the individual are far from having their origin only in goods which that individual sells for production. The public debt of civilized peoples is enormous; only a very small part of that debt has been used in production, and often very poorly. The individuals who enjoy the interest on that debt certainly cannot then be considered as persons who have surrendered economic goods to production. Similar observations could be made with regard to the salaries of the ever increasing bureaucracy of modern states, with regard to expenditures on war, naval forces, and many of the expenditures on public works. We are not investigating here whether, and in what measure, these expenditures are more or less useful to society, and in which cases they are indispensable to it; we simply claim that their utility, when it exists, is a different species from that which results from economic production.

28. Furthermore, the expenditures of individuals are far from being restricted to the economic goods which they purchase. Taxes make up an appreciable part of them.

By a very rough calculation, but one which is perhaps not so very far from the truth, it is estimated that in certain countries of Europe about 25 percent of the income of individuals is taken by taxes. Hence the theory which we have expounded would only be of value for at most three-fourths of the total income of a nation.

29. It is easy to modify that theory so as to make allowance for the phenomena we have just pointed out. To do so it is sufficient to distinguish the part of individuals' incomes which comes from economic phenomena and the part which does not, and to do the same for their expenditures.

30. The part of the income which is left to the individuals is spent by them in accordance with their tastes; and its allocation among the various expenditures comes within the theory of equilibrium regarding tastes which we have already given. The part taken by the public authority is spent according to other rules which economic science does not have to study. Economic science should assume that these rules are part of the given data of the problem

to be solved. The laws of demand and supply will follow from the consideration of both of these categories of expenditures. If only one of them alone were to be considered, the divergence from the concrete phenomenon could be considerable. For example, for iron and steel the demands of government involve a considerable part of the output.

31. So far as the equilibrium of obstacles is concerned, allowance must be made for the fact that the expenditure by the enterprises is not equal to the total income of the individuals as before, but that the former constitutes only a part of the latter since the rest has another origin (public debt, government salaries, etc.). The allocation of the part destined to purchase goods transformed by production is determined by the theory of equilibrium with reference to obstacles. The allocation of the other part of incomes is determined by considerations which, as in the analogous case above, lie outside the investigations of economic science, and which consequently must be borrowed from other sciences; hence this allocation should appear among the given data of the problem.

32. **Properties of equilibrium.** Depending on the conditions in which it occurs, equilibrium possesses certain properties which it is important to be familiar with.

33. We will begin by defining a term which is desirable to use in order to avoid prolixity. We will say that the members of a collectivity enjoy *maximum ophelimity* in a certain position when it is impossible to find a way of moving from that position very slightly in such a manner that the ophelimity enjoyed by each of the individuals of that collectivity increases or decreases. That is to say, any small displacement in departing from that position necessarily has the effect of increasing the ophelimity which certain individuals enjoy, and decreasing that which others enjoy, of being agreeable to some and disagreeable to others.

34. **Equilibrium in exchange.** We have the following theorem:

For phenomena of Type I, when equilibrium takes place at a point where the indifference curves of the contracting parties are tangent, the members of the collectivity under consideration enjoy maximum ophelimity.

Let us note that this position of equilibrium can be reached either by a rectilinear path, that is, with constant prices, or by any path whatsoever.

35. A rigorous demonstration of this theorem can only be given with the help of mathematics (Appendix); here we shall merely give a sketch of it.

Let us begin by considering exchange between two individuals [Figure 50]. The axes are ox and oy for the first, and ωa and $\omega \beta$ for the second. Now let us arrange them so that the paths traveled by the two individuals merge into a single line as in Figure 16 (III, 116). The indifference lines are $t, t', t'', \ldots$ for the first individual, and $s, s', s'', \ldots$ for the second. For the first one the hill of pleasure rises from o toward ω, and for the second, on the other hand, it rises from ω toward o.

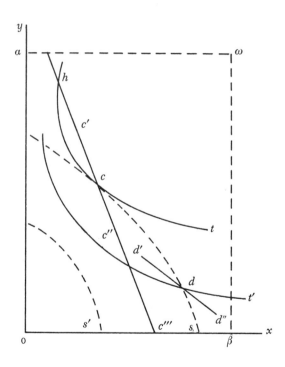

FIG. 50

For phenomena of Type I, we know that the equilibrium point must be at a point of tangency of the indifference curves of the two individuals. Let c be one of these points. If we move away from it following the route cc', we ascend the first individual's hill of pleasure and descend that of the second; and conversely, if we follow the route cc''. Hence it is not possible to move away from c helping, or harming, both individuals at one and the same time; but necessarily, if it is agreeable to the one, it is disagreeable to the other.

It is not the same for points, such as d, where two indifference curves intersect. If we follow the route dd' we increase the satisfaction of both individuals; if we follow the line dd'' we decrease it for both.

36. For phenomena of Type I equilibrium occurs at a point such as c; for phenomena of Type II, equilibrium occurs at a point such as d; therein lies the difference between these two types of phenomena so far as maximum ophelimity is concerned.

37. Returning to Figure 50, we see intuitively that, in extending the path cc' towards h, we always descend the second individual's hill of pleasure, whereas on the other hand, we do begin by climbing the first individual's hill of pleasure, but then we descend when we are beyond the point where $cc'h$ is tangent to an indifference line. Consequently, if we move away from the position of equilibrium a finite distance along a straight line, the ophelimities which the two individuals enjoy can vary in such a way that the one increases while the other decreases, or so that they both decrease together; but they cannot increase together. That is only true, however, for goods whose ophelimities are independent, or in the cases where these goods have a dependence of the first kind (IV, 42).

Mathematics alone (Appendix) enables a rigorous proof to be given, not only in this case, but also in the general case of several goods and several individuals.

38. If we were able to conduct experiments on human society such as the chemist performs in his laboratory, the preceding theorem would enable us to solve the following problem:

A given collectivity is considered; the indices of ophelimity of its members are unknown; it is known that with the exchange of certain quantities there is equilibrium; we ask whether the conditions in which it is obtained are those of free competition?

It is necessary to perform an experiment in order to see whether, the manner in which exchanges are made remaining the same, we can add (note carefully: add and not substitute) other exchanges, made at constant prices, which satisfy all the individuals. If so, equilibrium does not occur as in free competition; if not, it does so occur.

39. **Equilibrium in production.** We must distinguish several cases here:

1° *Selling prices constant.* (a) Coefficients of production variable with total output, that is, goods whose cost of production varies with output. (β) Coefficients of production constant with respect to output, that is, goods whose cost of production is constant. 2° *Selling prices variable.*

40. 1° (*a*). This case is given by Figure 46 (§4). The equilibrium points *c* and *c'* are not those which give maximum ophelimity for this transformation (Appendix). Consequently, there can be a point which is not on the line of complete transformations and such that the transforming enterprise has a profit there, while the consumers are better off than at *c* or *c'*. This case, in real life, is occasionally encountered with trusts.

41. 1° (*β*). This is the case of Figure 44 (§1). The equilibrium point *c* gives the maximum ophelimity for the transformations (Appendix).

42. 2° The variable prices can be such that they produce a phenomenon analogous to that of case 1° (*a*).

But if these prices can be arranged to obtain the maximum ophelimity for the transformations, we thereby can reach the point *e*, Figure 51, which gives this maximum (Appendix).[2]

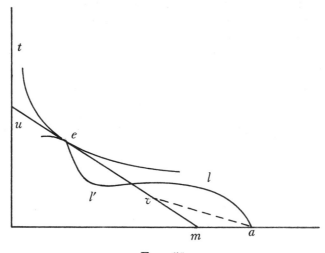

FIG. 51

43. One certainly arrives there if the path of complete transformations, *amu*, is followed; similarly if we follow a path *avu*, which coincides with that line only along the segment *veu*; or finally a path *all'e* tangent at *e* to the line of complete transformations and to the indifference line *t*.

In reality, this last path is very difficult to follow because it is necessary to surmise precisely where point e is located; on the other hand, the first two paths can be followed without knowing precisely where point e is.

44. It is probable that the greatest part of production is of the type in which the cost of production varies with the quantity produced; consequently we can assert that the system of constant prices, which is generally used in our society, does not yield maximum ophelimity; and if we take into account the great number of products to which this conclusion applies, it appears that the loss of ophelimity must be very great.

45. It is because of this that, even in our social organization, producers benefit from the use of variable prices; and since they cannot do it directly, they endeavour to do it indirectly by expedients which can only very roughly approach the solution which would give maximum ophelimity.

Generally, variable prices are achieved by dividing consumers into classes; this device is better than nothing, but it is far from the solution in which the prices for all consumers would vary.

46. The very serious error of judging economic facts according to moral standards leads many people, more or less consciously, to think that the profit of the producer can be only the loss of the consumer, and *vice versa*. Consequently, if the producer gains nothing, if he is on the line of complete transformations, it is imagined that the consumer cannot suffer any loss.

Without dwelling on the fact that, as we have already seen (§ 10), the line of complete transformations may be obtained with an excess cost of production, it is well not to forget the very frequent case indicated in § 39, 1° (a).

47. Assume, for example, that a country consumes 100 of a good X and that this good is produced by domestic factories at a cost of 5 per unit. The total cost is 500; and if the total selling price is also 500, the domestic producers make no profit.

Now assume that they produce 200, which lowers the cost of production to 3. They sell 120 within the country at a price of 3.50, and 80 abroad at a price of 2.50. In all they receive 620 for a good which costs them 600, and consequently they make a profit. The domestic consumers moan because they pay more for the good than foreigners do; but, at bottom, they pay less for it than they paid before, and consequently they profit rather than lose.

It is possible, but it is not certain, that a similar phenomenon occurs occasionally in Germany, where the producers sell abroad at a price below what they charge within the country, because in this way they can increase the quantity produced and reduce the cost of production.

48. The phenomena which we have just studied suggest, in an abstract way and without taking into account the practical difficulties, an important argument in favor of collectivist production. Much better than production partially subject to competition and partially to monopolies, which we have now, it could make use of variable prices which would permit the line of complete transformations to be followed, and consequently would permit point e of Figure 46 (§ 4) to be attained, whereas at present we have to stop at point c', or even at point c. The advantage which society would have could be so great that it would offset the inevitable harm arising from production of this kind. But to accomplish that the sole purpose of the collectivist production would have to be the pursuit of ophelimity in production, and not the procurement of monopoly profits for the workers, or the pursuit of humanitarian ideals.[2] As earlier economists had clearly seen, the study of greatest advantage for society is that of the problem of production.

Even cooperative societies could take us onto the line of complete transformations, but that does not happen because they allow themselves to be diverted from their purpose by ethical, philanthropic, and humanitarian views. One cannot pursue two hares at once.

If the phenomenon is considered from the point of view of economic theories exclusively, an arrangement for private enterprise in railroads which exacts from the companies which operate them, as has been done in Italy, a fixed charge on the gross receipts (or even on the net receipts) for the benefit of the state, is a poor one. This is because, instead of being induced to approach the line of complete transformations, they are prevented from doing so.

49. Free competition determines the coefficients of production in a way that assures maximum ophelimity (Appendix). It tends to equalize the net incomes of such capital as can be created by means of saving; indeed, savings obviously are transformed into that capital yielding the most income, until the abundance of such capital makes the net income from them fall to the common level. This equality of net incomes is likewise a condition for obtaining the maximum ophelimity from the use of such capital. Even in this

---

[2] Among the socialists, G. Sorel has the great merit of having understood that the problem which collectivism must solve is principally a problem of production.

case, rigorous proof can be given only with mathematics[3]; here we can only point out briefly the course taken by the phenomenon.

50. With regard to the income of capital, we can remark that if savings obtain a greater income in one use than in another, that signifies that the first use is more "productive" than the second. Consequently there is an advantage for "society" in decreasing the second use of savings in order to increase the first, and the equality of the net incomes is thereby achieved in the two cases. But this reasoning is certainly not very precise, not at all rigorous, and consequently it alone could indeed prove nothing.

51. Reasoning which, without making use of mathematics, brings in the coefficients of production is a little better, but not much so.

Enterprises determine them so as to achieve minimum cost; but competition drives them onto the line of complete transformations; consequently, it is those who buy from and sell to them, who after all benefit from the activity which the enterprises carry on.

The short-coming in proofs of this kind is not only that they lack precision, but also, and principally, that they do not give a clear idea of the conditions necessary for the theorems to be true.

52. **Equilibrium in the collectivist society.** We must now discuss phenomena of Type III, to which we have so far simply alluded (III, 49).

In order to give them a concrete form, and using an abstraction analogous to that of the *homo oeconomicus*, let us consider a collectivist society whose purpose is to procure maximum ophelimity for its members.

53. The problem is divided into two others which are completely different and which cannot be solved with the same criteria: 1° We have a problem of distribution: how should the goods which the society possesses or produces be divided among the members? (III, 12, 16). It is necessary to bring in different kinds of ethical and social considerations, comparisons of ophelimity of different individuals, etc. We do not have to deal with that here. Therefore we will assume this problem solved. 2° We have a problem of production: how to produce the economic goods in such a way that, distributing them according to the rules obtained by the solution of the first problem, the members of the society obtain maximum ophelimity.

---

[3] *Cours*, § 724.

54. After all that we have said, the solution of this problem is easy.

Prices and the net interest on capital can disappear as actual entities, if that is possible; but they will remain as accounting entities; without them the *ministry of production* would proceed blindly and would not know how to plan production. Plainly if the state owns all the capital, all net interest goes to it.

55. In order to obtain maximum ophelimity, the collectivist state will have to equalize the different net interests and determine the coefficients of production in the same way that free competition determines them. Moreover, after having made the distribution according to the rules from the first problem, it will have to permit a new distribution which the members of the collectivity can effect among themselves, or which the socialist state can make, but which, in any case, will have to be made as if it were effected by free competition.

56. Hence the difference between Type I phenomena and those of Type III rests principally in the distribution of incomes. In phenomena of Type I, this distribution takes place in accordance with all the historical and economic contingencies in which the society has evolved; in the phenomena of Type III, it is the result of certain ethico-social principles.

57. Furthermore, we must investigate whether certain forms of production are more easily brought about in real life with phenomena of Type I or with those of Type III. Theoretically, nothing prevents assuming, for example, that in free competition the line of complete transformations is followed, but in practice that may be more difficult with free competition than with collectivist production (§ 48).

58. The collectivist state, more so than free competition, appears to be able to carry the equilibrium point onto the line of complete transformations. Indeed, it is difficult for a private company to follow precisely the line of complete transformations in its sales. To do so, it first would have to charge its customers the overhead expenses, and then sell the goods at cost, overhead expenses excluded. Except for some special cases, we do not see how that could happen. On the other hand, the socialist state can levy, on the consumers of its goods, a tax equal to the overhead expenses of the production of that good, and then sell at cost; accordingly it can follow the line of complete transformations.

59. The socialist state can relinquish to the consumers of a good the rent (V, 95) produced by that good. When the maximum profit

line intersects the line of exchanges, that is, when competition is incomplete, and with simple competition of private producers, equilibrium takes place at this point of intersection. The socialist state can bring this equilibrium point back onto the line of complete transformations, as if competition were complete.

60. In the economic state based on private property, production is managed by entrepreneurs and property owners; hence there is a certain expense which is included in the obstacles. In the collectivist state, production would be managed by employees of that state; the expense which they would give rise to could be greater, and their work less efficient; in that case, the advantages pointed out could be offset and changed into a loss.

61. To sum up, pure economics does not give us a truly decisive criterion for choosing between an organization of society based on private property and a socialist organization. This problem can be solved only by taking other characteristics of the phenomena into account.

62. **Ophelimity maxima for segments of collectivities.** Phenomena of Type III may refer to a more or less restricted part, rather than the entire collectivity. If a single individual is considered, Type III merges into Type II.

For a certain number of individuals considered collectively, there are values of the coefficients of production which procure such quantities of economic goods for that collectivity that, if they are distributed according to rules determined in the problem of distribution, they provide maximum ophelimity for the members of that collectivity.[4]

The proof of this proposition is similar to that which was given when we considered the entire collectivity.

63. In real life, labor unions, producers who enjoy customs protection, and syndicates of merchants who exploit consumers, provide numerous examples in which the coefficients of production are determined with the purpose of favoring certain segments of collectivities.

64. It must be noted that, save for certain quite exceptional cases, these values of the coefficients differ, and often differ considerably, from the values which provide maximum ophelimity for the entire collectivity.

65. **International trade.** Except in the preceding case, we have up to now considered only closed [*isolées*] collectivities. In order to

---

[4] *Cours*, § 727.

move closer to reality, it is now necessary to consider collectivities with reciprocal relationships. This theory is called the theory of international trade, and we will preserve that name.

The preceding case differs from the present case. In the former it was assumed that certain coefficients of production could be imposed on the whole collectivity, made up of sub-collectivities A, B, C . . . ; and we sought the values of these coefficients which provide maximum ophelimity for the members of collectivity A. Now we do not assume that collectivity A can impose the coefficients of production on the other collectivities B, C, . . . directly, but, on the contrary, we assume that each of these collectivities is independent, and that consequently each one is able to regulate its own production, but not that of the others, not directly at least.

Even when we only study a single collectivity, it is necessary to take transportation expenses into account, but that necessity is still more obvious when one deals with collectivities separated in space. Consequently, it can be seen that the price of the same good is different in two different collectivities.

66. After what we have said for a single collectivity, the conditions of equilibrium for several collectivities are easily obtained.

Let us consider a collectivity X which deals with other collectivities which we will call Y, and which, for simplicity, we will regard as a single collectivity. For each of these collectivities, we already know the conditions of equilibrium of tastes and of obstacles; but now they are not enough to solve the problem because there are other unknowns, specifically the quantities of economic goods exchanged between X and Y. Assume there are 100 of them; then one hundred more conditions are needed in order to determine them.

67. First we will get the balance sheet of X for its dealings with Y; in order to set it up it will be necessary to account for each receipt and each expenditure, as we have pointed out in § 27 *et seq*. The balance sheet of Y is not necessary for reasons already given (III, 204). In the dealings between X and Y, the receipts of X are the expenditures of Y, and *vice versa*. Consequently, if receipts and expenditures balance for X, they balance for Y also. Hence consideration of the balance sheets gives us a single condition which we will call (*a*).

68. Next, the prices, taking into account transportation and other necessary expenditures (for example, insurance, exchange expenses, etc.), must be equal for the quantities exchanged, because there cannot be two prices on the same market. One of the goods may be chosen as an international money; consequently, in this case,

only 99 prices are left; hence the equality conditions, which we will call (β), are 99 in number.

If condition (α) is added to the 99 (β) conditions, we have 100 conditions in all, exactly what is necessary to determine the 100 unknowns.

69. But, in general, we cannot assume that there is only one money, identical for X and for Y. It must be assumed that X and Y have monies which are peculiar to themselves even when these are identical and are struck from the same metal. In this case, the money of Y has a certain relation to the money of X, that is, has a certain price expressed in the money of X, and this is an additional unknown. If it is added to the 100 others, we have 101 unknowns. But since we now have 100 prices, there are 100 (β) conditions, and by adding condition (α) there are 101 conditions, that is, as many conditions as unknowns.

It remains to be seen how equilibrium is established, but we will be able to do that only after the study of money (VIII, 35 *et seq.*).

70. **Equilibrium of prices.** In all our reasoning so far we have chosen one good as money; the rates of exchange of this good with the others, that is to say, the prices, depend on tastes and obstacles, and consequently are determined when the latter are.

There must be an initial modification of that theory due to the quantity of money in circulation. Indeed, it must be noted that the money-good has ophelimity not only in consumption, but also because it is used for currency. In order that all prices may increase by 10 percent, for example, it would be necessary not only that there occur a corresponding change in the ophelimity of the money-good, compared to the ophelimity of other goods, but also that there be enough money for circulation with the new prices.

71. **Quantity theory of money.** Let us assume that the quantity of money in circulation must vary proportionally with prices; this can be approximately so if, while prices change, the velocity of circulation does not change, and if the proportion of substitutes for money does not change either. This hypothesis is the basis of what has been called the quantity theory of money. If it is accepted, it would then be necessary, as prices increase 10 percent, that the quantity of the money-good increase in a way not only to enable it to be consumed in a greater quantity so that the elementary ophelimity decreases, but also in such a way that the quantity of money in circulation increases 10 percent.

Hence prices would be determined ultimately by the ophelimity of the money-good and by the quantity of it which would be in circulation.

72. If, instead of a good, we had for money any convenient thing whatsoever, for example paper money, all prices would depend only on the quantity of that money in circulation.

73. The hypotheses which we have just made are never fulfilled completely. Not only do all the prices not change at the same time in the same proportions, but in addition the velocity of circulation surely varies, and the proportion of money-substitutes also varies. It follows from this that the quantity theory of money can never be more than approximately and roughly true.

74. Thus in the case of paper money it is possible to have two positions of equilibrium for which all the circumstances are identical except for the following: 1° All prices are greater, by 10 percent for example, 2° the velocity of circulation is increased, and the proportion of substitutes for money may have increased also, so that the same quantity of money suffices for circulation with the new prices.

75. In the case of a money-good, it would be necessary that this velocity and this proportion of substitutes increase in such a way as to make the quantity in circulation excessive, so that the consumption of the money-good can increase in order to decrease the elementary ophelimity.

76. The hypothesis which we made regarding paper money can be fulfilled approximately; but the one which we made for the money-good seems difficult to verify in the proportions indicated although it may often occur in smaller proportions. We conclude that identical positions of equilibrium with different prices would be possible in the first case, impossible in the second.

77. This last conclusion is perhaps too categorical. It would be difficult to attack if the consumption of the money-good were nearly as great as the total of other consumption. Let us assume that in a collectivity of farmers who consume wheat, wine, oil, wool, and a few other goods, wheat is chosen as the money-good; the conclusion in question certainly would stand. But does it still stand if, as in our societies, the money-good is gold, consumption of which is very small in comparison with other consumption? It is difficult to see why all prices should be regulated in a precise and rigorous fashion by the consumption of gold in watch cases, jewelry, etc. The correspondence between these two phenomena cannot be perfect.

78. It must be noted that here we are leaving the domain of pure economics and entering that of applied economics. Similarly, rational

mechanics shows us that two equal and directly opposed forces are always in equilibrium, whatever be their intensity; but applied mechanics tells us that, if a solid body is moved in between these forces, allowance must also be made for the resistance of the materials.

79. Let us assume that, all other circumstances remaining the same, all prices increase by 10 percent. In order for the equality of the weighted ophelimities to establish the subsisting equilibrium, the quantity of gold which can be consumed must increase; and it is because that quantity cannot increase that the prices must return to what they were before. But the following facts must be noted here: 1° The equality of the weighted ophelimities does establish itself approximately for goods of extensive and daily use, not quite so well for goods of limited use and which are purchased only from time to time. Consequently, in real life, there is a certain leeway in the equality that the ophelimity of gold must have with the others. 2° If all prices increase, gold mining would have to become less profitable, and consequently decrease. But that mining is so uncertain that it is regulated by entirely different considerations; and, within certain limits, variations in the prices of other goods have no effect, or almost no effect. 3° Finally, a change in conditions regarding circulation may also have a certain action (§ 73). We conclude that with gold money, identical positions of equilibrium are possible, within certain limits, with different prices. Within these limits they then would no longer be completely and exclusively determined by the formulas of pure economics (§ 82).

80. **Relations between equilibrium and the prices of the factors of production.** 1° Let us assume that all the prices of the factors of production change, but that the existing indebtedness in the society (the public debt, commercial credit, mortgages, etc.) does not change. For example, if the prices of all the factors of production increase by 10 percent, the prices of products also increase by 10 percent; consequently, from this point of view, nothing would be changed in the real situation of the workers and of the capitalists who contribute to production. They receive 10 percent more and they spend 10 percent more for consumption. From another point of view their situation does change because, in continuing to pay the same nominal sum to their creditors, they in fact give up 10 percent less than before, in goods. Consequently, the assumed change favors those who take part in production, and harms those who have a fixed income independent of production. It is unnecessary to add that an opposite change would have opposite effects.

81. For the change in prices to be possible, it must not be constrained by money; hence we must repeat the considerations pointed out in § 71 *et seq*. In the case assumed, and when gold is the money, those who participate in production will consume perhaps (§ 79) a little more gold and those who have fixed incomes a little less; in total, there will be perhaps a small increase in its consumption, which will easily be furnished by the mines. Regarding circulation, its velocity may increase, and greater use could be made of substitutes if that is necessary. Prices, however, could not increase beyond certain limits, because the quantity of gold available would become insufficient.

82. In real life, the obstacles to price changes come from the competition of independent collectivities, either in the same country or abroad (international trade), and from the difficulty in making all prices move at the same time; consequently, those which do not change restrain the movement of the others. These are the things which, within the limits permitted by the forces which give rise to the variation in the consumption and production of gold (§ 79), determine prices.

83. If the prices of the majority or of all the goods of a country rise, exports decrease, imports increase, and gold leaves the country to go abroad; as a result, prices end up by falling and returning to their original state. The opposite facts can be shown in the case of a general decrease in prices.

84. 2° The prices of the factors of production never all change at the same time. Let us assume that wages increase by 10 percent; the interest on new capital and on some of the old will be able to increase 10 percent also, but for some of the latter, the interest will not be able to change, or not increase in proportion to the increase in wages, or may even decrease; and, if they cannot be withdrawn from production, they will get a negative *rent*. Consequently, an increase in wages will profit the workers; it could be of no consequence to the owners of new capital and to the owners of some of the old capital; but it will hurt the owners of another part of the old capital and all those who have fixed incomes.

85. Let us assume now that it is products which, as the result of certain measures—for example protective custom duties—have increased in price; and let us see what the consequences are. If, by hypothesis, the prices of all products increase, the prices of all the factors of production can increase in the same proportions if fixed incomes and indebtedness are disregarded, and equilibrium will again be established as in § 71. Similarly, by taking into account

fixed incomes and indebtedness, results similar to those of § 80 will be obtained. As for the phenomena of § 84, it must be noted that when the prices of products increase, all capital, the old as well as the new, benefits, and we see positive rents appear.

86. The hypothesis we have just made is never realized in practice. It is not possible that the prices of all products increase; consequently, the production of certain goods is stimulated, that of others is discouraged. The new capital can flow into the favored production and the old capital, which cannot be withdrawn from whatever production has suffered, yields negative rents.

87. Up to now we have considered successive positions of equilibrium; we must also see what develops in passing from one to the other. A change in one part of the economic organism does not spread instantaneously to all the other parts; and during the time that it takes to spread from one point to another, the phenomena are different from those which exist after equilibrium is established again.

88. If wages increase, it is not easy, except in some particular cases, for entrepreneurs to increase product prices correspondingly; and consequently, until that increase is obtained, their position deteriorates. In the interim, the increase in wages brings the workers a greater benefit than that which they will have when the operation is completed because their incomes have increased whereas their expenditures on consumption have not yet increased proportionally. Those who have fixed incomes suffer less while the movement is taking place than when it is completed.

89. In addition, the movement can never be general. Wages, and even product prices in one branch of production, can increase a good deal, but at the same time prices in other branches of production will not increase at all or almost not at all; and it is only after successive wage increases, in many branches of production, that the price increases which correspond to a general increase in wages are realized. The process is such that by the time the effect is seen, the cause often is already forgotten.

90. Here is the subjective version of these phenomena. Man's actions are influenced much more by sensations resulting from present circumstances than by those due to anticipations of the future, and much more by the pressure of facts which act on him directly than by that of those which act only indirectly. Consequently, in the case which we are considering, the workers will be much more inclined to press for an increase in wages than they would be if they felt the effects of a general increase in wages; similarly entrepreneurs will be much more inclined to resist the workers. As for those who

have fixed incomes, and who must, in the end, bear the expense of the struggle between the workers and the entrepreneurs, they show themselves to have less good sense than sheep who, led to the slaughter and frightened as they are by the odor of blood, do resist. They imagine that strikes are directed against the "capitalists," whom they do not even know how to distinguish from entrepreneurs, and they do not see that in the last analysis strikes hit those who have fixed incomes and debts owed to them much more than the entrepreneurs and the capitalists.

91. The entrepreneurs always press for increases in the prices of the goods they produce, and in that they are pursuing their own interest because these increases certainly obtain an advantage for them during such length of time as is necessary to arrive at a new position of equilibrium. Each one, moreover, imagines that he enjoys all the advantage of the increase in price of his own good, without seeing the partial offset which will follow the increase in price of other goods. It is the same for property owners who endeavor to obtain positive rents. In general the workers are indifferent to these price movements because they do not have immediate repercussions on wages; they think that only the "capitalists" have to be concerned about these price changes. As a result, they do not resist those which, in the last analysis, will be harmful to them, and they do not promote those which, in the last analysis, will be advantageous to them. Nevertheless there are exceptions, and, contrary to this general case, the workers in Germany have spoken out against protective duties on foodstuffs, and have understood that these duties would turn against them in the end. In part, perhaps, that comes from the education which the socialists have given the workers in that country.

92. **Economic circulation.** Production and the means of payment form a circle. Every modification at one point of the phenomenon has repercussions, but not all the same, on all the others. If we make the prices of products increase, we will, as a consequence, also make the prices of the factors of production increase. On the other hand if we make the latter increase, we will, as a consequence, make the former increase. In this form, the two operations appear identical; but that is not the case because the pressure exerted on the prices of products does not spread to the prices of the factors of production in the same way that the pressure exerted on those prices spreads to the former. In sum, in one way or the other, we arrive at a general increase in prices; but this increase is not the same for the various economic goods, and these changes differ as between

the first and the second way. Different individuals enjoy it or suffer from it, depending upon whether the operation takes place in the first or the second way.

93. **Erroneous interpretations of competition between entrepreneurs.** Competition between entrepreneurs manifests itself by their *tendency* to supply, at a certain price, more goods than the consumers demand; or, what comes to the same thing, by their *tendency* to supply a certain quantity at a price lower than that which consumers are paying (IX, 84).

It is the observation of these facts, wrongly interpreted, which has given rise to the erroneous notion that there is a permanent excess of production. If that excess really existed, one would have to identify an ever growing mass of goods; for example, there would have to be a constant increase in the world's *stock* of coal, iron, copper, cotton, silk, etc. This is not the case; hence the claimed excess of production can exist only as a tendency, and not as a fact.

94. Having accepted excess production as true, some have asserted that it would be advantageous for entrepreneurs to increase the wages of workers because in that way, they say, the "purchasing power" of the workers, and consequently consumption, would be increased.

95. The only truth in that proposition is this: The entrepreneur who, for example, pays double wages, double interest on capital, and who sells the goods produced at a doubled price, finds himself in the same situation afterwards as before. But neither these double wages, nor this double interest on capital will make the total consumption of goods increase, the only effect they will have is to divide this total differently: a greater part going to certain factors of production and a smaller part to those who have fixed incomes. Furthermore, the production of certain goods may increase, whereas that of other goods may decrease.

96. In addition some people profess, and by means of a new and more gross error, to deduce the cause of economic crises from this alleged excess production (IX, 82, 83).

97. **Erroneous conceptions of production.** People used to say, and still do frequently, that there are three factors of production, *nature*, labor, and capital, meaning by this last term savings, or even mobile capital. This proposition has little, if any, meaning. It is not clear why *nature* is separated from labor and capital, as if labor and capital were not natural things. In short, they are simply saying that in order to produce, some labor, some capital, and another thing, which is designated by the word *nature*, are neces-

sary. This is not false, but it is of no great use to us for understanding what production is.

98. Others say that the factors of production are land, labor, and capital; others trace everything back to land and labor; others, to labor alone. Completely false theories come from that, such as the one which asserts that the worker enters the service of the capitalist only when there is no more *free land*[5] to cultivate, or the one which claims to measure value by "crystallized" labor.[6]

99. All these theories have a common defect; it is forgetting that production is nothing else but the transformation of certain things into certain other things, and thinking that the different products can be obtained thanks to those abstract and general things which are called land, labor, and capital. It is not those abstract things we need for production, but certain concrete and special kinds of things, often very special, depending on the product which one wants to obtain. In order to get Rhine wine, for example, land situated on the banks of the Rhine is necessary, not just any land whatever; in order to get a statue, we do not need just any kind of labor, but rather the labor of a sculptor; in order to get a locomotive, we must have not just any mobile capital at all, but rather that whose form is such that it gives precisely a locomotive.

100. Before their land was discovered by Europeans, the Australians did not know about our domestic animals; they had *free land* to take at will; but, whatever labor they may have been able to apply to it, it is quite certain that they could not have obtained either a sheep, or an ox, or a horse. At the present time, immense flocks of sheep live in Australia, but they do not come from *free land* in general, nor from labor, nor even from capital in general, but from a very special capital, that is, from the flocks which existed in Europe. If some individuals who know how to work the land have a field where wheat can grow, if they have wheat seeds and in addition some mobile capital, plows, buildings, etc., and, finally, enough savings to be able to wait for the next harvest, they will be able to live and to produce wheat. Nothing stands in the way of saying that this wheat is produced by land, labor, and capital; but one then is talking about the genus instead of the species. All the land, all the labor, all the capital existing on the globe is unable to give us a single grain of wheat if we do not have a very special capital, the wheat seed.

---

[5] *Systèmes*, II, p. 285 *et seq.*
[6] *Systèmes*, II, p. 342 *et seq.*

101. These considerations should be enough to show the error of these theories; but, in addition to that, these theories are irreconcilable with historical and present facts on more than one score. They are simply a product of the sentiment which rebels against the "capitalist," and they remain foreign to the investigation of uniformities which is the sole concern of science.

CHAPTER VII

POPULATION

1. Man as producer is the point of departure for the economic phenomenon which in the end leads to man considered as consumer; thus we have a stream which flows into itself in a circular fashion.

2. **Social heterogeneity.** As we have already indicated[1] in II, 102, society is not homogeneous, and those who do not deliberately close their eyes have to recognize that men differ greatly from one another from the physical, moral, and intellectual viewpoints.

To these inequalities of human beings *per se* correspond economic and social inequalities, which we observe among all peoples, from the most ancient times to the present, everywhere in the world, and such that this characteristic is always present. Human society may be defined as a hierarchical collectivity.

We will not pause to investigate whether or not it is possible for the collectivity to remain and the hierarchy to disappear since the data for such study are not available. We will confine ourselves to the consideration of such facts as have developed up till now and which we still observe.

3. **The mean type and the distribution of deviations.** The distribution of men from the point of view of their quality is only a particular case of a much more general phenomenon. One can observe a large number of things which have a certain mean type; those which deviate from it only a little are very numerous, those which deviate considerably are very limited in number. If these deviations can be measured, a graph of the phenomenon can be constructed. Let us count the number of things whose deviations from the mean type are between zero and one; set *aa'* [in Figure 52] equal to 1, and

---

[1] On population, see R. Benini, *Principii di demografia*, Florence, 1901, a little known work, but excellent from all points of view.

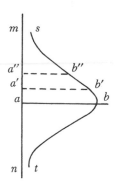

FIG. 52

the area *abb'a'* equal to the number [of such deviations]. Similarly we count the number of things whose deviations from the mean type are between 1 and 2; set *a'a''* equal to 1, and the area *a'b'b''a''* equal to this number. Continue in this way for all the positive deviations, which go from *a* toward *m*; we do the same thing for the negative deviations, going from *a* toward *n*; thus we obtain a curve *tbs*.

4. An analogous curve is obtained in many other cases among which we can note the following.

Assume that we have an urn which contains 20 white balls and 30 black balls. Ten balls are drawn from the urn, returning the ball to the urn after each draw; this operation is repeated a large number of times. The mean type will be the one in which the group of 10 balls drawn from the urn is composed of 4 white balls and 6 black balls. Many of the drawings will differ very little from this type; a very small number will diverge considerably. The phenomenon would give us a curve analogous to that of Figure 52.

5. From this observation many writers conclude, without anything more, that the two phenomena are identical. That is a very serious error. From the resemblance of these two curves it may be concluded only that the two phenomena have a common character; namely, that they depend on things which have a tendency to concentrate around a mean type. To be able to consider the two phenomena the same, the comparison of the two curves must be pushed further, to see whether they truly coincide.

6. This has been done in a particular case. If the same quantity is measured a large number of times, the measurements will be different; and the amounts by which they diverge from the true measure-

ment may be called *errors*. These errors yield a curve called the *curve of errors*, the form of which is analogous to the one in Figure 52. Observation shows us that this curve is the same as the one obtained by drawing balls from an urn by a procedure such as the one in § 4.[2]

7. This result is not so simple, and at bottom begs the question. In reality, it is not correct that the curve of errors always has the form indicated. In that case the deviation is said to follow from "constant errors"; these are eliminated and the curve in question obtained once more. From this it is concluded that the curve of errors has a certain determinate form when all the circumstances which may give it another form are eliminated; this proposition is very obvious, but one has only reproduced in the conclusion what was contained in the premises.

8. We need not concern ourselves any further with the theory of errors. Let us observe, though, that in certain cases, due to the lack of data, it cannot be ascertained whether the curve for a phenomenon is, or is not, the same as the curve for drawings from an urn, and in this situation the phenomena cannot be considered to be the same.

9. It often happens that natural phenomena give not one hump as in Figure 52, but two as in Figure 53, or even more. In this case

FIG. 53

writers usually assume that the two humps of Figure 53 result from superimposing two curves of the type of Figure 52, and without further ado they consider the phenomenon shown in Figure 53 as equivalent to drawings from two urns of given composition.

---

[2] On this same problem, considered from another point of view, compare Bertrand, *Calcul des probabilités*, §§ 149, 150.

This is going a bit too fast. It is enough to note that by choosing a suitable number of curves such as the one in Figure 52, and superimposing them, any curve whatsoever can be obtained; consequently the fact that a curve may result from superimposing a certain number of curves analogous to the one in Figure 52 tells us nothing about the nature of that curve.

10. Study of these laws for wages gives us in many cases a certain mean wage with deviations distributed according to a curve analogous to the one in Figure 52, but which, however, is not symmetrical with respect to the line ab. But from this single analogy one cannot conclude that these deviations follow the so-called law of *errors*.

11. **Distribution of income.**[3] By analogy with facts of the same type, it is likely that the curve for incomes should have a form similar to that of Figure 54. If we set mo equal to a certain income x and set mp equal to 1, the area $mnqp$ gives us the number of individuals who have an income between x and $x + 1$.

But for all incomes, statistics provide information only for the cqb segment of the curve, and perhaps, in a very few cases, for a small portion bb'. The segment ab', or, better, ab, remains purely hypothetical.

12. The curve is not symmetrical with respect to sb; the upper part, bc, is very elongated, the ba segment is quite compressed.

From this simple consideration one cannot conclude that there is no symmetry in the qualities of the individuals who are above and below the mean s. Indeed, of two individuals who deviate equally from the mean of the qualities, the one who has exceptional aptitudes for making money may have a very high income; but the one who has qualities equally different from the mean but in the negative direction, cannot, without dying, drop below the minimum income sufficient to sustain life.

13. The curve $abnc$ is not the curve of the qualities of men, but a curve of other facts related to these qualities.

14. If we consider the curve for student examination scores, we get a curve analogous to ABC [in Figure 55]. Assume now that for some reason the examiners never give less than 5 points, because a single point below the mean is enough to fail a candidate. In this case, for the same students, the form of the curve will change and become quite similar to curve abC.

---

[3] *Cours*, Book III, Chapter I. To the facts given in the *Cours* we can add those in the *Giornale degli Economisti*, Rome, January 1897.

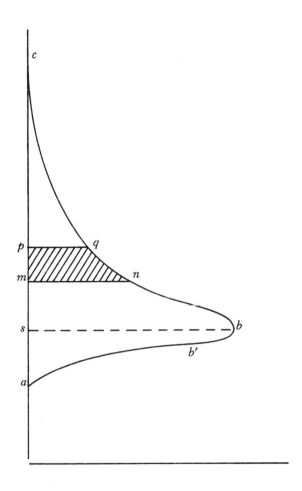

Fig. 54

Something similar occurs with respect to incomes. There is no limit to distance above the mean, there is a limit below.

15. The form of the curve cqb, Figure 54, which statistics give us, does not correspond at all to the curve of errors, that is, to the form the curve would have if the acquisition and conservation of wealth depended only on chance.[4]

16. Moreover, statistics show us that the curve cqb, Figure 54, varies very little in space and time; different peoples and different

---

[4] *Cours*, § 962.

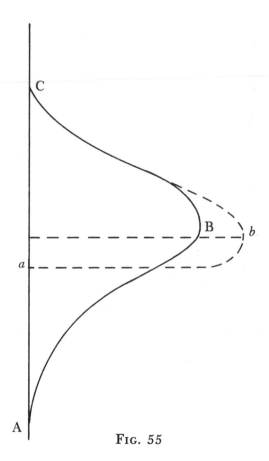

Fig. 55

eras yield very similar curves. There is a remarkable stability in the form of this curve.

17. It seems, on the other hand, that there may be more diversity in the lower and less known part of the curve. There is a certain minimum income *oa* below which men cannot fall without perishing of poverty and hunger. The curve may coincide more or less with the line *ak* which indicates this minimum income (Figure 56). Among the peoples of antiquity, for whom famines were frequent, the curve took form (I). Among modern peoples it takes form (II).

18. The area *ahbc*, Figure 56, gives a picture of society. The outward form varies little, the interior portion is, on the other hand, in constant movement; while certain individuals are rising to higher levels, others are sinking. Those who fall to *ah* disappear; thus some

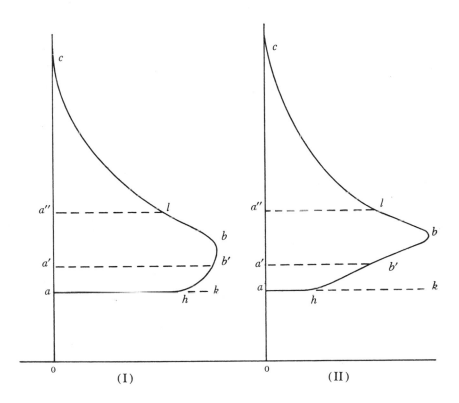

FIG. 56.

elements are eliminated. It is strange, but true, that the same phenomenon occurs in the upper regions. Experience tells us that aristocracies do not last; the reasons for this phenomenon are numerous and we know very little about them, but there is no doubt about the reality of the phenomenon itself.

19. We have first a region $ahb'a'$ in which incomes are very low, people cannot subsist, whether they be good or bad; in this region selection operates only to a very small extent because extreme poverty debases and destroys the good elements as well as the bad. Next comes the region $a'b'bla''$ in which selection operates with maximum intensity. Incomes are not large enough to preserve everyone whether they are or are not well fitted for the struggle of life, but they are not low enough to dishearten the best elements. In this region child mortality is considerable, and this mortality is probably a powerful

means of selection.[5] This region is the crucible in which the future aristocracies (in the etymological sense: ἄριστος = best) are developed; from this region come the elements who rise to the higher region $a''lc$. Once there, their descendants degenerate; thus this region $a''lc$ is maintained only as a result of immigration from the lower region. As we have already said, the reasons for this fact are numerous and not well understood; one important reason may well be the non-intervention of selection. Incomes are so large that they enable even the weak, the ill-adapted, the incompetent and the defective to survive.

The lines $a'b'$ and $a''l$ serve only to fix ideas, they do not actually exist. The boundaries of these regions are not sharply defined, we move gradually from one region to the other.

20. The inferior elements of region $a'b'la''$ descend into region $ahb'a'$, where they are eliminated. If this region were to disappear, and if nothing else could fill its role, the inferior elements would contaminate region $a'b'la''$, which would thus become less suitable for producing the superior elements which move into region $a''lc$, and the whole society would fall into decadence. This decadence would be still more rapid if serious obstacles were placed in the way of selection operating in region $a'b'la''$. The future will show our descendants whether such are not the effects of the humanitarian measures of our era.

21. It is not only the accumulation of inferior elements in a social stratum which harms society, but also the accumulation in the lower strata of superior elements which are prevented from rising. When, at the same time, the upper strata are full of inferior elements and the lower strata full of superior ones, social equilibrium becomes highly unstable and a violent revolution is imminent. In a way, the social body may be compared to the human body, which soon perishes if the elimination of toxic matter is prevented.

22. The phenomenon is very complex. It is not sufficient only to take income into account, we must also take into consideration the use which is made of it and how it is obtained. Among modern peoples incomes in region $a'b'la''$ are increased in a way which could seriously obstruct selection; but a significant part of these incomes is now spent on alcohol or otherwise squandered so that conditions which make selection possible remain nevertheless. Moreover, alcoholism itself is a powerful agent of selection and causes the disappearance of individuals and races who do not know how to resist it.

---

[5] *Systèmes*, I, Chapter IX.

The objection is usually raised that alcoholism harms not only the individual but also his descendants. This is a very strong objection from the ethical point of view, but it is nothing from the point of view of selection. This objection even works against those who use it. It is obvious, in fact, that an agent of selection is so much the better when its action applies not only to individuals but also to their descendants. Tuberculosis is also a powerful means of selection, since only a small number of the strong are affected, while it destroys a very large number of the weak.

23. The data we have for determining the form of the curve *blc* refer principally to the 19th century and to civilized peoples; consequently the conclusions drawn from them cannot be applied outside these limits. But it is possible, as a more or less probable inference, that in other times and among other peoples a form fairly similar to what we find today would be obtained.

Similarly we cannot assert that the form would not change if the social structure were to change in some radical fashion, if, for example, collectivism were substituted for the system of private property. It seems unlikely that there would no longer be a hierarchy. The form of that hierarchy could be similar to that given by the incomes of individuals, but it would not correspond to income in money.

24. If we stay within the limits indicated in § 23, we see that during the 19th century the curve *blc* has slowly changed form in certan cases. The curve is still of the same type but the constants are different. This change has been in a certain direction.

In the *Cours*, the term "decrease in income inequality," which was in common use, was used to identify this direction. But this term has given rise to ambiguity,[6] just as had the term *utility* which we were obliged to replace by the term *ophelimity*. Similarly with the term "income inequality," it must be replaced by some neologism which would be given a precise definition. Political economy, unhappily, is not yet far enough advanced to use new terms at will, as is done with no difficulty in chemistry, physics, etc. Hence we will use a terminology which is still somewhat imperfect. "Decrease in the inequality of the proportion of incomes" will mean a specific phenomenon which we are about to define.

Let there be a group A made up of one individual having a 10,000 franc annual income and nine individuals each having an annual income of 1,000 francs. Let there be another group B made up of

---

[6] See C. Bresciani, *Giornale degli economisti*, January 1907.

nine individuals each having a 10,000 franc annual income and one individual with only a 1,000 franc income. For the moment let us call the individuals who have 10,000 francs annual income "rich" and those who have 1,000 "poor." Group A has one rich and nine poor, group B has nine rich and one poor.

Ordinary language expresses the difference between A and B by saying that the inequality of income is greater in A, where there is only one rich person among the ten individuals, than in B where there are, on the contrary, nine rich persons among the ten individuals. To avoid all ambiguity, we will say that moving from A to B there has been a decrease in the proportion of inequality of incomes.

"In general, when the number of persons having an income less than x decreases[7] compared to the number of persons having an income greater than x, we will say that inequality *of the proportion* of incomes decreases.[8]

That being settled it can be said that during the 19th century the curve of income distribution in certain countries has moved slightly in the direction of a decrease in the proportion[9] of inequality of incomes.

25. The fact which has been rigorously elucidated by mathematical study of the curve of incomes was established earlier, empirically and by induction, by M. Paul Leroy-Beaulieu, who made it the subject of a celebrated work. Some have wanted to derive from it a general law according to which income inequality would con-

---

[7] The *Cours*, § 964, reads "increase." That is a typographical error discovered just after the publication of the *Cours*.

[8] This definition is just like the one given in the *Cours*, § 964, except that we now add the words: *of the proportion*.

Following this definition, the *Cours* reads: "But the reader is well and duly warned that by these words we intend to mean this thing and nothing else." And in a note it is indicated that where N_z is the number of individuals having an income of x or more, and N_h is the number of individuals having income of h or more, set

$$u_x = \frac{N_z}{N_h} \cdot$$

"Following the definition we have given, inequality of incomes decreases when u_x increases."

This really ought to be sufficient to dispel all ambiguity.

[9] The addition of this term to the name of this fact will no more prevent additional ambiguity than the substitution of the term *ophelimity* for the term *utility* if people obstinately insist on seeking the meaning of terms in their etymology, instead of holding to the rigorous definitions, especially mathematical ones, which are given. See on this subject: "L'économie et la sociologie au point de vue scientifique," *Rivista di Scienza*, No. 2, 1907.

tinue to decrease. But such a conclusion goes far beyond what can be drawn from the premises. Empirical laws such as this one have only slight or even no value beyond the limits within which they have been observed to be true.

26. In certain countries, for example England, at least during the 19th century, considerable variation may be seen in the lower part, *ahb*, of the curve [Figure 56]. It coincides with the line *hk*, which represents the minimum income necessary to sustain life, to a much lesser extent.

27. If we replace the form in Figure 54 by a different one in which the squashed down line [*cqnb* in Figure 54] is replaced by an almost straight line, we get a curve *clb* [in Figure 57] which coincides with what the statistics [of incomes] give us; and the lower part *bka* [in Figure 57], for which we have no data, will be replaced by the straight line *sb* corresponding to a minimum income *os* which is substituted for the actual minimum income which is somewhere between *os* and *oa*.

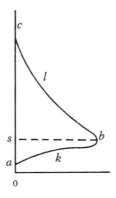

FIG. 57

28. Given the above, if it is conceded that, as is the case for certain peoples of the 19th century, the curve type *blc* does not change but that only the constants change, we arrive at the following proposition:

1° *An increase in the minimum income, and* 2° *a decrease in the inequality of the proportion of incomes* (§ 24), *cannot take place, separately or together, if the total income is not growing more rapidly than the population.*

29. The converse of that proposition is true save for one theoreti-

cal exception which is difficult to verify in practice,[10] and we can take the following proposition to be true:

Whenever total income increases more rapidly than the population, that is, when the mean income increases, the following effects, separately or jointly, can be observed: 1° an increase in the minimum income, and 2° a decrease in the inequality of the proportion of incomes (§ 24).

Proof of these two theorems requires the use of mathematics, hence we refer the reader to our *Cours.*

30. Given the tendency of population to be distributed, with respect to income, according to a certain form, it follows that any change in one part of the curve has repercussions on the other parts; and eventually the society reassumes the customary form, just as a solution of a known salt always yields the same crystals whether they are large or small.

31. If, for example, the wealthiest citizens were deprived of all their income, thus suppressing the area *edc* [in Figure 58], the curve would not retain the form *abde*, but sooner or later would reestablish itself in a form *ats* similar to the initial curve. In the same way, if a famine or some other eventuality of the same type were to wipe out the lower part of the population, *akb'f*, the figure would not retain the form *fb'dc*, but would return to a form *ats* resembling the original one.

32. **Relationships between economic conditions and population.** It is clear that man, as all living creatures, multiplies more or less according as the conditions for life are more or less favorable. The agricultural population will be more dense where the soil is more fertile, and less so where the soil is less fruitful. The subsurface itself, depending on whether it is richer or poorer, will permit the development of a larger or smaller number of people. The relationships are less simple when they concern industry and commerce, whose relations with telluric and geographical conditions are much more complex. Moreover, the population itself reacts upon the very conditions which enable it to live; consequently the density of population is the effect of certain economic conditions and the cause of some others.

33. Countries where population density is greatest are far from being the richest countries. For example, as M. Levasseur points out, Sicily has a density of 113 inhabitants per square kilometer, and France has only 72. Clearly Sicily is not wealthier than France.

---

[10] *Cours*, II, pp. 323, 324.

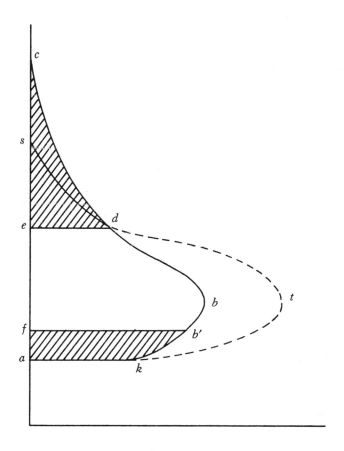

FIG. 58

Similarly, the valley of the Ganges has a density two times greater than that of France.

34. But if density is not directly related to the wealth of different countries, it is related to the variations in wealth within a given country. This is an example of a very general phenomenon. The reasons for this fact are the following. The total number of individuals living in a given territory is related to many facts A, B, C, . . . which are somewhat different, A', B', C', . . . for example, for another territory. Assume that A represents wealth; it varies from one territory to another, but facts B, C, . . . also vary, for example the mores, the greater ease of providing for wants in warm countries, etc. There can be a trade-off between the effects of one of these facts

and those of another, and the total effect differs from what it would have been if only one of the facts had changed.

35. When the variations in wealth, A, within the same country are considered, there are two states of affairs, A, B, C, . . . , and A', B, C, . . . , in which the most important, if not the only, variation is in A. Thus the total effect, which alone we can observe, more or less coincides with the effect of the variation in A alone.

36. That is not all. If only variations in wealth are considered, it can and does in fact happen that the absolute value of wealth and the amount of variations in wealth act on the population in opposite directions.

37. For example, in certain countries the wealthiest part of the population has a lower birth rate than the poorest part[11] (§ 53); this does not mean that an increase in wealth may not have an initial effect of increasing the number of marriages and births.

38. In the 19th century, in civilized countries, a considerable increase in the wealth per capita was observed. At the same time, *nuptiality* (number of marriages per 1,000 persons), *natality* (number of births per 1,000 persons), and *mortality* (number of deaths per 1,000 persons) have fallen. Total population has increased, but the annual rate of increase has tended to fall.

39. These facts are reciprocally related. Increase in wealth has promoted the increase in population; it very probably has helped to limit nuptiality and natality; it certainly has had the effect of reducing mortality by making important and costly hygienic measures possible. Very probably by accustoming men to an easier life, it tends to decrease the rate of increase of the population.

40. The decrease in nuptiality contributes directly to the decrease in natality, and consequently to the decrease in total mortality, which is considerably influenced by infant mortality. M. Cauderlier even considers that changes in natality are solely the result of variations in nuptiality. Hence the decrease in nuptiality, directly or indirectly, through the decrease in births, has influenced the growth in wealth per capita.

41. The decrease in natality is in large part a cause of the decrease in mortality, and it has had an influence, as we have shown, on wealth; in short, it is a direct cause of the decrease in the annual rate of growth of population.

42. The decrease in mortality operates in the opposite direction, and insofar as the size of the total population is concerned it has

---

[11] *Systèmes*, II, p. 139.

offset in part the decrease in natality. Infant mortality indubitably has decreased; decrease in adult mortality is less important and less certain.

43. Population seems to be almost stationary in France; it is growing considerably in England and Germany, but even in these two countries the rate of growth has a tendency to diminish. In the 19th century the population of England grew in geometric proportion in a ratio such that the population doubled every 54 years.[12] Since the wealth per capita has increased, and considerably so, this means that in England the increases in wealth have been greater than those of the geometric progression above.[13]

44. Improvement and deterioration of economic conditions in a country are related to population phenomena. To see this clearly, we must establish a criterion for the state of economic conditions. For agricultural peoples in our part of the world we can use the price of wheat; for industrial and commercial peoples we must consider other data. According to Marshall, nuptiality in England in the first half of the 19th century depended principally on agricultural production; on the other hand, in the second half of the 19th century it depended principally on commercial fluctuations. This change results from the fact that England has become mainly an industrial country rather than mainly agricultural, as it was at the beginning of the 19th century.

45. At present, in England, nuptiality is related to the amount of foreign trade and to the total amounts cleared at the Clearing-House; the latter are simply indices of industrial and commercial fluctuations.

46. There are certain general phenomena called economic crises (IX, 73). Prosperous years are followed by years of economic depression, which are followed by more prosperous years, and so on. We can tell approximately when prosperity is at a maximum or a minimum, but the precise dates of the high and the low points cannot be determined. Hence comparisons may be made only in some approximate way.

47. If the preceding considerations were not taken into account, anything desired could be deduced from the statistics. For example, if one wanted to prove that nuptiality is decreasing in England, one would compare the nuptiality of 17.6 for the year 1873, which is a year which ended a period of prosperity, with the nuptiality of 14.2 for the year 1886, a year of economic depression. If, on the

---

[12] *Cours*, § 211.
[13] *Cours*, § 212.

other hand, one wanted to show that nuptiality is increasing, one would compare a nuptiality of 14.2 for the year 1886 to nuptiality of 16.5 for the year 1899. Obviously we must guard against such reasoning.

48. The mathematical theory of coincidences or correlation tells us whether two facts which are observed together a certain number of times are linked by chance or whether they occur at the same time because they are interrelated. It is only with difficulty, however, that this theory can be used in our subject matter. We are not dealing with facts one expects to coincide in an instantaneous way, but rather with facts which operate reciprocally but with a certain latitude, and the number of coincidences in that case means little. Economic prosperity decreases or increases gradually, and the indicators we have represent the phenomenon only very roughly. Moreover, a decrease or increase of prosperity does not have an immediate effect on marriages; it influences births and deaths still more slowly. If the curves of the phenomena which one wants to compare are represented graphically, it can be seen whether there is any relationship between their oscillations. This method, although very imperfect, is perhaps still the best we can use in practice for the time being.

49. The first effect of an increase in economic prosperity is an immediate increase in nuptiality and natality, and a decrease in mortality. The first phenomenon is notable and manifests itself clearly. The second is less pronounced, and perhaps, according to the theory of M. Cauderlier, is a mere consequence of the first, in large part at least. The third is somewhat doubtful for civilized and wealthy peoples; for poverty stricken peoples we do not have any precise statistics, but it is difficult to deny it if famines, which were frequent in former times, are taken into account.

50. A rapid increase in the wealth of a country is favorable to selection because it provides individuals with good opportunities to grow rich and rise to higher levels of society. A similar result is obtained without an increase in wealth when economic conditions in the society are changing rapidly.

51. Until now we have spoken only of changes in wealth; we should also consider the level of as well as the variations in wealth, and compare two social conditions which differ in that the wealth per capita is higher in the one than in the other.

52. We have seen in § 29 that such a difference corresponds to a difference in the distribution of income, and to a difference in minimum income; but the wealth per capita is related to many other very important facts.

53. Some very wealthy peoples have a very low natality, from which it could be concluded that the absolute level of wealth operates in a way directly contrary to changes in that wealth. It remains, however, in doubt. It is possible that there is no cause and effect relationship between absolute wealth and natality, but that these two phenomena are both the result of other things, that is, that there may be certain causes which increase wealth and decrease natality at the same time.

54. Economic conditions affect not only the number of marriages, births, deaths and the total size of the population, but also all the characteristics of the population, its customs, its laws, its political organization. Certain things are possible only if there is a considerable increase in wealth. Among peoples who have scarcely enough to feed their adults, infants are killed readily enough, and the elderly are systematically destroyed.[14] Nowadays, among wealthy peoples, pensions are established for old people and invalids. Among very poor peoples women are treated with less regard than domestic animals; among civilized peoples, especially the very wealthy population of the United States of America, women have become objects of luxury who consume but do not produce.[15] Obviously for such

---

[14] *Cours*, § 247.

[15] For a view favorable to American *feminism*, see Th. Bentzon, *Les Américaines chez elles;* an opposite view is taken in a study by Cleveland Moffet of New York, reprinted in *Mercure de France*, 1904. "Our country, certain Americans say, is one in which women receive the most from men and give them the least. Men are for them nothing but money-making machines. A woman knows almost nothing about what her husband does but only what he earns."

It must not be forgotten that writers always exaggerate in one way or another.

M. G. B. Baker, in an article published in the February issue of *Everybody's Magazine*, writes: "The American society woman is a creature of luxury and leisure. Her sole duty in life is to be amused and to be decorative. She has had time to acquire the accomplishment of society and the delicacies of refinement. Vastly superior in appearance to her mother, she is even superior to her father and brothers."

The situation was very different in earlier times, when the level of wealth in America was much less than that now attained. For example, Mistress Trollope, who traveled in that country from 1827 to 1831, wrote: "Except for balls . . . women are excluded from all the pleasures of the men. The latter have numerous and frequent gatherings . . . but the former are never admitted. If such were not the established custom, it would be impossible that someone had not devised some means of sparing the wealthy women and their daughters the pain of performing the thousands of ignoble household duties which they nearly all do in their homes."

a thing to be possible a country's wealth must be very great. This condition of women reacts in turn on customs.

Feminism is a malady which can only beset a rich people, or the rich portion of a poor people. With the increase of wealth in ancient Rome, depravity in the lives of women also increased. If certain modern women did not have the money necessary to parade their idleness and their concupiscence, the gynecologists would be less busy. The stupid compassion for malefactors, which has spread among certain modern peoples, can only exist among wealthy peoples for whom some loss of wealth is no great hardship. On the other hand, an increase in wealth, accompanied generally by a greater density of population and by better means of communication, causes brigandage in the countryside to disappear; the profession of brigand becomes impossible. This is not the effect of moral progress because precisely the opposite result is observed in the large cities; there assaults become more frequent.

With the increase in wealth the laws dealing with debtors can become much less severe. It is also known that socialist sentiments increase in the wake of a long period of peace and increase in wealth. Among a very poor people the scarce capital is very precious, human labor very abundant and cheap; consequently political power is held by the capitalists, most frequently the landowners. As the wealth of a country increases, the importance of capital diminishes and that of labor increases; little by little the workers acquire the power and privileges which formerly were held by the capitalists. At the same time changes in customs, morality, sentiments, literature, and art are to be observed. Among poor peoples, writers flatter the rich; among wealth peoples, they flatter the common people.

Ancient writers were not ignorant of the profound changes that an increase in wealth brings in the social organization, but ordinarily, due to the necessities of moralistic declamations, they called these changes "corruption." Sometimes, however, the facts were better described. The author of the *Republic of the Athenians*, which is usually attributed to Xenophon, saw clearly the relation between an increase in wealth and greater concern for the lower classes of the population. He shows how, as a result of the development of their commerce, the Athenians were led to improve the condition of slaves and aliens. In order to provide stability in the organization of his Republic, Plato took great care to prevent the citizens from becoming too wealthy.

It was not by chance that democratic organization developed in the wealthy cities of Athens and Rome. Later, in the Middle Ages, chance had no part in the rebirth of democracy where wealth again appeared, as in Provence and the Italian republics, and in the free cities of Germany; nor did it have any part in the disappearance of democracy in those countries when wealth began to diminish. The Albigensian heresy seemed to be a purely religious matter, whereas at bottom it was in large part a democratic movement which was destroyed by the crusaders of the countries to the north where, because per capita wealth was much lower, the social organization was different.

The great plague which devastated Europe toward the middle of the 14th century, killing many people, raised the wealth per capita temporarily; the lower classes found their condition improved and as a result democratic movements developed in certain regions, for example, Wat Tyler's revolt in England. The latter was put down, but since the repression was mild, only a small amount of wealth was destroyed; the causes remaining, the effects continued to be felt, and as Thorold Rogers points out, "although the rebellious peasants had been defeated and dispersed, and their leaders imprisoned or hanged, basically the victory was theirs."

Villani remarks[16] that after the great number of deaths which accompanied the plague in Florence "men were less numerous and, enriched by the goods and property which came to them through inheritance, they forgot the events which had taken place as if they had never happened and lived most dissolute and disorganized lives. . . . The common people, men and women, because there was such an abundance of everything, no longer wanted to work at their accustomed trades and demanded the dearest and most delicate foods. . . ."

It was the same in England. In Florence, where prior to the plague wealth was already great and institutions democratic, no one dared to oppose the claims of the workers; in England, where due to the greater poverty these institutions did not exist, it was sought, by the celebrated *Statute of Laborers*, to oblige workers to be content with the wages they had before the high mortality brought on by the plague, but that attempt failed.

Recent well conducted studies have shown that in France and Germany the years preceding the birth of Protestantism were years of very great economic prosperity. That prosperity favored the extension of religious reform and the democratic movement which originally accompanied it. But the long wars which followed, by destroying a large amount of wealth, caused the conditions which

[16] *Cronica di Matteo Villani*, I, 4.

had given birth to the democratic movement to disappear; and so the latter disappeared entirely, or almost entirely,[17] to reappear later in England, in France and in the rest of Europe with the next increase in wealth. And if now it is more intense in France than elsewhere, it is not by chance that that circumstance occurs together with the increase in wealth in that country, at a time when the number of inhabitants is almost constant and the wealth per capita is increasing.

55. We must not forget that the phenomena which we have seen follow a path parallel to the increase in wealth, operate in their turn to modify the phenomenon of increased wealth itself, and thus a certain equilibrium is established between them.

This set of actions and reactions may also be conducive to the rhythmical movement which is characteristic of social phenomena. Increase in the wealth per capita fosters democracy; but the latter, at least according to what we have been able to observe up to now, entails great destruction of wealth and even eventually dries up the sources of it. Hence it is its own grave-digger, it destroys what gave it birth (§ 83).

History abounds with examples which could be invoked to support this assertion, and if it seems that it is not so today, that is first of all because the time during which the work of the destruction of wealth has taken place has not been long, and also because the amazing improvements in production techniques in our era have enabled a larger amount of wealth to be produced than has been destroyed. But if the destruction of wealth continues and if additional improvements are not found, improvements of a type such that production exceeds this destruction, or at least equals it, the social phenomenon could change completely.

From an objective point of view, the phenomena we have been studying plainly are related by mutual dependence; but from the subjective point of view they are ordinarily interpreted as if they were related as cause and effect. And thus even though, objectively, there may be something which comes close to such a relation, it is curious to observe that often the subjective interpretation reverses the terms. Thus it seems very probable, almost certain, that humanitarian sentiments, legislative measures on behalf of the poor, and other improvements in their conditions do not contribute, or contribute very little, toward an increase in wealth, and often diminish it. The relation of mutual dependence between these phenomena

---

[17] In Florence, the Medici, by a progressive tax, got rid of their adversaries, and at the same time weakened the democracy by removing the conditions on which it was based.

approaches a relation in which the increase in wealth is the *cause*, and the development of humanitarian sentiments and improvement in the condition of the poor are the *effects*. The subjective interpretation, on the other hand, considers the humanitarian sentiments as a cause, and imagines that they are the cause of the improvement in the conditions of the poor, that is, of the increase in the portion of wealth they consume.

There are good people who imagine that if today's workingman eats meat every day, whereas there was a time when he ate it only on holidays, it is because of the development of ethical and humanitarian sentiments—others say it is because socialism's "great truths" have finally been recognized—and they do not understand that increased wealth is an absolutely indispensable condition in order that popular consumption, that is, consumption by the greatest number of people, be able to increase.[18]

Usually, so far as improvement in the people's economic conditions is concerned, humanitarians simply play the role of the busybody.

56. The result of all the preceding is that wealth per capita is, at least in part, a good index of the economic, social, moral and political conditions of a people. It goes without saying that other factors may enter in and that this correspondence can only be approximate. Moreover, we must take into account the fact that people imitate each other more or less. Consequently, certain institutions which among a wealthy people are directly related to wealth, may be copied by another people among whom they would not have arisen spontaneously.

57. **The production of human capital.** Like all capital, man has a certain cost of production; but this cost depends on the mode of living, on the standard of life.

58. If it is assumed that the cost of production of a human being is given by what is strictly necessary to keep him alive and train him, and that for human capital there is also an equality between the cost of production and the price of the capital obtained, then

---

[18] I have been criticized for not having taken up the improvement in the condition of the poorer classes at the same time as the succession of the *elites*. I did not do so because, given the facts that I knew, it did not seem that the former phenomenon was a consequence of the latter; it is a consequence of the increase in wealth, at least in large part. A ship is going down the river, swept along by the current; now the one dominates, now the other. The two phenomena are concomitant, they are not related as cause and effect.

It is well known that only the main part of a phenomenon is seen in such a case. The poorer classes may derive some advantage, as a by-product, from the struggle between the *elites*.

by regarding the price of labor as interest (V, 88), one comes to the conclusion that the condition of men can never be improved in any way; all improvement obtained for the benefit of laborers would simply have the effect of reducing their cost of production. This is the core of Lassalle's *iron law*,[19] from which many of the errors of other economists have come.

59. The two premises of this argument have not been confirmed by the facts. We have already discussed the first. As for the second, one may indeed invoke in its favor the fact that the immediate result of an improvement in economic conditions is an increase in the number of marriages and consequently of births; but against it is the other fact that a permanent increase in wealth is linked to a decrease in the number of births; and the second effect greatly outweighs the first.

60. Increase in wealth does not proceed uniformly; there are periods of rapid increase, others of stagnation, and even of decrease. The increase in the number of marriages when the tide is rising is at least partially offset by the decrease in this number when the tide is ebbing; in addition there is the steady reduction which is linked to a permanent increase in wealth.

61. The cost of production of an adult obviously depends on child mortality; but contrary to what one might think, a decrease in mortality in early childhood does not produce a corresponding decrease in this cost.[20] This is because many of those who have survived early childhood die a little later, before becoming adults.

62. **Obstacles to the generative force.** Increase in population results from the opposition which exists between the generative force and the obstacles it may encounter. Two hypotheses are possible: it may be assumed that these obstacles do not exist and that consequently the number of births is always at the maximum, the number of deaths a minimum, the increase in population maximum. Or it may be assumed that the generative force does encounter obstacles which diminish the number of births, increase the number of deaths and limit (ignoring migration for the moment) the increase in population.

63. The first hypothesis is obviously contrary to the facts. It is enough to point to the oscillations in the number of marriages and births shown by statistics. It is impossible to believe that they correspond precisely to variations in the reproductive instinct. Moreover, more important oscillations are found among all peoples.

[19] *Systèmes*, II, p. 235.
[20] *Cours*, § 255.

Famines, epidemics and wars have considerably diminished the size of some populations, which after a few years have returned to their original state.

64. Hence only the second hypothesis remains, and it can be rigorously demonstrated that it does correspond to the facts. Writers who implicitly accept this hypothesis usually state it in another form; they specify the obstacles and then declare that the means of subsistence limit population. They are thus led into a discussion of how to increase the means of subsistence, whether by decreasing waste or by increasing the means of subsistence by any measures appropriate for this purpose. And so the debate gets off the track. We must abandon these considerations and instead of an elastic limit, such as the means of subsistence, consider a fixed limit, that of space.

65. In Norway, the difference between births and deaths, from 1805 to 1880, yields an annual increase in population of 13.48 per thousand; for England from 1861 to 1880, it was 13.4 per thousand; for the German empire, 12.3 per thousand. Assume that the population of these three countries, which was 72,728,000 in 1880, continued to increase at the lowest of the three rates above, that is, at 12.3 per thousand per annum. In 1,200 years the number of human beings would be 1,707 followed by eleven zeros. The [inhabitable] surface of the earth being about 131 [million] square kilometers, there would then be one inhabitant per square meter, which is absurd. Thus it is absolutely impossible that the population of the three countries under consideration could continue to grow in the future at the same rate as in the period 1861 to 1880.

66. As for the past, it can be remarked that if the population of the earth had been only 50 million at the beginning of the Christian era, and if it had increased at the rate observed in Norway, in 1891 the number of human beings would have been equal to 489 followed by sixteen zeros. Assume that in 1086 the population of England had been about two million persons; if it had increased at the present rate there would have had to be 84 thousand millions in 1886. If the population of England continued to grow according to the rule observed from 1801 to 1891, in about six and a half centuries England would have one inhabitant per square meter.

All this is absurd; therefore it is certain that population could not have increased in the past, and cannot increase in the future, at the present rate; thus it has been proved that there have been and there will be obstacles to such increase.

67. In seeking that proof of our proposition we also found another one along the way. We see that the 19th century was exceptional

from the point of view of the growth in Norway, England and Germany (IX, 37), and that neither in the past nor in the future could these countries have a similar growth over a long period of time.

68. **The means of subsistence and population.** Lack of means of subsistence, then, obviously can be an obstacle to increase in population; it operates in different ways on different social strata, Figure 54 (§ 11). In the lower part, where the level of incomes almost coincides with the line of minimum income, the lack of means of subsistence operates principally by increasing mortality. This phenomenon is illustrated by many of the facts collected by Malthus in his book. In the upper part, the effect of lack of means of subsistence is only indirect. We have seen that the form of the income distribution curve varies little; consequently if one of the lower levels in Figure 54 is suppressed, all the higher levels fall correspondingly, and the total area of the figure becomes smaller. It is easy to understand that if the workers were to disappear the owners of the factories where they worked and those who, in the so-called liberal professions, derive their income from these factory owners, all fall into poverty. The lack of means of subsistence, which is felt directly in the lower levels, operates in the middle social strata by holding down the number of marriages and by raising the age at which persons marry, thus leading to a decrease in births. The peasant who has only a little property does not want to have too many children so that this property will not be divided into too many parts. The bourgeois who is short on the usual sources of income limits the expenditures of his family and the number of his children. In countries where a large part of the patrimony goes to the eldest son, the younger sons often do not marry. These same effects are observed in the highest levels of society, but there we also find the very powerful phenomenon of the decadence of *elites*, which causes all select groups to disappear more or less rapidly.

69. Sismondi, worthy precursor of our *humanitarians*, believed he could prove the absurdity of the theory that the means of subsistence limits population by citing the case of one family, the Montmorency's, which was on the verge of disappearing in Sismondi's day, although, having always lived in abundance, they should, according to the theory Sismondi was refuting, have filled up the countryside with inhabitants. With this type of reasoning, someone who wanted to prove that the tortoise is a very fast animal could cite the example of a race horse.

70. It is useful to note the lack of precision in this term "means

of subsistence." Though different as between peoples and countries, it certainly includes, in addition to food, protection from the elements, that is, clothing and shelter, and also fuel in cold countries. And all these components vary according to circumstances. They certainly are not the same for the European and the Chinese, for example, nor for the Englishman and the Spaniard.

71. **Nature of the obstacles.** Following the example of Malthus the obstacles may be classified into PREVENTIVE which operate before birth and up to that moment, and REPRESSIVE, which operate after birth.

72. Preventive obstacles can operate in two ways: α) by diminishing the number of marriages; and β) by diminishing the number of births, whatever be the number of marriages. Obstacle (α) can have an effect on legitimate fecundity, obstacle (β) on illegitimate fecundity. Part of the population may remain celibate, but this decrease in the number of marriages (α) can be offset by an increase in the number of births for the marriages contracted (β).

73. (α) 1° Statistics show that among some modern civilized peoples the number of marriages does decrease without illegitimate fecundity increasing. 2° Celibacy, when it is actually practiced, decreases the number of marriages. The large harems of the great lords of the orient and the polyandry of Tibet have similar effects.

74. (β) 1° The custom of marrying later in life diminishes the number of births. This obstacle operates among some civilized peoples. Malthus preached recourse to this method only; he would have had men and women delay marriage, and live completely chaste lives before marriage; this is what is called *moral restraint*. 2° Marriages may be numerous and at an early age, but the partners use direct means to decrease the number of births. This is what is called *Malthusianism*, an improper term, for Malthus never displayed any support for these practices. 3° Certainly for many ancient peoples, for barbarian or savage peoples even today, and probably for the inhabitants of some large modern cities, abortion must be considered an important preventive obstacle to births. 4° Incontinence and prostitution perhaps should be counted as preventive obstacles also. 5° Some people claim, but this is not certain, that great intellectual activity militates against reproduction. Many other causes which decrease the number of births could be listed, but this is a subject which goes beyond the object of our present study.

75. Repressive obstacles can come: (α) From an increase in the number of deaths which follow directly from a lack of food (poverty, famine) or indirectly from illnesses caused by poverty,

or which are a result of the absence of the hygienic measures which, not just through ignorance but also because of high cost, may not be practiced. This cause operates continuously as well as in a discontinuous way *via* epidemics. (β) From an increase in violent deaths, such as infanticide, murder, and deaths due to wars. (γ) From emigration.

76. Obstacles to the increase of population do not necessarily decrease the disproportion between population and wealth, because they may also decrease wealth. For example, war can increase that disproportion by destroying relatively more wealth than men; emigration can take less people, relatively, than wealth out of a country.

77. The indirect effect of the obstacles may be different from the direct effect (§ 80).

Note that a population A and a population B may have the same annual increase, resulting from a large number of births and a large number of deaths for A, and from a small number of births and a small number of deaths for B. The first case is typical of barbarian peoples and also, in part, of civilized peoples up to the present century; in contemporary Europe, Russia, Hungary and Spain approach this case. The second case is that of wealthier and more civilized peoples; in contemporary Europe, France, Switzerland and Belgium approach it.

78. Even if the increase is the same for A and for B, the composition of their populations would be different. In A there would be many children and few adults; the opposite for B.

79. The equilibrium between the number of births and the number of deaths, from which the increase in population results, depends on an infinite number of economic and social causes; but once established, if a change takes place in one direction, it immediately produces a change in the opposite direction, thus reestablishing the original equilibrium. To tell the truth, this observation is a tautology[21] because it is this fact itself which is characteristic of and defines equilibrium (III, 22). Hence we must modify the form of the observation and say that experience shows us that in reality there is an equilibrium, which, however, can slowly change.

---

[21] Certain writers have seen in these facts indications of a mysterious law to which they have given the name "law of compensation." They will find their so-called law in all cases where an equilibrium exists.

Levasseur, *La population française*, II, p. 11: "When a demographic phenomenon departs sharply from the mean . . . it usually produces an equally sharp reaction . . . ; the following year, sometimes even several years later, this phenomenon still remains different from its mean and returns to its level again only after several oscillations, thus obeying a *law of compensation*."

It is a well known fact that following a war or an epidemic, marriages and births increase, and the population which the war or the epidemics had decimated quickly returns to its original level. Similarly an increase in emigration may not produce a decrease in population but have the effect rather of stimulating marriages and births. Conversely, an increase in the number of marriages and births can be rapidly offset by an increase in the number of deaths and in emigration.

80. Certain practices intended to diminish the population but which can also affect customs in a permanent way and consequently change the equilibrium itself, have a totally different effect. This is involved in the claim that emigration, by providing an outlet for excess population, increases improvidence in its generation; consequently in certain cases emigration can be, in the end, a cause not of a decrease but of an increase in population. Similar observations have been made on the subject of abortion, the exposure of infants and infanticide. Material for giving a rigorous proof of these things, however, is lacking.

81. **Subjective view of phenomena related to population increase.** The question of population growth and the obstacles to it is one which men seem unable to consider without becoming emotional; the reason for this is that they are concerned about championing a preconceived theory rather than with devoting themselves to scientific research; and they regard those who contradict them with the same anger with which believers regard infidels.

We have here a good example of the way in which economic considerations combine with others to determine men's opinions. The ratio of wealth to the number of men is a very powerful social fact. And social facts, through the effects they have on men living in society, determine their opinions of it. Thus the fact of the ratio of wealth to the number of people operates indirectly and nearly always without the knowledge of those affected (§ 54).

82. It is to the interest of the wealthy classes and political oligarchies that population increase as much as possible, because an abundance of labor makes it easy to hire, and because a larger number of subjects enhances the power of the politically dominant class. If other factors did not enter into the situation the phenomenon would then be very simple. On the one hand, the wealthy and politically dominant classes would preach in favor of increasing the population; on the other hand, the poor classes would be in favor of its restriction. Such would be the theory, but in the real world the opposite might take place, the wealthy limiting the

number of their children in order to keep their patrimony intact, and the poor having many children in order to profit from them or simply because of improvidence. A phenomenon of this type may be observed in France, and it is not by chance that the *nationalists* and the conservatives are warm champions of measures for increasing the population (§ 86). The radical-socialists are less well advised, and their leadership has shown itself disposed to approve legislative measures tending to promote population increase (§ 86). It is true that usually these measures have been devoid of all efficacy; but if they were effective they would destroy the power base of the radical-socialists.

83. The phenomenon is, moreover, much more complex than it seems at first. As far as the influence of any economic principle is concerned, we know that it can have different effects because of the ignorance of individuals and their needs of the moment.

Do revolutions take place more easily when the poor classes are suffering considerable poverty, or when they are relatively well-off?

84. If this question is answered in favor of the first hypothesis, at any given time the wealthy classes and the dominant classes would be preaching limitation of population for fear of seeing the power of their adversaries increase, and the leaders of the populace, on the other hand, would be advocating unlimited population increase precisely in order to increase the number of their troops. This is what took place toward the end of the 18th century and the beginning of the 19th, and was the basis of the debate between Godwin and Malthus.

85. If the question is answered in favor of the second hypothesis, which although it seems paradoxical at first is indeed more in accord with the facts as shown by careful study (§ 54), the effects of the economic element will be entirely different. The dominant classes sometimes understand this, but sometimes they do not and seem to know nothing about the reason for the facts. And so, although de Tocqueville has clearly given, in a special case, the correct answer to the question, today we see many members of the dominant class behaving in a way which is prejudicial to the future of their own class. As a blind man groping along, they seem to have no notion of the course they ought to follow, and end up pursuing their own ruin. In addition, ethical grounds and also physiological decadence contribute to this result. The leaders of the common people, in a word the members of the new *elite* who are getting ready to oust those of the old *elite*, have sometimes understood that an excessive amount of poverty simply led to riots easily suppressed by the

dominant class and that, on the other hand, an increase in well-being is better preparation for revolution. This is why some of them are supporters of population limitation, while others do not concern themselves with this question, or exert only a little effort on behalf of measures which would increase population (§ 82). But the leaders who would be well disposed toward limitation encounter a serious obstacle in the fact that they must satisfy their followers' sentiments (§ 87). The common man is especially concerned with his present needs, he wants to eat, drink and satisfy his sexual desires; and the leaders are compelled to promise that when "capitalism" has been destroyed and the golden age arrives, all these needs, all these desires, can be satisfied without restraint.

86. There are not only economic motives, there are also ethical, religious, metaphysical, aesthetic, etc., motives. Quite apart from any economic motive, religious conservatives are indignant at the mere idea that anyone might want to act contrary to the divine precept of increase and multiply. In modern times everything concerning sexual relations has been covered by a chaste veil, but often hypocritically. The idea that man be so audacious as to calculate the consequences of his sexual satisfactions and, looking ahead, regulate them, appears to certain people to be such a monstrous thing that it is difficult for them to consider it dispassionately. These are the motives, and there are still others it would take too long to enumerate, which induce many members of the upper classes of society to oppose vigorously everything which would tend to limit the size of the population. Sometimes these motives are an addition to the economic motives we have spoken of, but often they are so strong that by themselves they can determine people's opinions. These doctrines come from sentiments alone, and instead of drawing their theories from the facts, their authors propose to subordinate the facts to the theories. They already know the solution to the population problem before having studied it, and if they resort to observation, it is not to search for the solution to the problem but to find arguments to justify their preconceived opinions.

87. Among the people, other causes have similar effects, as we have already indicated in § 85. The promise of great abundance of economic goods, thanks to a new social organization, seems insufficient to some, who wish to add unlimited license for their passions; some go so far as to claim that man will be able to give free rein to his sexual instinct because he will no longer have to fear any unpleasant consequences, and Fourier, more logical than the others, allows for the satisfaction of all human instincts for the same reason.

Sometimes these fantasies are given a pseudo-scientific garb and it is claimed that the sexual instinct can be indulged without fear because it will diminish with increased intellectual activity. Note that the results remain the same if there are a small number of children born because the sexual instinct is strong but men do not let it dominate them, or because the sexual instinct is weak and men do not curb it. Thus all this debate has no other purpose than speculation about whether, in some future centuries, certain acts will be voluntary or not.

88. The facts we have just been examining are psychic facts, facts of opinion, of doctrine. It must be added immediately that these beliefs and opinions have had no effect, or have had only a slight effect, on the actual increase in population; it appears that it is this increase which has influenced the psychic facts we have just mentioned, rather than the latter influencing the former. In the first half of the 19th century scholars and statesmen in France extolled the advantages of population limitation, *Malthusianism*, and the population increased; now they preach the necessity of pushing for an increase in population, and the population remains stationary.

89. **Malthus and his theories.**[22] Even today prevailing custom in the study of political economy does not permit us to study the problem of population without mentioning Malthus; and, though not approving of this custom, we cannot ignore it as long as it exists. Besides, a study of this type can be profitable. The theories of Malthus will provide an example of the errors one inevitably falls into when theory and practice, when scientific research and the preaching of morality, are mixed together.

90. Malthus's work is unclear. It is often difficult to know precisely what questions this author is posing. All in all four parts can be distinguished in this work.

91. 1° A scientific part, that is, research on the uniformities of phenomena. Malthus has the great merit of having suggested and tried to demonstrate that the generative force by itself would have led to a greater increase in population than that observed in real life, from which it follows that this force is restricted by certain obstacles. But Malthus added some less certain details to the study of this general theory. He wanted to establish that population tends to grow according to a geometric progression, and the means of subsistence according to an arithmetic progression; in addition he

---

[22] For a criticism of *malthusianism* see the work of M. Tullio Martello, *L'economia politica antimalthusiana e il socialismo*, Venice, 1894; this study is full of penetrating observations and profound thoughts.

estimated that this geometric progression was such that the population would double in about 25 years.

There have been an unbelievable number of controversies and useless debates dealing with these two celebrated progressions.

In some cases the ideas of Malthus have been so misunderstood by his detractors that one can question their good faith.

92. If we compare this theory of Malthus with the facts, we see that in one particular case, that of England in the 19th century, the population has grown according to a geometric progression, doubling about every 54 years; but wealth has grown according to an even greater progression, and in this case the arithmetic progression does not correspond in any way to reality (*Cours*, § § 211, 212).

93. Similarly Malthus does not restrict himself to observation alone when he asserts that the obstacles necessarily belong to one of the following three classes: moral restraint, vice and poverty-stricken conditions of life (misery). The sole objective of this classification is to oblige men to resort to moral restraint.

94. 2° A descriptive and historical part in which the author proposes to demonstrate the existence and effects of the last two types of obstacles. He says that the first one "has very little effect on men in the present state of society," although abstaining from marriage, considered independently of its moral consequences, does operate strongly, among modern peoples, to reduce the number of births.

95. 3° A part of the work is polemical. The author wants to show that man's economic and social condition, good or bad, depends almost exclusively on how much or how little people restrict the number of births, and that it depends very little, or even not at all, on governmental action and on the social organization. This part is manifestly false.

96. 4° A part whose purpose is to preach certain rules of conduct. The author has discovered the universal panacea; namely, moral restraint, or to put it in current terminology, he has solved the "social question"; he mounts the pulpit and reveals the new faith. This part can be disregarded. One more sermon, added to all those which have already been given, showing all that is useful, beautiful and noble about chastity, really adds nothing new to our knowledge.

97. **Human society in general.** As we have already pointed out (II, 102) society appears to us as a heterogeneous mass, hierarchically organized.[23] This hierarchy always exists, except perhaps

---

[23] M. R. Bennini has published some excellent studies on *social hierarchies*.

among savage populations which live scattered about like animals. It follows from this fact that society is always governed by a small number of men, by an *elite*, even when it seems to have a completely democratic organization; this has been recognized since earliest times. In the Athenian democracy there were demagogues, "leaders of the people,"[24] and Aristophanes, in his *Knights*, depicts them as achieving dominance over a people lacking in good sense. In our time the democracies in France, England, the United States, etc., are in fact governed by a small number of politicians. Similarly, absolute monarchies, save in the very rare cases where the monarch is a genius of the first order, are also governed by an *elite*, which is often a bureaucracy.[25]

98. One could conceive of a society in which the hierarchy were permanent; but such a society would not be real. In all human societies, even in those organized in castes, the hierarchy eventually is modified. The principal difference between societies consists in this: that the change can be more or less slow, or more or less rapid.

The fact, of which we are so often reminded, that aristocracies disappear, emerges from all the history of our societies. It is a fact which has been known from the earliest times;[26] it has been confirmed scientifically by the studies of Jacoby, Ammon, etc.[27] This history of human societies, in large part, is the history of a succession of aristocracies.

99. All species of living beings would degenerate but for the intervention of selection; the human race does not escape this law. The *humanitarians* can close their eyes and deliberately ignore this truth, but that in no way changes the facts. Some degenerate elements which have to be eliminated by selection are born in every species. The unhappiness caused by this destruction is the price paid

---

[24] δημαγωγός comes from δῆμος and ἄγω.

[25] *Equites*, 62: ὁ δ' αὐτὸν ὡς ὁρᾶ μεμμαχχοηχότα, "when he sees the stupidity in that state." See also the scholiast. Moreover, the entire comedy elaborates on this point.

[26] Dante, *Purgatorio*, VII, 121-122:
> Rade volte risurge per li rami
> L'umana probitate . . .

Paradiso, XVI, 76-78:
> Udir come le schiatte si disfanno
> Non ti parrà nuova cosa nè forte,
> Poscia che le cittadi termine hanno.

[27] Paul Jacoby, *Etudes sur la sélection dans les rapports avec l'hérédité chez l'homme*, Paris, 1881; Otto Ammon, *Die Gesellschaftsordnung und ihre natürlichen Grundlagen;* Vacher de Lapouge, *Les sélections sociales*.

for perfecting the race; it is one of those many cases where the good of the individual is at variance with the good of the species (II, 30). Certain forms of selection may disappear; but they must be replaced by others so that the race does not degenerate. At present some people think that from now on the human race can dispense with selection which operates through war. They may be right but they may also be wrong. This much is certain, that they have furnished no solid proof for their belief; their declamations on the evils entailed by war and the suffering of human beings resulting from it cannot be considered as such proof.

100. Finally there is a very important fact which, as we have already explained, is related to a large number of social facts and even partially determines them. This fact is the ratio of wealth, or better, capital, per capita. The larger this ratio, the more highly developed is the civilization. We must remember, however, that we are obliged to evaluate wealth in *numéraire*, and the unit of *numéraire* is in no way fixed; it follows that wealth per capita is known only more or less approximately.

A great many people believe that new social forms are determined much more by variations in the distribution of wealth than by variations in the amount of wealth per capita. This view is absolutely wrong; we have shown that changes in the distribution are of little importance (§ 16), while variation in the average amount can be very important (§ 92).

101. We have mentioned four types of facts, namely: the hierarchy, the succession of aristocracies, selection, and the wealth or capital per inhabitant. These facts are by far the most important in determining the character of a society, that is, in determining other social facts. But, in reality, it is not a relation of cause and effect which is involved. The first facts influence the second, but the latter, in their turn, react on the former; and in the final analysis, we have a relation of mutual dependence.

102. **Quantitative conditions regarding usefulness to society and to the individual.** It does not seem, at the moment, that there is any point in examining the appropriateness of setting a limit to the growth of capital per inhabitant; but it is possible that the day may come when this problem might arise.

103. With respect to the hierarchy, succession of aristocracies, and selection, the problem of maximum utility is principally quantitative. Human societies cannot exist without a hierarchy; but it would be a very serious error to conclude from this that they would be more prosperous the more rigid is the hierarchy. Similarly, change

of aristocracies is useful; but a certain stability is not to be disregarded. Selection must be kept within limits such that its advantageous effects for the species are not purchased with too much suffering by individuals.

These considerations raise many very serious problems which we cannot go into here. It will suffice to have indicated that they exist, which many people still do not know, or doubt, or refuse to admit.

104. **Stability and selection.** One could imagine a human society in which each individual each day behaved independently of the past; the faculty for change or mutability would then be very great. In absolute terms this state of affairs is impossible, for it is impossible to prevent an individual from relying, at least in part, on his own past activity and the circumstances in which he has lived, if only for the experience which he may have acquired. The most poverty-stricken savage peoples only approximate this condition, for they always have some shelter, some weapons, some capital.

105. At the other extreme we can conceive of a society in which each person is assigned his role, from birth to death, and from which there can be no escape. Stability here would be very great, society would be crystallized. This extreme case does not exist in real life either; societies organized into castes only approximate it more or less.

106. Societies which have existed, and which exist now, are intermediate cases of various types. In modern societies the elements of stability are provided by private property and inheritance; the elements of change and selection come from the opportunity everyone has to rise as far as he can in the social hierarchy. To tell the truth, there is nothing to indicate that this state of affairs is perfect, nor that it ought to continue indefinitely. If some type of private ownership, of capital, for example, and inheritance could be effectively abolished, in whole or in part, the element of stability would be greatly weakened, and the element of change and selection strengthened. It cannot be decided *a priori* whether that would be advantageous or detrimental to society.

107. Starting from the premise that in the past it has been advantageous to decrease the strength of one of these two elements and increase that of the other, some people conclude that it would be equally advantageous to continue the same thing in the future; but such reasoning is worthless, for in all quantitative problems of this type there is a maximum. To reason in that way is like starting with the fact that a seed germinates better when the tempera-

ture rises from 6° to 20°, and concluding thereby that it would be better still if the temperature were to rise to 100°.

108. Reasoning which concludes that, because a diminution in one of these two elements and an increase in the other have been observed in the past, the same thing will be observed in the future has no value either. Changes in societies are not constantly in the same direction, they are generally oscillatory.[28]

109. The advantages of mutability, which is one reason for selection, and the drawbacks of stability, follow in large part from the fact that aristocracies do not endure. In addition, because of man's characteristic misoneism and his reluctance to exert himself too much, it is desirable that the best ones be stimulated by the competition of those who are less capable; hence even the mere possibility of change is useful. On the other hand, change pushed to extremes is very painful to man, it disheartens him and reduces his efforts to a minimum. Someone whose situation is less desirable than another's naturally desires change, but after having succeeded he desires even more to conserve what he has acquired and stabilize his condition. Human societies have a very strong tendency to give a certain rigidity to any new organization, to become crystallized in any new form. Therefore it very often happens that the passage from one form to another is not by a continuous movement, but by jumps; one form breaks up and is replaced by another, the latter in its turn will break up, and so it goes. This is observable in all forms of human activity, in language, for example, in law, etc. No living language is immutable; but on the other hand, a language composed exclusively of neologisms would be incomprehensible; an appropriate middle course is necessary. The introduction of neologisms does not proceed uniformly, it takes place at intervals on the authority of well-known writers, or other literary authority, such as the French Academy or the Accademia della Crusca in Italy. Analogous phenomena can be observed in the field of legislation; and it is not only in countries where the law has become codified that changes end up as a new rigid system, but even in those where it would seem that legislation ought to be much more flexible.[29]

110. In social economy mutability may take various forms, and these may be replaced in part by others. Mutability could work in

---

[28] *Cours*, II, § 258; *Systèmes*, I, p. 344.

[29] H. Sumner Maine, *Ancient Law*, London, 1861, Chapter III, compares the systems of Roman and English *equity*: "In Rome as in England, the jurisprudence of equity leads, as always happens, to a state of law similar to that which the old common law constituted when equity began to modify

opposition to selection, but we will consider only changes which aid it. Violent revolutions often have this result. When active, energetic, intelligent elements have accumulated in the lower strata, and on the other hand, the higher strata include an overly large proportion of degenerate elements (§ § 20, 21), a revolution which replaces one *aristocracy* with another breaks out. The new social structure then becomes rigid, and will be broken up itself by a similar revolution.

These violent revolutions can be replaced by a percolation process in which the select, the most apt, elements rise and decayed elements move downward. Some such movement is almost always taking place but it can be more or less intense; and it is this variation in intensity which permits the accumulation, or the non-accumulation, of decayed elements in the higher strata and of superior elements in the lower strata.

111. In order that this movement be sufficient to prevent such accumulation it is not enough that it be permitted by law and that there be no obstacles put in its way (caste for example), but circumstances must be such that movement can become a reality. For example, among war-like peoples, it is not enough that law and custom permit a simple soldier to become a general, it is further necessary that war furnish him the opportunity. Among commercial and industrial peoples, it is not enough that law and custom permit the poorest citizen to become wealthy and rise to the highest positions in the state, it is also necessary that there be a commercial and industrial development intensive enough that this becomes a reality for an appreciable number of citizens.

112. Measures which, directly or indirectly, reduce debts weaken the stable element, and consequently indirectly reinforce the elements of mutability and selection. The effect is the same for anything which causes a general rise in prices, but only for the time during which they are rising. If, for example, all prices double, economic equilibrium ends up, after some length of time, identical to what it was originally; but during the passage from the one state to the other debts diminish and mutability and selection are facilitated. Debasement of the currency, increase in the quantity of

---

it. There always comes a time when the moral principles adopted have supported all their legitimate consequences; and then the system based on them becomes as rigid, as incapable of development, and as likely to fall behind progress in mores as the most strict legal codes." [French] translation, Courcelle-Seneuil, Paris, 1874, p. 66.

precious metals (after the discovery of America for example), issues of paper money, protective tariffs, trade unions obtaining increases in wages, etc., have in part the effect of facilitating mutability and selection. But they also have other effects, and it remains to be seen in each particular case whether the damage they cause is not greater than the advantageous results.

113. It has been noted that in Athens, after the reforms of Solon, there was no longer any need to resort to debt reduction, money was not debased, and no other process was initiated to raise prices. The principal reason for this fact should be sought in the intense commercial activity of Athens, which by itself alone was sufficient to insure the circulation of the *aristocracies*.

114. From the days of classical antiquity up to our own times, we observe among the peoples of Europe a series of revolutions, of legislative measures, of intentional or accidental events, all of which cooperate to reinforce the element of mutability and selection. It can be concluded, with high probability, that the element of stability, or even of mutability opposed to selection, was extremely strong; and as a result the factors tending to weaken it were brought about by reaction. For other societies this conclusion could be different. The necessity of providing changes favorable to selection is also related to the proportion of superior elements produced in the lower strata. It may be that the greater stability of certain oriental peoples is due, at least in part, to the fact that this proportion is lower among them than among western peoples.

115. If among our western populations the element of stability were exclusively the result of the institution of private property and inheritance, that would be very strong evidence of the necessity for reducing, or even abolishing, the institution of private property. It is strange that the socialists have not perceived the support which this manner of viewing the phenomena could bring to their theories.

But the element of stability which is opposed to change *via* selection is, in our societies, far from being exclusively the result of the institution of private property Laws and customs have divided men into classes, and even where these classes have disappeared, as among modern democratic peoples, wealth assures advantages which enable certain individuals to beat back competitors. In the United States of America, politicians and judges often sell themselves to the highest bidder. In France, the Panama affair and other similar ones have shown that European democracy, from this point of view, does not differ essentially from American democracy. In general, from ancient times up to our own, the upper classes of society have used political power to despoil the poor classes; but at present, in certain democratic countries, a diametrically opposite phenomenon seems to have begun. We have never been able to observe, for a long enough time period, a state of affairs in which the government remains neutral, neither aiding the latter to despoil the former, nor conversely. Thus we cannot decide empirically whether the considerable strength of the element of stability which opposes selection of elements from the lower classes has its origin in the institution of private property or in political oppression by the upper classes. To be able to draw correct conclusions, it would be necessary to be able to separate the two types of facts and study their effects separately.

116. **Subjective interpretation of the preceding facts.** Up to now we have observed the facts objectively. But they appear in a quite different way to man's feelings and to his intellect. We have shown elsewhere how the circulation of *elites* is subjectively interpreted, and we cannot dwell on this point. In general, men are prone to give their private demands the form of general demands. A new aristocracy which wants to supplant another older one ordinarily gives battle, not in its own name, but in the name of the greatest number. A rising aristocracy always wears the mask of democracy (II, 104).

The state of mind produced by the accumulation of superior elements in the lower strata and inferior elements in the upper strata often manifests itself in religious, moral, political and pseudo-scientific theories about the equality of men. And from this comes the paradoxical fact that it is precisely the inequality of men which has induced them to proclaim their equality.

117. Peoples of antiquity reduced debts and the interest on loans without theoretical discussions; governments in times past debased the currency without invoking economic theories, and took measures for economic protection without knowing what it is. The facts have not been the result of theories; but just the opposite, the theories have been constructed to justify the facts. Nowadays people want to provide a theoretical foundation for all these facts. A religious basis has been provided for reducing, or even abolishing, interest on money, and from it have come great theoretical debates whose practical effects are just about nothing because they in no way influence the real causes of the facts.

Let us assume that it could be demonstrated rigorously that interest on money is not "legitimate," or, on the other hand, that it is perfectly legitimate. Neither in the one case nor in the other would the facts be changed, or rather they would be changed only in a quite negligible manner. The same for the protective tariff. All the theories for or against it have not had the slightest practical effect. Some studies or discourses on this subject may indeed have had some effect, not by reason of their scientific content, but because they evoked certain sentiments and were able to unite people who had certain common interests. The theoretical debates which took place for some years on bimetallism were completely useless; they are now ended because an increase in prices has occurred for reasons other than the free coinage of silver. Marx's theory of value has become antiquated in our day since the socialist leaders have little by little come into the management of public affairs. The assertion that value is crystallized labor was nothing other than the expression of a sentiment of unrest felt by the superior elements of the new aristocracy, compelled as they were to remain in the lower strata. Consequently, it is quite natural that as they enter the higher strata, their sentiments change, and as a result their mode of expression changes too. This is particularly true of a class taken as a whole, since for some particular individuals sentiments persist even when the circumstances which gave rise to them have changed.

It must never be forgotten (II, 4) that ordinarily men are not conscious of the origin of their sentiments, and therefore it often happens that they believe they are yielding to the clarity of theoretical reasoning when they are acting under the influence of quite different reasons.

CHAPTER VIII

LAND CAPITAL AND MOBILE CAPITAL

1. **Land capital.** This capital should be considered in the state in which it exists; the ground cannot be separated from the mobile capital which has been, as they say, "incorporated" into it.

Land capital is composed of agricultural land, mines, industrial sites, sites for dwellings, for country homes, etc.

2. Competition among segments of land capital manifests itself indirectly by means of their products or their users who go where they find land capital which suits them. For example wheat from land in the United States of America is shipped to Europe and competes with wheat from land on this continent. Similarly, thanks to the development of modern means of transportation, men who work in the center of large cities can live in the suburbs, whose land thus competes with that in the center of the city.

3. It is difficult and often impossible to produce additional land capital by means of saving; consequently the phenomenon of *rent* will manifest itself most clearly with respect to land.

4. Land capital does not enjoy any economic precedence over other capital; it is neither more nor less indispensable to production than other capital. On the other hand, it often is of greater importance than other capital from the political viewpoint. For a very long time, and among a large number of peoples, political power has belonged to the owners of the land.

5. Land ownership may take numerous forms. Real life furnishes examples of many varieties within the main classes of ownership: collective, family and individual.

6. Similarly the forms of relationships between the owners of the land and those who work it are quite varied. Several of these forms may exist side by side and may be more or less appropriate to the circumstances. The search for the best form of ownership

321

in abstracto is an insoluble problem. In modern agriculture we encounter the following forms which are quite widespread: direct working of the soil by the owner and his family, cultivation by laborers who work under the direction of the owners, renting, *metayage*. Each of these forms is better suited than the others to certain types of farming and to certain economic and social contingencies.

7. It can be socially advantageous for land not to change ownership too easily; it is, in general, economically advantageous if it is able to pass easily into the hands of those who know best how to exploit it. It is also advantageous for the nominal owner of land to be the actual owner as well. This is not the case when the land is encumbered with mortgages for an amount almost equal to the value of the land itself. In this case the nominal owner is in reality the manager for his creditors, and he cultivates the land on their behalf.

8. **Mobile capital.** This category includes all capital which is left when human capital (people) and land capital have been subtracted. Factories, houses, supplies of all sorts of things, domestic animals, machines, means of transport, household goods, metallic money, and the like are the principal kinds of mobile capital. Most of these things are readily obtained *via* the transformation of savings. Some of such capital can be transported readily from one place to another and as a result competition among these elements of mobile capital takes place directly. The cases of *rent* which can be observed are often less important than those involving land capital.

9. **Savings.** Savings are made up of the economic goods which men abstain from consuming. Because such goods are ordinarily valued in money, people often imagine that savings are made up of money.

10. The goods saved do not accumulate, but are promptly transformed; as a result, the sum total of savings in existence in a country at any given time is made up of stocks only to a small extent; for the most part it exists in the form of mobile capital, in the form of improvements in land capital, or even is incorporated in human capital.

It is necessary to be careful not to confuse simple savings with savings transformed into capital, that is, transformed into things which are used in production, nor with *capital-savings*[1] which is that part of savings which, although not transformed into other capital, is nevertheless used in production. Wheat in a granary, for

---

[1] *Cours*, § 90.

example, is simple savings; the moment a part of this wheat is used to feed the laborers who work the land—a part which, consumed in this fashion, will be replaced at harvest time—it is *capital-savings*; the part which is used to buy cattle to work on the land, or the machine which threshes the wheat, will cease to exist in the form of savings, and be transformed into *capital*.

Let us not forget that this classification has the same character as the one we gave to the concept of *capital* in V, § 21; that is, it is not very rigorous and is partly arbitrary; nevertheless, it is convenient for conveying an idea of many phenomena without using mathematics; its lack of rigor is not inconvenient because we will make no use of it in the formulas of pure economics, which alone furnish us with rigorous proofs.

11. Saving is only partially determined by the income one receives from it; it results in part also from man's desire to have in reserve goods which can be consumed from time to time; it is also the result of an instinctive act of man, who behaves in this respect like many animals. This is why, even if the interest on savings were to fall to zero, men would not cease to save; it can even happen that certain individuals save more, within certain limits at least, when the interest on savings decreases. Assume an individual who intends to stop working when he has saved enough to have an income of 2,000 francs for the rest of his life. If the interest on savings decreases, he would have to work a greater number of years, or save more each year, or both. We note that from the beginning of the 19th century to the present time, in civilized countries, the income from savings has been decreasing, and at the same time saving has been increasing.

In summary, within the limits of our observations, which of course are very restricted, we can in no way assert that the annual amount of saving depends exclusively, or even principally, on (is a *function of*) the interest on savings; and still less can we say that saving increases with an increase in interest, or *vice versa*.

In the transformation of savings man is influenced by a very great number of considerations; one of these is the gross interest which he will receive from the savings; if other things are equal, given two possible transformations, he will choose the one which provides the larger gross interest; but if the circumstances surrounding these two uses are different, he might choose the one which provides lower gross interest but has other favorable aspects.

We have already (V, 30) taken some of these circumstances into account, and have eliminated them by deducting certain sums for insurance and amortization of the capital from the gross interest; what remains is approximately the net interest.[2]

By proceeding in the same way, certain other circumstances could be eliminated; but sometimes that would be very difficult, and not very useful.

12. In addition it should be noted that the elimination we have just indicated is only approximate. It corresponds to some objective considerations, whereas subjective considerations are what largely determine the use of savings. We already noted this fact when we spoke about the profit which enterprises may yield (V, 68). Let us add an example. Here are two uses for 1,000 francs: 1° the probability of loss in the year is $\frac{1}{4}$, consequently the insurance premium is 250 francs; gross interest is 300 francs, thus net interest is 50 francs; 2° the probability of loss is only 1/100, consequently the insurance premium is only 10 francs; gross interest is 60 francs, net interest is 50 francs.

---

[2] Some literary economists, who have the bad habit of discussing things they do not understand, see a tautology in this. Naturally, they say, if one eliminates from two gross prices everything which makes them different, one obtains equal residuals.

That is not the case at all. The rate of interest is related to a large number of facts; i.e., (A) the insurance premium; (B) the amortization charge; (C) the difference in price between a future good and a present good, or the net rate of interest; (D, E, F, etc.) an infinity of other objective and subjective circumstances. The theorem asserts that in a given time and place and for certain classes of use of capital (for example purchases of securities on the Exchange): 1° the group of factors D, E, F, . . . , although they may have a predominant influence in special cases, in general and on the average have only much less influence than factors A, B, and C, so that the former group can often be disregarded compared to the latter group. 2° A and B are essentially variable, and in any case more variable than C, which, under the stated conditions, remains almost constant. Thus as a first and rough approximation the residuals which remain after subtracting A and B from the gross prices are nearly equal.

These explanations are given here only for a didactic purpose, for all polemics with persons unaccustomed to scientific reasoning can be only a waste of time.

For example, it is useless to refute the assertion of Professor A. Graziani, who believes somewhat naively that "to include place and time in one category of transformations amounts to a purely verbal unification." If observation of facts has not apprised him that, far from being united only verbally, these transformations always exist together in concrete phenomena, so that most often they can only be separated by means of abstraction, he must be abandoned to his lucubrations which have only remote connections with scientific reality.

Net interest is equal in the two cases; hence both uses are equivalent objectively; but the first will be preferred by certain individuals, and the second by others. Thus, in reality, there is a certain type of savings which is directed toward each of these uses, and there is no, or very little, competition between them.

12b. There is an infinite number of quite varied circumstances which operate to make rates of gross interest different.

For example, on the Exchange a new security issue which is completely identical in every respect to the securities of older issues, can nevertheless, for a certain time, until they are well "seasoned" ["classés"], have a lower price than the securities issued earlier.

Sometimes there are curious anomalies. For example, 1906 5% Russians during the entire year 1907 had been quoted in London 3 to 4 points lower than in Paris. Thus, on the 20th of January 1908 these securities could be purchased in London[3] at 91.5, while in Paris one paid 96.1. These securities have absolutely the same guaranty, and are transferable at short notice in London and Paris alike. The difference between the two prices could be accounted for, if absolutely necessary, at least in part, by speculation, by the circumstance that one who buys these securities for resale has an advantage operating at Paris where only one price is quoted. But it is inconceivable why the Frenchman who wants to use his capital to buy 5% Russians pays 96.1 in Paris when he could get them for 91.5 in London. It is probably due to psychological causes, habit, etc.

But here is an even more curious anomaly. Two series of 4% Argentines, with interest payable at the same time, April and October, are traded in Paris and in Brussels. It is absolutely impossible to establish the slightest difference in intrinsic value between the 1897-1908 4% Argentines and the 1900 4% Argentines. But the second series was quoted both in Paris and in Brussels in 1907 at several points above the first. On August 10, 1907, the first series was worth 84.05 at Paris and the second 91.70. Here then is what appears to be one good and which on the same market, at the same time, has two prices. It is possible that it is a matter of seasoning [classement] of the bonds, but the complete explanation of these phenomena is yet to be given.

The sale of goods at retail presents still more numerous anomalies.

---

[3] In London two prices are quoted, one for securities the public wants to sell, the other for securities the public wants to buy. These two prices were 91 and 91.5.

For example, it is not unusual to find two neighboring shops selling identical goods at different prices.

The conclusion to be drawn from these facts is the one we have already mentioned many times. Political economy, as many other sciences, is concerned only with phenomena in general and on the average. Meteorology can tell us the average amount of rain which falls annually in a given locality; it is and will always remain incapable of informing us of the fate of each drop of rain.

13. The different ways of using savings can give rise to different classes of savings, which form nearly as many commodities of different qualities.

One of the circumstances we have to examine here is the time during which the savings will remain in the use, that is, whether the loan of the savings—or any other equivalent operation—is for a short or a long term. In reality, savings do not constitute one homogeneous mass. One part may be employed only for a rather short time, another part for a more or less long time. All possible varieties are found on the financial markets of our societies, ranging from savings which may be lent only for a few days to those which may be lent for several years.

14. The modern organization of joint stock companies, whose securities may be easily bought and sold, has made the differences between savings which may be advanced for a short time and savings which may be advanced for a very long time much less pronounced, because those who buy securities which have a large market on the exchange are always certain of being able to resell them the moment they need their savings. They are not sure, however, of being able to get their purchase price. This explains why governments generally pay a lower interest on their treasury bonds than on their *Rentes*. For the former, one will get exactly the sum lent; for the latter, it may be larger or smaller.

15. Just like differences in time, differences in space differentiate certain categories of savings. Ordinarily, to induce savings to emigrate, the interest offered must be greater abroad than in the saver's own country.

16. Many other psychological factors affect the interest on savings. In France, the alliance with Russia has been advantageous for Russian government bonds, and consequently interest on them is lower than it would have been without that friendly attitude on the part of French buyers.

Finally, psychological factors which accompany economic crises also influence the determination of interest on savings.

17. Interest on savings and social organization. Interest on savings comes from the difference between a thing available today and a thing available after a certain time, just as the difference in the prices of wine and oil comes from the difference in the qualities of these two goods. In order to determine quantitatively the interest on savings—just like the price difference between wine and oil—we must draw on all the conditions of economic equilibrium.

18. Consequently, whatever be the social organization (V, 48), given that what man can enjoy today will never be exactly equal to what he can enjoy only after a certain time—just as wine will never be the same as oil—interest on savings will always exist—just as there will always be, at least in general, a difference between the price of wine and the price of oil; but this interest and these prices will vary quantitatively depending upon the social organization, because the latter is one of the conditions of economic equilibrium (V, 48).

19. One can conceive of a social organization in which each person would make use only of the savings which he produces and which he owns; in such a social organization one could say, to use a certain modern jargon, that the producer is not separated from his means of production. Certain people would have more savings than they could use, and for them the interest on savings would be almost zero; there would be others who would have a very small quantity of savings, and for them the interest would be very high. On the other hand, when there can be commerce in savings, interest acquires a value in between these two extremes. This commerce naturally entails certain expenses, but neverthless the economic advantage to the society is very great, and that is why all societies end up by having commerce in savings.

20. Similarly one can conceive of a social organization in which the State has a monopoly of commerce in savings, just as in certain countries it now has a monopoly in tobacco. Taking the strictly economic point of view, it is difficult to decide whether such a monopoly of savings would raise or lower interest; one can only say that up till now, in general, the State has a higher cost of production in its industries than does private industry, which is proved by the fact that state industries have never been able to withstand the competition of private industry, and the State has always had to resort to compulsion to eliminate that private competition. But it can be objected that something which was not true in the past may be so in the future, and nothing prevents anyone from believing that the organization of State industries may become improved. In addi-

tion, the monopoly could be partial. For certain uses of savings private commerce may remain superior to the monopoly, for others it may be that there would be no great difference.

21. But two systems for the utilization of savings can be equivalent from the economic point of view, and differ enormously from the social point of view. These two things must not be confused. The existence of a shopkeeper class gives a society a different character from the one it would have if retail trade were conducted by department stores, by cooperatives, or by a State monopoly. Similarly, a society where there is private commerce in savings, and another society in which such commerce does not exist, either because it is a state monopoly or because each person uses only his own savings, differ enormously from the social point of view, apart from the differences which there may be from the economic point of view.

22. **Subjective version of the phenomena.** The most proximate obstacle to the acquisition of a good is the one which makes the greatest impression on us. The child believes that the only obstacle to obtaining some toys is the ill will of the merchant, who demands money. Similarly the adult believes that the cupidity of merchants is the only obstacle to obtaining goods cheaply; *maximum* laws, which fix the prices of some goods, are based on this sentiment. Someone who needs to transform future goods into present goods believes that there is no other obstacle but the dishonesty of the usurer, or "exploitation by the capitalist."

23. To these sentiments are added others which stem from the social organization. The great majority of men consider only the practical, and consequently synthetic, problem, and are absolutely incapable of dividing it into its different parts.

24. The sentiments we have just spoken about are primitive; they arise in man directly as a reaction against the obstacles he encounters, and as a result they will always remain, even though they be considerably weakened.

As we have often pointed out, man feels an extreme need to give an appearance of logic to his sentiments, to regard as the result of reasoning what is really the result of instinct, to give a logical theory for his non-logical actions. The form taken by his sentiments is the one which accords best, in part with the times in which they occur, and in part with the character of their author.

Theories are developed more or less according to the nature of things. With regard to the obstacle which comes from the price which a merchant must be paid for a good, it does not seem that they have ever been very complex; but there are numerous theories regarding the obstacle which comes from the price of transforming future goods into present goods.

25. There is something mysterious in this transformation of future goods into present goods; moreover it is a subject which lends itself to subtleties. Precisely because of this characteristic, it often has been governed by religious precepts, and it has given birth to metaphysical, legal and economic theories. These theories may be studied if one wants to know the way human concepts arise and develop, the evolution of social psychology; but they tell us nothing about the objective phenomenon of interest on capital. The polemics they have stirred up cannot have the least efficacy in changing the objective phenomenon; or, to put it very rigorously, that efficacy is so slight we can take it as nil. Indeed, let us assume, by means of an impossible hypothesis, that one of these theories could be proved false, and that it could be done so clearly that the proof would be accepted by everyone. The sentiments which had given birth to it would not be shaken; they would simply generate other similar theories. Without the intervention, however, of any polemics, but just because of change in the times and circumstances, these sentiments do assume a different form. Thus the Middle Ages produced theological and metaphysical theories, and our era economic theories, such as that of Karl Marx's *more-value* [*surplus-value*], that of *free land*, etc., without, however, making legal theories, such as that of Anton Menger, disappear. That good man, being only slightly acquainted with economic theories, invented certain *fundamental rights*[4] which are truly quite amusing; but after all everyone does what he can with his capabilities and knowledge.

26. **The so-called law of the decline in interest on capital.** It is certain that in the past interest on capital has sometimes gone up and sometimes gone down, without anyone being able to point out a general direction of movement. Some persons have claimed that nowadays this movement should be in the direction of a decline in interest. We have here a good example of confusion between science and practice.

M. Leroy-Beaulieu thinks there are three reasons for a decline in interest: 1° the safety of transactions; 2° the increase in the quantity of savings and the fact that all savings are now put on the market; 3° the decrease, with a given technology, in the productivity of additional capital. On the other hand there are three reasons which

---

[4] *Systemes*, II, p. 107.

operate to raise interest: 1° important discoveries suitable for practical application; 2° the emigration of capital to new countries; 3°
wars and social revolutions.

He concludes that the latter three items have less strength than
the first three, and as a result there should be a decline, little by
little, in interest on capital.[5]

27. There are two quite distinct parts in this reasoning. The
first has a scientific character; the second, a practical character.

In the first part the author establishes some relations between
certain facts and interest on capital; and although there is more
literary elegance than scientific rigor in this tripartite division of
favorable and unfavorable forces, one can accept this first part.

In the second part the author gazes into the future and tries to
foresee coming events. But how can he assert that there will be
no more great discoveries such as that of the railroad, that prolonged wars no longer menace the human race, that we are safe
from profound social upheavals? And yet, according to his own
words, in order to accept his conclusion, it is necessary to assume
that nothing like that will happen. But even if his claim is correct,
it is so by means of an extraordinary insight, by divination, and
not by scientific reasoning, because no reasoning of that type can,
given the knowledge we possess, enable him to know whether,
within a few years or after a long time, there will or will not be
prolonged wars, social upheavals, great discoveries, etc.

28. Already the facts show that our author has not been a good
prophet. He predicted that twenty or twenty-five years after 1880,
thus around 1900 to 1905, interest on capital would have dropped
to $1\frac{1}{2}$ or 2 percent[6] in western Europe. On the contrary, in 1904
the French 3 percents, the German 3 percents, the English $2\frac{1}{2}$ percents were all below par, and at the beginning of 1908 the German
empire floated a large loan at 4 percent.

29. **Money.** A good which serves to express the prices of other
goods is an IDEAL MONEY (*numéraire*), or a CONCRETE MONEY
(or simply money). The latter plays a physical role in exchanges;
the former does not.[7]

---

[5] The author again made this prophesy in 1896 in his *Traité théorique et
pratique d'économie politique*, II, p. 166.

[6] "But the result of all these movements is the normal tendency for a
gradual decrease in the rate of interest on capital." *Traité théorique et pratique
d'économie politique*, II, p. 105.

[7] We can point out an excellent work by Professor Tullio Martello, *La
Moneta;* unfortunately the book is out of print.

It is a case of a TRUE MONEY when the exchanges in which it enters are free. When a good is a true money, one kilogram of that good not having the monetary form can be exchanged for one kilogram (a little more or less) having the monetary form. For example, 10 twenty franc pieces are put in a melting pot; the gold ingot obtained can be exchanged for 10 twenty franc pieces, or just about that; thus the twenty franc pieces are true money. Into the melting pot are put 40 silver *écus*; the bit of melted down silver that is obtained can only be exchanged for much less than 40 *écus*; at present it would exchange for 20 *écus*. Thus the silver *écu* is not a true money at the present time.

All money which is not true money is FIDUCIARY MONEY, or even FALSE MONEY. The former is accepted voluntarily by the parties to the exchange without fraud or coercion, the latter is accepted only because the person who receives it is obliged to do so by law, or because he is deceived.

Between these two types of money is fiduciary money which is convertible legal tender [has *cours légal*]. For example, the notes of the Bank of England must be accepted by the public at their face value, but they can be exchanged immediately for gold at the Bank of England. In the Latin Union, silver *écus*, in practice but not by law, can be exchanged for gold with little or even no loss; thus they are convertible legal tender fiduciary money. Inconvertible legal tender notes [*billets à cours forcé*], when they cannot be exchanged at par for gold, are false money.

30. Money fills two principal roles: 1° it facilitates the exchange of goods; 2° it guarantees that exchange. The first role can be performed equally well by a true money or by a false money; the second can be performed only by a true money.[8] Since sometimes only the first role has been taken into consideration, some people have looked upon money only as a token without intrinsic value.

31. **Foreign exchange.** One kilogram of gold in London and one kilogram of gold in New York are not two identical things; they are differentiated by space. Consequently an individual may give something more or less than a kilogram of gold in London to get a kilogram of gold in New York. This more or this less is the EXCHANGE, unfavorable to London in the first case, favorable in the second.

32. Other less important circumstances operate to differentiate these two equal weights of gold. It may be necessary to have that

[8] *Cours,* § 276 *et seq.*

gold coined, or it may already be in the form of coined money; not only space, but also the time necessary for transport, etc., must be allowed for.

33. In taking account of all these circumstances, the expenses necessary to transport to New York—and have available in the money form in use there—one kilogram of gold which is in bullion form in London, can be calculated. This expense gives us the GOLD POINT.

34. Someone in London can use one of the following two procedures to make a payment in New York. He can buy a credit on New York (check, bill of exchange, etc.) by paying the exchange; or he can actually send the gold, paying the necessary expenses. It is clear that he will use the less expensive method, consequently he will buy credits as long as the exchange remains below, or at most equal to, the expenses of transportation and transformation of the gold. Hence the gold point is the one where gold begins to be exported from a county in order to make payments abroad.

We have sketched the main lines of the phenomenon; many details must be added. The gold point can vary according to circumstances: for example whether the gold is being exported simply to pay a debt, or with a view to speculation, etc.

35. **Exchange and international trade.** Given that equilibrium in international trade has been established, let us assume that it is disrupted by an increase in imports of goods. This increase in imports will have to be paid for with the country's gold; the exchange will become unfavorable to that country, the price of its money expressed in foreign money will decrease, consequently prices of domestic goods, which remain nominally the same, will decrease if expressed in foreign currency. From this it follows that exports will be stimulated and imports discouraged. Thus there are two forces which tend to reestablish equilibrium. That is not all; for us to obtain gold from abroad a higher interest will have to be paid; in practice, banks of issue must raise the discount; that will be an obstacle to further transformations of savings into capital, and to additional consumption, and thus there will be, on this score also, a tendency to return to the position of equilibrium.

If the equilibrium is disturbed by an excess of exports, obviously the phenomena are exactly opposite to those we have just sketched.

36. In a country with a paper currency, if equilibrium is disturbed by an excess of imports, the price of the paper money expressed in gold decreases; that stimulates exports, discourages imports, and

these forces operate, as in the preceding case, to reestablish equilibrium.

Certain governments—to protect, they say, commerce and industry—attempt to maintain the discount rate nearly always the same. To accomplish this, they decrease the amounts discounted, which ends up having an effect similar to increasing the discount rate since it tends thereby to discourage consumption and additional transformations of savings into capital. Or else they achieve it by increasing the quantity of paper money in circulation, which depresses its price and, as a result, augments the intensity of the forces which stimulate exports and discourage imports.

37. It is essential not to confuse the dynamic effects which result from a movement from one position of equilibrium to another, with the static effects of any position of equilibrium.

It is because of such confusion that certain writers have imagined that a depreciated money favors exports and discourages imports. This is not correct; these effects occur only while the money is depreciating.

Let us assume a position of equilibrium in which a sum of paper money is worth 80 of gold; and another position in which 100 of the paper money is worth 50 of gold. These two positions can be identical, and even—save for secondary phenomena depending on the uncertainty in the value of the money—identical to the equilibrium position which would prevail under a gold regime. They are identical because prices have varied precisely in inverse proportion to the depreciation of the money; what was worth 100 in the position of equilibrium under a gold regime, is worth 125 when 100 in paper money costs 80, and is worth 200 when 100 in paper money costs 50. As between these three positions of equilibrium, exports are no more stimulated, imports are no more discouraged, in one than in another.

But during passage from the first to the second, or from the second to the third, certain prices remain nominally the same; that is, they decrease if expressed in gold, and it is because of this fact that exports are stimulated, and imports discouraged.

38. It is precisely because the positions of equilibrium which we have just mentioned are identical, that a country which has a paper money can return to gold by changing the value of the monetary unit, assigning to it its real value. This was done in Russia and in Austria-Hungary.

39. On the other hand, if conditions in the country are not changed at all and if there is simply a borrowing of gold to end

the inconvertibility, it is in vain; gold is scarcely brought into the country when it leaves. If it were otherwise, this borrowing would have the power to change all the economic conditions in the country and to bring it to a new position of equilibrium.

One does not make gold circulate in a country by introducing it in an artificial manner, but by attracting it there by means of trade.

40. **Gresham's Law.** This law states that "bad money drives out the good"; but this is an elliptical way of speaking. In order for the bad money to drive out the good, there must be a sufficient quantity of it in circulation; otherwise the two types of money can circulate at the same time, and that is what occurs in real life with respect to small change of copper or nickel which circulates at the same time as gold.

Gresham's law is only a corollary of the principle of the stability of economic equilibrium. Since the quantity of money in circulation which corresponds to equilibrium cannot be arbitrarily increased, if an additional quantity of money is put into circulation an equal quantity must leave which will be exported abroad or melted down to secure the metal. Obviously it will be the best money, that which has the highest price, which will be withdrawn from circulation in this way, and will be replaced by the less good money.

41. **Bimetallism.** Within narrow limits, two moneys can be in circulation, gold and silver, for example. Let us assume now that the price of silver expressed in gold falls; a greater quantity of silver will be coined, the increase in the demand for this metal will cause the price of silver to rise, and it may rise enough to reach the price it had prior to the original fall. But the limits within which this phenomenon is possible are very narrow; and it is easy to see that if the production of silver exceeds these limits, the increase in the demand for silver for minting will not be enough to restore the old price of silver; all the gold will disappear from circulation and only silver will circulate. Indeed, bimetallism, in France, has always been unstable; it sometimes had a tendency to become gold monometallism, and sometimes silver monometallism. At present it would be a silver monometallism, if the coinage of silver had not been prohibited.

42. **Money substitutes.** Among civilized peoples, money is used very little in exchanges; it is replaced by bank notes, checks, bills of exchange, various clearing transfers, etc. In England, the Clearing House, where credits and debits of certain bankers are offset against each other, gives rise to enormous transactions, which would be physically impossible if it were necessary to use metallic money.

The amount of metallic money in circulation in England has remained almost constant, while commercial transactions have assumed colossal proportions. It has been replaced by money substitutes.

Among modern civilized peoples money plays a less and less important role in exchanges, almost all of which tend to be handled without the intervention of money, as when the latter did not yet exist and goods were obtained by direct exchange (barter).

43. Metallic money constitutes a very modest part of the wealth of a country. For example, the wealth of England is estimated at 251 billion francs, whereas the metallic money has not reached 3 billion. Thus we see how great is the error of those who think that wealth or even just capital is made up of gold.

44. According to the estimates of the Director of the Mint of the United States there is about 26 billion francs worth of monetary gold in the world. It is unnecessary to remark that this figure is very uncertain.

45. The figures for industrial consumption of gold and silver are still more uncertain.

Here, however, are the estimates of the United States Director of the Mint for the year 1901:

Silver	....	1,370,685 kilograms
Gold	....	119,271 kilograms
Francs	....	411 millions

46. **Banks.** Banks of deposit receive deposits and make loans; thus they are entrepreneurs who transform simple savings into capital-savings, or sometimes into capital, and who play an important role in production.

Banks of issue issue bank notes and hold the metallic money which must be used to convert the notes, so that these remain fiduciary money and do not become false money. Hence they contribute to public order, insuring the monetary circulation of metal and economizing on the use of metal and the consumption of it which results from its circulation.

47. It is putting it in an incorrect way to say that gold in the vaults of banks of issue serves as a *guaranty* for the notes. What constitutes the sole and unique guaranty for the notes is always being exchanged for gold without the least difficulty. The gold metal which the banks have in their vaults is simply a means of making that exchange. The price of bank notes in gold has no direct

relation to the quantity of gold in the vaults of the bank, but only to the ease, or the difficulty, of exchanging the notes for gold. If a bank has a large amount of gold in its vaults but does not redeem its notes, the latter may be below par; while for another bank which has much less gold but which does redeem its notes, they will be at par. The Scottish banks, when they were unrestricted, continued for some time to ensure the redemption of their notes with a metallic money reserve equal to one-seventh of the value of the notes.

48. By means of the discount rate large banks of issue are able to modify the state of the money market in their countries, within certain limits. But it is an error to believe that where a true money exists, they can set the discount rate where they wish; the latter must be just about equal to that rate which corresponds to equilibrium. When the Bank of England anticipates future monetary difficulties and wishes to raise the discount rate in order to avoid them, it borrows money on the market giving as security English consols; and in that way the quantity of money available for loans diminishes.

49. When the vaults of a bank of issue are drained of metallic money, it can remedy that state of affairs only by raising its discount rate; all other means have little or no effectiveness, and can cause serious harm. Among the means to be avoided is that of borrowing to put gold into the vault; if the causes which made the gold flow out continue to exist, the vaults will rapidly be emptied again (§ 39).

50. An increase in the discount is detrimental to entrepreneurs; so they put pressure on the government, and the government on the banks, in order to avoid it. If they succumb to that pressure, inconvertibility of bank notes comes about fairly easily.

CHAPTER IX

THE CONCRETE ECONOMIC PHENOMENON

1. When one wants to study crystallography, he begins by studying geometry, not because he believes that crystals are perfect geometric bodies, but because study of the latter furnishes elements which are indispensable to the study of the former. Similarly, we began with the study of pure economics, not because we think the abstract phenomena of that science are identical to concrete phenomena, but simply because that first study is useful to us in understanding the second.

In Chapters VII and VIII we have already begun the study of concrete phenomena by exploring the character of certain capital; we come now to concrete phenomena concerning the economy in general.

2. In consumption the concrete phenomenon differs from the abstract phenomenon. This is so especially because certain types of consumption are determined by custom, and because for other types man is a very imperfect scale for weighing ophelimities. Hence the equality of weighted ophelimities only occurs approximately.

3. Many goods produced on a large scale must later be sold at retail. Some economists show a certain disdain for dealing with retail prices, as if that were something beneath the dignity of the science. They think they can discuss the price of wine at wholesale, but not the price of a liter of wine sold by an innkeeper. Almost all wine produced, however, ends up being sold by an innkeeper, a restaurateur, a retail merchant, or by the producer for household consumption.

In retail sales there often is no competition, or very little. Retail merchants are quite numerous and their capital is a much greater amount than what should be necessary for distribution of the goods.

It is these circumstances which assure the success of consumer co-operatives and department stores.

4. In the most civilized countries retail merchants form syndicates and fix common prices, which are generally much higher than the wholesale prices of goods or the costs of production; they are often double or triple or even more.

5. The number of retail merchants and their capital increases until, despite the elevated prices, these merchants do not earn any more than they could in some other endeavor.

6. It must be noted that the harm caused by this imperfect organization of distribution is much greater than that which results from the expense necessary to maintain this inflated number of merchants and to pay the interest on the superfluous capital. Let us assume that, in a certain country, these two amounts add up to a total of 100 per year; it would be much to the advantage of consumers to pay this sum of 100 directly to their parasites, provided that they could have the prices which would result from a good organization of the distribution system. This observation is general and applies to all similar cases (VI, 8 *et seq.*).

Likewise, one of the main evils caused by labor unions, syndicates of capitalists and sales syndicates, is the alteration of the coefficients of production resulting in values different from those which provide maximum ophelimity. The wealth thus destroyed is often much greater than what the syndicates appropriate to themselves.

7. The wholesale price of many goods varies daily; retail prices remain constant over fairly long periods. For example, the wholesale prices of flour, coffee and cotton vary each day, whereas the retail prices of bread, coffee and cotton do not. The consumer does not like it if price changes are too frequent, and the retail merchant accommodates him by making use of an average wholesale price. The concrete phenomenon again differs from the abstract phenomenon.

8. Phenomena which come closer to those studied in pure economics are found in large scale production. The organization of such production often is good, and this explains why producer co-operatives have only rarely been successful. Syndicates, trusts and monopolies are also found in large scale production. In Europe, however, consumers suffer less harm from them perhaps than from shopkeepers and trade unions. In the United States of America that harm is perhaps equal or even much greater.

9. Subjectively, the phenomenon seems different because most people who give attention to it are impelled by the contemporary humanitarian mania to excuse not only all harm caused by workers

or by persons of little affluence, but even to excuse the legal offenses which any of these worthy people may commit. Hatred blinds them, however, when they talk about well-to-do persons and especially about "capitalists," and even more so if it concerns "speculators."

M. Pantaleoni aptly remarks that "it is truly singular that this crusade against these would-be monopolies, and hence in favor of the free competition which some find menaced, is led by people who, when it is not a question of syndicates (trusts), do not cease to point out the harm, as serious as it is imaginary, done by that same competition, and to demand legal remedies for it no less rigorous than those they would like to devise for the syndicates (trusts). It is also strange that the same people who see a monopoly character in an agreement between entrepreneurs that the sales of a good be made at one price rather than another, and who also find this characteristic when it is a case of the sale of certain services, for example, railway or ship transport, do not see this same characteristic in an agreement among individual sellers of personal services, for example, among masons, ditch-diggers, etc."[1]

10. **"Trusts."** Modern syndicates have two principal goals: 1° To give enterprises the size which corresponds to minimum costs of production. We have already talked about this in connection with enterprise in general, and it is unnecessary to return to this subject. M. Pantaleoni adds that they also have the goal of uniting related enterprises into one economic unit. It is quite certain that this is sometimes true, but for the present at least it is quite subsidiary a purpose compared to the one which remains to be given. 2° To escape free competition, in whole or in part.

11. At bottom, this last goal always exists, but it is often hidden. It will be said, for example, that the goal of the syndicate is not to raise prices, but to prevent them from becoming *ruinous*. But it is precisely such prices, ruinous for entrepreneurs, which are advantageous to consumers, not only directly, but also indirectly, because it is under the pressure of such prices that enterprises introduce improvements in their production. By protecting them from that pressure, the syndicate shields them from the need for such innovations. It is true that the desire to make greater profits still encourages such improvements, but man works more energetically if it is a case of escaping imminent ruin than if it is a case of seeking greater profits. It is precisely for this reason that industries run by the

---

[1] *Giornale degli economisti*, March 1903, p. 240.

State, which are sure to survive thanks to revenues from taxpayers, are not as progressive as private companies which struggle for life itself.

12. In some countries the syndicates claim that their only purpose is to oppose *unfair* competition (against which they often ask for the intervention of the law); but looking at things a little closer is enough to see that the competition which they call unfair is simply competition, nothing more. In May of 1905, the Swiss newspapers published the following "communique" from the lithographers: "The general assembly of the Swiss Society of Master Lithographers met on the 20th and 21st of May at Lucerne. Unfair competition continuing to spread its effects, it has been decided to institute a committee on ethics, . . . charged with appraising unfair conduct, *especially offers of ridiculous prices*. . . . The assembly has been obliged, reluctantly, to expel one house which has made itself conspicuous, on various occasions, by ridiculous prices."

13. It cannot be denied that there have been some trusts which have prospered without enjoying any privilege, without the aid of customs protection; but they are few in number compared to the trusts which owe their birth and their success to measures of this type.

14. Note that for the small syndicates, which are perhaps most detrimental to consumers because there is a large number of them and because they inflate prices substantially, the good will of the authorities and the indifference of consumers often are enough to make monopoly possible.[2] This is what makes for the success of cooperative societies, which would be still greater if they had the courage to sell at prices low enough to get rid of the economic parasites who keep prices high. That is what the department stores have done, and what they would continue to do if in certain countries they did not have to submit to the oppression of the law and the public treasury which interferes to prevent consumers from buying merchandise cheaply.

---

[2] A cotton producer advertises his merchandise in the papers, adding, to be acceptable to the syndicate of retail merchants, that "he does not sell directly to consumers." If the consumers also organized themselves into a syndicate and replied that they will not buy this cotton, the producer would change his ways. Meanwhile, in certain Swiss cities, darning cotton is three times (*sic*) more expensive than in Italy.

One could cite similar examples *ad infinitum*. It is certainly possible that all these syndicates have some sublime virtues, but it is equally certain, even more certain, that they make consumers pay much more dearly for goods than they would cost under a regime of free competition.

15. In sum, there is no reason to believe that the trade unions, the industrial syndicates, etc., are necessarily detrimental to consumers; they are so only as a consequence of certain of their practices, and only in so far as the latter are the cause of higher prices.

16. Collective contracts for production, for labor, etc., can be useful; and consequently, in certain cases, they can be advantageously substituted for individual contracts; this will depend above all on the ways in which they are drafted and on the certainty that they will be carried out. The lack of this certainty is the principal obstacle encountered by collective labor contracts.

At present there is a very marked tendency to put the workman above the laws, civil and even penal. The latter only obligate the bourgeois. Thus any workman can arbitrarily break off his work contract under the pretense of a strike. The employers who dare to follow this example are unfailingly ordered by the courts to pay damages. If a dispute between employers and workers is submitted to arbitrators, the decision of the latter binds the employers; but not so the workers who disregard it if it does not suit them.

17. In all periods of the history of our country we find facts similar to the practices we have just pointed out, permitting certain persons to use stratagems to appropriate to themselves the goods of others; hence we can assert, as a uniformity revealed by history, that the efforts of men are utilized in two different ways: they are directed to the production or transformation of economic goods, or else to the appropriation of goods produced by others. War, especially in ancient times, has enabled a strong nation to appropriate the goods of a weak one; within a given nation, it is by means of laws and, from time to time, revolutions, that the strong still despoil the weak.

18. It must be noted that this division of human activity is not peculiar to the division which results from free competition, it is one of general applicability. Let us assume a society in which goods are distributed according to any rule whatsoever; for example, each member of the society receives an equal share. We would still find that division of men's efforts: one part of them would be engaged in producing the goods which then have to be distributed in an equal manner, and one part would be engaged, not in producing, but in appropriating to themselves the goods produced by the others.

19. It is obvious that the maximum economic advantage for society is not obtained in this way. We cannot be so positive on the subject of the social advantage since the struggle to appropriate the goods of others may be favorable to selection (§ 35).

20. At the beginning of the 19th century economists believed

that this uniformity revealed by history was about to disappear; they believed that it was a case of ignorance, and that if the cause were abolished through the diffusion of economic knowledge, the effect would also disappear.[3] This was also an era in which people habitually repeated "open a school and you will close a prison." Quite the opposite, education has become general, but criminality has not diminished. In France, juvenile criminality has increased parallel to education. All cultivated persons have studied political economy, but the society they are part of is not moving in the direction which J. B. Say hoped; at this moment it even is going in the opposite direction. Theories have only a very limited effect in the determination of man's actions; self-interest and passions play a much greater role, and some obliging theory is always found in the nick of time to justify them.

21. Of many examples, it will suffice to mention that same *balance of trade* for which Say has provided the theory. It is not possible to find a clearer and more rigorous proof, theoretically and practically, than the one which shows that a country does not grow rich if its total exports exceeds its total imports, and, conversely, that it is not impoverished if the latter surpasses the former. Nevertheless, even in our day, there are some people who never cease repeat-

---

[3] The reasoning of J. B. Say, *Cours complet d'économie politique pratique*, pp. 9-11, is characteristic: "Political economy, by enabling us to understand the laws according to which goods can be created, distributed, and consumed, thereby leads effectively toward the preservation and well being not only of individuals, but also of society, which, without that, is only able to provide disorder and carnage . . . what a sad spectacle history presents us! Nations without industry, lacking everything, driven by need to war, and slaughtering each other in order to live. . . . That was society among the ancients. . . . I do not mention the barbarism of the Middle Ages, the feudal anarchy, religious proscriptions. . . . But from the moment that people acquire the conviction that a state can grow and prosper without it being at the expense of another . . . from that moment nations can resort to means of existence which are more certain, more fruitful, less dangerous; and each individual, instead of groaning under conditions of general misfortune, has his share in the progress of the body politic. This is what we can expect from a more widespread knowledge of the resourcefulness of civilization. Instead of building public prosperity on the exercise of brute force, political economy gives it enlightened self-interest as a foundation. From that time men no longer search for happiness where it is not, but where it is certain to be found. . . . If the nations had not been and were not still infatuated with the balance of trade, and with the view that one nation cannot prosper if it is not to the detriment of another, fifty years of war during the last two centuries could have been avoided. . . . Hence it is education which we lack, and especially education in the art of living in society."

ing that nonsense that the enrichment or impoverishment of a country depends on whether the balance of trade is *favorable* or *unfavorable*.

22. Say can be excused for having made a mistake because he could not know the facts, future facts to him, which unfolded in the second half of the 19th century and showed that the uniformity he had observed in the past has continued into the present, and has not been at all changed by the diffusion of education in general, and by the knowledge of political economy in particular.

23. In past centuries, high prices were considered bad, low prices good; it is the opposite today. Formerly governments endeavored to insure low prices for the benefit of their subjects; today they try to raise prices. Formerly, obstacles were placed in the way of exporting grains in order to maintain low prices within the country; today obstacles are put in the way of importing them in order to raise the domestic price.

Near the middle of the 16th century, in France, people complained so much about the rising prices, that the king was disturbed and directed Malestroit to study the matter. In the second half of the 19th century, because prices were slowly falling, or more precisely, did not continue to rise, statesmen, the universities and learned men set out to search for the cause of that calamity. The contrast between these two facts, which are types of the same species, illustrates clearly the difference between the two eras.

24. It is desirable to look for an explanation of this phenomenon. As usual we will not find it in a single fact, but in a great many of them. One of the principal ones is the difference in social organization. Heretofore, the majority of those in the government of the nation had fixed or nearly fixed incomes, and the rise in prices was disadvantageous to them (VI, 80). Today, the majority are entrepreneurs and workers, and the rise in prices is advantageous to them. We must add some special reasons which could act in a direction opposite to the general reason we have just mentioned, or in the same direction. When the sovereign needed money, he imposed some taxes without asking whether that would raise prices since the direct advantage in this case was greater than the indirect harm; and similarly he conferred privileges having the same effect. On the other hand, for grain there was a particular reason which strongly supported holding prices as low as possible. Because of the low level of wealth of the people of that era, a high price of grain was synonymous with a food shortage and disorders and riots of all sorts would result from that. Hence it would be very difficult for the

government to accede to the wishes of the landowners who generally have an interest in the prices of grain being high, in order to obtain rents.

As long as the rise in prices is only for some goods and as long as it is less than the rise in wages, the workers do not suffer from it. But towards the end of 1906, the rise in prices became general in England, France and Italy, and the workers began to suffer from the high cost of living. The rise in prices no longer appeared to everyone as a benefit then; but since no one wanted to deal with the causes which had brought it about, seeking government subsidies for the workers was all that was done.

In Italy migration from the countryside to the cities and a considerable increase in prices of construction materials and wages of construction workers have been the cause of a considerable rise in rents. Instead of allowing this force to operate, which would deter the migration from the countryside to the cities and lower the wages of construction workers, the government and the banks are asked for subsidies in order to build additional houses in the cities; and since that will take place, in part, at the expense of the country areas, the migration to the cities will increase instead of diminishing. Agriculture in southern Italy lacks capital; instead of supplying it there and increasing production, capital is diverted to the cities, where it does not contribute to economic production.

25. About the middle of the 14th century, a famous *Statute*, which remained in force until the reign of Elizabeth, was promulgated in England. By virtue of that *Statute* all able bodied men who did not have a private income, had to work at a wage fixed by the *Statute*.[4]

Despite that, agricultural wages increased and continuous attempts were made to resist that increase. A statute of the 5th year of the reign of Elizabeth entrusted to justices of the peace, assembled in their quarter sessions, the task of fixing wages of craft workers and agricultural workers; this law remained in effect until 1814; at that time competition was allowed to operate, but associations of workers were prohibited. In 1825 the latter were permitted in

---

[4] No individual less than sixty years old, whether of free or servile condition, could refuse to work the land at the usual wage of the twentieth year of the reign (1347). This could be done only by those who lived on income from trade or from some craft, or who possessed sufficient rent, or who themselves worked their own land. . . . The old wages were to serve as a norm; those who asked more were to be prosecuted. . . . Masters who paid higher wages were to be subject to a fine equal to triple the excess paid.

part, but there were still some restrictions which were removed in 1875. Then there was a very short period of freedom. After that the workers, the oppressed becoming the oppressors, imposed their conditions, and the law assisted them. In 1904, all the parties, in view of the approaching elections, vied with each other in flattering the workers. The liberal party, which has kept its name but given up its principles, moved to socialism, and promises, if victorious, to put all the power of the law at the service of the workers. The conservative party, which is in power, can not only promise, but can propose and get the House of Commons to pass, a law by virtue of which the labor unions no longer have responsibility in the strikes which they incite and strikers can persecute the *krumirs* with impunity; and it is understood that this is only a first payment on larger favors.

26. In France, the phenomenon is still more marked. A few years ago the workers could not even organize themselves into a union; now the unionists enjoy extraordinary privileges; strikers can with impunity assault workers who are willing to work, set fire to factories, and wreak havoc on banks and private homes.

The character of the taxes, as well as, in part, the types of expenditures of the national government and the communes are one of the surest indicators of the economic and social condition of a country, because the dominant class always, as much as it can, lays the weight of taxes on the subject class and turns the expenditures to its own benefit. It is a daydream to speak of "justice in taxation"; so far this earth has never seen it.

The speech against the income tax given by M. Ribot early in 1908 has truly comical portions. That eminent politician, after profound thought, has discovered that the income tax would divide citizens into two classes: those who vote the tax and those who pay it. That he did not make this discovery sooner is certainly not the fault of his adversaries, for they have proclaimed in every way that their purpose was precisely what M. Ribot believes he has discovered and that, insofar as the income tax attains this end, it brings a country a little more "social justice."

M. Paul Leroy-Beaulieu[5] describes the present development in France very well: "Thus the main indirect taxes have been the object of considerable reductions for about twenty years, for the last ten years especially; nevertheless the exemptions from the habitation

---

[5] *Journal des Débats*, July 1904. [In the second paragraph of the quotation brackets inserted by Pareto.]

tax [*contribution mobilière*] for persons of small and average incomes have been entirely maintained.

"Moreover, several years ago for small assessments a reduction was granted in whole or in part in the portion of the land tax going to the national government. . . . Let us now consider the categories of average and large tax-payers. For twenty years the legislature has increased their share of taxes, not only absolutely but also relatively, by rate revisions and by new taxes and also by an introduction of the principle of progression into certain taxes. . . . The progressive character of the habitation tax in the cities has been greatly accentuated; the tax from which small and moderate rentals were exempted has been levied on the higher rentals by a recent law. Moderate size license fees, and large ones more so, have been steadily increased, whereas the small ones have been constantly decreased. Inheritances have been subjected to a very progressive tax rate, which becomes, for large collateral inheritances, tantamount to pure extortion, a kind of confiscation. . . . In earlier times, and even not so long ago, the national budget allocated nothing or almost nothing to relief and philanthropy. . . . The budgets of the communes indeed had some expenditures of a humanitarian character, but they were rather limited. Primary education was not yet free or only rarely so; today not only is it free everywhere but the schools give [subsidies].

"The national government budget and especially the budgets of the communes abound in all kinds of subsidies and grants having a philanthropic and humanitarian character. The result is that each day more and more of the public resources are used, not for general services for the country, but for the special benefit of the lower income groups in the population."

A writer of great talent, and one who is the antitheses of M. Leroy-Beaulieu from the point of view of economic theory, states that: "The objective of the party, in all countries and at all times, is to take over the State and use it for the best interest of the party and its allies. Until recent years the Marxists taught, on the contrary, that they wished to suppress the State. . . . Things naturally changed when electoral success led the socialist leaders to find that the possession of power offers great advantages. . . ."[6] "In order to truly comprehend the transformation which has taken place in socialist thought, it is necessary to examine the composition of the modern State. It is a body of intellectuals which is invested with privileges

---

[6] Georges Sorel, *La décomposition du Marxisme*, Marcel Rivière, 1908, p. 48.

and which possesses the political means to defend itself against the attacks made on it by other groups of intellectuals avid to take over the benefits of public office. The parties organize themselves for the purpose of capturing offices and they are analogous to the State itself. The thesis which Marx proposed in the *Communist Manifesto* could be expressed as follows: 'All social movements until now, have been carried out by minorities for the benefit of minorities.' We would say that all our political crises consist of the replacement of intellectuals by other intellectuals. . . .'[7]

It could not be said better; G. Sorel describes very accurately what is taking place in our societies.[8]

27. Objectively all these facts can be summed up in a general way, without going into specific details, by saying that every economic phenomenon tends to be regulated according to the interests of the social classes which have a preponderance in the government.

Subjectively, it is in the name of "justice" or of "morality" and at the present time of "progress," that the adversaries array themselves for combat. But, among those who mount the assault on the old society, only the masses believe in the new religion in good faith. The leaders who make up the new elite fully recognize its complete lack of substance. The blind faith of the masses and the skepticism of the leaders is one of the most important causes of victory. On the other hand, on the side of the decaying elite, the leaders themselves more or less believe in that "justice," that "morality," that progress"; thus they are constrained in their movements and lead their troops to certain defeat.[9]

28. If the real man were solely a *homo oeconomicus* the phenomenon would differ from reality much less. And all those who deliberately aim at a certain end would often be able to acknowledge frankly that they act in such and such a way because they find it to their advantage. But the real man is also a *homo ethicus*, and every

---

[7] Georges Sorel, *loc cit*, p. 50.

[8] See also the numerous works of G. de Molinari.

[9] This is what has happened to Marshal MacMahon and his ministers. Such bungling of a situation so eminently favorable has rarely been seen in history. If these people had had the least energy, the least firmness of character, their victory and that of the bourgeoisie would have been assured. But these were honest and good humanitarians, incapable of taking the least advantage of the circumstances which presented themselves.

After its defeat, the bourgeoisie is only able to moan and lament, appealing to the "justice" of its conquerers, whose *vae victis* resounds in its ears. Thus it justifies the social usefulness of the victory of its adversaries. The world belongs to the strong.

private interest seeks to conceal itself under the guise of the public interest (II, 105, 106).

Certain facts in connection with this are typical. At a certain point of evolution, those who want to change the social organization change certain laws, but do not yet dare to change others for fear of offending the dominant prejudices too much. From the political point of view this is what took place in Rome at the time of the emergence of the empire. From the economic point of view, we can see this in our own time.

Our laws and our codes still draw inspiration from certain principles which some people want to change. The provisions of the law are replaced by others as far as possible, but when this cannot be done, the judges are asked to make decisions according to their conscience and not according to the letter of the law. This has given rise to some very beautiful theories in France, Italy and Germany. In the last two countries this point of evolution has not yet been passed. In France it is beginning to be. The same persons who enthusiastically applauded the decisions of the "good judge" deliberately ruling counter to the law in order to follow—so he said—his conscience, now applaud with the same enthusiasm minister Briand's declaration that the judge is not to concern himself with his conscience but only with the letter of the law.

Looking only at the manner in which they are expressed, there appears to be an obvious contradiction between these two points of view. That contradiction really does exist for those people for whom the thought is not different from the form which it assumes. But these are, in general, the faithful of the new religion, and the intensity of their faith prevents them from perceiving the contradiction between two absolutely opposite propositions (II, 48). But for the leaders this contradiction does not exist at all, since for them it is a question of means and not of an end, and it is perfectly natural that means change when circumstances change. As for the theorists, it is not for nothing that casuistry was invented, and when their masters wish it, they will turn back from "law freely interpreted" to law literally interpreted with the same ease with which at present they are willing to substitute the first for the second. The law has always had, and always will have, theories adapted to the promotion of the interests of the dominant class.

29. There are innumerable similar facts which could be cited, and truly they make up the fabric of the history of societies. But it would be wrong to believe that only the interest of the dominant class is involved. Other facts also contribute to changing the form

of the phenomenon, and that is because these actions are non-logical and are in part taken under the pressure of circumstances outside of man, without his seeing the consequences clearly.

30. This is understood clearly when the transformation which is now beginning is studied, a transformation which is giving birth to a new privileged class. History furnishes other examples of these transformations about which we have a general impression but know very little in the way of details. On the other hand, we know the details of what is taking place before our eyes very well, whereas we see the still undetermined general outlines quite poorly. Thus study of the past and study of the present complement each other.

The facts pointed out in § 28 are only a particular case of much more general facts.

Societies are continually being transformed, and that transformation is particularly rapid for civilized societies in our day; often it is more a matter of form than of substance, but it exists none the less. Everything changes, even the form of novels and plays; conceptions of ethics and of law assume new forms.

Trifling changes in a society may be made in a day, the day the law is changed. For more important changes a legal state A indeed changes into a legal state B, but under system A the decisions of the courts already lean toward system B and form a transition from A to B. Finally, for profound transformations, there is a transitional state which often lasts many years, during which the law is still nominally A but where little by little it comes to an end because it no longer has any weight. And state B in fact already exists when the law finally recognizes it.[10]

This phenomenon is so well known in Roman law, in English law and in other legal systems that we need not point out the transformations which these systems have undergone in this way. We will just mention one recent fact because it throws light on a transformation which is in process in our societies.

A decision[11] of the Swiss federal court is as follows: "As the federal court has already recognized in many previous decisions, the guaranty of property rights such as in Article 12 of the Constitution

[10] Aristotle had already noted a similar fact examples of which were supplied by the great laboratory of the Greek republics (*Politics*, IV, 5, 2): ὥσθ' οἱ μὲν νόμοι διαμενοῦσιν οἱ προϊπάρχοντες, κρατοῦσι δ'οἱ μεταβάλλοντες τὴν πολιτειαν "so that the laws previously established continue in force for some time, although the power already belongs to those who have changed the government of the city."

[11] Mourlevat c. Conseil d'Etat de Fribourg, June 1, 1904, (*Journal des tribunaux et Revue judiciaire*, Lausanne, 1905).

of Fribourg[12] and also either in that form or in another, in the constitution of all the other cantons (with a single exception),[13] is not an absolute guaranty. The court has always held that constitutional provisions of the type such as in the aforementioned Article 12 guarantee the inviolability of property only to the extent to which that property is determined and defined in the internal legislation of the cantons; in other words the legislation of a canton can, without infringing on the constitutional principle above mentioned, limit the content of the right of property, determine the particular rights of which the latter is composed, modify, extend, or limit the regulations concerning property, with the sole condition (note it is the only one) that it do so in a general way, equal for all."

With this last condition, the restriction of the right of property can extend as far as its abolition. According to this kind of reasoning, a law which would declare that private property is abolished, without any indemnity, for all citizens equally, would in no way be in conflict with an article of the constitution according to which the right of property is inviolable and cannot be abolished without indemnity.

The reason for this contradiction is quite obvious. We are in a state of transition in which already some people are striking out at private property but do not yet dare to do so too openly.[14]

---

[12] Here is Article 12 of the Constitution of Fribourg of May 7, 1907: "Property is inviolable. This principle can be derogated only in cases of public benefit determined by law and by the prior payment of or the guaranty of a just and complete indemnity."

In 1857 socialist principles were not yet welcomed into legislation. It is very easy to change the constitutions of the cantons; thus this article could easily be removed or modified, but that would perhaps be premature and it would not take place without trouble for it would thereby stimulate the resistance of those who are not yet converted to socialism; therefore, until the article can be changed in an explicit fashion, they content themselves with changing it implicitly, by straining the meaning of the words.

[13] The exception is that of the canton of Tessin, which does not contain an article analogous to the one we have just cited.

[14] In 1908, G. Sorel published a book entitled: *Réflexions sur la violence*. It is the most remarkable scientific work on sociology in many years. We are thus quite pleased to find in it confirmation of several of the theories of the Italian edition of this *Manuel*, published in 1906. G. Sorel arrives at his conclusions in a way both independent of and different from that which we followed. This circumstance increases the probability that the theories in question correspond accurately to the facts.

See also, by the same author, *Insegnamenti sociali della economia contemporanea*, Palermo, 1906.

"Although the Carolingian state," says Pertile,[15] "was not as yet a feudal state, under its rule the elements were already developing from which were to emerge the fief of private right and political feudalism."

The historian of the future will say: although France at the beginning of the 20th century was not yet a state dominated by a privileged caste drawn from the working class, nevertheless the elements were already developing from which was to come the domination of that caste.

"Between the 6th and the 9th century," says Fustel de Coulanges,[16] "between the age of Clovis and that of Charlemagne, the history of political institutions is very obscure. This is not for want of documents. We have chronicles. . . . Life in those times is described in clear and precise terms. We can see how men lived, spoke, and thought. But despite all that, it is still very difficult to know how the populations were governed. These documents are not in agreement with each other. . . ."

This lack of concordance exists at present in France. Legally, the privileged caste[17] does not yet exist, and if only the laws are studied, we must say that the worker is subject to the law just as is the bourgeois, the striker just as the workman who is willing to work, and that the law punishes anyone who infringes on another's right to work. But if we study the facts directly, we are led to quite different conclusions.[18] We see that until very recently these con-

---

[15] *Storia del diritto italiano*, I, p. 191.

[16] *Etude sur les origines du système féodal du VIᵉ au VIIIᵉ siècle (Académie des sciences morales et politiques).*

[17] Fustel de Coulanges, *Les origines du système féodal; le bénéfice et le patronat pendant l'époque mérovingienne*, Paris, 1890, p. 429. "The feudal regime existed as early as the 7th century with its characteristic features and its complete organization. Only it did not exist alone. . . . Legally it was the monarchical institutions which governed the people. Feudalism was outside of the ordinary rules of law. The laws were no longer against it as in the time of the emperors; at least they did not yet sanction it. Vasselage already held an important place in custom and in diverse rights; it amounted to almost nothing in public law."

[18] G. Sorel, *Réflexions sur la violence*, p. 41: "Onto the degeneracy of the capitalist economy is grafted the ideology of a bourgeois class, timorous, humanitarian, and claiming to free its thought from the conditions of its existence. The race of bold leaders who had produced the grandeur of modern industry has disappeared, to give way to an ultra-refined aristocracy which asks only to live in peace. This degeneracy fills our parliamentary socialists with joy. Their role would be nothing if they faced a bourgeoisie which would energetically fling itself onto the paths of capitalistic progress, which would regard timidity as a disgrace, and which would take pride in thinking

clusions, which in fact were being applied, were not accepted and were even resisted in theory, and that only now are they beginning to be approved theoretically. Thus we are approaching the last period of the evolution in which they will acquire a legal form. At the same time, if we arrive at that point, those who will belong to the privileged caste will be determined. This is still uncertain today. It is not and probably will not be all the workers, but only the workers organized into unions or perhaps only the unions sympathetic to the government.[19]

31. These workers are above the law because the public authority does not resist their claims, or because, what comes to the same thing, it only resists them in an ineffectual way. If they commit offenses, they are not prosecuted; if they are prosecuted, the government compels the judges to acquit them. Moreover, there are never any witnesses for the prosecution, because those who could give evidence know that they would not be safe from the vengeance of the accused; if, by chance, a court convicts them, they are soon pardoned; finally, very frequent amnesties assure complete impunity.[20]

---

[19] *Privilege*, which is precisely one of the main factors giving birth to the feudal system, was granted by the sovereign to those who seemed to him to be worthy. There was no fixed rule to determine the persons who ought to enjoy it. Fustel de Coulanges (*op. cit.*, § 30) p. 424: "For several centuries, it [privilege] has been one of the facts a thousand times repeated which imperceptibly modified and in the end transformed the institutions of a people. By changing the nature of the allegiance of great persons, and by shifting the allegiance of small and powerless persons, it changed the structure of the body social." [The insertion in the quotation above is Pareto's.]

[20] G. Sorel, *Réflexions sur la violence*, p. 28, speaks of France, but what he says also applies perfectly to Italy: "Nearly all the union leaders know how to take advantage of this situation and they teach the workers that it is not a question of seeking favors and that they must capitalize on *bourgeois cowardice* in order to impose the will of the proletariat. There are too many facts supporting this tactic for it not to take root in the world of the worker."

P. 30: "A social policy founded on bourgeois cowardice which consists of always giving way before the threat of violence cannot fail to engender the idea that the bourgeoisie is condemned to death and that its disappearance is only a question of time. Each conflict which gives rise to violence thus becomes an early battle. . . ."

---

of its own class interests. Their power is enormous in the face of a bourgeoisie which has become almost as stupid as the nobility of the 18th century. If the degradation of the upper bourgeoisie continues to increase regularly at the pace which it has for some years now, our socialist officials can reasonably hope to attain the object of their dreams and sleep in sumptuous town houses."

At Lorient in 1903 the court convicted a striker guilty of serious violence; his companions besieged the court, shattered the windows and wounded a judge. Twenty-seven of them were tried and convicted, but the under-prefect intervened immediately, threatened the president of the court that he would "hold him responsible" for the disorders that this judgment might provoke, and the president reopened the hearing which had been adjourned, and in agreement with the judges, changed the judgment. At Armentières most of those who had engaged in pillages, arson and unprovoked attacks were not even disturbed. Only persons not belonging to the privileged caste were prosecuted, and the public prosecutor himself, in his indictment, was forced to admit that "the investigation found it almost impossible to gather useful testimony, the majority of those whose houses were invaded and sacked having fled or hidden themselves in terror, the others hesitating or refusing to speak through fear of reprisals."[21]

32. Many facts of this type could be cited; the following is typical. In June 1904, there was a strike of tramway workers at Nice accompanied by the usual violence; we borrow from a French newspaper the story of the outcome of that event:

Nice, 28 June.—"This evening, at seven o'clock, the prefect and the public prosecutor were advised by dispatch that the pardon of five demonstrators, convicted at the beginning of the strike of the tramway employees, had just been signed by the President of the Republic. It will be recalled that the strikers had consented to return to work on the express promise that a pardon for those convicted would be granted within forty-eight hours. In a meeting held last night, the tramway employees, dissatisfied with the delays in the signing of the clemency order, had decided to stop work again today, Monday, if their imprisoned comrades were not free by that time. There would then have been a general strike because all the associations of workers had declared that they would join with the tramway workers. The prisoners were set free this evening at nine-thirty. The public prosecutor himself went to the jail to carry out the formalities of their release. The news of the release of the prisoners has caused the greatest joyfulness among the workers."

---

[21] Pertile, *op. cit.*, p. 259: ". . . the right of appeal was often illusory. And that is so whether because of the difficulties which came from distance or obstacles put in the way by the baron; or because of the procedure followed in certain countries which seemed well devised to keep even the most courageous from trying it; or finally because, even if one obtained a better judgment, the king frequently lacked the means of carrying it out even if the baron would not take vengeance because of the boldness of his vassal."

It is a current practice of strikers to return to work only after having imposed the condition that those who have been arrested and convicted by the courts be released; the government humbly obeys.

In May 1905, at Limoges, with the assent of the police who stood by, inert and benevolent, the strikers besieged for several days the Beaulieu company's factory, in which eleven persons, four of them young children, were suffering from hunger. The mayor, a socialist deputy, intervened, but cautiously, by entreating the strikers to allow at least a little bread to be sent into the building so that the besieged people would not die of hunger. But the besiegers, who did not disdain the irony, permitted only a single loaf to be sent in for the eleven starving people. The latter, taught by the events of Cluses, did not even attempt to defend themselves; if they had tried it, the police would have immediately gone into action, arrested them and they would have been convicted by the court, as happened to the unhappy industrialists of Cluses (II, 92). A child, the son of the concierge, driven by hunger, wanted to go search for a little milk. He was beaten by the strikers, who were protected by the authorities, and had two ribs broken; not content with that, the strikers forcibly drove back the doctor who wanted to go to the aid of that unfortunate wounded child.

The *humanitarians* naturally take the side of the excellent strikers who abuse the bourgeois. The minister M. Etienne told a delegation of Limoges merchants, who came to Paris to ask that the persons and the goods of citizens be protected, "that they were the elder sons of the democracy and that they ought to give proof of their feeling of good will and affection toward their younger brothers, the workers, so as to bring their misguided minds back to calm and reason."

The French government, however, was obliged to use force to defend itself against these "younger brothers," but the Chamber immediately voted aid to the injured among the aggressors and to the injured among the government force which had been attacked, thus putting the criminals and those who had defended the law on the same basis, without any distinction.

In Italy the railroad employees abuse at will the public which pays and maintains them.[22] They have not been punished; they even receive praise from persons belonging to the upper social classes;

---

[22] Among Italian politicians, M. Napoleone Colajanni has had the courage to recognize the exaggerations in the claims of the "ferrovieri," and the very great courage to say so plainly.

and the citizens must resign themselves to enduring their whims.[23]

In Italy, in France and in Russia,[24] the strikers have put forth another claim, namely, that they be paid for days on strike just as if they had worked, and in certain cases they have found people weak enough, cowardly enough, to give in on this point. If that arrangement becomes generalized, it is hard to see why the workers, under various pretexts, would not remain on strike all year round; they would stroll about and draw their pay nevertheless. What is astonishing is not that they make this claim, for after all everyone tries to obtain the most he can; what is strange is the lack of good sense and strength on the part of messieurs-the-humanitarians who invent sophisms upon sophisms to justify these claims.

There is still more. Where the evolution is more advanced, that is to say, in France and Italy, we see taking root a doctrine according to which members of law enforcement agencies should allow themselves to be insulted, scoffed at, beaten, stoned and knocked about by the rioting strikers without making use of their arms. Up to now it has been thought that such conduct was more worthy of a saintly anchorite than of a soldier, but the 20th century is seeing the contrary opinion born. The soldiers and police who dare to defend themselves and, weapons in hand, repulse their attackers, are accused of "lacking cool heads"—that is the hallowed term; on the other hand, if, injured by the bricks, paving stones, iron bolts or other projectiles, and streaming with blood, they endure everything without giving blow for blow, their conduct is declared to be "admirable." Where the evolution is not yet as far advanced, for example in Germany, a completely different meaning is given to the term "admirable conduct" as applied to soldiers and to members of law enforcement agencies. The sport of throwing stones at them would be extremely dangerous for those who would want to pursue it there; so strikers and rioters carefully abstain from it, whereas they engage

---

[23] Additional events have confirmed the observations expressed in these lines published in 1906.

[24] The *Moniteur des intérêts matériels* of June 7, 1905, said with respect to Russia: "Some have gone so far as to claim that they be paid during the days on strike, and some employers in the north having had the weakness to agree, that absurd demand is now raised in all departments."

At the time of the agricultural strikes in Upper Italy in 1908, the "demands" of the agricultural workers included this: The workers shall have the right to abstain from work every time they receive the order for it from the directors of their leagues, and the owners must pay the wages of these workers just as if they had worked.

in it freely in countries where they can secure that pleasure almost with impunity.

The decadent bourgeoisie of our era wants two contradictory things. On the one hand they expect their goods and their persons to be protected by the police; on the other hand they demand that the latter abstain from any act which would offend the exquisite sensitivity of the bourgeois nerves and that, especially, on no account are the police to shed the blood of the adversaries whom they are supposed to restrain and contend with. Such a state of things is unstable and cannot last. If some day some energetic and ambitious man finds himself in the army, he will put himself and his comrades on the side of the adversaries of the bourgeoisie, who at least do not make such absurd contradictory demands, do not have such sensitive nerves and, desiring the end, know enough to desire the means.

Some have presented as proof of the energy of the bourgeoisie the lust for gain which it still displays in our time; but that lust for gain could not replace the bellicose courage which tends more and more to be lacking. From among innumerable proofs, it will suffice to recall here the fate of usurers, Jews and Lombards, of the Middle Ages. Steel more than once deprived them of their gold; a similar fate awaits those who find themselves in similar conditions.

32b. The humanitarian religion has spread so far nowadays, it so imbues all theory and all reasoning, that just pointing out acts of violence is synonomous with censuring them. But on the contrary, there are many cases in which one intends neither to censure nor to approve these acts, but simply to take account of them in studying the direction in which a certain social evolution is going.

Two classes are facing each other at present; let us call them A and B. The struggle between them grows sharper from day to day, and it can end only in some decisive battle. The members of the first class seek, each in his own way, to enrich themselves, with little concern for the common interest of their class; the members of the second class put that interest ahead of everything, and look forward, rightly or wrongly, to the improvement of their particular situation by a joint victory for the entire class. Among the A's treason, far from being censured, is praised and admired. The A's regard the most highly those of their number who best know how to promote the interests of the B's,[25] and this is so in all branches of human activity. The politician who wants to please the A's must above all busy himself bestowing favors on the B's; the magistrate, the his-

---

[25] The humanitarian bourgeoisie has made a saint of Waldeck-Rousseau, the politician who betrayed them and delivered them to their enemies.

torian, the writer and the dramatist will obtain success among the A's only if they make fun of them and extol the merits of the B's. Among the B's, on the other hand, anyone who betrays the interest of their class is despised, disgraced, beaten if necessary and punished by every lawful and unlawful means available. All public or private activity is judged by the B's from the point of view of their class interests, and any man who gives offense is condemned by a much more formidable judgment than those of the bourgeois judges.

The A's live from day to day, concerned only with avoiding boredom and with postponing as long as possible a battle which those among them who have not lost all good sense still recognize to be inevitable; to achieve that they give in always and about everything; they humble and lower themselves, they descend to the basest flatteries and voluntarily let themselves be trampled on by their adversaries. They moan and complain that their good intentions are not recognized; they declare, more or less hypocritically, that they live only to make the B's happy; for that reason they have been created and put into the world, it is their "social duty," their religion. Those among them who call themselves Christians no longer believe in the divinity of Christ, rather they believe he was the first socialist and that satisfies their needs for religiosity; they declare that "religion is a way of life," and "a way of life" is socialism. Although there are some clever humanitarians who, while declaiming on "Progress, Science, and Justice" do not neglect to line their pockets, there are others who take these declamations seriously and who aspire to become good ascetics.[26] The B's have a far sighted and very firm

---

[26] Facts proving *humanitarianism* is a religion are very numerous; we have cited a few; the following can be added: The humanitarians' need for proselytizing is similar to the need for proselytizing of impassioned believers of other religions, the Christians of the Middle Ages, for example.

It is understandable that revolutionaries are concerned that, even outside their own country, there not exist centers of resistance to the revolution, or even social organizations which escape their domination. But what interest can a good Italian, French or English bourgeois properly have, for example, in whether or not there is a parliament in Russia or in Persia? Yet these good bourgeois treat this subject with a passion comparable only to that of the Catholic missionary desiring to convert the infidels. We have seen the bourgeois press, with pious fraud, systematically and in silence pass over the crimes of the Russian revolutionaries and dwell at length on the repressive measures which these crimes made necessary. The Shah of Persia, for having brutally suppressed his revolutionary parliament, has incurred the censure and the wrath of our excellent humanitarians. They even rewrite history. It was believed until the present that someone named Julius Caesar had

plan; they wish to substitute themselves for the A's. They accept everything from the A's and concede them nothing; they feel bold and arrogant in their strength, in the indomitable energy which they know how to use to obtain their goal. Never do they stoop to flattering their adversaries, still less to saying that they live only for the latter's well-being. Asceticism does not attract them at all, and the dreams of the humanitarians leave them more or less indifferent. It is indeed to no avail that the ingenious "intellectuals" have created the marvelous theory of "solidarity"; that prodigious effort of their mind has been entirely wasted, the B's have not even deigned to bother about it. The A's can feel "solidarity" with the B's as much as they please; but the B's do not feel the slightest "solidarity" with the A's.

Looking only on the surface, the philanthropic activity of the A's takes us into a strange world where each person seems to look after the interests of others but neglect his own interests; but looking more closely we see that it only appears that way. In reality this activity of the A's often has the purpose of satisfying certain of their immediate interests, certain of their passions, certain sentiments, certain prejudices. But the philanthropic form is not neutral, it reacts on the character of the A's and prevents them from being aware of the results which the activity they engage in will have in the end.[27]

Some of them, having completely forgotten the important lesson of 1789, busy themselves "extinguishing the lights of the sky," and until that work has effects similar to those it already has had, they

---

[27] A simple bit of good sense would have been enough for the Russian ruling classes to understand that *Tolstoyism* could lead only to defeat in the Russo-Japanese war and to the revolutionary Saturnalia which was the consequence of it. But among the leaders some enriched themselves through customs protection and corruptions, others were besotted by their humanitarian faith.

---

been a rather good commander. It seems that there is nothing to that at all and that we had been wholly mistaken about him. This story is not without some analogy to the one in the Middle Ages, among Christians, which numbered the Mohammedans among idolators and made Virgil a celebrated sorcerer.

Hypocrisy, the plague of all religions, is not lacking in certain manifestations of the humanitarian religion. The same English statesmen who cried "The Douma is dead, long live the Douma," take good care not to grant a parliament to Egypt or to India. It is for heaven to reconcile these contradictions.

obtain as payment a smile and praise from M. Viviani. Others have
devoted themselves to the destruction of institutions, such as the
army[28] and the magistracy, which can prevent social dissolution;
with all their ability they clear the way for the triumph by the B's.
Others dedicate themselves to work of secondary importance; they
have a mania for protecting everything and everybody. They protect children and young people, adults and old people, men and
women, honest workers, strikers, petty crooks, malefactors of all
kinds, prostitutes, pimps, *Apaches*, swindlers—all sorts of people,
except themselves.

Each year, in the months of July and August, the flies and the
humanitarian congresses swarm, without interfering with the insects
and the congresses which infest the other months of the year. The
B's take no part at all in these saturnalias, but the A's are full of
solicitude for public aid, for national and international protection
of workers, for prohibiting night work by women in industry, for
preventing people from drinking what they please, for preventing
lovers from corresponding with each other, and for an infinity of
other similar things. A great number of A's live in terror of germs
and in respectful fear of the *sawbones*. The latter has replaced the
spiritual director of old, he rules the drinking, the eating and even
the love making of his subjects, who dream only of forcibly imposing
this regulation on other persons, exactly the way the believer of past
centuries wished to impose his faith on unbelievers by force.

But it is especially to the malefactors that all the tender solicitude
of the A's is devoted.[29] By means of laws regarding first offenders,

---

[28] G. Sorel, *Réflexions sur la violence*, p. 82: "Syndicalism in France is
engaged in an antimilitary propaganda which clearly shows the great distance
separating it from parliamentary socialism on that issue of state policy. Many
journalists believe that it is solely a case of an exaggerated humanitarian
movement . . . that is a gross error. One should not believe that they are
protesting against the harshness of the discipline, or against the length of
military service, or against the presence in the upper ranks of officers hostile
to present institutions; those are reasons which lead many bourgeois to applaud declamations against the army . . . but they are not the reasons of the
syndicalists. The army is the clearest manifestation . . . one can have of the
state. The syndicalists do not propose to reform the state . . . they wish to
destroy it."

[29] A very remarkable case, typical of this class, is that of Jeanne Weber
in France. This woman was accused of having killed several children. Several
excellent doctors concluded that the deaths were natural. France has two
courts of appeal: the one which has that name and the *League of the rights
of man and the citizen*. The latter naturally took up the cause of Jeanne
Weber, and the magistrates continued to bow down and released this woman.

pardons, etc., there will soon be placed among the rights of man and of the citizen the right to commit at least a first offense with impunity. To benefit delinquents, in certain cases their convictions are not entered in their judicial record; they are thus enabled to take advantage of the good faith of persons willing to employ them, to deceive them and commit additional offenses.

All this foolishness about degenerates has in no way taken hold of the B's. If they agree with the A's with regard to "putting out the lights of the sky," it is only because, rightly or wrongly, they think that it is advantageous to their class. Never have they been seen to call a congress for the "social protection" of the A's nor, to tell the truth, for any other sort of protection for their adversaries. They are energetic and robust he-men who want to eat when hungry, drink when thirsty, make love when it suits them and who laugh at M. Purgon. They let their adversaries *drink the water of slaves.*[30] They will have indulgence for the *Apaches* as long as the latter remain their allies, just as Julius Caesar protected Claudius and his men as long as he found it to his advantage. It is self-interest which rules the conduct of the B's, not sentimental twaddle. When the leaders of the B's become the masters, they will know how to get rid of those who disturb the order which they will have established, and they will destroy them without the least scruple.[31] Male-

---

[30] Ovid, *Amores*, VI, 25-26.
     ... *Sic unquam longa relevere catena,*
     Nec tibi perpetuo serva bibatur aqua.
[31] The numerous cases in which the mob wants *to lynch* malefactors demonstrate clearly that the populace still retains the vigor of the race, vigor which the upper classes have lost.

Note along the same lines that when the religious congregations in France were despoiled, it was only one of the common people who gave his life for his faith. In Italy, the socialists who risk their lives in the riots are all common people.

And so she was permitted to continue her exploits, but she made the mistake of allowing herself to be caught in the very act. Rochefort had the courage to point out that the protectors of Weber were responsible for that last offence; but that was only the whim of a brilliant writer, and the serene foolishness of the humanitarians has not been disturbed by it.

It must be noted that the learned Faculty of Medicine which does not even know how to tell whether a child has died by strangulation or by natural causes, does know, on the other hand, to the nearest unit, the exact number of deaths which, in a given country, are due *indirectly* to the use of alcoholic drinks! Quite unlike experimental science which seeks only to find uniformities in facts, the *Science* of the humanitarians possesses these astounding mysteries.

factors will do well to hasten to enjoy the terrestial paradise which the simple-minded imbecility of the decadent bourgeoisie provides them, for this state of things will soon end and will not reappear for a long time.

Finally, and this fact alone is as important as all the others, the A's have a morbid dread of bloodshed. The B's are ready to shed as much as is necessary to attain their goal, and they certainly will not do without the victory just because it can be purchased only by climbing over piles of bodies.

In Europe the A's include the largest part of the bourgeoisie and attract a large number of egalitarian socialists, parliamentary socialists or other similar types; the B's today call themselves syndicalists, tomorrow they will have another name and probably still others before the day of victory. The issue of names has no importance at all; the distinction between the A's and the B's is established not by words but by facts.

Those which we have just cited are enough to be able to foresee which side will probably be victorious. The course of events could, it is true, be changed by widespread wars or, what is infinitely less probable, by a change in the character and sentiments of the bourgeoisie.[32]

All known historical facts confirm that no social class can for long hold its property or its power if it does not have the strength and vigor necessary to defend them. In the long run only power determines the social forms; the great error of the 19th century will be to have forgotten that principle.

33. At the present time we are seeing the passage from one position of equilibrium to another take place. A degenerate bourgeoisie no longer has the courage to defend the possessions it still holds. Its situation can be compared to that of the Carthaginians on the eve of the third Punic War, when each day Masinissa seized

---

[32] G. Sorel, *Réflexions sur la violence*, p. 35. "A disturbance, wisely channeled, is extremely useful to the parliamentary socialists who are close to the government and rich bourgeoisie, and who boast that they know how to moderate the revolution; thus they can promote the success of financial affairs in which they are interested, and obtain minor favors for many important voters . . ." pp. 36-37: "The great mass of voters understand nothing of what takes place in politics and have no comprehension at all of economic history; they are on the side which seems to them to have the strength; and one can get anything he wants from them as long as he can prove to them that he is strong enough to make the government yield. It is necessary, however, not to go too far, because the bourgeoisie could wake up and the country could place itself in the hands of a resolutely conservative statesman."

additional pieces of their territory and Rome prevented them from defending themselves,[33] until finally their city was destroyed and they themselves reduced to slavery. Their humble submission to their enemies was of no use at all.

The submission of the bourgeoisie to its enemies and its cowardly servility will be just as useless.[34]

In our day there plainly exists a privileged caste which alone imposes its will on the government, although it does not support that government and would not support a government of the bourgeois or of any other social class. And equally clear is the change in public opinion which precedes and paves the way for a change in the laws since these facts, instead of provoking resistance, are accepted with a stupid resignation by that same bourgeois class. The Court of Appeals in France has decided that a strike dissolves the labor contract, thus the present law is still enforced; but already public opinion demands a change and Jaurès proposes that it be amended so that a strike does not dissolve the labor contract. When that has been obtained, a very important privilege will have been set up in favor of the workers. The latter will be able to walk out of the factory for months and months, and the entrepreneur will still remain bound by the labor contract. But if, for example, a landlord where workers live stopped providing them meals, it would be found just, and rightly so, that the contract had been broken, and the workers could make other arrangements.

34. Among the changes which are underway, not the least remarkable is that of an *entente* between entrepreneurs and workers. The entrepreneur is not the capitalist, he hires the services of capital as well as those of workers on the market. What does it matter to him if he pays high prices for these services if he can sell the products at a price such that his profit is assured? Naturally he would prefer to sell the merchandise he produces at high prices,

---

[33] In June 1908, during the agricultural strike at Parma, the government prevented the bourgeois from defending themselves, although it allowed all latitude to their adversaries in attacking them. The latter went so far as to stop the railroad trains in order to hunt down the *Krumirs*.

[34] G. Sorel, *Réflexions sur la violence*, p. 169: "The beautiful reasoning of these gentlemen, pundits on social obligation, assumes that violence will no longer increase or even that it will decrease as the intellectuals pay more compliments, utter more platitudes, and do more simpering in honor of the union of the classes. Unhappily for these great thinkers, things take place altogether differently. It so happens that violence continues to increase as fast as it ought to be decreasing according to the principles of this lofty sociology."

and pay low wages; but since that is not possible he makes a virtue of necessity and turns to the line of least resistance. But the latter unquestionably, at least in our era, lies with the consumers. The spinelessness of some of them surpasses all belief. They have conceived of forming so-called buyers' leagues. According to the name, it would seem that these fine people join together in order to get merchandise of the best possible quality at the least price. Not at all! Their sole aim is to obtain from entrepreneurs preferential treatment for workers and clerks, all the rest is of little importance to them.

A concrete example of the possibility of an accord between entrepreneurs and workers at the expense of consumers is furnished by a recent law in Australia. The manufacturers of agricultural machinery have obtained a prohibitive tariff directed against the importation of American machinery, but with the condition that if they do not pay "equitable and reasonable" wages to their workers they must pay, on the products of their manufacture, half the duty imposed by the customs.

It must be noted that these laws are efficacious only insofar as they create privileges. If they were general, the consumers being then identical with the producers, the result would just be a nominal rise in prices. It is true that there would be a period of transition in which creditors and annuitants would be despoiled, but afterwards there would be a return almost to the original equilibrium.

35. Widespread European wars or other events of that type can arrest the course of the evolution taking place in our time; but if these events do not come about, and if that evolution reaches its end, it will result in an economic state which, except for its form and the names of things, will not be very different from the present state. We will still have an economic state in which monopolies of certain privileged persons will exist side by side with free competition between other citizens. The principal change in the final analysis will be in those who are privileged; in sum there will be, under another name, a new bourgeoisie.

Georges Sorel believes a complete change is possible; he says: "In the Marxist conception, the revolution is accomplished by the workers, who, accustomed to the regime of the large industrial factories, reduce the intellectuals to being no more than clerks carrying out their jobs, and as few of them as possible. Indeed, everyone knows that a business is regarded as the better managed insofar as it has the fewer administrative personnel."[35]

---

[35] G. Sorel, *La décomposition du Marxisme*, p. 51.

We would not dare to assert that such organization is impossible; the future can be full of surprises. Who, in the time of Aristotle, could have foreseen the parliamentary regimes which now rule almost all civilized peoples? But what we know of history and of contemporary facts seems to us contrary to the possibility of a change of that type, at least in the near future.

We are, on the other hand, in agreement with Sorel on the subject of the means which may lead to this evolution. "In trying to understand how minds have always been prepared for revolutions, it is easy to see that there has always been recourse to social myths, the formulas of which have varied according to the times."[56] "One must expect to encounter many deviations which will seem to call everything into question again; there will be times when everything which had been regarded as definitely acquired will be thought lost. ...It is precisely because of this characteristic of a new revolutionary movement that it is necessary to avoid giving formulas other than the myth formula: discouragement could result from the disillusion produced by the disproportion between the actual and the expected condition. . . ."[37]

These are indeed the characteristics of a faith and a religion, that is to say of forces which can act effectively to bring about a social change; and we ought to recall here what we have already said in I, 43, and, in general, our often repeated observations on sentiments and non-logical actions.

The error of the humanitarians, however, is not in having a religion, for it is by means of a religion that society is influenced, but in having chosen a religion which is appropriate only to weak beings lacking in all energy and courage, and which, if it should triumph, would lower European societies below the Peruvian society at the time of the Incas.

35b. Let us try to extend to the concrete phenomenon and even to the social phenomenon the considerations we developed in III, 11, 12 and in VI, 33.

Any economic or social state is in general neither absolutely rigid nor is it such that any movement whatsoever can occur. Some conditions, which we will call *restrictions* [*liaisons*], prevent certain movements and permit others. For example, a society which has castes permits certain movements within the same caste and prevents movements between different castes. A society in which there is private property and inheritance prevents certain movements

36 G. Sorel, *La décomposition du Marxisme*, p. 55.
37 G. Sorel, *La décomposition du Marxisme*, p. 63.

which would be possible in a society where those institutions did not exist.

There are two types of problems: 1° Choosing among restrictions in order to attain a certain end; 2° Given the restrictions, choosing, from among all possible movements, those to be carried out.

The objective sought obviously can be anything whatsoever. It could be to attain the largest possible population, or the happiest, or the most moral, etc.; but these terms, except for the first, are vague and need to be defined if it is desired to employ scientific reasoning.

Let us observe that the first problem can, in a strict sense, be included in the second; for that to be so it would be enough to consider a society without restrictions, and then the restrictions which are to be determined, the first problem, would be given by the second.

But generally there are some restrictions which everyone endorses, and it would be a waste of effort to debate about them. For example, it would be completely absurd to consider cannibalism as a possibility in civilized societies in our era.

Let us assume, then, that certain restrictions are given and take up the second problem.

We must study two types of quite distinct movements. 1° Certain movements can be advantageous to all the members of the society, or to some of them without being disadvantageous to others. 2° Certain other movements can be advantageous to some of the members of the society only by being disadvantageous to others.

As long as movements of the first class are possible, the material well being or the moral or religious qualities or any other qualities of the society can be increased, at least for some of its members, without detriment to the others. This cannot happen when only movements of the second class are possible.

Hence the situation in which movements of the first class are no longer possible can be considered as a certain maximum situation. We have done this with respect to ophelimity in VI, 33; and in that case the reasoning has all the rigor desirable (Appendix). It can have this characteristic whenever it is a question of something which can be measured; when it is a question of things which cannot be measured, the reasoning can only be more or less vague.

Even in this last case, however, much reasoning which has always been done and which continues to be done about social organization in reality reduces to more or less imperfect remarks about that maximum. It is in part disregarded by other, basically metaphysical and religious, reasoning; even the latter kind of reasoning, however, almost always wishes to reconcile the two things and to claim to attain this maximum.

Consider slavery. If the masters say simply and brutally, "It pleases us that things be so, and we are imposing our will," it is clear that it is not a case of a maximum for the entire society.

Aristotle starts out by basing slavery on metaphysical considerations, but he hastens to add that it is useful to the slave to serve and to the master to command (*Politics*, I, 2, 20). So doing, he deals with precisely one case of our general problem.

Some authors have maintained that slavery was useful because it was the only means of obtaining leisure for those men who, by their discoveries, have enabled civilization to develop. This is still an instance of our problem; but here the end is different than in the previous one; it is not a matter of the present utility of the masters and the slaves, but of the future utility of the society.

From the economic point of view, every effective monopoly, every poor choice of the coefficients of production, every poor use of the economic goods available to the society, take us farther away from the position of maximum ophelimity. This fact may be expressed in various ways. For example, one can say that the social organization might be changed in such a way that all the members of the society could enjoy greater well-being, or at least that some of those members could enjoy greater well-being without harming any others. Or one can say that the people who suffer from the social organization not being at maximum ophelimity could, if they were allowed to reach that maximum position, pay an amount such that everyone would find the new organization advantageous. This is how in former times the redemption of certain seigneurial rights could be advantageous to both villeins and lords. One can also say that in a position which is not one of maximum ophelimity there is a conflict between the interest of people who derive an advantage from that situation and the general interest. It can be added that as long as the position of maximum ophelimity is not reached, the growth, the gain of a given branch of economic activity is not necessarily a gain for society. It becomes such only when the position of maximum ophelimity is reached.

At bottom all these propositions, and still others, are concerned with the same facts but consider different aspects of the problem of maximum ophelimity.

36. The present economic organization is in part similar to the one which preceded it, and probably it will not change much, at least in the near future. It is an organization consisting of free com-

petition with some monopoly, some privileges, some prohibitions. What varies are the proportions in which these elements are combined.

37. At the beginning of the 19th century, large industry began to develop, and it has progressed more rapidly than the restrictive legislation which now affects it. It is partly to this circumstance that we owe the extraordinary growth in the wealth and in the population of civilized countries in this century (VII, 67).

The movement has now greatly slowed down; there is a strong tendency for a part of the present social configuration to become crystallized through constraints of all kinds, and we are moving closer to the rigid organizations[38] which had broken up at the end

---

[38] Man is restricted even in his smallest acts. For example, the law requires workers to rest on Sunday. In Switzerland the members of a religious sect, the *Adventists*, demand the right to rest on Saturday; that option was denied them by the authorities. But it is not enough that the law imposes on man the day and the manner of his repose, it is equally concerned with what he ought to eat and what he ought to drink, often under the pretext of hygiene, and sometimes without any pretext at all. In certain wine producing countries it is forbidden to make wine from raisins. There is no pretext of hygiene in this case; the only purpose of the law is to serve the interests of the wine producers. Why not require women to wear silk dresses instead of woolen ones in order to favor the spinners and weavers of silk?

Those rather senseless people who are anti-alcoholists are demanding new laws to prevent people from drinking what they please. Then along come other fanatics who have condemned the use of tea, of meat and even of milk.

Under the pretext of stamping out pornography, some would like to prevent the publishing of any book which could not be placed, without danger, into the hands of children. New congregations of the Index operate mysteriously close to the administration of the state railroads and prohibit the sale in stations of newspapers and books which do not appear moral enough to these worthy inquisitors.

The laws claiming to be directed against the "white slave traffic" are most often only a way of protecting domestic prostitution. A woman is permitted to sell her charms within the country, but is forbidden to put them on a market which would be more advantageous for her.

A campaign has been undertaken against the *poste-restante* under the pretext that it is used by lovers! A multitude of fanatics study day and night ways to remove all liberty from their fellow man and reduce society to a vast convent, of which these marvelous specimens of the human race naturally would be the superiors.

The law on the weekly rest, in France and Italy, is degenerating into a meddling and encroaching tyranny.

After having regulated factory work some want to regulate outwork in the home, and in England a law was proposed to fix the minimum wage also. An individual can die of hunger if he wants; but he may not work below this wage. For certain people, the ideal social organization appears to be one

of the 18th and beginning of the 19th century—those of a kind such that the theory in which it is assumed that man can act freely in following his own tastes applies only to an ever more limited domain, since each day sees an increase in the constraints which are imposed on man and which determine his actions in a rigid fashion.

38. Another consequence of such restrictive organization is that it would be a serious error to try to predict practical results, even in a purely economic matter, by means of economic theories alone.

Restrictive measures tend to become the main part; this matter properly belongs to the theory of non-logical actions.

39. **International trade.** The subject is very complex and it would require a whole volume to treat it in a suitable way. Hence we must resign ourselves to some very brief suggestions.

40. **Economic theory.** Consider two collectivities, each of which has certain capital which, at least within certain limits, cannot be transported to the other to compete with the capital of the latter.

Goods and certain services of capital can be exchanged by these two collectivities, and there may be imports and exports of certificates of public debts, securities of industrial companies, etc., as well.

41. Let us begin by considering only the exchange of goods and the import and export of money. We have already seen that, in civilized countries, the amount of gold in circulation is a very small part of the national wealth, and that the quantity of gold does not vary much. Imports and exports of gold serve to establish equilibrium when it is disturbed, but in the long run they approximately offset each other; they can be disregarded and only the exchanges of goods and of capital services need be taken into consideration. This is essentially J. B. Say's *theory of markets*.

42. Each collectivity will employ its own capital in the uses which are most advantageous to it. Suppose there are only two goods A and B. The first collectivity produces A, for example, and obtains B *via* exchange; the second collectivity produces only B, and obtains A *via* exchange. From this fact it can be deduced only that the first collectivity benefits more from producing A for its consumption, and obtaining B by exchange, than in producing both A and B for

---

where each citizen would be escorted by an inspector who would regulate his work, his recreations . . . and his pleasures.

Now some people dream of passing, each year without exception, a large number of laws taking away from man the right to do things which formerly were legal. They will end up regulating all man's actions from the moment of birth until his death.

its consumption. The same, *mutatis mutandis*, for the second collectivity. But it cannot be concluded from this that B is produced more easily by the second collectivity than by the first, and that A is produced more easily by the first collectivity than by the second. Ricardo's theory of comparative costs at bottom comes down to that.

Moreover, everything we have just said is very imprecise; no one knows clearly what it means to say that one thing is produced *more easily* than another. Professor Bastable warns us that the comparison between the costs of A and of B should be based not on the prices, but on the *sacrifices;* but he does not, and he could not, tell us in a precise way what these *sacrifices* consist of. In reality, this theory can be set forth rigorously only with the aid of mathematics.

43. Ricardo gives a very simple example in which each collectivity is reduced to one individual. "Assume," he says, "two workers who know how to make both shoes and hats. One of them is skillful in both of these trades, but if he makes hats his advantage over his competitor is only one-fifth; his advantage is one-third if he makes shoes. Is it not better for both if the more skillful worker makes only shoes, and the less skillful one makes only hats?"[39]

Professor Bastable, who cites this example, adds: "A simple calculation is enough to see that both workers benefit from this arrangement."

44. But that is not quite correct. It is strange that he does not see that this is true only in certain cases, and that it is not true in others. Ricardo's reasoning is good only to illustrate one possible case.

45. Let A and B be the two goods which Ricardo talks about, and assume that in one day the less skillful worker produces 1 of A, or 1 of B. According to Ricardo's example, the more skillful worker will in one day make six-fifths of A or four-thirds of B. This is shown by the following table in which I and II identify the workers.

	I	II
A	6/5	1
B	4/3	1

Let us assume that the two workers each work thirty days pro-

---

[39] In this example we see immediately what the *sacrifices* to which Ricardo's theory alludes consist of, because we consider not two collectivities, but two men, and because we assume that labor alone enters into the production of the goods. But reality is quite different, being varied and complex.

ducing A, thirty days producing B, and that thereby their wants are satisfied. We will have:

		I	II	Total Quantities
(α)	A............	36	30	66
	B............	40	30	70

Then, still following Ricardo, let us assume that I produces only B, and II only A; we will have:

		I	II	Total Quantities
(β)	A............		60	60
	B............	80		80

The total quantity to be divided between the two people is greater for B, but it is smaller for A, and we do not know whether, taking account of the tastes of the individuals, there is, or there is not, compensation. If there is compensation (§ 51), Ricardo's proposition is true; if there is not compensation, the proposition is false (§ 52). For example, if A is bread and B coral ornaments, it could very well happen that the deficit of 6 bread will not be compensated by 10 more coral.

46. In order for Ricardo's conclusion always to be true, it is necessary that, when I produces only B and II produces only A, the total quantities produced both be greater than in the case where, for the direct satisfaction of their tastes, I and II both produce both A and B.[40]

47. For example, let us again assume that I works 30 days making A and 30 days making B; but that II works 22 days making A, and 38 days making B. Moreover, and this is the main point, let

---

[40] While II is making 1 of A, let us assume that I makes x of it; and while II is making 1 of B, I makes y of it.

Let (μ) be a combination in which, in time t, I produces B only and II produces A only; and (π) another combination in which I produces A in time $t\text{-}\theta$, and B during the time θ; II produces A during the time $t\text{-}\theta'$, and B during time θ'.

If we desire that the quantities of A and of B produced in the combination (μ) be greater than those produced in the combination (π), we must have:

$$t > (t\text{-}\theta)x + t\text{-}\theta'$$
$$ty > \theta y + \theta',$$

or

$$\theta' < (t\text{-}\theta)y, \qquad\qquad \theta' > (t\text{-}\theta)x$$

These formulas have been used to construct the table in the text. Note that in order for them to hold it is necessary to have

$$y > x.$$

us assume that the tastes are satisfied by the quantities produced in this fashion; we will have:

		I	II	Total Quantities
(γ)	A	36	22	58
	B	40	38	78

The quantities produced when I only makes B and II just A are greater than the total quantities above. Consequently the amounts to be distributed are definitely more advantageous to each of the two individuals. They could be divided, for example, in the following way:

		I	II	Total Quantities
(δ)	A	37	23	60
	B	41	39	80

It is obvious that combination (δ) is more advantageous for each individual than combination (γ).

48. Let us make a calculation which will be useful in what follows. Assume that in combination (β) the price of A is 1, and the same for the price of B. In combination (δ), I exchanges 37 A's for 39 B's, and consequently the price of A in B is 39/37; individual II exchanges 39 B's for 37 A's, and consequently, for him, the price of B in A (assuming the price of A is 1, that is) is 37/39. But the price of A should be the same on the two markets (there are no transportation expenses); and similarly for that of B. Hence it is necessary to multiply the prices for II by 39/37, and we have the following prices:

(δ)

	I	II
A	39/37	39/37
B	1	1

In combination (α), if the price of B is 1, as we have assumed, the price of A, for I, will be 10/9; and if II protects himself from the importation of B by a customs duty of 1/9, we will have the following prices:

(α)

	I	II
A	10/9	10/9
B	1	10/9

The fraction 10/9 is greater than the fraction 39/37, consequently in our example, and this is merely one possibility, the prices in combination (a) which is the protection combination, are higher than in combination (δ), which is that of free trade.

49. In practice, the prices refer not to the produced good B, but rather to good A (money) which circulates freely. On this hypothesis, the prices of the free trade combination (δ) are:

$$(\delta')$$

	I	II
A..........	1	1
B..........	37/39	37/39

The prices of the protection combination (a) are:

$$(a')$$

	I	II
A..........	1	1
B..........	9/10	1

And consequently II's protective tariff for good B raises the price of B for II, and lowers the price of B for I.

50. Let us return to case (β), and assume that the tastes of the individuals are satisfied in such a way that these individuals are better off than in case (a) when the distribution is made as follows:

		I	II	Total Quantities
(ε)	A..........	29	31	60
	B..........	49	31	80

That is, for I the increase in B more than compensates for the decrease in A; and as for II, he gets greater amounts of both goods, hence he definitely is better off than before.

In this case, but thanks only to the hypothesis made with regard to the tastes of I, Ricardo's conclusion still stands.

Note that if the two collectivities do not trade with each other and collectivity I still wants to obtain 49 B's, it will have only 27.9 of A, whereas collectivity II will have only 30 A's and 30 B's, as a result of which, to sum up, they will both be worse off than before.

51. Reasoning as in § 49, we start by observing that the prices are proportional to the following values:

	I	II
A..........	31/29	1
B..........	1	29/31

But the prices of A on the two markets should be equal (transportation expenses are assumed equal to zero), similarly for those of

B; for that to be so it is necessary to multiply the prices for II by 31/29, and we have the following prices:

$$(\varepsilon')$$

	I	II
A..........	31/29	31/29
B..........	1	1

As a consequence we again reach the same conclusion as that in § 49. But let us note carefully that this is only one possibility, and that, by choosing some other values, this conclusion would no longer be true.

52. For example, if the tastes were satisfied not by combination (ε), but by the following:

		I	II	Total Quantities
(θ)	A..........	28	32	60
	B..........	45	35	80

the prices in terms of B in combination (α), which is that of protection, would be lower than the prices in combination (θ), which is that of free trade; and if the prices are expressed in A, II's protective tariff on good B would raise the price of B, not only for II, but also for I. But, in fact, even with free trade, combination (α) is the one which will occur. Indeed, if I, in order to satisfy his tastes begins by producing 45 B's he has the time needed to produce 31.5 A's left. Then it is more advantageous to him to produce A and B, than to produce B alone and obtain A *via* trade with II. We have here a case in which Ricardo's proposition cannot be accepted (§ 45).

Everything we have just said merely provides some indications, in the form of examples, which enable us to discover certain possibilities by induction. A rigorous proof can be given only by employing the formulas of pure economics and making use of mathematics.

53. If a collectivity has a monopoly of a good and if the members of the collectivity compete in the sale of this good, it may be useful to the collectivity to replace the monopoly price by the competitive price, and this can be done by putting a tax on its export.

54. A duty on importation is essentially different from the preceding case. When this duty actually decreases the importation of a foreign good, which is then partly or totally replaced in consumption by a domestic good which is itself then produced in greater quantity, there is, in general, a destruction of wealth.[41]

---

[41] *Cours*, § 864 *et seq.*

The exceptions are of little importance; it would not be so, in general, for the case which we described in VI, 47; that is, when, in place of a given price for all portions of the good, the price inside the country may be different from the one abroad, and when this can bring about a reduction in the cost of the good, because, in that case, the price is lower in the second situation than in the first, which is precisely the opposite of the effect of a protective tariff.

The case studied in VI, 47, can be modified; we can assume that, with free trade, 100 units of a good X will be produced at a cost of 5, and will be sold at this price of 5. The entrepreneurs thus make no profit. Then, upon the imposition of a protective tariff, they sell 90 units within the country at a price of 6, and 60 units abroad at a price of 4. Thus they sell 150 units in all and take in 780.

The cost of production of these 150 units must be higher than 4.67, otherwise the entrepreneurs would not need a protective tariff, and they could sell 100 units within the country at a price of 5, and 50 units abroad at a price of 4, taking in 700 in all, a sum equal to the cost. Let us assume then that the cost is 4.80. The 150 units will cost the entrepreneurs 720, and since they take in 780, they make a profit of 60. But the consumers lose 90, and this is a greater amount than the producers gain. This conclusion is general.[42]

Thus we can *grosso-modo*, and as a first approximation, conclude that every protective tariff is the cause of a destruction of wealth within the country which levies this duty on a good.

This conclusion will stand, if, in addition to the exchange of goods, we include the numerous other things which make up the balance of debits and credits between the two countries under consideration.

------

[42] Let a be the quantity produced under free trade, at a price p; then when, due to a protective tariff, the domestic price is p', let b be the quantity sold within the country, and c the quantity sold abroad at the price p''. Finally, let q be the cost of production of one unit when $b + c$ is produced. For the producers to derive a profit due to the protective tariff, it is necessary that
$$p'b + p''c > (b+c)q.$$
In order that there be no profit in this combination when there is free-trade, it is necessary that
$$pa + (b+c-a)p'' < (b+c)q.$$
Finally, in order that the profit of the producers be greater than the loss to consumers, it would be necessary to have
$$p'b + p''c - (b+c)q > (p'-p)b.$$
From these inequalities we derive
$$b > a;$$
which is impossible. Since the protective tariff raises the price, the amount sold within the country decreases, and as a result b must be smaller than a.

Among the evils caused by protection, it is necessary to count the change in the values of the production coefficients which would yield maximum ophelimity. For example, in England free trade has been favorable to the intensive cultivation of grain; in certain states of continental Europe protection has favored the extensive cultivation of grain.

Trade unions and producer associations have analogous effects.

55. **Indirect economic effects.** One of these effects, if not real, at least supposed, is famous. It has been said that protection could be useful to protect infant industries, which, later, having become adult, would no longer need it. It cannot be denied *a priori* that such could sometimes be the case, but there is no known example of it. All the industries born under a system of protection have always sought more and more protection, and the day has never come when they declared they could do without it.

The theoretical possibility indicated in § § 49 and 51 seems to be a real phenomenon in many cases, and a large number of facts impel us to believe that for certain countries protection has raised a large number of prices of protected goods in such a way that a general rise in the cost of living has been the result. We have already talked about the effects of a general rise in prices (VI, 80), and it is not necessary to go into that again.

If one country produces certain goods, and if other countries put protective tariffs on those goods, their prices decrease in the country which produces them (§ 49). The experimental verification of this theoretical deduction, however, is not nearly so easy as that of the preceding deduction.

Finally, the destruction of wealth which is the effect of protection has, in its turn, a number of economic and social effects (VII, 54 *passim*), which appear as indirect effects of protection.

56. **Distribution effects.** Obviously protection changes the distribution among certain individuals. The combinations which can occur are infinite; we can say roughly and in a very general way that agricultural protection especially favors landowners for whom it increases *rents*. Industrial protection favors the owners of industrial sites in a permanent way, and entrepreneurs in a temporary way. The latter, at first, get some temporary *rents* which the competition of other entrepreneurs reduces and nullifies more or less rapidly. It favors skilled workers, who get wages higher than those they would have been able to get if the protected industries had not been established, but it is a detriment to the workers who work in the unprotected industries or in agriculture. Finally, a part

of the bourgeosie belonging to the liberal professions also benefit; industry, more than agriculture, has need for engineers, lawyers, notaries, etc.

These conditions vary with the conditions of production in different countries. In Russia, for example, industrial protection is at the expense of agriculture. In Germany, both industry and agriculture can be protected, and they are. As a result agriculture benefits from protection and does not suffer too much from industrial protection.

57. **Social effects.** Industrial protection in agricultural countries, and free trade in an industrial country, both have the effect of developing industry. Consequently, depending on the country, these contrasting measures can have similar effects, which consist especially in providing or increasing the power of the working class and of democracy—and of socialism too. Protection in Russia has such effects, just as does free trade in England.

Where there is a landed aristocracy, as in Germany, agricultural protection strengthens that aristocracy, and helps it avoid being destroyed by other aristocracies. It is for this reason that agricultural protection is perhaps indispensable for the preservation of the present social organization in Germany.

Industrial protection in essentially agricultural countries and free trade in essentially industrial countries, by aiding industry, constitutes a powerful means of selection from the worker class and also from the bourgeoisie, which provides clerks, engineers, etc., to industry.

Protection is also, in general, a means of selection for those who, by various artifices in buying voters, journalists and politicians, obtain the protective tariffs. But in truth, this selection yields a very decadent aristocracy, even inferior to one which would be provided by brigandage, which at the very least would produce courageous men.

58. **Fiscal effects.** Among modern peoples it is not a question of protection pure and simple; fiscal measures are always intermingled. All modern states which are subjected to protection derive enormous sums for their budgets from customs duties; customs duties are the principal source of receipts in the United States of America and in the Swiss Confederation.

59. Within every country, modern democracy tends to replace indirect taxes with direct taxes. The citizens who make up a majority of the population can be reached only by means of customs duties, whereas direct taxes, especially progressive taxes, exploit the well-

to-do classes, which always make up only a small fraction of the population. In certain cases, protection restores to a part of the well-to-do people a portion of what has been taken from them by progressive taxes, or even by other taxes, the proceeds of which are in part spent to carry out measures of state socialism.

60. From all the preceding it can be seen how complex is the practical and synthetic problem of knowing whether protection is preferable to free trade, or *vice versa*. In this general form, the problem is insoluble anyway because it has no precise meaning. It is necessary to state the specific problem, which can be expressed thus: given all the economic and social conditions of a country at a given time, to find, for that country at that time, which system is preferable, protection or free trade.

61. The following reasoning is incorrect because it neglects some essential conditions of the problem: protection entails a destruction of wealth, accordingly in every era and for every country protection is detrimental and free trade advantageous.[43]

62. **Reasons for protection.** These reasons certainly do not include the theoretical solution of the economic problem we have just spoken of. Even if it were very clearly demonstrated that protection always entails the destruction of wealth, if that were taught to every citizen just as they learn the abc's, protection would lose so small a number of partisans and free trade would gain so few of them that the effect can be almost, or even completely, disregarded. The motives which lead men to act are quite different.[44]

63. Protection generally is established by a coalition whose principle members are: 1° those who hope to reap an immediate and

---

[43] The author of this book has been wrong in occasionally expressing himself in some polemic work—which has no scientific value anyway—in a manner which leads one to believe, at least implicitly, that he reasoned similarly. In 1887, however, he wrote: "Finally, the social effects and their economic consequences, which one could call doubly indirect effects of protection, are the primary issues involved and, in my opinion, the only ones which could sometimes raise serious doubts about the more or less considerable usefulness of free trade, in certain special cases." (*Sulla recrudescenza della protezione doganale*; paper read at the Academy of Georgofili, May 28, 1887).

[44] M. Bordeau, who follows the evolution of socialism with much perspicacity, writes: "How inadequate is the work done by all of us concerned with socialist questions when we restrict ourselves to explaining and refuting abstract theories, which most workers are ignorant of, or about which they care little! The common people's notions come from their sentiments, the sentiments from their sensations, and their sensations themselves flow from their way of life, from the nature of, the duration of, and the gain from their work." *Socialistes et sociologues*, p. 164.

considerable benefit from protection; that is, proprietors who will obtain some permanent *rents*, entrepreneurs who will get some *rents* which actually will be temporary, a fact which causes little concern provided they last long enough to provide a profit, and those persons with occupations which may be protected. 2° The politicians who hope, thanks to the tax receipts from protection (§ 58), to enrich the budget which they control. All those who hope to profit from the expenditures which the State will make, and who are intelligent enough to understand that in order to increase expenditures it is necessary to increase receipts. 3° Those whose *nationalistic* sentiments are successfully aroused in such a way as to make them believe that protection serves to defend the fatherland against the foreigner. It is necessary to include once more the "ethical ones," few in number when it is a question of protection *via* customs duties, in greater number when it is a question of other restrictive measures; the latter imagine or pretend to believe that these measures are in accord with their ethics. This is a rather peculiar type of man; when they are in good faith, they are easily gulled; and when they are in bad faith, they are the ones who do the gulling. 4° Finally, but small in number at present, those who are informed, intelligent and foresighted enough to see that democracy tends more and more to despoil the rich, and who having neither the will, nor the courage, nor the strength to resist directly, choose this indirect means of recovering a part of what has been taken from them and, in any case, of avoiding being the only ones to pay taxes.

64. It is a coalition of this kind which established the alcohol monopoly in Switzerland; the fourth category was not included, however, and the third was a little different. Taking part were: 1° Those from whom the management of the monopoly buys alcohol at a much higher price than the ordinary market price.[45] Farm operators, who can distill without restraint the products of their harvests and who then sell the alcohol produced at a price above what they would obtain if the monopoly did not exist. 2° The public authorities, whose budget is increased from the proceeds of the monopoly. 3° Anti-alcoholists who, good sectarians that they are,

---

[45] Numa Droz, *Essais économiques. Le monopole de l'alcool en Suisse*, p. 577: "Since it is the confederation which passes on the contracts for delivery of the alcohol, people appeal to it, especially in election years, to demand that . . . it improve the terms of the contracts, so that higher amounts can be paid for the native potato, or else the elections will turn out badly. This is how the *potato vote* came about."

The ethical anti-alcoholists do not notice or pretend not to notice these things.

approve everything which may or which they think may strike a blow against their enemy, alcohol.

65. In England, the present protectionist movement is the work of the fourth category of § 63. The third category is very large; nationalistic sentiment is consumed by the pursuit of a closer union with the colonies. The first and second categories hide behind the third, which carries the standard of the coalition.

66. In order to explain how those who champion protection make themselves heard so easily, it is necessary to add a consideration which applies to social movements generally. The intensity of the work of an individual is not proportionate to the benefits which that work may bring him, nor to the harm which it may enable him to avoid. If a certain measure A is the cause of the loss of one franc to each of a thousand persons, and of a thousand franc gain to one individual, the latter will expend a great deal of energy, whereas the former will resist weakly; and it is likely that, in the end, the person who is attempting to secure the thousand francs *via* A will be successful.[46]

A protectionist measure provides large benefits to a small number of people, and causes a very great number of consumers a slight loss. This circumstance makes it easier to put a protection measure into practice.

It must also be noted that a total sum generally has a stronger impact than the total of the impacts of the parts of that sum. The sum of one hundred francs is equal to one hundred times one franc arithmetically; but this equality is no longer true when it is a matter of an individual's sensations; a sum total of one hundred francs can make a stronger impression than one hundred times one franc. This is truer still if the one hundred francs is received directly, and if the different francs whose total is equal to one hundred francs are obtained indirectly; the difference is greater still if there is some doubt about who gets each of these francs.

The producer can estimate quite accurately the profit which he will derive from a customs duty on the goods which he produces; let us assume that he estimates he can obtain one hundred francs. It matters little that the goods will be sold over a period of time; so far as the customs duty is concerned it is just one operation, and the sum of one hundred francs is viewed in its totality. As a consumer he will have to bear the burden of the protection accorded to other goods. Let us assume that he buys for his consumption one hundred of these goods each one of which will cost him one franc

---

[46] *Systèmes*, I, p. 128; *Cours*, II, § 1046 *et seq.*

more because of the protection. Here again it matters little whether the purchase of these goods be made on one or several occasions. In total, the person of whom we are speaking will have lost one hundred francs, exactly what the protection gains for him. The impression, however, which the one of these facts will make on him will be quite different from that made by the other. Not only does the total of one hundred francs which he gains on his goods make a greater impression on him than the hundred francs which he loses one by one, but in addition, the former is much more certain, or, if one prefers, much less uncertain than the latter. Protection almost certainly makes the price of the protected good rise; but it is not certain that the prices of non-protected goods do not rise for quite different reasons. In short, the additional amount which our individual will receive is nearly certain, the additional amount which he will spend is highly uncertain.

That is not yet all. The hypothesis which we have just made is not always fulfilled, and often a producer gains more from the protection accorded his good than he loses *via* the protection accorded the goods of other producers.

Let there be one economic state in which causes A, B, C, . . . of destruction of wealth operate, and another in which none of these causes are present. There is no doubt that in the second economic state (distribution remaining the same) all the people will be in a better position than in the first. But if we compare, on the other hand, an economic state in which the causes A, B, C, . . . of destruction of wealth are present, with another state in which the causes B, C, . . . exist, we no longer can assert that in the second state all individuals are in a better position than in the first, because the destruction of wealth which results from B, C, . . . can develop in a way such that it offsets and even surpasses the destruction produced by A in the first state.

The opinion of liberal economists, that protection laws are imposed on a country by a coalition of politicians and a small number of producers, cannot be accepted in a general way, because we have at least one particular case in which that is contradicted by experience. Indeed, in Switzerland, protective tariffs have been approved by a popular *referendum*, that is, by a majority of the voters who took part in the balloting.

Similarly, the opinion that protection laws are tolerated only as a result of public ignorance has no foundation, because those who benefit from these laws often give evidence of having very keen minds and a good sense of the opportune, and those who bear the cost sin less because of ignorance than from lack of courage and energy.

This is seen still better by observing consumers who act no differently in similar cases where the excuse of ignorance cannot be used. For example, when a league such as that of the lithographers notifies everyone that it expels and persecutes the producer guilty of working at prices advantageous to consumers (§ 12), the latter could defend him and attack those who are trying to hurt him. If they do not do even that, how could they undertake the much more arduous task of changing the laws and escaping the burdens of the protective tariffs! The world, in short, belongs to those who know how to seize it.

67. To condemn protection it is not enough to point out that it is established by those who find a direct advantage in it and, in large part, by those who intend to appropriate to themselves the goods of others, because even if those are the motives which induce them to act in such a way, the end which they attain could be to the good of the country. We have seen that in the determination of the coefficients of production producers have in mind only their own advantage, yet they end up organizing production for the greatest good of the consumers. Something analogous could take place with respect to protection (§ 35).

68. It is not possible to judge the effect of protection, or of free trade, by comparing the countries where they exist, because these countries differ on many other points. One can only, and with much caution, make this comparison for a given country, and for a length of time which does not exceed two or three years, at a time when a country is going from protection to free trade, or conversely. In this case, the other circumstances vary little in comparison to the change which has occurred in the realm of foreign trade, and one can, with some likelihood, at least partly connect the variation in the effects with the variation in the circumstance which has changed most.

69. In this way one obtains a practical confirmation of the assertion that protection, in reducing imports, also decreases exports. This phenomenon has been observed in a great number of cases and for many countries.[47]

70. According to what we said in § 68, it is an error to cite the prosperity of the United States as evidence of the usefulness of pro-

[47] *Cours*, § 881.

tection, or the prosperity of England as evidence of the usefulness of free trade.[48]

Nor can England and Germany be compared as if there were no other difference between those two countries than the practice of free trade in England and protection in Germany.

71. Let us note, moreover, that if, in England, free trade increases wealth, the trade union demands destroy it. The widespread and lengthy strike of the machine workers was the result of the latter's demand that employers not be allowed to introduce improved machines except with the permission of the workers, and with the condition that the gain resulting from these machines accrue to the workers. In practice, this prevented the introduction of these machines, which would have been a cost to the employers without providing them any profit.

In this situation there is a contradiction between the behavior of the humanitarian and decadent bourgeosie,[49] who took the side of the workers, and the wailing of that same bourgeosie because German industry is surpassing English industry. When one wants a thing, he must not complain about its consequences.

If English industry has made less progress than German industry in recent years, that is certainly due in part to the negligence of the employers who relied on their long standing renown, without being concerned about moving forward; but much more still is it due to the tyranny which the trade unions exercise over the employers, whereas German industry escapes it for the moment, or does not feel it with the same intensity.

72. If the protectionist policy triumphs in England, it will certainly entail a certain destruction of wealth; but if, in addition, the new social organization which will result from this policy curbs

---

[48] Thus this proposition in the *Cours*, § 891, is incorrect: "England, thanks to its faithfulness to the principles of liberal political economy, continues to see its prosperity increase. . . ." The author was wrong to accept, without submitting it to a sufficiently strict examination, a proposition current among the liberal economists and which seemed to them to have the value of an axiom. Moreover, it was expressed badly, because it is quite true that at the time when he wrote, England practiced free trade and had a monetary system consistent with the principles of the liberal school, but already municipal socialism, which has progressed so much since that time, was beginning to sprout and the system of humanitarian restrictions was flourishing. To be precise, the author should not have been so positive about the fidelity of England to the principles of liberal economics.

[49] Among the latter there have been some bishops and archbishops who would have done better to have kept busy with theology rather than with political economy.

municipal socialism and the system of humanitarian constraint, or even simply cuts down the power of the trade unions, a considerable amount of wealth will be saved, which could offset, or even more than offset, the loss due to protection. Thus the final result could be an increase in well-being.

73. **Economic crises.** The economic complexus is composed of molecules which vibrate continuously; this is a consequence of the nature of man and of the economic problems which he has to solve. These movements may occur in different directions, and in that case they partially offset each other. Sometimes we note that certain industries and types of business activity are prospering while others are languishing. On the whole there is a compensation and it cannot be said that there is either a general state of prosperity or a state of economic depression.

But from time to time, whatever the causes, almost all of these movements of the elements of the economic complexus occur in the same direction. We then observe that nearly all industries, types of business activity and occupations are prospering, or that there is stagnation and they are languishing; in that case there is a general state of prosperity or of economic depression.

74. The latter, when rather marked, are called CRISES. But since observation shows that a state of depression is always preceded by a state of extraordinary activity, the meaning of the word crisis ought to be extended to the whole of these two phenomena, calling the period of extraordinary activity the *upswing* [*période ascendante*] of the crisis and the period of depression the *downswing période descendante*] of the crisis.

This definition of the crisis is not very precise, however. The movements of the elements of the economic complexus are incessant. Trifling movements are not called crises, more important movements are. But how to distinguish between them? It would be necessary, at the very least, to have a reliable measure available. But that is impossible. Even if there is no doubt about the extreme cases, we cannot make use of this terminology for the intermediate cases. It is the same as with the words young and old which are used to indicate different ages.

75. The crisis is only a particular case of the great law of rhythm which dominates all social phenomena.[50] The form of the crisis reflects the social structure, but the latter does not affect the underlying basis, which depends on the nature of man and economic problems. There are crises not only in commerce and in

---

[50] *Systèmes*, I, p. 30.

private industry, but in public enterprises as well. Municipalities go through some periods during which the cities are transformed, and some periods during which no new works are undertaken. Countries have never built railroads in a uniform way; in some periods they have done a great deal of construction, in others very little. In England, from time to time, a *naval panic* can be observed. When the nation fears a foreign invasion, every expenditure on the fleet is hastily approved. Then some periods of calm follow during which new ship construction slackens.

76. Goods must be produced a certain length of time, and sometimes a very long time, in advance of consumption. In order for production to be perfectly adapted to consumption it would be necessary: 1° that forecasts of consumption could be made; 2° that the results of production could be accurately foreseen. It is impossible to do this with precision.

77. In the present organization, it is the producers and merchants who try to make these forecasts. If they predict accurately, they grow rich; if they make a mistake, they are ruined. In a socialist system, employees of the State would have to do this work; it is probable that they would make more mistakes and do so more often than private persons. To be convinced of this it is enough, among other things, to recall the difficulty with which governments provision their armies in the field, whereas business provides marvelously for the far more varied and complex consumption in large cities such as Paris, London and Berlin.

In its efforts to adapt to consumption, production is sometimes ahead, sometimes behind, and oscillation in one direction is often the cause of oscillation in the opposite direction. When *philoxera* overran the French vineyards, production remained below consumption, and the price of wine rose; there was much to be gained by producing more; everyone began to replant the vineyards with American vines, and production, due to the very fact that it had been too low, surpassed consumption and now more wine is produced than is called for, at practicable prices, by consumption. And so we see an oscillation in the opposite direction taking form.

78. Crises have two main types of causes, namely: (a) Any objective change in the conditions of production, if extensive enough, can give rise to a crisis. The food shortages of former times were related to this cause. (β) Subjective synchronism of economic movements turn movements which otherwise would have given rise to smaller departures from economic equilibrium into intense crises.

79. The subjective cause is powerful. In certain periods men are full of confidence, in others they are extremely discouraged. Nowadays these states of mind are modified by experience. The memory of the downswing of past crises diminishes the exaggerated faith in complete success during the upswing of a new crisis; the memory of the upswing of past crises diminishes the excessive discouragement during the downswing of a new crisis.

All writers who have studied crises carefully have seen the role played by men's imagination. Montesquieu talks about it very clearly in connection with the subject of the crisis which took place in the time of Law.[51] But generally people take to be an effect of the crisis what is, on the contrary, one of the principal reasons for it.

80. During the upswing everyone is content and no one talks about a crisis. That period, however, is surely preparing the way for the downswing which distresses everyone and which alone is given the name crisis. The upswing usually lasts longer than the downswing. Things go up little by little, they are hurled down in a single stroke.

81. People attribute much greater harm to crises than they actually produce. That is because man feels his misfortunes acutely, but easily forgets the good things he has enjoyed. It seems to him that the latter are his due, and that the former strike him unjustly. The troubles of the downswing of the crisis weigh heavily on man's imagination, and he forgets the gains he realized during the upswing.

In the final analysis it has not been demonstrated that the oscillatory movement which we call crisis causes only harm to human society. It could be that it is more advantageous than harmful.

82. Events which are concomitant with crises have been regarded as causes.

During the upswing, when everything is on the road to prosperity, *consumption* increases, and entrepreneurs expand *production;* in order to do so they *transform savings* into fixed and circulating capital, and draw heavily on *credit; circulation* [of money] is more rapid.

Each of these facts has been regarded as the exclusive cause of the downswing, to which the name crisis is given. What is true in

---

[51] *Lettres persanes, CXLII.* He pretends that Law is speaking as follows: "People of Baetica, do you want to be rich? Imagine that I am very much so, *and that you are very rich also;* every morning tell yourself that your fortune has doubled during the night, and if you have creditors, go pay them with what you have imagined, and tell them to imagine it in their turn."

this is simply that these facts are observed in the upswing which always precedes the downswing.

83. What is called excess consumption during the upswing is only the greater consumption which is due to the economic prosperity of that period; and that excess will be changed into a deficiency of consumption, that is to say, into less consumption, when economic prosperity diminishes in the downswing.

Similarly, production increases during the upswing in order to satisfy the growing demands of consumption. There is then a deficiency of production; for example, "shortages" of coal are almost always observed in the upswing. Then when the downswing comes, consumption decreases and production becomes overabundant; for a while, that is, until a decrease in production has taken place, there is an "excess" of production.

It is pure fantasy to speak of a permanent excess of production. If that were so, somewhere there would have to be, as we have already said, some ever increasing stockpiles of goods whose production exceeds their consumption. This is not observed.

Similar remarks could be made on the subject of transformation of savings, and about the demand for credit.

When someone speaks of the "circulation crisis," he usually is taking the effect for the cause. It is because of the crisis that circulation is sometimes rapid (in the upswing), and sometimes slow (in the downswing); it is not the crisis which is produced by the variations in circulation.

84. In addition there are some phenomena independent of crises which, misinterpreted, have given rise to the errors which we just pointed out.

The permanent phenomenon which is called excess consumption is nothing but man's tendency to consume as much as he can to satisfy his tastes; this is the force which stimulates production.

What is generally called excess production is the tendency of entrepreneurs to supply, at a certain price, more goods than consumption demands; this is the force which stimulates consumption.

Since consumption and production never are, and never can be, perfectly equal, there is, from time to time in real life, an excess of the one or the other, soon offset by a corresponding shortage.

For example, assume there are certain producers who have a good in stock and who, in one year, produce 100 units of it. If consumption is 120, the 20 extra units will be taken out of stock. The following year the producers, inspired by this excess consumption, will raise prices and produce 110, whereas the buyers, restrained precisely by that rise in prices, will consume only 90; consequently there will be excess production of 20 units, which will replenish the stock. Thus there has sometimes been an excess of consumption and a deficiency in production, and sometimes a deficiency in consumption and an excess of production.

Similar phenomena may be observed in the production and consumption of coal, cast-iron and many other goods; but generally the oscillation lasts more than one year.

85. **Symptoms of the crisis.** Clement Juglar sees them in the balance sheets of banks of issue; Pierre des Essars in the velocity of circulation of deposits in banks of issue.

The quantity of available savings and the oscillatory movements of crises are related. In the upswing this quantity decreases; in the downswing it increases.

Just as a pond connected with the sea can indicate the level of the latter, the quantities of money available in the vaults of the banks of issue can give an idea of the quantity of savings available in the country.

We must take care not to confuse the effect with the cause, and not imagine that by holding gold in the vaults of the banks by artificial means the crisis would be prevented. Anyone who reasoned like that would be like someone who would break his thermometer to prevent the temperature from rising.

When the beginning of a downswing of a crisis appears, there are always some people who claim that the crisis is due to a deficiency of the circulating medium, and all sorts of projects are hatched for reorganization of the banks and even of the monetary system. But what appears as a shortage in the circulating medium is precisely the force which is acting to restore the equilibrium which has been disturbed. Let us suppose that just before the downswing the quantity of the circulating medium is considerably increased. The result will be simply to prolong the upswing; this will have the effect of moving the economic aggregate still farther from its position of equilibrium and, consequently, making the crisis which must inevitably occur more serious. There is only one way to stop the speculators, the producers and the consumers, who move farther and farther away from the equilibrium position. It is to cut off their means; in other words, to bring about a shortage in the circulating medium which they need in order to continue their operations.

The fantastic notions of President Roosevelt, accusing the trusts and the market speculators of being the cause of the crisis which raged in the United States near the end of the year 1907, belong in the realm of fable. The crisis has been general; it has struck some countries, such as England, where the trusts are only exceptions, and some countries, such as Germany, where extremely severe legislation reduces speculation in securities on the exchange to a minimum. In Paris there is much more speculation than in Berlin, and if France has been relatively unhurt by the crisis it is because, not having taken part in the upswing, she has thereby avoided the downswing. Where there is no flood-tide there is no ebb-tide.

We must distinguish carefully between the financial crisis which is observed on the exchange, and the economic crisis which hits production.

The financial crisis occurs suddenly at the beginning of the downswing. It is severe, but it passes quickly. The discount rate of the Bank of England is, in these circumstances, abruptly raised to a great height, but a few months is enough for it to return to its normal rate.

The economic crisis occurs slowly, developing over several years, only coming to an end little by little, and then a new upswing begins.

On the exchange, during the downswing, securities with a fixed income, mainly government bonds of the highest grade, increase in price; the shares of industrial enterprises are depressed. The contrary takes place during the upswing.

When the downswing occurs there are some governments which attribute it to the criminal manoeuvres of the market speculators. Thus the Italian government, in 1907 and 1908, took police measures against people who committed the offense of selling, instead of buying, industrial securities. These measures generally produce an effect opposite to what is wanted, for indeed far from restoring confidence they contributed toward increasing distrust.

Moreover, it should be understood that in reality the bearish speculator is not very harmful, except to another speculator, that is, to a bullish speculator. If the bearish speculators are selling securities below their value, this is an excellent occasion for people who have some money available to buy them.

As for those persons who keep their securities in their strong boxes just to collect the dividends, the battle taking place between the speculators on the market is a matter of complete indifference to them.

Indeed, far from always being harmful, bearish speculation can be very useful in certain cases. It prevents the upswing from being prolonged and thereby moving the [economic] aggregate always farther away from the equilibrium position. When the downswing comes it paves the way for the upswing. It is well known on the market that the *buying back in by the bears* is one of the most powerful causes of a rise.

Finally it must be noted that *bullish speculation* and *bearish speculation* are often only two terms for the same thing. How could those who are speculating on a fall sell if no one bought? And how could those who speculate on a rise buy if no one sold?

86. Clement Juglar has noted that in the upswing the quantity of money in the vaults of banks of issue diminishes, and their portfolios increase; during the downswing, opposite effects are observed. That writer has made a technical study of the maxima and minima of cash balances and portfolios, and he was able to establish definite relationships between these phenomena.

87. Pierre des Essars has calculated, for an 85 year period, the velocity of circulation of deposits in the Bank of France, and (for a somewhat shorter period) in the Bank of Italy, and he has been able to confirm that the [velocity of] circulation is a maximum at the time when the upswing is ending and the downswing beginning, and a minimum during the period of liquidation in the crisis.

88. W. Stanley Jevons believed he could determine approximately the length of the periods of crises. According to him there would be three years of business depression, three years of brisk business activity, two years of very great business activity, one year of maximum activity, one year for the catastrophe; and then there would begin again other periods identical to the preceding. Thus there would be some ten years from one crisis to another.

The real phenomenon does not occur with that regularity and the periods are not all of the same number of years; Jevons's description can only provide a vague notion of the facts.

APPENDIX

1. The sole purpose of this appendix is to provide further explanation of the theories set forth in the text. It is by no means a treatise on mathematical economics for which considerably more space than is available here would be necessary.[1]

2. Let x and y be the quantities of economic goods X and Y possessed by an individual. Assume that there is no reason to take account of the order in which these goods are consumed (IV, 7), that is, consider the arrangements xy and yx to be identical.

Choose any combination x_1y_1 whatsoever, and find all the others x_2y_2, x_3y_3, ..., which, for the individual under consideration, are equivalent, among which the choice is, for him, a matter of *indifference* (III, 52). By interpolating, we can obtain an equation

$$f_1(x, y) = 0 \qquad (1)$$

such that if x is given the values

$$x_1, x_2, x_3, \ldots,$$

we obtain for y the values

$$y_1, y_2, y_3, \ldots.$$

Equation (1) is that of an *indifference line*[2] (III, 54). Starting from another combination (x_1', y_1') which is not included among the

---

[1] The results, partly new, of our latest studies of the economic problem are presented here. Hence this appendix should be substituted for our previous works; it replaces them.

[2] The notions of indifference lines and of preference lines were introduced into the science by Professor F. Y. Edgeworth. He started with the notion of *utility* (ophelimity), which he assumed to be a known quantity, and from it deduced the definition of these lines. We have inverted the problem. We have shown that by starting with the notion of indifference lines, a notion given directly by experience, we can arrive at the determination of economic equilibrium and work back again to certain functions, among which will be ophelimity, if it exists. In any case *indices* of ophelimity will be obtained.

preceding ones, the equation of another indifference line will be obtained, and so on. Assign an index, I, to each of these indifference lines as described in Chapter III, § 55. The indices

$$I_1, \ I_2, \ I_3, \ \ldots$$

will correspond to the functions

$$f_1, \ f_2, \ f_3, \ \ldots.$$

If we interpolate the parameters in these functions, we will obtain a function f, which will generate the functions $f_1, f_2, \ldots$, for the different values of I. With suitable values assigned to I, the equation

$$f(x, y, I) = 0 \tag{2}$$

will give us all the indifference curves.[3]

3. If equation (2) is regarded as the equation of a surface, the projections of the contour lines of that surface onto the xy plane will be indifference lines. This surface is in part arbitrary because the indices I are in part arbitrary, that is, it is any one of the surfaces which have for a projection of their contour lines the indifference curves given by the equations

$$f_1 = 0, \quad f_2 = 0, \quad \ldots,$$

and those which are in between them.

In sum, we only know the projection of the contour lines, and that is not enough to determine the surface which has these contour lines. This surface remains in part arbitrary.

In order to simplify, equation (2) can be put into the form

$$I = \Psi(x, y). \tag{3}$$

We will get an indifference line by giving I a fixed value.

The same considerations obviously apply to any number of goods whatsoever and in that case we have

$$I = \Psi(x, y, z, \ldots). \tag{4}$$

4. Whenever a system of indices (3) or (4) has been obtained, we get an infinite number of others, given by the equation

$$I = F(\Psi), \tag{5}$$

where F is an arbitrary function.

---

[3] For more details, see P. Boninsegni, "I fondamenti dell'economia pura," in the *Giornale degli economisti*, Rome, February 1902.

When one moves from a combination $(x, y, z, \ldots)$ to the combination $(x + dx, y, z, \ldots)$, the index I increases by

$$\frac{\partial I}{\partial x}dx = F'\Psi_x dx, \qquad (6)$$

where Ψ_x is the partial derivative of Ψ with respect to x. The individual will prefer the second combination to the first since it will contain more of X and just as much of the other goods. If we want a higher index to indicate a combination preferable to one which has a lower index, the increase in I given by (6) must be positive when dx is positive. Hence it is necessary to restrict the arbitrary choice of F somewhat, so that the right hand side of (6), and of the analogous equations in $y, z, \ldots$, be positive. We will always assume this to be the case.

5. If equation (5) is differentiated with I taken as constant, we obtain

$$0 = \Psi_x F' dx + \Psi_y F' dy + \Psi_z F' dz + \ldots \qquad (7)$$

or

$$0 = \Psi_x dx + \Psi_y dy + \Psi_z dz + \ldots \qquad (8)$$

An equation equivalent to the last mentioned could be obtained directly from observation. To do so we would look for the positive quantity $\triangle_1 x$ by which x must be increased in order to offset the decrease represented by the negative quantity $\triangle y$. Similarly we will look for the $\triangle_2 x$ which corresponds to $\triangle z$, etc. Then by setting

$$\triangle x = \triangle_1 x + \triangle_2 x + \ldots$$

we would get an equation of the form

$$0 = q_x' \triangle x + q_y' \triangle y + \ldots,$$

and, taking the limit, we will get

$$0 = q_x dx + q_y dy + q_z dz + \ldots \qquad (9)$$

This equation is equivalent to equation (7) or (8). Hence it should have an integrating factor in the case we are considering, but not in other cases.

6. Strictly speaking, equation (9) is the only one which we need in order to establish the theory of economic equilibrium; but that equation contains nothing which corresponds to ophelimity, or to the indices of ophelimity. Hence the entire theory of economic equilibrium is independent of the notions of (economic) *utility*, of

value in use, or of ophelimity.[4] Only one thing is needed, that is to know the limits of the ratios

$$\frac{\triangle_1 x}{\triangle y}, \quad \frac{\triangle_2 x}{\triangle z}, \quad \ldots$$

where the quantities $\triangle_1 x, \triangle y, \triangle_2 x, \triangle z, \ldots$ are such that the choice among the combinations $(x, y, z, \ldots)$, $(x + \triangle_1 x, y + \triangle y, z, \ldots)$, $(x + \triangle_2 x, y, z + \triangle z, \ldots)$, etc., is a matter of indifference.

Hence a whole treatise on pure economics could be written starting with equation (9) and the other analogous equations, and it is even possible that some day it will be appropriate to do so.[5]

By integrating equation (9), equation (4) or equation (5) would be obtained. In that case it is possible that, in order to make things a little more concise, some people might think it appropriate to give some name to the quantity I; thus in mechanics it was considered appropriate to give the name *kinetic energy* to a certain integral, and the name *entropy* to another in thermodynamics. Nevertheless, since there is so little to be gained by doing that, we could give no name at all to function (5), and designate it simply by the letter I; nothing would be changed in the economic theories.[6]

7. But just as in mechanics, after having mathematically defined the work of a force, kinetic energy, potential, energy, etc., there is room for investigating the relationships between these quantities and the facts of experience, so in economic science we are led to investigate what relationships there are between the quantity I and the facts of experience.

That is what we are going to do now; but the reader must not forget that this is a digression, that the study we are undertaking is

---

[4] We too began by basing the theory of economic equilibrium on these notions, just as all economists were then doing. But then we recognized that they could be bypassed, and we developed the theory of choice, which gives greater rigor and clarity to the entire theory of economic equilibrium.

[5] This is one of the numerous grounds on which our theories depart completely from those of the Austrian School.

[6] This is quite inconceivable to the literary economists and metaphysicians. One of them, a professor of political economy in an Italian University, cites another most learned professor who has dedicated himself to profound etymological research on the subject of ophelimity, without being able to find out (alas!) what that quantity is.

Can anyone imagine a professor of thermodynamics devoting himself to etymological researches among the ancient Greek writers in order to discover what entropy can indeed be?

This observation is enough to give a good idea of the backward state in which political economy still finds itself in relation to sciences such as mechanics, astronomy, physics, chemistry, etc.

not at all necessary in order to establish the theory of economic equilibrium, and that it is even outside of it.

8. The differential equation (9) has an integral (§ 5). When the latter is put in the form of (5), and the arbitrary function chosen as explained in § 4, it possesses the following two properties: 1° the values of I which correspond to two combinations between which the choice, for the individual, is a matter of indifference, are equal; 2° if a certain combination (α) is preferable to another combination (β), the value of I corresponding to (α) is greater than that which corresponds to (β), (§ 134).

9. If the pleasure given by a combination (x, y) is considered, it can be said that choosing the one or the other of two combinations which give the same pleasure is a matter of indifference and that, of two combinations giving different pleasure, the individual chooses the one which gives him the most.

A correspondence is thus established between the quantity I and pleasure. The former may serve as an index of the latter.

But this correspondence is not unambiguous, since an infinity of values of I can correspond to the same combination (x, y), depending on the form adopted for F. If the correspondence were unambiguous I could be adopted as a measure of pleasure in the sense that only one value of I (except for the unit of measure) would correspond to a given pleasure, and that two equal values of I would correspond to two equal pleasures, and that to one pleasure greater than another would correspond a value of I greater than that which corresponds to this other.

10. Let us assume that we can find an integrating factor such that Ψ_x is solely a function of x, Ψ_y of y, etc. In this case, among the infinite number of systems of indices, there is one which is such that the partial derivative of Ψ with respect to x, Ψ_x, is a function only of x, the partial derivative Ψ_y is a function only of y, etc. We obtain this system by assuming in equation (6) and the other analogous equations that F' is equal to a constant A. Then

$$\left. \begin{array}{l} \dfrac{\partial I}{\partial x} = A\Psi_x, \quad \dfrac{\partial I}{\partial y} = A\Psi_y, \quad \cdots \\[2ex] I = A\Psi, \quad \Psi = \displaystyle\int \Psi_x dx + \int \Psi_y dy + \cdots \end{array} \right\} \quad (10)$$

If for these goods the pleasure obtained from the consumption of dx depends only on x, that obtained from the consumption of dy depends only on y, etc., only the values given by equations (10), among all the values given by equation (5), correspond to the pleasure obtained from the consumption $x, y, z, \ldots$ This correspondence is unambiguous, except for the value of A which fixes the unit of measure. Hence in this case, the quantity I, given by equations (10), can be regarded as the measure of the pleasure obtained from the combination $(x, y, z, \ldots)$, or if one wants, for the measure of the value in use, of the utility, of the *rareté* (Walras), of the ophelimity, of that combination.

11. But if Ψ_x is not solely a function of x, Ψ_y of y, etc., the correspondence between I and the pleasure is no longer unambiguous; the quantity I can no longer be regarded as the measure of the pleasure; it is only an index of it.

It must not be forgotten that we are speaking here only of goods the order of consumption of which is a matter of indifference. Otherwise the conclusion we have just stated would be different.

12. When there are only two economic goods, the function I always exists, whether the order of consumption is indifferent or not.

"The transition from the case of only two goods to the case of three or more goods would merit a more detailed examination than in the *Manuale*. Indeed, we know that a differential binomial expression

$$X dx + Y dy$$

always has an infinite number of integrating factors, whereas a trinomial expression, or one with still more terms, may have none."[7]

That is what we are now going to take up.

Let us note first of all that if we assume that the individual can choose the order of consumption (IV, 7), he will choose the order which is most agreeable to him. Then every differential polynomial expression is integrable because the path of the integration is fixed. Hence, this case reduces to the preceding one. Here we only have to deal with the case in which, for some reason, the individual may consume the goods in any order, without sticking to the one which is most agreeable.

---

[7] Professor Vito Volterra states this, referring to the Italian edition of this book, in the *Giornale degli economisti*, April 1906.

The criticisms of the literary economists have no value; but the observations and criticisms of a scholar such as Professor Volterra have great value and are important for the progress of the science.

Following that observation, we published an article in the *Giornale degli economisti*, July 1906, in which we tried to clear up the point to which Professor Volterra very rightly called attention. It is that article which we are summarizing now in the text; but the lack of space obliges us to give only the principal results and to omit the details; on the other hand, we are adding several new considerations.

13. Let us assume that the individual is at the point $(x, y, z, \ldots, t)$ and that he consumes the quantities $\triangle x$ and $\triangle y$, determined in such a manner that the choice between the above combination and the combination $(x + \triangle x, y + \triangle y, z, \ldots, t)$ is a matter of indifference. We will find, from observation, the equation

$$\triangle x + b_y' \triangle y = 0$$

We shall assume in all that follows that a_x', b_y', and the other analogous quantities, depend solely on the $x, y, z, \ldots$ coordinates of the point to which they refer, and that they do not depend at all on the order of consumption.

If we take the limit, and set

$$\triangle x = \frac{\partial x}{\partial y} \triangle y$$

we will have

$$\frac{\partial x}{\partial y} dy + b_y dy = 0 \qquad (11)$$

Other analogous equations will be obtained by varying x and z, x and u, $\ldots$, x and t. Sum these equations, and by virtue of

$$dx = \frac{\partial x}{\partial y} dy + \frac{\partial x}{\partial z} dz + \ldots + \frac{\partial x}{\partial t} dt,$$

we will get:

$$0 = dx + b_y dy + c_z dz + \ldots + n_t dt. \qquad (12)$$

If we multiply this equation by an arbitrary factor, we will give it the form:

$$0 = A_x dx + B_y dy + \ldots + M_s ds + N_t dt. \qquad (12b)$$

The quantities b_y, c_z, $\ldots$, m_s, n_t are supplied by observation; hence the quantities A_x, B_y, $\ldots$, N_t are supplied, except for a factor, by observation.

When the order of consumption does not affect the individual's consumption choices, equation (12) has an integrating factor; when the order of consumption does affect his choices, equation (12) does not have an integrating factor.

14. Let us assume that the order of consumption does influence the choice. Consider a fixed order of consumption, for example $x, y, z, \ldots, s, t$. We find an indifference *variety* (in hyperspace) by experiment, and write its equation in form (5). Equation (5)

differs, however, from the equation of the same form which we now
obtain, in that equation (5) is valid whatever be the order of consumption and the one we obtain now is valid only for the fixed order
under consideration.

Hence we see that in the two following cases, 1° if the order of
consumption is a matter of indifference, and 2° if the order of consumption has an influence on the choices but the order is fixed in
advance, we obtain an equation of form (5), or the corresponding
differential equation, which can be written:

$$0 = \varphi_x dx + \varphi_y dy + \varphi_z dz + \ldots + \varphi_t dt. \qquad (13)$$

Observation does not give the functions φ_x, φ_y, $\ldots$, φ_t precisely,
but only their ratios to one of them, for example:

$$\frac{\varphi_y}{\varphi_x}, \frac{\varphi_z}{\varphi_x}, \ldots, \frac{\varphi_t}{\varphi_x}.$$

Following the order fixed, the individual starts from the point
$(0, 0, \ldots, 0)$ and arrives at the point $(x, y, \ldots, s, t)$ traveling the
path

$$(0, 0, \ldots, 0), (x, 0, \ldots, 0), (x, y, \ldots, 0), \ldots$$
$$\ldots, (x, y, \ldots, s, t). \qquad (\alpha)$$

If he then travels another route,

$$(0, 0, \ldots, 0), (x + dx, \ldots, 0), \ldots$$
$$\ldots, (x + dx, y + dy, \ldots, t + dt), \qquad (\beta)$$

he will again find himself on the indifference variety which passes
through the point $(x, y, \ldots, s, t)$, provided that equation (7), obtained by differentiating (5), is satisfied.

The routes $(0, 0, \ldots, 0)$, $(x, 0, \ldots, 0)$ and $(0, 0, \ldots, 0)$,
$(x + dx, dy, \ldots, 0)$ are particular cases of the preceding routes.
Hence we should have:

$$0 = \Psi_x(x, 0, \ldots, 0) F'(\Psi(x, 0, \ldots, 0)) dx$$
$$+ \Psi_y(x, 0, \ldots, 0) F'(\Psi(x, 0, \ldots, 0)) dy. \qquad (14)$$

But in addition, the choice between the combinations $(x, 0)$ and
$(x + dx, dy)$ being a matter of indifference, we must have an equation which only differs by a factor from the following

$$0 = A_x(x, 0, \ldots, 0) dx + B_y(x, 0, \ldots, 0) dy.$$

Since this equation and the preceding one must hold at the same time, we must have:

$$\Psi_x(x, 0, \ldots, 0) F'(\Psi(x, 0, \ldots, 0))$$
$$= A_x(x, 0, \ldots, 0) G(x),$$

$$\Psi_y(x, 0, \ldots, 0) F'(\Psi(x, 0, \ldots, 0))$$
$$= B_y(x, 0, \ldots, 0) G(x),$$

$$(15)$$

where G is an arbitrary function.

By similar reasoning about the routes $(0, \ldots, 0)$, $(x, \ldots, 0)$, $(x, y, \ldots)$ and $(0, \ldots, 0)$, $(x, 0, \ldots, 0)$, $(x, y + dy, dz, \ldots, 0)$ we will get:

$$\Psi_y(x, y, \ldots, 0) F'(\Psi(x, y, \ldots, 0))$$
$$= B_y(x, y, \ldots, 0) G'(x, y),$$

$$\Psi_z(x, y, \ldots, 0) F'(\Psi(x, y, \ldots, 0))$$
$$= C_z(x, y, \ldots, 0) G'(x, y),$$

$$(16)$$

where G' is an arbitrary function.

But if we set $y = 0$ in the first part of (16), we obtain an equation which differs from the second part of (15) only in that $G'(x, 0)$ is replaced by $G(x)$. Hence we must have

$$G'(x, 0) = G(x)$$

and, in general, the functions G, G', G'', $\ldots$ can be replaced by $G(x, 0, \ldots, 0)$, $G(x, y, \ldots, 0)$, $\ldots$, $G(x, y, \ldots, t)$. But since A_x, B_y, $\ldots$ are known except for a factor, the functions G can be understood as included in that factor. In that case we have

$$A_x(x, 0, \ldots, 0) = \Psi_x(x, 0, \ldots, 0) F'(\Psi(x, 0, \ldots, 0))$$

$$B_y(x, y, \ldots, 0) = \Psi_y(x, y, \ldots, 0) F'(\Psi(x, y, \ldots, 0))$$

$$\cdots\cdots\cdots\cdots\cdots\cdots\cdots\cdots\cdots\cdots\cdots\cdots\cdots\cdots$$

$$N_t(x, y, \ldots, t) = \Psi_t(x, y, \ldots, t) F'(\Psi(x, y, \ldots, t)).$$

$$(17)$$

Such are the relations which must hold between the quantities A_x, B_y, $\ldots$, and Ψ_x, Ψ_y, $\ldots$, given by observation.

15. Let us assume that pleasure can be measured and see if we can establish a correspondence between that pleasure and the quantities found in equations (17).

When the individual is at the point $(x, y, \ldots, s, t)$, let $P_x dx$,

$Q_y dy, \ldots, S_s ds, T_t dt$, be the pleasure which is yielded by the consumption of $dx, dy, \ldots, dt$, respectively.

If the choice between the combination $(x, y, \ldots, t)$ and $(x + dx, y + dy, \ldots, t + dt)$ is a matter of indifference, we must have:

$$0 = P_x dx + Q_y dy + \ldots + T_t dt. \qquad (18)$$

Comparing this equation to equation (12b) we will have:

$$P_x = A_x H, \; Q_y = B_y H, \; \ldots, \; T_t = N_t H, \qquad (19)$$

where H is a function of $x, y, \ldots, t$.

The pleasure which the individual will get by following route (α) of § 14 will be:

$$G = \int_0^x P_x(x, 0, \ldots, 0) \, dx + \int_0^y Q_y(x, y, \ldots, 0) \, dy + \ldots$$
$$+ \int_0^t T_t(x, y, \ldots, t) \, dt,$$

or again:

$$G = P(x, 0, \ldots, 0) - P(0, 0, \ldots, 0) + Q(x, y, \ldots, 0)$$
$$- Q(x, 0, \ldots, 0) + \ldots + T(x, y, \ldots, t) - T(x, y, \ldots, s, 0).$$

If we differentiate and compare to equation (7), we will have:

$$\left.\begin{array}{l}
\Psi_t F' = T_t(x, y, \ldots, t), \\[6pt]
\Psi_s F' = T_s(x, y, \ldots, t) - T_s(x, y, \ldots, s, 0) \\
\qquad\qquad\qquad\qquad + S_s(x, y, \ldots, s, 0) \\[6pt]
\cdots\cdots\cdots\cdots\cdots\cdots\cdots\cdots\cdots\cdots\cdots\cdots \\[6pt]
\Psi_x F' = T_x(x, \ldots, t) - T_x(x, \ldots, s, 0) \\
\qquad + S_x(x, \ldots, s, 0) - S_x(x, \ldots, 0, 0) + \ldots \\
\qquad\qquad\qquad\qquad\qquad + P_x(x, \ldots, 0).
\end{array}\right\} \quad (20)$$

The $\Psi_t, \Psi_s, \ldots F'$, of the left hand sides are all functions of all the variables $x, y, \ldots, s, t$.

Comparing the first of equations (20) to the last of equations (17) shows that we have

$$H = 1;$$

which follows moreover from the fact that F', being arbitrary, can always be assumed to include H.

Equations (20) and (17) are satisfied by setting

$$T_t = \Psi_t F', \; S_s = \Psi_s F' + \chi_s, \; \ldots, \; P_x = \Psi_x F' + \chi_x. \quad (21)$$

All the functions which are found in these equations are functions of all the variables $x, y, \ldots, s, t$. In addition, χ_s is zero for $t = 0$; χ_u is zero for $t = 0, s = 0; \ldots; \chi_x$ is zero for $t = 0, s = 0, \ldots, y = 0$.

In fact, the first of equations (21) is the same as the last of equations (17); the second of (21), if we let $t = 0$, becomes the second to last of (17); etc.

Integrating (17), and taking (19) into account, gives us

$$T(x, \ldots, t) - T(x, \ldots, s, 0) = F(\Psi(x, \ldots, t)) \\ - F(\Psi(x, \ldots, s, 0)),$$

$$S(x, \ldots, s, 0) - S(x, \ldots, 0, 0) = F(\Psi(x, \ldots, s, 0)) \\ - F(\Psi(x, \ldots, 0, 0)),$$

$$\ldots \ldots \ldots \ldots \ldots \ldots \ldots \ldots \ldots \ldots \ldots \ldots$$

$$P(x, 0, \ldots, 0) - P(0, \ldots, 0) = F(\Psi(x, 0, \ldots, 0)) \\ - F(\Psi(0, \ldots, 0)),$$

and these values satisfy equations (20).

16. Equations (21) show that, as long as we do not have other data from observation, we cannot establish an unambiguous correspondence between the ophelimities $P_x, Q_y, \ldots, T_t$ and the quantities $\Psi_x, \Psi_y, \ldots, \Psi_t$ given by observation. The latter can indeed serve as indices of the former, but they do not measure them.

17. The values (21) can be divided into two classes.

1st Class. All the $\chi_s, \chi_u, \ldots, \chi_x$ terms vanish. In this case the quantities $P_x, Q_y, \ldots, T_t$ turn out to be the partial derivatives of the same function. But in that case these quantities can represent the pleasure resulting from the consumption of goods when this pleasure is independent of the order of consumption. Thus the goods, $X, Y, \ldots, T$, whose consumption yields pleasure which does depend on the order of consumption, can hypothetically, *when they are consumed in a fixed order*, be considered equivalent to goods the consumption of which yields pleasure independent of the order of consumption. But precisely because of that, these hypothetical pleasures are different from the real pleasures.

2nd Class. All, or part of, the $\chi_s, \chi_u, \ldots, \chi_x$ terms are different from zero. In this case the pleasure $P_x, \ldots, T_t$ vary depending on the order of consumption. Hence it is in this second class that we must attempt to find the expressions for the real pleasures.

18. To do so we must find a way to get rid of the arbitrary function, as we did in § 10.

Let us assume that the individual travels the path
$$(0, 0, \ldots, 0), (h, 0, \ldots, 0), (h, k, \ldots, 0), \ldots$$
$$\ldots, (h, k, \ldots, m, n), (x, k, \ldots, n), (x, y, \ldots, n), \ldots \quad (\gamma)$$
$$\ldots, (x, y, \ldots, t).$$

If we determine, by experiment, the indifference variety which corresponds to paths of this kind, we will get, as usual, an equation of the form

$$I = F(\varphi); \tag{22}$$

or

$$0 = \varphi_x F' dx + \varphi_y F' dy + \ldots + \varphi_t F' dt. \tag{23}$$

The quantities φ_x, φ_y, ... are given by observation.

The pleasure, ophelimity, which the individual will enjoy in this case, will be

$$G = \int_0^h P_x(x, 0, \ldots, 0) \, dx + \int_0^k Q_y(h, y, \ldots, 0) \, dy + \ldots$$

$$+ \int_0^n T_t(h, k, \ldots, m, t) \, dt + \int_h^x P_x(x, k, \ldots, n) \, dx \tag{24}$$

$$+ \int_k^y Q_y(x, y, l, \ldots, n) \, dy + \ldots$$

$$+ \int_n^t T_t(x, y, \ldots, t) \, dt.$$

If we differentiate this equation we will get an equation

$$0 = \frac{\partial G}{\partial x} \, dx + \frac{\partial G}{\partial y} \, dy + \ldots + \frac{\partial G}{\partial t} \, dt, \tag{25}$$

which must be equivalent to equation (23); but we have, according to (24),

$$\frac{\partial G}{\partial t} = T_t(x, y, \ldots, t)$$

and this value is independent of $h, k, \ldots, n$. Hence equation (23), or an equivalent equation, obtained by observation, should have an integrating factor such that the last term of that equation is independent of $h, k, \ldots, n$.

Moreover, there is only one of these factors for, where Γ denotes this factor, we know that the others will have the form

$$\Gamma F(\varphi)$$

where F is an arbitrary function. But φ depends on $h, k, \ldots, n$, and consequently $F(\varphi)$ does too. Only the factor Γ, then, is independent of these quantities. Multiplying the equation given by observation by this factor Γ, we will get a value, without the arbitrary function, for T_t multiplied by a constant a.

It must be remembered that we do not know the functions A_x, B_y, ... but only the ratios of these functions to one of them, because they contain an arbitrary factor (§ 13). Equations (19) give

$$P_x = \frac{A_x}{N_t}T_t, \quad Q_y = \frac{B_y}{N_t}T_t, \quad \ldots, \tag{26}$$

or

$$P_x = \frac{1}{n_t}T_t, \quad Q_y = \frac{b_y}{n_t}T_t, \quad \ldots, \tag{26b}$$

and, since the quantity T_t is determined by observation, except for a constant, all the other quantities P_x, Q_y, ... are too.

Thus an unambiguous correspondence has been established between the pleasures, or ophelimities, P_x, Q_y, ..., T_t, and the quantities given by observation. The latter can then serve as a measure of the former.

19. Let us summarize the results obtained. Abstracting from a constant, which serves to fix the unit of measure, an unambiguous correspondence can be obtained between the quantities given by observation which serve to determine the indifference lines, or *varieties* (in hyperspace), and the pleasures (ophelimities) enjoyed by an individual who, having reached the point $(x, y, \ldots, t)$, consumes dx, dy, $\ldots$, dt, in two cases: 1° When the order of consumption is a matter of indifference, and the pleasure resulting from the consumption of dx depends only on x, that resulting from the consumption of dy depends only on y, etc.; and 2° When the pleasure is different depending on the order of consumption and we take it to be possible to perform the experiments necessary to determine the order.

Still remaining, then, is the case in which the order of consumption is a matter of indifference and the pleasure resulting from the consumption of dx depends on x, y, $\ldots$ t, or that resulting from the consumption of dy depends on x, y, $\ldots$, t, etc.[8]

In the case where the order of consumption is a matter of indifference, there exists a function of x, y, $\ldots$, t, such that the partial derivatives of that unique function represent the indices of the

---

[8] These results were published for the first time in our article in the *Giornale degli economisti*, July 1906.

pleasure or the pleasures from the consumption of $dx, dy, \ldots, dt$, when starting from the point $x, y, \ldots, t$.

In the case where the order of consumption influences the pleasure, this unique function does not exist, as long as the path to be followed is not determined.

20. It is convenient to give names to the quantities which we have considered.

The quantity I may, in all cases, serve as an index of pleasure. We will call it the *index of ophelimity*.[9] When this quantity can be used to measure the pleasure it is the *ophelimity*. If it corresponds to the consumption of a finite quantity of goods, it will be called *total ophelimity*. Its partial derivatives $I_x, I_y, \ldots$, with respect to the variables $x, y, \ldots$, will be called the *elementary ophelimity* of the goods $X, Y, \ldots$.

If we consider a consumption path which starts from a point $(x, y, \ldots, t)$ and comes back to that point, we will say that we travel a *closed cycle* if we return to that point with the same index of ophelimity with which we left it. This case corresponds to indifference in the order of consumption.

We will say that we travel an *open cycle* if we return to the starting point with an index of ophelimity different from the one with which we left it. This case corresponds to that in which the order of consumption has an influence on the pleasure.

21. Making use of this terminology we can state the results of § 19 in the following way.

Except for a constant, which serves to fix the unit of measure, ophelimity can be determined, thanks to observations which provide the indifference varieties, in two cases:

1° If the cycle is closed and if each ophelimity depends only on the variable to which it corresponds. 2° If the cycle is open.

The remaining case is that of closed cycles when the elementary ophelimities are functions of two or more variables.

Total ophelimity always exists in the case of closed cycles. It still exists in open cycles if the path is followed in a fixed order. It does not exist in open cycles when the path is not fixed.

---

[9] M. Gide proposes the name *desirability*. There is nothing to prevent adopting it. But it is a little odd to speak of the *desirability* of a thing which has already been consumed. In general it is what has not yet been consumed which is desired.

All these names are of little consequence. What does matter is that the thing designated be understood clearly and that no misunderstanding be possible.

Here we end the digression announced in § 7, and go on to deal with some basic notions of economic equilibrium.[10]

22. **Equilibrium in the case of one individual and two goods.**[11] Let us assume that the individual starts from the point (x_o, y_o) and that he is obliged to follow a certain path the projection of which on the xy plane (III, 74) is

$$f(x, y) = 0. \qquad (27)$$

Let us assume next that starting from the point (x_o, y_o) the indices given by equation (3) begin to increase. Since a combination having a greater index than another is preferred to the latter, the individual begins to move along the path indicated, and he will continue up to the point where the indices stop increasing and begin to decrease. But this point is the one where the path is tangent to an indifference line, that is, where the curve (27) is tangent to the projection of an indifference curve. Hence this point will be determined by the two equations

$$f_x dx + f_y dy = 0, \quad \varphi_x dx + \varphi_y dy = 0; \qquad (28)$$

and by equation (27). Hence, to determine the two unknowns x and y, we will have the two equations

$$f = 0, \quad f_x \varphi_y - f_y \varphi_x = 0. \qquad (29)$$

The partial derivatives of the function which gives the index have been denoted by φ_x and φ_y.

---

[10] A remarkable study on the generalization of the concept of ophelimity has been published while this book was in press. See: *Giornale degli economisti*, Rome, September 1908: V. Furlan, "Cenni su una generalizzazione del concetto d'ofelimita." [This footnote appears in the French text in the list of Additions on page 684.]

[11] It is only useful to consider this case as a preparation for the study of the general case of economic equilibrium.

We completely part company not only with the economists called the Austrian School, but also with other economists such as Professor Marshall, in that, in our opinion, only the necessity of considering the systems of simultaneous equations which determine equilibrium in the general case justifies the use of mathematics in political economy.

We think the use of mathematics for problems of the type such as that of one individual and two, or even several goods, does not give results the importance of which can be compared to those which are obtained in the cases of general economic equilibrium.

In our opinion it is the interdependence of economic phenomena which obliges us to make use of mathematical logic.

This way of viewing things may be good or bad; but in any case it must not be confused with that of economists who formulate theories omitting precisely this interdependence.

It is appropriate to note here that the equilibrium is determined without making use of the notions of *utility* (ophelimity), price, etc.

23. Let us assume we have a concave surface having contour lines the height of which above the horizontal plane *xy* is given by (3). On that surface let us draw a line whose projection is (27). Imagine a weight on that line. The point where it will be in equilibrium is precisely the one which is given by equations (29). The equilibrium of this weight and economic equilibrium are similar phenomena.

24. **Several economic goods.** Let us assume we have any number of goods whatsoever. The individual must move on the *variety* (in hyperspace)

$$f(x, y, z, \ldots) = 0; \qquad (30)$$

he will stop when the choices which he could make, if he continued to move, are a matter of indifference.

We have seen in § 14 that when the order of the choices is immaterial or, if not immaterial, is fixed in advance, we have the differential equation (13) of an indifference variety. That equation is equivalent to the following

$$\frac{\partial x}{\partial y} = -\frac{\varphi_y}{\varphi_x}, \quad \frac{\partial x}{\partial z} = -\frac{\varphi_z}{\varphi_x}, \quad \ldots;$$

and observation supplies the values of the right hand sides.

Furthermore, equation (30) yields

$$f_x\frac{\partial x}{\partial y} + f_y = 0, \quad f_x\frac{\partial x}{\partial z} + f_z = 0, \quad \ldots \qquad (31)$$

Combining these equations with the preceding ones we will have

$$\varphi_x = \frac{f_x}{f_y}\,\varphi_y = \frac{f_x}{f_z}\varphi_z = \ldots \qquad (32)$$

If the number of goods is *m*, the number of equations (32) is $m - 1$, and with equation (30), we have the *m* equations which are necessary to determine the *m* unknowns $x, y, \ldots$.

25. When the order of consumption affects the choices, this order necessarily must be fixed before the point of equilibrium can be determined. When this order is fixed, we have a function of $x, y, \ldots$ which may be used as an index for the choices, and we revert to the preceding case.

26. Equations (30) and (32) are fundamental to the theory of economic equilibrium. Equation (30) is the one for the obstacles;

it is in specifying it that we will find the innumerable cases of that equilibrium.

We have considered the obstacle to be given by the equation of a curve, a surface, a variety. It is often given by families of curves, of surfaces, of varieties. In that case equation (30) is replaced by $f_1(x, y, \ldots, \mu_1, \mu_2, \ldots) = 0$, $f_2(x, y, \ldots, \mu_1, \mu_2, \ldots) = 0$, $\ldots$, where $\mu_1, \mu_2, \ldots$ are parameters which must be determined. To do that we must have additional equations.

27. Let us consider a case of equilibrium analogous to that of (VI, 4).

The individual transforms X into Y.

He possesses x_o of X. He begins by using up a of X, without producing anything; then, to produce each unit of Y, b of X is required. We will have, then,

$$x_o - x = a + by,$$

or

$$a + by - x_o + x = 0. \tag{33}$$

This is equation (27). The second equation in (29) becomes

$$\varphi_y - b\varphi_x = 0. \tag{34}$$

Equations (33) and (34) give the quantity of X which will be transformed into Y.

28. We have just dealt with a problem of *individual economy*. Next assume that there are several individuals. If one of them has the power to fix the path which the others must follow, the latter only have problems of the kind which we have just solved. There is a different problem for the individual whom we have assumed to dominate the economic phenomenon, and whom we will call 2. To begin, we will assume that he has to deal with only one other individual,[12] whom we will call 1.

29. The quantities of goods the first individual has are x_{10} and y_{10} prior to any exchange, x_1 and y_1 at the point of equilibrium; the partial derivatives of the index which determines the choices are φ_{1x} and φ_{1y}. For the second individual these quantities are x_{20} and y_{20}, x_2 and y_2, φ_{2x} and φ_{2y}.

---

[12] Again this is a problem the study of which is useful only as preparation for the study of the general case of economic equilibrium.

Moreover, the case of only two traders does not occur in reality; it is only one of the elements of the real case of several traders and several goods.

When the total quantities of each good remain constant during the exchange, we have

$$x_{10} + x_{20} = x_1 + x_2, \quad y_{10} + y_{20} = y_1 + y_2. \qquad (35)$$

30. If the tastes of both individuals have to be satisfied, the equilibrium points can only be the points of tangency of an indifference curve of the first individual and an indifference curve of the second. But there are an infinity of these points, so some other conditions are necessary to make the problem determinate.

If individual 1 is left free to travel along the path which is fixed for him, he will only move on it where it is above the indifference line which passes through (x_{10}, y_{10}), and at the most, at the limit, he will travel along that line. Hence the equilibrium point most advantageous for 2 will be found at a point of tangency of that path and an indifference line of 2.

We will have

$$\varphi_1(x_1, y_1) = \varphi_1(x_{10}, y_{10}), \quad \varphi_{1x}\varphi_{2y} - \varphi_{1y}\varphi_{2x} = 0, \qquad (36)$$

which, with the two equations (35), give four equations, and thus the four unknowns x_1, y_1, x_2, y_2 can be determined.

31. It is possible that individual 2 simply intends to obtain the greatest possible amount of X. In this case, he will again compel individual 1 to move along an indifference line, but he will allow exchanges on that line to continue as far as is possible. If it intersects the x axis, equilibrium will take place at that point.

32. Individual 2 may only have the power to oblige 1 to follow a path chosen by 2 from among the family of curves

$$f(x_1, y_1, \mu) = 0, \qquad (37)$$

rather than any path whatsoever determined according to what pleases 2.

That is, individual 2 can only determine μ.

First of all, for equilibrium it is necessary to have equations (29); let

$$f_1(x_1, y_1, \mu) = 0, \quad f_{1x}\varphi_{1y} - f_{1y}\varphi_{1x} = 0; \qquad (38)$$

and then μ must be determined in accordance with the conditions which individual 2 will set.

33. 1° If the condition he fixes is stopping at the most favorable combination among all those which he can obtain, we must express

the fact that, for him, the index is a maximum when μ is varied; hence we will have

$$\varphi_{2x}\frac{dx_2}{d\mu} + \varphi_{2y}\frac{dy_2}{d\mu} = 0, \tag{39}$$

and, by virtue of equations (35),

$$\varphi_{2x}\frac{dx_1}{d\mu} + \varphi_{2y}\frac{dy_1}{d\mu} = 0. \tag{39b}$$

Combine this equation and one obtained by differentiating the first of equations (38) with respect to μ, by eliminating

$$\frac{dx_1}{d\mu}, \quad \frac{dy_1}{d\mu}.$$

Thus we have, with equations (35) and (38), the 5 equations needed to determine the 5 unknowns x_1, y_1, x_2, y_2, and μ.

2° If individual 2 sets the condition of having the maximum of Υ, we must express the fact that the value of y_2, given by equations (35) and (37), is a maximum when μ varies.

When y_2 is a maximum, y_1 is a minimum, by virtue of equations (35). Hence it will be necessary to differentiate equations (37) with respect to μ, to set

$$\frac{dy_1}{d\mu} = 0,$$

and to eliminate $\dfrac{dx_1}{d\mu}$; thereby we will get the fifth equation, which

is needed in order to determine μ.

34. Finally, we can assume that neither of the two individuals has the power to impose a certain value of μ on the other. During the exchange, each one only is concerned with making choices which are most advantageous to him without thinking about modifying the value of μ *directly*. This is the case of free competition (III, 41, 46).

For individual 1 we again have equations (38). If, in the first one of these equations, we substitute the values of x_1 and y_1 given by (35), we will have the equation of the path which individual 2 follows, and it is this path which must be tangent to an indifference curve of individual 2. Hence we will have

$$\varphi_{2x}dx_2 + \varphi_{2y}dy_2 = 0; \tag{40}$$

and, by virtue of equations (35)

$$\varphi_{2x}dx_1 + \varphi_{2y}dy_1 = 0.$$

Consequently

$$f_{1x}\varphi_{2y} - f_{1y}\varphi_{2x} = 0.$$

Since this case is very important, we write out the set of equations which correspond to it.

$$\left.\begin{array}{ll} x_{10} + x_{20} = x_1 + x_2, & y_{10} + y_{20} = y_1 + y_2, \\ f_{1x}\varphi_{1y} - f_{1y}\varphi_{1x} = 0, & f_{1x}\varphi_{2y} - f_{1y}\varphi_{2x} = 0, \\ f_1(x_1, y_1, \mu) = 0. & \end{array}\right\} \qquad (41)$$

These are the 5 equations which determine the 5 unknowns x_1, y_1, x_2, y_2, μ.

35. The following remarks are useful.

We considered two cases in which individual 2 acts with absolute power. He imposes on 1 the path to be followed, §§ 30, 31.

Next we considered two cases in which the power of individual 2 is less extreme. He can only determine a parameter of the family of curves which 1 must follow. These are cases of monopoly, § 33.

Finally individual 2 has no power over 1, nor 1 over 2. This is the case of free competition, § 34.

The parameter μ is determined at the pleasure of 2 in the cases of monopoly; it is determined indirectly by the action of both individuals in the case of free competition.

If we compare equation (39) and equation (40), we see that the first assumes that one goes from one to the other of the curves of the family (37), and the second assumes that one always stays on a given curve of that family, (III, 41 and 42).

It is necessary to be careful that μ is not treated as variable when equation (37) is differentiated in order to determine the point of tangency with an indifference line, otherwise one would pass from one line to another. This observation is so elementary that it may appear superfluous; it is made only because one writer has fallen into the silly error of allowing μ to vary.[13]

Equations (35) and (37) hold for any values whatsoever of the variables x_1 and y_1, whereas the equation

$$f_x\varphi_y - f_y\varphi_x = 0,$$

holds only for the values of x_1 and y_1 corresponding to the equilib-

---

[13] That is, of allowing the price, which corresponds to μ, to vary. What is more, that writer imagined that it is by error that in these circumstances we always differentiate with price held constant!

rium point. It is the same, in general, for equations (32). Some authors have fallen into serious errors by having disregarded this very elementary observation.

If the fourth equation in (41), which pertains to individual 2, is suppressed, the other equations give, as a function of μ, the quantities of goods exchanged by individual 1. These functions may be regarded as expressing the *law of supply and demand*, for any value of μ whatsoever.

36. In the case of three goods, there is no need to resort to considerations of hyperspace.

For an individual, we have indifference surfaces instead of indifference curves. The obstacles give the equation

$$f(x,y,z) = 0$$

of a surface instead of the curve (27).

Equilibrium takes place at the point where this surface is tangent to an indifference surface. When the order of consumption is a matter of indifference, any line drawn on the surface which represents the obstacles and touching a point where this surface is tangent to an indifference surface, leads to a point of equilibrium.

37. The equation

$$f(x, y, z, \ldots) = 0, \qquad (42)$$

partially differentiated, gives

$$-\frac{\partial x}{\partial y}dy = \frac{f_y}{f_x}dy, \quad -\frac{\partial x}{\partial z}dz = \frac{f_z}{f_x}dz, \quad \ldots$$

The left hand sides of these equations represent the quantities of X which the individual must give up, when equation (42) applies, in order to receive dy of Y, or dz of Z, etc.; and vice versa. It is handy to give a name to the quantities

$$\frac{f_y}{f_x}, \quad \frac{f_z}{f_x}, \quad \ldots; \qquad (43)$$

they are called the *prices of* $Y, Z, \ldots, in$ X, and we write

$$p_y = \frac{f_y}{f_x}, \quad p_z = \frac{f_z}{f_x}, \quad \ldots. \qquad (43b)$$

When X is money, the quantities (43) also are called *prices* in ordinary language.

When it is a question of exchange, these are the prices which are observed on the market; hence these are the quantities which observation gives, and it is from these quantities that equation (42) must be deduced. If the price of Y in terms of X is denoted by p_y, the price of Z in terms of X by p_z, etc., we will have

$$\frac{\partial x}{\partial y} = -p_y, \quad \frac{\partial x}{\partial z} = -p_z, \quad \dots; \tag{44}$$

and these are the equations which must be integrated to obtain equation (42).

38. Often the prices vary with the quantities $x, y, z, \dots$. When it is a case of studying certain phenomena, such as monopolies, we would not be able to abstract from this circumstance. But in a great many other very important phenomena, the prices may be regarded as constants.

When the prices are constants, equations (44) may be integrated immediately and give for equation (42)

$$x + p_y y + p_z z + \dots = c,$$

where c is a constant. But, where $x_0, y_0, z_0, \dots$ are the initial values of $x, y, \dots$, we must also have

$$x_0 + p_y y_0 + p_z z_0 + \dots = c,$$

and as a result equation (42) becomes

$$x - x_0 + p_y(y - y_0) + p_z(z - z_0) + \dots = 0. \tag{45}$$

This equation has a special significance in political economy. It gives the balance sheet of the receipts and the expenditures of the individual under consideration (III, 175).

Whether the prices are constants or variables, the balance sheet of the individual, for the exchange quantities $dx, dy, \dots$, is always given by

$$dx + p_y dy + p_z dz + \dots = 0. \tag{46}$$

39. When the prices are variables, this equation may not be integrable. In that case the balance sheet of the individual, for the final quantities $x, y, \dots$, depends on the order of consumption. We no longer have a function such as (30) to express the effects of the obstacles, these effects are expressed by (46). The order of consumption must be fixed if we want to know the balance sheet of the individual. That order being fixed, equation (46) becomes integrable, and we get an equation of the form (30), but which is valid only for that order.

40. To avoid being too lengthy, we restrict ourselves to a few special cases. Let us assume we have three goods, denote constants by a and b, and put

$$p_y = \frac{ay}{x}, \quad p_z = \frac{bz}{x}.$$

The equation

$$dx + \frac{ay}{x} dy + \frac{bz}{x} dz = 0$$

is integrable and gives

$$x^2 - x_o{}^2 + a(y^2 - y_o{}^2) + b(z^2 - z_o{}^2) = 0. \tag{47}$$

Now let us choose values such that it is not integrable, for example

$$p_y = \frac{ay + cz}{x}, \quad p_z = \frac{bz}{x}.$$

Suppose that one begins by buying Y and then buys Z. In this case the integration path is determined and we will have

$$x^2 - x_o{}^2 + a(y^2 - y_o{}^2) + 2cz_o(y - y_o) \\ + b(z^2 - z_o{}^2) = 0 \tag{48}$$

On the other hand, if one begins by buying Z and then buys Y, we will get

$$x^2 - x_o{}^2 + b(z^2 - z_o{}^2) + a(y^2 - y_o{}^2) \\ + 2cz(y - y_o) = 0. \tag{49}$$

If we have

$$y_o = 0, \quad z_o = 0,$$

equations (47) and (48) become identical, and take the form

$$x^2 - x_o{}^2 + ay^2 + bz^2 = 0.$$

But they are identical only in appearance, for in equation (47) the path of integration may be any one whatsoever, whereas it is fixed in equation (48). If this path is changed and Z is bought prior to buying Y, the form of equation (47) does not change, whereas instead of equation (48) we have, in the case we are considering

$$x^2 - x_o{}^2 + bz^2 + ay^2 + 2czy = 0$$

These values of p_y, p_z, ... only specify the law for successive purchases. They must not be confused with the values which the prices acquire at the point of equilibrium, and which are expressed as a function of the coordinates of that point (III, 169).

For example, at the equilibrium point we have

$$p_y^0 = f(x', y', z', \ldots);$$

where x', y', z', $\ldots$ are the values of x, y, z, $\ldots$ which correspond to that point. This price may remain the same during the whole series of purchases which lead to equilibrium (III, 169, γ); and it is in this sense that we say it is constant. Or it may vary during the successive purchases (III, 169, α) and behave according to a law expressed by

$$p_y = F(x, y, z, \ldots);$$

it is in this sense that we say the price is variable. Naturally at the point of equilibrium we must have

$$F(x', y', z', \ldots) = f(x', y', z', \ldots). \tag{50}$$

These principles are very simple, but forgetting them can and has entailed serious errors.

41. **Equilibrium for one individual, any number of goods, and constant prices.** Equilibrium is determined by equations (45) and (32); and by taking equations (43b) into account, we can write out this system of equations

$$\left.\begin{aligned} \varphi_x &= \frac{1}{p_y}\varphi_y = \frac{1}{p_z}\varphi_z = \ldots, \\ 0 &= x - x_0 + p_y(y - y_0) + p_z(z - z_0) + \ldots \end{aligned}\right\} \tag{51}$$

There is a total of m equations which determine the m quantities x, y, z, $\ldots$ at the point of equilibrium.

The equations in the first line of this system can be written

$$p_y = \frac{\varphi_y}{\varphi_x}, \quad p_z = \frac{\varphi_z}{\varphi_x}, \quad \ldots \tag{52}$$

There is an essential difference between these equations and equations (43b) which also give values of p_y, p_z, $\ldots$. Equations (43b) are valid for all the values of the variables. Equations (52) are valid only for the values of x, y, z, $\ldots$ which correspond to the point of equilibrium. In equations (43b) we can take the derivatives of the prices with respect to the variables x, y, $\ldots$; we cannot take these derivatives in equations (52). This observation is similar to the one already made in § 35.

To simplify the notation, the values x, y, z, $\ldots$, valid for any point whatsoever on the path traveled, and the values x', y', z', $\ldots$, referring to the point of equilibrium, will not always be written differently as was done in § 40. But it is a distinction which must never be forgotten.

If Y is a good which the individual is selling, y_o obviously cannot be zero. On the other hand, if it is a good which he is buying, y_o generally is zero.

42. Let us digress again in order to sketch briefly a new way of finding ophelimity.

Instead of conducting experiments to determine the indifference lines, or varieties, let us make some experiments to find out what quantities of goods the individual will buy at certain given prices. We set

$$y_o = 0, \quad z_o = 0, \quad \ldots$$

and give x_o a certain value; the experiment will reveal the quantities y, z, u, $\ldots$ which the individual purchases by disposing of a part of his x_o amount of X. Let us repeat these experiments varying x_o; we will get the values of y, z, u, $\ldots$ as a function of x_o, p_y, p_z, $\ldots$. If we eliminate x_o, by means of equation (45), the values of y, z, $\ldots$ will be given as functions of x, p_y, p_z, $\ldots$. Thanks to these operations we will have $m - 1$ equations in the $2m - 1$ quantities and prices, x, y, z, $\ldots$, p_y, p_z, $\ldots$; hence we can assume that these equations give the values of the $m - 1$ prices as functions of the m quantities, that is, that the experiment gives us p_y, p_z, as functions of x, y, z, $\ldots$. If we substitute these values in equations (52) we will thus have, through observation, the ratios of the quantities φ_x, φ_y, φ_z, $\ldots$ to one of them. This is precisely what we obtained (§ 14) by considering the indifference varieties.

After that the reasoning is identical to that which we used above.

The fairly great difficulty, the impossibility even, that may be found in carrying out these experiments in practice, is of little importance; their theoretical possibility alone is enough to prove, in the cases which we have examined, the existence of the indices of ophelimity, and to reveal certain of their characteristics.

43. We could deduce the theory of economic equilibrium directly from the experiments which have just been indicated. Indeed, these experiments give us

$$p_y = a_y, \quad p_z = b_z, \quad \ldots,$$

where a_y and b_z are known functions. These equations replace those of the first line of system (51), and the point of equilibrium is determined. But in this method, as long as the experiments are not actually performed, we do not have the few notions about the quantities a_y, b_z, ... which at least are furnished by the consideration of choices.[14]

44. **Properties of indifference lines.** Let us see exactly what everyday experience reveals about this subject.

Let

$$\varphi(x, y) = 0 \qquad (53)$$

be the equation of an indifference curve.

1° First of all we know that a decrease in x must be compensated by an increase in y, and vice versa. Hence we must have

$$\frac{dy}{dx} < 0. \qquad (54)$$

2° In general, and if we leave aside certain exceptional cases, the variable quantity dy which one is willing to give up, along an indifference line, for a constant quantity dx, diminishes as x increases. Thus we have the second characteristic of indifference lines, expressed by

$$\frac{d^2y}{dx^2} > 0. \qquad (55)$$

3° However, the greater is x, the less dy decreases which means that, still save for some exceptional cases, we should have

$$\frac{d^3y}{dx^3} < 0. \qquad (56)$$

There are a few reservations to make about goods having a dependence of the second kind, as we will see better in the following paragraph.

45. Now let us assume a movement from one indifference line to another. Let us call the variation parallel to the x axis δ_x, and the variation parallel to the y axis δ_y.

Reasoning as before, we will have

$$\delta_x \frac{dy}{dx} > 0, \quad \delta_y \frac{dy}{dx} < 0. \qquad (57)$$

---

[14] This point of view is developed in a scholarly article by E. Barone. See *Giornale degli economisti*, Rome, September 1908: E. Barone, "Il ministro della produzione nello stato collettivista." [This footnote is given in the *Additions* on page 684 of the French text.]

If *abc* represents [Figure 59] a part of one indifference line and *a'b'* a part of another, the inclination α' of *a'b'* with respect to *ox* is greater than the inclination α of *ab*, and less than the inclination β of *bc*.

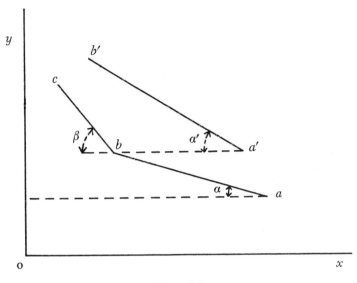

FIG. 59

This characteristic certainly seems to belong to goods whose consumption is independent. For example, if one has 5 of *X* and 5 of *Y* and after moving to another indifference line, he still has 5 of *Y* but 10 of *X*, it indeed seems, according to everything we know about consumption, that in the second position he will be inclined to give up more *X* for one *Y* than in the first position. The same conclusion is reached for goods which have a dependence of the first kind. But it is questionable for goods which have a dependence of the second kind. If *X* is a *superior* good and *Y* an *inferior* good (IV, 19), and if an individual is consuming both of them, we believe that he may exchange a certain quantity of *X* for a certain quantity of *Y*, for example 1 of *X* for 3 of *Y*; but when the individual has an abundance of *X*, and *Y* is on the verge of disappearing from his consumption, it is possible that he will refuse to give up one *X* for even a very large amount of *Y*, which is contrary to the hypothesis expressed by

$$\delta_x \frac{dy}{dx} > 0.$$

In fact, since $\dfrac{dy}{dx}$ is negative, this inequality indicates that dy decreases in absolute value when X increases.

Still, it is difficult to claim, in general, that for values of X between zero and the value of X when it completely replaces good Y in consumption, it does not happen that, good X becoming less valuable as it is more abundant, the individual is of a mind to be satisfied with decreasing quantities of Y when the quantity of X increases.

Hence some further observations are necessary to clarify this matter. They probably lead to establishing several categories of goods having a dependence of the second kind.

It is not so much the direct as the indirect observations which may be useful. Following the example of what is practiced in the physical sciences, we must make different hypotheses about the magnitudes in (57) and compare the inferences from these hypotheses with reality.

46. **Characteristics of the indices.** Let the index be

$$I = \varphi(x, y).$$

Along an indifference curve we will have

$$\frac{dy}{dx} = -\frac{\varphi_x}{\varphi_y},$$

and since dy and dx must be of opposite signs, φ_y and φ_x must have the same sign. We may choose the positive sign, which corresponds to the condition that a combination preferred to another has a larger index. If dx is positive, the combination $(x + dx, y)$ will be preferred to (x, y), and as a result $\varphi_x dx$ must be a positive quantity (§ 134).

Accordingly the first characteristic of the indices (IV, 32) is given by

$$\varphi_x > 0, \quad \varphi_y > 0.$$

Inequalities (57) can be expressed by

$$-\frac{\partial}{\partial x}\frac{\varphi_x}{\varphi_y} > 0, \quad -\frac{\partial}{\partial y}\frac{\varphi_x}{\varphi_y} < 0$$

and consequently

$$\left.\begin{array}{l} \varphi_{xx}\varphi_y - \varphi_{xy}\varphi_x < 0, \\ \varphi_{yy}\varphi_x - \varphi_{xy}\varphi_y < 0; \end{array}\right\} \tag{58}$$

where φ_{xx}, φ_{xy}, and φ_{yy} are the second order partial derivatives.

When the system of indices is such that

$$\varphi_{xy} = 0,$$

the inequalities (58) become

$$\varphi_{xx} < 0, \quad \psi_{yy} < 0, \tag{59}$$

and we have the second characteristic of the indices (IV, 33).

According to the same hypothesis, the third characteristic of indifference lines yields the following with regard to the indices

$$\varphi_{xxx} > 0, \quad \varphi_{yyy} > 0, \quad \ldots$$

47. If we assume that the quantities $dx, dy, dz, \ldots$ are all positive, the combination $(x + dx, y + dy, z + dz, \ldots)$ will be preferable to the combination $(x, y, z, \ldots)$; consequently we must have

$$d\varphi > 0.$$

But

$$d\varphi = \varphi_x dx + \varphi_y dy + \varphi_z dz + \ldots, \tag{60}$$

and [where dx^2 denotes $(dx)^2$, etc.]

$$d^2\varphi = \varphi_{xx} dx^2 + \varphi_{yy} dy^2 + \ldots + 2\varphi_{xy} dx dy + \ldots \tag{61}$$

We have three cases to examine. 1st case. φ_x depends only on x, φ_y depends only on y, etc. (IV, 8). In this case we have

$$\varphi_{xy} = 0, \quad \varphi_{xz} = 0, \quad \ldots, \quad \varphi_{yz} = 0, \quad \ldots \tag{62}$$

2nd case. The goods have a dependence of the first type (IV, 9). Save for a few exceptions in the sub-type (β) pointed out in (IV, 35), we have in general (IV, 39)[1]

$$\varphi_{xy} > 0, \quad \varphi_{xz} > 0, \quad \ldots, \quad \varphi_{yz} > 0, \quad \ldots \tag{63}$$

3rd case. The goods have a dependence of the second type (IV, 14). In this case we have in general (IV, 40)

$$\varphi_{xy} < 0, \quad \varphi_{xz} < 0, \quad \ldots, \quad \varphi_{yz} < 0, \quad \ldots \tag{64}$$

In all three cases, the indices have the characteristic indicated by equations (59), and we have

$$\varphi_{xx} < 0, \quad \varphi_{yy} < 0, \quad \varphi_{zz} < 0, \quad \ldots \tag{65}$$

If all the quantities $dx, dy, \ldots$, are assumed to be positive, or merely to have the same sign, we have in the 1st and 3rd cases[2]

$$d^2\varphi < 0. \tag{64*}$$

This inequality could not hold if the quantities dx, dy, ... did not all have the same sign. This case, which is very important, will be studied later (§ 124).

48. In the second of the cases which have just been considered, the preceding is not enough to determine the sign of $d^2\varphi$ when dx, dy, ... all have the same sign. We must resort to additional considerations. We have seen (IV, 42) that in this case, a good composed of fixed proportions of X, Y, Z, ... can be treated as if it were a simple good, and that, as a result, we have inequality (64*). That entails a certain consequence in regard to the partial derivatives of φ.

In order to have the good composed of x, y, z, ... we must set

$$y = \alpha x, \quad z = \beta x, \quad \ldots \qquad (65^*)$$

where α, β, ... are positive constants. In that case inequality (64*) becomes

$$\varphi_{xx} + \alpha^2 \varphi_{yy} + \ldots + 2\alpha \varphi_{xy} + \ldots + 2\alpha\beta \varphi_{yz} + \ldots < 0 \quad (66)$$

We know that for (66) to be true we must have

$$\varphi_{xx} < 0, \quad \begin{vmatrix} \varphi_{xx} & \varphi_{xy} \\ \varphi_{xy} & \varphi_{yy} \end{vmatrix} > 0, \quad \begin{vmatrix} \varphi_{xx} & \varphi_{xy} & \varphi_{xz} \\ \varphi_{xy} & \varphi_{yy} & \varphi_{yz} \\ \varphi_{xz} & \varphi_{yz} & \varphi_{zz} \end{vmatrix} < 0, \quad \ldots; \qquad (67)$$

which gives, in the case under consideration, an additional characteristic of the indices.

In (67) the variables x, y, z, ... must be permuted in all possible ways, which gives other inequalities similar to inequalities (67).

In the case of two goods, inequalities (67) become

$$\varphi_{xx} < 0, \quad \varphi_{xx}\varphi_{yy} - \varphi_{xy}^2 > 0.$$

We know that the second inequality is the condition that the *indicatrix* of the surface

$$1 = \varphi$$

be an ellipse.

49. Let us assume for a moment that inequalities (58) do hold for goods having a dependence of the second type.

The product of two negative quantities is a positive quantity; hence by multiplying together the two expressions in (58) we will get[3]

$$(\varphi_{xx}\varphi_{yy} - \varphi_{xy}^2)\varphi_x\varphi_y - (\varphi_{xx}\varphi_y^2 + \varphi_{yy}\varphi_x^2 - 2\varphi_{xy}\varphi_x\varphi_y)\varphi_{xy} > 0.$$

For goods having a dependence of the second kind we have

$$\varphi_{xy} < 0;$$

consequently the quantity which must be subtracted from the first term of the expression above is positive, and the result must be positive. Hence we must have

$$\varphi_{xx}\varphi_{yy} - \varphi_{xy}{}^2 > 0$$

But this is precisely the condition for the sign of

$$\delta^2\Phi = \varphi_{xx}dx^2 + \varphi_{yy}dy^2 + 2\varphi_{xy}dxdy$$

to be always the same, in this case minus.

Hence if we could agree that inequalities (58) hold for goods having a dependence of the second kind, we see, for the case of two goods, that the second variation of the ophelimity would be negative (§ 124).

50. We can proceed in a direction opposite to the one we have adopted; and, starting with the properties of ophelimity, we can deduce the characteristics of indifference lines.[15]

51. The forms of indifference lines are certainly very complex, and the examples which we have given in the text show how difficult it is, aside from a few particular cases, to subject them to algebraic analysis.[16] The difficulties arise from the fact that the analysis does not handle discontinuous functions very well, for example, those in Figure 31 (IV, 55) or Figure 33 (IV, 57).

Hence it would be fruitless to attempt to deal with the problem in its full extent; we must be satisfied with studying it in a small neighborhood of the point which we want to consider (IV, 67). In addition, it is necessary to replace functions which would represent the ophelimities rigorously with other functions which often will be only very rough approximations.

52. **General laws of supply and of demand.** Equations (51) determine the equilibrium point for an individual.

Let us set

$$\varphi_x = m;$$

m is the elementary index of the good whose price is one, that is, of money.

---

[15] See the Italian edition for details.

[16] In the *Giornale degli economisti*, Rome, September 1904, Prof. Boninsegni published a very good study of supply and demand functions in the case where the elementary ophelimities are linear.

Write the first line of equation (51) in the form

$$\varphi_x = m, \quad \varphi_y = p_y m, \quad \varphi_z = p_z m, \quad \ldots \qquad (68)$$

If we take the derivatives of all these equations with respect to p_y, we will have

$$\left. \begin{aligned}
\varphi_{xx}\frac{\partial x}{\partial p_y} + \varphi_{xy}\frac{\partial y}{\partial p_y} + \cdots &= \frac{\partial m}{\partial p_y} \\
\varphi_{xy}\frac{\partial x}{\partial p_y} + \varphi_{yy}\frac{\partial y}{\partial p_y} + \cdots &= p_y\frac{\partial m}{\partial p_y} + m \\
\varphi_{xz}\frac{\partial x}{\partial p_y} + \varphi_{yz}\frac{\partial y}{\partial p_y} + \cdots &= p_z\frac{\partial m}{\partial p_y}
\end{aligned} \right\} \qquad (69)$$

$$\cdots\cdots\cdots\cdots\cdots\cdots\cdots\cdots\cdots\cdots\cdots\cdots$$

Let R denote the Hessian

$$R = \begin{vmatrix} \varphi_{xx} & \varphi_{xy} & \varphi_{xz} & \cdots \\ \varphi_{xy} & \varphi_{yy} & \varphi_{yz} & \cdots \\ \varphi_{xz} & \varphi_{yz} & \varphi_{zz} & \cdots \\ & \cdot & \cdot & \cdot & \cdot \\ & \cdot & \cdot & \cdot & \cdot \end{vmatrix} \qquad (70)$$

Substitute $1, p_y, p_z, \ldots$ for the first column, the second, etc. of this determinant, and denote the determinants which result from these substitutions by $R_1, R_2, \ldots$. In addition, let H_{in} be the minor which is obtained by suppressing the elements of the ith row and the nth column of R, this minor being taken with the sign which it should have in the expansion of R so that

$$R = \varphi_{xx}H_{11} + \varphi_{xy}H_{21} + \cdots.$$

Also, due to the form of R,

$$H_{in} = H_{ni}.$$

We will have

$$\left. \begin{aligned}
R\frac{\partial x}{\partial p_y} &= mH_{21} + R_1\frac{\partial m}{\partial p_y} \\
R\frac{\partial y}{\partial p_y} &= mH_{22} + R_2\frac{\partial m}{\partial p_y} \\
R\frac{\partial z}{\partial p_y} &= mH_{23} + R_3\frac{\partial m}{\partial p_y}
\end{aligned} \right\} \qquad (71)$$

$$\cdots\cdots\cdots\cdots\cdots\cdots\cdots\cdots\cdots$$

If we take the partial derivative of the last equation in (51), we will have

$$0 = \frac{\partial x}{\partial p_y} + y - y_o + p_y \frac{\partial y}{\partial p_y} + p_z \frac{\partial z}{\partial p_y} \qquad (72)$$

Now form the determinant

$$M = - \begin{vmatrix} 0 & 1 & p_y & p_z & \cdots \\ 1 & \varphi_{xx} & \varphi_{xy} & \varphi_{xz} & \cdots \\ p_y & \varphi_{xy} & \varphi_{yy} & \varphi_{yz} & \cdots \\ p_z & \varphi_{xz} & \varphi_{yz} & \varphi_{zz} & \cdots \\ \cdots & \cdots & \cdots & \cdots & \cdots \end{vmatrix}$$

As before, let M_{in} be the minors of this determinant, each with the sign which is appropriate in the expansion, so that

$$M = M_{21} + p_y M_{31} + p_z M_{41} + \cdots$$

We will have

$$\left. \begin{array}{l} M = R_1 + p_y R_2 + p_z R_3 + \cdots \\ M_{31} = H_{21} + p_y H_{22} + p_z H_{23} + \cdots \end{array} \right\} \qquad (73)$$

If we substitute values from (71) into equation (72), we will obtain

$$0 = (y - y_o)R + m M_{31} + \frac{\partial m}{\partial p_y} M$$

or

$$\frac{\partial m}{\partial p_y} = - \frac{(y - y_o)R + m M_{31}}{M}; \qquad (74)$$

consequently

$$\frac{\partial y}{\partial p_y} = \frac{- (y - y_o) + m \left(\dfrac{M H_{22}}{R R_2} - \dfrac{M_{31}}{R} \right)}{M} R_2 \qquad (75)$$

This formula tells us how the demand (or the supply) of a good Υ varies with its own price p_y and does so in the most general case, where the elementary indices are functions of all the variables $x, y, z, \ldots$.[17]

---

[17] We gave these formulas for the first time in the *Giornale degli economisti*, August 1892.

For another good, for example Z, we will have

$$\frac{\partial z}{\partial p_y} = \frac{-(y - y_o) + m\left(\dfrac{MH_{23}}{RR_3} - \dfrac{M_{31}}{R}\right)}{M} R_3 \qquad (76)$$

53. For the first case of § 47, that is, if we have

$$\varphi_{xy} = 0, \quad \varphi_{xz} = 0, \quad \ldots, \quad \varphi_{yz} = 0, \quad \ldots,$$

we obtain

$$R = \varphi_{xx}\varphi_{yy}\varphi_{zz}\ldots, \quad H_{11} = \frac{R}{\varphi_{xx}}, \quad H_{22} = \frac{R}{\varphi_{yy}}, \quad \ldots$$

$$H_{23} = 0, \quad \ldots \quad R_1 = R\frac{1}{\varphi_{xx}}, \quad R_2 = R\frac{p_y}{\varphi_{yy}}, \quad \ldots$$

$$M_{31} = p_y H_{22}, \quad \ldots$$

$$\frac{M}{R} = \frac{1}{\varphi_{xx}} + \frac{p_y^2}{\varphi_{yy}} + \frac{p_z^2}{\varphi_{zz}} + \ldots \qquad (77)$$

For brevity we will let

$$\frac{M}{R} = T$$

And then we will have

$$\left.\begin{array}{l}
\dfrac{\partial m}{\partial p_y} = -\dfrac{y - y_o + m\dfrac{p_y}{\varphi_{yy}}}{T} = -\dfrac{y - y_o + \dfrac{\varphi_y}{\varphi_{yy}}}{T}, \\[3em]
\dfrac{\partial y}{\partial p_y} = \dfrac{-(y - y_o)p_y + m\left(T - \dfrac{p_y^2}{\varphi_{yy}}\right)}{T\varphi_{yy}}, \\[3em]
\dfrac{\partial z}{\partial p_y} = \dfrac{\partial m}{\partial p_y}\dfrac{p_z}{\varphi_{xx}}, \quad \ldots
\end{array}\right\} \qquad (78)$$

And in addition

$$\frac{\partial p_y (y - y_o)}{\partial p_y} = -\frac{\partial m}{\partial p_y}\left(T - \frac{p_y^2}{\varphi_{yy}}\right). \qquad (79)$$

54. In these formulas, m is essentially positive, as are the prices p_y, p_z, $\ldots$. Since φ_{xx}, φ_{yy}, $\ldots$ are negative, T is a negative quantity,

and $T\varphi_{yy}$, $T\varphi_{zz}$, ... are positive; finally, by virtue of formula (77), the quantity

$$T - \frac{p_y^2}{\varphi_{yy}}$$

is negative.

If good Y is *demanded* by the individual, the quantity $y - y_0$ is positive; it is negative if the good is *supplied*.

It follows from this that formulas (78) give rise to the following conclusions.

1° If good Y is demanded, we always have

$$\frac{\partial y}{\partial p_y} < 0.$$

The demand decreases when price increases.[18]

Since the numerator of $\dfrac{\partial m}{\partial p_y}$ is composed of a positive term and a negative term, nothing can be concluded about its sign. But equation (79) shows that this sign is the same as that of the left hand side of (79). But this left hand side represents the variation in the expenditure

$$p_y(y - y_0)$$

which the individual makes to obtain Y.

When the price of Y increases, three cases may appear: (α) The individual reduces his expenditure on Y; in that case he has more money available for his other purchases; hence the index of ophelimity of money should decrease. And this is what our formulas indicate by the negative value of $\dfrac{\partial m}{\partial p_y}$. The third line of formulas (78) shows that the quantities of Z, U, ... demanded all increase

(β) The expenditure on Y remains the same. In this case we have

$$\frac{\partial m}{\partial p_y} = 0,$$

and the quantities of Z, U, ... demanded all remain the same.

---

[18] This general proposition, obtained for the case where the price of a good depends on all the quantities exchanged and, vice versa, where the quantity of a good exchanged depends on all the prices, must not be confused with the propositions, superficially much the same, which were obtained under the hypothesis that the price of a good depends solely on the quantity of that good purchased, or sold. A table which lists the price of a good on one side and on the other the quantity of that good which an individual buys, or sells, without taking account of other goods, does not correspond to reality; it is only a hypothetical case.

(γ) The expenditure on Y increases. In this case the individual has less money available. He reduces his expenditures on other goods and, as our formulas indicate, the elementary index of the ophelimity of money increases.

2° If good Y is supplied, the numerator of the second of formulas (78) has a positive term and a negative term. Nothing may be concluded about the sign of $\dfrac{\partial y}{\partial p_y}$. On the other hand we always have

$$\frac{\partial m}{\partial p_y} < 0, \quad \frac{\partial z}{\partial p_y} > 0, \quad \ldots;$$

and, by changing the sign of $y - y_0$ in formula (79) we will have

$$\frac{\partial p_y (y_0 - y)}{\partial p_y} > 0$$

Hence the individual receives a larger total amount for the good Y which he is selling. We cannot say whether he sells more or less of it. The index of the ophelimity of money decreases.

55. These results have been obtained for the case where

$$\varphi_{xy} = 0, \quad \varphi_{xz} = 0, \quad \ldots, \quad \varphi_{yz} = 0, \quad \ldots,$$

but when these quantities have small enough values, which in practice corresponds to a very large number of cases, equations (78) and (79) still hold approximately and consequently the results do not differ from those which we have just pointed out.

But we must not forget that there are other cases where the values of $\varphi_{xy}, \ldots$ may be large enough to modify these results.

56. Following Professor Marshall, many economists have believed it possible, in general, for small variations in prices and quantities, to consider the index of ophelimity of money, m, as constant, which amounts to setting

$$\frac{\partial m}{\partial p_y} = 0.$$

The formulas which we have just given show that we could not accept that proposition.[19]

Even when the quantity

$$\frac{\partial m}{\partial p_y}$$

is very small, it could not be disregarded if care were not taken to

---

[19] We have stressed this point in the *Giornale degli economisti*, March 1892, April 1895, and in the *Cours*, § 84.

show that the error thereby committed does not change the results obtained.

57. After we have a few notions about the variations in demand and supply, formulas (74), (75), (76), and (78) can be used to obtain some notions about the indices of ophelimity, and vice versa.

58. Assume that, in the case represented by equations (78), we have

$$\frac{\partial m}{\partial p_y} = 0. \tag{80}$$

In order that this equation be satisfied, the denominator of this expression, as given by (78), must be infinite, or the numerator must be zero.

The absolute value of the denominator T can be fairly large, even very large, when we have a very large number of goods; but it is not infinite, at least in general. If it is assumed that $\frac{\partial m}{\partial p_y}$ can be disregarded because T is very large, it will follow that all the $\frac{\partial z}{\partial p_y}, \frac{\partial u}{\partial p_y}, \ldots$ can also be disregarded. For $\frac{\partial y}{\partial p_y}$, we get

$$\frac{\partial y}{\partial p_y} = \frac{m}{\varphi_{yy}}.$$

Hence, the hypothesis is tantamount to assuming that when p_y varies, only the quantity y varies, while $z, u, \ldots$ remain constant. This assumption may be admissible in certain cases, but in general it is inadmissible.

The equation

$$0 = \frac{\partial x}{\partial p_y} + \frac{\partial (p_y y)}{\partial p_y} + p_z \frac{\partial z}{\partial p_y} + \cdots$$

expresses the variation which the budget undergoes when p_y varies. Under the hypothesis we have made, all the terms but one vanish, and we have

$$\frac{\partial (p_y y)}{\partial p_y} = 0;$$

but that is false, for if on the one hand the terms which we have assumed to be zero are actually very small, on the other hand there is a very large number of them, so that their sum is not negligible.

In all the problems relating to exchange, the budget equation and consideration of its variations are essential, at least in general. It follows that, in these problems, we cannot assume that the index of ophelimity, m, is constant, except in very special cases which must be justified.

59. Let us now consider the other hypothesis, that is, that the numerator vanishes.

In that case we have

$$y - y_o + \frac{\varphi_y}{\varphi_{yy}} = 0,$$

and consequently

$$\varphi_y = \frac{B}{y - y_o},$$

where B is an arbitrary constant. But we could not agree, in general, that the index of ophelimity of the consumption of the quantity y depends on the initial quantity y_o possessed by the individual. In the cases of goods supplied, y_o cannot be zero, and as a result the form which we have just found for φ_y, and the hypothesis which led us to it, must be rejected.

In the cases of goods demanded, y_o can be zero, and the form

$$\varphi_y = \frac{B}{y}$$

becomes admissible. But let us examine its consequences.

Assume an individual who supplies X and buys all the other goods $Y, Z, \ldots$, for which we assume

$$\varphi_y = \frac{B}{y}, \quad \varphi_z = \frac{C}{z}, \quad \ldots \tag{81}$$

We will have

$$x_o - x = p_y y + p_z z + \ldots$$

$$\varphi_x = \frac{B}{p_y y} = \frac{C}{p_z z} = \ldots,$$

and consequently

$$(x_o - x)\varphi_x = B + C + \ldots \tag{82}$$

This equation states that the individual's expenditure $x_o - x$ does not vary when the prices of the goods which he buys vary. That is hardly admissible, in general.

In addition there is φ_x; and if we do not want to accept the form

$$\varphi_x = \frac{A}{x_o - x},$$

the index of ophelimity is no longer constant. If we assume, for a moment, that φ_x does have this inadmissible form, we arrive at consequences less admissible still.

Indeed, in that case, equation (82) becomes

$$A = B + C + \ldots$$

If this relationship between the constants of the indices of ophelimity does not hold, equilibrium is impossible. If, by some extraordinary chance, it is satisfied, the equilibrium would be indeterminate. We could choose a value for x arbitrarily and then set

$$y = \frac{B(x_o - x)}{Ap_y}, \quad z = \frac{C(x_o - x)}{Ap_z}, \quad \ldots$$

and equilibrium would exist.

In every case, then, we arrive at results which oblige us to reject, at least in general, the hypothesis that the index of ophelimity, m, is constant.

60. Where $\alpha, \beta, \gamma, \ldots$ are very small quantities, let

$$\varphi_x = \frac{A}{x^{1+\alpha}}, \quad \varphi_y = \frac{B}{y^{1+\beta}}, \quad \varphi_z = \frac{C}{z^{1+\gamma}}, \quad \ldots$$

We will have

$$p_y y = \left(\frac{B}{A}\right)^{\frac{1}{1+\beta}} x^{\frac{1+\alpha}{1+\beta}} p_y^{\frac{\beta}{1+\beta}}$$

and then

$$p_y y = \frac{B}{A} x (1 + \varepsilon_y).$$

In a similar manner we will obtain

$$p_z z = \frac{C}{A} x (1 + \varepsilon_z), \quad \ldots,$$

where $\varepsilon_y, \varepsilon_z, \ldots$ are very small quantities.

If we let

$$h_o = x_o + p_y y_o + p_z z_o + \ldots,$$

the last equation in (51) becomes

$$h_o = x + p_y y + p_z z + \ldots.$$

We will get

$$h_o = x(H + K),$$

where $H = 1 + \dfrac{B}{A} + \dfrac{C}{A} + \ldots$, and $K = \dfrac{B}{A}\varepsilon_y + \dfrac{C}{A}\varepsilon_z + \ldots$.

Consequently

$$x = \frac{h_o}{H + K} = \frac{h_o}{H}(1 + l).$$

Since the quantity K is very small, the quantity l will be also. Then we will have

$$
\left.
\begin{aligned}
p_y y &= \frac{B}{A}\frac{h_o}{H}(1 + l)(1 + \varepsilon_y), \\[2mm]
p_z z &= \frac{C}{A}\frac{h_o}{H}(1 + l)(1 + \varepsilon_z), \\[2mm]
&\cdot\cdot\cdot\cdot\cdot\cdot\cdot\cdot\cdot\cdot\cdot\cdot\cdot\cdot\cdot\cdot\cdot\cdot\cdot\cdot\cdot
\end{aligned}
\right\}
\tag{83}
$$

61. The value of T, given in § 53, becomes

$$
\begin{aligned}
-T &= \frac{x^{2+a}}{(1+\alpha)A} + \frac{p_y^2 y^{2+\beta}}{(1+\beta)B} + \cdots \\[2mm]
&= \frac{x^{2+a}}{(1+\alpha)A} + \frac{p_y^2 B x^2 (1+\varepsilon_y)^2 y^\beta}{(1+\beta)A^2} + \cdots \\[2mm]
&= \frac{x^2}{A}(H + q),
\end{aligned}
$$

where q is a very small quantity.

Now equations (78) give

$$
\left.
\begin{aligned}
\frac{\partial m}{\partial p_y} &= -\frac{y_o A H}{h_o^2}(1 + m_y) \\[2mm]
\frac{\partial y}{\partial p_y} &= \frac{B}{A}\frac{p_y y_o - h_o}{H p_y^2}(1 + n_y) \\[2mm]
\frac{\partial z}{\partial p_y} &= \frac{C y_o}{A H p_z}(1 + r_y) \\[2mm]
&\cdot\cdot\cdot\cdot\cdot\cdot\cdot\cdot\cdot\cdot\cdot\cdot\cdot\cdot\cdot\cdot\cdot\cdot\cdot\cdot
\end{aligned}
\right\}
\tag{84}
$$

where m_y, n_y, r_y, $\ldots$ are all small quantities.

These formulas can also be obtained directly from equations (82) and (83).

62. If Y is a good which is demanded, there must be at least one other good which is supplied. If we assume that this is Z, z_o must not be zero, but must be a positive quantity, consequently

$$p_y y_o - h_o < 0,$$

and by virtue of equations (84), we once again have

$$\frac{\partial y}{\partial p_y} < 0.$$

If Y is supplied, there must, it is true, be at least one good which is demanded; but for the goods demanded the initial quantities can be zero. If Y is the only good supplied, and if all the other goods are demanded with their initial quantities being zero, we have

$$\frac{\partial y}{\partial p_y} = 0.$$

If another good, for example U, were supplied, u_o could not be zero, and consequently

$$\frac{\partial y}{\partial p_y} < 0.$$

When y decreases, the quantity $y_o - y$ which is supplied increases. Hence the increase in price would always make the supply increase. In order that the supply decrease after having increased, the factor $1 + n_y$ must change sign, which is not possible as long as n_y remains a very small quantity. Hence the hypothesis which has just been made is not compatible with the hypothesis that $\alpha, \beta, \ldots$ be very small quantities, unless, by compensation, other quantities do not become very large.

When Y is demanded and $y_o = 0$, the principal part of $p_y y$ in formulae (83) is independent of p_y; hence it remains constant when p_y varies. In that case the variation can only come from terms in l and in ε_y, which are disregarded when it is assumed that the indices of ophelimity have the form (81).

63. **General case of exchange with constant prices.** Assume we have θ individuals, whom we will indicate by $1, 2, \ldots, \theta$, and m goods $X, Y, Z, \ldots$.

Assume that all the individuals follow Type I in their exchanges, that is, free competition (III, 4). That means that each of them accepts the market prices although in reality the latter are *indirectly* modified by the exchanges made by these individuals.[20] Accordingly, for each individual, we will have equations similar to equations (51). We assign the index i to all symbols which refer to individual

---

[20] As we have already remarked, this condition must never be forgotten. Its omission would make the proposition, of which it is an essential part, false.

We often repeat certain things because they are constantly neglected, forgotten, and ignored by some persons who write about economic theory.

i. Equations (51) and those which state that the total quantities of goods do not vary during the exchange, give

$$\left.\begin{array}{l} \varphi_{1x} = \dfrac{1}{p_y}\varphi_{1y} = \dfrac{1}{p_z}\varphi_{1z} = \ldots, \\[2ex] \varphi_{2x} = \dfrac{1}{p_y}\varphi_{2y} = \dfrac{1}{p_z}\varphi_{2z} = \ldots, \\[1ex] \cdots\cdots\cdots\cdots\cdots\cdots\cdots \end{array}\right\} \quad \text{(A)}$$

$$\left.\begin{array}{l} x_1 - x_{10} + p_y(y_1 - y_{10}) + p_z(z_1 - z_{10}) + \ldots = 0, \\[1ex] x_2 - x_{20} + p_y(y_2 - y_{20}) + p_z(z_2 - z_{20}) + \ldots = 0, \\[1ex] \cdots\cdots\cdots\cdots\cdots\cdots\cdots\cdots\cdots\cdots\cdots \\[1ex] x_{\theta-1} - x_{\theta-1,0} + p_y(y_{\theta-1} - y_{\theta-1,0}) + \ldots = 0. \end{array}\right\} \quad \text{(B)}$$

$$\left.\begin{array}{l} x_1 - x_{10} + x_2 - x_{20} + \ldots = 0 \\[1ex] y_1 - y_{10} + y_2 - y_{20} + \ldots = 0 \\[1ex] \cdots\cdots\cdots\cdots\cdots\cdots\cdots \end{array}\right\} \quad \text{(C)}$$

Note that the equation which corresponds to the index θ is not written in system (B) because it follows from the other equations (B) and (C). If one wanted to include that equation, it would be necessary to suppress another one.

The equations which we have just written correspond to categories (A), (B), and (C) of the conditions which were described in (III, 199 *et. seq.*).

The unknowns are: 1° The $m - 1$ prices, and 2° the $m\theta$ quantities $x_1, x_2, \ldots, y_1, y_2, \ldots$, which is $m\theta + m - 1$ in all.

The equations are: 1° The $(m - 1)\theta$ equations (A), 2° the $\theta - 1$ equations (B), and 3° the m equations (C); hence $m\theta + m - 1$ in all.

The number of equations is the same as the number of unknowns and the problem is fully determined.

As has already been noted (§ 35) in an analogous case, it must not be forgotten that equations (B) and (C) are valid for all the values of the variables $x_1, x_2, \ldots, y_1, y_2, \ldots$, whereas equations (A) are valid only for the values of those variables which correspond to the point of equilibrium.

In system (A), $\varphi_{1x}, \varphi_{2x}, \ldots$ may be functions of all the variables, $x, y, z, \ldots$, as can $\varphi_{1y}, \ldots, \varphi_{1z}, \ldots$, etc.

64. If we return the equation which is missing from (B), and, to compensate for that, suppress one of equations (C), we can handle equations (A) and (B) as system (51) was handled to obtain the laws of supply and of demand. The $m\theta$ quantities x_1, x_2, $\ldots$, y_1, y_2, $\ldots$ will be functions of the $m - 1$ unknowns p_y, p_z, $\ldots$; and the $m - 1$ equations (C) will provide the means for determining these unknowns.

65. It may happen that the owner of a good supplied, Y for example, does not use it to satisfy his tastes; we then say that he *supplies the entire quantity* at his disposal. If we indicate this by $y_{10} = y_1$, individual 1 being the owner of that good, there will be one less unknown. In addition, in system (A), the equation in which the quantity φ_{1y} appears must be suppressed. Thus the number of equations remains equal to the number of unknowns.

66. Money, being a good, must have an ophelimity of its own for some individuals; but it may not have it for others. Let us assume that X does not have ophelimity for individual 1. In that case we must suppress the equation in φ_{1x} in system (A); in that way one equation is lost.

But in addition since X does not have ophelimity for individual 1, he does not consume any of it. He uses the entire amount he receives to obtain goods Y, Z, $\ldots$, among which is included a good which represents savings. Hence we will have

$$x_1 - x_{10} = 0,$$

which determines x_1. We then have one less unknown, and the number of equations is again equal to the number of unknowns.

67. **Operations according to Type II.** Assume that individual 1 does not accept the prices as he finds them in the market, but endeavors to modify them, with a view to achieving a certain end.

This case includes the one which is commonly called monopoly. The individual sells Y and buys the other goods. He does not take the index of ophelimity of Y into account either because Y has no ophelimity for him, or because having an excess of Y is of no consequence to him, provided he attains other ends.

Among these ends we consider two principal ones: (α) The individual tries to obtain the maximum receipts, expressed in money, from his monopoly. (β) The individual tries to obtain maximum ophelimity.

68. **One monopolist and one good.** Since the individual does not take the index of ophelimity of Y into account, the equation in

φ_{1y} is missing from system (A). In order to restore the equality between the number of equations and the number of unknowns, one of the unknowns must be given; if we assume that this is p_y, we will then have

$$y_{10} - y_1 = f(p_y).$$

(α) If individual 1 has in mind obtaining the greatest amount of money possible from his monopoly, he will have to maximize

$$(y_{10} - y_1)p_y = p_y f(p_y),$$

and that will require setting

$$\frac{d(p_y f)}{dp_y} = 0. \tag{85}$$

This equation serves to determine p_y, and the problem is solved.

If there were a stopping point which preceded the value of y determined in this way, the individual will have to stop at that stopping point. That is the case where he does not possess the quantity of Y which corresponds to the maximum given by equation (85).

(β) If the individual has in mind obtaining maximum ophelimity, he must set

$$\frac{d\varphi_1}{dp_y} = 0;$$

or

$$0 = \varphi_{1x}\frac{dx_1}{dp_y} + \varphi_{1y}\frac{dy_1}{dp_y} + \varphi_{1z}\frac{dz_1}{dp_y} + \cdots \tag{86}$$

We know $x_1, y_1, \ldots$ as functions of p_y; hence equation (86) includes only known quantities; and it solves the problem.

In order to return to the case of free competition, we must express the condition that $d\varphi_1$ is zero, not when p_y varies, but rather when p_y remains constant and y varies. Then instead of equation (86) we have

$$0 = \varphi_{1x}dx_1 + \varphi_{1y}dy_1,$$

and, recalling the definition of price, we will have

$$0 = \varphi_{1x} - \frac{1}{p_y}\varphi_{1y},$$

which is precisely the equation which was missing because it had been suppressed.

The case where individual 1 would also have a monopoly of Z is dealt with in a manner similar to that just indicated.

69. **Two monopolists and one good.**[21] Assume that 1 and 2 sell Υ, operating according to Type II, and that they buy the other goods.

Now system (A) lacks two equations, and as a result it is necessary that two unknowns be given. Let us specify p_y and y_2; all the other unknowns will be expressed as functions of these; and if we set

$$s_1 = (y_{10} - y_1)p_y, \quad s_2 = (y_{20} - y_2)p_y,$$

we will get an equation of the form

$$F(s_1, s_2, p_y) = 0 \tag{87}$$

(α) In order to have maximum money receipts, s_1 and s_2 must be maximized.

Let us give s_2 an arbitrary value. The condition for maximum s_1 is

$$\frac{\partial F}{\partial p_y} = 0. \tag{88}$$

If we eliminate p_y from equations (87) and (88), we will have

$$f(s_1, s_2) = 0. \tag{89}$$

If we had been given arbitrarily the value of s_1, and looked for the condition for maximum s_2, we would still have gotten equation (88), consequently we would have ended up with equation (89). Hence the latter gives the maximum value of s_1 for an arbitrary value of s_2, and vice versa.

Geometrically equation (89) represents the contour of surface (87) on the $s_1 s_2$ plane.

We chose s_2 arbitrarily, and found equation (89) in order to determine maximum s_1, when p_y varies. Now let us allow s_2 to vary and determine maximum s_1; we will have

$$\frac{\partial f}{\partial s_2} = 0. \tag{90}$$

If we want to determine maximum s_2, when s_1 varies, we would have

$$\frac{\partial f}{\partial s_1} = 0. \tag{91}$$

We thus would have three equations to determine our two un-

---

[21] Professor F. Y. Edgeworth, making certain hypotheses, was the first to deal with a particular case of this problem. *Giornale degli economisti*, July 1897.

knowns. Hence the hypotheses which have led us to this result are not, in general, compatible; and it cannot be assumed that the two individuals both act according to Type II.

Geometrically, the two equations (90) and (91) can be satisfied only at special [*singuliers*] points of the curve (89). Equations (89) and (90) determine the point (α) where the curve qr, the equation of which is (89), has a tangent parallel to the s_2 axis [Figure 60]. Equations (89) and (91) determine the point (β) where that curve has a tangent parallel to the s_1 axis. These two points are in general different; and consequently the three equations (89), (90), and (91) are not compatible.

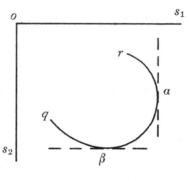

FIG. 60

From the mathematical point of view, it is not correct to say, as is often done, that, in the case of two monopolists and one good, the problem of equilibrium is indeterminate. On the contrary, it is over determined, because conditions are imposed which are incompatible.

70. (β) Suppose that it is a case of maximizing the index of ophelimity. Replace the two equations which are missing from system (A) by equations

$$t_1 = \varphi_1, \quad t_2 = \varphi_2, \tag{92}$$

where t_1 and t_2 are new variables. The expressions for φ_1 and φ_2 are known as functions of x_1, y_1, ..., x_2, y_2, ... Hence we will obtain expressions for all the unknowns as functions of t_1 and t_2; and we will have an equation of the form

$$F(t_1, t_2, p_y) = 0.$$

The rest of the reasoning is now similar to the preceding, and leads to the same results.

71. **Two monopolists and two goods.** Let us assume that individual 1 sells Y and buys all the other goods, and that individual 2 sells Z and buys all the other goods.

System (A) again lacks two equations, and as before two unknowns must be given. Let us choose p_y and p_z. All the other quantities will become functions of p_y and p_z; hence we will have

$$F_1(s_1, p_y, p_z) = 0, \quad F_2(s_2, p_y, p_z) = 0, \tag{93}$$

or

$$f_1(\varphi_1, p_y, p_z) = 0, \quad f_2(\varphi_2, p_y, p_z) = 0. \tag{94}$$

Now we must maximize s_1 *when p_y varies*, and s_2 as well, not when p_y varies, as before, but *when p_z varies*. Therein lies the main difference from the preceding problem; and this difference is the source of the difference in the conclusions.

When maximum ophelimity is considered, it is likewise necessary to maximize φ_1 *when p_y varies*, and to maximize φ_2 *when p_z varies*.

In the case where the monopolists want to obtain the greatest money receipts from their monopoly, we will have to set

$$\frac{\partial F_1}{\partial p_y} = 0, \ \frac{\partial F_2}{\partial p_z} = 0.$$

These two equations, along with the two equations (93), enable us to determine the four unknowns s_1, s_2, p_y, and p_z. Hence the problem is solved.

In the case where the monopolists seek maximum ophelimity, we must set

$$\frac{\partial f_1}{\partial p_y} = 0, \ \frac{\partial f_2}{\partial p_z} = 0.$$

These two equations, along with the two equations (94), solve the problem.

The difference between this problem and the preceding lies essentially in the fact that, in the preceding problem, the objective was to maximize s_1 when p_y and s_2 varied, and likewise s_2 when s_1 and p_y varied. That is impossible.

In the present problem, it is a question of maximizing s_1 when p_y and p_z vary, and s_2 when p_y and p_z vary. That is not at all impossible, at least in general, and the problem is fully determined.

The same conclusion is reached in looking for maximum φ_1 and maximum φ_2.

72. The following considerations are so elementary that they probably are superfluous.

In the problem in § 71 we could take the unknowns p_y and p_z as given. That obviously should not change the conclusions.

Accordingly, let us assume that in that problem, we have the two equations

$$F_1(s_1, p_y, p_z) = 0, \quad F_2(s_2, p_y, p_z) = 0. \tag{95}$$

If we arbitrarily fix the amount s_2 which individual 2 derives from his monopoly, the second one of the equations just written determines p_z as a function of s_2 and p_y. Hence we will have

$$\frac{\partial F_2}{\partial p_y} + \frac{\partial F_2}{\partial p_z} \frac{\partial p_z}{\partial p_y} = 0.$$

The condition that s_1 is a maximum when p_y varies gives

$$\frac{\partial F_1}{\partial p_y} + \frac{\partial F_1}{\partial p_z} \frac{\partial p_z}{\partial p_y} = 0.$$

These two equations lead to the following

$$\frac{\partial F_1}{\partial p_y} \frac{\partial F_2}{\partial p_z} - \frac{\partial F_2}{\partial p_y} \frac{\partial F_1}{\partial p_z} = 0.$$

Eliminate p_y and p_z from this equation and the two equations in (95); we will obtain an equation having the form of (89). The rest of the reasoning is identical to that which has been made about that equation, and gives the same results.

73. From the economic point of view, in the case of the problem in § 69, it can be pointed out that in assuming a position in which one of the monopolists obtains s_1 from his monopoly, and the other obtains s_2, the first one need only lower his price by a very small amount in order to increase his gain and reduce the share of his competitor to zero; and vice versa. Hence the solution of the problem which we have posed is impossible, because no s_1, s_2 position is a position of equilibrium.

74. By reasoning in that manner, we are tempted to believe that the problem is indeterminate, contrary to what we said in § 69.

The source of this contradiction is found in the way in which the problem is presented. It is necessary to distinguish between an individual's *power* to exercise a monopoly, and the *fact* that the individual does exercise it, acting according to Type II.

In the problem in § 69 we assume that two individuals do *in fact* behave according to Type II, with regard to selling good Y, and we arrive at the conclusion that our hypothesis cannot be realized.

In the problem in § 73 we assume that two individuals have the *power* to act according to Type II, with regard to the sale of the same good Y, and we arrive at the conclusion that the problem is indeterminate, for we do not know what use each of these two individuals will make of his *power*.

This conclusion is identical to the preceding one. If the two individuals could use their monopoly, we would have no need to know what use of it each would make in order that the problem be determinate.

75. It is idle to ask pure economics what will happen when two individuals, having the power to exercise a monopoly in the sale of one and the same good, find themselves face to face. Pure economics, by showing us that it is impossible for these two individuals in fact to make use of their monopoly, both acting according to Type II, has said everything that it could tell us. It is for observation of facts to tell us the rest.

Pure economics cannot even tell us that the two individuals will shuttle back and forth indefinitely between two extreme positions of equilibrium. That does not follow at all from the fact that the equilibrium is determined by two incompatible equations.

76. Still less should we imagine that observation of facts is going to lead to a unique solution. On the contrary, there are an infinite number of them.

First of all there are quite numerous and very diverse cases in which the two *potential* monopolists amount to one monopolist in fact. If the two monopolists come to an agreement, there no longer is more than one. The cartels, the trusts, etc., have made us well acquainted with the ways of achieving such agreement. Similarly there no longer is more than one of them if the second monopolist accepts the prices fixed by the first, who alone is acting according to Type II in that case.

This last case is frequent in real life. When a company "controls" (that is the technical term) a considerable fraction of production, for example 80/100, it often happens that it is that company which sets the prices; the producers of the remaining 20/100 accept them.

Next there are the very numerous cases in which good Y, which appears to be homogeneous, is in reality divided into several goods. Thus a lady of fashion is not accustomed to buy her clothes in department stores; she goes to a couturier. There are incidental circumstances, of credit, certain attentions given to the customers, etc., which can differentiate otherwise identical goods.

Finally the objective of monopolist 1 may be to ruin his competitor 2; or, on the other hand, to allow him to just get along so as not to provoke him into running the risk of a fight to the finish. There are an infinite number of other circumstances of this kind, all of which vary the nature of the problem posed.

Moreover this variation may, in exceptional cases, arise from the problem itself. Assume, for example, that the sum $y_{10} + y_{20}$ of the amounts of Y possessed by individuals 1 and 2 is less than the amount which, if they were a single monopolist, would correspond to the maximum amount of X which they could derive from their monopoly. In this case individuals 1 and 2 both have stopping points (III, 62); it will be expedient for each to offer the entire quantity at his disposal. We no longer have the case of individuals acting according to Type II, but the case of individuals acting according to Type I (§ 65).

It is well to recall that the majority of the cases which we observe in real life are cases of monopolies in production rather than cases of monopolies in exchange.

76b. An example will be useful for clarifying certain points,

Let us assume we have two monopolists who sell Y and buy X and Z. To simplify, we will consider a single consumer; the case where there are several consumers is similar, however. This consumer buys y of good Y, and sells $x_0 - x$ of X, and $z_0 - z$ of Z. We are assuming that the indices of ophelimity have the forms given in the following equations.

For the two monopolists we have equations

$$\frac{1}{x_1} = \frac{1}{p_z} \frac{c'}{z_1^2}, \qquad \frac{1}{x_2} = \frac{1}{p_z} \frac{c''}{z_2^2},$$

$$p_y y_1 = s_1 = x_1 + p_z z_1, \qquad p_y y_2 = s_2 = x_2 + p_z z_2.$$

From these equations we derive

$$s_1 = p_z \left(z_1 + \frac{z_1^2}{c'} \right), \qquad s_2 = p_z \left(z_2 + \frac{z_2^2}{c''} \right).$$

For the consumer we have

$$\frac{1}{x^2} = \frac{a^2}{p_y y^4} = \frac{b}{p_z z},$$

$$x_0 - x = x_1 + x_2, \qquad z_0 - z = z_1 + z_2.$$

Hence we will have

$$p_z z = \frac{b}{a^2} p_y y^4, \qquad x = \frac{y^2}{a} \sqrt{p_y}.$$

If we let

$$s = s_1 + s_2,$$

the equations of the monopolists yield

$$s = x_1 + x_2 + p_z(z_1 + z_2)$$

$$= x_0 - \frac{y^2}{a}\sqrt{p_y} + p_z z_0 - \frac{b}{a^2} p_y y^4;$$

hence

$$p_z = \frac{1}{z_0}\left(s - x_0 + \frac{y^2}{a}\sqrt{p_y} + \frac{b}{a^2} p_y y^4\right).$$

But

$$y = y_1 + y_2 = \frac{s_1 + s_2}{p_y} = \frac{p_y}{s};$$

and, by substituting that value in the preceding equation, p_z is obtained as a function of p_y and of s. Consequently, the equations which we have obtained for the monopolists

$$z_1 + \frac{z_1^2}{c'} = \frac{1}{p_z} s_1, \qquad z_2 + \frac{z_2^2}{c''} = \frac{1}{p_z} s_2,$$

have their right hand sides made up of s_1 and s_2, multiplied by a function of p_y and of s, that is to say, that the left hand sides are functions of p_y, s_1, and s_2. Obviously it is necessary to choose the positive roots of these expressions, which are

$$z_1 = -\frac{c'}{2} + \sqrt{\frac{c'^2}{4} + \frac{c's_1}{p_z}},$$

$$z_2 = -\frac{c''}{2} + \sqrt{\frac{c''^2}{4} + \frac{c''s_2}{p_z}}.$$

But

$$z = \frac{b p_y y^4}{a^2 p_z} = \frac{b s^4}{a^2 p_z p_y^3} = z_0 - (z_1 + z_2);$$

therefore finally

$$z_0 - \frac{b s^4}{a^2 p_z p_y^3} + \frac{c' + c''}{2} - \sqrt{\frac{c'^2}{4} + \frac{c's_1}{p_z}} - \sqrt{\frac{c''^2}{4} + \frac{c''s_2}{p_z}} = 0$$

This is equation (87) of § 69.

If there are only two goods, X and Y, this equation takes a particular form, which it is desirable to examine.

We have for the consumer simply

$$\frac{1}{x^2} = \frac{a^2}{p_y y^4}, \qquad x_o - x = x_1 + x_2;$$

and for the monopolists

$$s_1 = x_1, \qquad s_2 = x_2.$$

Hence we will have

$$\frac{y^2 \sqrt{p_y}}{a} = x_o - s;$$

and

$$x_o - s - \frac{s^2}{a} p_y^{-3/2} = 0.$$

This is equation (87) of § 69, which in this case takes the form

$$F(s_1 + s_2, p_y) = 0.$$

If p_y is eliminated from this equation and equation (88), we obtain for equation (89)

$$f(s_1 + s_2) = 0; \tag{89b}$$

and the two equations (90) and (91) become identical, that is

$$f'(s_1 + s_2) = 0. \tag{90b}$$

But in this case, it is equations (89b) and (90b) which are in general incompatible with the data given. The rest of the reasoning is the same as that of § 69, and the conclusions are identical.

77. **Production.** Let us assume that certain goods $A, B, C, \ldots$, or certain capital services, are transformed into other goods $X, Y, Z, \ldots$. Let us call

θ, the number of individuals,

n, the number of goods, or capital services $A, B, \ldots$

m, the number of goods $X, Y, \ldots$

$\pi_x, \pi_y, \ldots$, the unit cost, for the producer of goods $X, Y, \ldots$

$p_x, p_y, \ldots$, their selling prices.

$p_a, p_b, \ldots$, the prices of goods $A, B, \ldots$; we will take A as money, and set

$$p_a = 1.$$

$x_1, y_1, \ldots, x_2, y_2, \ldots$, the quantities of the products which are consumed, in an intermediate position.

$x_1', y_1', \ldots, x_2', y_2', \ldots$, these same quantities for the position of equilibrium.

$a_1, b_1, \ldots, a_2, b_2, \ldots,$ and

$a_1', b_1', \ldots, a_2', b_2', \ldots,$ will have analogous meanings for A, $B, \ldots$

To simplify, it is assumed that the initial quantities of goods $X, Y, \ldots$ are zero. As for the initial quantities of $A, B, \ldots,$ they will be denoted by $a_{10}, b_{10}, \ldots, a_{20}, \ldots$

In addition we will adopt the following designations. We will call

$x, y, \ldots,$ the total quantities of goods *produced*, in an intermediate position, before reaching the position of equilibrium.

$X'', Y'', \ldots,$ these same quantities *produced*, when we have reached the position of equilibrium.

$X, Y, \ldots,$ the total quantities *consumed*, in an intermediate position, before reaching the position of equilibrium.

$X', Y', \ldots,$ these same quantities *consumed* when we have reached the position of equilibrium.

$a, b, \ldots,$ the quantities *supplied* to the enterprise, in an intermediate position.

$A, B, \ldots,$ the quantities *transformed* by the enterprise, in an intermediate position.

$A', B', \ldots,$ the quantities *consumed*, when we have reached a position of equilibrium.

$A'', B'', \ldots,$ the quantities *supplied* to the enterprise, when we have reached a position of equilibrium.

$A''', B''', \ldots,$ the quantities *transformed* by the enterprise when we have reached a position of equilibrium.

$A_0', B_0', \ldots,$ the initial quantities of $A', B', \ldots$

We will have

$$\left.\begin{array}{ll} a_1' + a_2' + \ldots = A', & b_1' + b_2' + \ldots = B', \quad \ldots, \\ a_{10} + a_{20} + \ldots = A_0', & b_{10} + b_{20} + \ldots = B_0', \quad \ldots; \end{array}\right\}(96)$$

$$A'' = A_0' - A', \quad B'' = B_0' - B', \quad \ldots \qquad (97)$$

$$\left.\begin{array}{ll} x_1 + x_2 + \ldots = X, & y_1 + y_2 + \ldots = Y, \quad \ldots, \\ x_1' + x_2' + \ldots = X', & y_1' + y_2' + \ldots = Y', \quad \ldots. \end{array}\right\}(98)$$

Having reached the position of equilibrium, we will have

$$\left.\begin{array}{lll} x = X'', & y = Y'', & \ldots, \\ X = X', & Y = Y', & \ldots, \\ A = A''', & B = B''', & \ldots. \end{array}\right\} (99)$$

But these equations are not valid for an intermediate position.

In the case of free competition (III, 44 to 46) we must have

$$X'' = X', \qquad Y'' = Y', \qquad \dots \qquad (100)$$

In the case of monopoly, of Y for example, Y'' can be greater than Y', the difference becoming monopoly profit. Or again some of the quantities A', B', ... will be different from the corresponding quantities A'', B'', ...; and the difference will be the profit of the monopolist.

78. **The coefficients of production.** The technical conditions of production will give us the quantities A, B, ... as functions of x, y, ...; that is to say

$$A = F(x, y, \dots), \quad B = G(x, y, \dots), \quad \dots$$

The partial derivatives

$$a_x = \frac{\partial F}{\partial x}, \quad b_x = \frac{\partial G}{\partial x}, \quad \dots, \quad a_y = \frac{\partial F}{\partial y}, \quad \dots \qquad (101)$$

are called *coefficients of production*. $a_x dx$ is the quantity of A which is necessary to produce dx of X, when x of X, y of Y, etc. have already been produced; a_y, ..., b_x, b_y, ... have analogous meanings.

In assuming the existence of the integral functions F, G, ..., we implicitly assume that the quantities of A, B, C, ... employed in production do not depend on the path followed to reach the point under consideration. This is indeed just how things take place in reality.

Let us assume that a_x, b_x, ... are functions of x only, that a_y, b_y, ... are functions of y only, etc. Assume further that there are fixed expenses [*frais généraux*] A_0''', B_0''', ..., independent of x, y, ... In this case the integral functions F, G, ... surely exist. We will have

$$\left.\begin{array}{l} A''' = F = A_0''' + \displaystyle\int_0^{X''} a_x dx + \int_0^{Y''} a_y dy + \dots, \\[3mm] B''' = G = B_0''' + \displaystyle\int_0^{X''} b_x dx + \int_0^{Y''} b_y dy + \dots, \\[2mm] \dots \dots \dots \dots \dots \dots \dots \dots \dots \dots \dots \dots \end{array}\right\} \qquad (102)$$

If we assume that the coefficients of fabrication are constant, and that there are no fixed expenses independent of the quantities produced, we will have

$$\left.\begin{array}{l} A''' = a_x X'' + a_y Y'' + \dots, \\[2mm] B''' = b_x X'' + b_y Y'' + \dots, \\[2mm] \dots \dots \dots \dots \dots \dots \dots \dots \end{array}\right\} \qquad (103)$$

If we assume that there are fixed expenses A_0''', B_0''', ..., we will have

$$\left. \begin{array}{l} A''' = A_0''' + a_x X'' + a_y Y'' + \ldots, \\ B''' = B_0''' + b_x X'' + b_y Y'' + \ldots, \\ \cdots\cdots\cdots\cdots\cdots\cdots\cdots \end{array} \right\} \qquad (103b)$$

79. Costs of production. We are assuming that the production of X, Y, ... is independent. The costs of production of dx, dy, ..., when x, y, ... have already been produced, will be

$$\left. \begin{array}{l} \pi_x dx = (a_x + p_b b_x + p_c c_x + \ldots)\, dx, \\ \pi_y dy = (a_y + p_b b_y + p_c c_y + \ldots)\, dy, \\ \cdots\cdots\cdots\cdots\cdots\cdots\cdots\cdots \end{array} \right\} \qquad (104)$$

These expressions may, or may not, be partial derivatives of the same function. If we assume that they are, we assume thereby that we always come to the same result whatever be the order, the sequence, of fabrications. Otherwise the costs of production would vary with that order. The question merits clarification by observation of what takes place in real life. Meanwhile we can assume the prices p_b, p_c, ... to be constant without departing too far from reality. With that hypothesis, and recalling that we have assumed that a_x, b_x, ... were functions of x only, a_y, b_y, ..., of y only, etc., the integral function, for which expressions (104) represent the partial derivatives, certainly exists. Moreover, we can integrate each of these equations, and get the costs of production of X'', Y'', ... separately, that is

$$\Pi_x = \pi_{0x} + \int_0^{X''} \pi_x dx, \quad \Pi_y = \pi_{0y} + \int_0^{Y''} \pi_y dy, \quad \ldots, \qquad (105)$$

where π_{0x}, π_{0y}, ... are fixed expenses independent of x, y, ... By taking equations (102) and (104) into account we obtain

$$\pi_{0x} + \pi_{0y} + \ldots = A_0''' + p_b B_0''' + \ldots \qquad (106)$$

It must not be forgotten that in saying that p_b, p_c, ... are constant, we only mean that the prices of the successive portions of B, C, ... employed in the same operation do not vary. This is case (δ) of (III, 169).

On the other hand, for certain investigations which we will have to make, it is appropriate to assume that the prices p_x, p_y, ... are variable for the successive portions.

80. **Equilibrium of the consumers.** Let us begin by assuming that all the prices are constant. Assume further that the consumers behave according to Type I (free competition). What we have said on the subject of exchange gives the following equations for equilibrium immediately.

$$\left.\begin{array}{l} \dfrac{1}{p_x}\varphi_{1x}(x_1') = \ldots = \varphi_{1a}(a_1') = \dfrac{1}{p_b}\varphi_{1b}(b_1') = \ldots \\[3mm] \dfrac{1}{p_x}\varphi_{2x}(x_2') = \ldots = \varphi_{2a}(a_2') = \dfrac{1}{p_b}\varphi_{2b}(b_2') = \ldots \\[3mm] \cdots\cdots\cdots\cdots\cdots\cdots\cdots\cdots\cdots\cdots\cdots\cdots\cdots \end{array}\right\} \text{(A)}$$

$$\left.\begin{array}{l} a_1' - a_{10} + p_b(b_1' - b_{10}) + \ldots + p_x x_1' + p_y y_1' + \ldots = 0 \\[1mm] a_2' - a_{20} + p_b(b_2' - b_{20}) + \ldots + p_x x_2' + p_y y_2' + \ldots = 0 \\[1mm] \cdots\cdots\cdots\cdots\cdots\cdots\cdots\cdots\cdots\cdots\cdots\cdots\cdots \end{array}\right\} \text{(B)}$$

$$\left.\begin{array}{c} x_1' + x_2' + \ldots = X', \quad y_1' + y_2' + \ldots = Y', \quad \ldots, \\[1mm] a_{10} - a_1' + a_{20} - a_2' + \ldots = A'', \\[1mm] b_{10} - b_1' + b_{20} - b_2' + \ldots = B'', \quad \ldots \end{array}\right\} \text{(M)}$$

Equations (A) are $(m+n-1)\theta$ in number,
Equations (B) are θ in number,
Equations (M) are $m+n$ in number.
Total ...... $(m+n)\theta + m + n.$

Summing equations (B) and taking account of (M), we will have

$$A'' + p_b B'' + \ldots = p_x X' + p_y Y' + \ldots \qquad (107)$$

If the prices $p_x, p_y, \ldots$ are variable, p_x being a function only of X, p_y of Y, etc., equation (107) will be replaced by the following

$$A'' + p_b B'' + \ldots = \int_0^{X'} p_x dX + \int_0^{Y'} p_y dY + \ldots \qquad (107b)$$

81. **Equilibrium of the enterprises.** We are assuming that the enterprises produce precisely the quantities of $X, Y, \ldots$ which they sell; their profits, or their losses, are expressed in quantities of the goods $A, B, \ldots$.

The amounts of $A, B, \ldots$ which the enterprises need in order to produce the quantities $x, y, \ldots$ have already been given in § 78. Thus we have the system

$$A''' = F, \quad B''' = G, \quad \ldots \qquad (108)$$

The total expenses Π_x, Π_y, ... necessary to produce x, y, ... are given by equations (105). Summing them, we will have

$$A''' + p_b B''' + \ldots = \Pi_x + \Pi_y + \ldots \qquad (109)$$

This equation, however, could be written directly, since each side represents the total amount spent for production.

82. **Equilibrium of production.** Now the problem is to relate the enterprises and the consumers to each other. We will have different economic situations depending on the manner in which the enterprises and the consumers are related.

83. (α) **Free competition.** The entrepreneurs and the consumers behave according to Type I. This situation is characterized by equality between the cost of production and the selling price of goods. We assume that this equality takes place for total receipts and total expenditures (§ 116). When the prices are constant and there are no fixed expenses, this equality also entails the equality of the cost of production and the selling price of the last portion produced (§ 92).

Hence we will have

$$p_x X' = \Pi_x, \quad p_y Y' = \Pi_y, \quad \ldots \qquad (D)$$

Addition of these equations gives

$$p_x X' + p_y Y' + \ldots = \Pi_x + \Pi_y + \ldots;$$

and if we take equations (107) and (109) into account, this equation will become

$$A'' + p_b B'' + \ldots = A''' + p_b B''' + \ldots.$$

It is possible for the quantities A'', B'', ... to be greater than the quantities A''', B''', ..., but they cannot be smaller, because the enterprise can receive the goods in question from no other source than the consumers. Accordingly the preceding equation implies

$$A'' = A''', \quad B'' = B''', \quad \ldots \qquad (E)$$

In the case of variable prices, it is sufficient to replace $p_x X$, $p_y Y$, ... by

$$\int_0^X p_x \, dX, \quad \int_0^Y p_y \, dY, \quad \ldots$$

If the π_{0x}, π_{0y}, ... are zero and the coefficients of production are constant,[22] equations (D) become

$$\left.\begin{aligned} p_x &= a_x + p_b b_x + p_c c_x + \cdots, \\ p_y &= a_y + p_b b_y + p_c c_y + \cdots, \\ &\cdots\cdots\cdots\cdots\cdots\cdots\cdots \end{aligned}\right\} \qquad \text{(D}'\text{)}$$

Thanks to equations (103), equations (E) become

$$\left.\begin{aligned} A'' &= a_x X'' + a_y Y'' + \cdots, \\ B'' &= b_x X'' + b_y Y'' + \cdots, \\ &\cdots\cdots\cdots\cdots\cdots\cdots \end{aligned}\right\} \qquad \text{(E}'\text{)}$$

Equation (107) follows from systems (B) and (M); equations (E) follow from equations (D), (107), and (109). Consequently in the system (B), (M), (109), (D), (E), there is one equation which must be suppressed.

This also can be seen directly in systems (D') and (E'), which include system (109). Indeed, these systems give

$$A'' + B'' p_b + \ldots = p_x X'' + p_y Y'' + \cdots;$$

or, since at the point of equilibrium we have $X'' = X'$, $Y'' = Y'$, ...,

$$A'' + B'' p_b + \ldots = p_x X' + p_y Y' + \cdots.$$

But this equation is identical to equation (107) which follows from systems (B) and (M).

Equations (109), (D), and (E), of which one is suppressed, give the values of X, Y, ..., A'', B'', ..., except for one of them which remains unknown. Systems (A), (B), and (M) then include only that unknown, the $(m+n)\theta$ quantities x_1, y_1, ..., x_2, ..., a_1, ..., and the $m+n-1$ prices; hence $(m+n)\theta + m + n$ unknowns in all. But we have seen (§ 80) that the number of these equations is precisely $(m+n)\theta + m + n$. Thus the problem of equilibrium is solved and fully determined.

84. (β) **Monopoly in production.** Let us assume that the producer of a good Y is able to behave according to Type II. System (D) lacks one equation, and that equation is

$$p_y Y' = \Pi_y.$$

---

[22] This is the case which has been studied by Léon Walras. Walras had the very great distinction of giving for the first time, in this particular case, the general equations of economic equilibrium. The path which he thus opened is very fruitful.

Consequently, the entire system (E) no longer exists. Indeed it must be so, for if the entrepreneur has a profit we must have some additional information to know what he will do with it. We can assume, as we please, that he will use this profit to buy X, Y, $\ldots$, A, B, or any other goods. All these cases, however, are treated in the same manner. In order to simplify, we will assume that the profit of the entrepreneur is converted into good A, whose price is one.

85. Following this hypothesis, we restore all the equations of system (E) except the first, which is replaced by an equation stating that the difference $A'' - A'''$, instead of being zero, is equal to the entrepreneur's profit; let

$$A'' - A''' = p_y Y' - \Pi_y.$$

If we denote this profit by ξ, systems (D) and (E) are replaced by the following

$$p_x X' = \Pi_x, \quad p_y Y' - \Pi_y = \xi, \quad p_z Z' = \Pi_z, \quad \ldots, \qquad \text{(D'')}$$

$$A'' - A''' = \xi, \quad B'' = B''', \quad \ldots. \qquad \text{(E'')}$$

Here again one of the equations follows from the others and must be suppressed.

Indeed (D'') gives

$$p_x X' + p_y Y' + \ldots = \xi + \Pi_x + \Pi_y + \ldots;$$

and substituting for Π_x, Π_y, $\ldots$,

$$p_x X' + p_y Y' + \ldots = \xi + A''' + p_b B''' + \ldots$$

In addition, systems (B) and (M) give

$$p_x X' + p_y Y' + \ldots = A'' + p_b B'' + \ldots$$

Using these two equations and taking into account equations

$$B'' = B''', \quad C'' = C''', \quad \ldots,$$

of system (E''), we obtain

$$A'' = \xi + A''';$$

this is precisely the first equation of system (E''), which thus follows from the others.

If we suppress one equation of systems (D'') and (E''), $m + n - 1$ are left. Systems (A), (B), and (M) furnish $(m + n)\theta + m + n$ equations. Thus we have

$$(m + n)\theta + 2m + 2n - 1$$

equations in all.

The quantities A''', B''', ... are still determined by equations (108). So then we have as unknowns:

$(m+n)\theta$	quantities $x_1, y_1, \ldots, a_1, \ldots,$
$m+n-1$	prices
$m+n$	quantities $X, Y, \ldots, A', B', \ldots,$
$\underline{1}$	quantity ξ.
$(m+n)\theta + 2m + 2n$	.... Total

Hence the number of the unknowns is one more than the number of equations; consequently all the unknowns can be determined as functions of one of them. The latter can be chosen arbitrarily; let us choose p_y.

All the other unknowns being expressed as functions of p_y, we will have

$$\xi = f(p_y).$$

The monopolist generally endeavors to maximize his profit ξ expressed in *numéraire;* hence we will have

$$\frac{\partial f}{\partial p_y} = 0. \tag{111}$$

This is the equation which was missing. Now the number of equations is equal to the number of unknowns, and the problem is solved.

86. Assume that the monopolist makes his calculations in ophelimity. He uses his profit to buy certain goods $X, Y, \ldots, A, B, \ldots$, and obtains the quantities x''', y''', ...

We will have the following equations for him

$$\frac{1}{p_x}\varphi_x(x''') = \ldots = \varphi_a(a''') = \frac{1}{p_b}\varphi_b(b''') = \ldots;$$

$$p_x x''' + p_y y''' + \ldots + a''' + p_b b''' + \ldots = \xi.$$

These equations enable the quantities to be determined as functions of the prices and of ξ. Hence the total ophelimity, φ, which the entrepreneur enjoys will be a function of the prices and of ξ, and since these quantities are themselves functions of p_y, we will have

$$\varphi = F(p_y).$$

For the entrepreneur to obtain maximum ophelimity, it is necessary that

$$\frac{dF}{dp_y} = 0,$$

and in this case, this equation replaces equation (111).

87. We can, as we have seen, choose the independent variable arbitrarily. Hence whether the monopolist acted to determine p_y, or any other variable, the result will be the same as far as the determination of the point of equilibrium is concerned. But there can be differences regarding other matters, among them the stability of the equilibrium. This point will be clarified later (§ 98).

87b. If we assumed that in the production of a given good there were two individuals acting according to Type II, the problem would be over determined, and the hypothesis just made cannot be realized. The proof is the same as the one given in § 69, and leads to considerations analogous to those of §§ 72, 73, 74, 75, and 76.

88. If we assume an individual behaving according to type II with respect to a good Y, and another individual also behaving according to type II with respect to another good Z, the problem is possible; and it is solved by considerations analogous to those which were developed in § 71.

It must not be forgotten that the enterprise generally makes its calculations in *numéraire* and not in ophelimity.

89. (γ) **Maximum ophelimity.** First of all it is advisable to define this term exactly. As we have seen (VI, 53), there are two problems to solve in order to obtain maximum welfare for a collectivity. Given certain rules of distribution, we can seek the position which gives, always in conformance with these rules, the greatest possible welfare to the individuals of the collectivity.

Consider any position, and assume that we move away from it by a very small amount, consistent with the restrictions [*liaisons*]. If in so doing the welfare of all the individuals of the collectivity is increased, it is obvious that the new position is more advantageous to each one of them; and vice versa, it is less so if the welfare of all the individuals is decreased. Moreover, the welfare of some of them can remain the same, without changing these conclusions. But on the other hand, if this small movement increases the welfare of certain individuals and decreases that of others, we can no longer state positively that it is advantageous to the entire collectivity to carry out that movement.

These considerations lead to defining the position of maximum ophelimity to be one from which it is impossible to move a very small distance, in such a way that the ophelimities of the individuals, except for some which remain constant, all increase or decrease (VI, 33).

Let us denote any variations whatsoever by δ, as for example when we move from one path to another (§ 22); and denote each individual's total ophelimity by Φ_1, Φ_2, ... Consider the expression

$$\frac{1}{\varphi_{1a}}\delta\Phi_1 + \frac{1}{\varphi_{2a}}\delta\Phi_2 + \frac{1}{\varphi_{3a}}\delta\Phi_3 + \ldots \qquad (112)$$

If we exclude the case where the $\delta\Phi_1$, $\delta\Phi_2$, ... are zero, it is clear that since the quantities φ_{1a}, φ_{2a}, ... are essentially positive, this expression (112) can become zero only if some of the $\delta\Phi$ are positive and some are negative, although some always can be zero. Consequently, if we set

$$0 = \frac{1}{\varphi_{1a}}\delta\Phi_{1a} + \frac{1}{\varphi_{2a}}\delta\Phi_{2a} + \frac{1}{\varphi_{3a}}\delta\Phi_{3a} + \ldots, \qquad (113)$$

the case where all the changes are positive, or negative, will be excluded. Hence equation (113) characterizes maximum ophelimity, according to our definition, for the collectivity under consideration. All the variations in this equation must be consistent with the restrictions in the system.

It is convenient to choose the definition of maximum ophelimity for a collectivity in such a way that it coincides with the one for a single individual. This indeed is the case for the definition which we have just given (§ 116).

90. Let us apply these considerations to production. If there is a positive difference between the sum realized from the sale of a good X and what it cost, that is, if

$$\int_0^{X'} p_x dX - \Pi_x > 0, \qquad (114)$$

the goods represented by this sum obviously can be disposed of by distributing them to some or all of the members of the collectivity. In that way all the terms of expression (112) become positive, or certain ones become positive, the others being zero. Hence the position of maximum ophelimity is not attained. In order for it to be reached, expression (114) must become zero; for then we no longer have goods available to make all the terms of (112) positive, or to make some of them positive, the others being zero.

The condition which we have just found is the same as the one which characterizes free competition (§ 83).

91. This condition is necessary, but, in general, it is not sufficient. There are other variations to consider.

The variations which at the point of equilibrium occur, for the consumers, on the path which has led to that point, merely reproduce equations (A). They have already been taken into account; it is unnecessary to dwell on this.

92. Let us assume that the conditions of production and consumption of a good X vary. If the variation in expression (114), which can be written

$$\delta\left(\int_0^{X'} p_x dx - \pi_{0x} - \int_0^{X''} \pi_x dx \right),$$

were positive, we would have a certain quantity to distribute to the members of the collectivity and we could make all the terms of expression (112) positive, except for those which are zero; and conversely we could make them negative if the variation considered were negative. Accordingly, for maximum ophelimity, the variation must be zero. Hence substituting for Π_x the value given by equations (105), we will have

$$\delta\left(\int_0^{X'} p_x dx - \pi_{0x} - \int_0^{X''} \pi_x d\dot{x} \right) = 0 \qquad (115)$$

Let us denote the values of p_x and π_x at the point of equilibrium by $p_x{}^0$ and $\pi_x{}^0$. At that point we have $X' = X''$. The preceding variation becomes

$$\left(p_x{}^0 - \pi_x{}^0 + \int_0^{X'} \left(\frac{dp_x}{dX'} - \frac{d\pi_x}{dX'} \right) dx \right) \delta X' = 0 \qquad (116)$$

Instead of considering any variations whatsoever, let us consider the variations which take place when the parameters (§ 26), which are found in the expressions for p_x and π_x, remain constant. In this case δ changes to d, and production is continued along the path which has led to the point of equilibrium. The parameters being regarded as constant, the derivatives of p_x and π_x with respect to X' are zero which gives

$$p_x{}^0 - \pi_x{}^0 = 0.$$

If this equation were not satisfied, that would mean that in making the quantity of X produced (equal to the quantity consumed) vary by $\delta X''$, the production of X leaves a certain residue. And the maximum ophelimity is not reached in such case because this residue can be used to make expression (112) positive, or negative.

The same result can be reached in another way. At the point of equilibrium we have

$$\delta\Phi_1 = \varphi_{1x}\delta x_1 + \varphi_{1a}\delta a_1 + \varphi_{1b}\delta b_1 + \ldots,$$

$$\delta\Phi_2 = \varphi_{2x}\delta x_2 + \varphi_{2a}\delta a_2 + \varphi_{2b}\delta b_2 + \ldots,$$

$$\cdots\cdots\cdots\cdots\cdots\cdots\cdots\cdots\cdots\cdots$$

If for φ_{1x}, φ_{1a}, ... we substitute their expressions taken from equations (A) of § 80, we will have

$$\frac{1}{\varphi_{1a}}\delta\Phi_1 = p_x\delta x_1' + \delta a_1' + p_b\delta b_1' + \ldots,$$

$$\frac{1}{\varphi_{2a}}\delta\Phi_2 = p_x\delta x_2' + \delta a_2' + p_b\delta b_2' + \ldots,$$

$$\cdots\cdots\cdots\cdots\cdots\cdots\cdots\cdots\cdots\cdots$$

Summing, and taking into account equations (96), (97), and (98), and the fact that, at the point of equilibrium, we have

$$X' = X'', \quad A'' = A''', \quad \ldots,$$

we will get

$$\frac{1}{\varphi_{1a}}\delta\Phi_1 + \frac{1}{\varphi_{2a}}\delta\Phi_2 + \frac{1}{\varphi_{3a}}\delta\Phi_3 + \ldots$$

$$= p_x{}^0\delta X'' - \delta A''' - p_b{}^0\delta B''' - \ldots$$

If the movement represents a continuation of the path along which production takes place, δ changes into d and we have

$$\frac{1}{\varphi_{1a}}d\Phi_1 + \frac{1}{\varphi_{2a}}d\Phi_2 + \ldots \qquad (117)$$

$$= p_x{}^0dX'' - dA''' - p_b{}^0dB''' - \ldots$$

In addition, let us investigate the cost of production of dX''. If the integral function of which the expressions (104) represent the partial derivatives exists, either directly, or because the path of integration is given, the cost of production of dX'' is obtained by substituting dX'' for dx in the first equation of (104), and we have

$$\pi_x{}^0dX'' = (a_x + p_b{}^0b_x + \ldots)dX''.$$

The equations give

$$dA''' = a_x dX'', \quad dB''' = b_x dX'', \quad \ldots;$$

consequently the preceding equation becomes

$$\pi_x{}^0 dX'' = dA''' + p_b{}^0 dB''' + \ldots .$$

Substitute this value in the right hand side of equation (117). The left hand side is zero when maximum ophelimity is attained, hence the right hand side must also be zero in that case, and we have

$$0 = p_x{}^0 dX'' - \pi_x{}^0 dX''$$

or

$$p_x{}^0 - \pi_x{}^0 = 0,$$

as before.

This theory is only a particular case of a more general theory which will be given later (§ 109 *et seq.*).

Obviously for $Y, Z, \ldots$, we have equations similar to those which we have just found. Consequently we can write

$$p_x{}^0 = \pi_x{}^0, \quad p_y{}^0 = \pi_y{}^0, \quad \ldots . \tag{118}$$

The values of $\pi_x{}^0, \pi_y{}^0, \ldots$ are those which correspond to the point of equilibrium.

92b. The results we have reached can be expressed in the following manner.[4]

The necessary and sufficient conditions for attaining maximum ophelimity are:

1° The equality of the integrals

$$\int_0^{x''} p_x dx = \pi_{0x} + \int_0^{x} \pi_x dx, \quad \ldots ;$$

2° The equality of the last elements of these integrals

$$p_x{}^0 = \pi_x{}^0, \quad p_y{}^0 = \pi_y{}^0, \quad \ldots .$$

When the $\pi_{0x}, \ldots$ are zero and the prices are constant, these two conditions reduce to just one. Indeed the first is expressed by

$$p_x X'' = \pi_x x, \quad \ldots ;$$

and the second by

$$p_x = \pi_x, \quad \ldots ;$$

and since $X'' = x, \ldots$, the first equation is identical to the second.

When the $\pi_{0x}, \ldots$ are not zero and the prices are constant, the first condition gives

$$p_x x = \pi_{0x} + \pi_x x, \quad \ldots ,$$

and the second

$$p_x = \pi_x, \quad \ldots .$$

These equations are incompatible. Thus, for phenomena of Type I, when there are fixed expenses π_{0x}, ..., it is, in general, impossible to reach maximum ophelimity with constant prices (VI, 43).

This occurs because with constant prices one cannot go on moving, while maintaining the equilibrium of the budgets.

In the case of free competition the two conditions indicated tend to be fulfilled. The first being satisfied, it is clear that manufacturers have a tendency to expand production as long as

$$p_x{}^0 > \pi_x{}^0, \quad ...,$$

but the state of the market can deter them.

Moreover, the second condition being fulfilled, competition operates to achieve the first; but that may not be possible.

93. **Numerical example.** The preceding will be clarified by a very simple numerical example.

Assume we have a group of identical consumers who sell A and B and buy X. Similarly, assume a group of enterprises which transform A and B into X.

For any point of equilibrium for the consumers, the quantities consumed will be x, a, and b.

We are changing the notation in order to simplify things. These quantities x, a, and b are the ones which were denoted before by X', A', and B' at the point of equilibrium.

If we assume

$$\varphi_x = \frac{1}{\sqrt{x}} - \frac{1}{x + 0.5},$$

the three characteristics of the indices

$$\varphi_x > 0, \quad \varphi_{xx} < 0, \quad \varphi_{xxx} > 0,$$

hold true for

$$x \geqq 4.$$

These three characteristics are also satisfied for the functions

$$\varphi_a = \frac{M}{a^{0.4}}, \quad \varphi_b = \frac{N}{\sqrt{b}}.$$

In addition, let

$$a_0 = 17, \quad b_0 = 28.$$

The quantities supplied to the enterprise will be

$$A'' = 17 - a, \quad B'' = 28 - b.$$

The equilibrium conditions for the consumers are

$$\left.\begin{array}{c} \dfrac{1}{p_x}\varphi_x = \varphi_a = \dfrac{1}{p_b}\varphi_b \\[2mm] p_x x = A'' + p_b B''. \end{array}\right\} \qquad (119)$$

The quantities transformed by the enterprise are A''' and B''', and we will let

$$A''' = 3 + 0.5x, \quad B''' = 5 + x.$$

These are equations (108).

94. In the case of free competition, systems (D) and (E) become

$$\left.\begin{array}{c} p_x x = A''' + p_b B''' \\[2mm] A'' = A''', \quad B'' = B''' \end{array}\right\} \qquad (120)$$

The first of these equations is identical to the last equation in (119) and therefore must be suppressed, as we already know.

Let us try to determine the parameters so as to have several points of equilibrium. There can be two of them. Assume that they correspond to the points given by $x = 4.2$ and by $x = 12$. We will have

$$\log M = \bar{1}.6413093, \qquad \log N = \bar{1}.1872683.$$

Let us see what takes place in the neighborhood of these points. For the first, we will have the following table:

x	$A'' - A'''$	$\log p_x$	$\log p_b$	B''
4	-0.08966	0.235354	$\bar{1}.339498$	9
4.2	0	0.228533	$\bar{1}.339099$	9.2
5	$+0.29028$	0.20422	$\bar{1}.338161$	10

The enterprise cannot remain at a point below $x = 4.2$ because it would have a loss, since $A'' - A'''$ is then negative. It can remain at the point $x = 4.2$, and at points for which $x > 4.2$.

On that side of the point $x = 4.2$ the equilibrium is unstable, for by decreasing the price p_x, the enterprise sells a greater quantity of X and increases its profit. Even if it is the only one, it will be motivated to move; it will be obliged to do so if it has competitors. The movement can continue until a point of stable equilibrium is reached.

For the point $x = 12$, we have the following table:

x	$A'' - A'''$	$\log p_x$	$\log p_b$	B''
11	$+ 0.25768$	0.056649	$\bar{1}.372788$	16
12	0	0.039397	$\bar{1}.386499$	17
13	$- 0.31643$	0.023980	$\bar{1}.403162$	18

The enterprise cannot go beyond the point $x = 12$ without entering a region where it would have losses. On the side where $x < 12$, it is driven by competition toward the point $x = 12$. Hence this is a point of stable equilibrium.

95. In this hypothetical case there are several circumstances which deserve to be noted.

If a syndicate of the suppliers of B required its members not to sell that good below a certain price, it could happen that the movement which starts from the point of unstable equilibrium would be arrested. Assume, for example, that the members of the syndicate must not sell their goods below the price which corresponds to $x = 4.2$. The equilibrium at this point would become stable, for in order to move away from it the enterprise needs to pay a lower price for the good.

We will see (§ 100) that the ophelimity which the sellers of B enjoy is greater at the point $x = 12$ than at the point $x = 4.2$. Thus their syndicate would have the effect of diminishing their welfare instead of increasing it.

This effect will occur as long as p_b decreases when B' increases. For

$$x = \qquad 4 \qquad\qquad 5 \qquad\qquad 6$$

we have

$$\log p_b = \bar{1}.339498 \qquad \bar{1}.338161 \qquad \bar{1}.338845$$

Thus the effect pointed out will extend up to a point located in the neighborhood of $x = 5$. Beyond this point, it will no longer occur.

96. Now assume a syndicate of enterprises operating according to Type II in the production and sale of X.

Assume that we still have

$$B'' = B''',$$

but that

$$A'' - A''' = \xi,$$

where ξ is the profit of the enterprise.

To facilitate the numerical calculations, it is convenient to take x as the independent variable. The profit ξ is 0 for $x = 4.2$, and for $x = 12$; between these two values there is a maximum.

First giving to x the values 5, 6, ... we find

$x =$	7	8	9
$\xi =$ 0.63607	0.65367	0.58997

Hence the maximum must be in the vicinity of the point $x = 8$. Substituting values of x which increase by a tenth, we have

$x =$	7.6	7.7	7.8
$\xi =$ 0.65709	0.65751	0.65706

We could fit a parabola to these three points. Setting

$$x = 7.6 + u$$

we would have

$$\xi = 0.65709 + u\Delta\xi + \frac{u(u-1)}{2}\Delta^2\xi;$$

or

$$\xi = 0.65709 + (\Delta\xi - \tfrac{1}{2}\Delta^2\xi)u + \frac{u^2}{2}\Delta^2\xi.$$

In order to find the maximum take the derivative and set it equal to zero; this will give

$$0 = (\Delta\xi - \tfrac{1}{2}\Delta^2\xi) + u\Delta^2\xi.$$

This equation replaces equation (111) and can be used to find an approximate value of x. But it is unnecessary to seek this precision in a hypothetical case, and we will simply assume that the maximum corresponds to $x = 7.7$.

We will have the following table:

x	ξ	$\log p_x$	$\log p_b$	B''
7.6	0.65709	0.129472	$\overline{1}.344071$	12.6
7.7	0.65751	0.126992	$\overline{1}.344565$	12.7
7.8	0.65706	0.124535	$\overline{1}.345120$	12.8

Hence the monopolists will have to stop at the price p_x which corresponds to $x = 7.7$. This price is lower than the one which corresponds to $x = 7.6$.

97. If the syndicate acts as a single monopolist, in order to stop precisely at the point $x = 7.7$, it must fix the price and the allocation of the quantities among its members.

If it only fixed a price below which the members must not sell, for example the price which corresponds to $x = 7.7$, the allocation of the quantities would remain undetermined. Assume, then, that the syndicate determines it, but allows a certain latitude for small variations.

The members of the syndicate cannot move toward $x > 7.7$, because the price p_x would fall below the fixed limit. That limit does not prevent them from moving toward $x < 7.7$, but the competition for sales drives them back to the point $x = 7.7$. Hence this is a point of stable equilibrium.

98. The choice of the independent variable is immaterial. p_b may be chosen. If the syndicate fixes this price p_b, and the quantities of B which its members can buy, there is no difference from the preceding case.

Nor is there any difference, at the point where we are now, if the syndicate fixes an upper limit for p_b, one which corresponds to $x = 7.7$, and allows a little latitude regarding the quantities.

98b. It would no longer be the same if, for some reason, the syndicate thought it to be in its interest to stop at a point at which B'' increases when p_b decreases.

Assume, for example, that the syndicate wished to stop at the point $x = 4.2$. If it fixed the price p_x corresponding to $x = 4.2$, below which its members could not go, the latter will not be able to move in the direction $x > 4.2$. Moreover, they would suffer losses if they moved in the direction $x < 4.2$. Hence the point $x = 4.2$ becomes a point of stable equilibrium.

But assume now that the syndicate acts on p_b instead of acting on p_x. It fixes the price p_b which corresponds to $x = 4.2$ and forbids its members to go beyond that limit. It also fixes the quantities, but with a little latitude.

The members of the syndicate cannot move toward $x < 4.2$, either because they would go beyond the limit which had been set for p_b, or because they would suffer losses. But they can move toward $x > 4.2$, and the competition for sales does not bring them back to that point.

Thus, if the syndicate acts on p_x, the point $x = 4.2$ is a point of stable equilibrium; it is a point of unstable equilibrium if the syndicate acts on p_b.

99. Let us look for the point where the consumers obtain maximum ophelimity. We know that the prices of the goods produced can no longer be constant. The equality of the last element of the integrals indicated in § 92 gives, for the point of equilibrium

$$p_x = 0.5 + p_b.$$

Indeed, the last portion dx is produced with $0.5dx$ of A, and dx of B.

Equilibrium will be determined by the following equations

$$\frac{1}{p_x}\varphi_x = \varphi_a = \frac{1}{p_b}\varphi_b, \quad p_x = 0.5 + p_b, \quad A'' = A''', \quad B'' = B'''.$$

Eliminating the prices, we have

$$\varphi_x = 0.5\varphi + \varphi_b$$

and expressing the quantities as a function of x, we obtain

$$\varphi_x(x) = 0.5\varphi_a(14 - 0.5x) + \varphi_b(23 - x).$$

This equation gives

$$x = 17.854;$$

and we then have

$$p_b{}^0 = 0.2967, \quad p_x{}^0 = 0.7967.$$

100. Let us now calculate the total ophelimities for the various points of equilibrium.

We have

$$\Phi = 2\sqrt{x} - \log{(x + 0.5)} + \frac{10}{6}Ma^{0.6} + 2N\sqrt{b};$$

the logarithm is Naperian.

Let us calculate the ophelimity in excess of that for the point $x = 4.2$, that is, calculate

$$\Omega = \Phi(x) - \Phi(4.2);$$

we will obtain

$x = 4.2$	7.7	12	17.854
$\Omega = 0$	0.355	0.854	1.062

According to what we have seen in § 92, maximum ophelimity is inconsistent with constant prices, it is attained only for $x = 17.854$. Starting from the origin, we no longer follow a straight line, as would be the case with p_x constant, but a bent line. The enterprise receives 3 of A and 5 of B, without delivering anything, then it delivers X at the rate of 1 of that good for 0.5 of A and 1 of B. It suffices, moreover, that it be the last portions of the good which are provided in that way.

101. **Variability of the coefficients of production.** Some of the coefficients of production are constant, or nearly constant, others vary with the quantity of product, and still others present a variation of a special kind; they form a group such that an increase in certain of these coefficients can be offset by a decrease in others. Finally an enterprise's cost of production may vary with the total quantity produced by that enterprise.

102. Expressions (105) for the cost of production can be written

$$\pi_{0x} + \int_0^{x''} (a_x + p_b b_x + \dots) dx, \quad \dots;$$

and in these formulas a_x, b_x, $\dots$ may be functions of x. Hence we have already allowed for the variability as a function of the quantities x, y, $\dots$; and we no longer have to be concerned with it.

103. Let b_y, c_y, $\dots$, e_y be a group of coefficients of production such that the variations in certain of them are compensated by the variations in others. The technical conditions of production apprise us of the law describing these compensations, which can be expressed by

$$f(b_y, c_y, \dots, e_y) = 0. \tag{121}$$

The enterprise must determine these coefficients, subject to the law indicated. In doing so, it can, as in other economic phenomena, operate according to Type I or according to Type II.

104. Let us begin by assuming that it operates according to Type I. The enterprise accepts the market prices without trying to

modify them directly; it makes its calculations with those prices and determines the coefficients. But, without intending to do so, it has modified the market prices. Consequently, it makes its calculations again with the new prices. And so on indefinitely. The path followed by the enterprise is analogous to a pursuit curve.

In other words, the coefficients of production under the integral sign should be regarded as independent of the integral's limits. This is characteristic of Type I phenomena, with regard to the prices as well as the coefficients of fabrication.

If the coefficients b_y, c_y, $\ldots$, e_y are varied, the variation of the expense incurred to produce Y will be

$$\delta \Pi_y = \int_0^{Y''} (p_b \delta b_y + p_c \delta c_y + \ldots + b_y \delta p_b + \ldots) \, dy \qquad (122)$$

In the present case, since the enterprise accepts the market prices, and does not take their variations into account, it operates as if we had

$$\delta \Pi_y = \int_0^{Y''} (p_b \delta b_y + p_c \delta c_y + \ldots) \, dy.$$

It is this expression which must equal zero in order for the expenditure Π_y to be a minimum, a minimum which would be attained if the prices would remain constant. But it will not be attained because the prices vary, which will oblige the enterprise to begin its calculations again with the new prices.

Hence in this case we will have

$$0 = \int_0^{Y''} (p_b \delta b_y + p_c \delta c_y + \ldots) \, dy. \qquad (123)$$

When this equation holds with the existing market prices, the enterprise will no longer have to revise its calculations; it will stop. Hence equilibrium will be attained when equation (123) holds along with the other equations of equilibrium.

105. If we have only equation (121) involving the group of coefficients under consideration, one of them, b_y for example, can be assumed to be a function of the others c_y, $\ldots$, e_y, which are then the independent variables. As a result equation (123) gives rise to the following equations

$$\int_0^{Y''} \left(p_b \frac{\partial b_y}{\partial c_y} + p_c \right) \delta c_y \, dy = 0, \quad \ldots .$$

But the δc_y, ... variations are entirely arbitrary; consequently the preceding equations can only be satisfied if

$$p_b \frac{\partial b_y}{\partial c_y} + p_c = 0, \quad \ldots, \quad p_b \frac{\partial b_y}{\partial e_y} + p_e - 0. \qquad (124)$$

We can take the partial derivatives of b_y in equation (121) and substitute them in this system, which, if the group $b_y, c_y, \ldots, e_y$ consists of r coefficients, contains $r-1$ equations. If we add equation (121) to these equations we will have r equations, that is, as many as there are unknowns. Hence the problem is fully determined.

These equations belong to category (F) conditions (V, 85).

If instead of one equation (121) we had several of them, the reasoning would be similar and would lead to the same conclusions.

When the coefficients of fabrication are constant with respect to the variables $x, y, \ldots$, equation (123) becomes

$$0 = p_b \delta b_y + p_c \delta c_y + \ldots,$$

and equations (124) are derived directly from it.

Replacing the partial derivatives of b_y in (124) by their values, and setting

$$f_b = \frac{\partial f}{\partial b_y}, \quad \ldots, \quad f_e = \frac{\partial f}{\partial e_y}$$

as usual, we will have

$$p_b f_c - p_c f_b = 0, \quad \ldots, \quad p_b f_e - p_e f_b = 0. \qquad (125)$$

106. If the enterprise acts according to Type II, it will endeavor to maximize its profit, either by simply reducing the cost of production to a minimum, or, if it is able to take the variations in the sale of Y into account, by endeavoring to maximize the expression

$$A'' - A''' = \int_0^{Y''} p_y dY - \Pi_y.$$

As has been explained in §§ 84 and 85, the equation which is thereby obtained will replace

$$A'' = A''',$$

which no longer exists.

In this case, not only the prices, but also the coefficients of fabrication, can, under the integral sign, be assumed to be functions of the limits. The enterprise acts, not with the current values of the prices and of the coefficients of fabrication in mind, but the values which they will acquire at the point of equilibrium.

This manner of operating assumes that the enterprise not only enjoys a monopoly but also is able to arrange things so as to attain this maximum. But the last condition is very difficult, one may as well say impossible, to realize, at least in general, in the present state of our knowledge. On the other hand, entrepreneurs know fairly well, if not in theory, at least in practice, the possible offsets between the coefficients of production. Through more or less repeated attempts, they have, or acquire, a certain knowledge of the nature of equation (121) and use it to make their calculations and reduce the cost of production as far as possible. Operations according to Type I are routine and continually carried out by enterprises.

107. The question of the division of quantities among the enterprises remains to be examined (V, 78). If an enterprise produces q_z of Z and increases its production by δq_z, the cost of production of Z will vary by a certain amount, which we must set equal to zero if the enterprise wants to have a minimum cost of production. Thus we will have the equation

$$0 = \frac{\partial a_z}{\partial q_z} + p_b \frac{\partial b_z}{\partial q_z} + \dots . \qquad (126)$$

There will be other similar equations, one for each enterprise, and they will determine the division of production.

108. It is advisable to note a few very common errors on the subject of coefficients of production.

Certain writers assume that all coefficients of production are constant; others assume that all of them are variable. Both ways of regarding the phenomenon are equally erroneous; some of these coefficients are constant, or nearly constant, and some are variable.

The literary economists have a marked tendency to transform the properties of the relationships between things into properties of the things; that results from the difficulty which they have in dealing with problems where the mutual dependence of phenomena comes into play, because they ignore the appropriate methods.

They have not failed to apply their erroneous method to the theory of the coefficients of production. They have thought that certain relationships which allow obtaining maximum "utility" from production exist between the factors of production;[23] and dominated by that idea, they believed that they had found a law in political economy analogous to the law of definite proportions in chemistry.[24]

All that is incorrect and misleading. First it is necessary to get rid of such vague conceptions as *utility* of production, useful effect, and other similar ones, and replace them with precise notions, such as those of minimum cost of production or of maximum profit. Next it must be clearly understood that the determination of the coefficients of production is not only a technical operation, but that it depends on prices, the state of the market, and in general on *all* the circumstances of economic equilibrium. It is a system of equations which must be solved; it is not a set of isolated, independent equations.

Because the literary economists do not have clear ideas, not only about the solution of a system of simultaneous equations, but not

---

[23] One author gives this definition of what he calls the law of definite proportions: *"to obtain a given useful result, the elements of production must be in a fixed relationship,"* or in other words: *"a useful result is associated with a fixed qualitative and quantitative combination of the elements of production."*

What is meant by this "useful result" is not at all clear; besides, it is not a question of any "useful result" whatsoever; it is a maximum and minimum problem which must be solved.

The manner in which the proposition is stated leads one to believe that the "useful result" depends only on the relationship between the elements of production, whereas it depends on their prices, and the latter depend on all the other circumstances which determine equilibrium. It is, in short, on all these circumstances that the "useful result" depends.

[24] Time should never be wasted wrangling about words. Hence, if one wishes, that terminology may be accepted, provided it is clearly understood that the law of definite proportions in political economy has absolutely nothing to do with the law in chemistry which bears the same name.

In production the proportions of the components can vary by imperceptible degrees, which is not the case for the proportions in which chemical elements combine. In political economy these proportions do not depend only on the components of production, but also on all the other circumstances which determine economic equilibrium. Hence, given the elements of production, the proportions are by no means definite, whereas they are in chemistry; they are indefinite, and remain so, as long as all the other circumstances of economic equilibrium are not taken into account.

There are, to be sure, some goods which combine in fixed proportions, either in consumption—for example a blade of a knife and its handle—or in production—for example the four wheels of a car. For these goods it is appropriate to reserve the term complementary goods; and in speaking of these goods one can quite correctly allude to the law of definite proportions. But since, by hypothesis, the quantities in which these goods combine are *fixed*, these are not involved when one has in mind determining the *variable* proportions of certain goods in order to assure certain properties of production, for example, maximum quantities produced, or minimum cost of production, or maximum profits, etc.

even about the nature of such a problem, they make desperate efforts to substitute for this system of simultaneous equations a system of equations which can be solved individually, since this latter problem is the only one which the state of their knowledge permits them to handle.[25] This is what has misled them on the subject of the general theory of economic equilibrium and which continues to mislead them in this particular case.

Finally there is an essential matter which cannot be neglected in the determination of the coefficients of production; it is the consideration of the types according to which the enterprise acts. The determination made according to the type which we have called I is essentially different from one which is carried out according to the type which we have designated by II. If that is passed over in silence, one gets a completely false idea of the phenomenon.

109. **Properties of economic equilibrium.** The consumers of $X, Y, \ldots$ are also the suppliers of $A, B, \ldots$. When the quantities of goods increase by $dX, \ldots, da, \ldots$, the sum of the budgets of the consumers can be written

$$p_x dX + p_y dY + \ldots - da - p_b db - \ldots \qquad (127)$$

Let us integrate following a fixed path; we must get zero, since the receipts must balance the expenditures (among which is included saving). The path being fixed, all the variables $X, Y, \ldots$, $a, b, \ldots$ can be assumed to be functions of one of them, of X for example, and if we set

$$V = p_x + p_y \frac{dY}{dX} + \ldots - \frac{da}{dX} - p_b \frac{db}{dX} - \ldots, \qquad (128)$$

---

[25] After the publication of the Italian edition of this *Manuel*, there was in Italy a considerable output of pamphlets, review articles, and elementary essays seeking to demonstrate that the theory of economic equilibrium was, to say the least, useless, and that relations of cause and effect should be substituted for relations of mutual dependence. One writer, by a stroke of genius, even found a sure criterion for identifying these relationships of cause and effect. Is it not obvious that if one fact precedes another chronologically, the first is the cause, and the second the effect?

It is a long time now since some persons, applying this principle, said that since the chicken lays the eggs, the chicken is the cause and the egg is the effect; but other persons replied that since the chicken comes from the egg, the egg is the cause and the chicken is the effect. *Adhuc sub judice lis est.*

Truly Dame Nature could have shown a little more consideration and could have established relationships adapted to the intelligence and understanding of these writers; in that way she would have spared them the unpleasantness of constructing theories which resemble a little too much the reasoning of the fox who, in the fable, had lost his tail.

we will have

$$0 = \int_0^{X'} V dX. \tag{129}$$

Let us vary the quantities X, Y, ..., a, b, ...; these variations are not wholly independent; they must be consistent with the restrictions in the system. If we allow for these restrictions, there remain a certain number of variations which are independent. Assume that the variation of expression (129) is identically zero, without establishing *at the limits* additional relations between the variations which remain independent.

If we write out the variation of the integral following the usual method, we will find

$$0 = \left[\delta U \right]_0^{X'} + \delta R + \int_0^{X'} \delta T dX; \tag{130}$$

$$\left.\begin{aligned}
\delta U &= V dX + p_y \omega_y + \ldots - \omega_a - p_b \omega_b - \ldots, \\
\delta R &= \delta X' \int_0^{X'} \frac{\partial V}{\partial X'}\, dX, \\
\delta T &= \left(\frac{\partial V}{\partial Y} - \frac{dp_y}{dX} \right) \omega_y + \ldots + \frac{\partial V}{\partial a} \omega_a \\
&\quad + \left(\frac{\partial V}{\partial b} + \frac{dp_b}{dX} \right) \omega_b + \ldots, \\
\omega_y &= \delta Y - \frac{dY}{dX}\, \delta X, \ldots, \ \omega_b = \delta b - \frac{db}{dX}\, \delta X, \ldots
\end{aligned}\right\} \tag{131}$$

We know that in expression (130) the sum of the first two terms on the one hand, and the integral on the other hand, must vanish separately. As we have just said, we are assuming that the first part vanishes without establishing, at the limits, additional relations between the variations. As for the second part, it can vanish establishing, or not establishing, some relation between the variations.

110. If we work out the value of δU, we will have, at the point of equilibrium X'

$$\delta U = p_x \delta X' + p_y \delta Y' + \ldots - \delta A'' - p_b \delta B'' - \ldots, \tag{132}$$

the value being zero at the point zero.

But at the equilibrium point we have

$$\frac{1}{\varphi_{1a}}\delta\Phi_1 = p_x\delta x_1' + \ldots + \delta a_1' + p_b\delta b_1' + \ldots,$$

$$\frac{1}{\varphi_{2a}}\delta\Phi_2 = p_x\delta x_2' + \ldots + \delta a_2' + p_b\delta b_2' + \ldots,$$

. . . .

$$A_0' - A' = A'', \quad B_0' - B' = B'', \quad \ldots,$$

$$-\delta A' = \delta A'', \quad -\delta B' = \delta B'', \quad \ldots;$$

and consequently

$$\frac{1}{\varphi_{1a}}\delta\Phi_1 + \frac{1}{\varphi_{2a}}\delta\Phi_2 + \ldots = p_x\delta X' + p_y\delta Y' + \ldots$$
$$- \delta A'' - p_b\delta B'' - \ldots;$$

hence, at the point of equilibrium

$$\delta U = \frac{1}{\varphi_{1a}}\delta\Phi_1 + \frac{1}{\varphi_{2a}}\delta\Phi_2 + \ldots \qquad (133)$$

111. We have seen (§ 89) that by setting expression (133) equal to zero the points where maximum ophelimity is realized are characterized.

When the value of δU, at the equilibrium point, becomes zero without introducing additional relations between the variations which remain independent, the right hand side of expression (133) is also zero, and maximum ophelimity is attained, at least in regard to this type of variations.

If, on the other hand, δU, at the equilibrium point, becomes zero only by establishing additional relations between the variations $\delta X'$, $\delta Y'$, ..., it would, in order to make expression (133) positive or negative, be enough to assume that these relations are not satisfied; and we would no longer have maximum ophelimity.

It is a matter now of finding the conditions under which the last two parts of expression (130) vanish.

As for the integral, we know that it vanishes if expression (127) is integrable, that is, if the budget does not change whatever be the path followed to reach the point of equilibrium. This is the only case which we will study here.

δR remains to be considered. If we assume, as a restriction of the system, that at every point where production stops, the sum expended for the production of the goods is equal to the sum which is realized from their sale, the variation of the difference between these sums will have to be zero, and, reasoning as we did in § 92 to obtain equation (116), we will have

$$\delta P + \delta Q = 0 \qquad (134)$$

$$\delta P = \left(p_x^{\,0} - \pi_x^{\,0} + (p_y^{\,0} - \pi_y^{\,0})\left(\frac{dY}{dX}\right)^{0} + \dots \right) \delta X',$$

$$\delta Q = \delta X' \int_0^{x'} \left(\frac{dp_x}{dX'} - \frac{d\pi_x}{dX'} + \left(\frac{dp_y}{dX'} - \frac{d\pi_y}{dX'} \right) \frac{dY}{dX} + \dots \right) dX.$$

In this last expression, let us replace π_x, π_y, ... by their forms in (104); note that the quantities supplied to the enterprise must be equal to the quantities transformed, that is, we must have

$$da = a_x dX + a_y dY + \dots,$$
$$db = b_x dX + b_y dY + \dots,$$
$$\cdots \cdots \cdots \cdots \cdots \cdots \cdots \cdots \cdots$$

Thus we obtain

$$\delta Q = dR;$$

and as a result

$$\delta P + \delta R = 0 \qquad (135)$$

It follows from this that if at the point of economic equilibrium we have

$$\delta P = 0,$$

we will also have

$$\delta R = 0,$$

and maximum ophelimity will be realized at that point.

When the fabrications of different goods are independent, the equation $\delta P = 0$ yields equations (118) of § 92.

If the equation $\delta P = 0$ is not inconsistent with the other data given for the problem, it is realized through operations of the entrepreneurs following Type I. And in this case, the point of equilibrium at which we arrive possesses the property of assuring maximum ophelimity.

If the equation $\delta P = 0$ were inconsistent with the other data given for the problem, equilibrium could take place at a point where this equation does not hold, or at a point where total receipts of entrepreneurs is not equal to total expenditures for production (III, 100, 135); in these two cases, we will not have maximum ophelimity.

The single condition that the receipts of the enterprise be equal to the expenditures gives only equation (134), which is insufficient to assure maximum ophelimity. It is still necessary that δP be equal to zero; and this is an important result of the theory which we have just developed.

112. Next, variability of the coefficients of fabrication must be taken into account. Assume that among a group of the latter there exists the relation indicated by equation (121), the meaning of which has been explained in § 103. Thanks to this equation (121), any one of the coefficients, b_y for example, is a function of the other coefficients in the group. The variations of the latter remain arbitrary. The variables not included in the group remain constant. We will indicate these new variations by δ'.

Let us change the independent variable in V. Choosing Y, we will have

$$V = p_x \frac{dX}{dY} + p_y + \cdots - \frac{da}{dY} - p_b \frac{db}{dY} - \cdots$$

Let c_y vary; since the quantities $X, Y, \ldots$ do not vary, we will have

$$\left. \begin{aligned} \delta'V &= \delta'H - \delta'K; \\ \delta'H &= \frac{dX}{dY}\delta'p_x + \delta'p_y + \cdots - \frac{db}{dY}\delta'p_b \cdots; \\ \delta'K &= p_b\delta'\frac{db}{dY} + p_c\delta'\frac{dc}{dY}. \end{aligned} \right\} \quad (136)$$

Since the quantities of $A, B, \ldots$ supplied must be equal to the quantities transformed, we will have

$$\frac{db}{dY} = b_y, \quad \frac{dc}{dY} = c_y;$$

hence

$$\delta'K = p_b\delta'b_y + p_c\delta'c_y.$$

In addition, equation (121) gives

$$\delta'b_y = \frac{\partial b_y}{\partial c_y}\delta'c_y$$

hence we will have

$$\delta'K = \left(p_b \frac{\partial b_y}{\partial c_y} + p_c \right) \delta'c_y.$$

If the enterprise acts according to Type I, as has been explained in § 104, we will have

$$\delta'K = 0. \tag{137}$$

This equation follows immediately from equations (124).
In addition the equilibrium of the budgets requires that

$$\delta' \int_0^{Y'} V dY = 0;$$

and, reasoning as in § 109, we obtain:

$$-\delta'K + \int_0^{Y'} \delta'H dY = 0.$$

Consequently, by virtue of equation (137):

$$\int_0^{Y'} \delta'H dY = 0.$$

But this quantity is none other than the one which we designated by δR in § 109, where Y is now the independent variable; and since it is zero, a repetition of the reasoning of § 109 will show that we also have:

$$\delta'U = 0.$$

113. The variations which result from these operations also reduce expression (133) to zero. Indeed, since only b and c vary, we have

$$\delta'\Phi_1 = -\varphi_{1b}\delta'b_1 - \varphi_{1c}\delta'c_1, \quad \delta'\Phi_2 = -\varphi_{2b}\delta'b_2 - \varphi_{2c}\delta'c_2, \quad \dots$$

If we sum these equations, and use system (A) as usual, we will have

$$\left. \begin{array}{l} \delta'U = \dfrac{1}{\varphi_{1a}}\delta'\Phi_1 + \dfrac{1}{\varphi_{2a}}\delta'\Phi_2 + \cdots \\[2mm] = -p_b\delta'B' - p_c\delta'C' = p_b\delta'B'' - p_c\delta'C''. \end{array} \right\} \tag{138}$$

Since the quantities supplied must be equal to the quantities transformed, we will have

$$\delta'B'' = \int_0^{Y''} \delta'b_y dy, \quad \delta'C'' = \int_0^{Y''} \delta'c_y dy.$$

The prices p_b and p_c are independent of y; hence we can write

$$\delta'U = \int_0^{Y'} \left(p_b \frac{db_y}{dc_y} + p_c \right) \delta'c_y dy;$$

and, by virtue of equations (124), we will have:

$$\delta'U = 0.$$

Hence maximum ophelimity is realized.

114. In a similar way the operations indicated in § 107 with regard to the division of the quantities would be shown to be compatible with the equilibrium of the balance sheets on the one hand, and to insure maximum ophelimity on the other.

115. Accordingly we arrive at the conclusion that operations carried out according to Type I, when they are possible, lead, in the cases we have just examined, to equilibrium points where maximum ophelimity is realized.

This is one of the most important theorems of economic science, and the use of mathematics gives it a generality and a rigor which, for the moment at least, could not otherwise be attained.[26]

115b. Expression (133) can have a different form. At the equilibrium points we have $X' = X''$, $Y' = Y''$, $\ldots$,

$$\delta A'' = \delta A''' = a_x \delta X'' + a_y \delta Y'' + \ldots,$$

$$\delta B'' = \delta B''' = b_x \delta X'' + b_y \delta Y'' + \ldots,$$

$$\cdots\cdots\cdots\cdots\cdots\cdots\cdots\cdots\cdots\cdots\cdots$$

Consequently equation (133) becomes

$$\delta U = (p_x - a_x - p_b b_x - \ldots)\delta X''$$

$$+ (p_y - a_y - p_b b_y - \ldots)\delta Y''$$

$$+ \cdots\cdots\cdots\cdots\cdots\cdots\cdots$$

or

$$\delta U = (p_x^0 - \pi_x^0)\delta X'' + (p_y^0 - \pi_y^0)\delta Y'' + \cdots$$

In order for that expression to vanish without establishing additional relations between the $\delta X''$, $\delta Y''$, $\ldots$, it is necessary that

$$p_x^0 = \pi_x^0, \quad p_y^0 = \pi_y^0, \quad \ldots;$$

which we had already obtained in a particular case (§ 92).

---

[26] We gave some proofs of this theorem, for some particular cases, in our *Cours*, 1897. Then we gave more and more general proofs in the *Giornale degli economisti*, November 1903; in the Italian edition of the *Manuale*, 1906; and another one is given here.

These equations follow from the condition that the balance sheets must remain in equilibrium when X'', Y'', ... are varied.

They become identical with the condition of the equality of the costs of production and the selling prices, when the prices are constant and there is no reason to take general expenses into account.

Finally, it must not be forgotten that the integral in expression (130) must vanish. Moreover it is well known that it will vanish identically when expression (127) is integrable.

The conditions which we have just found, and which assure equilibrium of the balance sheets, must be added to the condition of operating according to Type I, in order to obtain maximum ophelimity.

116. If the individuals of the collectivity are reduced to a single one, the condition by which we have defined maximum ophelimity for a collectivity,

$$0 = \frac{1}{\varphi_{1a}} \delta\Phi_1 + \frac{1}{\varphi_{2a}} \delta\Phi_2 + \dots,$$

reduces to

$$\delta\Phi_1 = 0$$

In that case it coincides with the definition of maximum ophelimity for an individual.

It follows from this that the conditions we have just obtained for maximum ophelimity of a collectivity reduce, in the case of a single individual, to the conditions for maximum ophelimity for individual production.

If we use d to denote the variations along a path, or a certain kind of paths (§ 26; III, 74), when the individual acts according to Type I, the equilibrium condition is given by

$$d\Phi_1 = 0.$$

It may, or may not, coincide with the preceding condition for maximum ophelimity. The purpose of the study we have just made has been precisely to investigate the conditions under which such coincidence does take place.

It does not take place when the path is imposed by one person acting according to Type II. Nor does it take place in other cases, for example in the one where the prices must be constant while there are fixed expenses, for, in that case, the consumers may indeed act strictly according to Type I, but the producers cannot realize the two conditions for Type I at the same time, namely the equality of the cost of production and of the selling price, not only for the entire amount of the good, but also for the last portion produced when the point of equilibrium is reached.

117. In general, for consumers who behave according to Type I, we always have, at the point of equilibrium,

$$d\Phi_1 = 0, \quad d\Phi_2 = 0, \quad \ldots;$$

and consequently

$$0 = \frac{1}{\varphi_{1a}} d\Phi_1 + \frac{1}{\varphi_{2a}} d\Phi_2 + \ldots, \tag{139}$$

where the d's have reference to the paths which have led to the point of equilibrium.

Then at this point we may, or may not, have

$$0 = \frac{1}{\varphi_{1a}} \delta\Phi_1 + \frac{1}{\varphi_{2a}} \delta\Phi_2 + \ldots, \tag{140}$$

where the δ's indicate any variations which are consistent with the restrictions. Hence the δ's include the d's; but the d's do not include the δ's.

Accordingly there are two kinds of equilibrium points. For the one, only equation (139) is satisfied; these points do not give maximum ophelimity. For the other, equation (140), which includes equation (139), is satisfied. These points do give maximum ophelimity,

In certain cases, for example for exchange with constant prices (§ 119) according to Type I, these two kinds of points reduce to a single one, and maximum ophelimity is always realized.

118. According to the results we have just obtained, the condition

$$0 = \frac{1}{\varphi_{1a}} \delta\Phi_1 + \frac{1}{\varphi_{2a}} \delta\Phi_2 + \ldots,$$

is the one which must be fulfilled if production is organized according to the type designated as III (III, 49; VI, 53); this would especially be the type which a socialist organization of production would have to follow.

119. In the case of exchange with constant prices, and when operations are according to Type I, the proof of the conditions for maximum ophelimity becomes remarkably simple.[27]

---

[27] We gave this proof for the first time in the *Giornale degli economisti*, November 1903.

If we take the variations of equations (B) of § 63, we will have

$$\delta x_1 + p_y \delta y_1 + \ldots + (y_1 - y_{10}) \delta p_y + \ldots = 0,$$
$$\delta x_2 + p_y \delta y_2 + \ldots + (y_2 - y_{20}) \delta p_y + \ldots = 0, \quad\Big\} \quad (141)$$
$$\cdots\cdots\cdots\cdots\cdots\cdots\cdots\cdots\cdots\cdots\cdots\cdots$$

Summing and taking equations (C) into account, we will have

$$\delta X + p_y \delta Y + p_z \delta Z + \ldots = 0$$

$$X = x_1 + x_2 + \ldots, \quad Y = y_1 + y_2 + \ldots, \quad \ldots . \tag{142}$$

But the first equation is none other than

$$\frac{1}{\varphi_{1a}} \delta \Phi_1 + \frac{1}{\varphi_{2a}} \delta \Phi_2 + \ldots = 0;$$

hence the conditions for maximum ophelimity are always fulfilled in exchange when operations are according to Type I.

Similar proofs can be given in some analogous cases for production.

120. It may be useful to relate this proof to the general proof which we have just given.

The sum of equations (141) is composed of two parts. One is expressed by

$$(Y - Y_0)\delta p_y + (Z - Z_0)\delta p_z + \ldots$$
$$Y_0 = y_{10} + y_{20} + \ldots, \quad \ldots ;$$

it vanishes identically because

$$Y - Y_0 = 0, \quad Z - Z_0 = 0, \quad \ldots .$$

The other part is the one which gives equation (142). It is the part which corresponds to the δU in expression (130). As for the part under the integral sign, it vanishes identically because

$$\frac{\partial V}{\partial Y} = 0, \quad \frac{dp_y}{dX} = 0, \quad \ldots$$

121. Let us consider an equilibrium point for which equation (140),

$$0 = \frac{1}{\varphi_{1a}} \delta \Phi_1 + \frac{1}{\varphi_{2a}} \delta \Phi_2 + \ldots, \tag{140}$$

is satisfied.

Assume a position of equilibrium, which we will designate by I, and for which we have the quantities $x_1', y_1', \ldots, x_2', y_2', \ldots$. Let there be another position, which may, or may not, be one of equilibrium, and which we will designate by II. For that position, the quantities will be designated x_1'', y_1'', ..., x_2'', ... Intermediate values will be x_1, y_1, ..., x_2, ...

Assume that we pass from I to II, not via any paths whatsoever, but via paths defined by the following equations

$$\left.\begin{array}{l} x_1 = x_1' + \alpha_1 t, \quad y_1 = y_1' + \beta_1 t, \quad ..., \\ x_2 = x_2' + \alpha_2 t, \quad .... \end{array}\right\} \quad (143)$$

where α_1, β_1, ..., α_2, ... are constants and t is a new variable which is assumed positive. We can also set

$$p_y'' = p_y' + \sigma_y t, \quad ..., \quad a_x'' = a_x + \omega_x t, \quad ...,$$

but it is necessary to bear in mind that σ_y, ..., ω_x, ... are not constants. These are functions of the variables and they follow from the equations which the prices and the coefficients of production must satisfy.

It is obvious that when the ophelimities at both given points are independent of the paths followed, another path having the same extremities as the path we have just considered will give identical results.

For an individual the second variation of ophelimity is

$$\delta^2\Phi_1 = \varphi_{xx}\delta x_1^2 + \varphi_{yy}\delta y_1^2 + ... + 2\varphi_{xy}\delta x_1\delta y_1 + ...$$

Thanks to equations (143), this expression becomes

$$\frac{\delta^2\Phi_1}{\delta t^2} = \varphi_{xx}\alpha_1^2 + \varphi_{yy}\beta_1^2 + ... \quad (144)$$

$$+ 2\varphi_{xy}\alpha_1\beta_1 + 2\varphi_{xz}\alpha_1\gamma_1 + ...$$

122. Assume, for a moment, that this quantity is always negative. In that case $\delta\Phi_1$ will always decrease when t increases, that is, when there is a movement from position I to position II. We have seen (§ 89) that at the point where maximum ophelimity is attained, some of the variations $\delta\Phi_1$, $\delta\Phi_2$, ... of expression (112) must be positive, and some negative. If one moves from this point with the values of $\delta^2\Phi_1$, $\delta^2\Phi_2$, ... continually negative, the preceding negative variations will increase in absolute value, the ones which are positive will decrease in absolute value and can become negative; but none of those which are negative can decrease in absolute value and become positive. Consequently we cannot move from position I to position II, following the paths indicated, and increasing the

welfare of all the individuals of the collectivity. The ophelimity which certain individuals enjoy will increase but it will decrease for other individuals.

Hence this proposition holds true, not only for infinitely small displacements, but also for finite displacements.

If the movement takes place in the direction in which all the $\delta\Phi_1$, $\delta\Phi_2$, ... are zero, all the ophelimities will decrease. This is what happens when we follow the path along which equilibrium of the consumers takes place.

123. The proposition stated in the preceding paragraph is subject to three conditions: 1° Equation (140) must be satisfied. Hence point I must be one of the points of equilibrium for which maximum ophelimity is obtained. 2° Finite movements must be made along the paths (143). 3° Along these paths, the second variations of ophelimity must be negative for each individual.

124. It is now a question of determining when this last condition is satisfied.

With that in mind let us go back to the considerations which were set forth in §§ 47 and 48. For brevity indicate the ophelimities φ_{1x}, ..., simply by φ_x, ... For an individual we will have

$$\delta^2\Phi_1 = \varphi_{xx}dx_1{}^2 + \varphi_{yy}dy_1{}^2 + \ldots + 2\varphi_{xy}dx_1dy_1 + \ldots. \quad (145)$$

1° If φ_x depends only on x_1, φ_y on y_1, etc., we have

$$\varphi_{xx} < 0, \quad \ldots, \quad \varphi_{xy} = 0, \quad \ldots$$

and expression (145) is always negative.

2° If the goods have a dependence of the first kind we have in general

$$\varphi_{xx} < 0, \quad \ldots, \quad \varphi_{xy} > 0, \quad \ldots.$$

But in that case, as we have seen in § 48, we can consider a good which yields inequality (66).

$$\varphi_{xx} + \alpha^2\varphi_{yy} + \ldots + 2\alpha\beta\varphi_{yz} + \ldots < 0, \quad (66)$$

where α, β, ... are positive constants.

The left hand side contains two kinds of terms. The first kind is composed of the ophelimities φ_{xx}, φ_{yy}, ..., multiplied by the squares 1, α^2, β^2, ... These terms are always negative whatever be the signs of α, β, ... The second kind of term is of the type $2\alpha\beta\varphi_{yz}$. These terms are positive when α, β, ... are positive quantities; some of them are negative if α, β, ... do not all have the same sign. When these terms are all positive, the sum of the positive terms and the negative terms of the first kind is negative, by virtue of inequality (66). Hence it will still be so, for all the more reason, if some of these terms are negative. Consequently expression (66) is always negative, whatever be the quantities α, β, ... Hence expression (145) will also always be negative.

3° If the goods have a dependence of the second kind (IV, 14), we have

$$\varphi_{xx} < 0, \quad \dots, \quad \varphi_{xy} < 0, \quad \dots$$

and expression (145) can be positive or negative.

For example, assume that there are only two variables and that we have

$$\delta^2\Phi_1 = \varphi_{xx}dx^2 + \varphi_{yy}dy^2 + 2\varphi_{xy}dxdy. \tag{146}$$

We know that the quadratic form which corresponds to the right hand side of this equation is definite if we have

$$\varphi_{xx}\varphi_{yy} - \varphi_{xy}{}^2 > 0,$$

and in that case expression (146) will always be negative. But if we have

$$\varphi_{xx}\varphi_{yy} - \varphi_{xy}{}^2 < 0,$$

the form is indefinite, and expression (146) can change sign.

If for one category of these goods we could accept inequalities (58), it would follow, as has been explained in § 49, that expression (146) is always negative. But the existence of inequalities (58) cannot be accepted, at least not without additional observations.

125. It follows from this analysis that in the case where elementary ophelimities of goods are independent, and in the case of a dependence of the second kind, the second variation of the ophelimities is negative, and consequently the third condition indicated in § 123 is satisfied.

126. In the case of exchange, and if all the exchangers behave according to Type I, the first condition of § 123 is always satisfied. Consequently, in this case and for the goods which we have just indicated, we cannot move away from an equilibrium point, following paths (143), without decreasing all the ophelimities of the individuals of the collectivity, or decreasing some of them while others may increase.

127. It is easy to understand what is meant, from the economic point of view, by expression (112), that is

$$\frac{1}{\varphi_{1a}}\delta\Phi_1 + \frac{1}{\varphi_{2a}}\delta\Phi_2 + \frac{1}{\varphi_{3a}}\delta\Phi_3 + \ldots .$$

If we set

$$\delta s_1 = \frac{1}{\varphi_{1a}}\delta\Phi_1$$

we have

$$\delta\Phi_1 = \varphi_{1a}\delta s_1;$$

that means that the consumption of the quantities of goods δx_1, δy_1, ..., yields an increase in ophelimity (or index of ophelimity), to individual 1, equal to what this individual would obtain by consuming the quantity δs_1 of good A.

Hence the expressions δs_1, δs_2, ... represent all the quantities of the good A, and if we set

$$\delta S = \delta s_1 + \delta s_2 + \ldots ,$$

δS will be a quantity of good A, and we will have:

$$\delta S = \frac{1}{\varphi_{1a}}\delta\Phi_1 + \frac{1}{\varphi_{2a}}\delta\Phi_2 + \ldots . \qquad (147)$$

128. We could not add the quantities

$$\delta\Phi_1, \quad \delta\Phi_2, \quad \delta\Phi_3, \quad \ldots ,$$

because they are heterogeneous; but we can add the quantities

$$\frac{1}{\varphi_{1a}}\delta\Phi_1, \quad \frac{1}{\varphi_{2a}}\delta\Phi_2, \quad \ldots ,$$

because they are homogeneous since they are all quantities of the same good A.

129. Hence expression (112) or its equivalent (147) represents the quantity of good A which, if distributed to the members of the collectivity, would provide each of them the same pleasure which he obtains from the actual consumption of goods δx_1, δy_1, ..., δx_2, ...

It is obvious that as long as we have positive values for expression (147) while following a certain path, we can increase the welfare of all the members of the collectivity by distributing that positive quantity δS; and if the values of δS were negative, we could decrease the welfare of all the members of the collectivity. When the value of δS is zero, we no longer have any goods to distribute to the members of the collectivity. If we want to increase the share of some of them, we can only do so by decreasing the share of some others in such a way that the sum of all the shares remains constant, since

$$\delta S = 0.$$

That is why this equation can be used to define maximum ophelimity for a collectivity.

The economic meaning of expression (112) would enable us to write directly certain equations which we have obtained in other ways. But it was useful to show how these equations could be obtained by consideration of expression (112) alone, and how they are linked to the general theories of the calculus of variations.

130. Looking at the theories which we have just set forth as a whole will better bring out the general lines which may sometimes be obscured in the study of details.

Pure economics, just as rational mechanics, began by studying particular cases, and then progressed little by little to the general study of economic systems. The latter is, however, by far the most important study in economic science; we still have only the beginnings, and an enormous amount remains to be done in that field.

131. A model economic system may be formulated either as a theoretical type of concrete phenomena, or as an ideal type of phenomena such as some reformers would like to achieve.

This first operation should be kept quite distinct from all others. In the case of concrete phenomena the objective of the operation is to obtain a theoretical phenomenon resembling the concrete phenomena in view as much as possible. There is a certain latitude, and one representation does not necessarily exclude another. Thus, by a similar operation, the earth may be represented by a sphere, by an ellipsoid, or by a spheroid.

In the case of an ideal phenomenon, the difficulty in the operation lies in the fact that often the notions of reformers completely lack precision; but that difficulty is itself useful, in that it apprises us that these conceptions must be either clarified or rejected as inconsistent.

For example, there is no difficulty in constructing an ideal system in which distribution is based on the principle "to each person equal shares of certain things." But it is absolutely impossible to construct an ideal system based on the principle "to each according to his merits," or "to each according to his needs." Hence before continuing the reasoning, it is necessary to state precisely what those terms mean.

132. The restrictions in the system and the equations which express them summarize our preceding study.

If the number of equations is equal to the number of unknowns, the system is rigid; everything is determined by the restrictions, and we have nothing more to do (III, 24).

The most interesting cases are those in which the number of restriction equations is less than the number of unknowns. In that case the system is flexible, and there is occasion to seek its equilibrium position.

133. The economic system can be divided into several others, which are connected at certain points, generally at the equilibrium points.

For example, consider a system of equations

$$F_1(x_1, y_1, \ldots) = 0, \quad F_2(x_2, y_2, \ldots) = 0, \quad \ldots, \quad (148)$$

with θ unknowns undetermined; and a second system

$$G_1(\xi_1, \eta_1, \ldots) = 0, \quad G_2(\xi_2, \eta_2, \ldots) = 0, \quad \ldots, \quad (149)$$

with θ' unknowns undetermined. These systems can and should be considered independently of each other; but suppose they are joined by equations valid only at the point of equilibrium. At one of these points let

$$x_1{}^0, y_1{}^0, \ldots, x_2{}^0, \ldots, \xi_1{}^0, \eta_1{}^0, \ldots, \xi_2{}^0, \ldots, \quad (150)$$

be the values of the variables. Systems (148) and (149) are joined together by some equations at points such as given by the quantities (150); let them be

$$H_1 = 0, \quad H_2 = 0, \quad \ldots. \quad (151)$$

In preceding paragraphs we have considered the case in which system (148) is that of the restrictions in exchange, and system (149) is that of the restrictions in production. In that case, system (151) expresses the relations between the quantities produced and the quantities consumed (§ 82).

Those restrictions which separate the system under consideration from the rest of the economic world must be noted. We have generally assumed that our system received nothing from the outside; but systems which do receive certain things could be considered as well.

The condition that the system receive nothing from outside is expressed, in the case of exchange, by the condition that the total quantity of each good remains constant; and in the case of production, by the condition that the quantities produced result from the quantities transformed.

134. In order to know the equilibrium position of a system such as system (148), we must know how the movements permitted by the system take place.

Assume we can find certain functions

$$R_i(x_i, y_i, \ldots), \qquad i = 1, 2, 3, \ldots, \qquad (152)$$

which possess the following property.

Let x_i be one of the variables which can be considered as independent, and give it a positive increment dx_i. If a positive increment in R_i results from that, the movement will take place in the positive x_i direction; if a negative increment results, the movement will take place in the opposite direction. Consequently no movement takes place if this increment is zero.

Hence at the points of equilibrium, we must have:

$$\left(\frac{\partial R_i}{\partial x_i}\right)^0 = 0, \quad \left(\frac{\partial R_i}{\partial y_i}\right)^0 = 0, \quad \ldots, \qquad (153)$$

$$i = 1, 2, 3, \ldots .$$

The ( )^0 denote the values of

$$\frac{\partial R_i}{\partial x_i}, \quad \ldots,$$

when, after taking the derivative, the x_i^0, y_i^0, ... values corresponding to the equilibrium points are substituted for x_i, y_i, ...

We will have similar equations for every system similar to system (148), and they will complete the number of equations necessary to determine the unknowns at the equilibrium point.

135. These considerations are extremely general; they apply as well to mechanical systems as to economic systems.

For the latter there are several kinds of index functions such as functions (152). The easiest to find are those which relate to the budget, especially in the case of monopoly; and this explains why, among the first works on mathematical economics, we find those of Cournot dealing with precisely analogous cases.

Let x' be the quantity of a good which a monopolist sells at the point of equilibrium, and let $F(x^0)$ be his profit per unit. His total profit will be

$$x^0 F(x^0);$$

and that expression can be taken for one of the index functions (152) when we are considering a monopolist who tries to obtain the greatest possible money profit.

The case of free competition is analogous, but a little more complicated (§ 140).

136. It is more difficult to find index functions which determine the direction of movement of consumers. But if we assume, for a moment, that we can measure the pleasure which some particular consumption yields to a man, and if we assume that this man tries to obtain the greatest pleasure possible, the functions which measure the pleasure will be precisely the index functions (152) which we are seeking.

Thus was born pure economics, thanks to the labors of Jevons, Walras, Marshall, Edgeworth, Irving Fisher, etc.

137. The result which we have just obtained contains something superfluous, and it is precisely that something which makes the result questionable. Specifically, in order to obtain functions (152) there is no need to measure pleasure; it suffices to have functions which increase when the pleasure increases, and decreases when it decreases. Besides, no one has been able to succeed in demonstrating that pleasure can be measured—that it is a quantity. Especially has no one been able to find how to go about measuring it.

Our theory of the indices of ophelimity arose from these considerations.

138. We can take a step further toward generality of the theories. It is not necessary that functions (152) be indices of ophelimity, it is sufficient that they be indices of the direction in which we anticipate that the individual will move. For example, find indices of asceticism, substitute them in functions (152), and you will have the mathematical theory of asceticism. Find the index functions of altruism, and you will have the mathematical theory of altruism.

At the same time as we thereby make the meaning of equations (153) more general, we also make the meaning of the restriction equations (148) of § 133 more and more general. This progress from the particular to the general is certainly not peculiar to the theories of pure economics; we also find it in rational mechanics and in other sciences.

Consideration of the *second kind* of obstacles (III, 73 *et seq.*), and the distinction between the types of phenomena (III, 40, 89), give a high degree of generality to the theories of mathematical economics.

139. If index functions (152) do not explicitly contain the x_i^0, y_i^0, ..., then x_i^0, y_i^0, ... can be substituted in these functions for x_i, y_i, ..., and we will have

$$\left(\frac{\partial R_i}{\partial x_i}\right)^0 = \frac{\partial R_i^0}{\partial x_i^0}, \quad \ldots$$

But these equations would no longer hold if the R_i contained the x_i^0, y_i^0, ... explicitly. In that case the system

$$\frac{\partial R_i^0}{\partial x_i^0} = 0, \quad \frac{\partial R_i^0}{\partial y_i^0} = 0, \quad \ldots, \tag{154}$$

$$i = 1, 2, 3, \ldots$$

is different from system (153).

140. A very important distinction in political economy follows from this observation.

Certain index functions contain constants, which, when equilibrium is assumed to be established, are determined as functions of the quantities x_i^0, y_i^0, ... But from the exclusively mathematical point of view, we should distinguish two types of index functions (152): (I) The constants are left in these functions, and equation system (153) is obtained. (II) We substitute for the constants their values as functions of x_i^0, y_i^0, ..., and equation system (154) is obtained.

These types are the same as those we already distinguished using the economic point of view (III, 39, *et seq.*) and (Appendix, §§ 35, 63, 67, 83, etc.).

More generally, Type I will correspond to all the cases in which the individual to whom the index function refers is not able, or does not desire, to modify the values of certain constants in the index function *directly*. Type II corresponds to the case where he has that power and uses it.

This division of economic phenomena, which we pointed out in 1896 in our *Cours*,[28] has become much more general in our more recent works.

141. Assume that, by selling dx of a good, an individual makes a profit

$$f(x)\,dx.$$

after he has sold the quantity x^0, his profit will be

$$\int_0^{x^0} f(x)\,dx. \tag{155}$$

Whether it is a case of free competition or of monopoly, every individual tries to obtain the greatest profit possible; hence in both cases function (155) can be regarded as one of the index functions (152) which will indicate the direction in which the individual tends to move. But in the case of free competition, the individual cannot vary the constants which will be expressed in terms of x^0, when equilibrium is established. Consequently, in taking the derivative of equation (155) we will obtain

$$f(x^0) = 0 \tag{156}$$

for one of equations (153).

In the case of monopoly, the individual has the power to vary these constants, hence it is necessary to substitute their values in terms of x^0 in expression (155), and then differentiate. We will thus obtain

$$f(x^0) + \int_0^{x^0} \frac{\partial f}{\partial x^0}\,dx = 0, \tag{157}$$

for one of equations (154).

The profit may be expressed in ophelimity (indices of ophelimity), or in money.

---

[28] *Cours*, § 59, note 1 and *passim*. After having given the equation of the budget

$$r_a + p_b r_b + p_c r_c + \ldots = 0$$

we add: "... if the exchanger is concerned only with the quantities of economic goods which he possesses, without attempting by any maneuvers to influence the prices, which is the case of free competition, it must be assumed that only the quantities r_b, r_c, ... are variable, and in the differentiation p_b, p_c, ... must be treated as constants. If, on the other hand, the objective of the exchanger is to regulate his demand and his supply in such a way as to make the prices vary, it will be necessary to consider as variables not only r_b, r_c, ..., but also p_b, p_c, ..."

Assume an operation according to the free competition type. If, for an exchanger, the profit is expressed in ophelimity, equation (156) gives equations (A) of §80. If, for an entrepreneur, the profit is expressed in money, equation (156) gives equation (116) of §92.

There are analogous considerations for equation (157), in the case of monopoly.

142. Next we need to consider the second derivatives of the index functions where the first derivatives are zero. This study is interesting for distinguishing the different kinds of equilibrium. It is a field of research which has as yet been very little explored.

143. Consideration of the restrictions and of the index functions finally gives us a certain system of equations

$$(\Omega)$$

which determines equilibrium.

What usefulness is there in having determined this theoretical equilibrium in this way? First of all it is useful for knowing whether the conditions set up are compatible with each other, whether, the number of the equations being equal to the number of the unknowns, equilibrium is fully determined, and finally, whether equilibrium is, or is not, possible under the assumed conditions. Moreover, we learn to distinguish points of stable equilibrium from points of unstable equilibrium, and we find some equilibria are stable in certain directions and unstable in others. All these considerations give rise to numerous and interesting studies.

Next, the equations (Ω) enable us to study the effects of variations in the constants in these equations and their economic significance. There is still a very extensive class of investigations which has been hardly touched.

Progress along these lines probably depends principally on the practical knowledge which we can acquire about the nature and values of the parameters in the index functions. It is perhaps an indirect route which will give us these notions. We can make certain hypotheses and then see if they give results which correspond to reality (§§45, 57, and 101).

It must be noted that the investigations of economic equilibrium made by the literary economists necessarily assume the existence of equations (Ω); the difference between these investigations and those of pure economics lies principally in the fact that the former are made blindly and by extremely imperfect and very often faulty methods, whereas the latter are made with a purpose in mind.

Finally, we must again refer to equations (Ω) in connection with all study of the properties of economic equilibrium.

144. One of these properties is very important; it is the one which relates to maximum ophelimity for a collectivity (§ 89).

We must investigate whether a certain position of equilibrium is, or is not, a position of maximum ophelimity as well. Economic antagonisms arise from the fact that it is to the interest of certain persons to establish equilibrium at a point which does not correspond to a point of maximum ophelimity for the entire collectivity. The most common case is that of monopoly; but there is an infinity of others, hardly glimpsed by the literary economists; and only the theories of pure economics can give us precise ideas about them.

The theory of the maximum ophelimity for a collectivity, outlined in our *Cours*, has been expanded considerably in the different works we have published since the *Cours*. Thereby it has become much more general.

145. For a collectivity, maximum ophelimity is determined by the equation:

$$0 = \frac{1}{\varphi_{1a}}\delta\Phi_1 + \frac{1}{\varphi_{2a}}\delta\Phi_2 + \ldots, \tag{158}$$

which will also be written:

$$\delta U = 0.$$

The values of the variables refer to the points of equilibrium.

If we assume that the quantities a_1', a_2', a_3', ... are constants, that is, that $\delta a_1'$, $\delta a_2'$, ... are zero and that there are no other restrictions, the variations $\delta x_1'$, $\delta y_1'$, ..., $\delta x_2'$, ... will be independent and equation (158) will entail:

$$\varphi_{1x}(x_1') = 0, \quad \varphi_{1y}(y_1') = 0, \quad \ldots$$

$$\varphi_{2x}(x_2') = 0, \quad \varphi_{2y}(y_2') = 0, \quad \ldots$$

$$\ldots \ldots \ldots \ldots \ldots \ldots \ldots \ldots \ldots \ldots$$

This is the case where every one of the members of the collectivity possesses sufficient amounts of all the goods X, Y, ... so as to reach satiety, plus a quantity of A which remains constant. This obviously is a position of maximum ophelimity.

146. When the consumers operate according to Type I, equation (158) becomes:

$$0 = p_x\delta X' + p_y\delta Y' + \ldots - \delta A'' - p_b\delta B'' - \ldots \tag{159}$$

as has been seen in § 110.

In the case of exchange the system has the restriction that the values of X', Y', ..., A'', ... must remain constant.

Hence their variations are equal to zero, and equation (159) is always satisfied.

147. A restriction which is generally imposed on economic systems is that the sum of all the budgets must be zero, which means that the economic system under consideration receives nothing from outside and provides nothing to the outside.

When the prices are variable, the sum total of the budgets is given by equation (129) of § 109. Not only is it zero for the point of equilibrium, but its variation must also be zero since with the δ's we pass from a point where the sum is zero to another point where it is likewise zero.

As has been seen in § 109, the variation of this sum total of the budgets consists of three parts, of which the last is an integral which equals zero when the value of this sum does not depend on the path followed to arrive at the point of equilibrium, which we will assume to be the case in the following. The first two parts are:

$$\delta U + \delta R$$

and we have:

$$\delta R = \delta X' \int_0^{X'} \left(\frac{dp_x}{dX'} + \frac{dp_y}{dX'} \frac{dY}{dX} + \dots \right) dX. \qquad (160)$$

In the case of exchange, and when there is Type I behavior, the prices p_x, p_y, ... must, under the integral sign, be assumed to be independent of the limit X'; consequently:

$$\delta R = 0$$

We have already seen that $\delta U = 0$, consequently the condition imposed by the restrictions given by the budgets is satisfied.

148. The case of production is a little more complicated.

The restriction involving the budgets of the consumers still exists, that is, in assuming, as always, that the integral of formula (130) vanishes, we must have:

$$0 = \delta U + \delta R \qquad (161)$$

but since the quantities X', Y', ..., A'', B'', ... are no longer constant, we do not know whether the two parts of the right hand side of equation (161) vanish separately.

These are the relationships between the quantities consumed or provided by the consumers, X', Y', ..., and A'', B'', ..., and the quantities produced, or transformed, by the enterprise, X'', Y'', ..., and A''', B''', ..., which give us one of the main restrictions relating consumption and production (§ 82).

Exactly the same thing is expressed by the following two conditions, which thus provide identical restrictions.

(α) The total quantities sold to the consumers are equal to the total quantities produced, and the total quantities supplied by the consumers are equal to the total quantities transformed:

$$X' = X'', \quad Y' = Y'', \quad ..., \quad A'' = A''', \quad ... \qquad (162)$$

The infinitesimal quantities which are produced, at the point of equilibrium, following the production path, are equal to the infinitesimal quantities consumed, at that point, along the consumption path:

$$dX' = dX'', \quad dY' = dY'', \quad ... \qquad (163)$$

(β) The total receipts from the sale of the goods by the enterprise is equal to the total cost of production:

$$\int_0^{X'}(p_x - \pi_x)\,dX = 0, \quad \int_0^{Y'}(p_y - \pi_y)\,dY = 0, \quad ... \qquad (164)$$

The receipts from the sale of the last portion of the good is equal to the cost of production of that portion

$$p_x^0 - \pi_x^0 = 0, \quad p_y^0 - \pi_y^0 = 0, \quad ... \qquad (165)$$

149. These restrictions are those of Type I for the enterprise. When they are satisfied, maximum ophelimity is attained.

The proof is given in two ways, depending upon whether the restrictions are expressed in form (α) or form (β).

Both these forms were used in § 91. Form (β) was used in § 115. In any case, it is shown that:

$$\delta R = 0 \qquad (166)$$

and as a result equation (161) gives:

$$\delta U = 0, \qquad (167)$$

which shows that maximum ophelimity is realized.

Similarly for the variation of the coefficients of fabrication, equation (166) is again established, and, by means of equation (161), we again find equation (167). This procedure is used in all analogous cases.

150. Equations (162) may not be compatible with equations (163); or, what amounts to the same thing, equations (164) may not be compatible with equations (165). In that case the enterprise cannot act strictly according to Type I. Depending upon the circumstances, one or the other of the incompatible equation systems will not be satisfied (§ 111). In that case maximum ophelimity is not realized.

151. After having considered the infinitesimal variations of ophelimity (index of ophelimity), we should consider the finite variations when we pass from one point to another, with certain restrictions. The study of the second variation of ophelimity can be used, in certain cases (§§ 121 to 126), to demonstrate that, under certain conditions, ophelimity cannot increase for all the persons making up the collectivity when we move a finite distance away from the point of equilibrium.

Obviously this is only a very particular case of a type of research as important as it is varied.

152. When, for an individual, there are several points of equilibrium at each of which maximum ophelimity is realized, we must look for the *maximum maximorum*. We can also investigate the differences in the ophelimities (indices of ophelimity) at different points at which maximum ophelimity may not be realized (§ 100). These investigations are of very great interest from the economic point of view; they can give us somewhat more precise ideas about phenomena which at present we perceive only dimly.

TRANSLATOR'S NOTES

Chapter III, [1], (§ 83, ¶ 1): In Chapters III through VI Pareto consistently uses the word *inclinaison* (inclination or slope)—which usually is translated slope here—rather than *pente* (slope). Of course, where prices are constant from one exchange to another, it would be quite satisfactory to say that a change in price is represented by a change in the inclination (*inclinaison*) of the path travelled. But certainly (III, § 154), the price of B in terms of A is not equal to the *inclination* of the straight line *dcm* with respect to the *o*B axis; rather, it is equal to the *slope* with respect to the *o*B axis. (With regard to the sign of the slope, see the succeeding paragraphs of this note.) Similarly, the (average) cost of production (III, § 194) must be the slope, not the inclination, and in IV, §§ 32 and 60, the elementary ophelimity must be the slope, not the inclination.

Pareto appears to have neglected to bother with signs, and, often perhaps, that is all there is to it. On the other hand, he does discuss the "essentially positive" character of prices (III, § 173); and he is explicit about being interested in acute angles (which, of course, have positive tangents) such as *oca*, *oma'*, . . . in Figure 25 and III, § 173. Furthermore, in IV, § 63, where the slope (*inclinaison*) of a linear consumer indifference line, having the usual slope, is identified in effect as the trade-off between two goods between two points on the line, Pareto considers only the positive character of the two quantities.

Sometimes the reference axis is given in the reverse of the usual direction, which is consistent with the approach pointed out in the preceding paragraph, for example *mo*, rather than *om*, in III, § 184, VI, § 4, and other cases. But this is far from a consistent practice.

Chapter III, [2], (§ 97, ¶ 1): In Figure 12 the alternative paths given by a series of straight lines starting from *m* would not yield the points of tangency, *c, c', c", c'''*, and the locus of these and analogous points shown in that figure. Nevertheless, Figure 12 is reproduced as found in the French text without change.

Chapter III, [3], (§ 122, ¶ 1): Many writers have observed that Pareto was sometimes careless in his exposition. The discussion in §§ 121

493

and 122 is one of which it is especially difficult to make sense. Indeed, Knut Wicksell's opinion was that it made none. See "Vilfredo Pareto's *Manuel d'economie politique*" in Wicksell's *Selected Papers on Economic Theory* (Erik Lindahl, ed.), page 173.

Chapter III, [4], (§ 154, ¶ 1): See note [1] to Chapter III.

Chapter VI, [1], (§ 8, ¶ 1): Pareto uses the term *simple coût*, translated "direct cost" here. See § 58 where he expresses his point more fully.

Chapter VI, [2], (§ 42, ¶ 2): Figure 51 has been redrawn to the following extent. The segment of *all'e* to the left of *l'* did not rise to a point of tangency at *e* and then curve down from the line *mu* as shown here. Rather, in the French text, it rose in an approximately linear fashion toward *t*, passing through *mu* at *e*. The result was then that the segment of the indifference curve *t* (shown here) to the left of *e* appeared to be merely a linear extension of the line *all'e*.

Appendix, [1], (§ 47, ¶ 3): The French text has the inequality signs reversed in equations (63) and (64). For consistency with the definitions they should be as given here.

Appendix, [2], (§ 47, ¶ 5): In the French text the equation numbers (64) and (65) were erroneously used twice. The second use is distinguished here by asterisks, but otherwise the same equation numbering is maintained.

Appendix, [3], (§ 49, ¶ 2): In the inequality given in this paragraph, the minus sign preceding $\varphi_{yy} \varphi_x{}^2$ of the second term left hand side has been changed to a plus sign for consistency with the description that the inequality is the result of multiplying together the two expressions in inequalities (58).

Appendix, [4], (§ 92b, ¶ 1): The notation in this section is puzzling. It is reproduced here exactly as in the French text.

ALPHABETICAL INDEX

The roman numerals refer to chapters, the arabic numerals refer to sections. Boldface characters indicate the main sections on a subject. [Erroneous section references have been removed and minor corrections made. Otherwise this index is the one given in the French text.—A.S.]

ABSTRACTION: Capital, V, 33. Its meaning in pure economics, III, 1 to 5. Faculty for abstraction varies according to the individual, II, 47. The enterprise, V, 4, 62, 65, 66. Types of abstraction, indispensable for constructing theories, I, 20, 21, **22**, 23 to 27; III, 37, 39 to 45, 110; IV, 31. Its use for putting some order into human actions, II, 2, **3**.

ACTIONS, LOGICAL AND NON-LOGICAL: II, **2**, **3**, 4, 5, **18**, 22 to 26, 49 to 51, 91 to 93, 101, 108. Men believe relations logical which are not, II, **4**, 9, 22, 108; VIII, 24, 25; IX, 20, 28, 29, 38, 62, 66, 79. Saving, VIII, 11.

AMORTIZATION: V, **30 to 32**; VIII, **11**.

APPROXIMATIONS, SUCCESSIVE: I, 13, **14**.

BANKS: VIII, 46 to 50.

BIMETALLISM: VIII, 41.

BUDGET OF THE ENTERPRISE: V, 7, 24, **29**, **43** to 47, 59 to 61, 66 to 69, 87. Appendix, 77 to 79.

BUDGET OF THE INDIVIDUAL: III, **175**, 200, 204. Appendix, 38.

BUDGET OF THE PRODUCER: III, 176, 205.

CAPITAL: V, **17** to 20, **21**, 22 to 32, 45; VIII, 1 to 8, 10, 25, 26 to 28.

CAPITAL, LAND: VIII, **1** to 7.

CAPITAL, MOBILE: VIII, 8.

CAUSE OF PRICE AND VALUE: does not exist, III, 225 to 227; V, 42.

CIRCULATION OF ARISTOCRACIES OR OF ELITES: II, 103 to 107; VII, **19** to 21, 55, 101, 109 to 114, 116; IX, 30 to 35.

CIRCULATION, ECONOMIC: V, 6; VI, **92**.

CLASS STRUGGLE: II, 103 to 109, 113 to 123; IX, 23 to 27, 29 to 36.

COEFFICIENTS OF PRODUCTION: V, **35**; Appendix, 78. How ———— are determined, V, 16, 37, 82 to 86; VI, 49, 51, 55, 63; Appendix, 101 to 106. Variability of ————, V, 15, **70** to 77, 82 to 86.

COLLECTIVIST ORGANIZATION: III, 49, 50, 165, 166; V, 12; VI, 48, **52** to 61; Appendix, 89.

COMPARATIVE COSTS, RICARDO'S THEORY OF: IX, 42 to 52.

COMPETITION: III, **46, 82,** 86, 105, 116 to 127, 137 to 151, **162,** 163, 170, 196 to 216, **208;** V, **73;** VI, 6, 10, 13, 49 to 51; VIII, 2; Appendix, 34, 83. Complete and incomplete, III, 100, 101, 105, **150.**

CONTRACTS FOR PRODUCTON, COLLECTIVE: IX, 16.

CORRELATION: VII, 48.

COST OF PRODUCTION: III, **177** to 179, 221, 224; V, 78 to 80, 94; Appendix, 79. Equality of ———— and selling price, III, 176, **205,** 221; V, 66 to 69, 88; Appendix, 83. Cost of production increasing with quantity, III, 102, **105;** VI, 3, 12 to 14, 23. *Idem* decreasing, III, 102, 103; VI, 3, 4, 10, 11, 23, 24.

COST OF REPRODUCTION: III, 221.

CURVE OF ERRORS: VII, 6.

CRISES, ECONOMIC: VII, 46, 47; IX, **73 to 88.**

DEPENDENCE BETWEEN GOODS: IV, 8 to 24, 35 to 42, 49, 50, 55 to 57; Appendix, 46.

DISCOUNT AND BANKS OF ISSUE: VIII, 49, 50.

DISCOVERY: I, 51.

DISTRIBUTION OF INCOME: VII, 11 to 31. Decrease in income inequality, VII, **24, 25.**

DIVERGENCE FROM MEAN TYPE: VII, 3 to 10.

DIVISION OF LABOR: V, 2, 3.

DYNAMICS, ECONOMIC: III, 7, 8.

ECONOMICS: Objectives of the study of ————, I, 1; III, 1 to 5, **14.** Morality should be taken into account, I, **24, 25, 26.** Its evolution, III, 29 to 31, 157, 189, 219 to 228; IV, 11; V, 93; VI, 15, 97, 101; VII, 69, 89 to 94; VIII, 21 to 27; IX, 20 to 22.

ECONOMICS, PURE: III, 3 to 7, 22, **228;** VI, 61; IX, 38.

ENTREPRENEUR, ENTERPRISE: V, 2, 4 to 7, 62 to 69; VIII, 50. The entrepreneur's capital, V, 61. Incorrect interpretation of competition among entrepreneurs, VI, 93 to 96; IX, 84. Goal of the enterprise, V, 8 to 12. Paths followed by the enterprise, V, 13 to 16.

EQUILIBRIUM, ECONOMIC: III, 14, 19, **22** to 24, **27,** 90 to 228; VI, 26 to 31; Appendix 22, 23. Stable and unstable, III, **123, 124,** 125, 126, 133, 215, 216. Successive positions of equilibrium, V, 89.

EVOLUTION: As the source of moral precepts, I, 44. Of morality, II, 20.

EXCESS CONSUMPTION: IX, 82 to 84.

EXCESS PRODUCTION: VI, 93 to 96; IX, 83, 84.

EXCHANGE: III, 40 to 51, 69, **70,** 82, 83, **97** to 99; VI, 8. Equilibrium of ————, III, 109 to 111, **112,** 114 to 119, **120,** 121 to 133, **196** to **204,** 208; VI, 34 to 38; Appendix, 63 to 67.

FACTORS OF PRODUCTION: V, 36.

FEMINISM: VII, 54.

FICTIONS, LEGAL: II, 12.

FINAL DEGREE OF UTILITY: III, 228.

FOREIGN EXCHANGE: VIII, **31** to **34**, 35 to 39.

FREE TRADE AND PROTECTION: IX, 42 to 72.

GENERATIVE FORCE: restrained by obstacles, VII, **62** to 67, 71 to 80.

GOLD POINT: VIII, 33, 34.

GOODS, COMPLEMENTARY: IV, 9, 12; Appendix, 49.

GOODS, ECONOMIC: III, 16.

GOODS, MATERIAL AND IMMATERIAL: V, 34.

GRESHAM'S LAW: VIII, 40.

GUARANTY OF BANK NOTES: VIII, 47.

HETEROGENIETY, SOCIAL: II, 102, 109, **110**; VII, **2** to 21.

HIERARCHIES, SOCIAL: II, 102; VII, **97**, 98, 103.

HIERARCHY OF GOODS: IV, **19**, 51, 66.

HILL OF PLEASURE OR OF OPHELIMITY: III, **58**, 59, 60, 127, 134; IV, **69**, 70; Appendix, 3.

HILL OF PROFIT: III, **81**, 84.

HISTORY OF ECONOMIC PHENOMENA: I, 33.

INCOME FROM CAPITAL: V, **48** to 60, 66 to 69, 91, 92; VII, 117; VIII, 11, 48, 49, 50. Gross income, V, **49**, 50. Net income, V, **52** to 58, 66 to 69, **88**, 90; VI, 50, 51, 54. Income from savings, VIII, 11 to 25. Alleged decrease in net income from capital, VIII, 26 to 28.

INDICES OF OPHELIMITY: III, 35, 36, **55**, 97; Appendix, 46 to 50.

INDICES OF PRODUCER'S REVENUE: III, **75**, 76, 78.

INDIFFERENCE LINES, PRODUCER'S: III, **76**, 77, 100, 103 to 105.

INDIFFERENCE LINES OF OBSTACLES: III, **75** to 81, 100 to 105, 114; V, 63 to 65; VI, 2 to 4.

INDIFFERENCE LINES OF TASTES: III, 52, 53, **54**, 55 to 59, 77, 80, 97; IV, 27, 43, 65, 67; VI, 19; Appendix, 2 to 4.

INSURANCE: V **30** to **32**; VIII, 11, 12.

INTERDEPENDENCE: See Mutual dependence.

INTERNATIONAL TRADE: VI, **65** to 69; IX, **39** to 72.

INTUITION: I, 45.

IRON LAW: VII, 58.

LAW OF SUPPLY AND DEMAND: III, 182 to 193, **222**, 223; Appendix, 52 to 55.

LAWS, SCIENTIFIC: See uniformities.

LINE OF COMPLETE TRANSFORMATIONS: III, **75**, 79, 108, 133, 141 to 151; V, 63, 65; VI, 3, 7, 10, 40, 43, 48, 58, 59.

LINE OF MAXIMUM PROFIT: III, **105**, 107, 113, 135 to 140, 147 to 150; VI, 12 to 25.

MALTHUS, HIS THEORY: VII, 89 to 96.

MARKETS, THEORY OF: IX, 41.

MAXIMUM COLLECTIVE UTILITY: VI, **33**, 34, 37, 38, 44, 53 to 61; Appendix, 89, 117. For segments of collectivities, VI, 62 to 64.

MAXIMUM INDIVIDUAL OPHELIMITY: III, 130 to 134; VI, 9, 41 to 48; IX, 6.

METHOD: I, **35**, 36; II, 1; III, **3**, 13, 189, 217, 218.

MONEY: V, 27, 46, 86, 87; VII, 112; VIII, **29**, 30. It is a small part of the wealth of a nation, VIII, 43, 44. Substitutes for — — — —, VIII, 42. Quantity theory, VI, 71 to 79.

MONEY, PURCHASNG POWER OF: III, 222.

MONOPOLY: III, 47, 48, 128 to 132, 151, **161**, 162, 164; V, 64, 83; VI, 10; IX, 53, 54; Appendix, 68 to 76b.

MORALS AND MORES: II, **18** to 20, 23 to 40.

MORTALITY: VII, 38 to 42, 49.

MOVEMENTS, REAL: II, 97; III, **22**.

MOVEMENTS, VIRTUAL: II, 97; III, **22**.

MUTABILITY, SOCIAL: VII, 104, 106 to 115.

MUTUAL DEPENDENCE BETWEEN PHENOMENA: III, 3, 219, 224, 225 to 228; V, 6; VII, 55.

NATALITY: VII, 38 to 42, 53.

NUPTIALITY: VII, 38 to 40, 45, 47, 49.

OBSTACLES: Chapter V. III, 14, 15, 19, 23, 25, 27, 37, **68** to 74, 106, 118, 147, 202. First kind of — — — —, III, 68, **69** to 72. Second kind of — — — — III, 68, 73, 74, 167, **168**.

OPHELIMITY: III, 30 **32** to 36, 58, 78, 196.

PAPER MONEY: VI: 72, 74, 76.

PATHS: III, **60** to 63, 74 to 91, 94 to 98, 117 to 120, 212; Appendix, 26, 27. Rectilinear paths, III, 96, 108, 133, **172**; Appendix, 38.

PHENOMENON, CONCRETE: Chapter IX. Divergence from the real phenomenon, III, 110; V, 27 to 31; IX, 2. Science is analytic, practice is synthetic, I, **26** to 30. A phenomenon cannot be known in complete detail, I, 10. It cannot be known by studying an *a priori* notion of it, I, **15** to 17. Theories about phenomena are always incomplete and only approximative, I, **11**, **19**, 20.

POLITICAL ECONOMY: See Economics.

PRICE: III, 152, **153** to 155, 158 to 174; VI, 7 to 9, 39 to 48, 54; Appendix, 37, 39. Relations between equilibrium and prices of the factors of production, VI, 80 to 91. High and low prices, VI, 90, 91; IX, **23**, 24.

PRIVATE PROPERTY: VI, 60, 61; VII, 106, **115**; VIII, 4 to 7.

PRODUCTION: III, 71, 78, 79, 82, 84, 100 to 105, 135 to 151, 205 to 216; V, 81 to 97; VI, 39 to 51, 97 to 101; IX, 8, 37, 38. Equilibrium of production, V, 81 to 87, 96; VI, 39 to 61; Appendix, 77, 82, 84, 88. Division of production, V, 78 to 80; Appendix, 107. Production of capital, V, 88, 89.

PRODUCTION OF HUMAN CAPITAL: VII, 57 to 61.

RARETÉ: III, 227.

RATE OF EXCHANGE: III, 226.

REASONING BY ELIMINATION: I, 18.

REDUCTION OF DEBT: VII, 112, 113, 117.

RELATIONS BETWEEN ECONOMIC CONDITIONS AND POPU-
LATION: VII, 32 to 56.

RELATIONS, SUBJECTIVE AND OBJECTIVE: II, **6**, 7 to 17.
Theories of two kinds of actions are essentially different, II, 18.

RENT: V, 62, 63, 69, **90** to 97; VI, 59; VIII, 3, 8; IX, 56, 63.

RESTRICTIONS ON ECONOMIC ACTIVITY: IX, 37, 38.

RETAIL TRADE: IX, 3 to 6.

RHYTHM: II, 55, 56, 57, 58; VII, 55; IX, 73, 74, **75**.

SAVINGS: VIII, 9 to 21. Capital savings, VIII, 10.

SCIENCE: Pure science, III, 4, 5. No scientific proposition is true
"absolutely," "within the limits of known experience" must always be
understood, I, 36. It is concerned only with experimental propositions,
I, 36, **37**, 38. A precept does not belong to science, I, 39. Science has
nothing in common with faith, I, 36, **41**, 101. Confusion between
science and faith, I, **42**, 43 to 48. Conflict between the conditions for
actions and those for knowledge, II, 101.

SELECTION: II, 30; VII, 50, 98, **99**, 104 to 115; IX, 19, 57.

SENSATIONS: of an individual, comparisons between them or with
those of other individuals, III, **11**, **12**, 16, 17.

SENTIMENTS, MORAL AND RELIGIOUS: II, 21, 22, 41 to 74,
81 to 87, 91, 110 to 123.

SERVICES OF CAPITAL: V, **33**, **35**, 45, 50, 52.

SOCIETY, HUMAN, IN GENERAL: VII, 97 to 101.

SOCIOLOGY: II, 75 to 80, 84.

SPECULATION: III, 171.

SPOLIATION: IX, 17 to 22, 25 to 27, 31 to 36.

STABILITY: VII, 97, 98, 103, **105**, 106, 109, 114, 115.

STANDARD OF LIFE: VII, 57.

STATICS, ECONOMIC: III, 7, 8, **9**.

SUBJECTIVE VIEW: II, **6** to 17, 91 to 96, 101, 104 to 109, 113 to
123; IX, 20, 22. ———— of variations in prices, VI, 90; IX, 23 to 27.
———— of population phenomena, VII, **81** to 88, **116**, 117. ————
of savings phenomena, VIII, 22 to 25. ———— of production phenomena, IX, 9, 12, 61, 62, 66, 79.

SUBSISTENCE, MEANS OF, AND POPULATION: VII, 68 to 70.

SUPPLY AND DEMAND: III, **180** to 195, 222, 223, 224.

SYNDICATES: VI, 63; IX, 4, 6, 10 to 16, 25, 26, 31.

TASTES: Chapter IV. III, 14, 19, 25, 27, 37, 78, 199. Direct and
indirect effects of ———— III, **39** to 42, 93 to 99.

TERMINAL POINT: III, **62**, 63, 94.

THEORIES: Nature and criterion of truth, I, 20; II, 6. Theories about concrete phenomena are only approximative, I, **11**, 32. Theories are incomplete, I, 10, **19**, 20; II, 7. Theories and direct or indirect experiments, I, 20. How they are contrasted with practice, I, 28. Science is analytic, practice is synthetic, I, 26.

THEORIES, QUANTITATIVE: I, 11, 31; II, 100, 110.

TRANSFORMATION OF ECONOMIC GOODS: III, 70.

TRANSFORMATION, OBJECTIVE: III, 71; physical transformation, III, 72; V, 48.

TRANSFORMATION IN SPACE: III, 72; V, **38**, 48; ———— in time, III, 72; V, **39** to 48, 53, 56.

TRUSTS: IX, 10 to 16.

TRUTHS, EXPERIMENTAL: I, 36. Whether the universal consent of men can replace experiment, I, 46. Always contingent, I, 36.

TYPES OF ECONOMIC PHENOMENA: III, 39, **40, 41, 42,** 43 to 45, 49 to 51, 92, 110 to 115, 117 to 132, 138 to 151, **160, 161,** 196 to 208; V, **8** to 12, 71 to 75, 81, 82 to 84, 86, 88; VI, 16, 52 to 61; Appendix, 35.

UNIFORMITY OR LAW: I, 4, 5, 6. Conditions of a ————, I, 8, 9, 30. Exceptions to laws, I, 7.

UTILITY: III, 28, 29, 30, 35. Utility for the individual and utility for the species, II, 30, 34, 36, 37; VII, 99, 102, 103, 109.

UTILITY, FINAL DEGREE OF: See final degree of utility.

VALUE IN EXCHANGE: III, 156, 157.

VALUE IN USE: III, 29, 35.

VARIATIONS, CONTINUOUS AND DISCONTINUOUS: III, 65 to 67; IV, 47.

WHOLESALE TRADE: IX, 7, 8.

TABLE OF AUTHORS CITED

The Roman numeral refers to the chapter and the arabic number to the section. [Except for minor corrections this list is the one given in the French text.—A.S.]

Aeschylus, II, 57.
Ammon, Otto, VII, 98.
Anaximander, I, 13.
Anaximenes, I, 13.
Aristophanes, II, 66, 68; VII, 97.
Aristotle, I, 47; II, 64, 100, 117; IX, 30.
Aynard, II, 118.

Baker, G. B., VII, 54.
Barone, E., Appendix, 43.
Bastable, IX, 43.
Bayle, II, 53.
Benini, R., VII, 2, 97.
Bentzon, T., VII, 54.
Bernard, C., I, 47, 48.
Bertrand, VII, 6.
Boissier, G., II, 42, 58.
Boninsegni, P., Appendix, 3, 51.
Bourdeau, J., IX, 62.
Bresciani, C., VII, 24.
Brunetière, II, 101, 6°.
Bulot, II, 50.

Cairnes, III, 222.
Cato, I, 2.
Cauderlier, VII, 40, 49.
Cicero, II, 14, 27, 73, 116.
Colajanni, N., IX, 32.
Combes, II, 50, 94.
Cournot, III, 30.
Croce, B., I, 7, 10, 17, 47.

Dante, I, 42; II, 48; VII, 98.
Darwin, Charles, II, 76.

Descartes, I, 47.
Diogenes Laertius, I, 47; II, 63.
Dionysius of Halicarnassus, II, 116.
Droz, N., IX, 64.

Edgeworth, III, 30, 54; Appendix, 2, 69.
Essars, Pierre des, IX, 85, 87.
Euclid, I, 7.
Euripides, II, 57, 64.

Fechner, IV, 33.
Ferrara, III, 221; V, 34.
Fisher, Irving, III, 30, 35; V, 17.
Funck-Bretano, II, 50.
Furlan, V., Appendix, 21.
Fustel de Coulanges, II, 56; IX, 30.

Gaius, II, 38.
Germain, II, 118.
Gide, Appendix, 20.
Godwin, VII, 34.
Graziani, VIII, 11.
Greef, G. de, I, 1.
Grote, II, 70.
Guyot, Yves, II, 50.

Hegel, II, 14.
Hesiod, II, 48.
Horace, II, 71.

Jacoby, Paul, VII, 98.
Jagemann, II, 122.
Jevons, W. S., III, 30; IX, 88.
Juglar, C., IX, 85, 86.

Kant, I, 47; II, 25, 38.

Lapouge, VII, 98.
Lassalle, VII, 58.
Lea, II, 58.
Leibnitz, I, 47.
Leroy-Beaulieu, P., I, 3; VII, 25; VIII, 26; IX, 26.
Levasseur, VII, 33, 79.
Lucas-Championnière, II, 50.

Machiavelli, II, 58, 99, 100.
Magnaud, II, 50.
Maine, Sir Henry Sumner, II, 81; VII, 109.
Malthus, VII, 68, 71, 74, 84, 89ff.

Marshall, III, 30; VII, 44; Appendix, 22, 56.
Martial, IV, 26.
Martello, Tullio, VII, 89; VIII, 29.
Marx, Karl, III, 226; VII, 117; VIII, 25.
Menger, Anton, VIII, 25.
Mill, John Stuart, I, 3; II, 25, 34, 38.
Molinari, IX, 26.
Moniteur des intérêts matériels, V, 69; IX, 32.
Montesquieu, II, 19; IX, 79.
Musset, Alfred de, II, 20.

Ovid, IX, 32b.

Pantaleoni, Maffeo, IX, 9, 10.
Pauthier, II, 39.
Pertile, IX, 30, 31.
Pidoux, II, 85.
Plato, I, 47; II, 28, 42, 48.
Pliny, I, 2, 12.
Plutarch, II, 63.
Poincaré, H., I, 17; II, 14.
Polybius, II, 73.
Post, II, 81.

Reinach, S., II, 51, 58.
Ribot, IX, 26.
Ricardo, V, 93, 94; IX, 43, 44, 45.
Rogers, Thorold, VII, 54.
Roosevelt, Theodore, II, 101; IX, 85.

Say, J. B., IX, 20, 21, 41.
Sextus Empiricus, II, 27.
Sismondi, VII, 69.
Smith, Adam, I, 3.
Sorel, G., I, 28, 30; II, 96, 107b, 118; VI, 48; IX, 26, 30, 31, 32b, 33, 35.
Spencer, Herbert, II, 29, 31, 50, 101, 2°, 6°.
Stahl, II, 123.

Tannery, Paul, I, 13, 51.
Tarde, II, 88.
Tertullian, II, 14.
Theognis of Megara, II, 82.
Theophrastes, II, 42.
Thornton, III, 223.
Thucydides, I, 6; II, 71, 93.
Tocqueville, VII, 85.
Trollope, VII, 54.

Villani, VII, 54.
Volterra, I, 21; Appendix, 12.

Waldeck-Rousseau, IX, 32b.
Walras, Léon, III, 30, 226, 227; Appendix, 83.
Wundt, IV, 33.

Xenophon, II, 67; VII, 54.

Zeller, II, 68, 70.